...the reaction to this... nature of the universe we in... curiosity of gods - it is up to us - none will... ghastly impression of the failure of our systems especially economic, educational, and political - the push button civilization we were gloating over suddenly became terror - but we soon got them going all... business the same as usual - a little blurry - that's all - The violence mind... a dead mind anyway. No surprise to... find that reaction as it was - the journalistic mind... reporters mind leaning to the humorous... the only attempt ready to arouse the people to what had really happened to them - not an explosive bomb but an... bomb - made them... quicker... than you can kill beneath a plough. She... in a fierce... so I say let's pause and consider. this... lack of vision that... only hide... our very... from ourselves but close... rob our any future we are able to see...

# FRANK LLOYD WRIGHT
# COLLECTED WRITINGS

*Volume* **4**

1939–1949

*Edited by*
*Bruce Brooks Pfeiffer*

*Introduction by Kenneth Frampton*

Rizzoli/New York in association with The Frank Lloyd Wright Foundation

First published in the United States of America in 1994 by
Rizzoli International Publications, Inc.
300 Park Avenue South, New York, New York 10010
Copyright © The Frank Lloyd Wright Foundation 1994
The drawings of Frank Lloyd Wright are copyright
© The Frank Lloyd Wright Foundation 1994

Library of Congress Cataloging-in-Publication Data

Wright, Frank Lloyd, 1867–1959.
[Selections, 1994]
    The collected writings of Frank Lloyd Wright/
    edited by Bruce Brooks Pfeiffer.
        p. cm.
    Includes index.
    Contents: v. 1. 1894–1930—v. 2. 1930–1932.
    including a reprint of his 1932 autobiography.—
    v. 3. 1931–1939—v. 4. 1939–1949.
    ISBN 0-8478-1546-3 (HC : v. 1).—ISBN 0-8478-1547-1 (pbk. : v. 1)—
    ISBN 0-8478-1548-X (HC : v. 2).—ISBN 0-8478-1549-8 (pbk. : v. 2)—
    ISBN 0-8478-1699-0 (HC : v. 3).—ISBN 0-8478-1700-8 (pbk. : v. 3)—
    ISBN 0-8478-1803-9 (HC : v. 4).—ISBN 0-8478-1804-7 (pbk. : v. 4).
    I. Pfeiffer, Bruce Brooks.
    II. Wright, Frank Lloyd, 1867–1959. Autobiography.
    NA737. W7A35 1992
    720—dc20                                          91–40987
                                                      CIP

Printed in Singapore

Designed by Sisco & Evans, New York

**Frontispiece: Frank Lloyd Wright, 1939, New York. Photograph by Edward Steichen.
Reprinted with permission of Joanna T. Steichen.** FLLW Fdn FA#6005.0024 [AV1136.052]

# CONTENTS

# INTRODUCTION

This volume of Wright's collected essays, covering the period 1939 to 1949, carries forward many of the themes that Wright had broached in the 1930s, above all the unremitting attacks on all his familiar aversions: his ambivalence toward the state, his antipathy for the monumental "grandomania" of the École des Beaux-Arts, now extended to its successor, the Art Deco movement, and his repudiation of contemporary architecture at its most abstract, the so-called reductive functionalism of the International Style that for Wright certainly included Russian Constructivism.

The early 1940s, however, introduced a new target, namely the inevitable involvement of America in yet another world war. In retrospect, it seems that this pending conflict traumatized him to such a degree that he felt compelled to reassert his categoric opposition to all war, along with the eccentricity of his own political position. Thus we find him writing, as early as November 1940 in an essay entitled "Wake Up America!", the following inflammatory declaration:

> During several months past I could "listen in" or read at any time anywhere and imagine myself back in the stupid days of 1914. But that previous catastrophe to the economy and morale of our democratic world was nothing compared to what now takes us in its grip. Shame enough to sell out our best thought at first sign of danger and see our nationals run pell-mell to play a second-hand imitation of the enemy when our power can never lie in saving empire unless we too are empirical. Imitation always base, never yet won a battle. No, our real enemy is not Hitler! Our real enemy lies in our own timidity and stupidity as seen in this frightful current so smoothly moved, coaxed in the direction of self-destruction. "To save Britain"? No, to maintain Britain as our only shield against our own slavery or destruction is the insane notion sold to mediocrity by way of its own salesmen, from chief executive to the journalistic horde. (p. 40)

Although this, in many respects, was only an extension of the pacifism that he had already expressed during the 1914–1918 conflict, there is a discernible if subtle allusion to his partiality for Teutonic culture, to such a degree that whereas he scrupulously disowned fascism as such, he nonetheless viewed the Third Reich as a distant, economic threat rather than as a totalitarian power bent on world domination. Moreover, he indulged elsewhere in sentiments touched by antisemitism:

> But, if as a people we are going on to ultimate victory over selfish or vengeful interests that infect us because those interests are unable to feel outside their own pockets, see beyond their own factory floors, or rise above their murdered European relatives, it will go on alive only because the country can see with the help of its own free minority the murderous character of "power-politics" as now played in unison by the two parties and realize the utter folly of such make-shift money-getting as is now in action. Why do our people not realize that it is this make-shift money-system that is the real danger now? That system is there at the bottom of this cry "save Britain." The system knows it well. Mass mediocrity does not know it. (p. 40)

**Sports club and play resort for Huntington Hartford (Project), Hollywood, California. 1947. Perspective. Pencil, sepia ink, and color pencil on tracing paper, 48 x 36".** FLLW Fdn#4731.019

Elsewhere, after Pearl Harbor, he expressed a certain sympathy for Japanese imperial claims, electing to see these as the natural fulfillment of the desire of the Orient to establish an imperium of its own.

Needless to say such views led him into conflict with many of his colleagues, including his faithful friend Lewis Mumford, who would eventually lose his only son in the war, and his cousin Richard Lloyd Jones, newspaper editor and blockhouse client, who, according to Wright, told him: "Hell, Frank, if you don't like the system on which this country's run, why don't you get out of it? Go somewhere else! God-dammit" (p. 124). Later, as Bruce Pfeiffer points out, he even fell foul of infamous Senator McCarthy from Wisconsin, who in the full flood of his demagogic career attempted to have Wright impeached as an anti-American communist.

To characterize Wright's attitude at this time as isolationism is to miss the complexity of his vision; above all his persistent evocation of what was surely an unprecedented form of capitalism, if it was capitalism at all. This was a hypothetically restructured economy that he would characterize as economic nationalism—the ramifications of which were surely as revolutionary as anything envisaged by Karl Marx, for whom Wright professed a marked distaste, if not total disdain. While professing after Emerson that the best form of government was the one that intervened the least, Wright nonetheless conjured up a utopia in which all useful inventions would at once enter the public domain, with the inventor being appropriately compensated by the state. An equally egalitarian provision would be to reserve for each citizen a certain quantum of interest-free national credit—a scheme patently modeled after C. H. Douglas's *Social Credit,* first published in 1924. Thus, as Wright put it, the state would assure that "neither land nor money nor creative ideas can be speculative commodities to be traded or held over by somebody against the common good" (p. 64). Hence the equally zany notion, as set forth in *The Disappearing City* (1932), of reserving an acre of land for every American at birth. A year later in 1941, in an article devoted to the work of G. Hickling, the editor of the English magazine *Reality,* Wright followed Hickling's views by arguing that since America was self-sufficient she could pioneer the Social Credit system with impunity, since she could feed her population and remain solvent irrespective of whether she had an excess of imports or exports.

Hickling was not the only British Social Credit theorist to whom Wright turned in these years, as one may judge from one Stanley C. Norton, who contributed an important short essay on economic theory to the second number of the *Taliesin* magazine. This was devoted to elaborating the economic implications of that which Norton called The New Frontier:

> The idea of the new system lies in a form of true "Economic Nationalism"—putting our own house in order first, making one's own country sound economically and financially. Briefly, instead of the issue of money and credit being the monopoly of private financier-money-lenders, it will become the function of the state. Credit will be socialized. Money will become a medium of exchange, of distribution, and not a commodity in the hands of private firms to be let out on hire. The government will create money for defense and for all public works and social services; this money being backed by the credit of the country, as is the case when government borrows from private banks, but it would be free of interest and it would not come out of the taxpayer's pockets. A form of National Dividend will replace relief and all social-security payments. The controlled "Just Price," which will replace the present prices swollen by overheads and selling costs, will be instituted for all necessaries. In place of the exchange of goods for gold, or gold for gadgets, there will be among the countries an exchange of needed goods for needed goods.

However naive and utopian this economic theory of need may have been—a theory notably missing in Marx—it was echoed by Wright, in what presumably was his own critique of American plutocratic capitalism. Like Le Corbusier, he was categorically opposed to the emergence of modern consumerism as a form of engineered wastage on a mammoth scale.

Thus we cannot judge Wright's pacifist tracts of the early 1940s—he wrote ten such essays between 1940 and 1942—without setting them against the frustration and anger he felt with regard to the fundamentally wasteful character of American civilization, particularly given the disaster of the Great Depression that, notwithstanding Roosevelt's New Deal, had had such a devastating effect not only on the country as a whole but also on his own practice. The full dimension of the burden that this imposed upon the sixty-five-year-old Wright as he attempted to both rebuild his aunts' Hillside Home School and to initiate the Taliesin Fellowship is compellingly set forth in Book Five of the second edition of *An Autobiography* (1943) under the section subtitled "Form":

> We needed, and desperately, lumber, stone, lime and laborers of all sorts. As you see in the lines (and between them), we had very little or no money at all to pay for these coveted desirables. . . . We were now where we had to have more lumber or stop work altogether. Standing around in the woods of our country, were many piles of sawed oak. I coveted them all as I coveted gravel, sand, and cement. . . . I tried to buy some of these lumber piles, pay part down, part on credit. But nothing could be done. The hard financial going all around had made everyone, especially the farmers, doubly suspicious, especially so of me, the spender of so much money with no visible means of support. . . . I drove over to see Herb, offered him a fair price and terms for four hundred acres of timber, on the stump. . . . Then I found a good sawer on the other side of the river who agreed to saw the logs at the regular price if we cut them and brought them in. . . . Forthwith, we went headlong into logging. The place became a logging camp. Soon, after overcoming innumerable difficulties of a time-consuming, painful but picturesque character, green-oak timber was going up into the walls and trusses of our coveted buildings. . . . But we had to have lime or stop. . . . The lumberyards were full of cement—but for us to keep our work going, deliveries were only for cash-down. The cement dealers, like the lumber dealers, all knew their way out of the scrape they were in: stick together. Keep prices up. . . . Strictly up against it again, under pressure, I remembered that lime for the original Hillside Home School buildings . . . had all been burned in the hills not more than several miles away. The old kiln might be there yet! . . . So up went the boys to bring the old wrecked lime-kiln back to life again and themselves learn how to burn lime: a bunch of greensters. I got an old-time lime-burner from Black Earth to instruct them. We fixed up the broken grates with old ones we took from the old buildings at Hillside—patched up the tumbled walls, stripped a section of the old stone quarry and filled the patched-up restoration with good raw lime rock; piled cords and cords of wood alongside in long ranks to feed the roaring fires. . . . We got good lime . . . hundreds of bushels of it. We could have gone into the lime business, and thought seriously of doing so. . . . There was no building. Little money was coming in to go into so many hands, and without any, some of the men began to get ugly. But they would go away with a little. During many ensuing weeks there were outrageous scenes. One, Jones, a troublesome ringleader, attacked me in the studio one late afternoon—got his hands well on towards my throat when Henry jumped at him, yelling so loud with anger that Jones was scared "into taking his hands off Mr. Wright." (pp. 136–154)

With such telling anecdotes as these, rather anachronically arranged, Wright patched together the fifth book of *An Autobiography,* published in its entirety in a revised format in 1943. In this version he elected to subdivide the original Book One into two books, dealing with Fellowship and Family separately, thereby transforming Books Two and Three into Books Three and Four, respectively, and summarily adding a fifth book, "Form," before going to press. A pending sixth book, listed as such here, added relatively minor details to the original account of the Broadacre concept as published in *The Disappearing City* in 1932. This book prepared, but presumably never added to, *An Autobiography,* because it was seen as rather superfluous to information already set forth in *The Disappearing City* and later reworked in *When Democracy Builds* of 1945. This in turn was reworked once again in *The Living City* in 1958, just one year before his death. What is not repeated here, nor anywhere else for that matter, is Wright's wholly ambivalent attitude toward state control, for although he remained opposed to bureaucracy in all its forms, and above all to building codes (p. 346), he nonetheless thought that government should intervene when it came to the provision of the basic infrastructure, particularly with regard to conserving his beloved Arizona desert and the panoramic site of his own Taliesin West. Even more specifically, he wanted the government to protect him from the U.S. Army Corps of Engineers who, notwithstanding his petitioning the president, still persisted in taking powerlines across the desert panorama of Taliesin West.

Despite his belief in the manifest destiny of the democratic state, Wright clearly felt that the present federation of the United States was too cumbersome and that the nation should be subdivided along regional and cultural lines into the three separate states—Usonia, Usonia South, and New England. This is set forth in an essay of that title written in 1941:

> If this union, now divided into forty-eight separate states, is ever to be freed from equivocal British domination . . . it would be far better, and much the lesser of all probable evils to rearrange the states into a more simple and characteristic federation, a grouping of all the states into three principal states. Allow New England to keep the national capital and the official buildings of the present city of Washington as a present from the greater part of the nation.
>
> There is now pressing upon us the need for a far greater national capital. . . . probably placed midway on the rolling prairies of the great Mid-West beside the Father of Waters—our Mississippi; there where the amplitude, rectitude and impartiality that might characterize the greater part of our nation, could, unhampered by congenital prejudice or the equivocal influence of foreign powers, be free to initiate and grow the ways and means to live a good life as the independent democracy this country was designed to be. . . . According to geography, climate, natural self-interest and sentiment, three general state-groupings are manifest. They are the New England states, the Southern states including Texas and the great intermediate body of the Union. . . . Were such equitable and better-fitting boundaries established in our country and this more simple and democratic system of election, one more directly responsible to the people, set up: my Lords, Ladies and Gentlemen, I give you USONIA, USONIA SOUTH AND NEW ENGLAND: THE UNITED STATES OF NORTH AMERICA (pp. 90–92).

With so many essays and books treating the same themes, repetition is unavoidable, and one often finds oneself wading through a great deal of reiterative material to get at the kernel of Wright's thought, which, once encountered, seems even now to be surprisingly fresh and insightful. That Wright needed much closer editing than that Olgivanna or Eugene Masselink or anyone could provide goes without saying. As the essay "Form" reveals, Wright was certainly not above mocking his editors by persisting with his romantic rhetoric in the face of their critical commentary (pp. 157–159).

These essays reveal only too clearly how Wright's anti-interventionist stance of the early 1940s was intimately bound up with his broader political views and how these in turn were inextricable from the socioeconomic and technical implications of his Broadacre City thesis; the full elaboration of which was first made available to *Taliesin* subscribers in 1941 in part as a series of negative slogans. Thus one learned in short order that Broadacre City was dead set against officialdom, policemen, slums, and landlords and that no suspended power or communication lines would be permitted on the surface. By a similar token, regarding utilities Wright insisted that coal should not be burnt, except at source. Hence Broadacre City projected a smokeless form of regional urbanization exclusively fed by automobiles and electrically powered monorails, with trains running at speeds of up to 200 mph. To these recommendations were added the recycling of sewage as fertilizer and the introduction of concave, floodlit roadbeds without ditches so that the storm-water would be conducted to a central grated gulley that would also serve as a dividing strip.

In the same year, in an essay entitled "Defense," he posited a further list of undesirable practices that were advanced as the sociopolitical corollaries, so to speak, of his deurbanization thesis. Among the barbaric sentiments and pursuits of the Western world that Wright would have liked to have seen proscribed, one may note militarism (and with it conscription), patriotism, imperialism, academics, journalism, fashion, organized sport, and mass entertainment of all kinds—from Broadway to Hollywood. Parts of this critique read like passages from Simone Weil's *The Need for Roots* of 1943, in which she would make similar arguments. She posited above all that one cannot expect ordinary people to sacrifice their lives for a homeland in which they have no ultimate stake.

Of all Wright's anti-interventionist essays, the most prophetic by far was his 1941 Taliesin Square piece entitled "Of What Use Is a Great Navy with No Place to Hide?", an essay that all too uncannily foresaw the Japanese destruction of the American fleet at Pearl Harbor on 7 December 1941. In the essay entitled "Good Afternoon, Editor Evjue," published in *The Capital Times* of Madison, Wisconsin, on 29 May 1941, Wright even anticipated Roosevelt's strategy of provocation—that is, his deliberate massing of the fleet as a sitting target (pp. 80–81).

Throughout these writings of the early 1940s, together with the fifth book of *An Autobiography*, a number of dyadic polarities are constantly alluded to. Wright insisted on the indisputable virtues of a mixed economy with the emphasis falling, as always, on the agrarian, on tillage, as he liked to call it, as the key to self-sufficiency. Aside from this particular antinomy, there is sufficient evidence of Wright seeing the world as a series of irreconcilable antagonisms. Thus he opposed nature to history, culture to education, apprenticeship to scholarship, salesmanship to statesmanship, and, last but not least, experiment to experimental. In a similar vein, he saw the master builder as one who was capable of conceiving everything from the landscape to the interior, as opposed to the professional architect, who in Wright's view was only capable of designing grandiloquent shells. At the same time deurbanization was the overriding credo that reappeared constantly in his writings from the early 1930s on; although on his official visit to the Soviet Union in 1937 he seemed to have been totally oblivious to the fact that the Russian avant-garde had been conceived with a very similar issue (pp. 228–239). At the same time that Wright was deprecating about the then official plan for the expansion of Moscow, he was surprisingly charitable to the young architects of the Soviet state, including Boris Iofan, who despite the "grandomania" of his winning design for the Palace of the Soviets was again in Wright's good graces for his streamlined USSR Pavilion, built for the Paris World Exposition of 1937.

Soon after receiving the Guggenheim Museum commission from Hilla Rebay in 1943, Wright encountered yet another protagonist with whom he could tussle for the hearts and minds of the world's most democratic state, namely the already infamous New York Commissioner Robert Moses, whose technocratic approach to replanning the New York region did not sit well with Wright. Needless to say, Wright's Broadacre City thesis did not find much sympathy from the bureaucracy of Moses's Triborough Bridge Authority. Antithetical to housing as any kind of solution to the social and environmental problems confronting the modern city, Wright had the temerity to be critical of Moses's high-rise, high-density housing proposals, while Moses lost no time cutting Wright down to size:

> While we were generally familiar with your publications and views, my little group of earnest thinkers, or rather constructors, have read the Taliesin Pamphlet and your more recent memorandum with considerable interest. The consensus of opinion is that we do not fully

understand them. Some of the implications are most interesting, and, of course, we respect your accomplishments in the field of architecture, but it seems to us you have taken on a little too much territory. Most of my boys would feel you would get further if you tried an experiment on a reasonable scale, frankly called it an experiment and refrained from announcing that it was the pattern of all future American living. (p. 268)

As it turned out, the Moses bureaucracy remained fairly hostile to Wright even as an architect, as one may judge from their sporadic but more or less continual opposition to the realization of the Guggenheim (which would have never seen the light of day had it not been for Rebay's persistence and Wright's determination, not to mention the decisive move made late in the day, in 1957, by Harry Guggenheim, after Solomon R. Guggenheim's death in 1949, when he elected to put the Guggenheim fortune fully behind erecting the building). Be this as it may, Wright was already locking horns with Moses over the building a decade before. In his 1947 essay "Prejudice, Sir, Is a Disease," Wright explained,

I suggest that Robert Moses (the man) actually see the model of the new museum designed as a great gift from a great New Yorker to his own great city for a great purpose. As an individual or an official Moses owed this to himself before, "carte blanche," he generalized so freely concerning this great thing which he reads about in the papers or only hears about from the boys in his backroom where there is ample reason to believe they are blind to the world-wide trend which they choose to see as "functionalism." (p. 309)

Despite Wright's lifelong ambivalence toward the university, he had sufficient cause to be grateful to this generic institution; in the first instance for sustaining him at a difficult moment in his career, to wit the Kahn lectures he gave at Princeton University in 1930; in the second, for the invitation he received in 1946 from his hometown university to participate in a seminar dedicated to the "Works of the Mind." For all that he prided himself on always speaking spontaneously without notes, he seems to have taken such formal presentations seriously, rising to this particular occasion with a well-crafted piece—as he would do again in 1949 in his AIA Gold Medal acceptance speech. However with this particular address, given at the University of Chicago under the title "The Architect," Wright is as perceptive and audacious on the subject of human creativity as anything from the pen of the French mathematician Henri Poincare, only now from a predictably different standpoint:

As for my share in this discussion (or presentation) of various phases of human activity said to proceed from the mind, it is my belief that for five hundred years at least we have had no architecture which did proceed from the Mind.

So here at the beginning we might as well clear up a little ambiguity concerning what we are in the habit of calling the Mind. Some of us laughingly (and wrongly) refer to our "minds." But the Mind should be not only a matter of the head (the intellect) but an affair of the heart and of the imagination and of the hand (or what we call technique). . . . As I have said, we mistake memory, association of ideas, rationalizations, ratiocination—we mistake all that hypnosis and hallucination for thinking. But none of it is thinking at all. Do you realize that a great musician, if he is a performer, does not really have to think? Very few professors ever have to think. A mathematician does not have to think. You can study mathematics all your life and never do a bit of thinking. . . . Thinking is an intense concentration of which few people are capable or even aware. It is a going-within, somehow, penetrating into the very nature of some objective: going in after gaining adequate experience of nature . . . and *staying in* there until you get what you went in after. You may not get it the first time, and you may not get it the second. And you may spend half your life trying to get into that place where the thing you are seeking really is—where it lives—finally to find the plane upon which what we call Reality really lives. But once you do find it—what a reward! (pp. 285–286, 289).

A comparable charm and wit was surely present in his 1949 AIA Gold Medal Address, only this time it was combined with an exceptional openness and warmth, all the more surprising and touching given Wright's lifelong hostility to the profession and his arrogant habit of expressing nothing but contempt for most of his colleagues. Above all one is struck by his magnanimity in graciously accepting this belated recognition from his peers, exactly a decade after the British had accorded him the RIBA Gold Medal in 1939:

No man climbs so high or sinks so low that he isn't eager to receive the good will and admiration of his fellow men. He may be reprehensible in many ways; he may seem to care nothing about it; he may hitch his wagon to his star, but however he may be circumstanced or whatever his ideals or his actions, he never loses desire for the approbation of his kind.

So I feel humble and grateful.

Upon this really fine occasion of our presence here I don't think humility a very becoming state for me.

But I really feel deeply touched by this token of esteem from the home boys.

Honors have reached me from almost every great nation in the world.

Honor has, however, been a long time coming from home.

But here it is at last. Handsomely indeed.

Yes . . . I am extremely grateful. (p. 325)

Wright did not leave the matter there, however, and those who were lulled into thinking they might only have to endure an entertaining and somewhat outrageous speech were led by degrees into a challenging—not to say extremely somber—discourse. Thus, halfway through his address, the audience was forcibly brought to ponder the fate of architecture in a techno-scientific epoch:

All was well established, especially during the Gothic period. So an architect in those days was pretty well furnished with everything in the way of ideas he needed to work with. He didn't have to be a *creator*. He merely had to be a sentient artist, with fine perception let's say and some practical knowledge of building, especially if he was going to engage in some monumental enterprise. But he didn't have to *create* as he must do now.

We live under entirely different conditions. We live by this leverage we call the Machine. Most of us are machines ourselves; not much higher in consciousness and mentality than the man in the garage. Anyhow, *we do live by the machine* and we do have the enormous product of all modern sciences in our toolbox.

But as a matter of fact it is Science that is ruining us in Architecture and Art as it has already ruined Religion, as it has made a monkey of Philosophy. Already Science has practically destroyed us spiritually and is sending us into perpetual war. (p. 327)

With *Genius and the Mobocracy* published under the sign of Wright's "red square" by Duell, Sloan and Pearce in 1949, the wheel would come full circle, and Wright at the age of seventy-two would return once again to the time he spent in the Auditorium Tower as "a pencil in the hand of the master." Written ostensibly as a gloss on a set of drawings Louis Sullivan had presented to Wright on 11 April

**Frank Lloyd Wright and Dr. Ludd M. Spivey, President, Florida Southern College, Lakeland, Florida. At construction site, 1939.**
FLLW Fdn FA#6801.0001

1924, just three days before Sullivan's death, *Genius and the Mobocracy* strayed from its ostensible subject in the usual Wrightian fashion before settling down to give an extremely personal account of the trials and tribulations of Sullivan's life, from the time he returned home from the École in Paris, as a Parisite (note the typical Wrightian pun), to his death at the age of sixty-eight. Much, as usual, floats to the surface in this text that is partly extraneous to the theme of the book—from the crucial importance of Nature as the source of all tectonic form as opposed to the eclecticism of History (p. 337), to the incapacity of photography to capture the essence of spatial depth (p. 340). And the text is as much a sympathetic portrait of Adler as an homage to Sullivan. We learn a good deal here about what it was like to live through the triumphant realization of the Adler and Sullivan Auditorium Building in 1890 and about how Sullivan, thereafter swollen-headed by this triumph at the age of thirty-four, would absent himself from the office for long periods of time with increasing frequency. "The master was working away in his rose garden down there at Biloxi by the Gulf, next door to his beloved friends the James Charnleys, for whom I had drawn a cottage which I liked better than lieber-meister's. Both were experiments that seem tame enough now. Later I designed the Charnley townhouse on Astor Street" (p. 357).

Needless to say we learn as much about Wright and his young colleagues in the Sullivan orbit as we do about the master himself; above all we are told of George Elmslie's all but saintlike fidelity to Sullivan, even in his later years, and about the open competition—not to say confrontation—that developed almost at once between Wright and Irving Gill, leading to the latter's prompt departure after having been insulted by Wright. We are also provided with a brief but touching portrait of the young German engineer Paul Mueller from Stuttgart, who shortly passed from Sullivan's employ to become the engineering partner in the Probst Construction Company, a firm that later realized a great deal of Wright's own work. Indeed, Wright was not beyond criticizing Sullivan for his misrepresentation of the presence of the steel frame in the elevations of the Wainwright Building—a critique that could be extended by implication to Wright's own high-rise exercise projected for the San Francisco Call Company in 1912, a work that Wright would remain inordinately proud of throughout his life. However ultimately appreciative, Wright's criticism of Sullivan did not stop with this, for as Wright would declare, "It is only fair to say, now, that in none of these Adler and Sullivan buildings are 'form and function' one or, excepting clay (called 'terra cotta'), is the nature-of-materials considered at all, either as a matter of fact or as determining organic form" (p. 361). This is Wright as the tectonic architect par excellence—an architect who like Pugin and Perret before him believed that materiality, structure, and construction were the absolute prerequisites for a great building culture. As he put it in *Genius and the Mobocracy,* "When I speak of architecture as organic I mean the great art of structure coming back to its early integrity: again alive as a great reality" (p. 336).

K.F.

# FRANK LLOYD WRIGHT
# A BIOGRAPHICAL SKETCH:
# 1939–1949

In the spring of 1939 Wright was extremely busy with some of his most ambitious projects. The administration building for the S.C. Johnson & Son Co. opened. Fallingwater was completed and furnishings were being installed. Plans were well under way for the campus of Florida Southern College in Lakeland, Florida, and the Community Church in Kansas City, Missouri, was about to break ground. Fees for some of these larger commissions made it possible for Wright to purchase 160 acres in the Arizona desert in 1937 and to start construction of Taliesin West, a winter home and studio. A crew was also at work during the summers to speed up the construction. Returning to Arizona in December 1939, Wright completed the main structures, including a drafting room, office, cabaret theater, kitchen, dining room and private living quarters. An apprentice court, providing further living quarters, was started in construction. *Arizona Highways,* a state-supported magazine, published a special issue on Taliesin West in May 1940.

Several Usonian homes, based on a prototype designed for Herbert Jacobs in 1937, were in construction throughout the nation, from New Jersey to California. To help cut costs and to aid in the construction of these houses, Wright sent out his apprentices to supervise the work and to establish subcontracts for masonry and carpentry.

By the winter of 1939–1940, amidst all this building, Wright was still lecturing and publishing. He was at work with his new publisher, Duell, Sloan and Pearce in New York, for a revised and extended edition of the autobiography he had first published in 1932 (reproduced in full in volume 2 of *Collected Writings*). As the editing of the revised first autobiography had progressed, Wright had written to his editor Max Putzel, "It seems to me that the expurgated edition is going to have the effect of making the original edition very valuable. Perhaps we should therefore strike off a thousand copies more of the book, as was, and keep them for a rise." The year 1940 marked the founding of The Frank Lloyd Wright Foundation, a non-profit corporation with tax exemption incorporated in the State of Wisconsin. To this foundation Wright gave his work, his homes, his property, and the art collections he acquired after 1940. In this way he made certain that his work as well as his intellectual property would be protected into the future.

Duell, Sloan and Pearce agreed, in 1940, that they would publish three books by or about him and his work. Frederick Gutheim came to Taliesin and went through Wright's manuscript file, both published and unpublished. In a book entitled *Frank Lloyd Wright on Architecture* Gutheim published excerpts, for the most part, of the those texts he found to be most pertinent. At the end of the same year, from 13 November 1940 to 4 January 1941, The Museum of Modern Art in New York held a large show of Wright's work entitled "Frank Lloyd Wright: American Architect." This was to date the largest exhibition ever held on Wright, and Henry-Russell Hitchcock, following the closing of the show, included Wright's material, but expanded, in the book *In the Nature of Materials: The Buildings of Frank Lloyd Wright 1887–1941.* By the end of 1942 Wright was under contract with Duell, Sloan and Pearce for the third book of this trilogy, a revised and expanded *An Autobiography* that would by published in 1943.

While the Second World War escalated in Europe, Wright became more and more outspoken about America's role in the conflict. When the war finally engulfed the United States, with architectural work again slowing down, Wright, as he had done during the depression, turned to writing. This time his subject was less architecture and more social, economic, and political in its scope, more a preachment of how mankind must learn to live without war than how mankind should build in peace. As the senseless destruction and loss of life grew to staggering proportions, Wright turned in his writings to his never-diminishing faith in democracy, in which he placed the utmost hope and trust. He pleaded with his nation to forego war and the type of nationalism that breeds further war and to embrace "this democratic faith" as its investment in the future.

Much of his writing in this period is thus devoted to antiwar sentiments, both before and after the entrance of the nation into the war. He was touched quite personally because of the apprentices under his care at Taliesin who were drafted. (He instinctively despised conscription.) Some apprentices enlisted; others stayed behind and ran the farm on farm deferments. But a few refused to go to war as a matter of principle and were sent to prison. He wrote,

> As for conscription, I think it has deprived every young man in America of the honor and privilege of dedicating himself as a free man to the service of his country. . . . Were I born forty years later than 1869 I too should be a conscientious objector.[1]

Understandably Wright supported the choice of the apprentices who were sent to Sandstone Prison, and went up to the prison in Minnesota to talk to them along with a group of other conscientious objectors imprisoned there.

Despite the ongoing war in both the European and the Pacific arenas and the resulting lack of architectural work, Wright, Olgivanna, and their children were spared the humiliation and deprivation that beset them during the years from 1924 to 1930. Taliesin was secure. A large farm guaranteed them all, including the apprentices, fine, healthy produce. The ongoing construction of their homes in Wisconsin, in the summer, and Arizona, in the winter, assured them a healthy, varied life-style, either working at the desk or drafting table, or doing hard physical work in construction and on the farm.

Furthermore, one very important commission came to him in the midst of the world conflict: The Solomon R. Gggenenheim Museum. During the war years Wright made the preliminary studies, presentation drawings, model of the structure, and the final working drawings, signed in 1945. But construction was deferred until the end of the war, and even then it was further deferred because Guggenheim believed, eroneously so, that building costs, at that time escalating, would soon go down.

By 1945 Wright was writing about the formation of the United Nations, which he regarded as nothing much more than an enormous police force that, through threat and force, could never assure the world of a fair peace. Also with the end of the war, work in the studio began to pick up. The campus at Florida Southern College was under construction. He was commissioned to design a civic center for Pittsburgh, which included two cantilevered bridges crossing the Allegheny and Mononagahela rivers; a hotel and play resort in Huntington Hartford in Hollywood; a fifty-story hotel in Dallas; a department store in Amedabad, India; a hotel, apartments, shops, and a theater complex in Washington, D.C.; and two banks in Arizona. None of these was constructed, but they illustrated that the demand for the vigor and force of his genius was even stronger as he approached his eighth decade. With the design of the Guggenheim Museum a new grammar of construction and form had come into his hand, and the great projects of those and following years reveal a corresponding new sense of design and treatment of detail. A simplicity of form along with a plasticity of materials, both welded together as one, came about as a result of his expanded use of reinforced concrete—seen earlier in the design for Fallingwater and, even more so, in the Johnson Wax administration building. One building, designed during the war years, went into construction when the war was over: the Johnson Wax research laboratory, adjacent to the administration building he had designed in 1936.

**The Wright family at Taliesin West, 1946. From left to right: Olgivanna, Wright, Svetlana (Mrs. Peters), William Wesley Peters, and Iovanna.** FLLW Fdn FA#6401.0050

Tragedy struck the Wrights in the fall of 1946 when their daughter Svetlana was killed in an automobile accident as she was driving from Taliesin to the neighboring village of Spring Green. She was Olgivanna's daughter by a previous marriage, and was herself married to apprentice William Wesley Peters. His wife was crushed by the sudden loss of her oldest daughter. But Wright urged her to go on and to keep active in life. Daily he supported and encouraged her. Years later, after Wright himself had died, she reflected that his support of her during this terrible time in 1946 had given her the strength and fortitude to cope with the death of her husband in 1959.

Meanwhile, as he urged her to move ahead, in his own work there was a renewed acceleration of commissions, both commercial and residential. But Solomon Guggenheim's death in 1949 dealt a serious blow to the commission, and it looked for a while as if the building would never come to fruition. Adding new parcels of land to their existing site necessitated new designs and new working drawings. The museum itself changed its mission, expanded its collections, and hired a new director. Wright was called upon to answer to all of these changes in terms of design. But 1949 saw one important event in his life: He was awarded the Gold Medal of the American Institute of Architects on March 17. On accepting the award, Wright acknowledged his gratitude to his colleagues for this rare recognition of his contributions:

> Honors have reached me from almost every great nation in the world. Honor has, however, been a long time coming from home. But here it is at last. Handsomely, indeed. Yes . . . I am extremely grateful.[2]

B.B.P.

1. An Open Letter to Patrick Stone (Judge) from Frank Lloyd Wright, 18 December 1942. FLLW Fdn AV#2401.262.

2. Taliesin Square-Paper Number 13.

# DINNER TALK AT HULL HOUSE: NOVEMBER EIGHTH, 1939

**A**lmost forty years after his first talk given at Chicago's Hull House, which was founded as a social settlement by Jane Addams in 1889, Wright was invited to return to deliver another lecture. His address reiterated some of the points he had made in the 1901 paper "The Art and Craft of the Machine." This time he spoke of how the machine had indeed taken over the twentieth century, not as he envisioned it as "a tool in the hand of the artist" but as a deadly force that was enslaving mankind rather than freeing it:

> The Machine owns the man now. The Man does not own the machine as forty years ago I hoped and believed he might. We know that machinery has put some 19,000,000 workers into the unemployment lists. We know that it is the machine that has done this thing, yet no one is willing to admit it. Therein lies our misfortune.

He also spoke about the role of government in the arts, particularly in housing. He recalled a conversation he had recently had with a government official in the field:

> Out of the slums of today, you are making the slums of tomorrow. Personally, I do not believe government should be allowed to spend one dollar for creative work like Architecture, Painting, Music, Sculpture, or the Theater. My faith is that given the opportunity, having the sincere interior impulse, what we call "Art" is best left to take care of itself—if only we will get the artificial lets and hindrances like Education and Government out of the way.

He further spoke of his belief in decentralization and explained how it was made possible, practical, and serviceable to people by way of such proposals as Broadacre City, his model of an organized community with the requirements of modern living in a spacious environment. Wright placed the emphasis, and the responsibility, of these cures on the shoulders of the nation's architects:

> Architecture is the great art and science of structure. As such it must be the centerline of any true culture. None of the great cultures of the world but evolved an architecture to match, fulfill, and fructify the life lived.

Fully supporting Emerson's dictum that the best government is the least government, Wright, an ardently independent political thinker and firm believer in the force of the minority, wrote,

> Government. I am naturally enough suspicious of anything "governmental" in art. The reason is that

**Wright at the construction site of S.C. Johnson & Son Administration Building, Racine, Wisconsin. 1937.** FLLW Fdn FA#6801.0017

*nothing "ipso facto" can be helpful and govern-*
*ment may be only ipso facto if it is to survive—*
*in other words, win the next election.*

*[Speech published in part in Frederick Gut-*
*heim.* On Architecture. *New York: Duell, Sloan*
*and Pearce, 1940.]*

LADIES AND GENTLEMEN: [ALL RISE TO THEIR FEET FOLLOW-
ing the introduction by William Deknatel[1]—Mr.
Wright, moving the audience to be seated] Please sit
down: [Choosing to give a wrong interpretation to
the gesture of respect] I am not quite that old . . .
perhaps I've lived about 125 years but somehow
that has little or nothing to do with the case. So,
let's sit down, please. I came to talk informally to a
group at a single table only to find myself addressing
a multitude, with no prepared address—but—let
me see . . . Well. . . . About forty years ago over
there in the old library [almost all Hull House people present at that meeting are no longer with us
tonight] we had a good knock-down and drag-out
"fight" over a new Arts and Crafts Society for
Chicago. The enemy at that time—there is always
the enemy—were Ruskin and Morris reactionaries.
Ruskin and Morris had imbued the young life of
Chicago with a worthy ambition to make things by
hand, pound their fingers and do all sorts of unbecoming handicraft—good in its way but entirely beside the mark in our Chicago day's work. I couldn't
see that ambition as worth any man's time when everything around us was, by and large, going hideous
because the machine was out of hand. Direction
was lacking. I saw it necessary to go to work on our
surrounding ugliness at its source. But in this I was
supported only by Jane Addams, Julia Lathrop and
Florence Kelley. The others present turned away
from such profane, workaday suggestions.

To that meeting came a university professor,
Charles Zeublin by name—sociologist of the first
rank, but Ruskin and Morris pattern. He could
speak splendidly, while I couldn't do any better
than my young friend has just done now. [A mischievous glance at Deknatel who had consulted a
manuscript as he spoke.] Another voluble member
of that group, incipient in the arts and crafts move-

ment, was by name, Professor Oscar Lovell Triggs.
You may remember him as the man who said in
the public prints that Rockefeller was a greater fellow than Shakespeare? Yet he didn't last long at
the University of Chicago. To make a long story
shorter, between the erudite Professors Zeublin
and Triggs, I got badly set down. But Jane Addams,
bless her, Julia Lathrop and Florence Kelley were
not content. They postponed organization and
asked me to bring in a paper. [Mr. Wright outlines
the gist of the paper. That paper, by the way, has
since been published around the world in some
seven different languages.] Reading from that paper
I declared, in no uncertain terms, that the machine
*was* an artist's tool if and when in creative artists'
hands. "In creative artists' hands" was the catch in
it as I look back upon it now. Well . . . the young
arts-and-crafters, eager to go in for socially accred-
ited self-indulgence in the Arts, didn't believe what
I said because Ruskin and Morris had believed no
such thing. But the mill of the Gods grinds this
time exceedingly fast and here I stand tonight God-
father to the inauguration of that organic idea in
practical form here at Hull House. I can assure you
that this is, therefore, more than a mere sentimental occasion for me. And we seem quite able to proceed upon the basis then proposed. My young
friend, Deknatel, having been poisoned by that ideology (now the new modern idealism) while working for a time with me, and swelled to proper dimensions in consequence (we all swell), it does
seem as though, at long last, the *nature* of such tools
as we have, the *nature* of materials, the *nature* of
opportunity and purpose and the *nature* of our life
as we must live it today . . . again, in short, it does
seem as if—the great simplicities—may get a break.

Because these simple integrities of thought and
action were lacking, the Arts have been independently at each other's throats these hundreds of years
and we find them dependent or moribund now if we
try to live as we conclude we ought to live. Meantime our youth have been sterilized by professional
theories, intimidated by scholarly armchair estheti-
cians until, because of such intimidation, Architecture itself, which ought to be flourishing because
of all the building needed by a new nation, has lan-

guished until it is about ready for burial as Architecture. Yes . . . the scholarly-aesthetician was the correct thing in our American Architecture, with his History of Art in his hand, teaching exactly as *he* was taught—while Life passed him by. So the only thing the new country could see to decently use in the circumstances was what we call "Colonial"—bastard of Classic tradition washed up on our Eastern shore.

Concerning the validity of that Colonial tradition: Invited to take the Sir George Watson Chair for the year 1939, I have just lately been in England. At the first meeting in the new Hall of F.R.I.B.A. I said England had had a Declaration of Independence from us, July 4, 1776, concerning taxes and now England was going to have another, May 1939, concerning the spirit. (A minority report I confessed.) And I politely invited cultural England to get off our cultural chest; I declared we had been harassed long enough by English "old-colonial" and that I didn't think it was ever worth much even to them because it was the dwindling end of a decadent French culture when they got it and it was all certainly worth less than nothing to us when we were confronted with the building of a new nation. Well, strange to say, they readily agreed with me. Another thing not so strange and that you should know, for reasons I will explain, is that Paris agreed, too. While I was still in England, the Director General of the Beaux Arts, the President of the International Society of Architects and the Mayor of Paris sent a delegate to London to invite me to attend a little dinner in Paris (in my honor, yes) . . . and lecture there. I declined the lectures because I will lecture in no language but my own, distrusting interpreters almost as much as stenographers. But I gladly attended the dinner and afterward spent three days in Paris going about with Beaux-Arts architects looking at recent architecture. I saw many extraordinary modern buildings there as I had also seen them in the Balkan cities. I don't think we have many as genuinely advanced as those. I was surprised because I was familiar only with reactionary Beaux-Arts attitudes in the schools of our own country, I saw I would have to reverse my feeling about the Paris Beaux Arts. Said I, "I have never thought much of the Beaux Arts training in our country." Said the President and the Director General,

"We don't think much of it in your country either." They probably didn't realize the brick they were handing to me. I suppose it is ungentlemanly to throw it now . . . but, just for good measure I will tell you that the Director General and the President said: "We have wanted to show you we are standing shoulder to shoulder with you."

Now you of the Arts and Crafts may take that as you may. I mention it to show you how much in line with modern progress in other countries you are at Hull House at this moment as we begin where I tried to begin so far back as about forty years ago? Here we are, not quite "forty years later," starting the work at Hull House that will make the buildings of today better buildings, better furnished, easier to build and easier to work and live in every day than ever buildings were before, just because of modern tools and our ways with them. The tenets of this Arts and Crafts Society today cannot be "aesthetics" in the old sense. They will not be "artistic" either. We won't call the tenets we hold "Art" perhaps. Long ago I began to suspect the term when I heard it and now do whenever I read it. Anyone following through with some understanding of means to ends and with the great desire of great purpose . . . not many such will feel deeply concerned today with the terms "aesthetic" or "artistic." Yes . . . the enemy forty years ago was Ruskin and Morris. They conquered then. Today, I hesitate to say it in the circumstances but . . . well . . . I believe I still see the enemy here again tonight . . . well, Government. I am naturally enough suspicious of anything "governmental" in art. The reason is that nothing "ipso facto" can be helpful and government may be only ipso facto if it is to survive—in other words win the next election. For instance, Government won't lend money on anything that is today or tomorrow. "They" won't lend money or give a hand to the builder of a house which is to be "the" better house ten years from now. Believe it or not, "they" will only lend to you upon yesterday . . . and then only in the middle of the road. Yes, our yesterday is their tomorrow. Now, lots of things can be done by way of committee meeting just as valuable and necessary things *must* be done by way of government. But you cannot do much that way in what we call creative art. So I fear it is going to be more than difficult to come through with the radical ideas which are the natural basis of all creative endeavor by way of "official" aid. No . . . nothing "official" in our new national experiment has ever encouraged original thinking in any cultural situation. Government cannot speculate nor can it experiment except at peril. On the other hand it can take hold and consolidate what gains have been made in spite of it. *But how to get on with it to where we must go from there?* As I have seen that necessity, that is no affair for Government. I may be looking the gift horse in the teeth and be embarrassing at the moment but frankly I am concerned about what might be the case with Hull House provided a Federal instructive movement were undertaken there and "took us over" in the Arts. How far *could* such minor officialdom "conscientiously" let us live? Because of the very radical nature of such creative effort as this must be no less than because of its own character, government would be bound to be afraid of anything so radical. I am one of those men, of course, who have never had luck with government nor with any committee meeting either, unless some one strong man was on the committee who could say what was to happen.

In passing, since I have dwelt at length on distrust of government, just for good measure there is one more occasion for distrust. [Mr. Wright here told of a conversation with Nathan Straus[2] starting with an account of how Mr. Straus, indicating the progress U.S.H.A.[3] had made, marked off a corner of a very large director's table, saying that "what had been done was as that small corner to the whole table."]

I felt thankful. I felt thankful that it had gone no further, for this reason: because we, you and I everywhere are called upon to pay a little more rent to unearned increment so these desolate people of the slums may have a shower, a flower box, and a patch of lawn. So far, so good, but what I saw in Government housing was the skyscraper laid down on its side—that's all—ourselves invited to help the poor into it to stay in it. I saw government making a national *institution* of poverty, poverty so subsidized by us that impoverishment must go on paying rent, forever. Mr. Straus kindly asked me to have dinner with him that night to meet some dozen other architects, most of them working for him. At dinner he asked

me what I thought about what I had seen of "housing" in his office that day. I hesitated. "Do you really want to know?" I asked. He did, so I told him the truth . . . "Out of the slums of today, you are making the slums of tomorrow." He didn't believe me nor like it. Pressed for reasons I said, "Flower boxes and tubs are good camouflage. Camouflage isn't really what the poor need." Now I believe that if you and I are going to pay this subsidy out of our own pockets why should we continue to pay more rent to Realty? Why not pay the money to *Transportation?* Make it easy for poverty to escape and cease to be poverty? Why not break down this iron ring that urban realty throws around poverty? Why not take "the poor" out and set them down where they can come and go rent-free someday and meantime learn to earn from the ground as well as at the bench?

Yes, U.S.H.A. Housing is (and Hull House should know it) just another basis for distrust of the Governmental where ideas are needed. The life of the people is here concerned and, of course, where the people should live their own lives in their own way. Personally, I do not believe government should be allowed to spend one dollar for creative work like Architecture, Painting, Music, Sculpture, or the Theater. My faith is that given the opportunity, having the sincere internal impulse, what we call "Art" is best left to take care of itself—*if only we will get the artificial lets and hindrances like Education and Government out of the way.* Or where they belong, somewhere in the background. I say, let's stand back and give indigenous culture a chance to live on its own feet! Shame to say nothing of the kind will soon have a chance to live that way in our "Free" country.

Here I am again using the term "creative art." Did I bring the term in here tonight or did my young friend Deknatel? But nevertheless at Hull House you should be on the radical ground the term necessarily implies. And if you are so *you will be so entirely on your own.* Unfortunately for you Art, though still Art, in our time has not been Art according to the spirit of great work but only living upon the letter—that is to say the History of Art. Look around you now and see the consequences in our establishments of great wealth.

In our culture power and boundless resources

everywhere but integrity of means to ends nowhere. I guess primarily our blood *is* financial, our mind money. But all around our nation the other countries of the world are beginning to see the great modern improvements that have cost us so much take effect in new cultural forms. We have mostly thrown them away because to use them has not been "historical" and to so use them "unbankable." *Authority* has allowed nothing to live in the way of culture that was indigenous except as this puny, silly little "Colonial tradition" might be so. And of course it is not so at all. Always I have seen cultural progress within us up against that precious remnant of would-be aesthetic self-righteousness. As for government's share in all this: observe the buildings at Washington. Every one of them is without exception superficially, expensively, falsely traditional. A monument to Abraham Lincoln? Gone to Greece. To Thomas Jefferson, the radical of his time, give him the latest thing from Rome. But I like to believe that the grand picture *that* spurious monument to Tom makes is the last defiant grandomania of scholastic obstruction: the natural end of the aesthetician's waste of life and opportunity to which we are officially bound and must call "Classic" or say "Colonial." Notwithstanding all well-meant official or educational abuse whatsoever I believe our national soul is our own but so far as culture goes I can see it only as way down underneath as in out of the way places. The States are, of course, in point of culture still a little one-horse-England, the more so the farther East we go. Hence this solicitude of a parent for a necessarily tender young effort such as this one dedicated here at Hull House tonight? Will it begin to be usefully felt, its native, well-intentioned ubiquitous enemies—governmental and educational—notwithstanding?

It *is* true that in any circumstances whatever Creative Art is not something you can go out and find when you will and then tell it where to get off as you please. Nor is it something schools can teach the masses. But you may inoculate the ground for it, widen the measure of appreciation of its coming. You may inculcate it too and government can buy the tools and furnish the materials. But the creative thing, I am sure, will come from the direction you least expect. Usually it comes out of the more simple things by way of men with unspoiled (that is to say not too sophisticated) minds. I do not mean simpleminded. I mean the mind that is simple, born with sincerity. Creative art is usually sincere, sometimes childlike, but never childish. Yet childishness we see everywhere, on the radio, in the movies, in painting especially. Almost never do we experience or see the feeling of joy in work and unselfish enthusiasm for the idea behind work that means the true creative spirit. Why? Democrats aren't we? Then why don't we trust life? Why is this great experiment in democracy so afraid of the consequences of the very thing we profess: freedom? Is it because there is yet much too much *property* at stake? Even so why are we so afraid of *ourselves?* Even the more intelligent and free among us dare not encourage radical freedom in this matter of culture. That is to say, actual freedom. How then can a government so elected and officialized or a university so endowed ever encourage individual life? Democracy?

What I have just given to you as provincial in our society is really at the moment the psychology of this nation. We are—look at our cultural acts—just provincials. That monument to Thomas Jefferson for proof! It is the latest evidence.

Now, what is the chief characteristic of the provincial mind? I say it is FEAR! Fear that we won't come off in good style. Any provincial will watch to see what everybody else is doing . . . and try to do it as though it were the way he would have done it anyway. That is why we are a little One-Horse England. When I went to England on a cultural errand I knew this. But only while there did I fully realize it. Few of us ever realize more than a small portion of what we know. But I have, somehow, found my way down the line for forty-five years nevertheless and notwithstanding because I do believe implicitly in the human soul and trust—myself. It is the first condition of trusting others. We could have had a great architecture of our own today which would mean a growing culture if we had allowed ourselves to learn something of Architecture. But Fashion still rules in Education and Government. So just as we have our clothes so we have our houses, we have our teaching and, no less so, our regulations. The Fashion has made up appearances throughout the country until the life of the nation is afraid to say its soul is its own. As an architect studying *structure,* his life devoted to combat this deadly cultural lag, one watchword I hand on to you tonight—the word *decentralization. Decentralize all along the line!* Exaggeration is not greatness nor anything like it. Time was when it was one of the wonders of the world with us. It is now our curse.

Well . . . at any rate, this isn't the voice of a mere dissenter. I do have genuine faith and enthusiasm for what I believe to be the first principles underneath true culture in this our country. Haven't I broken both fists over opposition to that? Before that hope is done and over with I would gladly throw the broken fists after the breaking. I desire the integrity of indigenous culture for our United States more than anything I can name outside love for those dear to me and I hope and believe Hull House will continue a pioneer in this field, no matter, now, where the enemy sits or how. And I see (meeting Miss Charlotte Carr for the first time) that you have a good general sitting here beside me to carry on wonderful Jane Addams' work for Democracy.

To get back, once more, to our art and craft thesis tonight, I want to say that the thesis has changed, somewhat, since that evening nearly forty years ago. The Machine owns the man now. The Man does not own the machine as forty years ago I hoped and believed he might. We know that machinery has put some 19,000,000 workers into unemployment lists. We know that it is abuse of the machine that has done this thing, yet no one is willing to admit it. Therein lies our misfortune. Yes . . . I stood at Hull House forty years ago championing the machine as a creative artist's tool, if placed in his hands to be used to make human life better worth living. But I have since seen it, by degrees, taken away from him and seen it fall instead into the hands, at best of schoolboys, or next best, of commercialized advertising experts, to be superficially streamlined or at worst dominated by professional exploiters of human life. And it has become apparent to me by now that almost anyone can speak the language of our modern architecture, but how few seem able to actually get inside by long devotion to the practical use of organic principle and do something about it that might be called organic?

I have done something about it along that line myself, and modeled a free pattern for Democracy. [At this point Mr. Wright told a story about a great friend of Jane Addams—his uncle Rev. Jenkin Lloyd Jones.] He said—Jenkin Lloyd Jones was building a settlement—Lincoln Center—a kind of church on the South Side of Chicago—"to do for the rich," so he said, "what Jane Addams' Hull House was doing for the poor." I tried to plan the building for him, but we couldn't agree. "Frank," he would say, "I've been all over the world; have seen more great buildings than you've ever seen. Can't you trust me?" (But he didn't say he'd seen more buildings than I had ever *imagined*.) "No . . ." I said—"not with *my* building." (The struggle for culture in Chicago was like that with some of us then and is sometimes now.) Sure enough, it was his building before he got through as you may see for yourselves down there on Oakwood Boulevard. But Jenkin Lloyd Jones' declaration that his settlement was to do for the rich what Jane Addams' "Settlement" was doing for the poor struck me and stayed right along with me to bear fruit—Broadacre City. My first concern, then as now, is with the rich. My work is done mainly in the real slums of our great country—the upper income brackets of the gold coasts, peacock alleys and penthouses of our cities. You laugh . . . but no, really, I mean what I say. Their plight is tragic. I well know the real poverty-stricken America today is our ultra-successful rich citizenry.

So . . . during the dreadful time when we all had nothing at all to do (the breakdown we politely call "depression" was severe for about seven years, I think) I knew most of my friends, those I had worked with and learned to love, had blood running down behind their dress shirt fronts—all dying a thousand deaths when they needed die but one. Having pinned their faith to "having" they must now "hold" simply because to *have* in that sense means to *hold*. Holding was now agony and futility. The circumstances were pretty tough for rich and poor alike—but toughest of all for the rich. And yet I lived to see at that time a number of my rich friends form a ring around me to keep me at work when "they" tried to drive me into the streets to get a worm's-eye view of society. Then why shouldn't *I* go to work for *them?* I did. I went to work on Broadacre City. A way out for the rich as well as for the poor. But the funny thing is that having attained a cross-section of our civilization and evolved a free pattern which would let my friends out of misery and uncertainty to enjoy and live in fruitfulness and peace, came their criticism: "He's just Communist" said some, or "He's a Fascist" said others, or "He's Escapist" still others said. They said anything and everything except to say what the City really was—a true basis for trying out genuine Capitalism. I believe that someday Capital will be honest enough so that honest Capitalism will really be tried out as the basis for honest Democracy. There in the models for Broadacre City I tried to establish a sound basis for trying it out. So, after the models of the City had gone around the country for a while, exhibited first in Rockefeller Center (a wonder the Center didn't fall in on the model) I took it all back to Taliesin.[4] But we are not through with it. Broadacre City is again going out on exhibition, soon, in important places with sharper, clearer explanations than before.

My young workers in the Arts! Nature-study is your study. Out of the nature of materials comes the nature of the thing to be done for the nature of the purpose for which it was intended. Incidentally I will say, as might be expected, that organic integrity was as lacking in these things we called the New York World's Fair and the Chicago World's Fair as it was in the Columbian Fair. Both were characteristic opportunities to express ourselves in our new conditions but nothing happened. Of course we could afford to throw *them* all away. But what, really, is our ideal? I have assumed all along that it was genuine freedom of life for the individual as an individual! Democracy? Well . . . instead of that greater freedom of thought and action in a culture of today, we are imprisoned by reactionary imitations finally at the mercy of these great improvements we haven't recognized in our culture at all. The city is becoming a hideous waste. Especially have we neglected the nature of the swift simple clean-cut elements of space and speed of our time, except to imitate their superficial aspects. Our culture is officially—educationally—bound eye, hand and foot to neglect these things best adapted to purpose today—Space and Speed. We may see the progress of both anywhere only as a confusing physical fact except in Organic Architecture. Otherwise nothing of either as cultural idea characterizes our life. We are unaware of the nature of the man now. He has changed so much in forty years. He is mobilized for one thing. And he is electronic. Before he had gone two or three steps forty years ago he has now gone several miles and is already by way of going ten more to every one of them. So, to catch up with him we need intensive Nature study of him, and within his new circumstances everywhere. Yes, more and better organic nature study in every expression of him. Such fundamental thinking in simples is what Culture needs and of course is most needed in this endeavor here. I urge you to be patient in this research.When I say "Nature" I do not mean the great out of doors merely (picking up a table knife), I mean the nature of this thing in my hand for instance. And in that same philosophic sense the nature of whatever is. This means that you must learn to see Life as *structure,* therefore see its *Architecture*. Architecture is the great art and science of *structure*. As such it must be the centerline of any true culture. None of the great cultures of the world but evolved an architecture to match, fulfill, and fructify the life lived. If only Usonians had had enough sense to see Architecture that way we too might have had great culture on the way.

The Architecture of yesterday, like the Architecture we need today, was timely and indigenous when it really was Architecture. If we would only understand that.

Now this rambling talk which I expected to give to a few around a single table and find myself giving to a multitude must come to an end. I am glad to give my blessing, such as it is, to this endeavor. I would like to see it well grounded and happily on its way. You may attribute any fears I have expressed to parental solicitude—not to disillusion. Anything I may do to help, I am going to do.

[Miss Charlotte Carr rose to champion Government at Hull House. When she had done Mr. Wright stood up beside her to say these concluding words after applause had subsided]:

In conclusion—Patriotic as we are here at this moment do you realize we have never even had an appropriate name for our own country? Samuel Butler gave us one: "USONIA," a word derived from Union. So why not name our nation USONIA?[5]

What the people of our country need most is beauty of environment. What we need most is some correlation in these things we, by habit, call Art. There must be some cooperation of effort between them all because the idea informing all is the same. Science, Art, Religion are one.

First of all our concern is to make more excellent use of modern advantages. They will otherwise destroy us. That concern may well begin in what we used to call but need no longer call the kitchen [pointing to the table]. Now this table is well furnished and set. But it is the usual collection of many too many articles for much too much of everything.

Just for a significant little example . . . no one in our nation, with all the teaching of art we have had, has ever been moved to abolish from the table this brutal butcher's tool (holds up again the knife he had previously taken in hand).

The great task today is one of elimination. First to eliminate the insignificant and then correlate what remains. Vital new forms are needed for environment, new expressions of life as now changed and as it will change continually. That is your task at Hull House. This task cannot be performed by painters. They paint. The same is true of sculptors. They sculpt. True of weavers and potters. They weave and pot. All, long ago, took a little shovel full of coals and went off somewhere to start a little hell of their own. Painting, the universal favorite, no longer contributes much to environment. As representation it is prostitute. The camera has disposed of it. Pictures are hung on walls or painted *on* them—they are not *of* them. The easel picture has become a kind of accomplished self-indulgence, sensual as eating or pessimistic as a Broadway wise cracker. Therefore such correlation as we desire can come, only, from the Architect.

In our culture we have no real sense of unity because we do not know this and have made no common cause with *structure*. We have not made *structure* the center line of culture nor of economics nor of education. And until we have made it so . . .

until we begin with a fundamental understanding of organic structure we have nothing to build a good life upon. This applies to music too, but it applies especially to anything at all in the Arts or in Civilization because it is especially essential to good life. Out of an endeavor such as this should come a certain get-together of the Arts and out of that needed correlation would in good time come noble environment for the people of our United States.

The creative mind must be trained afresh in *structure* by masters of the *altogether* and the Architect is today, more than ever before, that master. In our provincial society any great architect must be termed a radical (the word means roots—at the root). Were our eyes opened we would see that the radical is the actual conservative. Cultivate that type of effort and that type of mind among you whenever you find it. You need the mind that can see at the root this thing we call life coming together as a whole and not merely know but *realize* that Science, Art, and Religion are indivisible. That mind will be an architect's mind. And so I say you are fortunate and right in having for your leader a young architect—the one who introduced me to you tonight. He will be helpful to you in this attempt to hold everything well together, giving to each thing its true proportion and right significance in the fresh synthesis good life must ever continue to be.

---

1. William Deknatel (1905–1972) was one of the earliest apprentices at Taliesin. He later opened his own firm in Chicago (1936–1971); active in urban renewal and social welfare, he served as president of Hull House from 1953 to 1962.

2. Nathan Straus (1889–1961), a journalist and public official, headed the U.S. Housing Authority from 1937 to 1942. The Straus family owned Macy's department store from 1896 until 1968.

3. One of a number of federal agencies, the U.S. Housing Authority coordinated urban low-rent and slum clearance projects.

4. The Broadacre City model, after being initially exhibited at Rockefeller Center, traveled to Pittsburgh; Washington, D.C.; Madison and Iowa County, Wisconsin; and Marquette, Michigan, before returning to Taliesin.

5. "USONIA" was an acronym for the United States of North America, which Wright first used in 1925. He credited Samuel Butler for its creation, but no one has yet been able to find the original quote.

# TO THE FIFTY-EIGHTH

**P**ublished in the October issue of the Journal of the Royal Institute of British Architects, *this article is a rebuttal to some of the criticisms brought about by Wright's lectures in London in May 1939.[1] He defended his position on man and the machine: "I began my work as architect by sensibly accepting the machine as the creative artist's inevitable tool, believing that only where such as he had it in control could it prove a blessing instead of a curse." But now forty years since his first address on the "Arts and Crafts of the Machine," he realized what the Machine had become:*

> *Have I "changed" because I used to say the machine is the artist's tool and now say that man should use the machine and not the machine use man? . . . The man is not using the machine! The machine is using the man and is using him so he is losing himself . . . becoming a "thing" beneath his push button and steering wheel. Neither are by him or for him. Already he is started and steered by forces beyond his control, owing to feudal hangovers society will not yet give up.*

*In addition to outlining his thoughts on community life, he also confronted in this paper the proponents of the International Style with a typically provocative proposal: "I suggest you put a gently sloping roof on any Le Corbusier or Gropius [building] just to see what you have left of the so-called International Style after proper deductions have been made."[2]*

IF PRINTED REACTIONS TO MY TALKS IN LONDON—NO speaker really—which should have reached me there but now reach me at Taliesin mean anything, I have succeeded in getting myself misunderstood and well disliked, especially by those who should have been quick to understand me. I refer to the 58th variety—"the fruit of my own orchard"? For such pains as I took in the circumstances I am accused of disowning the "fruit of my own orchard" when I intended only to cut down saplings interfering with good fruit. Therefore certain intellectualists (saplings) are saying I am changed to "escapist." A bad word, their word "escapist"? Why call names? Why not go to work? *Do* something on their own that doesn't take refuge with the incompetent in a "universal" pattern for

something that (should it abide with principle) ought to be as alive and various as human character is itself!

And have I "changed" or only smashed myself as idol? I intended to smash that idol but only to let idol worshippers a little closer than they now seem to want to go. Hero worship is sometimes pretty awful. That any of mine can now bear hide or hair of me would surprise me.

But, can't they be sports and smart as they, and I, think they are? Don't they know that every word of their own European creed, every form they use at least if not the every way they use it, came either directly or indirectly from my own "*escape*"?

Can they really believe Taliesin turning its face away from life because it refuses to see any pattern as "fit for the establishment of any contemporary vernacular" whatsoever and lives out in the country instead of some urban backyard or city slum? Can they believe that we at Taliesin advocate a "back-to-the-land" movement? Do they really imagine that I build self-indulgences for capitalistic parasites in the name of esoteric philosophy and work for the rich, that my buildings are expensive, etc., etc? I would like to compare the cost of them with the cost of theirs. Is the idea that good architecture must be, first of all, good building and the architect a master-builder first and an aesthetician afterward—heresy? Is the idea that good community life is the life of the individual raised to the *n*th power rather than the life of the individual reduced to the lowest common denominator—idealistic hallucination? Cake? In this connection I ask M.A.R.S.[3] . . . again . . . which came first—hen or egg? Well—if the egg is the *Idea* then the egg came first—and, just so—society. First the great Individual (the Idea or Egg) then Society (the Hen). After that what have you?

Do they advocate abandoning women and children to be bombed in English, German, or Russian slums? All great cities are slums now—communism or no communism. They like them. Why?

Are they so in love with intellectualizations they can't see any true surface, or see any surface true, because of obliterating reflections? Then what hope to escape some universal pattern for the individual human soul named after some European?

I could only prove to them that today my building is as far in advance of my building, 1893–1911, as my building of that period was in advance of that around about it at the time, by teaching them to put two and two together so they will not make just *one* "four" but make *infinite* fours?

Once and for all concerning this constantly repeated reference to my contribution to Architecture as a kind of romanticism: because any attempt on their part to establish a "contemporary vernacular" is defied by the revelations of principle eternally fresh and new in every building I build—they drag in the term "Romanticism" to conceal their own importance whereas it really only explains it.

I love Romance as I love sentiment. But just as I dislike sentimentality I would dislike their "Romance." I suggest you put a gently sloping roof on

any Le Corbusier or Gropius just to see what you have left of the so-called International Style after proper deductions have been made.

Boys, you are all going knowing *why* but not knowing *where*. Then why do you speak so much and so surely of *how?*

And I see some chance remark of mine led a few to draw the absurd conclusion that we at Taliesin don't keep in touch with "life as is" because we aren't newspaper addicts.

Have I "changed" because I used to say the machine is the artist's tool and now say that man should use the machine and not the machine use man? Believing that I see, now as then, the only way he can use it I took the idea to them. Amused . . . a little bored . . . I observe the fact that those who got the seed and raise the flowers now consider themselves creative-par with the seed they use. Is this why some form of imitation in their generation is more acceptable than the original? Is that why my own thought and work must go home by way of some derivative, not by me? I accept that backwash as European reaction on the way toward the "International Style": a style that could never be Democratic because it is *the use of man by the machine.* Are "they" striving to perfect that? Why thus fail to distinguish between the economies of living and the forces of life? That distinction is only *"Romantic"* to them? Is it?

If only "they" would take as much pains to really understand me as I have in trying to justify their presence in the "orchard"—we might go places together, mutual help . . . first aid to a desperate world in dire need.

Well—what do "they" say?

I began my work as architect by sensibly accepting the machine as the creative artist's inevitable tool believing that only where such as he had it in control could it prove a blessing instead of a curse. I saw the consequences of machinery: standardization, extreme urbanization, human life becoming more and more vicarious and so more and more removed from the ground. I saw that life might be made dependent upon push button and steering wheel—saw it without flinching. I saw human energy reduced to ohms and K.W., germs and glands—saw life centralized until it was at the mercy of the push button

**Members of the Taliesin Fellowship making the model of the Herbert F. Johnson House, "Wingspread," 1940. Photograph by Pedro E. Guerrero.** FLLW Fdn FA#6504.0051

and steering wheel—still believing salvation lay in creative artist control. I had faith in that.

I still have faith. But, *where is that creative force to-day?* The man is not using the machine! *The machine is using the man* and is using him so he is losing himself . . . becoming a "thing" beneath his push button and steering wheel. Neither are *by* him or *for* him. Already he is started and steered by forces beyond his control, owing to feudal hangovers society will not yet give up.

I see now as I saw then—that the only way man can use the machine—not let it use him—is to get it as a working principle into work by way of the great human force we used to call creative-artist. Well . . . again, where is he?

If he exists now he will probably be found under some other name, because, as he stood in no-man's land, the machine has already wiped him out as any constructive element in social life today. I foresaw this possibility. I did not accept it.

Le Corbusier, Gropius, *et al.*, are yet where I stood in 1900. I do not recant nor resign the position I then took but I have *experienced* my own philosophy. I have seen it taking partial effect by way of the generations following me. What I started to do, with high faith, and confidence in human-creative forces, I see giving way to certain sterilizing factors in my original equation. Instead of mastering those

factors on the side of creation, Europe has seen only a new aesthetic for academic consumption in a foolish effort to establish a contemporary vernacular. So, bid to England, I came with another "Declaration of Independence." This time one concerned, not with taxes, but with independence of any aesthetic whatsoever where this matter of *life as structure* is concerned—social, political, or artistic. I said that the only way man can use his machine and *keep alive what is best in him* is to go by means of it to the larger freedom the machine makes possible—go toward *decentralization* instead of continuing the centralization the machine exploits and, so far as any great human benefit goes, will soon explode.

Simple enough?

Do I continue to befog the issue? If so the Machine itself will prove me right. Meantime I can wait and work.

1. See *Frank Lloyd Wright Collected Writings Volume 3,* "An Organic Architecture," (1939), pp. 299–334.

2. For more on Wright's opinions about the International Style see "To My Critics in the Land of the Danube and the Rhine" (1931); "To the Neuter," "Of Thee I Sing," "For All May Raise the Flowers Now For All Have Got the Seed" (1932); and "Architecture of Individualism" (1934) in *Frank Lloyd Wright Collected Writings Volume 3.*

3. The Modern Architectural Research Group was founded in London in 1933. Advocating the introduction of rationalism, one of their projects was a plan for completely rebuilding London.

# CHICAGO'S AUDITORIUM IS FIFTY YEARS OLD

**O**n the fiftieth anniversary of the completion of Adler & Sullivan's great building, The Architectural Forum published this article by Wright in its September issue. A logical and integrated composition, the auditorium was the genesis of Sullivan's mature style. Although a commission for the firm of Adler & Sullivan, the concept, design structure, and engineering of the building was singularly Adler's. Wright emphasizes this point: "Sullivan, designing partner, was novice in those days. The respect and affection of the two partners for each other seemed unbounded. . . . The dramatic expression of the interior was Sullivan's." By 1887, when the commission was underway and Sullivan needed draftsmen to carry out his ideas for the interior decorations, the twenty-year-old Wright had arrived in Chicago and applied for a job at the office of Adler & Sullivan. At Sullivan's request he returned some days later with a selection of his own drawings and sketches. Sullivan had no prior inkling of who this young man from Madison, Wisconsin, was, but he recognized Wright's drafting skill and hired him immediately. Many of the drawings for the ornamental features throughout the auditorium's interiors are by Wright but are in the idiom of Louis Sullivan, whom he came to call Lieber Meister. Wright worked in the firm for nearly seven years before leaving to open his own office.

Adler was unquestionably a formidable personality. But his remarkable sense of engineering, and especially of acoustics, won Wright's admiration from the moment Wright came to work for the firm. The greatness of their buildings was due, without doubt, to Adler as the engineer and Sullivan as the designing partner. One without the other could never produce the same remarkable oeuvre. When Wright was elevated to the position of Chief of Design, he had, along with Louis Sullivan, Dankmar Adler, and the contractor Paul Mueller, his own private office. The other members of the firm worked in the main drafting room or the general office. Adler would occasionally bring in to Wright's office a design or detail drawn by one of the draftsmen and exclaim, "Here, Wright, can't you nift this up a bit?" And when he witnessed the result of Wright's "nifting it up a bit," he would remark, "Well, Wright, I see you are still snatching victory from the jaws of defeat!" [Published in The Architectural Forum, September 1940]

**Adler and Sullivan Auditorium Building, Interior, Chicago, Illinois. 1890. Photograph courtesy Chicago Architectural Photographing Company, David R. Phillips.** FLLW Fdn FA#8801.0001

THE AUDITORIUM WAS THE LARGEST AND MOST IMPORTANT commission Adler & Sullivan, or any architect in America, had had up to that time. The building became famous before it was completed.

We used to call Dankmar Adler "Chief" in those busy days when the Auditorium was building, and he stood squarely in the midst of the great turmoil, solidly dominating the whole building process, from the trenches where the footings were going into a floating foundation, to the great trusses that later spanned the greatest room for opera the world has ever seen.

Contractors would take a drink before they came to "get it" from the Chief. I've heard him take one of them on as a mastiff would pick up a rat, shake him and drop him. I've seen them red-faced and perspiring leaving his little place next the outer office, mopping their brows, but jacked up to better work and more of it. Or perhaps condemned to tear out what they had done and do it over again as he had told them to do it in the first place. Most of the profit had gone out of the job because they had tried and failed to fool the Old Man. These would be green ones. Those who knew him feared and respected him mightily. He was master of their craft and they knew it. His bushy brows at that time almost hid a pair of piercing gray eyes. His square gray beard and squarish head seemed square with the building, and his personal solidity was a guarantee that out of all that confusion would issue the beauty of order.

During that constructive war time I've heard Louis Sullivan's cry of "Adler! Adler!"—the cry rising every now and then in emergency appeals to the chief. In emergencies, not only *lieber meister* but all of us always turned to Adler. "Adler!" was the common cry in the drafting room as on the works. And Adler never failed anybody. We used to feel him back of us just as the gangs on the building did. He would range up alongside the boards and put a heavy point straight without hesitation. At other times he would ponder, with a guttural growl, and invariably come out with what was needed to straighten out the problem. And tough problems were coming up day in and day out for years.

Sullivan, designing partner, was novice in those days. The respect of the two partners for each other—and affection too—seemed unbounded. Adler, master of that particular plan for the Auditorium, was Sullivan's best critic, and his judgment quieted and strengthened greatly the final result.

Adler himself had never developed the facility in design naturally possessed by Sullivan, but Sullivan himself at that time had no such grasp of building technique as was necessary to build this vast, complicated building, and had acquired no power at all over either the men building it or the men owning the enterprise.

The Chicago Auditorium was entirely Adler's commission and more largely Adler's own building than Sullivan's—where its constitution and plan were concerned. The dramatic expression of the interior was Sullivan's; and that of the exterior, Richardson's influence, I should say, except the square tower developed by Adler's criticism and, after the footings were already in, raised by Sullivan to a more dominating mass. This tower was the best feature of the outside, the one causing most trouble and receiving most careful study from both men. They were both satisfied with it, but the additional height caused serious settlement that never ceased to worry the Chief.

The receding elliptical arches spanning the great room were the best feature of the interior, and they were a development by Sullivan of Adler's invention of the sounding board or sloping ceiling above the proscenium; it had marked all Adler auditoriums before he took the young genius Sullivan in.

Most of this work in planning the Auditorium took place in the Borden block, now destroyed, but long before the opening we all moved into the new offices in the tower, where we were in constant touch with what went on below, an industrial world under a great architect.

Stagecraft has not advanced much since that day. Adler's Auditorium stage would stand up with the best stages in the world today. Acoustics were Dankmar Adler's specialty. There is no house in the world equal to the Auditorium in that respect. Among all the theaters built by Adler, and later by Adler & Sullivan, there were no failures acoustically.

A pity that the great room should not now be the Chicago home of grand opera!

# TO ARIZONA

**W**right first went to Arizona during the winter of 1928–1929, when he was called in as consulting architect for the design of the Arizona Biltmore Hotel. Phoenix, where he and his family lived for that period, was a small town at that time, and the desert, with its surrounding rim of mountains, was close at hand. He immediately fell in love with the region, which at that time was sparsely populated and unspoiled:

> Here all is sculptured by wind and water, patterned in color and texture. Rocks and reptiles no less so than the cacti. A desert building should be notably simple in outline as the region itself is sculptured.

He returned the next year, this time to design and build a new resort hotel near the town of Chandler, some miles south of Phoenix. Given the choice of renting space for his family and corps of seven draftsmen or building something of his own, he naturally elected to build. The resulting wood and canvas tentlike structure was called Ocotilla. There he made the preliminary drawings and construction documents for the resort, San Marcos-in-the-Desert. Living in a structure of his own design, close to the life and drama of the desert again, enthralled him.

In the winter of 1934–1935 he again migrated to Arizona, but now with the members of the Taliesin Fellowship (about thirty young men and women), and rented a space in Chandler called The Hacienda, set up shop, and prepared the models of Broadacre City and related structures.

In 1935 he sketched out an article entitled "To Arizona," in which he extolled the environment and warned the citizens of Arizona not to endanger, destroy, and thereby sacrifice the state's remarkable natural features, including the desert. He reminded them of its value as a playground with clean air and pure sunlight, and that, as such, it was a place where the touring public would come each winter to escape other, colder, zones.

By 1936 he was again in the Phoenix region, this time to recuperate from pneumonia. During that trip his wife encouraged him to think about building a permanent home in the desert, one to which he, his family, and the Taliesin Fellowship could migrate each winter from the unbearable cold of Wisconsin:

> To live indoors with the Fellowship during a Northern winter would be hard on the Fellowship and hard on us. We are an outdoor outfit; besides it costs thirty-five hundred dollars to heat all our buildings at Taliesin, so it is cheaper to move Southwest. The trek across the continent began November, 1933. Each trek was an event of the first magnitude. The Fellowship's annual hegira with sleeping bags and camping outfit, big canvas-covered truck, cars and trailers for thirty-five, was an event even in Fellowship

*life. The first several years we stayed at Dr. Chandler's hacienda at Chandler, Arizona. Very happy there, too, but crazy to build for ourselves.*[1]

*By 1940 Taliesin West, the name chosen for this winter camp-home-studio, had been in construction for two years and was nearly completed. Drafting room, studio, office, dining room, and galley were up and in use; quarters for the Wrights and their apprentices were nearing completion as well. Up to that time, they had all lived on the desert in tents or temporary wood and canvas shelters. Life was primitive, to say the least: no water, no electricity, no heat, no plumbing.*

*In May 1940, the "camp" was published for the first time in the magazine* Arizona Highways. *For this article, Wright edited his first draft of "To Arizona," and included the first published photographs of Taliesin West.*[2] *[Published in* Arizona Highways, *May 1940]*

I, TOO, HAVE DISCOVERED THIS AMERICA THAT IS ARIZONA. It will seem strange to the small group of fortunate people who intelligently live here that anyone in their nation should have to "discover" Arizona after seeing the Grand Canyon. But the remarkable beauty peculiar to this southern Arizona region is quite undiscovered by the grand-average American, or for that matter, by the super-American. This I believe is about to change, and the inevitable boom accompanying such discoveries of the picturesque and of climate in the United States will soon come to set Arizona backward a decade or so. That doesn't matter much, if Arizona clings faithfully to its inheritance and takes care of it. The desert with its rim of arid mountains spotted like the leopard's skin or tattooed with amazing patterns of creation, is a grand garden the like of which in sheer beauty of reach, space, and pattern does not exist, I think, in the world.

It is the grandeur of this great desert-garden that is Arizona's chief asset. Of course, water poured on certain portions of it will send cases of grapefruit, oranges, lettuce, and melons rolling east to market

just as they go from other states. But the American people will not come rolling in here for things like that. If they come, they will come because of great desert beauty made accessible and a way of life belonging to it. They will come to breathe the incomparably pure air here on account of the desert but must find Arizona a good host. They will come to get away from "weather": come to play and some of them come to stay in the invigorating sunshine . . . but they should find civilized entertainment too, second to none. All of Arizona is not a large enough playground for the United States. So it may well remain caviar to the average and yet prosper mightily.

Compared to the intoxicating air, sweeping mountain vistas and astonishing cactus plant-life especially created on the rocks and in crannies, or at large on the ranges of this desert-garden, all else in Arizona is insignificant—even if considered by way of the realtor as "property." Los Angeles has oversold by billions a winter climate wholly inferior to this one of the Salt River Valley which lay quietly undiscovered behind the mountain ranges that cut it off from the too-well-known California Coast until, now, even Californians are coming here to winter.

In the Salt River Valley winter climate is in unexampled perfection, due, almost wholly, to the vast surrounding desert. I, for one, dread to see this incomparable nature garden marred, eventually spoiled by candy-makers, cactus hunters, careless fire-builders and the fancy period-house builders, as well as the Hopi Indian imitators, or imitation Mexican "hut" builders. They will soon destroy the most accessible parts unless Arizona people have the sense to stop them. Where the oasis laboriously extends itself and desert growth has to die that man may prosper, there the candy-makers and cactus-hunters should be confined with the "period" imitations.

All those who come here to live must eat. Some must go out and dig irrigation ditches to earn more money to make them strong to go out to dig more ditches. And date palms and fig trees, grapefruit and orange groves are all desirable and beautiful things in themselves, where they belong, but not to be compared in money-getting value to the noble Saguaro, the wicked Cholla, the desert-well called the Bisnaga. Whoever has seen the golden

**The Arizona desert, Taliesin West, and the McDowell Mountains. Photograph by Marian Kanouse.** FLLW Fdn FA#3803.2010

Palo Verde, Mesquite, Creosote bush and the flaming Ocotillo, the Ironwood's violet profusion under the canopy of Arizona blue never gets over the experience and always longs to see it again.

What a scientific marvel of construction that long-lived Saguaro! Or the latticed stalk of the Cholla! Nature, driven to economize materials by hard conditions, develops in the Saguaro a system of economy by reinforcement of vertical rods, a plaiting of tendons that holds the structure bolt upright for six centuries or more.

And go study the stalk of that wicked Cholla for a pattern of latticed steel structure. You will find it in the plaiting of the stalks. Or study the stem of the fibrous Ocotillo waving its red flag from the tops of a spray of slender plaited whips fifteen feet long.

What a building might be that had a proper respect for Arizona's streamlined spaces, its structure walled like the Saguaro, textured like it too, by the nature of its construction.

No. The Arizona desert is no place for the hard box-walls of the houses of the Middle West and East. Here all is sculptured by wind and water, patterned in color and texture. Rocks and reptiles no less so than the cacti. A desert building should be nobly simple in outline as the region itself is sculptured: should have learned from the cactus many secrets of straight-line-patterns for its forms, playing with the light and softening the building into its proper place among the organic desert creations—the man-made building heightening the beauty of the desert and the desert more beautiful because of the building. A dream, but realization is coming.

We do not yet understand such pattern in form because it is an attribute of a very high and perhaps older Culture. We are just now trying to think ornament useless or continue to go wrong with it by trying to *emphasize* with it when Nature intended it to soften, conceal, and harmonize. Nature herself does just that very thing with it, always, as you will see if you will go to school to the Desert.

Nature never sticks ornament onto anything. She gets it all out from the inside of the thing the way it grows. It is always *of* the thing. Integral. Plain white house walls defy the sun and jump to your eyes from the desert forty miles or more away. They are not true desert buildings in any cultivated sense.

Nor is the Indian Hopi-house a desert house in any true sense. Even were the Hopi imitation no base imitation for us, it is too loud. The projecting poles soften it with shadows a very little; the native Indian got that far with it. But the Indian learned from the desert when he made pots or mats or beadwork or clothed himself. He got something of the spirit of the desert into all those things as we may see. The rattlesnake, the Gila Monster, and the Cacti may have taught him something we don't learn.

But, Architecture, the great art, except on very primitive terms, was beyond him as Music and Literature. The Fine Arts are in themselves a finer civilization—or ought to be. They once were and will be again. What better opportunity to throw off the old shackles and begin than right here in Arizona, now?

I suggest that the dotted line is the line for the desert; not the hard line nor the knife edge. And in the line comes a new type of structure for the Arizona spaces to save the desert from the invasion of the fashionable builder with his now famous 57 varieties.

Anyone may see that the desert abhors sun-defiance as nature abhors a vacuum. This universal sun-acceptance by way of pattern is a condition of survival and is everywhere evident. That means integral-ornament in everything. Sun-acceptance in building means that dotted-line in outline and wall-surfaces that eagerly take the light and play with it and break it up and render it harmless or drink it in until sunlight blends the building into place with the creation around it. Man's imagination is none too lively, at best, but the task is not too great to harmonize his building masses with topography and typify his building-walls with the nature-creation they consort with, by taking the abstract design inherent in all desert fabric of his own work whenever he, himself, makes anything. That is to say, he should be able to make the essential spirit of the thing, however or whatever it is, come through as objective.

The ever-advancing human threat to the integral beauty of Arizona might be avoided if the architect would only go to school to the Desert in this sense and humbly learn harmonious contrasts or sympathetic treatments that would, thus, quietly, "belong." The climate of this region abhors the "box."

Is this organic abstraction, as expression, too difficult for us at this stage of our development? All right then. Cover up your walls, plant trees and vines and water them well. But plant trees and vines native to the condition here. Be quiet—will you—at any cost. Blot out your clumsy intrusions as you best can. It is the only apology you can make to Arizona.

Now, I believe that Arizona mountain ranges, her "draws" and "washes" and her grand square miles of desert floor are worth more eventually (even in terms of the antiquated gold standard) than all the land "reclaimed" or that can be reclaimed by irrigation ditches. I admit that an irrigated oasis is necessary to the human life coming into the desert to remain. But I hope Arizona won't, as California did, get the cart before the horse. That is to say, I hope ranching and vigorous enterprise concerning drinking and eating won't go far enough to spoil in any degree the grand garden that the state really is, an asset that will soon bring wealth to the various Arizona pioneers if only they will learn to use it as intelligent hosts just as it already brings beautiful life to millions of faded, jaded refugees from our American cities. All cities are increasingly slums. So this conservation of desert creation grows even more important. It is more important to government than the conservation of the forests and is important as any conservation of water in mountain streams. Should the legislature of the state neglect to protect its true reserves in this—eventually yes, its *greatest financial resources*—the Federal Government should take Arizona over and protect it or future Arizona may yet live to curse its short sighted—too long-lived legislators.

Arizona already needs less salesmanship and more statesmanship as it needs less building and more good roads and good Architecture. It needs also to qualify itself to be a gracious, competent host to a great Nation. A great road program is part of that. And I doubt if it can be the needed host to the nation by putting into effect any such slogans as "Arizona for the Arizonans"—for instance.

The best in the world is none too good for Arizona if she is going to live up to her marvelous gift.

1. Frank Lloyd Wright. *An Autobiography*. New York: Duell, Sloan and Pearce, 1943. p. 452.

2. See also "Why I Love Wisconsin" in *Frank Lloyd Wright Collected Writings Volume 3*, p. 134.

**Taliesin West, Scottsdale, Arizona.** FLLW Fdn FA#3803.0006

**Arch Obler House, "Eaglefeather" (Project), Malibu, California. 1940. Perspective. Pencil and color pencil on tracing paper, 36 x 23".**
FLLW Fdn#4018.001

# WAKE UP AMERICA!

**F**rank Lloyd Wright was a dedicated pacifist and isolationist when it came to the foreign policy of the United States of America, as illustrated by his response in a televised interview with Mike Wallace:

> They're professional warriors, aren't they? I'm against war—always have been, always will be. And anything connected with it is anathema to me. I've never considered it necessary, and I think one war only breeds another, and I think I've been borne out by a reading of history, haven't I? One war always has in it, in its intestines, another—and another has another. So why be for war? And if you're not for war, why are you for warriors?

Although he hated having labels attached to him, and berated terms that ended with "ists, ites, and isms," it is abundantly clear from this article that he wholeheartedly wanted the nation to steer clear of the European conflict:

> During several months past I could "listen in" or read at any time anywhere and imagine myself back in the stupid days of 1914. But that previous catastrophe to the economy and morale of our democratic world was nothing compared to what now takes us in its grip.

Wright believed that the incentive to get the nation into the war was based on a false premise:

> No, our real enemy is not Hitler! Our real enemy lies in our timidity and stupidity as seen in the frightful current so smoothly moved, coaxed in the direction of self-destruction. "To save Britain"? No, to maintain Britain as our only shield against our own slavery or destruction is the insane notion sold to mediocrity by way of its own salesmen from chief executive to the journalist horde. . . . The false standards we have been aiding Britain to maintain, or have ourselves been aided by Britain to maintain, are played out! They are all senile: a demonstrated bottle-neck without issue except war. . . . England is one thing. English culture is in no danger. But British Imperialism never was anything but a foolish challenge to the world.

His plea for America to seek a deeper definition of true democracy rings throughout the article. Obviously it was a controversial point of view, but at the end of the text he concluded, as a footnote,

> Originally written as an editorial for the Capital Times of Madison, Wisconsin, to follow my first editorial for that paper, the foregoing text was first printed in the Christian Century, issue of November 13, 1940. Some pretty strong reactions reached Taliesin, well worth printing someday.

WAKE UP AMERICA! OUR COUNTRY'S MOST CREATIVE minds were shut out of any decisive vote in the last election by the bi-party pact "save Britain." As current nationalism now runs to murder, any plan for defense of our own way of life according to our best genius has been handed over to the old worm's eye view of war, a "foreign-policy" prolonging war toward ruin of any way of life we could or should defend.

By way of popular "easements" (call them publicity) again we have been newsed, radioed and scared out of Democracy. During several months past I could "listen in" or read at any time anywhere and imagine myself back in the stupid days of 1914. But that previous catastrophe to the economy and morale of our democratic world was nothing compared to what now takes us in its grip. Shame enough to sell out our best thought at first sign of danger and see our nationals run pell-mell to play a second-hand imitation of the enemy when our power can never lie in saving empire unless we too are empirical. Imitation always base, never yet won a battle. No, our real enemy is not Hitler! Our real enemy lies in our own timidity and stupidity as seen in this frightful current so smoothly moved, coaxed in the direction of self-destruction. "To save Britain"? No, to maintain Britain as our only shield against our own slavery or destruction is the insane notion sold to mediocrity by way of its own salesmen from chief executive to the journalistic horde.

The only safe-guard Democracy can ever have is a free, morally enlightened, fearless minority. Unfortunately for our country such enlightenment and courage is (and it may ever be) a minority. But Democracy deprived of either the vote or the voice of that minority will stay in infancy, a pushed, helpless mediocrity. Democracy's very life depends upon entire freedom to continually choose from among its free minority the best and bravest thought. Party pacts made to end or continue the way of life we call Democracy silencing that vote and voice, and what has democracy? Any influence whatsoever, designed to keep the mediocrity ignorant of the real issue by falsifying or stultifying the enlightened minority, is not only dangerous to democracy. It is soon fatal.

I maintain that our non-interventionist, isolationist if you like, American minority is characterized by the strongest and most valiant men and women in the world where work with creative ideas is concerned. But, they have been put out of participation by this undemocratic pact to save empire, in order to save us from "worse than death." And that cry for salvation has been political bogey in every match ever played in our country between the enlightened minority and the make-shift business, petty officialism and political-power-push-overs. Must manipulated mediocrity again overwhelm the real issue in our democracy? If so, let's say our mobocracy, not our democracy. Dictatorship is inevitable to mobocracy. We have it already in conscription in peacetime.

But, if as a people we are going on to ultimate victory over selfish or vengeful interests that infect us because those interests are unable to feel outside their own pockets, see beyond their own factory floors, or rise above their murdered European relatives, it will go on alive only because the country can see with the help of its own free minority the murderous character of "power-politics" as now played in unison by the two parties and realize the utter folly of such make-shift money-getting as is now in action. Why do our people not realize that it is this make-shift money-system that is in real danger now? That system is there at the bottom of this cry "save Britain." The system knows it well. Mass mediocrity does not know it.

Wake up America! The false standards we have been aiding Britain to maintain, or have ourselves been aided by Britain to maintain, are played out! They are all senile: a demonstrated bottle-neck without issue except war. We can recognize that to beat the law of gravitation (a relatively simple matter) is impossible without consistent structure on a good foundation. But to beat our enemy his way we have not got one foundation at all. We cannot get one with extravagant preparation for war no matter how far we go. England is one thing. English culture is in no danger. But British Imperialism never was anything but a foolish challenge to the world. Democracy might be the foundation needed for both ourselves and England were democracy now really England's friend more than the exploiter's refuge. But fortunately for Hitler nothing is further from world democracy at this moment than any real grasp of the meaning of democracy. The Democracy of the moment is a depravity, the inevitable consequence of the term continually used for trade diplomacy and exploitation. Can't we understand that what alone can keep democracy a valid force working for the freedom of the world is courage to trust the truth; the will to tell the people the whole truth; the honest practice of our own principles without fear or favor; continually wide-open access to our best and bravest thought? Then only are we in this country, safe! Without that practice what hope for democracy now or ever. Any influences, public or private, intended to block these practices, those are the influences that are our real enemies.

Unhappy old Tolstoi wrote that present forms of government are inseparable from war. He may have been right. Anyhow, this is the second war these United States have been frightened into within the past twenty-three years not honestly knowing what it is all about. We are now publicly pushed to spend our labor and young lives afresh with all the dated paraphernalia for shedding blood now all too familiar to the enemy while the ways of sound economic democracy lie wasted or untried. By the two party pact we lose real opportunity to beat the enemy. We lose it when we throw the old monkey-wrench of war into the only means of salvation we ever really had: staunch faith in the way of life we are sworn to maintain. Cut off from its salient minority. All, regardless, must now accept this pattern set by force, a force already senile—and profanely call the insanity "democracy" or go to jail for five years . . . if the objector hasn't got ten thousand dollars. Thus doomed to defeat.

Democracy! Democracy is a way of life in which the individual and what makes him one—his character—has, owing to a way of government wherein choice is free to the human soul, open chance to develop. A democratic government that recognizes an inner realm of choice belonging by inalienable right to every individual and that within that inner realm of conscience there can be neither invasion nor compulsion. No dictatorship on earth could vanquish this nation were it grounded that way. But where is that way of manhood now? How pleased the enemy to see democracy confessing and preparing its own defeat by wasting its resources to meet the enemy on his own terms! In a word by force committing its manhood to force

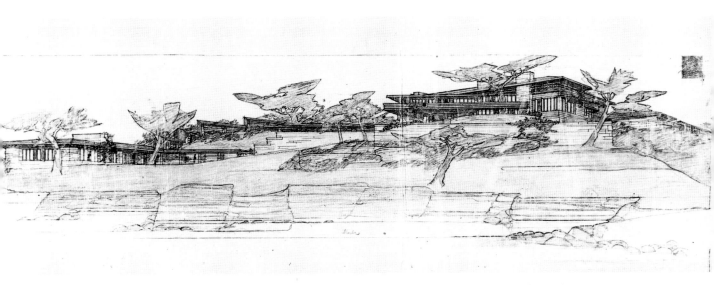

**John Nesbitt House, "Stoneweb" (Project), Los Angeles, California. 1940. Perspective. Pencil, ink, and color pencil on tracing paper, 48 x 21".** FLLW Fdn#4017.003

**Lloyd Lewis House, Libertyville, Illinois. 1940. Perspective. Pencil and color pencil on tracing paper, 37 x 23".** FLLW Fdn#4008.002

before force has any validity. Rationalize conscription how we may, any true faith in democratic ideas is swamped by the act. A pleasant smile and a please for sugar-coating do not change the fact. Slowly but efficiently the frightened huddle is moved along toward legal self-destruction. Unless democracy is going down to stay down we must wake up! True defense for us must be a matter of putting better ideas than Hitler's total-state and total-war-among-states into practical effect here and now. The total-man and peace-among-men are ideas that democracy is being ruthlessly exploited to fear now.

But the exploiter of men is always first to turn upon manhood and take refuge in the State. That is where the exploiter is now asking for blood. State-

hood versus Man-hood! Must our people wake up now to see the two as enemies?

A newspaper man can order the navy about. A pleasant president can gather information-men about him, arm the boys and order them about, getting just as many of them war-minded and killed as any plug-ugly could. But nothing of that sort can save our country when the democratic principles on which our national life rests go wrong or rotten. Lacking the practice of consistent principle, democratic ways and means are going wrong just when the world needs help most as the great forces of life here on earth again surge forward in this ceaseless tide of change. Fearful and reluctant as we are, thus exploited we must face these great organic changes, face them on our own merits. We cannot face them on

Britain's! If we try to go on in that old way of life—we are lost anyway. Can mediocrity "take it" led by push-over power-politics concerned with make-shift money? No. Can Democracy meet the total-state on that enemy's own terms as we continually extend the democratic front to be defended? No.

But wake up America! Nature, by placing us where we are, has done better by us than we do for ourselves. Honestly invoke the democratic princi-ples we now only exploit, slam the doors shut where need be, call meddling diplomats off their perches, and, minding our own business here at home, withstanding all alien influences whatsoever, tackle the job of becoming fit to live for the life that is now our own if we only knew how to appreciate and use it. If we knew that, we would know how to defend it—our way as we have known before when the time came. We would make no enemies, then. Our billions upon billions for murder will be wast-ed with the gold it is already useless for us even to try to defend.

These United States would have been impreg-nable by now were we content with honest democ-racy and had not tried to set ourselves up as a mighty plutocracy. The only trouble we would have with the interior kind of defense for which I plead is that it would require the greatest of courage: great moral courage. The kind our forefathers had when they turned their backs on the senility of the total-state and its total-wars-among-states and came over here to found and to foster a new order for the total-man and peace-among-men.

**Members of the Taliesin Fellowship preparing the model of Broadacre City, Chandler, Arizona. 1935. Photograph by Cornelia Brierly.**
FLLW Fdn FA#3402.0058

# THE NEW FRONTIER:
# BROADACRE CITY

Constructed by the Taliesin Fellowship in winter residence at Chandler, Arizona, during the winter of 1934–1935, the Broadacre City model then went on tour to major cities such as Pittsburgh, New York, and Washington. Along with the main model of the city, other models related to the general plan were constructed: a suspension bridge, a highway interchange, a farm, a group of small houses, a service station, as well as the model for a theater, made two years earlier. Wright and the Fellowship had begun a magazine called, simply, Taliesin as an organ for their work and thought. In 1940, five years after the tour of the model, all the various texts and articles on Broadacre City were compiled together in this publication and sent out to the subscribers.

Realizing there was much repetition in these articles, Wright explained,

Each time I attempt to put the scheme for Broadacres into words a new aspect of many details not considered before occurs to me. So no two discourses concerning the future have all in common. There is more between the lines still than appears in the lines.

In his articles throughout the publication he responded to some of the reactions to the tour of the models in the various cities, such as to those of Mies van der Rohe and the Mayor of Pittsburgh.

Broadacre City was not a model of buildings but rather a scheme for buildings set into the countryside. The buildings themselves were represented by blocks, as were the masses of forestation. Only certain buildings reflected previous designs: the Gordon Strong Planetarium and Automobile Objective at the far corner of the model, and the several St. Mark's Towers scattered throughout. The drawings for the model are likewise schematic, not detailed, except for some housing designs labeled "Sustenance Houses" where Wright addressed the problem of the low-cost house as an individual unit rather than housing as it was generally known. Some of his bridge designs were more fully developed, as well as his design for the service station. Even as early as 1934 he envisioned the service stations throughout the nation as more than mere gas stations, as small stores of convenience with food, produce, and assorted articles—what today has evolved into the mini-mart.

The theme of Broadacre City, its underlying ideas and principles, would return constantly throughout Wright's life from the time the model was first built in 1934 to the last book he wrote, entitled The Living City, in 1958, some six months before his death. In fact, all of the principles of his work, all of his thought *about planning, building, and environment, would be connected to this concept of a decentralized, liberated society, the centerline of which would be architecture. Now, some sixty years later, the message of Broadacre City becomes especially pertinent as we face life on a planet that has steadily and consistently been destroying its natural resources, its natural features, and its very existence. New generations are now turning to these concepts of Wright's in realization that the message he preached some decades ago is fully applicable to today as we witness our environment being destroyed.*

*Broadacre City represented, in 1935, a definite solution that can even now be observed if life—one worth living—is to survive on this planet. Many ideas first instigated in this model plan of fifty-eight years ago have indeed already become part of our daily life, among them the shopping center accessed by the automobile, the highway motel, and the general trend toward decentralization. [Published in* Taliesin *magazine, October 1940]*

NO INSTITUTES
No petty officialism
No Landlord—No tenant
No politicians—No academicians
No traffic problem
No back and forth haul
No poles—no wires in sight
No ditches alongside the roads
No headlights—No visible lamps
No policemen
No minor axis—No major axis
No yards for raw materials
No smoke—No hardrails
No radio or billboard advertising
No slum—No scum

## A NEW SUCCESS IDEAL

By the simple exercise of several inherently just rights of man—freedom to decentralize, redistribute, and correlate the properties of the work of man on earth to his birthright, which is the ground itself, Broadacre City becomes reality.

One of the deadly efficiencies, the one in which we have taken most pride—most damnable of all—has been what education has called "academic." The "academic" is the major and minor axis of classic architecture in human dress, or in human terms, which makes all symmetry a fixation. No chrysalis, this. At best we see it as a crystal, and any crystal is a finality—fixation at the end of growth. As I see Architecture, the best architect is he who will devise forms nearest organic, these forms features of human growth through changes natural to that growth. Civilization itself is inevitably a form; but (if Democracy is sanity) it is now the fixation called academic. All regimentation is a form of death which may sometimes serve life, but which more often imposes upon it. In Broadacres all is symmetrical, but it is seldom obviously, and never academically, so. Whatever forms issue are capable of normal growth without the destruction of their pattern. Nor is there much obvious repetition in the new city. Where regiment and row serve the general harmony of arrangement both are present, but generally both are absent except where planting and cultivation are naturally a process, or where walls afford a desired seclusion. Rhythm is the substitute for such repetition. Wherever mere repetition (standardization) enters it has been modified by inner rhythms, either by art or nature, as it must be modified to be of any lasting human value.

The three major inventions already at work building Broadacres, whether the powers that overbuilt the old cities like it or not, are: (1) The motor car: increased general mobility of the human being. (2) Radio, telephone, and telegraph: electrical intercommunication becoming complete. (3) Standardized machine-shop production: machine invention plus scientific discovery.

The price of the major three to America has been the exploitation we see everywhere around us in waste and in the ugly scaffolding left by utilities and commercial exploitation that may now be thrown away. The price has not been too great if, through popular government, we are able to exercise the use of three inherent rights of man: (1) His social right to a simple direct medium of exchange in place of gold as a commodity: some form of universal social credit. (2) His social right to his place on the ground as he has had his right in the sun and air: land to be held only by use and improvements. (3) His social right to the ideas by which and for which he lives: that is to say public ownership of invention and scientific discoveries that concern the life of the people.

The only assumption made by Broadacres as an ideal is this: that these three rights will become the possession of the citizen as soon as the folly of endeavoring to cheat him of their democratic values becomes as apparent to those who hold, (feudal survivors or survivals), as it is becoming apparent to the thinking people who are held, blindly abject or subject against their will. In short, as soon as the meaning of Democracy becomes clear to America

The landlord is really no happier than the tenant. The speculator can no longer win much at a game that is about played out. It is becoming more evident every day that the present success-ideal, (placing as it does, a premium upon the wolf, the fox and the rat in human affairs, and above all, upon the parasite), is a false ideal, and just as injurious to the "successful" as to the victim of such success.

Well, sociologically, Broadacres is release from all this fatal "success" which, after all, is only excess. So I have called it a *new freedom for living in America*. It has not only thrown the scaffolding aside, but it has set up a new ideal of success.

In Broadacres, (so far as simplified government goes) by the elimination of cities and towns petty and minor officialdom has been reduced to one minor government for each county. The waste motion, the back and forth haul that today makes so much idle "business," is gone. Distribution becomes automatic and direct, taking place mostly in the region of origin. Methods of distribution of anything and everything are simple and direct. From the maker to the consumer by the most direct route.

Coal (one third the tonnage of the haul of our railways) is eliminated by burning it at the mines and transferring net power. This will make it easier to take over those great rights of way, the railroads; and to take off the cumbersome rolling stock and put the right of way into general service. These rights of way will become the arterials on which truck traffic is concentrated on lower side lanes, with many lanes of speed traffic above, and monorail speed trains at the center, continuously running. And since traffic may take off or on the traffic ways at any given point these materials are not dated—traffic but fluescent traffic. And the great arterial, as well as all the highways, become in themselves great architecture. Automatically they afford concealed within their sub-structure all necessary storage facilities of raw materials. Here we have the elimination of all unsightly piles of raw materials. In the hands of the state, but by way of the county, all redistribution of land will be had—a minimum of one acre going to the childless family and more to the larger family as determined by the state. The agent of the state in all matters of land-allotment or improvement, or in matters affecting the harmony of the whole, is the architect. All building is subject to his sense of the whole as organic architecture. Here architecture as landscape takes on the character of architecture by way of the simple process of cultivation.

All public utilities are concentrated in the hands of the state and the various county governments as are also matters of administration, patrol, fire, post, banking, license and record, thus making politics a vital matter to everyone in the new city instead of the present hopeless indifference that makes "politics" a grafter's profession.

In the buildings for Broadacres no distinction exists between much and little, more and less. Quality is in all, for all, alike. The thought entering into the first estate or the last estate is of the best. The difference is only in individuality and extent. There is nothing poor or mean anywhere in Broadacres.

Nor does Broadacres issue any dictum or see finality in any matter either of pattern or of style.

Organic character *is* style. Such style has myriad forms inherently good. Growth is possible to Broadacres because Broadacres is a fundamental form and not able to destroy the city as a mere accident of change. Growth is welcome as integral pattern unfolding from within.

In the models may now be seen in actual form all the elemental units of our social structure: the correlated farm, the factory (its smoke and gases eliminated by using coal at the mines); the decentralized school; the various conditions of residence; the home offices; safe traffic; simplified government; and all common interests taking place in a single coordination wherein all are employed: *little* farms, *little* homes for industry, *little* factories, *little* schools, a *little* university going to the people mostly by way of their interest in the ground, *little* laboratories on their ground for professional men. And the farm itself, notwithstanding its animals, becomes the most attractive unit of the city. The husband of the animals is a last indecent association with them, and with all else as well: true Farm-relief.

Broadacres as conceived here would automatically end unemployment and all its evils forever. There would never be labor enough, nor could there be under-consumption. Whatever a man did would be well done—obviously and directly—because done mostly by himself in his own interest under the most valuable inspiration and direction: under experience preferably, certainly, if necessary. Economic independence would be near every man who worked; a subsistence certain. A life varied and interesting is the inevitable consequence. Nothing too good for anybody—and no substitute sought for quality.

Every kind of builder would be likely to have a jealous eye to the harmony of the whole within broad limits fixed by the county architect, an architect chosen perhaps by the county itself. Each county would thus naturally develop an individuality of its own. Architecture, in the broad sense of the term would thrive naturally.

In any organic architecture the ground itself predetermines all features, climate modifies them, available means limit them, and function shapes them.

Form and Function are one in Broadacres; therefore Broadacres is no finality. The main model shows four square miles of a typical countryside in the temperate zone, developed on the acre as unit and accommodating some 1400 families. It could swing north or swing south. The type, according to conditions, climate, and the topography of the region would change somewhat.

In the models the emphasis has been placed upon diversity in unity, recognizing in the necessity of cultivation a need for formality in most of the planting. By a simple government-subsidy, certain specific acres or groups of acre units are, in every succeeding generation, planted to useful trees, meantime beautiful masses of greenery giving privacy and forming various rural division. But there are no rows of trees alongside the roads to shut out the view. Where rows are planted they are perpendicular to the road, or the trees are planted in groups. Useful trees like white pine, walnut, birch, beech fir, etc., would come to maturity as well as would fruit and nut trees, making a profitable crop; meantime giving character, privacy, and comfort to the city. The general park, a flowered meadow beside the stream, is bordered with ranks of trees forming a great be-flowered wall gradually rising in height above the flowers at ground level. A music-garden is sequestered from noise at one end. Much is made of general pastimes by way of the circus, aquarium, arboretum, and of the various arts and crafts.

The traffic problem has had especial attention, for the sooner mobility is made a comfort and a facility the sooner will Broadacres arrive at its destiny. Every Broadacre Citizen has his own car or more. Multiple-lane highways make travel safe and enjoyable. There are no grade crossings nor left turns on grade. The road system and construction is such that no signals nor lampposts need be seen. No ditches alongside the roads. No curbs either; an inlaid purfling, over which the car cannot go without damage to itself, protects the pedestrian. The roads have no ditches and are concave rather than convex—drainage and utilities in conduit at the center.

In air transport Broadacres goes beyond the present aeroplane and substitutes the aerotor, capable of rising straight up, and by reversible rotors able to travel in any direction under radio control at a maximum speed of say 200 miles an hour, able to descend safely into the hexacomb from which it arose or anywhere else, by any Broadacre doorstep if desired.

The only fixed transport trains kept on the arterial are the long distance monorail cars traveling at a speed (already established in Germany) of 200 miles per hour. All other traffic is by motor car on the twelve-lane levels, or the triple truck lanes on the lower levels—these lanes having on both sides the advantage of delivery direct to warehouse or from warehouse to consumer. Local trucks may get to warehouse-storage on lower levels under the main arterial itself. A local truck-road parallels the swifter lanes.

Houses in the new city are of course as varied as the individuals choosing them but generally harmonious they make much of fireproof synthetic arrangement, but the houses do not neglect the older nature-materials wherever they are desired and available. Householders' utilities are nearly all planned in prefabricated utility stacks or units, simplifying construction and reducing building costs to a certainty. There is the professional's house with its laboratory, the minimum house with its workshop, the medium house ditto, the larger house, and the house of machine-age luxury. We speak of them as a one-car house, a two-car house, a three-car house and a five-car house. Glass is extensively used, as are roofless rooms; and the roof is used as a trellis or a garden. But where glass is extensively used it is usually for domestic purposes in the shadow of protecting "overhangs."

Copper for roofs is indicated generally on the model as a permanent cover capable of being worked in many appropriate ways and giving a general harmonious color effect—blue—to the whole.

Electricity, oil, and gas are the only popular fuels, each land allotment having a pit near the public lighting fixture, where access to the three may be had; and to water and sewer without tearing up the pavements.

The school problem is solved by a separate group of low buildings in the interior spaces of the city where the children can directly and conveniently walk to and from home. The school building group includes galleries for loan collections from the museum, a small concert and lecture hall, small gardens for the children for gathering in small groups, and many well-lighted cubicles for individual outdoor study. There is a small traveling zoo, large pools, green playgrounds, and each pupil has a small garden plot allotted to him.

This Kindergarten school group is at the very center of the model, and contains at its center the higher school adapted to separation of the students into small groups.

This tract of four smiles square, by means of this general liberal allotment determined by acreage and type of ground, including apartment buildings and hotel facilities, provides for about 1,400 families, say an average of five or more acres to the family.

To reiterate: the basis of the whole is general Decentralization as an applied principle and harmonious architectural reintegration of all units into one fabric: ground held only by use and improvements; public utilities and government itself owned by the people of Broadacre City; privacy for every man on his own ground; and a fair means of subsistence for all through their own work on their own ground or in their own laboratory or shop or in common offices serving the life of the whole.

There are too many details involved in the model of Broadacres to permit a complete explanation. Study of the model itself is necessary. Most details are explained by collateral models of the various types of construction shown. Highway construction, left turns, crossovers and underpasses and various houses and public buildings are shown in detailed models.

Anyone studying all these models should bear in mind the thesis upon which the design has been built up by the Taliesin Fellowship. Built carefully, not as a finality in any sense, but as an interpretation of the changes inevitable to our growth as a people and a nation that are taking place around us everywhere today.

Individuality established on such terms must thrive and can survive. Unwholesome life would get no encouragement; and the ghastly heritage left by wars and overcrowding in overdone ultra-capitalistic centers would be likely to disappear in three or four generations. The old success ideals having no chance, new ideals, natural to the best in man would be given fresh opportunity to develop. Growth becoming the law of the land.

Any totalitarian or communist threat would have little significance in such circumstances. Fear would be hard to arouse in a people so situated. What I have been describing here is really a capitalist society but a capitalist society broadly and firmly based upon the ground, let its apex be whatever it may, and not as now—apex on the ground, base in

**Broadacre City Model. 1935. Photograph by Skot Weidemann. Copyright © FLLW Fdn.** FLLW Fdn FA#3402.0091

the air. When the models of Broadacres were first exhibited at Rockefeller Center some of the newspapers assured their readers that the scheme was pure communism, others that it was totalitarian or state socialism, others that it was plain socialism. Not one critic could see in it the fact that it was a plastic form of a genuine democracy.

Any form genuinely democratic would be a plastic form—therefore non-academic in the sense that we are academic at the present time. Freedom of the sort however is about the last thing the socialized state would care to encounter or try to conquer. The very solidarity of a true Democratic success would terrorize them more than their planes and guns could terrorize us.

## MR. WRIGHT TALKS ON BROADACRE CITY TO LUDWIG MIES VAN DER ROHE

I am sorry, Mies, that we have no time to do more than touch upon the few features that may happen to come into my mind at this moment, because we have here before us in these models a complete cross section of our entire Usonian civilization as it might easily and soon be—I might say as it is going to be. The model section is taken at a typical county seat of government. This design presupposes that the city is going to the country, and assumes the country to be a characteristic four square miles of some future American county where the hills come down to the plains and a river flows down and across the plain. As you see here in the model there is some high ground running down to the plain. A river or stream cuts its way across the plain. This, being fairly characteristic topography is chosen to model the development you see here of a typical section of an American (or Usonian) county. The ultimate Broadacre City would be made up of these counties as they are now, but grouped into states; the counties and states would all be federated then just as they are now. Broadacre City is the entire country and predicated upon the basis that every man woman and child in America is entitled to "own" an acre of ground so long as they live on it or use it and every man at least owning his own car, or plane. So the portion we see here as a whole is really only a minute part of the future Broadacre City which eventually would include these Untied States. But in this small part you may find most of the ideas at work that would eventually shape the whole and hold it all together.

Like every other architectural scheme which is real, Broadacre City as here presented is a transitional scheme. All genuinely great building is transition building. Only as we can plan to take advantage of the law of change in process of growth can we do justice to human-nature. Through the law of cause and effect, we must proceed to interpret the present in terms of the future. So this is not intended to be an ultimate pattern but one so free of major and minor axes as never to become the usual academic fixation, and always to have sufficient reflex to accommodate inevitable organic change. In other words, it is not "classic." It is organic.

Here the agrarian, the industrialist, the artist, the scientist, and the philosopher meet on the ground itself. It may not be logical. But is the rising sun logical? It is natural and that is better. What Broadacres proposes is psychological and natural—now. The social forces of mankind have been dammed up long enough to see what must be coming.

All government services come from the county seat, from which postal deliveries are made and the necessary official distributions effected, direction and protection being given by aerotor from the official field near by the town-hall. Public utilities like gas, light, water and gasoline, conducted in channeled roadways and available by meter at the curb. As to other utilities, telephone poles and telegraph wires

are obsolete, our airplanes are still splendid stunts; our system of building utterly unscientific, and the poor old railroads out-of-date. We have had to find new ways to do what they did. The railroad is not adapted to the fluid traffic that is now a characteristic of modern life. So we have taken the railroad right-of-way (it belongs to the people anyway, and have made architecture out of its double track central speedway from coast to coast express traffic—a great triple-lane two-way automobile highway, paralleled on either side by county highways connecting every half mile with the countryside. Cars go one way only, in one portion; trucks go two ways lower down, one way in one portion but can take on or off every half mile. These ideal hard roads without ditches or gutters support speeds up to one hundred miles per hour. At county seat intersections we find stations for aerotor take-offs and every half mile you may see pass-overs and cross-unders for the main county cross-roads. Beneath this road construction (probably Federal) there is vast space for the continuous storage and delivery of building materials, fuel, etc. This main artery—the converted railroad—connects the counties of the states and the states themselves into the ultimate Broadacre City. All of course are owned and operated by the people's government.

Now, the counties of the U.S.A. average from thirty to fifty square miles each—and each already has a county seat. No need to change the location of these county seats nor change much that of the railroads nor change much the locations of the state and federal capitals. But we do abolish minor village governments to cut down minor officialdom. Government will be more highly centralized, the county government being more closely knit with federal administration, but there will be far less of it needed. State government still serves as an intermediary but becomes less and less needed as the process of government control becomes more organic because life is so. What is now the policeman is here automatic. Otherwise through this emphasis or government centralization of the common needs this is a decentralization of all man-made concerns, based upon the modern use of materials, glass, and steel, mobility and electrification. All owned or controlled by the general people whom they serve.

In determining the spacing of the city we assume every man is to have a car—or two. Or four or five. So we can build one-car houses, two-car houses or five-car houses. The space scale therefore has changed throughout. Changed in the ground allotments as in the dwellings themselves. The planning norm has ceased to be a man on his feet or a man seated behind a horse in a buggy. A mile to our man with the motor or ten miles in the air makes only a moment's distance. Space can be reckoned by time rather than feet and inches. But as this particular model is laid out we are still space-crowded.

On the basis of spacing shown here, the whole population of the U.S. could be accommodated in Texas alone. So let us consider this as a congested area, compared to what might actually take place. The fact is that the model shows here a condition not too unlike the development already taking place in the regional fields of our great cities themselves, except that the haphazard of that circumstance is here correlated and completed.

To allow for growth of population we reserve at the beginning certain tree-covered areas, trees being valuable crops subsidized by state government. The government by setting aside, say one third of the tillable areas takes care of future growth by providing more ground to work, the trees being cut down as crops when needed, to provide for growth.

These tree masses are a great landscape feature of Broadacres. Many kinds of useful trees (fine woods or nuts), all suited to the climate, may be planted by the acre. The ground thus conserved coming back into tillage when and as needed. Tilled ground could be returned to wooded area in this same way. In our model, the tree areas bear too small a relation to the whole area because we want to show as many features as possible in the small space at our disposal. So you will see more taken up in houses and gardens than would really be necessary in actual development.

In every society in Broadacre City, there are certain special functions like the arts, artcrafts, and small household manufactures such as weaving and dyeing and other small utilities. These are carried on in small factory units where the workers live. Everyone may live where he works if he wishes to do so.

The function of education (now more devoted to true culture than the acquiring of information) is still found in what we call the new University. Radio is one of the city's active assets. But radio is built into Broadacres as one of the assets controlled by the people themselves. Related to the new University, a decentralized unit, are the arboretum, aquarium, and zoo. All phases of nature are to be collected here for special nature study. The university, as you will see, has changed its character. A "classical" education would be worse than useless even more so than it is now. Instead, man studies man in relation to his birthright the ground, and man in relation to men.

He starts his earthly career with his feet on the ground, but his head may be in the clouds at times. When he is conceived in his mother's womb his place is ready here, as much ground as he can use is being reserved for him. Broadacres follows Henry George in the belief that a man should not only hold his land by way of his own use and improvements, but dedicate himself to it in the best sense of the spirit. There can be no absentee ownership of land. But meantime we cannot expect everyone to become bona fide tillers of the soil, particularly not the citizens of such urbanized population as we have at present. So we have made provision for the people who have been divorced from nature by excessive urban idealism and parasitic living. As I said, this must be a transition scheme because we must provide for people whose education and way of life has unfitted them for the more rounded life planned for here.

Understood rightly industry, art, science, and agriculture all have a common basis. We have not seen in our age that common basis with any constructive vision. If we have seen it, we have not acted upon it. No sense of the whole is anywhere evident in our modern life; thus, not only are all the many Usonian industrial and social activities uncorrelated but in every aspect of our activity there is a wasteful to and fro, a restlessness without purpose. Senseless concentrations are everywhere exaggerated. Concentrations are just as useless and meaningless as, for instance, the hauling of coal. One third of our yearly railroad tonnage is the coal haul. There is now no good reason why coal should not be burned at the mines, and the resultant heat and light distributed from the place of origin. Nor is there good reason to separate agriculture and manufacturing from residence districts or from each other, provided we take the curse off these operations, as is done in Broadacre City. In Broadacre City, every man is nearer every other man when he wants to be than he is in the present city. And the scaffolding still destroying our landscape—poles and wires, sign boards, railroad and lumber yards, etc., etc., do not exist in Broadacres.

Especially is the curse taken off farm and factory. The farm becomes a most desirable and lovable place in which to live, the most lovely to see. Animals are housed in fireproof sanitary quarters. The farmer is no longer an isolated human unit in the non-social hinterland. The curse has been taken off industry, as well. The curse has been taken off poverty of all kinds (except spiritual poverty) because there is the highest standard of quality in everything available for use, and there is left no inferior way of using anything. Differences now are only a matter of extent or of character. There is however a double curse on disorder.

Grouping may have true individuality, however. Both have been made a blessing by three principal freedoms: free ground, free education, and a free medium of exchange for all labor or commodities. This means entire freedom from speculation. There can be no speculation in any three of these essentials to the commonwealth essentially by way of which the commonwealth lives. Broadacre City is still a true capitalist system but one wherein private ownership is based upon personal use and public service: genuine Capitalism. Capitalism made organic since it is broadly based upon the ground and the individual upon the ground. After meeting the needs of all then according to the contribution of each, so may each receive. And any man's contribution, whatever the character or extent it may assume, must here be integral with the life of the citizen with the circumstances by and for which he lives; and concerning which he cannot lose the freedom of personal choice if he will work. If he will not work he becomes a charge upon the state and treated accordingly.

This, of course, is not the capitalism we have now, any more than it is communism. Let us call it

"Organic Capitalism," because a citizen of Broadacre City is an actual capitalist, not merely a potential one. He is no longer a mere gambler although there is still romance with which he may "gamble." The fact is he owns himself first of all (the first condition of an organic capital); and he may then choose and own if he pleases all that makes his life and the lives of those he loves worthwhile. He may own the fruit of his own labor or adding his unit of effort to a whole effort become entirely sympathetic and cooperative. He gives up to government only those matters into which no individuality can possibly enter, where there can be no question of sacrificing that in his nature which is himself. And that is the promise of true Democracy.

Government would especially be concerned with such things as public utilities. Government would be more an affair of business administration than meddling in politics. For instance, there is no longer need for one man to in some way regulate the money-getting of the other four. Competitive concerns are not needed to employ the citizenry. For instance, in Broadacre City, gasoline is at the curb, so is water, gas, electricity and compressed air. Sewage is handled on a nation-wide basis to be redistributed to the soil as fertilizer. Any society is much better off if these material things are thus organized as features of government in which every man has a direct business interest. Government would not then be as now a matter of politicians. This is a much more economic and effective basis for the development of industries and arts that are human and desirable, as well as the growth of efficiencies that have real and happy human value. The citizen would have about one-tenth of government which he has now; and that government would be the business administration of popular necessities, together with impersonal social affairs of a great nation. He would take an active interest in such government because it would be his own business.

The major problem of the means of distribution-mobility comes in here. We have to solve the vexing traffic-problem. It is one of the most important problems. First, the speed involved in general automobile traffic requires much space. And in solving these various problems we have made architecture out of roads. We have turned the road the other way up. We have made it concave with no ditches, so that one may stay on it, instead of the usual convex road with ditches. The road also serves for good drainage with a single deep grating-covered gutter in the middle draining to a conduit below. Beside this central conduit are smaller ones which are the conduits for wires and service pipes—all easily reached by removing a section of the continuous iron grating at the center of the road. The grating takes the place of the white or yellow road line now on the highways.

The top-turn intersection which we have devised, as architecture good to see, reduces the possibility of accident to pedestrian or motor traffic to one-tenth of one percent. Left-turns overhead in full sight are this one tenth and chance of accident there is small. Stop-and-go lights are eliminated. The road itself is lighted from the sides by low flood lights contained in floral features two feet above the ground, thus becoming a bright well-lighted ribbon with no lights glaring in the eyes of the driver. Wherever you see a road surface in Broadacre City it is a luminous surface at night and a dull red-toned surface in the daytime. Steel in tension is extensively used for the passovers and for all other construction where side spans are desirable; and wide spans are now desirable everywhere.

An interesting thing to consider in studying this model of Broadacres is the way distribution is effected. It is a fact that there is little or no back-and-forth haul and but little wasted to-and-fro. At the same time the scaffolding of our present social set-up (especially telephone wires and poles, billboards, storage yards for coal and building materials etc.) is all gone from this future city. To the ugly scaffolding of our present life the telephone and telegraph companies have contributed the worst features, and no longer needed, they disappear in this city of the future.

It follows naturally from all this genuinely constructive way of life that in the administration of Broadacre City the county architect is important. He has a certain disciplinary as well as cultural relationship to the whole, and since he maintains the harmony of the whole his must be one of the best minds the city has; and it will inevitably become the best trained. He could hardly be very young nor could he

be much educated by present standards. With the necessary apprentices the county architect is located in a workplace which is also an exhibition gallery placed by or near the county seat. He and his staff design the new buildings, develop and preserve the landscape of the county, and decide all questions affecting such matters. Nothing is left without continual provision for a better plan, keeping the way open to consistent growth. For this purpose careful studies and designs are prepared in advance for the better thing—that which has truest relation to the whole. The people themselves would be likely to express an interest in these things, because these future citizens of Broadacres would all be learning the features of that fundamental relationship at the university while young, and are growing up in it here. So the county architect would never lack for effective criticism. Wherever there is a nature-feature he would be sure to take advantage of it, as we have done here, and develop it through his knowledge of the principles and the way of life of an organic architecture.

As to what is called landscape, here are the parks. Because Broadacre City is a different type of architectural expression, one much more abstract than usual, we now make a great rising tree-wall for the park. The trees which make up the wall rise in height from the ground-level inside, up and out toward the surrounding streets. The tree-wall slopes upward from blossoming shrubs, to higher blossoming trees, then to conifers, and finally to elms and onto other majestic trees. Inside there is a more informal relationship. There are acres of flower beds, mosaics of color. At one end of these great spaces, thus sequestered, is a spacious out-of-doors music garden with enclosed spaces for dancing and refreshment.

The block-like effects seen in this model would not be so apparent as "block-like" in reality. But here we have presented everything in the abstract, it is the architect's way. But in the ultimate Broadacres it is true that landscape becomes architecture just as architecture becomes a kind of landscape. But both are integral with the ground and are an orchestration of form according to nature. Right in the midst of the future city we have fields of flowers and grain. Right in the farming section are the buildings of industry, culture, recreation and residence. Right in the midst of all is the market-place, a perpetual fair. And anywhere in it all folk may live happily at work.

Most landscape architects would say "But I love the natural scenery." Well, so do we. We augment natural "scenery." We develop for it by way of human nature, a collateral complementary scenery in the block of tree plantings in the ordered fields, even more beautiful than "nature." No, we outrage no "scenery." We aim to make it complementary to whatever we do—or the other way round adding the cleverest of human occupation as a feature in keeping with it. All the various features of life in Broadacres are appropriate to each other because the curse of ugliness and confusion has been removed from them all. Nothing can offend anything else even if it would. There is nothing offensive to either the rich man or the farmer in the proximity of each to the other nor the proximity of industry. The spacing of all is ample for all purposes and it is remarkable that it is all so simple and that it is, in the main, all so *right here now*. We need only the slight concerted political effort to remove the key-logs from the jam.

Of course there will be religion. Protestants, Catholics, Darkies and the Synagogue will be with us. Instead of each taking a little shovel full of coals and going off to start a little hell of his own in discord, we have under construction—as always, the great cathedral which is in fact a group of cathedrals. In the center, there is a great concourse or meeting place where all groups gather together to worship by way of the elements—fire, music, water, and pageantry. In this way they might grow toward

unity. But perhaps not. That depends more upon education as it would be in the future city where culture would largely take its place.

Speaking of education, notice that the children go in toward the inner spaces away from the highways and find their way from peaceful homes to peaceful schools along peaceful byways. Each school-boy and school-girl has his garden at school. Each has to begin with a hoe in his hand. In each one-story school place there is a little outdoor classroom, a little cinema, a little museum. But museums are all traveling museums. In Broadacres you will find most things decentralized, traveling continually, kept in continual circulation. All the personal, individual concerns of life are decentralized wherever possible to be applied at the desirable places as time and circumstance may give opportunity or vary the need. We begin at the root of society with culture of the children. Everything here seeks to begin again at the beginning hoping to avoid the mistakes that have all but put our Democracy to flight by now.

And the citizens must die here as elsewhere. Life is still a coming in and a going out. As man approaches death he usually becomes sentimental. He likes to see where his is to lie. So the cemetery here is mainly another greater forest reservation adjoining the cathedral. When a man dies, the trees which cover the place in which he is to be buried are cut down. His plot may be then made into a flower-bed or become a marble pavement—the choice being his, or what may be in his mind? And the crematory and columbarium is near by as another choice. Thus ends the exploitation by the monument mak-

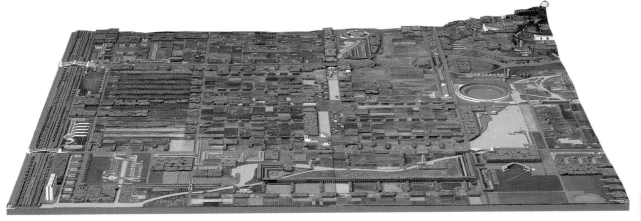

**Broadacre City Model. 1935. Photograph by Skot Weidemann. Copyright © FLLW Fdn.** FLLW Fdn FA#3402.0088

ers in common with most forms of exploitation. We have planned to end it.

Over here we have the commercial center, the marketplace a perpetual fair where the citizen and his wife come to buy and sell and see and learn. There is no reason why this still necessary barter function shouldn't be beautiful too. Flowers and vegetables picked fresh every hour are displayed here. Meats, game and fish are supplied fresh from farms and pools. And beside this market every little community center has its exhibition gallery where the finer things made by workers of all kinds are displayed to be sold. This market, as you see, is a perpetually functioning county fair of a finer sort. There would be demonstrations all the time of better ways of keeping house, planning, preserving, conserving. And there will be cultural exhibitions, examples of fine art and the universal crafts for sale. The curse is taken off commerce by its mutuality and here again—beauty. And I have not yet touched upon the beauty parlors, wayside inns, sanatoriums, hotels, skyscrapers in the country, various apartments, the clubs, cinema houses, race courses, aerodromes and various public memorials.

The traffic problem being solved, Broadacres is a delightfully safe place to live and to work in or go places near by or far away. Social intercourse is facilitated not impeded by the increased spacing and the freedom gained. Whatever you want to be or do there is an appropriate place for either. But the greatest thing here is to be able to do them all in harmony with a great altogether. The way of life as planned here kills off the specialist, eventually. But there are little compounds, with clinics or studios in gardens for doctors, scientists, architects and artists. Every professional man has his own little place of work and the people come to him. He does not waste his time and energy going to the city and back again as now.

So here, in this little model and in its collaterals, you have a definite cross-section and new form for every thing needed for a complete modern Usonian civilization. A true Culture. But the model you see here is only for this particular type of ground in these particular circumstances. Never would the same plan be imposed on land that is otherwise or when the circumstances changed. Instead, the re-sources of the land would be brought out and new forms wrought according to the circumstances.

[Postscript:] As the foregoing matter went along it was translated into German for Mies van der Rohe, the distinguished European architect now in charge of the Armour Institute of Architecture at Chicago. Many young architects were gathered together about the model listening as many thousands have listened from first to last—eagerly and intelligently as subsequent questions would show.

But, each time I attempt to put the scheme for Broadacres into words a new aspect of many details not considered before occurs to me. So no two discourses concerning the future have all in common. There is more between the lines still than appears in the lines.

## BROADACRE CITY LANDSCAPE

1. The plan for Broadacre City places the ground in human possession for human purposes instead of collecting humanity into congested narrow quarters, and viewing the ground around it.

2. Broadacres would have the landscape integral with human occupation and use, and so design its occupation and use that another landscape in human scale, no less beautiful than the natural one—even if different—must be the result. Tillage and consideration for the ground make a fresh and vitally humanized landscape.

3. Broadacres would not only preserve the integrity and beauty of the great nature-features that happened to be its site, but would add to them another beauty, considered and designed. This would come about as the natural result of a new integrity of planning and building, with appropriate systems of planting and cultivation in harmony with nature, but not "naturalistic." The outdoor extent of a man's place on the ground would become the open-air part of his house. All this a nature culture.

4. Broadacres rejects the idea that balance and rhythm are directly related to the ideal of freedom which democratic Broadacres desires to preserve. Standardization and repetition are not in themselves unbeautiful—witness a colonnade. Nor are they undesirable until they enter the domain where human life and individuality should be alive and working,

for there they stultify both life and individuality. The degree to which both standardization and repetition may be allowed to enter life-concerns (architecture is first among these concerns) depends upon the degree to which human individuality is already absent or willing to be sacrificed. Modern schools of aesthetics split upon this matter of degree. Those—the left—with less life and imagination prefer negation. Those—the right—with more life and imagination prefer the affirmations; self-expression being to them a natural expression which is needlessly sacrificed in relation to any truly liberal whole.

But the principle of an organic architecture must work neither from this "left" nor from this "right" but must go straight on. Broadacres tries to exemplify this principle at work for humanity and working not outside man but within him.

5. These models for the City of the Future—the new city in the country, Broadacre City—are all based upon the belief that there can be no lasting value in organic human nature as a mere negative or a negatived force. The Broadacres plan is motivated by the belief that everything that is true in human nature is of value—qualified by art, a force to be affirmed. Essentially man is a ground animal. Individuality is the great premium creative humanity places upon itself. Therefore, in all things concerning the individual, Broadacres plans individual free use of the ground; stands for the unification of public means to private ends in all uses of the ground. What best serves to preserve quality in the whole is accepted as best in every part. The design of the new city also sees no value in the part except as the part is harmoniously related to the whole in this sense of man and ground as one.

A great synthesis, worthy to be called a modern civilization, is implicit in Broadacres. The synthesis is attempted; and what form there is, is definitely in keeping with the nature of time, place, and Man today. That is to say, it is all in practicable Form. Broadacres is free-Form, but it is not form-free as might be supposed at first glance. It clings to what is left of liveliness in a world made ugly by ruthless exploitation—a world where the man-made outrages the God-made. Urban exaggeration has proved a curse; it is not growth. In perversion and decay lies the end of every civilization, as history records. In Broadacres urban and rural developments are made as one. And if modernity has advantages, then the modern opportunity to use them must lie in the direction of Broadacre City.

## BROADACRE HOUSES

Broadacre City houses have no basements, no attics, no separate dining rooms or kitchens, no radiators, no lighting fixtures. Yet the houses in Broadacre City are all more complete in mechanical equipment and economical in construction than any of the houses we have or any we yet know. They are one process instead of five process homes. Nevertheless they would be especially suited in plan and outline to the ground where they would stand and would make more of gardens and fields and nearby woods than now, insuring perpetual unity in variety. Just as the houses would be close to human scale in proportion so there would be a texture scale and a color scale natural to the materials used and to the way they were used. By means of sympathetic regard for nature, the houses would vary continually. "Decoration" would only be the natural result of the way in which all was used, and quite natural to modern industry.

Whether a one-car, two-car, or five-car house, there would be no differences in "Quality." The cottage next to a mansion would not seem inappropriate nor, were either next to farm, factory, studio or clinic, would the cottage be out of place. The Grandomania of egomania would find no place in the city. Yet every home would be a gentleman's house from grade to coping.

Regimentation would be gone except in public utilities and the affairs of government where individuality could not enter.

All the cars driven, all utensils and furnishings used, like the house—would express the nature of their purpose, not by mere association of ideas but by being valid gracious forms taking outward shape from interior conditions according to materials, process of making, and their purpose. Working properly together this would produce endless variety. Most of them lie long and low, emphasizing horizontal lines, but well open to views and garden.

So throughout Broadacre City there would be a true economy harmonious with the life of our century taking honest advantage of modern opportunity. All that Broadacre houses ask of society is that they be genuinely Democratic, and of all government that it be strictly impersonal. This city of the future does, however, ask for a quality of thought and a kind of thinking on the part of the citizen that organic architecture, alone at the present time represents or seems to understand; although it goes back through Jesus himself to the Chinese philosopher Lao Tze, who lived 500 B. C. A new reality in our way of living and building, an environment in our democracy.

## BROADACRES AT THE WISCONSIN STATE HISTORICAL LIBRARY, MADISON, 1937

The time lag is too great. The back-drag is becoming too heavy. Somebody has got to do some thinking which is neither politics, borrowing or lending. Why not you, my fellow citizens? Our government is doing what it can, but politics, though too willing to do so, *can't* think for you Mr. Citizen. As our government was planned, politicians dare not really lead. American politics is mostly a shrewd guess, with an eye on the politician's future. At their best, politicians can only read the writing on the wall! So the greatest good of which they are capable is to execute the will of the people—but seemingly, the people have no will. "The people" seem only to desire that more money-miracles be worked for them so that they may go on eating and sleeping in order to work and sit, as usual.

Well, Broadacre City is the living idea in these desperate circumstances of a builder and citizen, helped by a faithful band of young enthusiasts. It has and seeks no other credit than internal evidence affords to the observer. Broadacres has nothing to sell—but it does ask you to think. And if you think even a little you will see how all the forces we call modern (automobility and electro-communication) are inevitably destroying the conditions we are now seeking to live by. You will see that just as an industrial plant goes out of date overnight when a new and better machine is invented, so our whole reactionary social set-up goes out when machinery comes to be our way of livelihood. I think you will see too that

the sudden liberation from toil, which the machine brought to so many was no unmixed blessing, and that machine-made efficiencies can be just as much a curse as they are a blessing to humanity. Outside of plenty to eat and wear and show off with, the rich man is not truly better off now than the poor man. The quality of his life is often inferior. Indeed, it is just this *Quality* that is lacking in our lives. Quantity is a poor substitute, as we are learning now.

I believe you will see that if our country is to become better worth living in, the *United States of America will have to go to work!* The white collarite, himself an enormous speculative commodity, has gone to wreck riding upon speculative commodities. You probably know what these "commodities" are. I believe you will come to see, as I have, that the ground itself is the true sociological basis, and, when rightly interpreted, the salt and savor of all good life. And you will see too that the true profit of our future life is bound to come more from a man's sense of his own ground in relation to all of life—if the machine and invention are to mean anything valuable to human beings. We need a new freedom, wherein a man can use and improve a plot of ground thereby making the ground his own as long as he uses it. Neither land nor man should lie idle, a mere speculative commodity.

If our boasted "progress" means anything human, the advantages of the machine age *must* have social correlation with the ground. It is here that drudgery is best conquered by the machine. We are having our ultra-urban days, our suburban reactions and our rural isolations. Now we need the rural action that will refresh and give new meaning to all of these. We must break down the artificial barriers that exist between the urban and the rural. If you will think about it seriously you will see that *out of the ground into the light* comes everything of structure that is *beneficial* to mankind. And neither money nor leisure, given to us by the machine, can permanently change this nature of wealth.

A human being, from the time he is born, is as truly entitled to a piece of ground with which he can identify himself by the use of it as he is entitled to the air he breathes or the water he drinks. If he will work on his ground, he should eat. But, barring physical disability he should *not* eat if he does not work—except when he can fairly trade his right to work for some other actual contribution which he can make to the welfare and happiness of those who do work. Money, today, is this immunity from work, a false privilege. And because of it there is insecurity, confusion, and loss of quality in all life-concerns.

You may think this is far afield from the exhibition of the Broadacre City models. Not so. Every work of genuine architectural art has its philosophy. The philosophy of every form in Broadacres is just this "out of the ground into the light," in circumstances that make a happy thing of a man's use and improvement of *his own* ground.

As to the motive of this work called Broadacre City, it is due to an architect's love of his work and it is done in hope of showing his people the folly of expending billions to patch up, fence and fix up obsolescence. It is braver and better to let senescence die, and work to save the future.

It should be borne in mind that the models for Broadacre City show only a small section (four square miles) of a development that may extend from coast to coast, from border to border, or our country. The section here is taken at a typical county seat, and shows the various buildings that may be needed by any single county. All local phases of government are concentrated here. These models are designed for the temperate zone, planned to accommodate about fourteen hundred families in the exercise of their economic, recreational, and aesthetic lives. A premium is everywhere placed upon work and aesthetics. It is designed to provide all citizens of such a county community with the utmost in health and convenience; thus joy and pride in work may be brought back. The plan seeks to insure perfect safety of highways and beautification of the byways. Sun and air are made available to all under conditions of utmost privacy. We seek to maintain the beauty of organic relationship, each to each and all in all. With each dwelling there is a plot for intensive cultivation. The plan assumes a motor car, or a share in one, to each person. It provides for approximately an acre of ground for each person. There may be ten acres maximum, say, for a farmer —unless in certain regions for specific purposes larger tracts are needed. Spacious parks are allowed to

factories. There is no smoke, coal is burned at the mines and electric power used. Pipes are at the curb for gasoline, natural gas, and oil. The confident Mr. Rexford Tugwell thought the scheme carried horizontality too far—but even so, the present population of these United States could be comfortably accommodated in the state of Texas alone!

Among the architectural solutions of the traffic problem, there would be no grade crossings even on the gridiron, which, in this plan, is robbed of its objectionable features. It would be impossible for pedestrians to be run down. I ask you, what solution is there of the car versus the man in the present city? The traffic problem is an architectural problem.

Broadacre children are students in no "knowledge-factory" to become "system fodder," but are placed at the heart of the whole arrangement. Growth is a feature provided for in the city by the absence of all axial academic pattern of any kind, except government.

A simple system of federal or state reforestation reserves and subsidizes the planting each year of a certain acreage in useful woods. About one-third of the total area might be devoted to this. Meantime the growing tree-masses automatically lend shade and provide privacy and beauty to the whole city. Thus a new type of landscape is developed, one more architectural than now but no less beautiful because of its ordered spacing.

And Broadacre road-building, lighting, and bridge building all become good architecture. The modern process of factory fabrication is at work in the design of all this. But it is no longer a fetish. Mass production is here used as a definite means to develop more individuality and provide more comfort. "Standardization" is so used everywhere, to widen the scope of individuality. You may see this by studying the great variety of forms that spring from this fresh contact with the ground when the ground itself becomes an inspiring factor in the designing of the form.

Now, to take these models as literal pictures would be to miss their effect. A certain symbolism has been used throughout. It is the artist's way of presenting his subject. And using this term "artist" reminds me of the time the technocrat, Howard

Scott, came to Rockefeller Center to see Broadacres. At a glance he dismissed the whole with a wave of his hand, saying to the surrounding reporters, "Just an artist's dream. What this country needs is technocracy—more and more technocracy."

Now *that,* I'm afraid, is pretty much our social concept of the artist and his function—the dreaming and posing of his dream. It is a fundamental misunderstanding, a misunderstanding that may rob us of a way out of the mess we are making for ourselves and of ourselves. The artist, the "dreamer," supplies an element which the scientist, the "expert," the statistician, cannot supply; and that element is *"vision."*

"Where there is no vision the people perish."

Broadacre City is an unusually definite creative artist's vision. We have made these models so that you can see and touch the future city. And we exhibit it because nothing seems more important at this time than to awaken thought along the lines I have just been talking about. I hope I am talking well into the minds of some few listeners in relation to this whole business of life. Some of us are pretty well askew and some of us are looking askance at the sight. We well may be.

But Broadacre City, at least, does see this business of life as a whole. It sees life, not as a burden but as a splendid privilege; and it sees that no part of life amounts to much unless that part is harmoniously related to the whole. Thanks to creative scientists like Einstein, the creative-artist and the creative-scientist may now agree in this.

I think you now have a picture of a conservative *interpretation* of our vast machine-age resources in terms of a sound structural ideal that is comprehensive. The whole nature and character of this civilization of ours has in these models been *interpreted* and executed in detail to show a profit to *humanity* out of our vast mechanical resources and material riches.

Broadacre City is, of course, no political expedient. Nor has it anything to sell to a people already so badly oversold as we are. But in this idea of the new city is something to provoke your own needed thought; and it is definitely up to you fellow citizens. You must do the thinking, or you will see a noble ideal of human freedom wrecked before it comes of age. You must save it from being wrecked

by those "captains" who are too blind to see any future beyond their system of financial profit, or loss.

## BROADACRES TO PITTSBURGH

I know little of Alleghany County, but what I've seen of it shows it very different from county sections typified by Broadacre City. Nevertheless, the principles working in Broadacres should work as well for Alleghany county. But Pittsburgh seems to have ignored all principle in getting itself born if it ever meant to be a human asset. I believe the county largely a human liability.

A fundamental Broadacre principle is that all features of this city of the future arise out of the "lay of the land"—in both character and topography; also out of the industrial conditions arising from contiguity to rivers, lakes, mines, and timber, as well as other sources of supply for industry. Obviously this principle has not entered into the planning of Pittsburgh, if indeed there ever was any thought at all for Pittsburgh as a place to live in, and not forced upon it, post mortem.

Another Broadacre principle is the decentralization of everything except government, the centralization of which would be increased but simplified. Pittsburgh has tried to centralize everything across a river, regardless of expense, and—if reports are true—has tried, with much success, to decentralize government when it could.

Alleghany County seems to have worked on "to hell with nature, we'll get what we want." And I guess the indomitable Pittsburgh spirit got it. But, as I can see, it has been a pretty expensive and troublesome work down there in the gorge, the bare hills crowding in upon the river; and it is now none too good a place to be in unless to get a bare living, which, of course, is the only motive for living there at all.

So Pittsburgh (the biggest part of Alleghany County) huddles uncomfortably on two sides of the river; and climbs up the hillsides of the gorge as far as it can, meantime looking not only dirty and drab, but uncomfortable, as it tries to tie itself together with bridges, more bridges, and again bridges, and have its being in spite of the river. "In spite of the river" ought to be a Pittsburgh slogan, "to hell with the hills" thrown in for full effect. But the blind forces that built Pittsburgh regardless are now turning against the city to destroy it as they will destroy all the ultra industrial crowdings we call urban, except the great ports, and they will probably change them altogether. These blind forces are the great modern forces of machinery. Thanks to them Pittsburgh is already no more than useless scaffolding for the life that must soon appear. I see that the best people (most fortunate anyway) have gone away into the hills or made a palatial ribbon development of their own on a highway or two going out of town. (Of course the highway still comes back into town). But Pittsburgh in common with all cities, becomes more and more a slum as it becomes less and less livable. And no doubt eventually—as new machines and processes are invented—the city will become wholly obsolete—as a factory may become obsolete overnight.

I wonder how far, right now, the poison-gas that pours into the air and the corroding acids that pour into the river from her great mills are necessary? I wonder how far, right now, the great mills themselves are necessarily brutal, big, barren of human interest and so far out of human scale? I suspect they too are now only needless scaffolding; and that their real purpose will soon go afield into great parks and take with them and plant roundabout them (within a radius of ten miles or more) the humanity that once suffered them to be inhuman. The mills might then become factors for broader and better living conditions and for work. If they fail to lead in that direction so much the worse for their "interests." Ask Henry Ford about that, he seems to have learned something from his experience.

Big fruits often die on the vine just as such centralized "interest" as Pittsburgh must die. At this late day it is no use, even as medicine perhaps, to imagine how the river might have been made into a beautiful feature by damming and pooling it, flood-controlling it above, with driveways made across the dams of the pools to the tune of waterfalls as the parkways lead into and up to terraced levels alongside the pools for building picturesquely in relation to the waters; or to imagine how the factories and merchandising might have spread out on these lower terraces in parks with direct access to calm waters;

how the dwellings might have had each their acre and their gardens in clean air and sunshine—both related to the sense of space that is growing up now as modern; how motorization itself might have been made a safe pleasure instead of a perpetual hazard for the people going places in it all? Now, Broadacre City is simply a pattern for the elimination of this hazardous confusion of idea and purpose.

To apply its principles to Pittsburgh may be idle speculation because Pittsburgh is obsolescent and as slowly dying as surely as humanity is growing. In all probability the town will have to be abandoned, eventually to become a rusty ruin and tumble into the river, staining the waters with oxide of iron for another half century, meanwhile marking the spot where one phase of human endeavor, the era of excess called efficiency ended, and another phase began— the new phase to be known as the era of decentralization: the era wherein man as the normal unit became more free by way of the very machines that under present day centralization came near to enslaving him: the new era wherein thousands are to become individual capitalists in their own right instead of continuing to be employees of a diminishing few until, ultimately, only one would remain as supreme capitalistic lord-of-all.

In terms of practical structure Broadacre City is in Pittsburgh to preach a new hope for people who live in places like Pittsburgh. It definitely plans a rescue for that oppressed human element living in ugliness and danger, and by rejecting the specious old success-ideal as well as the complex old academic harness for it, uses the human birthright of the ground, as it ought to be used. Broadacre City proposes to use it as the greatest resource, for social progress in the making of a better mankind, in a true Democratic state.

## BROADACRE CITY IRKS THE MAYOR

*[A reply to the Mayor of Pittsburgh, 1935. "Democrats won't go there," says he.]*

Being mayor of Pittsburgh, or of any American city, must be a disqualification for seeing anything but bugaboos in Broadacre City. But if "Hizzoner" will take it from me, Broadacre City is not socialistic in any sense that he knows. Thomas

MODELS MADE B
FRANK LLOYD

Craven came to see the models at the Center in New York. He was amused because some of his friends had declared the new city to be "communism," some had declared it plainly "fascism," and some were sure it was a socialistic Utopia.

Since others have misconstrued, as the mayor does, here is the cat out of the bag! Broadacre City is "capitalism" carried to a humane conclusion, its base broadened, and placed firmly on the ground. In the new city every man is an actual capitalist with his feet on his own ground. He is free to choose the work best suited to him because economic independence enables him to say "no" as well as "yes." Today every man is only a potential capitalist, a petty gambler and the devil take the loser. Broadacre City is Organic Capitalism.

Broadacre citizens are no hirelings. They are free citizens, entirely on their own and *in* their own too where individuality has any concern. The Broadacres plan proceeds from generals to particulars; it assumes that neither land nor money nor creative ideas can be speculative commodities to be traded in or held over by somebody against the common good. If that necessarily means the Mayor's brand of Socialism, then God help Pittsburgh.

Nor does Broadacres believe that "politics" should be any more than the policy of the people themselves concerning the public utilities about which we hear continual wrangling among our mayors and politicians. There is a lot of snarling going on over that bone of contention. Another feature is thrown in for good measure, it is this— Broadacres' citizens who won't work shall starve. Through the right use of one's own faculties instead of through the use of money, is the Broadacre way.

The aged, the lame, halt and blind are, of course, another matter. They are well protected in the future city—and not by charity. The mayor says it would be no place for babies to be born in, and that a bunch of drunks would wreck the town. But there would be a place for every baby born there whereas the only right a baby has now is to the air it breathes. As for drunks, a home in Broadacres would be its own saloon if the Broadacre citizen so wished but a more decent one than any the mayor can show in his Pittsburgh. So why does Hizzoner think he could handle a bunch of drunks better than Broadacre citizens? I suspect that the "drunks" who owned their own homes would deal with rough and reckless drunks permanently. Plain drunks are not the only consequences of urban depravity Broadacres will reckon with. Yes, Broadacres, I am sure, would be better for babies and more devastating to plain drunks that even the mayor of Pittsburgh himself could ever be in his bailiwick.

"Democrats won't go there," Hizzoner says, probably with the Democratic Party of Pittsburgh in mind. And I don't know why any politician is going to go anywhere where he would be seriously required to think about the *rights of man,* or else be an intruder. I am afraid "Democrats" that try to get on to tickets nowadays wouldn't get very far in this city of the future because in this city they would have to be of a real service or starve.

Yes . . . the Broadacre idea means, quite simply, that these United States of America would have to go to work. As to money, they have had it and they have spent it or they have got it and mean to keep it or they are in line for it they think. Before all else Broadacres does mean just that: the citizens of the United States of America (as a whole) really will go to work without hindrance, putting into shape some good ideas, instead of sitting around waiting for their own government to feed them, think up jobs for them, pat them on the back or put them in the "workhouse" as Hizzoner says he does when they get drunk.

Mr. Mayor: How about a place in America where every man was his own jobber on his own job, and in his own way was doing something worthwhile for himself and his country at the same time? Would that be no place for your Democrats? That is just what the city of Broadacres would mean to our country. Our country has too long swung from Right to Left or from Left to Right, according to the direction in which the citizen thought his personal fortune to lie. Hizzoner says that our President Roosevelt knows nothing about human nature either, and wants to do for *us* such as Broadacres represents. "Us" is the Mayor's world.

Well, I don't know what the President intends but I don't believe he has yet seen or, if his cousin Delano has anything to say about, will ever see Broadacre City. But certainly the President knows

**Previous pages: Broadacre City Model. 1935. Photograph by Skot Weidemann. Copyright © FLLW Fdn.** FLLW Fdn FA#3402.0090

enough of human nature to be elected President of the United States, and to have dealt summarily with a situation so complex that it makes no sense at all. Least of all does that situation make sense to those who criticize him most. If any man ever had the most thankless job on earth, Franklin Roosevelt has that job. That job as he sees it is to save the capitalist system. He has my deepest sympathy and complete loyalty in that vain endeavor. But, before all, our president is an executive. Where is the will of the people? As to what will he must be continually guessing. If the people knew anything, or could talk intelligently about their own affairs, they might have some right to criticize their executive. But what right have they in the circumstances of having no ideas. The Roosevelt guess can't be worse than their own.

Money miracles have always come to an end. I think they are nearing an end for us all. Broadacre City seeing it so, plans a sane use of what was best in our old so-called system and kicks out the rest: overgrown cities and their mayors for instance, small towns aping big cities, the poor old telephone and telegraph companies, surcharged utility companies, senescent railroads, mass production in education or other human interest, all and sundry. This is done in order that we may have thousands of thousands of bona fide capitalists—instead of a few bona fide, with millionaires and millions of merely petty gamblers hanging to them or around them in bunches like grapes of wrath. Our president is up against a rotten remnant that politically has no other thought than to try to persuade the American people that a satisfied plutocracy and a contented democracy can live happily together. Insanity!

Well, Broadacre City is sanity. Sanity sees that great changes have already taken place and sees more taking place under our very eyes throughout the country, a complete lack of planning for present or future notwithstanding. Nothing looking that way has at this time been intelligently designed.

Well, Broadacres is a plan, so free in pattern that consequent or subsequent destruction to allow for growth is made unnecessary. It has come to town that you might see it and touch it; to show how the changes taking place can work for the citizen be he rich or poor. Neither from the Left nor

from the Right but Straight-on is all the politics or politicians Broadacres knows, yes, your Honor, or ever wants to know.

## A NEW FREEDOM FOR LIVING IN AMERICA

*[Broadcast by Mr. Wright at the opening of the National Exposition of Arts and Industries, Rockefeller Center, New York, April 1935, where the models of Broadacre City were shown.]*

Upon an occasion like this, to say that I love America and her initial ideal of Democracy is to set myself down as the usual sentimentalist or as a mere politician. Nevertheless I say it. It is my first line as I believe it will be my last sentiment. But even if the first forefathers of our Democracy could have foreseen the kind of success we were to have by way of the machine they could not have set up the necessary mechanism needed to defend their ideal of democracy. Let us admit it—our forefathers lacked the technique. Nor have statesmen with the needed fundamental technique and the necessary nerve yet appeared.

Meantime what hope of Democracy we have left to us goes from bad to worse, until almost no one now believes it practical. Here we are, an enormous nation of "ites," "istic" with all the "isms" which make the also-ran, busily inventing new isms—tragic breakdown staring us in the face. The present success-ideal proves to be a bad one for all but the few.

Now an architect should at least see life as organic form continually. His work should take shape according to the fundamentals of human nature and nature otherwise. As an architect I can see no such organic form in the life of our people today, but I can see forces working together or separately in that direction. As everyone knows, we live in economic, aesthetic and moral chaos, for the reason that American life has achieved no organic form. As our civilization moves on it becomes more of an agonizing economic struggle than a happy realization.

But this architect knows, too, that all true forms are born of some inner struggle. So far as our struggle has been, and is, sincere, we may hope to find the forms architectural and economic that will finally let Democracy come through to us.

Out of an experience somewhat extensive in getting organic forms evolved in our architecture, it is with the great hope to make clear an organic form for the Democratic city of the American future that I have tried to grasp and concretely interpret the whole drift of great change taking place in and around us, in order to help create a human state more natural than the one that present cupidity and stupidity will allow. This means, of course, that through these models we have set up you may see a new success ideal for your own America.

In Broadacres you will find not only a pattern for natural freedom for the individual as individual. You will find there structure based upon decentralization of nearly everything big business has built up to be "Big," and you will find an economic ground-structure aimed at more individuality and greater simplicity, and at more direct responsibility of government where human individuality is not concerned. So Broadacre City is no mere "Back-to-the-Land" idea but is, rather, a breaking down of the artificial divisions set up between urban and rural life. By a more intelligent use of our developed scientific powers we establish a practical way of life that will bring the Arts, Agriculture, and Industry into a harmonious whole. And, I believe that there are harmonious elements of any city that really has a democratic future. Whether we yet know it or not we are about ready to throw away the costly but ugly scaffolding of which present urban life is the worst example, and let the horizontal city appear together with a system of creation and distribution more corresponding to the natural conditions to our life here on earth. Naturally the new city will appear because of, and by way of, the great development in science that we have so dearly bought as the physical basis for our present life. We ought now to use that basis for the purpose of a greater freedom instead of our growth being hampered and our souls enslaved by its consequences.

So here, in the entrails of final enormity, Rockefeller Center, New York City, you may see concrete ideas of a fresh way of life—man staying with the ground, his imagination creating new forms firmly based on the ideals that were intended to found this country in new freedom as a democracy.

Certainly, the new forms that Broadacres proposes do represent a new success-ideal but the forms are not mere invention. By anyone inclined to pa-

tiently study them they will be found to be conservative *interpretations* of actual circumstances today. I do not say that Broadacre City is the ultimate form. But I say it might well be that if we could honestly call our lives our own we are going forward to the freedom of which the forefathers well dreamed.

Great nature mocks man-made efforts, throws the man aside to take a little here and a little there to go on with her work. I could point to history to prove that to work with her is wisdom, to go against her is failure or even worse, catastrophe. And it no longer requires a seer to realize that America now knows the punishments that are the result of going recklessly against nature. Broadacre City not only perceives that failure, but with the belief that quantity can never be a satisfactory substitute for quality gathers together the net result of our best world-efforts to this time, and goes forward to a new cultural form more firmly and generously based upon enlightened human egoism than any yet conceived. Superficially you will see it as a form of architectural order but you may see it as *inherently* a safer basis for our democratic society than the substitute for civilization we have achieved in our quite complete commercialization of life.

It is high time that some fundamental radicals among us gathered together the loose ends of opportunity lying waste all about us, and instead of laying more, by means of them, project some such sensible plan for life as our forefathers hoped and believed would be ours. It is some organic sense of the whole seen as entity that is now the greatest social need.

Because the psychological moment is here, the models are here to show you the future that is now. Really to grasp the significance of our work on this cross-section of our civilization requires considerably more intelligent and unselfish application on your part than most of you will yet be either prepared, or be willing to give. But the making of these models required just that kind of application for a life-time and also the fruit of a life-time of experience. Many months of devotion on the part of the Taliesin Fellowship—the young men and women who unselfishly made them—has brought the models here, where their worth for the future may be judged.

# OUR WORK

The article "Wake Up America!" appears as an editorial in the February 1941 issue of Taliesin. The major part of this issue of the magazine is devoted to describing the activities of the Taliesin Fellowship, including articles by Wright's wife and several of his apprentices.

The issue opens with Wright's text entitled "Our Work" and is a description of the aims of the Taliesin Fellowship. The fellowship had existed for nine years. It was started in 1932, at the worst point of the Great Depression. Wright's friends, relatives, clients, and neighbors were all of the opinion that the school would not survive longer than a year; but the school survived and expanded, which can be seen as a tribute to the Wrights and to the apprentices who, hand in hand, worked hard and long to keep Taliesin afloat.

As the Taliesin Fellowship approached the end of its first decade, Wright stated the values and principles upon which it was founded:

A short-time ex-apprentice asked an apprentice still working at Taliesin, "Is Mr. Wright only interested in turning out men—or is he really interested in turning out architects?" I should answer him by saying, that in spite of feudal hangovers and the abuses the machine is piling up on top of them, both time and tide are so running that unless we have the man we cannot have what I have been calling the architect. The very idea of an organic architecture is of such integrity that you are the thing you do or you can't do much. So I believe that the builder who will eventually take the place of the old broker in architecture must interpret Life in terms of actual building, and in a democracy do so out of himself. But not knowing life from within, how is he going to make life objective by any building whatever? I say he must become an all-around man no longer content to be a man-achine. At the moment this is a dangerous heresy. . . . Art has been left out or far behind in these shifts. And that means that the greatest human element of all life in all time has been left out, especially left out of the thing we miscall education. Foolishly we imagine our brand of education to be culture. By way of the omission—notwithstanding the teaching and practice of the "History of Art," education and culture in America are no longer on speaking terms.

At Taliesin we hope to make them one.

Wright's inspiring ability to communicate to young people is well expressed in several passages in this article:

To this end the Taliesin novitiate is decentralization, a mobile way of life wherein "servant" has ceased to exist. "Service" is not sales talk at Taliesin but a natural condition. Everyone's hands are in the mud from which the bricks are made. And they are made from early rising bell until all tumble into bed, not quite worn out.

But he also showed his humor:

But unfortunately for architecture and for you, young man, Democracy in America is unnecessarily slow *and becoming troublesome. Plutocracy is swifter, and here. Temporarily.*

*[Published in* Taliesin *magazine, February 1941]*

WHY DO YOU WANT TO BECOME AN ARCHITECT?

If you can truthfully say you love building and want to know buildings from the inside out, how do you expect to become the kind of builder we call an Architect?

What do you expect to learn in the schools that will help you to build good buildings? Mathematics? History of Art—Design?

Experience in actual planning and actual building with materials, learning the nature of materials by actual work with materials is needed. But the contractor and builder is not an architect. Then, where is the characteristic creative inspiration of all true architecture to be found?

Of what possible use to you there are schoolbooks and art history or school "styles" or any mere technique, where all that is concerned?

Poor, patchwork America needs no more "period" architecture. She needs integral architecture. She needs organic character in all her institutions. Experience, inspired, could furnish the data for true interpretation of her own life. University education with its armchair styles and armchair historical points of view can't give this needed inspiration to the young man today. At best, the university as it stands can have but a small place in the development of any creative ability. At worst it can ruin what the young man has. The young man in architecture must seek experience under inspired leadership—seek the guidance of men who know building from the inside out, content to build from the ground up. And I mean spiritually as well as outwardly. Master-minds to whom the philosophy of structure is a natural consequence of learning from the great book of books—creation itself, knowing that a style is the graveyard of all Style.

So, find a master young man! He will be the better for you and you for him in any democracy, if Democracy works. At Taliesin we believe it will work.

But unfortunately for architecture and for you, young man, Democracy in America is unnecessarily slow and becoming troublesome. Plutocracy is swifter, and here. Temporarily.

## THE FELLOWSHIP

I should say that present systems of government-spending and popular education are exactly wrong if architecture, radical structure, is the genuine concern of education or government.

To justify this statement I point to consequences: the imitations and general sterility that make of America a place wherein you will be hard put to it to find anything from the hand of any professional manifestly inspired by the country itself or true to any life in it that might be called native.

Taliesin has no choice but to reject nearly all the tenets that would maintain such national characteristics as the "cultural lag." We have set up in Wisconsin an experiment which volunteers something so simple as to be amusing to the complex mental processes that expect to get enlightenment by cerebratious studentry, pseudo Beaux-Arts training in high and higher schools; training looked upon with contempt by the French Beaux-Arts itself as I have learned from the Director of the Beaux-Arts—himself.

For eight years past, a small, changing group of about twenty-five (young men and women—all volunteers) have formed the working group of apprentices to myself. During that time the overeducated novice has met at first from me, neglect, in the hope that he might "relax" and so let such natural perception as he might have get a good "break." The novitiate soon finds the familiar books and the information they afford left behind. The Fellowship must and does stand together in atmosphere free from pretense. It stands upon "soil" which will nourish sincerity of character and purpose. Each Fellow may honestly possess that, at least, as a basis for cultivation of talent. Genius is something added to this from within and we can neither furnish nor gainsay it.

Previous education is usually a hindrance. All begin afresh (if they begin at all) to think about building as interpretation of life as lived now or soon. The novice cannot avoid the implications of such thinking nor can he ever get away from its effects. All are here together with me in a spontaneous way of life in surroundings pointing in the direction of that interpretation. They are the working comrades of one who has been "seeing it through" long enough to have gained some little wisdom from the actual experience of getting the principles of integral architecture into concrete form. That "one" is my-self. In this I think I have been tried by my time al-most as much as I have been a trial to my time?

But in any case apprenticeship back there in the feudal middle-ages was something like this one at Taliesin but with an important difference: the ap-prentice then was his master's servant: at democratic Taliesin he is his master's comrade. The apprentice is actively engaged with his master, together with a closely limited group of others like-minded, in the spirit of timely creation. While up to the present some one hundred and sixty young men now prac-ticing around the world have been with me for some time as employees, only during the past sev-eral years have any been here in the give-and-take of apprenticeship as we know it here now.

Young men have come and gone with appar-ently no deeper intention than to pick up whatever they could and turn it over to their advantage out in the "cash and carry" system as quickly as possible. I was then willing, but none too cooperative. Even so, some few of them managed pretty well.

But now, I expect these more intimate young co-workers, we are calling them apprentices, to be valuable workmen to their master's idea of work, knowing something of the nature of the whole, grow-ing able to utter it in building, or able to write, sing or play it in terms of the spirit of our own time, using well the manifold new opportunities of that time.

Unfortunately, the novice must bring some money to Taliesin with him to begin with in order to take his living off us while he is still a beginner. But we are not, even so, interested in getting him ready to earn money on the present basis of architectural brokerage or wagery. I have seen the damage that has done to a good cause. All the new methods have so far outrun the understanding of architect or artist that the feudal hang-overs of our economic system (cash and carry) kill his new effort just as they have killed the old culture and brought on the cultural lag.

I believe the old-style practitioner—broker of the styles (he was really a coroner) is dead anyway. A more creative individual capable of going through from start to finish with his own building as a master-builder is on the way to take his place. At

Taliesin apprentice Eugene Masselink making the model of the S.C. Johnson & Son Co. Administration Building, 1937. Photograph by Edmund Teske. FLLW Fdn FA#6511.0025

Taliesin we are trying to get him ready.

It will be the Master-builder in this sense and not an Architect in former sense who is going to make America a genuine Broadacre City, in due course.

Then, any architect will do perhaps only sever-al buildings but he will do them completely. Where predecessors did several hundred carcasses turning all over to office boys and an equivalent of the hairdress-er, or couturier, as a kind of "master of ceremonies."

In the Future that I believe to be the Present this master-builder will be a better balanced creative factor in Usonian society. He will be a single factor taking the place of realtor, contractor, decorator, landscapist and financier. All responsibility for his client's building will be actually placed in his hands. Professional predecessors worked for six percent— say. This architect of the future will work for thirty percent. What we are trying to do at Taliesin is sim-ply to make a little human material more fit for such increased individual responsibility, and qualified to see life as a whole. Part of our work is to awaken Usonian society itself to the immense service archi-tecture on that basis could render now. The new frontier lies right there.

To this end the Taliesin novitiate is decentral-ization, a mobile way of life wherein "servant" has ceased to exist. "Service" is not sales talk at Taliesin but a natural condition. Everyone's hands are in the mud from which the bricks are made. And they are made from early rising bell until all tumble into bed, not quite worn out. The inexperienced gradually get the sense of design and the feeling of materials into their hands after working upon plans and details to be executed in the nature of those materials aware of the purpose of the building planned. They find new uses to be made of new materials; get correlation of hand and brain where any plan or any necessity for planning is concerned. Meanwhile they are developing mastery over self through hard work and clear thinking along center lines Principle lays down. Those laid down by Tradition (with a capital T) are preserved here only in the spirit in which they were made. Traditions with a small "t" are lying around here almost entirely out of use. Taliesin is probably preaching and practicing again the old gospel of hard-work: adding tired to tired and adding it again.

The unpopular gospel of Work. And at a stage in our growth as a nation where all work is more or less prostitute to "wages." The worker a wage slave. Therefore I lay myself open to peculiarly invidious implications for the system. One of them, "getting my work done for nothing."

But—never mind. All it costs me to get my work done is all I have ever learned or earned or ever expect to earn or learn.

Work, work with new light for human-nature upon the nature of work, more especially where it concerns good building. A dream? Well, real enough to those who get into action here. Here is action, more action, and some more action all the while. Continual emergency at Taliesin! Not so much to work with here yet, even after eight years, but all the more necessity to work with thought, actuated by thought to germinate a better thought and a better way of doing whatever may be at hand to do.

Workers here become the thing they would do for their living. But the "job" and money-getting are set aside for years. We know that if our premise is right there will be no need to worry about that.

So this kind of life is no longer current "education." It is culture, instead. Organic growth is slow growth indeed—but the growth is real. While growth is going on we are all pretty well content.

Few scholastic "graduates" seem fitted to enter this sort of life. I mean there are few universities still able to make the necessary surrender to Reality instead of looking at prospects in the "cash and carry" system. University men either hopelessly in love with the romantic aspect of the pluto-democratic capitalist gamble or educated to imagine certain hard facts of the system to be reality do not constitute our reality. Too many graduates similar to those who first came here are therefore in the same case as any poor squirrel who might mistake the shell of the nut for the kernel. That squirrel wouldn't live well or live long in the circumstances. And exactly that is happening to the "graduate" today.

Similarly, the architects who made our present Architecture and left it to us as a predicament, are dead. Most of them were at best "designing partners." If anything is needed to prove that our present Architecture is their unburied corpse the late monuments at Washington erected to the memory of our beloved great, prove it.

We do not advocate a style at Taliesin, believing (I reiterate) that a style is the grave of Style. But what we do we practice in the nature of Style, and do so all the while.

Abstraction, the real form-pattern seen behind appearances really making them what they are, is continually being treated afresh.

We are learning to think and see in simples. And simples are always "abstract"?

Workers at Taliesin—whenever the spirit moves—record abstractions, what they see behind the outward aspect of their surroundings. They make such abstractions into buildings eventually as the deeper side of their labors. All are so minded and encouraged by me as to learn to see the outward form inside. Likewise see the inside from inside. Occasionally we exhibit such drawings by the Fellows in our little gallery. We often indulge in talk—sometimes encourage it. We write, and play too. When the spirit moves talk is pretty good.

Meanwhile, to work with, we have Taliesin itself; a spacious new draughting room; a new little playhouse made out of the old Hillside Home School gymnasium; likewise two small galleries for intimate exhibitions. We have made many fine models: good workmanship. We have it all upon about a thousand acres where Wisconsin is most beautiful. Taking our work along with us we leave it for the five winter months of each year to get fresh contacts with other soil and other scenes while we work: each year five months of Arizona desert. Seven months at Taliesin in pastoral environment. Next year maybe Russia or Japan or Mexico because any real architect, now, must be a citizen of this world. No narrow nationalist can exist in the light of this ideal of architecture as organic expression of organic social life. But nationalism as such as we know it now, goes to seed as it continually goes to war. We shall not escape. But the way of escape lies in the way of life at Taliesin and that is less eye upon the outside and more upon the inside. Less ambition for ourselves where others are concerned and more where we are concerned with ourselves—isolationist until intervention has some real basis. It would not then be intervention—but, even in participation, minding one's own business.

The unpardonable sin at Taliesin is to rest unless you are doing something while you "rest." We believe in recreation—not rest—and believe that change of the right kind of work in the right way is itself a valid sport. We believe too, that the pause to observe and reflect is often clearest in perspective when action is swiftest and most certain. Organic growth is slow growth and an obstruction, no doubt, in this age of the quick "turnover" and "intervention" for self-interest. But organic growth is not merely a garment to be hastily put on as current education tries to put it on in four years. No, it is of the thing, not on it, at Taliesin and it stays.

A short-time ex-apprentice recently asked an apprentice still working at Taliesin, "Is Mr. Wright only interested in turning out men—or is he really interested in turning out architects?" I should answer him by saying, that in spite of feudal hangovers and the abuses the machine is piling up on top of them, both time and tide are so running that unless we have the man we cannot have what I have been calling the architect. The very idea of an organic architecture is of such integrity that you are the thing you do or you can't do much. So I believe that the builder who will eventually take the place of the old broker in architecture must interpret Life in terms of actual building and in a democracy do so out of himself. But not knowing life from within how is he going to make life objective by any building whatever? I say he must become an all-around man no longer content to be a man-machine. At the moment this is dangerous heresy.

We are "turning out a lot of little Frank Lloyd Wrights," are we? And "none of them can get a license to practice architecture because the schools have legislation to their credit making only their product eligible for one."

That too.

Let's wait and see.

Neither, as impediment, exists for us at present.

Faith in knowledge of Principle made the practice of the Frank Lloyd Wright who speaks now and whenever he speaks to his apprentices or works alongside them. He is working continually. Principle doesn't make imitators in any long run. As for a "license to practice," well, no real builder needs any legal license that can't be had by his showing what he has actually done. Which is the only way any master-builder should be able to get a license to practice architecture at all.

Meantime, the services of the Taliesin Fellowship under my own direction are for sale to industry in the crafts or building for those who may have some special detached interest in any one of them, in planning, planting, and furnishing a home. We now have some reason to hope that a Fellowship at Taliesin may be valuable as "a living."

All of which causes people to regard Taliesin, "the foundation" and its Fellowship of apprentices, as some kind of "institution." But as time goes on the tendency will grow to regard Taliesin as less and less the home and workshop of a creative architect and more and more an endeavor in the direction of an indigenous culture.

Really Taliesin is yet no more like an institution than it was when I first built it as a place in which to live and work, myself. Employees in the Studio were then never more than seven. Even with enlarged facilities apprentices will—I hope—never be more than thirty. At one time the danger of institution did loom ahead but that was in the days when the first Taliesin prospectus was issued.

The danger soon became apparent and those plans promptly discarded. Others were made to preserve individuality, flexibility, and original integrity or let us say, the integrity of originality that primarily characterized Taliesin. Work and life here will never be "established" in the current sense of the term nor will Taliesin ever be an "institution" if I can help it. Nor will it become a popular success while I am living. Taliesin must remain, as it is, a slowly growing performance for creative work in America, but more especially is it a place in which to work together with me. Taliesin does have a tradition; perhaps the place has the only cultural tradition America can call its own: the tradition that is the birth and growth on American soil of the philosophy and ideals of an integral (or organic) architecture.

To live this organic philosophy is to live completely but dangerously and, as things are, more or less at the mercy of the misunderstanding and prejudice which must have its "bogey men."

No, the Taliesin Fellowship is in no danger of becoming a radical "cult." Its leader despises cults far too much for that to happen to us now.

So then to regard Taliesin as an individual attempt to produce the creative performance America so sorely needs (a need developed rather than satisfied by any of her academic systems) is to be able to quite completely understand its aims, their essential integrity and simplicity. We are not only building our own buildings at Hillside and steadily improving our quarters at Taliesin but we are building thirty or forty interesting houses for interested and interesting people in many different states. Besides this we have just taken the second Fellowship contract for a complete work. If we are American in spirit at Taliesin we must be un-American in method. Where technique is concerned, and it is always a concern, we are making new ones, techniques that we can honestly call our own and use well because we grow to understand them thoroughly by practice.

The strongest element in America today is no longer the city, nor the factory element. Nor the winners of the gamblers-game as set up and deified by national advertising; but it is the now neglected, strongest coming element: the agrarian.

The ground and what it holds for men in health and strength and inspiration, it is this that America has most neglected. Therefore she has neglected the true basis for any Culture she can call her own.

Organized manufacture has its "communism" and its prophets.

Organized "capital" has its success-ideal, its captains and its universities and all the profits and losses, and miscalls itself—democracy.

Science impartially serves both and as impartially is returning toward organizing the life of the ground in new cultural forms to express and enrich the life of today.

Time is here when a new sense of human values awakens in America and turns prophets, and such profits as we have known, to basic human values richer in content—turning forward toward our birthright—the ground. The true poet, of whatever kind, will now best serve the ground.

The ground! One unfailing human resource never "dated." For whatever great life or great art the world has won or will ever win the ground is the one unfailing source of inspiration. No matter how far away man drifted nostalgia made him suffer, weep and return—to the ground!

Unhappily all we can call America's culture has been the parasite's exploitation of other culture or some divorce from nature fatal to any sincerity of mind no matter how successfully civilization such as ours makes-shift with Science. Art has been left out or far behind in these shifts. And that means that the greatest human element of all life in all time has been left out, especially left out of the thing we miscall education. Foolishly we imagine our brand of education to be culture. By way of the omission—notwithstanding the teaching and practice of the "History of Art," education and culture in America are no longer on speaking terms.

At Taliesin we hope to make them one.

# OF WHAT USE IS A GREAT NAVY WITH NO PLACE TO HIDE?

The Taliesin Square-Papers (seventeen published from January 1941 to February 1953) served as a vehicle for Wright to voice his views and make them public. On the byline of the paper was printed,

A TALIESIN SQUARE-PAPER

A NON POLITICAL VOICE FROM OUR DEMOCRATIC MINORITY

A FREE FEARLESS ENLIGHTENED MINORITY IS THE CONSCIENCE OF A DEMOCRATIC NATION. WHEN THIS IS STIFLED, DEMOCRACY IS GONE FROM THE LIFE OF THE NATION.

The first Taliesin Square-Paper, published in February 1941, was Wright's response to a cablegram that came from the News Chronicle of London asking him to reply, in 1,500 words, to the statement "How I Would Rebuild London." As well as making it a Taliesin Square-Paper, he later incorporated the reply into the 1943 edition of An Autobiography.[1] Since London was being destroyed by constant bombing, his advice concerning rebuilding was strongly based on the various themes and elements of Broadacre City, foremost among them decentalization.

The second Taliesin Square-Paper, from May of the same year, further expounds on Wright's idea about the United States and the Second World War. Here he amplified his objections and concerns that were first published a year earlier in the article "Wake Up America!":

The democratic people must know, at heart, that going to war is the natural basis of Empire. Going to War is a lot easier than going to work, for all the boys who are to kill or be killed, maim or be maimed. And the spenders know how to make, even that, exciting to the boys: lots of badges, gilt buttons, gilt braid, brass bands, fine horses, great battleships, big forts and guns and many other dated but still picturesque paraphernalia including pocket money and medals for bravery, hostesses in camp, etc. Meantime papas and mamas throbbing and sobbing with pride, grief and ecstasy; church bells ringing, preachers preaching, sweethearts exciting, the news-sheets citing. And off we go again on the well-worn bloody trail to Nowhere and Never. Forever.

[Taliesin Square-Paper Number 2, May 1941]

HITLER IS WINNING THIS WAR WITHOUT A NAVY. WE ARE facing a new kind of warfare that the British Empire, owing to traditional faith in a great navy, cannot learn in time even if we furnished the equipment. We couldn't furnish the equipment because we don't yet know how to make it. So aid to Britain is impossible except to prolong the death agony of a great empire. Meanwhile we are deliberately weakening our own chance of survival if and when our time comes. Our frontier is no longer England nor, in any sense, is it European. Our frontier is our own shores. And the shorter these shores the better. Any realistic view of what goes on in Europe must make this plain to all but experts, officials, and news-sheet strategists. This war cannot be won on the sea. War has shifted its center!

England needed a strong friend and we might have been that strong friend to England but we have failed her as the Empire in desperation has now failed so many nations. A liberal individualist and moderate democratic nationalist myself, I am no believer in world-conquest nor have I any faith in so-called world-power. I hate the thought of Empire.

So long as I am governed by my choice of government I concede to others their right to be governed as they choose to be governed. I will prepare to defend this, my right, as their right and I will fight only when attacked. If this were lived up to honestly by us as a nation our United States would be impregnable and we would be a fatal stumbling block in the path of any plan for "world-conquest" either from within or from without. Because I honestly believe in democracy I think any form of world-power or sea-control both dated and doomed.

The shift in the center of warfare is in our favor. But once actually committed to England's past we are a bygone tradition ourselves.

Our danger lies not so much in far-reaching German Geopolitik as in the fact that the judgement of our leader nods, taxed beyond human endurance. He has lost common-sense and touch with his people in the arduous decisions of a rash third term. He sees himself the vis-a-vis of Hitler—his own country a hinterland growing dim.

Our danger lies in the fact that our best belligerents know so little of the world forces they affront in purely imaginary self-defense, and wish to see conquered in order that we may call them, too, "democratic." A complete loss of perspective.

Our danger lies in the publicity-politics of frightened interests that have no genuine experience from which to determine what or how we should fight if we fought: able to think only in terms of billions of dollars at a time when all dollars are on the way down and out.

Our danger lies in perpetually propagated advertising slogans that amount to lies fed to our people by newsheet and radio, lest the people use their common sense. All, so help me God, in the name of democracy! The worst element in our body politic, as usual, becoming the most "patriotic."

And, of course, not only our danger but our end as a democratic nation lies in any attempt whatsoever to take over this world-war on foreign shores. We have nothing to take over with except deflated dollars, conscript green cannon-fodder, and a vast, already dated, arsenal on order.

Well, again coming home across the hinterland, I see vast empty spaces of good ground affording occasional gas-stations and auto-camps opportunity to testify to our great country as mostly a backward empty-place, but being made ready to go to other shores to fight for something we haven't got at home, something that is only to be found at home if it is ever to be found at all. Fighting over there again might be worthwhile if only we could get that something (call it democratic prosperity) and bring it back with us. Of course we won't get it that way, but fear does funny things to the human psyche if it can raise a hue and cry. It can. The hue and cry is rising and the same old funny things are being done to us, right now, in the same old name of patriotism and democracy. Yes, we are passing up our native land by way of an overstressed president who now says it is "over there" and if we want it we will have to go over there to get it. There is a limit to the important decisions any human being can make. Evidently our president is fagged or bogged down to reflect his Harry Hopkins, Wendell Willkie, Hull, Stimson, and Knox,[2] amateur strategists all, some of whom have been abroad quite recently but also others, hangovers from early days still trying to keep our eastern states loyal English colonies.

Oh yes, . . . our President says "It"—Democracy—is "over there" and we must go over there to save it: by "there" meaning Dakar, Suez, Abyssinia, Singapore, Egypt, Greece, Finland, Norway, Holland, Belgium, Denmark, France—to all and sundry of whom (we will say nothing of Spain and the others) he has sent assurances of support even as the great Empire has given to all and sundry, promises of military aid. Principle being utterly lacking in all this we can only turn to policy to account for it. If we turn there we find only the policy found in a good old U.S.A. game: the good old game of poker.

But playing poker with no cards in the hand above a two spot and the joker is not "policy" at all. There is another name for it, out there in the barn.[3]

When William Allen White found he was in with a lot of gangsters making war-whoopee he got out and I say he got out just in time to save himself as we know him.[4] But Will still believes that the longer we keep the great Empire up against Warrior Germany, the less able Germany will be to molest us. And so Will is for all out aid to the great Empire, short of war, as an American shield. Just as the Empire has been doing that same thing to seven or eight other nations—British "shields" that have all given up. Willing to fight to the last Englishman then, is it our turn?

This attitude may be pre-eminently British, but it is utterly not American. This little fellow who hides behind the big fellow's back is not so much nobler than the big fellow who hides behind the little fellow. Is he?

But, American politics as played at present, imitating English politics, is a sorry equivocation with not one element of honest democracy in it. I can see nothing even decent in this frightened nation thus upsetting itself to give a pell-mell imitation of the great Empire.

Why can't we, the democratic people, see that the weakness of the Great Empire lies in the fact that it is dated if not senile and see for ourselves that it is no longer a great power? And see the world rapidly going beyond the fetish of great Empire either commercial, moral, or real-estate. The democratic people must see that Empire is no more than the apotheosis of Money and see the world slowly waking to realize that work is the miracle—not money. Work can do without money if it has ideas and leadership. Money can't do without work no matter what leadership it has unless it can conscript and go to war. Therein (at last) is really where this world-struggle simmers down for us in these United States. Tell our democratic people that truth! I say, tell them that where we are concerned our oncoming tragedy is going to lie in the fact that our enemies champion work while we champion money—we the great would-be democracy caught on the wrong side of the economic problem, and now getting ready to fight to keep on being wrong!

How well our universities have done their work! They have tried to make the beautiful people money-makers to raise a horde of spenders. And we see it coming clearer every day that there is no use in being money-minded any longer if Empire, the apotheosis of money, is going down.

And we see that if we would save Empire, we the democratic people must go to war because if we can't save Empire everybody, the money spenders especially, must go to work. Now, going to work shouldn't seem so bad even in the kind of democracy we think we are. But to that Eastern part of us that is already an out-and-out pseudo-fascist empire reflecting the great disappearing British empire, the thing must look fearful and hateful enough.

The democratic people must know, at heart, that going to war is the natural basis of Empire. Going to War is a lot easier than going to work, for all but the boys who are to kill or be killed, maim or be maimed. And the spenders know how to make, even that, exciting to the boys: lots of badges, gilt buttons, gilt braid, brass bands, fine horses, great battleships, big forts and guns and many other dated but still picturesque paraphernalia including pocket money and medals for bravery, hostesses in camp, etc. Meantime papas and mamas throbbing and sobbing with pride, grief and ecstasy; church bells ringing—preachers preaching, sweethearts exciting, the news-sheets citing. And off we go again on the well-worn bloody trail to Nowhere and Never. Forever.

Why does the damned thing keep on working? Is it because Work as an Ideal of the Good Life

**John Nesbitt House, "Sijistan" (Project). Remodel of Charles Ennis House, Los Angeles, California. 1941. Perspective. Dining Room. Pencil and color pencil on tracing paper, 25 x 19".** FLLW Fdn# 4119.001

has gone heavy and stale and Money is now the universal means that has already superseded work to achieve the supreme reward?

No. In a democracy we won't give up so easily. We can be flim-flammed for a while, bam-boozled a good deal—but I still believe we are more intelligent than we were last big money-war. And I believe that as a whole we the democratic people of this nation love the ideal of a free country well enough to go to work for it, even for wages. But how much better instead of going to work for wages to go to work for ourselves on our own ground in our own way? Silly as it may seem to excited and inciting authority just now that is our new

frontier—that and cooperative manufacturing and merchandising. Hitler could not cross that Frontier.

Policies can never supplant principles for long though the beautiful people are confused, bedeviled and debauched by the prevailing conspiracy of news-sheet lies, radio talks and phoney social rewards for wage-labor and for conventional moral conduct. No—all this can not obscure the real issue. Because this nation keeps sound at heart if the face does get dirty. And I say it is this decency at home, our common decency, that keeps the children clean, well-dressed and on the way to the district school: our married folk keeping decently together to keep a pleasant home to live in—all free to be honest with themselves and each other and all others—hating (as I believe most of our "beautiful people" do hate) the hypocrisy that goes with all these money-standards that are driving a great idea of life crazy and are now trying so hard to waste the whole future of a great new nation in another phoney war; on the lips the same hypocrisy that we inherited; and a conscience using ad libitum, ad nauseam, high sounding slogans for any and every dirty expedient. I say this, our common decency at home is our best national asset. If it got a fair break.

America! Wake up! The tragedy that will be our doom lies in the fact that such hypocrisy as this conceals, even from itself, that the worm's-eye view of war is past; this hypocrisy conceals even from itself the fact that to cling for salvation to out-moded engines of destruction like battleships, infantry, calvary, and forts, whether floating or forever fixed, is to cling for salvation to pure illusion. We the democratic people in these United States should see that the new agencies of our future were they "joined up" with ideas and labor, not money, would be better able to protect life than ever those new agencies were or ever will be able to destroy it? Yet here again in all this our nation is setting itself aside, not trusting to the advice of military experts, but ordered about by politicians, resorting again to out-moded war engines just as obsolete as the horse and buggy and the urban manure pile. "National defense" seems unable to see that this nation's defense no longer consists in fool man-toys that modern science has already rendered useless to the future. It is the democratic people themselves who must see that national defense and salvation lie ahead of these United States of America in ordered decentralization, in social reintegration with the ground, in a natural capitalist economy: in effective solidarity of will and the purpose to grow independent and strong here at home.

Only because we have run out of good ideas do we want to fight.

Yes, the old order rises again like a ghoul from the grave to reach the sap in our veins. If it is reached by conscription and war it will be solely because we the democratic people are too proud of our old stock and shop to learn to see Reality anew. We stated that reality ourselves when we were ourselves. It is not so long ago. Reality will be ours again. A great upsurge of resentment against the forces that tried to push this war over on us is going to rise from our soil and popular anger will sweep this country with disastrous results—when the "beautiful people" find out how they have been lied to again. And for what purpose.

I love England but I hate Empire as much as the more enlightened English people themselves hate it. And how I deplore the weakness that cannot stand against it with the better English thought of today.

Again I say to our own beautiful people . . . hell—let's be ourselves. Yes, if we die for it. To die is better than living as a cheap imitation of something that should have died a natural death of enlightenment a half-century ago instead of being now forced to its knees or to a bloody disgraceful end.

Is going to war the only way the United States can meet an enemy to its principles?

1. See *An Autobiography* "Book Five: Form" and "Book Six: Broadacre City," in this volume.

2. Harry Hopkins (1890–1946), first administrator of the lend-lease program inaugurated during World War II; Wendell Wilkie (1892–1944), defeated by Roosevelt in 1940, he became the President's personal representative abroad in 1941–1942; Cordell Hull (1871–1955), Secretary of State 1933–1944; Henry Stimson (1867–1950), Secretary of War 1940–1945; Frank Knox (1874–1944), Secretary of the Navy 1940–1944.

3. Horse manure.

4. William Allen White (1868–1944), liberal Republican owner and editor of *Emporia Gazette* (Emporia, Kansas), 1895–1944.

# GOOD AFTERNOON, EDITOR EVJUE

**W**illiam T. Evjue, editor and publisher of The Capital Times, *a Madison, Wisconsin, newspaper, was a good friend to Frank Lloyd Wright. For nearly twenty-five years Evjue published editorials and articles by Wright in his newspaper. Both men were liberals, but Evjue was the more political of the two and strongly supported President Roosevelt. Wright, on the other hand, believed that the president was poorly informed on foreign affairs:*

> *Our president, ignorant of the ground swell of foreign world power, is informed only by his special travelers abroad. His "inside" information has enabled him to see only political (not even cultural) England in trouble and probably in fatal disorder.*

*Wright referred to himself as British—"I am as 'British' as they ought to make them in these United States"—acknowledging his mother's Welsh background and his father's English heritage. But he makes a strong distinction between "British" as a cultural value and Great Britain as a force. In short, he despised the "empire," and this paper constantly reminds us of that fact.*

> *In the second part of this two-part publication, he explains his loathing for military conscription. This topic surfaced again later, in a much more personal context, when the draft took its toll on his apprentices in the Taliesin Fellowship. He also sounded a note of caution that is still in currency today:*

> *I believe in preparing adequate home-defense, not only now, but yesterday and tomorrow. When defense becomes necessary we should be automatically ready because defense would be an integral affair with us: not a grand splurge or an hysterical spending orgy whenever we get scared.*

*[Taliesin Square-Paper Number 3, June 1941]*

THE FOLLOWING TEXT, AN EXCHANGE BETWEEN MYSELF and William T. Evjue, editor, is reproduced from *The Capital Times* of Madison, Wisconsin, Thursday, May 29th, 1941. A second article replying to the accusation he had made that, pressed for a better plan than the President's I had been only "vague," was printed in the *Times*, Friday, June 6, 1941. A friendly gibe at the thought of Americas salvation coming from the green hills of Taliesin was his conclusion.

I have great respect and considerable affection for the editor of this paper. The fact that I deplore the violence of his anti-Hitlerism does not diminish this fact.

Deploring the extremity of his anti-Hitlerism does not mean that I am pro-Nazi. It means that I think he is trying to shoot the weathervane off the steeple when the congregation in the church below is his real enemy. And I admire his loyalty to our president because he believes the president's foreign policy is right. He is fortunate. I believe the president's foreign policy is dangerously wrong so I can only say so honestly. I am unfortunate. There is no need for me to say that I believe every Nazi utterly wrong for our United States because every principle I advocate, every act of my life is by nature, as I am myself, anti-Nazi.

Believing in democracy, however, I fail to see what right we have as a nation to say to that nation or any other nation, "You are all wet. Get democratic or we'll blow you out of the water—or to hell and gone with you before you get us." I can look with perfect confidence and calm upon a world entirely undemocratic provided I and my friendly neighbors, if I happen to have any such, are not directly molested. And if undemocratic ways of living and making a living are not forced upon me where I live.

The problem of meeting any threat of that kind I should say should not be met by abandoning what I believed in to get tough with the prospective enemy but by meeting him with actual proofs that my democratic faith and way of life was a better way than his way, were the enemy fascist, communist, empirical or capitalist. For the life of me I can't see how I could show that to an enemy by imitating his own faults and committing murder to match his own murdering.

Nor can I believe in Franklin Roosevelt's placing himself vis-a-vis with Hitler as the self-appointed saviour of the world. I don't believe in a saviour of the world. If I did I don't know what right he would have to save it from itself unless it appealed to him for salvation. It has not and probably will not, now. The world might have done so once upon a time, before Franklin made us a mere accomplice. England however, has appealed to us for salvation and if the English dominion itself were in danger and had openly declared for democratic government instead of kingly-empire I should be inclined to give neighborly aid. But even then I should not jeopar-

dize my home and my people's future by deliberately setting my own house on fire trying to put out the fire in the house appealing for aid, etc., etc., etc., etc.

I am as "British" as they ought to make them in these United States. I have been greatly honored by the British nation [for the award] but I do not think that a sufficient reason for me to abandon my principles or see my nation's welfare jeopardized without protest. It may be that I owe all this backwardness to lack of an early education at Groton under Dr. Peabody and a subsequent confirmation at Harvard. Unfortunately I am a native product from the tall grass of our midwestern prairies, finally endorsed by British culture itself. In my bones I feel that I am a truer friend to English culture than President Roosevelt. I have been around in this old world quite a lot—having myself, recently, spent six weeks in London, where I learned from very many enlightened British men and women that they thought no more of empire than I did but could no more get rid of it, owing to their politicians, than we can get rid of speculative Wall Street, on account of our politicians. I agreed with Ambassador Kennedy then and I agree with him now. Probably he has more intimate knowledge of the situation than President Roosevelt.

So what, my dear Bill? I say, adding violence to violence by us will not save democracy at home or abroad. Our president, from the day he got into congress for 50,000 airplanes down to the present moment, has turned his back on my country to face Hitler for the British empire. To me a foolish shortsighted act ignoring the nature of the currents of thought abroad in the world at this time. Our president, ignorant of the groundswell of foreign world power, is informed only by his special travelers abroad. His "inside" information has enabled him to see only political (not even cultural) England in trouble and probably in fatal disorder. Unbelievably ignorant of what is taking place in the thought of this new world we are to meet, our own president is largely responsible for our inability to take it in. We are becoming an exceedingly provincial egotistic nationality.

Our provincial columnists and wise-crackers: MacLeish, Sherwood, Max Anderson, Walter Lippmann and Dolly Thompson, et al, may be included in this egotistic provincial exaggeration, just for good measure. Killers all. And the kind of killer less pardonable than a Hitler because we profess a faith that should stand for principles otherwise. We are trying to live by a faith we have no good right to break with, just because a great neighbor, even an ancestor, if you like, is in wrong with four-fifths of the world. When, after working four years in Japan, I returned home in 1919, I wrote "eventually, I believe we are going to see a great new alignment of world-power: we will see Russia, China and Japan—Asiatics—led by the greatest technician of the world, Germany." I said we would do well to prepare. It seemed to most of our people worth no more than a laugh then. Japan was at war with Russia. But now?

Why not go to work to meet the oncoming tide if and when it comes instead of, frightened, fighting only to give four-fifths of the world a strangle-hold on us? Even were going to war a temporary solution, when I think of going to war under the good men and true provincials in the seats of power in Washington—I feel about going to war as little Susie must have felt about going to Heaven when the goody-goody Sunday school teacher asked all the little children who wanted to go to Heaven to please raise their hands. All raised their hands and waved wildly except a little pug-nosed, freckle-faced redhead on the back seat—Susie. Teacher, shocked, said, "Why, Susie! Don't you want to go to Heaven?!" "No, I don't," said Susie, "Not if that crowd's a-goin'!"

As little Susie felt about going to Heaven so I feel about going to war with political, provincial Washington as it is today. Another politically made and politically led war is ahead of us now. There is a better way to meet the enemy. I have devoted thirty-five years of my work-a-day life to that organic way. It is now called Broadacre City, a plan for decentralizing the United States of America and establishing a real democracy.

Bill has challenged me to put it down where it can be read—but I have already made a great model of it and have written a volume or two explaining it in detail. Not being a politician, I can't put it into a newspaper article. Being only a technician I suffer

the same disadvantage as Lindbergh, another and famous technician. He can fly it. I can build it. In time we might both learn to say it in the political arena. Meantime, I will try to write it down more simply and send it in to Bill. He might then acknowledge that at least I have a more practical immediate plan for saving democracy intact than Franklin Roosevelt's war for saving it in pieces, if at all.

## AGAIN "GOOD AFTERNOON," MR. EDITOR:

Just for the sake of the argument, here are a few "good afternoons" occasioned by your own "good afternoon." Bill, I was with Franklin Roosevelt in the early days you mention. I talked and wrote in his defense. I believed I understood his effort until he became entangled in the European conflagration by stampeding congress. With only hearsay information, he misjudged the world situation and did universal harm by destroying our democratic economy and morale.

1. I believe Voltaire taught Frederick the Great the true principle of democratic defense when he taught him to abolish the conscript and make an integral militia of citizen volunteers.

Because the democratic spirit is not in it, I believe conscription cannot provide victorious defense against slave-empire for any democratic nation.

By making lottery conscripts: A-1 to Z-1,270,090, we are demoralizing, not inspiring, American youth. Why must haphazard lottery take the place of free will and circumstantial evidence in selecting the defenders of this nation when human life is the pawn? In a democracy.

2. Unless our craven politicians' officious interferences deliberately provoke attack from our opponents Germany, Russia, France, Italy, and Japan, I do not believe we are in any immediate danger of attack even in case of the defeat of Great Britain's war. Except economic danger.

I believe we are, at present, in more immediate danger within our own nation than from the combined military forces of Germany, France, Italy, Russia, and Japan. I believe we have at least five years time to prepare to defend ourselves against slave-empire or any possible attempt at armed conquest by Germany, France, Italy, Russia, and Japan should the present alignment of slave-empire last that long and be hostile.

3. I believe in free labor as I believe in a free militia. If both are not superior—what in hell are we fighting to preserve?

4. Yes, I believe we could meet slave-production by a genuine natural economic order if, finally, "German Geopolitik" did reach for us. Economically we would have to get new form and a different style, one genuinely democratic. We need it for our own sake. We need it regardless of Germany, Russia, France, Italy, and Japan or anything they may do. If we can't get it, then why fight? We are licked anyway from within by our own guns, ships and planes.

How stupidly we are endangering our capacity to meet slave competition by wasting our resources upon fantastic preparations to "control the seas" and repel imaginary invasion!

Frightened by Hitler and using Hitler to frighten the nation, our president has stampeded congress and a craven congress has sold out democracy in these United States of America. The place of these congressmen in the ground swell rising on our great west and midwestern prairies will be odious, I believe, in any historic perspective.

5. I believe that the foolish haste in which defense is being prepared will result in obsolescence of our entire national defense investment before we can use it. We are too hastily investing billions in outmoded implements of destruction.

Our time and money should be spent more freely upon experiment and research not wholly by "experts" before we plunge into quantity production. Oh yes, there is yet time. "Haste makes waste" was never more apt than applied to this huddle of the frightened sheep around the bell wether.

6. I believe in preparing adequate home-defense, not only now, but yesterday and tomorrow. When defense becomes necessary we should be automatically ready because defense would be an integral affair with us: not a grand splurge or an hysterical spending orgy whenever we get scared.

Eventually we should have the best air force on earth, and be able to use it within five years time, meantime maintaining a superb submarine flotilla. But we should let it all go at that—except 350,000

men in a citizen militia, and we should learn to use these three defense arms together. Correlation is the most important thing to learn.

We should not prepare to invade or to conquer. But these things I know well would constitute more a danger than a defense until we had worked out a sound domestic economy independent of slave-labor that would use our resources in developing our own backward country. This nation should be no parasite on foreign trade as it seems to think it is now.

7. Our position might have looked very different from that of the small monarchies, Norway, Holland, Belgium or the republics, Czechoslovakia, Poland, because all these were English accomplices forming the famous "iron ring" around Germany. Later the small monarchies and Greece fell when they invested in empirical Britain. These now-conquered nations were really volunteer empirical-aid?

We have offered ourselves likewise. Was this good world-politics? We shall see if robbing our neutrality of integrity was the right way to help "the democracy of the world."

8. For the next five years I believe the shorter our shores, the more likely we are to defeat slave-empire by establishing and keeping a sound economic life to defend at home. "Hemisphere defense" is another vicious newspaper slogan. I believe South America on any present basis, either economic or military, should be reckoned lost while trying to make friends with the Latins, if we can. "The Allies of today are the enemies of tomorrow."

9. I believe military conscription is a political, economic, and social crime not only against our form of government but against the very life of our people.

Since I believe that voluntary citizen-militia is the only valid defense for us because we stand for democracy, I suggest that all conscripts be released by congress to see how many would volunteer after they have had a chance to look the old worm's-eye-view of war in the face.

Gibe, Bill, while you may, for it is certain that the solution of our world problem in the face of Germany, Russia, France, Italy, and Japan, slave-empire, does lie in the green hills of the Taliesins of our great nation and will be found there if ever found at all.

# DEFENSE

*This paper and "To Beat the Enemy" (pages 85–87) were written only a few weeks apart. They continued Wright's bitter diatribe against the United States entering the Second World War:*

*Democratic despotism is losing visibility rapidly as we sneak toward total war.*

*As with his several texts on Broadacre City, there is much repetition in these papers, but—also like the Broadacre texts—each has a different approach along with new material. [Taliesin Square-Paper Numbers 4 and 5, July 1941]*

No matter by what evidence the truth may be confronted, mankind in these United States is more individualized from day to day. Men are getting more and more concerned for their individuality. They do take increasing pride in the personal element. Universality is, therefore, losing importance and power as quality rises above quantity. Notwithstanding such success as we are seeing in European warfare and American big-business, general formulae prove themselves increasingly insufficient in human affairs as destruction and inane wealth gain headway. Human significance is more and more revealed to the individual by the individual in more and more highly specialized forms because "God becomes mightier in the process." And now, we the people of these United States should stop this vain bluffing with outmoded murder-machines and prepare to defend ourselves permanently by building up defense from the beginning on a solid foundation. Build defense as straightforward as possible.

Build up our own peculiar strength as single-mindedly from within as it is possible for us to build it. And build it unconcerned for everything remote or external as we can. The more we do this as individuals the purer and stronger we will become as a united people championing human Freedom. The less we ally ourselves with alien forces; the less we rely upon these forces; the more we take of ourselves upon our own shoulders; the more nature will smile upon us in our effort to build an impregnable free nation. Our true defense is not military now nor will be ever if we know the truth about ourselves. Let this truth come through: Democracy is far stronger than Fascism or Communism or any other ism if allowed to work. *The idea of the absolute autonomy of a free man has created a power in this world mightier than anything that can be opposed to it!*

We of the American democracy are the natural bearers of this power. Let us stop wasting it and make it felt. Military leaders equipped with all the planes and guns in the world couldn't make it take effect.

Our national weakness lies in the fact that with us Faith and Being are yet to become one: that "state of unhappy consciousness" as Hegel said. Nevertheless we are the one genuine constructive individuality that can now build upon earth the inner strength to empower the world against degeneracy. Were it not for our confusing rulers and were we not betrayed by a craven Congress we would stand here a power at this moment in world-history.

Being and belief coincide or nothing happens. The one great significance that will lead to this noble self-realization on our part is that the developed individual believes in himself, believes implicitly that innate Good is in him. The more we the people of these United States discover of the hidden forces of nature the more we will realize that self-realization, a noble selfhood, alone matters.

Being and belief must coincide—be one power. Our country then is forever a great power and, nevertheless, a free country. God does become mightier in that process. And it is irrelevant whether there are gods or not. In other words, whether Fascism or Communism or all isms whatever, win or lose. These United States will live to see the end of this era of American plutocracy and ambiguous British Empire if and when:

WHEN we end this storm of waste and death overhead by taking the white man's burden off his shoulders for good and all or leave the burden-bearer to put it down himself;

WHEN the private money-power of London and New York now expediently warring in the name of Democracy is exposed, expelled and Congress outlaws further false political credit or labels in America;

WHEN the people, in self-defense, refrain from installment buying or any form of borrowing at interest in any form whatsoever—social credit and a demurrage currency their first step in this direction: their legitimate capital a pyramid, base on the ground not in the air;

WHEN this tedious, perpetual prevarication of news—a cheap kind of diplomacy for private-profit, is ended by cancelling all newspapers or magazines with too much advertising or a private political point of view. Honest news can now be honestly free to an honest people only if the people manage to own the

**Roux Library, Florida Southern College, Lakeland, Florida. 1941. Ink on tracing paper, 37 x 18".** FLLW Fdn#4118.002

radio. By the Eternal, buy it now and show the huckster in the parlor up and show him out;

WHEN in this era of wonderful patriotism the people brand patriots as the worst enemies of the country they patriotize, their artful glorification of death no longer any part of life, recognizing that only disastrous policies make death expedient;

WHEN this business of reducing humanity to a problem in Arithmetic is stopped, dead, the people refusing to believe that freedom and liberty can be had or upheld by any methods whatsoever that demand their surrender. Such surrender can only get us killed as a nation. Body and soul!

WHEN we stop making courage and the spirit of sacrifice nothing at all by acts like conscription. The time is long past when Crucifixion can be substituted for discipline;

WHEN we end this servile era of the servant-mind in high places; Congress in particular; the inferiority complex. Down and out with all European hangovers. And indigenous roots for our Usonian culture or no culture;

WHEN we the people close the chronic university. Let the arm-chairs grow cold and put the innumerable four year loafers back to work at place of origin. Make the university-plants civic centers for the people;

WHEN we the people of these United States of America realize that any "expert" has stopped thinking in order to be wrong for more than fifty years—if he can live that long;

WHEN the tyrannized waste by Fashion will end by caging the fashion-monger and the "boulevardier" with the monkeys and we exchange this universal gadgetry of ours for main strength and awkwardness. Just for a healthy change!

WHEN our national entertainment, the cinema, demands names incidental to performance and refuses names to which performance is incidental: the box office star banished with the box-officer-producer to live together on a desert island. Fair trial demanded for a work of art on its own merits or no show;

WHEN we smack the wise-cracker with the gagster;

WHEN we end this era of the ultra-mobilized: a Nation all dressed up and no place to go. Some place to go or don't go;

WHEN, realizing what is now happening to them, the people end this era of the hard-pavement by trading the pavement in for grass;

WHEN the beautiful people end the slum-of-tomorrow in these United States by housing the houser in his own dam'd housing. And that goes for Uncle Sam; enable the people to own their own!

WHEN we the people end this internecine strife between the world of work and the world of money. Down with these two fists up and at each other all the time instead of clasping hands;

WHEN we the people heartlessly walk out on the military strategist—either specialist, columnist, corner grocery, politician or ruler;

WHEN we the people worship money-symbols no more but know the realities behind the symbols or refuse to use the symbols;

WHEN we the people end these wars of the rulers by letting peace declare itself.

For Democracy is of such sense and courage; the highest form of Aristocracy the world has ever known because it is integral. In the nature of materials. Who would want to fight a nation built that way?

Certainly not Hitler.

# TO BEAT THE ENEMY

THESE CRIMES MUST CEASE:

Crime 1.   Chronic artificial-scarcity.
Crime 2.   Real poverty.
Crime 3.   The general frustration of the people.

On account of these three crimes this nation has now utterly unrepayable money-debt, thousands of billions of hours of perfectly good man-power steadily unemployed year in and year out, lottery-conscripts by the million and countless billions wasted on exploited fright, again betrayed into a war with neither top, bottom nor sides.

No matter who wins this war, we, the people will eventually have to resolve this clash between two despotisms: the visible despotism of the axis powers and the invisible despotism of the so-called Democratic powers. Why not resolve it now? If not, all must accept this rapidly rising tide of despotism.

Democratic despotism is losing visibility rapidly as we sneak toward total war. Let the people on both sides ask their rulers now why we are at war and how they are conducting the war. If we ask we will find the answers to be the same. Winning the war is not going to help the people if either set of rulers win if orthodox-finance governs their use of the victory as it most surely will, unless the people act NO. If the people do not act no, democracy is no longer a living issue! If Hitler wins he would have to remain a visible despot. If Churchill wins he would have to become one with Franklin Roosevelt a likely second.

The ancient fable of David and Goliath might come in for a little national attention. The nation able to buy the most planes and guns the fastest and rank-and-file the most conscripts is Goliath! Where is David? He, with the pebble in his sling, is the people. It is time for David to find the weak spot in the Goliath armor. Essential factors of victory for the people

never did lie in this foolish trust in Goliath, the murder-machine. Outrageous bluff has already gone too far. We the people must get into effect a few ideas square with the form of government we profess. Victory for us lies in that direction.

What would the essential factors of our victory be? As always in a democracy: popular initiative. Buy back these United States of America for the people! Call back this one and elect a Congress that will capitalize this nation as planned by the constitution and at whatever sum is the essential need of the whole people—a fair appraisal made of the share due its present owners—issuing stock to them, making them co-partners in a genuine capitalism of the people, by the people, and for the people. Instead of going on with this unconstitutional futile money-gamble now staked on gold. Then our subservience to foreign influence would end. Call back the vassals of the present order for cause. Send others more capable and loyal. And if the Supreme Court proves to be disloyal to the constitution—well—there is a name and a remedy for that.

This is counter-revolution by popular initiative: a counter-revolution that is now our only salvation. Only democratic dynamics can put an end to this outmoded international control by the out of date, abstract, big-money-industry of London and New York busy now easing us into bigger and better wars whichever side wins this one.

Buy back the United States of America for the people! We the people need not wait to do this until the price has been raised by victory or marked down by defeat. We can make terms now and thus start the backfire now essential to save democracy from oncoming orthodox conflagration. And we the people must make such terms that no interest-bearing-mortgage can ever take the country away from the people again. Rich and poor alike would be the gainers. The whole world would see light coming into darkness.

But to make this transfer from the established feudal-gambling-game-for-gold-stakes to a genuine medium-of-exchange for-the-whole-people compatible with democracy, we the people must lay aside all party allegiances. If we are to keep democracy alive we need a higher courage than any we display in our military preparations to meet murder by murder. We can win the necessary economic freedom by exercising that higher courage in the genuine democratic dynamics that belong to us by right. We once believed that right to be dynamic—"mightier than the sword." And it was. We are already defeated if we do not believe it now.

Unfortunately, where we the people are most vitally concerned for our strength as a people the great newspapers and magazines can no longer help us. They have shot their bolt. We know that we have a genuine democratic press in our midst no longer. We now realize that if we are ever to get our country back into democratic character and uses again the electors themselves must themselves formulate specific demands for economic freedom, themselves collect signatures from other constituents of all congressmen. We have a few upright congressmen left. We can seat others without violence and thus upheld by the men we have definitely employed to represent us in Congress, secure coordination—or else!

We defended our lives with that Freedom soon after we were born and without a president. It is again necessary and we can do it again! We must do it now while there is a shred of Freedom left to democracy because Democracy is fast disappearing from our government. We the people are mightier than our rulers or else we accept this defeat slipped over on us with such insulting arrogance that Democracy already means less than Fascism as the visible-enemy openly declares it does and as the invisible enemy confesses by its subservient acts, that it does.

We the people can still declare that we are free. And we can prove it!

The possession of a right without the power to exercise it has no meaning. The only thing that power-financiers and power-politicians fear is this personal initiative of the people. We have this "sling and pebble" yet. It is our power in these tragic circumstances. If we have the moral courage of a David we still have a voice in our fate! By use of our characteristic power we can quit being the yes-men of conflicting ideologies of rulers and the anonymous power-financiers, before it is too late. We know this war to be the inevitable result of a policy inspired and desperately upheld by the power-financiers of London and New York. Never in the history of the civilized world have so many bowed so low to so few. We are too slow to give our share in all this foreign-policy its right name: Plutocracy. Why should American democracy fight with the blood of its own sons or with ballots either except to defeat Plutocracy and defend our faith from all insidious forms of Empire?

Democracy still means just what the constitution of the United States of America says it means: "government accord with the will of the people." If now the will of the people by persistent concerted action, awakens civic-pride and assumes with true courage individual responsibility in this matter of independent economic-freedom, a Hitler, a Churchill, a Stalin, or a Roosevelt—no matter how mechanized a Goliath—are no more a threat to us as a united people than tigers loose over there in the African jungle.

Now that we know the true economic alternative to economic slavery, we know there can be economic peace in this world. And so we know that any form of the despotic principle is anachronism. Get this basic truth well into our mind as a people and freedom is ours in deed and in truth. Aim that truth at Goliath-in-armor and the victory is with David.

But the insinuation that the poor are poor because the rich are rich is plain mischief in our democracy. Why believe that when the hills are lopped off the valleys will exalt themselves? And, where even the richest individual now needs all his income to subsist—no power to change the law in order to test it can exist. He too is a slave within a vicious circle. Personal initiative will disappear with any deliberate destruction of big private money-reservoirs upon any other plan than that of a natural economic order of freemen: the social credit established by the birth certificate of the United States. Our constitution.

Upon the one hand is the visible democratic enemy: Fascism. Upon the other hand is the invisible democratic enemy: Plutocracy.

The United States of America can choose neither. If she cannot make her principle of Democracy work now by way of genuine economic freedom and, in the circumstances buy the country back again for the people before it is too late, all will have to take the blackest despotism the world has ever seen. It is growing right here!

Higher education has failed our democracy. Arm-chair ignorance or cowardice has avoided all knowledge of the fundamental economic order essential to democracy. In consequence we are half-slave and half-free. With what reason can we now call a man or woman educated when neither has mastered the fundamental economics of the life they choose to live.

Democracy can win this war only if we can take up this fatal slack.

Our feudal money-system is the "Trojan Horse" standing strong within our gates! To look that gift-horse in the teeth is the duty of all who earnestly desire to defend the well-being of our Faith. Desire for democratic well-being must get into the democratic head. To have the desire at heart is not enough now. It never was enough. Fatuous well-meaning rulers buying planes, guns and running a lottery for conscripts can't put wisdom there in the democratic head any more than any mechanized military power on earth can ever take it away once we the people do put it there and proceed to use it as David used the pebble in his sling aimed at the fatal weakness in Goliath's armor . . . his low brow!

A better part of the civilized world still looks toward our country hoping to see intelligence, the shining brow of democratic freedom, at work in the lives of our people. From Calcutta to Dublin they want to believe we are strong. They do not believe our nation is an "also-ran" or our democracy only a form of economic license. They must be alarmed and ashamed to see us run to employ the same animalistic military expedients that have destroyed all the nations ever putting their trust in them, making haste to employ them because we have no intelligent faith in our own principles nor any real knowledge of how to apply them when the country is in danger. The friendly nations hope to see us meet the oncoming animalistic, orthodox world-revolution with intelligent radical counter-revolution requiring more courage than any mechanized military attack in the name of defense: economic freedom defeating economic slavery. This revolution alone can prevent our nation from throwing itself into the futile, universal military scrapheap, Goliath victorious. Heroic David a mechanized suicide—another mechanized idiot. Yes, my people, this counter-revolution is the true war against war.

This economic counter-revolution by the people is, world wide, the true war against all wars! It is moral-courage, vision, and skill pitted against animal-courage employing machines with cunning but with stupid brutality. A worldwide revival of orthodoxy pitted against democracy: Democracy the radical. But now that we the people know the true economic alternative to economic slavery we know there can be peace in this world. And, knowing that, we the people, yes, can make any form of the Despotic-principle—Anachronism; itself the scrapheap of humane civilization. And soon.

> Our time to unite is now.
> To a President
> All you are doing and saying is to America
> Dangled mirages,
> You have not learn'd of nature—of the
>     politics of nature you have not learn'd
>     the Great
> Amplitude, rectitude, impartiality,
> You have not seen that only such as they
>     are for these States,
> And that what is less than they must
>     sooner or later
> Lift off from these States.
>                                 —Walt Whitman[1]

A grain of hard sense. The ruler of a self-sufficing empire who finances it scientifically by way of social credit does not need to export anything at all, nor to put obstacles in the way of imports.

This would apply to a Hitler-Despotism.

It would apply to a Roosevelt-Democracy.

---

1. Walt Whitman, "Messenger Leaves," from *Leaves of Grass*.

**Map of Usonia, Taliesin Square-Paper Number 6. Newsprint.** FLLW Fdn#AV1001.008

# USONIA, USONIA SOUTH, AND NEW ENGLAND

*Decentralization, the chief principle in Wright's planning for Broadacre City, is here applied to the nation's process of governing itself. [Taliesin Square-Paper Number 6, August 1941]*

### A DECLARATION OF INDEPENDENCE . . . 1941

Here in our national home, the U.S.A., the atmosphere is becoming so loaded with false implication and impurities, now so heated and close that any voice telling truth is like an open window letting in fresh air. Already the open window is regarded as a danger, so, shut or obscured by fear. An Independent is named an Isolationist and patriotism is degraded to a level where no true Patriot would stand: where a convoy becomes a patrol.

Never during our national life-time have evil influences of foreign interests upon the natives so pervaded our national living-rooms as now. Never have the windows been so obscured nor the open doors so well shut—from the outside! The doors were first slammed shut by undemocratic pre-election concord between F.D.R. and W.W. one of whom was elected by the people on a promise that is becoming manifest as a lie.

With this elected president cheerfully making a role for himself never intended for the president of this republic in any circumstances whatsoever, the role of ruler, we the people of this country, unable to see clearly, are sinking deeper into fatal coma—we are less and less able to recognize ourselves as a free, independent nation. Instead of honest forthright in-dependence, all we know is what we read in the papers and all the papers know is what they think is good for the people to know in the circumstances.

We are now dependents in order that a "ruler" may make a bid for world-power and for commercial-supremacy. Both were, and always will be, a despot's mirage. Commercial supremacy is a foolish challenge to war even were it openly arrived at. Both world-power and commercial-supremacy belie and betray our democratic principles and any hope we may have for peace and prosperity among us is gone if we choose either. Britain is fighting like a predatory animal at bay to keep what she already had of both these bones of contention—world power and commercial-supremacy. She is unable to see that because modern warfare has shifted its center to the air her empire is already impracticable.

Because we believed that her Freedom of the Seas meant freedom of the seas for us we say, after her, "Freedom of the Seas."

She calls her Empire a "commonwealth of nations," but at the same time we are taught that if she cannot keep all she has, intact, then our own nation must go under. Why? Ask Franklin D. Roosevelt.

Once upon a time policing the seas was a necessity were England to keep her Empire. But on those terms she cannot keep it now and we cannot help her.

England, the most class-conscious country on earth, tough and seasoned in all this rough and tumble for sea-power has in the course of events inevitably again set herself up for a world target and at a time when, unluckily for our own republic, we have an ambitious executive, wistful preserver of "Freedom of the Seas" on British terms; one, by education and predilection, pro-British; a native who sees his own country in distorted perspective as a nation led and protected by the great liberal British Imperialism which he is pleased to call a great Democracy.

Now it is true enough that such culture as we have, our language, our antique money-system, our Roman laws, are a servile imitation of Britain's. If a matter of finance, then derived from the Bank of England; if a matter of culture, then copied from Oxford; if an affair of conscience, then we took over from British morals as they were and are now.

And of our North Eastern States, originally English this is true in Architecture, habits of thought and at this moment particularly true in world-outlook. All this is a servile imitation that the English themselves do not really respect but which they are willing to exploit, as usual. The precious opportunity for independent development we secured from the English by revolution in 1776 has already gone reactionary in these states. If you do not believe this go and see for yourselves or listen attentively to your Ruler. Now this were not so greatly important to our future as a nation were it not for the fact that this small block of States includes our National Capital, is also the seat of the financial management of the bulk of our nation's industrial wealth together with our greatest voting concentrations on hard pavements.

If this union, now divided into forty-eight separate states, is ever to be freed from equivocal British domination; if the people of this nation are ever able to listen to truth; if we are to not only see but act with clear vision in behalf of our independent destiny, it would be far better, and much the lesser of all probable evils to rearrange the states into a more simple and characteristic federation, a grouping of all the states into three principal states. Allow New England to keep the national capital and the official buildings of the present city of Washington as a present from the greater part of the nation.

There is now pressing upon us the need for a far greater national capital. One more adequate. One better able to express the genius of our modern spirit and allow scope for the growing Science and Art of our great people as a whole. This greater-federal-capital, call it USONIA, should be built now by Congressional edict (we are going to elect a new congress soon). This great tri-state federation, a new arrangement of the social body, should have a greater capital-city founded somewhere near the center of the nation; probably placed midway on the rolling prairies of the great Mid-West beside the Father of Waters—our Mississippi; there where the amplitude, rectitude and impartiality that might characterize the greater part of our nation, could, unhampered by congenital prejudice or the equivocal influence of foreign powers, be free to initiate and grow the ways and means to live a good life as the independent democracy this country was designed to be. The world has yet no idea so powerful as that of the absolute autonomy of a free man. Our Democracy must truly represent and defend that Idea.

We are so situated that Nature herself is on the side of our complete independence.

These North Eastern States were never really agrarian. They were, and still are, chiefly industrial. Evidently they are desirous and concentrated upon this one-ninth of our national business, the relatively insignificant part which we call "foreign trade" and upon a foreign policy according to that concentration. But while the country at large is by nature chiefly agrarian, these industrial states, already overcrowded, are surcharged with refugees inciting the nation to warfare until War by fair means or foul is now the order of the day. Meantime the power-groups of national money-power are hopelessly tangled up with the politics and industrial power under pressure in these states. And it is well for the nation to consider that the money from this one-ninth of our national business—foreign trade—does not reach the people at large. It mostly remains in power-finance money-bags of the power-finance system of

New York, an alias of the power-finance system of London. Both are masters of our Federal Banking System; the ever-threatening economic bottle-neck of what we laughingly call the Capitalistic System. So, this N.E. group of states is influential far beyond its deserts in shaping the destiny of this now greatly extended nation, especially so at this crucial time in our national life.

The "four freedoms" recently cited by our present "ruler" chanting in unison with the present ruler of the British, are not enough for our nation. Give us, for our country at large, at least, one more freedom: freedom from foreign influences; freedom to live openly and without equivocation our own national life! We want no meddling foreign domination either slanting or direct in our affairs at home. If foreign-trade has this curse fixed upon it then we need no foreign trade. This is why, we, the people at these coming elections must vote congressmen into power, who are able to stand and deliver us from these unduly influenced personalities and localities. Deliver these North Eastern States, and soon, to responsibilities of their own allowing them to decide their own fate without involving, too far, the lives of the greater part of our people. It is easy and expedient to do this by using ways and means already designed if we were to apply them to that end. A simple enlargement of existing states rights would be sufficient.

A tri-state United States comprising a more characteristic grouping of our people, each larger state formed according to special interest and problems peculiar to them, as well as to geography and climate would be an important first step in creating the greater freedom for all the states, needed if this nation is ever to decide its own destiny. If our economic order is become a chronic disorder continually forcing this equivocal liability upon us as a nation, as it now appears to be, then let us also change that economic order. Now is the time to begin again at the beginning correcting manifest mistakes. Let us end this equivocation and return to the people the credit they alone create.

There need be no rancor nor loss of convenience nor any loss of power on the part of anyone of the present United States. All the now existing separate states would retain their present names and individualities but their status would be as principal districts only of the larger state to which they belonged.

Were such relegation of this growing impasse in the affairs of our nation, the Union would be far better able as a whole to preserve itself and pursue its own manifest destiny. To preserve this Union by Force has proved a most unfortunate policy. The South today is a living example of such folly. "One law for the Lion and the Ox is oppression." Democracy cannot long survive such oppression.

According to geography, climate, natural self-interest and sentiment, three general state-groupings are manifest. They are the New England states, the Southern states including Texas and the great intermediate body of the Union. Allow each of these groups, as a greater solidarity, to follow manifest destiny and still cooperate in the greater commonwealth of a greater nation—THE UNITED STATES OF NORTH AMERICA. Differing so widely in sentiment and self-interest, were we as a whole people to be properly divided and re-federated all could live more amicably together in a more simple and characteristic freedom were such re-federation effected. The tri-state Union could cooperate as a great federation more efficiently than the forty-eight separate states would do or ever, separately, could so cooperate under the equivocal circumstances now existing.

And it is more than merely important that the citizens of each tri-state group elect their own congress as the individual states do now, but the congress elect its own President or chairman. The President or chairman thus elected to be an executive of Congress merely. The Federal Union would establish a general or fourth congress, an arbitrative body the members of which would not be directly chosen by popular vote except as they were elected by the congresses directly chosen by the people of the several states. The evil of a popularly elected president is manifest now. It is become a hangover from the kingship of kingdom. A National Congress thus chosen, an arbitrative body, would again elect its own chairman or president, and elect him as its own executive, merely. Such questions as "balance of power" need arise no more than they have arisen between the existing forty-eight separate states. No species of foreign-influence would be so likely to endanger or become so great a menace in this larger and more free grouping of the states as now. These influences would be less feared as they became more open and direct, more honestly concerned with their own life-interest as they would then become. All special interests and sentiments would be fairly out in the open. Were such equitable and better-fitting boundaries established in our country and this more simple and democratic system of election, one more directly responsible to the people, set up: my Lords, Ladies and Gentlemen, I give you USONIA, USONIA SOUTH AND NEW ENGLAND: THE UNITED STATES OF NORTH AMERICA. The manifest economy of such re-federation would be stupendous. The gain in national spirit tremendous.

GREAT THINGS ARE DONE WHEN MEN AND MOUNTAINS MEET.
THIS IS NOT DONE BY JOSTLING IN THE STREET.
WILLIAM BLAKE[1]

NEITHER POVERTY, WAR, TYRANNY, TAXES, SLUMS, OPPRESSION OR AGGRESSION ARE NECESSARY. THE MOBILIZATION OF ALL OUR RESOURCES FOR WAR SHOWS THAT IF THESE RESOURCES WERE MOBILIZED FOR THE ABOLITION OF POVERTY AND SERVITUDE, PEACE, PLENTY AND FREEDOM COULD ACTUALLY BE WON.

1. William Blake, "Poems," from *Blake's Notebook*.

# CALL THE DOCTOR

*Similar in vein to "The Man Who" series, Wright's short, witty fables,[1] this dialogue between "P" (American Public) and "J" (Thomas Jefferson) afforded Wright a vehicle through which to air his thoughts about the nation in the early months of 1941 and its impending, and inevitable, entrance into the Second World War. [Unpublished]*

YES, YES, CALL THE DOCTOR. WE, THE AMERICAN PUBLIC, are sick with fear and confusion. Whom shall we call for advice and help? Washington D.C.? Oh—No—that's half the trouble with us now. We've listened to Washington too much already. But that name does suggest someone, of course, "Father George." Show me to the telephone.

Operator? Get me Heaven, Presidential Row, and make it snappy.

Hello—Who's this?—John Middleman? How'd you get in up there? Of all places to find you. Say, get George Washington Coffee—I mean Mr. George Washington to the phone. (Damn—I wish I could get those "commercials" out of my head). Quick now, We're in horrible trouble down here. What's that? He isn't in condition to speak to anyone? Why? What's the matter with him?

JM (John Middleman): Oh, He's pacing back and forth, and running around like his head was off, either frantically waving his arms or holding them up against where his head is supposed to be, and all the while demanding of himself—"Oh, Why did I do it? Why did I do it again?"

P (American Public): What's he done, John? What is the mat . . .

JM: He's about to become the father of another country.

P: Oh, well then, Get me some other Fellow-countryman who is more at ease and able to talk.

JM: I see Old Tom Jefferson just over there, whiling away his time drawing house plans. Will he do?

P: He's kind of liberal isn't he? Maybe someone less pro-Hitler and "Red"—Yes, yes, all right. He'll do. I'm in a hurry. Call him.

P: Hello, Tom? Hitler's on his way over here. Our Production's jammed. He's laying siege to Washington, New York and Boston right this minute. He's got the Capitol's dome in his bomb-sight. Some pro-Hitler isolationists are holding up our National Defence. We can see the whites of his eyes from here, but we've given our guns away. Our fifth-column won't let our President get in there and fight barehanded. Hitler's on us. The President—, Congress—, Those "Reds." . . .

J: Wait, Wait, Calm yourself, "Pub." Take it easy. You're in a terrible state. What's all this about fighting, being invaded, being unprepared, and Hitler? Now say your piece again, but slowly and one thing at a time.

P: Say, are you pro-Hitler too? If I thought for a moment you were I'd send the F.B.I. . . .

J: Never heard of him.

P: Hitler's beatened up all Europe and is now murdering England. We must help England stop him there.

J: I thought you said he was invading this country?

P: Well he practically is. You see . . .

J: Nonsense, he's still over 2,000 miles away isn't he? What's this about helping England?

P: Yes, yes, we must save England to save ourselves. Best line of defence you know. We're just alike. We're the only Democracies left. It's Democracy we've got to save, to save the world from utter ruin.

J: What, save Democracy again? And why do you have to keep going back to England? If you're still not old enough to live without milk, why don't you learn to drink from a bottle? What do you think we broke the hold she had on us for? For you to rush back into her waiting arms? Stay home and grow up. What's this about your Defence Program getting jammed up? By the way, who's paying for this call?

P: Well, to be honest with you, I was going to reverse the charges, but I'll credit it to National Defence; that has room for everything and everybody. It's democratic.

J: All right then, now proceed to explain this mess you've scared yourself into. Why can't you manufacture what you want and need?

P: It's so hard to start up again. It wasn't until we heard that Hitler was on his way over here that business conditions picked up.

J: Leave Hitler where he is, in Europe. I don't know who and what and why he is, and could care less at the moment. I want to find out what is the matter with you.

P: But Hitler's got Italy on his side, and both together . . .

J: Oh, Stop, will you? You make me tired. How's Washington these days? Improved the architecture any lately?

P: Washington is very beautiful, green and white. Every building is white. God protect it from the coming bombs.

J: Any new buildings?

P: Oh, yes, Lincoln Memorial, Supreme Court, Commerce Building, all have beautiful white columns all around them. Our newly designed Bombshelter has seven columns leaning against and around the outside.

J: Still using columns, and more columns? I only used columns because I didn't know of anything better at the time. The plan for my next Monticello didn't have one column on it, and it wasn't to be a glaring and naked white either. No wonder the Italians are so anxious to come over here, they certainly would feel right "At Home" in Washington. Cooled off yet "Pub"? Or am I burning you up again with these insults? To repeat, why can't you make the things the people want and need?

P: (silence)

J: Don't sulk.

P: Well . . .

J: Come on, I'm trying to help, but you had to be cooled off before you could gather your wits enough to concentrate on yourself and not on that bird Hitler you shout so much about.

P: You see . . .

J: That's better.

P: We haven't been doing much lately, that is, for the last ten years and the machinery has got rusty and is hard to start. And besides it costs a lot of money to fix it up and we have spent so much during that time feeding those who were starving . . .

J: Feeding the starving? What kind of a mess have you got yourself into? Are the men that lazy? Aren't they willing to work to eat?

P: You see, when production started closing down ten years ago, it threw men out of work.

J: Oh, too many men for the amount of work to be done.

P: Yes, in a way . . .

J: Why didn't you send them out west where they could settle down on some new land and work out a living for themselves?

P: There isn't any more free land out in the west. It's all owned. In fact it's overflowing in one place called Hollywood.

J: Hollywood? What kind of a forest is that?

P: There are a lot of big heads there. Movie . . .

J: Oh, must be one of those Petrified Forests I've heard you had. Now, to return to the little matter of our country. It's so hard to analyze and then correct one's own faults, isn't it? What I want to know is why you closed down your shops in the first place. Did everyone all at once have to take vacations and cultural excursions to Europe? It seems to me that it wouldn't do any harm to keep working and have everyone getting more and better things.

P: Our production slowed up and almost stopped because prices suddenly started downward.

J: What had that to do with it?

P: The businessmen became afraid to buy when prices went down because it meant losing money buying at one price and having to sell at a lower one.

J: Yet the people needed those things and finally had to go hungry, ill-clothed and sheltered. Was that it?

P: Yes.

J: What caused the prices to go down in the first place?

P: As nearly as I can make out, it was this way. For some reason we kept having periods of business prosperity which were suddenly ended by a crash, a business collapse, then followed a long period of idling activity, mental depression and public distemper. After years of wrestling with the angel of despair for self mastery (as prescribed by Washington, D.C.) we managed to arouse enough self-confidence to make an attempt to get around some "corner" or other on to the main street known as "Prosperity Drive." Some say that it was our native zest of pioneering in a great new industry, such as automobile manufacturing, that lured us around "the corner," but really in most cases we were stampeded around it through Fear caused by a small gang in the back row shouting: "WAR, WAR, DEFENCE—We must go back to work to build guns and armaments to defend ourselves. HURRY, HURRY, or it will be too late." Incidently, I once looked back to see who was doing all the shouting and saw "our drivers" gleefully reach for their money bags and race after us not failing to snatch up every penny dropped by the scrambling and terrified people.

J: There now, so that's the picture, is it? Now I want to know what causes these crises you speak so distressingly about.

P: It seems to be this way. When our production machine is running along "swell" on the oil (money) supplied, or rather loaned out at a "profit" by individuals and bankers as individuals, there comes a time when some one of these investors, a big hand in the oil-pumping station at Wall Street, suddenly remembers that it must be about time for the recurrence of the inevitable crisis. The realization striking him so suddenly makes him think it to be a genuine premonition. So he pulls his huge investments out of danger. When the others get wind of it, they frantically rush in "to get" and "get out" in time too. The result is an oil-pumping station circulating terrific blasts of paralyzing foul air into our machinery. As the oil, money, flowing to the distributors of the products of our machines, slows down, becoming of insufficient quantity to buy from the producers, they buy less. Then those with the goods to sell begin to lower the prices to tempt sales. Then this price lowering oscillates up and down throughout the entire economic structure, causing such a drop in prices in selling and buying that industry approaches a standstill as it can not even get rid of what it already has on hand. Of course when the factories cease to operate, workers are dismissed, resulting in our serious unemployment problem.

J: Well, well. That is distressing and extremely dangerous to peace and contentment within your own ranks. Starving people know no limit to crime and hate. As the Doctor that was called in on this case, I would say your trouble is likely to be either in the fuel-pump or the source of the oil. If the fuel-pump is operated for personal profit I can understand that it would be rather temperamentally run. As to the source, when did the creation of money get out of the hand of the government? Wait, don't interrupt me, I realize the inefficiency and so the danger of bureaucratic control of such an active and alive thing as money. It would still be in the tempted hands of human beings. The temptation to graft would still be—Oh, oh, here it is. I got it. Why not take the temptation out of money, make money controllable even in human hands? Say, Mr. Public, ever notice the unusual, peculiar and un-natural characteristic of money, that distinguishes it from all other man-made fabrications? It is the only one not subject to rust, rot and decay. It has been made indestructible and deathless. Why it has even been endowed with the power to increase and grow, nourished only by time. It has been imbued by man with life eternal. Amazing facts. No wonder everyone prefers the possession of money to any other material thing. No wonder it is withdrawn from dangerous circulation, and hoarded. The hoarder can not suffer loss. And to think it is this storing of money when it is needed that paralyzes your production, resulting in great human misery from lack of work.

As Dr. Jefferson, I diagnose your ailment to be: Periodic starvation, due to economic indigestion, resulting from devouring "live-money." Money in a live state being very poisonous.

The Cure I recommend is: Not to give up eating money, but first "kill" it before attempting to take it into your system. Extract its venom "interest" and assign to it the nature of all other dead things—the ability to deteriorate and devaluate, by periodic taxation of the same. Then money will be no more desirable to hoard than any materials or goods. In fact less so, for it can not be eaten, worn as clothing or be made into good buildings.

Furthermore, I suggest that steps be taken immediately to cure this disease of yours. To run off to war while in your weakened condition is to court serious battle-blows with little power behind the ones you will deliver in return. At the same time you will be aggravating your uncured "disease," overtaxing yourself to the point of collapse.

P: But, Dr. Jefferson, that's change, against the Constitution.

J: Against the Constitution? Why, room for change was the very spirit of it. In regard to money itself, we have written words into the effect that it shall be the power of government to create and regulate our currency.

P: But, there would be so many against such a change.

J: Yes, I know, but not so many as you think; for if YOU (the public) knew it was absolutely necessary still having the power to vote, you would bring this change about democratically and peaceably. This change has got to come eventually and if not now, there is danger that it may soon come by revolution. By Gad, I'd give nine-tenths of this peaceful Heaven to be down there again. First, I'd have all the Italian columns torn down and dumped into "The Bay" and make Washington look like it was located in the U.S. Then I'd go to work on this currency curing business and get the "Right to Work," that we apparently left out, into the Constitution. So that the other "rights" would have meaning, worth and value.

Then let this fellow, what's his name—Hitler, or anyone else foolish enough to attack us on Our Own Soil come over. We would show him how we Americans could fight on a full stomach. Show him how much better men can fight with the will and courage derived from fighting to protect what they know is a higher culture in contrast to fighting with the fear of losing a social condition which they know has failed to afford many even the bare essentials of existence.

1. For "The Man Who" series, see *Frank Lloyd Wright Collected Writings Volume 3*, pp. 250–264.

# MUMFORD LECTURES

After their first meeting, in the late 1920s, Frank Lloyd Wright and Lewis Mumford, the social reformer and critic for The New Yorker, became good friends. It was due to Mumford's influence that Wright agreed to keep his work in the 1932 Museum of Modern Art show "Modern Architecture—International Exhibition," which Wright felt was "more propaganda than exhibition."[1] But suddenly, in August 1941, Wright attacked Mumford for a series of lectures he gave in Alabama on "The South in Architecture." The criticism focuses mainly on the work of Thomas Jefferson as an architect and on Henry Hobson Richardson. Remarks that Wright made here he later altered entirely:

> Thomas Jefferson was the man who did the one-brick thick serpentine wall. That was modern architecture. That was organic architecture. He knew that it would not stand up, four inches thick, but if he made it serpentine that way, it would stand there and be rather interesting to look at. Well, I maintain that the man who was capable of that, notwithstanding Monticello and the University of Virginia and all the rest of it, would have been sitting very close to where we are now in architecture today.[2]

Richardson, too, later won his admiration:

> Among the architects practicing in America when I entered Adler and Sullivan's offices, Richardson had the high honor of the field; Beaux-Arts graduate, Bostonian well-connected with the better elements of society, the Adamses, etc. But Richardson had robust appetite for romance. His Romanesque soon overthrew prevailing preferences for Renaissance. Eventually he became the most productive and successful of those men, the eclectics of their time.[3]

In fact, the intense disagreement with Mumford was a result of their differing opinions about the United States entering the war in Europe. The dispute over the war seriously injured, in fact almost shattered, their friendship for years, and accounts for much of the negative response Mumford's lectures drew from Wright in this article. [Published in The Saturday Review, 13 August 1941]

Lewis Mumford. Photograph courtesy of Mrs. Sophia Mumford. All rights reserved.
FLLW Fdn FA#AV6702.0004

I DON'T KNOW WHAT HAS HAPPENED TO MR. MUMFORD unless it is the war. How can he manage to be so right in the details and so wrong in the sum or so right in the sum and so wrong in the details of such erudition as he seems pleased to waste in the process of expanding Jefferson into a great architect, shrinking Richardson into a characteristic Southerner, and blowing him up many times life-size?

Contrary to Mr. Mumford's thesis in the first of these lectures, styles are necessarily created from within—each in its own good time and not because of any exterior influences of a universal character. A style is a particularity or it has no style. The drama of human development proceeds from within outwards—and there is no "tension between the regional and the universal." They are one when they are either.

What makes the pseudo-classic building a social and economic crime is that it knows nothing of the life that builds or inhabits it except as to a main hole to crawl in and out of and various holes in the walls to peep out of. All else is fashionably "trim" and cornice. It is at best a gigantic makeshift. It was entirely moral but wholly unethical. Neither Jefferson nor Richardson sought to change this.

If the pseudo-classicists believed in a "universal order" as Lewis says they did, it was because they were so uncreative as to have to accept one ready-made. One may dwell upon the unities of the Logos and the Cosmos, be persuaded that two times two equals four, and yet never get nearer Reality than that we like applesauce because it is universal and dislike apples because they are merely individual. Applesauce seems to be Lewis Mumford's growing "taste" in architecture.

I should say that Mr. Mumford's analysis of Jefferson the Architect in his second lecture is artificial writing just as Jefferson's Monticello was artificial architecture. Unfortunately, where architecture is concerned Lewis, like Thomas, remains the man of "taste." And there never is nor can there ever be one so far removed from the nature of the thing as the man of taste. He is like one blinded by the pleasing play of light on the surface of an object, never realizing, nor wishing to realize, the nature of that at which he gazes. But Thomas Jefferson could bring to America the fine rebellious mind of the highest form of aristocracy the world has ever seen: the Jeffersonian Democracy. To call any building he designed a great work of art could not be intelligent, however pleasing the architectural intonation or elegant the gesture. As a man of taste Jefferson, unfortunately, had only the tail-end of an utterly servile eclecticism for his inspiration. Lewis, unfortunately, has no such alibi. And I feel that he limits the author of "the Declaration" by trying to account him a great architect. When Jefferson was seventy-three years old he (the jack-of-all-trades were he on a lower plane) wrote:

> Some men look at constitutions—(or architectural styles?) with sanctimonious reverence and deem them like the ark of the covenant, too sacred to be touched.
>
> They ascribe to the men of the preceding age a wisdom more than human and suppose what they did to be beyond amendment. I knew that age

well. I belonged to it and labored with it. It deserved well of its country. It was very like the present, but forty years of experience in government is worth a century of book reading, and this they would themselves say were they to rise from the dead: "laws and institutions must go hand in hand with the progress of the human mind."

It is of course "regional" twaddle to say, as Mr. Mumford does in his third lecture, that the South, or any form of sectionalism, gave Thomas Jefferson or H. H. Richardson to the architecture of this country. Richardson was a robust romanticist of large caliber, the last grand-gesture of an architectural epoch: the most gorgeous picture-maker of the dying era of the eclectic.

I am mildly mortified to learn from Mr. Mumford's final lecture that I "widened and carried along the Richardson principles" because I never believed Mr. Richardson had any "principles."

No, Lewis! While I am hardly looking, you can't bring this man Richardson up on me from behind, slip in a coupling pin, and ask me to take him along! Moreover, can't you see, Lewis, that according to your view of me you are only turning him over to the Japanese?

With Lewis we are indeed back to the "Seven Lamps of Architecture" and the imperative need of throwing the lives of American boys at Hitler—*at once*. Blood, sweat, and tears have been promised to the British lads by Churchill. He is keeping his promise. Lewis Mumford now promises all these to us. In this connection may I quote Jefferson's last words as printed in these Mumford lectures as my own last words in this small review? "It is part of the American character to consider nothing as desperate."

1. See "Of Thee I Sing," *Frank Lloyd Wright Collected Writings Volume 3*, p. 113–115.

2. Frank Lloyd Wright in a talk to the Taliesin Fellowship, 1 May 1955.

3. Frank Lloyd Wright, *A Testament*. New York: Horizon Press, 1957. p. 39.

# HICKLING

*That Frank Lloyd Wright subscribed to various political and social journals from overseas, such as* Reality, *edited by G. Hickling, suggests that he was not insular in his reading even though he was certainly isolationist in his thinking. He never professed to be an expert on economics or political science, but he was keenly aware of those disciplines and avidly read their theorists: Silvio Gesell and Giuseppe Mazzini in particular. He was a close friend of Harold Groves, professor of economics at the University of Wisconsin. Wright's article "Hickling" was never published, but it clearly explains his isolationist views in response to Professor Hickling's theories:*

> *The noteworthy English editor of* Reality *pointed out that America was self-sufficient. And, for that reason, was able to take the lead of the world by adapting social-credit principles.*

*[Unpublished]*

IT IS A FUNDAMENTAL PRINCIPLE OF OUR DEMOCRACY THAT the Government be responsible to the people. *The Government derives all its authority from this principle!* This essential principle of Democracy needs special and sustained emphasis at the present time because ideas have been continuously proposed in Congress by the President himself designed to destroy democracy in the name of democracy. And a majority of our Congress seems to be willing to work for the destruction of the essential democratic principle. The net result of all this confusion of idea is to substitute an abstract external authority *above* the people's government, reducing the democratic responsibility of Congress to an international servility, and eventually occasion the loss of national and constitutional sovereignty.

This is Fascism? What else can it be?

The people of these United States, as in each and every other nation, are becoming completely helpless because nominal *leaders* are become *rulers* out of hand, engaging in mutual conflicts none of them have clearly thought through to a conclusion—their technique such as only to get the best, one of the other, their policy and acts all finally coming down to the psychology of a prize fighter in the prize-ring.

It is evident that the members of this present Congress of the United States are not instruments of their constituents but dominated by a ruler and, instead of themselves dominating an executive, are subservient to the invisible but powerful despotism of international financial interests whose aims are unannounced. This is as true of England as it is of us. We might correctly say that *because* it is true of England it is true of us. We may be smarter than the English but we are less shrewd. We still take our original pattern from the Island Empire overseas.

But, unless all signs that reach us fail, England will march to a concluded peace as a Socialist Commonwealth. Will that conclusion suit the "invisible despotism" over here?

This invisible despotism over us here, "is a great and potent world that governments do not control. That is the world of finance, the men who guide the ebb and flow of money. The men who control that river, as things are, have the ultimate word." Lord Tweedsmuir (late Governor-general of Canada).

As against this control the Isolationist (so-called) believes that while international trade is desirable it is not necessary. He believes that during the time that the world is inimical to us we can build a wall around America and that America can be made self-sufficient and still retain the free way of life: a wall especially desirable while the nations of Europe are, as usual, at each other's throats.

But the internationalists of the Willkie-Roosevelt type declare: "To remain free, nations must trade with one another; must trade freely in goods, in ideas, in customs, and traditions and values of all sorts and declare that regardless of the dangers of involvement this nation, to remain free, must enter the European debacle in order to come out with commercial supremacy."

Well, two days before the war, September 1, 1939, in an article entitled "Peace without Penury," G. Hickling, the noteworthy English Editor of *Reality* pointed out that America *was* self-sufficient. And, for that reason, was able to take the lead of the world by adapting social-credit principles. The article pointed out that she could then feed her population and keep solvent irrespective of whether she had an excess of imports or exports or an exact balance between both or even more of either. In short, that "economic supremacy" was a false and dangerous ideal.

And those who look carefully at the reactions of lend-lease activities can see adhesion to that "false and dangerous ideal" already driving a wedge between what might be a helpful united English-speaking alliance between the United States and Great Britain.

It would appear that the so-called Isolationists with their economic sufficiency are the true friends of England in this war—the only ones ultimately enabling the United States to offer her assistance and in the end to step in and dictate a reasonable peace instead of herself cutting England's throat by a carefully planned commercial-supremacy!

Interventionist rhetoric can't hide this truth eventually. What the Willkie-Roosevelt interventionist is really saying is, "If you *don't* sell your dinner to the foreigner you will have to borrow the dollars to eat it yourself." What happens if we *do* sell our dinner to the foreigner neither Willkie nor Roosevelt have explained. Presumably you get the dollars without borrowing them but to eat what? Unless you eat the foreigner who has eaten the dinner!

So much for the Willkie-Roosevelt "commercial supremacy"! Their blind belief in the exploded axioms of high Finance can only ruin this democracy.

Suppose this nation had a money system compatible with Democracy instead of the one we have which is inevitably only one for a Plutocracy? What enemy government could hope to maintain the support of its people in a war against us as a nation if we put this natural and practicable object as our peace aim: all possible abundance allowed to flow freely through the channels of industry converted from war to peace purposes so that there shall never again be any want? Nor any war.

No compulsion would be required to make every citizen of this country strive of his own free will for its attainment. And I ask, "what government could retain the support of its people in a war with a nation which put this natural and practicable object as its peace aim?"

This is the desire of every normal individual, and that desire would be rendered hopeless by Interventionist success in this war.

1942

# THE BASEMENT OF A DEMOCRATIC STATE

**A**lthough the nation was at war by the time this article was written, Wright was steadfastly convinced that the United States of America had no place in that conflict and was brought into it by the machinations of Churchill and Roosevelt. He does not go so far as to name the "Big Noises," as he refers to the powers in this text, but his intent is obvious. Needless to say, this article remained unpublished.

THE WORST OF ALL VILE POWERS ARE THOSE WHICH ROB A man of his individuality. Repeating the lie that the individual is less than the mass is becoming the daily common crime. If a man can be made to believe that lie he can be used for sacrifice fodder by the evil powers, and to any extent, as we may now see on any front in this all-out world war. Men have surrendered their own power (we call it initiative) and have given themselves over to moral stink and carnal filth in the swine-trough of this world through a servitude forced upon them through doubt of themselves and of their own powers. When confronted by what seems to them a superior power they have permitted doubt of their own to paralyze their own action and initiative.

Say they: "What can one man do against such power?" And it is because they believe themselves powerless that they *give* such power superiority. The power the man thus surrenders is all that distinguishes him from an animal. We call this human power "initiative."

Today the world is full of Big Noises: prominent men trying to give everybody who will listen inferiority complexes. They strive to make men forget that they have individuality; they create bogeys and images that exist only for and within their own servile imaginations; they call upon mankind to fall in and fight these bogeys. Millions are exhorted to surrender their personal interests in favor of national interests which in turn are to be surrendered to international interests. And all this is designed to concentrate and clamp down upon men more power, power more and more remote from them as individuals. Boiled down it exactly means that a manly man is expected to give up the bird of what personal freedom he has in favor of two to four bigger imaginary ones in the International bush.

To those who listen, the Big Noises are really thus presenting the Devil as the good God Almighty, calling on the listeners to bend the knee, worship, and die. Millions obey. But observe: the

**Anne Pfeiffer Chapel, Florida Southern College, Lakeland, Florida. 1939.** FLLW Fdn FA#3816.0073

power of these millions is not increased thereby—as they imagine. The flaw in it all lies in the fact that the Devil is not really Almighty and a little bit of Reality can overcome all illusory vanity of the sort.

There are more than a few who know this. The Medicine men have no power to confuse or betray them. When a man is once aware of his worth and dignity as an individual he has "*come to*" and is henceforth endowed with a conquering power. He can neither be scared by bogeys or deceived with lies or fancy labels. And it is difficult to carry him away with pious words or high-sounding protestations. Regardless of what they *say* he is likely to watch what the "prominent men" *do*.

Against this acid test the Medicine men have no defense. They are all afraid of this light that can be acquired without filling out any official forms. It is outside the control of would-be restrictors and so-called "planners." And believe it or not, *it is the greatest power in this world!* It is the only great stumbling block feared by the evil powers themselves.

This biggest attempt that has ever been made in the History of the World to subordinate humanity to the degrading level of a world-herd penned in by a wire fence of financial debt—will fail because of the few initiates aware of the truth: a consistent, unfailing light from within—let the pushful, artificial light of power-propaganda beat upon it as it will.

These evil planners: obsessed by the idea that they know what is good for everybody else and who have not hesitated to invoke carnal violence to enforce their own arrogance are fighting hard. But they are fighting against the truth! No lie like theirs can stand.

**Herbert Jacobs House, Madison, Wisconsin. 1937.** FLLW Fdn FA#3702.0027

# AN OPEN LETTER TO PATRICK STONE ET AL.

**H**ere Wright severely criticizes the judge, Patrick Stone, who sentenced Marcus Weston to Sandstone (a prison for political dissenters in Wisconsin). Wright felt that both the charges and the trial were a mockery: "The quality of American fair play is sunk pretty low when a judge on the bench uses his office (however he came by it) to sound off his prejudice against another man on mere hearsay." [Unpublished]

YOU DO NOT KNOW ME. I KNOW YOU ONLY AS YOU DEBASE your judgeship to throw stones at me. The quality of American fair play is sunk pretty low when a judge on the bench uses his office (however he came by it) to sound off his prejudice against another man on mere hearsay.

And we have too much of it taking refuge under the name of government when it is no more than a passing administration of our government. I have occasion to know well the arrogant prejudice raised against any man who refuses to run with the pack. But it is seldom in our country that it comes from the place all American citizens hoped, and still hope, to keep free and impartial.

So I believe you are another one of the things that is the matter with America. I think for the safety of this Nation such men as yourself should be deprived of any administrative authority whatever, right now.

In the case of Marcus Weston, a true conscientious objector, you have judged him only as a draft-evader and sentenced him as a criminal because he knew no better than to plead guilty to the charge lodged against him, a charge which was itself a willful evasion of his real status.

I have no more use for a draft-evader than you have.

The Taliesin Fellowship is a tax-free Democratic establishment wherein young men are recognized as responsible human beings with consciences of their own. I would never take it upon myself to advise them what to do where their own lives were the stake, even were I consulted. It would not be in the spirit of our Fellowship.

But young architects come here because of a common interest and faith. I often learn more from them than they learn from me. It is not surprising therefore that their feeling about war should independently, somewhat resemble mine? Independence is their status here because they are all volunteers as they will, I am sure, gladly testify. Nineteen of them are in the service.

As for conscription, I think it has deprived every young man in America of the honor and privilege of dedicating himself as a freeman to the service of his country. They were all condemned without a hearing and enslaved.

Were I born forty years later than 1869 [sic] I too should be a conscientious objector.

# ADDRESS AT SANDSTONE PRISON

*There can be no doubt that Frank Lloyd Wright's strong antipathy to war in general, and to the Second World War in particular, influenced the apprentices of the Taliesin Fellowship, although he maintained that was not the case. "Nor am I in the habit of telling young men who come to work and study with me what to think concerning their own personal views of their own private lives. Whenever I have done so, I have regretted it."[1] And, "Independence is their status here because they are all volunteers as they will, I am sure, gladly testify. Nineteen of them are now in the services."[2] Several of the apprentices were granted deferment because of their participation in farming the Taliesin Farmlands; others were sent to special camps where they were "excused" on religious grounds, for being Quakers, for example. Three apprentices were sent to Sandstone prison for being conscientious objectors. In 1942 Wright drove up to Sandstone to deliver a talk to an assembly of prisoners who were incarcerated there because of their belief that war was wrong and therefore they would not participate in it. Wright was especially appalled by the judges and courts that tried the young men of the Taliesin Fellowship in the first place. Concerning his views on these events and institutions, he wrote a tract entitled "Concerning Marcus Weston's Fellowship at Taliesin" and sent it to his friend and editor William T. Evjue of the* Capital Times *with the note, "Dear Bill— Will you see that this gets to the A.P. [Associated Press] and others. I hope you can publish it yourself— FLLW." [Unpublished]*

GOOD MEN AND BAD MEN IN THESE UNITED STATES HAVE been thinking and talking about the world as it may be after the second great war. No doubt you at Sandstone are involved more. I myself wanted to come here to see how the democratic principle works with the individual during wartime. Or more accurately to see what happens to the individual when it does not work.

Society will always be inferior to the individual in human worth and dignity. In the mass, society will resort to acts of which any individual compos-ing it would be ashamed. All of the national suicides and crimes against itself which society has committed have been committed in the name of the crowd or the so-called majority, although many bad Kings have committed atrocities of justice that a republican government could seldom match. But most of you boys are here at Sandstone because our own society took fright and to save itself decided to sacrifice its individuality and its individuals and seek survival by murdering before it was itself murdered as it believed it would be.

Because we live in a "to have and to hold" society which is readily alarmed and quickly huddles, it is hard to have both peace and what you want to have and hold if the other fellow wants to have it and hold it as badly as you do. War is the only means yet found and is no solution at all. It only ensures worse and more of it. But, to get back to you in this well-ordered, well-conducted prison which more resembles a monastery than the horrible places into which society used to throw its citizen to make examples of them when afraid for its own safety: I am interested in you not so much as casualties as I am interested in you as men responsible to yourselves for yourselves—men, who realizing that you have to live with yourselves all your lives long on good terms with yourself before you are fit to live with anyone else—have asserted your right to be on good terms with yourself.

I know something of the struggle to defend these rights of the individual that live on in him to higher purpose than any conformity to any corporeal command of self-interest. And I know the nature of the decisions a man has to make in those circumstances. Therefore I am here with you in Sandstone in spirit at least. And I want to reassure you that no punishment judges may inflict with the whips and penalties provided them for this purpose by law can ever destroy that inner man. They can make that man suffer. But what power is it that sits in judgement, finally, upon that man's judges? If that man is true to himself he will grow in power. His sufferings add to his stature and his strength. When the day of liberation comes he will be again free to use for his fellows the strength he has gained. The use of this inviolate inner strength of the man is the only salvation democracy will have in this world after war has spent its fear and fury. If peace comes to mankind—such inner strength will bring it. Nothing else known can keep it. Heroes are not what they used to be. Something in this world, perhaps the slowly rising level of intelligence which cannot be wholly bound down to the herd in a free republic has made the old style hero rather too obvious and his heroism questionable. Something is making of punishments, seen as "justice," a something as yet out of court.

It is becoming more and more evident to all men that like returns to like. "Judgement is mine saith the Lord. I will repay." We shall see more clearly every day that this is true and that every offense against himself committed either by the man or committed by society against him carries within itself its own natural punishment—the punishment that fits the crime of either the judged or the judging.

Have faith in that, boys, it will never fail you! War can make it fail only temporarily, as you will know.

But this is a world of expedients. Most of you are in Sandstone in what disgrace the law can inflict because of those expedients. While since the world we live in only knows how to work with such expedients you must be patient. We must all work within ourselves for that better world after the insane rage of war for which we have all been hoping and waiting. Some of us are working for it while the boys at the front are fighting and you are forced to "stand and wait!" Milton said—"they also serve who do but stand and wait." We need and want a world wherein what you can have and hold and get a little bit more of depends on how you got it, a world wherein success means more than it does now; a world wherein the old having-and-holding habit is seen as a warmaker, a pestilence rejected in favor of a free distribution of ground and a medium of exchange (we call it money) free of speculation. Trade barriers anywhere make trouble. There must be no bar to the employment of the man by himself at work that he loves best to do because he can do that work best. Especially we want a world beyond war—a world wherein there will be no chance to enslave any man for pseudo social ends and drive him to carnal victory over others or drive him to social suicide.

Well—Taliesin was dreaming of the practical plan and details for such a world when the billions of dollars that could have made it began to roll into our factories to roll out on to ships to find its way to the waste and horror of the old classic success-ideal, Victory.

We called the new world Broadacre City for lack of a better name . . . it is the city that is native and is nowhere except everywhere. Decentralization of everything was the general key to its freedom in manifold forms. And its ground was for all mankind wherever the inner strength of which I speak had a dwelling and the man would work for himself.

True independence was the soul of that new world and not the degeneracy of Interdependence we now hear so much about as the new fashion to come in worlds.

A witty Frenchman said—that "the people of the United States were the only people in history to have proceeded from barbarism to degeneracy with no civilization of our own in between." We now discover we had the billions to make that world but would only spend them for war. So we will have to make this new world by ourselves. And between us, it will be easier to make that new world because these billions have gone to the bottom of the sea or gone up in agony and the smoke of battle, because it is now more than likely that we will have to abandon the idea that Money plus Authority can rule the world and get down to earth with the idea that Work plus Ideas is wealth and *can* rule the world.

Intelligence with vision is rare, though. Possessive passions are like the rage of carnal battle and obscure the simple truths of life. The battle rages and destroys us in our attempts to destroy others until we learn, painfully little by little that civilizations always have and always will perish that way.

1. Document 2401.262, FLLW Archives, 16 January 1943.

2. Frank Lloyd Wright. "Open Letter to Patrick Stone," 18 December 1942.

# CONCERNING MARCUS WESTON'S FELLOWSHIP AT TALIESIN

*W*hen the United States entered the Second World War, nineteen of Wright's apprentices were inducted into the armed services. Another was excused on the basis of his religious upbringing, and three others were sent to prison on grounds of being conscientious objectors. When one of the conscientious objectors, Marcus Weston, was sentenced, twenty-five apprentices got together and signed a document—a plea—to the local draft board at Dodgeville, Wisconsin. Judge Patrick Stone accused the apprentices of submitting a document that was seditious. Wright responded with this article, and ended it with a poem by the English poet and patriot Wilfrid Blunt.[1] Wright pointed out in his text that Taliesin, as a training field for young builders, was involved in a work of great importance: "They believe (and I believe, too) that their constructive work at home to help make the country a country worth fighting for—a genuine free democracy—employing their real talent and highly specialized training, their own real gifts in their own way was better militancy than languishing in jail which is where they felt when they signed that paper they might land if their plea was not considered." [Unpublished]

JUSTICE IN WARTIME CONSISTS IN A WHIP FOR THE DRAFT board? And in this case, a draft board that is itself an evader of justice if ever one was.

The trial of Marcus Weston by a judge confessing his own prejudice at the trial was utterly equivocal. The so-called "judgement" should be set aside. The Court decree declares the young man was being punished for his association with me and punished as an example at the whipping post in sight of his fellows who were there in Court and were up against the same draft board conducting the same unconstitutional lottery Weston encountered. And conducting it in the same regardless way where they, too, are concerned.

Appeal from the "judgements" of this local draft board are heard in Madison before another board, a so-called "appeal board," with an irresponsible appointee for chairman. This irresponsible chairman declared to me that so long as his own son was in the army, every boy not in the army was a slacker and if any conscientious objectors (the sons of bitches) ever got before him he was going to slap them in . . . by God. And, yes sir.

Well—this document twenty-five of the Taliesin boys prepared was a plea (not to their proper local boards, unfortunately) to the local board at Dodgeville because they were here at Taliesin instead of at home. This Dodgeville draft board looked upon their plea to be considered of greater value to their country as a highly-trained and organized constructive-unit than a scattered destructive one, as a document that "smacked" of sedition, as the Judge says. If the perverse stupidity of the lay-mind can best that, the best has yet to get to the record.

The document that "smacks of sedition" is one these young men signed in good faith stating their honest conviction that deferment was better in their case than soldiery or jail. I knew nothing of the meetings among them at the time and now do not know who the prime-movers were or who finally framed the petition. But when the plea was presented to me I said I thought it was a well-written statement of their position and their views. And I still think so. Those who brought the statement in to show it to me all decisively declared themselves ready and willing to go through with it and that was that, so far as I was concerned. This place is militant but not a military academy. Nor am I in the habit of telling young men who come to work and study with me what to think concerning their own personal views of their own private lives. Whenever I have done so, I have regretted it.

In that respect I differ greatly from the present administration of their government and most of their friends, not to mention their families. It has been enough for me to respect them when in the case of my own children (eight in all) they were faced with a decision affecting their own personal lives. And I may mention that for the same reason I have never sought a job "by influence" or otherwise. If I did I knew I would be in the hands of the job—not the

**Marcus Weston at work on model of Press Building, Taliesin, 1940. Photograph by Pedro E. Guerrero.** FLLW Fdn FA#6504.0055

job in my hands. These facts can easily be proved.

Taliesin is a training field for young builders. The work here *is* of great importance, so we all believe, to the country that is fighting—for what?

They believe (and I believe too) that their constructive work at home to help make the country a country worth fighting for—a genuine free democracy—employing their real talent and highly specialized training, their own real gifts in their own way was better militancy than languishing in jail which is where they felt when they signed that paper they might land if their plea was not considered. They would land in jail because they were all opposed to this war. And, as I understand it, each (and nearly all of them) prepared statements of their own to this effect which are now on file with the local lottery office at Dodgeville.

The document that "smacks of sedition" was not intended by them as entitling them to status as "conscientious objectors" because that status has been narrowed down to the tag of some prenatal religious sect and any man having a conscience otherwise is doomed.

But the manly appeal fell before an unintelligent group of provincials who felt the whole affair of "artiteture" was a funny business anyway and a luxury at the best. So they laughed, or probably sneered, at the "draft-evaders" and slapped them all back in 1A, by God and Yes Sir.

But when a U.S. District Attorney knows no better and an amateur lawyer undertaking to defend young Weston begins and ends his defense by saying he too always thought "there was something wrong out there at Taliesin"—why, what have you?

And no better in "judgement" than this sort of thing is what is compelling with "the whip of scorpions" millions of young lives to be herded like sheep and driven by "judges" to slaughter their kind, or go to jail. Is this what they are asked to fight for? No. I think not. I believe the sort of thing these fine, and yes, noble young men are willing to go to jail to preserve is worth more than that would indicate.

And there is no doubt in my mind that young men like these are the bricks in a solid wall being painfully erected against all future wars and with greater suffering than in being wounded or killed in battle.

This neck of the woods has mighty occasion to honor one Marcus Weston—or be ashamed of itself. It is a good thing to fight for your country if you believe in fighting. But I say it is a greater thing to fight for the future of your country by going to jail, if necessary.

Now much is being made of the circumstance that many of the young men signing this plea that "smacks of sedition" did not go through with it but were beaten down by fear of the judicial whips that were held over them or their views were changed by our getting into actual war, or by who knows what? Not I.

But all are welcome here at Taliesin, either from the armed forces or from jail so long as they are doing their best in the circumstances—whatever they are. We do not all have the same moral stamina. And while Taliesin detests a moral coward above all, Taliesin knows itself well enough to be kind to weakness.

## TO MARCUS WESTON

A prison for a man who goes there to uphold his faith is like:

> A convent without God.
> Poverty, Chastity, Obedience are the
> precepts of these walls of grief.
> Nor shall I hear the vain laughter and
> tears of those who love me still.
> Lying cold in hunger, nights of wakeful-
> ness.
> Harsh orders given, no voice to soothe
> or please.
> Poor thieves for friends; for books,
> rules . . . meaningless.
> This is the grave . . . nay, hell. Yet Lord
> of Right
> Still in Thy light my spirit shall see light.

Lines from the Irish patriot, Wilfrid Blunt, Jan. 3, 1889, who was himself in jail.

1. Wilfrid Blunt, 1840–1922.

# O GOVERNMENT!

*In this unpublished manuscript Wright challenges a society that erects monuments to the nation's Founding Fathers by encasing their images in neoclassical garb. Referring to the Jefferson Memorial, designed by John Russell Pope and in construction at the time this was written, Wright avowed, "Thomas Jefferson had a mind and would certainly have kept pace with his country's growth. Had he lived until now we could not find his face turned toward the rear to encourage the gangrene of sentimentality, his mind closed to the superb advancement of the scientific art of building." And, "the architecture of the nation's capital belongs to the toga and the civilization that wore it."*

WHY WASTE MORE AMERICAN SUBSTANCE ON REACTIONARY monuments? Our bureaucratic architecture is already hard enough for the growing spirit of America to bear without adding more.

I refer to J. Russell Pope's arrogant insult to the memory of Thomas Jefferson, a cultured democrat adored by many of us and honored by all. With Mr. Pope—he is apparently growing fashionable in Washington—we are never fair and square with fine sentiment but must ever be preening the fine feathers of sentimental affectation or present at the morgue.

Thomas Jefferson? Were the gentleman alive today he would be first to scorn the stupid erudition mistaken in his honor and, abreast of the advanced thought of today, as he was leader of the advanced thought of his own time, he would promptly condemn both the folly and the waste. Life has changed, almost beyond belief, since Thomas Jefferson came to lend his abilities to our Great Experiment—bringing with him the clothes, furniture, and books on building familiar to the Georgian period he turned his back upon.

He was not an architect except as every gentleman of his day had book smattering of the Arts to whet his taste and abet his leisure. But Thomas Jefferson had a mind and would certainly have kept pace with his country's growth. Had he lived until now we could not find *his* face turned toward the rear to encourage the gangrene of sentimentality, his mind closed to the superb advancement of the scientific art of building. Architecture—a hobby of his, especially.

I imagine I see the sarcastic smile with which his shade must receive this fashionable design proposing to draw his mortal remains to the surface of the present and their own millions spent to memorialize him to his own people in terms of the feudal art and thought that clung to him then, deliberately to make of him now a fashionable effigy of reaction instead of a character appreciated by his own people as a noble spirit of progress and freedom. Were the great man living he might well say, "What folly to spend millions to preserve the letter of a man and not one dollar to mark his living spirit!"

Similar blunders have made our official buildings in Washington a dead weight upon the spirit of our progress. Our official monuments are shameful waste betraying the future of our architecture into the hands of sycophants, dilettantes, or boys educated far beyond their capacity—coming down soon to a mere matter of the fashions of some passing period. Meantime, indigenous creative art has gone begging for its life while the whole world of culture has laughed and laughs now at the erudite ignorance of such performances. Official America—alone— seems not to know it. Why, I ask, should easy money, even if taken from too easily rich Americans, be so wantonly spent to advertise to posterity that American authority is neither scholar nor gentleman? No scholar because unaware of the trend of honest advanced thought in the world of culture: no gentleman because willing to betray its own youth to senility or deserved ridicule.

How many Americans living and loyal to Jeffersonian ideals, understanding and loving the spirit of the man Jefferson, could tolerate this Johnny Pope masquerade in his honor?

Name one capable of such treachery!

And "government" would put this latest betrayal of Thomas Jefferson, another shameful mortgage on our future, beside government's other travesty of a great memory—the Lincoln Memorial. Beside the two put the stupendous folly erected to caricature the Supreme Court of the United States and see what all add up to. No more than the disease—provincial grandomania.

Sacrifice of the living spirit to the dead letter? Yes. And all add up to a total confession of impotence that no ignorance whatever can excuse to the young America that will be taxed to pay the bills. Add to that tax, the tax still later generations will pay to get rid of it all as it would be glad, even now, were it taxed to get rid of the army and navy building, the Congressional Library, the Union Station, the senseless "classic" and General-Grant-Gothic conceits generally adorning the government's monumental seat.

I, for one, sadly familiar with the sterile results of officialdom where works of art are concerned, am yet astonished at the effrontery in presuming to commit our people to one more world-famous miscarriage of grace to add to the disgraces already handed on to posterity by "government."

My earnest protest as an architect and an American herewith. Government, my government, let us up! Have we not suffered enough vain unreality? Take your unfeeling bulk off our progress in architecture by showing us now that American millions can be spent to nobly characterize the immortal spirit of a noblest American and that you are, at last, able to respectfully allow his clothes, his bookarchitecture, his furniture and utensils, his tastes to remain with his mortal body in his tomb. They too are his mortal remains.

O Government, if you cannot yet learn how to say honor to Thomas Jefferson with true significance and grace as architecture—say it with green spaces, noble trees and splendid masses of verdure and brooks. Or say it simple by way of a great forum where his own people may find a voice or consciously be one.

# THE NEW DISCRETION

**W**right, who never received a commission from the U.S. government, was, however, presented with a federal job early in 1942: the design for housing for defense plant workers in Pittsfield, Massachusetts. The scheme he proposed was a quadruple housing project based on the Sun Top homes he had built in Ardmore, Pennsylvania, three years earlier. Complete working drawings were prepared and signed, and work was about to begin but was suddenly halted. Wright explained the situation when the work was later published in the January 1948 Architectural Forum:

> In Washington all were quite generally delighted with it. . . . But sometime later word reached me that the local architects of Massachusetts had taken the matter up with their congressmen and that only local architects as provided for in a statute covering the matter would be allowed to handle the project. Although the government offered to buy what I had done, I declined to sell it because I would have no positive control over execution. And so this project is still one of the best shots in our locker. In this scheme, standardization is no barrier to the quality of infinite variety to be observed in nature.[1]

Even as this article was being written, at the close of 1942 and the beginning of 1943, the United States was desperately, and at great cost to human life and resources, involved in the Second World War. To Wright this war, more than any other that preceded it in history, only proved that war was obsolete and that it could and would solve nothing. To quote Wright from an interview with Mike Wallace in 1957, "I think one war only breeds another, and I think I've been borne out by the reading of history, haven't I? One war always has in it, in its intestines, another, and another and another."[2]

But in this paper he urges his readers to search for deeper values and reminds them that military and political forces are basically against the truly democratic principles. As he speaks of war, in relation to the current conflict, he throws no blame on any one particular side, either Allies or Axis, but keeps to the idea of its obsolescence. In one rather prophetic statement he observes:

> We in these United States, strangely unwilling to see the truth, are witnessing the arrogant hypocrisies of Foreign Policy and the brutal atrocities of Empire played to a dismal end. Should the great West persist in thus destroying itself by trying to live in the horse and buggy era and fight, then the ancient, more spiritual wisdom of the East, Russia, a free India and a free China, perhaps together with a chastened Japan, may

*combine to ensure of more humane world. If, un-hindered, the East were to take its own way with itself, would Central-Asia, because air-ways are already superseding sea-ways, again become the pivot of the civilized world? But should the Orient be unable to see the gigantic forces now released as Armageddon to all imperial-designs and fail to see how and that Nationalism and Imperialism are at an end, then the Son of the Morning goes the way of the Son of the Evening. Both go into the historic Night.*

*[Unpublished]*

AN ENGLISH GENERAL WRITES TO THE LONDON TIMES: "There is nothing so wearing as hate. There is nothing so destructive of coolness and judgement in a moment of crisis when these virtues are essential—as hate.

"Perhaps the real reason for this hate propaganda today—which continues unabated in political circles, is just to paralyze calm judgement amongst the people. In any case preachers of hate (military or political) are in reality sappers of strength, seeking to substitute bestiality for culture, mistaking viciousness for courage. All such advocates are a public danger.

"Those propagandists who are advocates of dire punishment, who are preaching a vicious hate of the enemy are making the same mistake as those who tried to introduce the sub-human blood-and-hate training for our soldiers." (from the *London Times,* February 3, 1943)

And to go on from where our ally, the English General, leaves off we must see that any military animus of man's primitive instincts is dated. Military animus was based upon a vast primitive world only partially explored and continually exploited by the steamship and the soldier.

We must look again and see that mechanical invention is now so vast and shrinking the spaces of this earth in Space-time so that war is already taken away from the soldier and the steamship. Distances are so shrunk by plane that all Empire, either by purchase or by conquest, becomes but "The Valor of Ignorance." The known science of war, all the world's best stock must be entirely thrown away!

To the military mind of today, as of yesterday, Democracy is still a heresy, or it is only the hypocrisy of commercial-empire, to be abandoned when attacked. But to the militant free mind of today the individual as a free man, the power-norm

**The Ardmore Experiment. Sun Top Homes for Otto Mallery, Ardmore, Pennsylvania. 1938. Perspective. Pencil on tracing paper, 35 x 18".** FLLW Fdn#3906.001

of Democracy, in the gigantic unexpected reactions of mechanized power has found release from Empire because no nation can longer confine and control this gigantic force or reckon with alchemy.

Just as teeming inventive-faculty (intending otherwise) made the car a mechanical thing to destroy the City from within so (intending otherwise) man has made the plans to destroy predatory-empire from the skies. Man did not so intend—but the development of the plane makes *organic* relations of race to ground and to native environment the only relations that can endure as Nations if, indeed, "Nationalism" on the old Military terms is not soon itself wholly obsolete.

This old military-game of holding Empire by violence, accelerated at first by the plane, has suddenly by way of re-revolution (the turnabout of the industrial revolution) become utterly *impractical* because Man assumed control of Monstrosity before he could control himself.

We will now hear man the alchemist and thinker, instead of man the hoarder and schemer.

Nature herself puts within man's every problem its own solution.

Nature herself never makes a thing without planting its congenital enemy beside it. Or within it.

Reactions are often more powerful and important than first-causes and we are seeing a great reaction take its course now to clear the way for a new form of action.

Newly liberated scientific force from within has gone so far beyond any nation's control from without that Political Science itself must wake up and compel a more liberal view of the future of mankind. That more liberal view may still be militant but can be "military" no more.

Vigilance is still the price of Liberty but "vigilance" is no longer a military affair! Vigilance is valid only in man's Vision, in his capacity to reason and his militant sense of justice.

Nations both great and small are compelled to disclose a better judgement or all will perish together!

The Industrial-revolution, the monster on which the West rode to power turns about. The Industrial-revolution re-revolves as alchemy appears.

We in these United States, strangely unwilling to see the truth, are witnessing the arrogant hypocrisies of Foreign Policy and the brutal atrocities of Empire played to a dismal end.

Should the great West persist in thus destroying itself by trying to live in the horse and buggy era and fight, then the ancient, more spiritual wisdom of the East, Russia, a free India and a free China, perhaps together with a chastened Japan, may combine to ensure a more humane world. If, unhindered, the East were to take its own way with itself would Central-Asia, because air-ways are already superseding sea-ways, again become the pivot of the civilized world?

But should the Orient be unable to see the gigantic forces now released as Armageddon to all imperial-designs and fail to see how and why Nationalism and Imperialism are at an end, then the Son of the Morning goes the way of the Son of the Evening. Both go into historic Night.

We can reasonably expect no more of this great emergency than a new Discretion. Plead for that Discretion at this time.

Not too late this Nation at least will learn that according to the inclination and ability of its people to mind their own business in the sphere of life directly their own, cultivating creative native-uses for human improvement; only so can our nation, for that matter likewise any other nation, now hope to be safe. The Safety of Nations can no longer lie in the old military power, from Outside inward. It can only be found in a new spiritual power exercised from the Within outward.

For that Reason Nature's *organic* law is now the only safe law for the United States of America. Organic law is the only law that can preserve Democracy. Jurisprudence does not yet furnish that kind of law. Politicians are afraid to "stock it"; Industry itself is none too familiar with it. Automatically organic-law destroys autocratic Rulers. Rulers? Not one of them has thought this thing through to more than a wishful conclusion.

Only by gaining familiarity with Organic law will we as a Nation learn that man may hammer heated iron but not a stick of dynamite!

And only then we will learn to see that bulldog tenacity is no fit substitute for Vision?

Is that "Non-interventionist"?

Well, if it is then the truly militant citizen of this tragic today is one because he will express this single, militant, non-military idea; *one organic law for every race and nation*; Nations bound each to the other only as all are bound to the interior development of their native-land; all Nations bound to ground that either Nature gave to each as their own destiny or ground inherited in trust for all who volunteer to join them *in the pursuits of peace*.

Empirical artificial frontiers are out! They are not yet out because man *wills* but because man *must* or mankind dies a prey to his own Monstrosity. Foreign "spheres of influence" can no longer converge toward War. All are compelled to converge toward Peace. Peace can no longer be imposed by the old external-power but in good stead it is a rising tide of enlightened self-interest: interior power supreme that will be called the Organic Law.

Only the commercialized fool clamoring for "freedom to produce," his Gods and his ministers pushing his goods, or endless boat-loads of blind warriors, could longer imagine any Empire, either one conquered or one bought, to be possible.

At first, then let us say, Peace comes to the peoples of the world because "all may raise the flowers (engines of destruction) now for all have got the seed" and therefore geopolitic barriers, fanciful or real, erected by the old militarism are dead, gone with the carriers of old-time transportation. Nevertheless Peace comes! And it comes to stay because no known militarism can ever be made over by any gang of ambitious Rulers to fit the new Time-space and the new alchemy which is now the circumambient air in which the cooling earth floats.

There can be no more "Have-not" nations because there can be no more "Have-alls."

What and where now are these *natural* bounds and barriers of Nations if any!

They may never be more in the future than a free approximation. But at least this comes clear—Freedom is no longer something to be divided up by a few Nations and the desired dividend counted on the fingers of one or even several Races. Democratic Freedom is by nature *organic*. And therefore Freedom is for Entity wherever Entity is found. Let it alone! Since no Nation can own the Universal air nor chart the universal highways, it lives.

The front doors of nations have become their back-doors. The sea-ways are not lanes of conquest. Open or shut, all doors are useless now.

Arrogance, my country, is become a suicidal luxury! No Nation dare longer afford to be arrogant on any Military or Production basis for conquest—either of the weak or of the strong. Herodotus, asked why all Nations perished, said, "First, Success, then as a consequence of success, arrogance and injustice; then as a consequence of arrogance and injustice: downfall."

But this world, even though so shrinking by diminished Time and magnified internal Force that monstrous destruction may be practically immediate, is yet large and rich enough for all races of men to thrive when its peoples may grow strong without fear of deprivation or violence, because Empire must cease its predatory roam and therefore—Industry be compelled to curb its inordinate voracity.

Through a new Fear (at first) a new era for the Science and Art of Creative-work is dawning. Construction is more man's joy than any he ever knew in conquest by purchase or by violence. Construction is more exciting and dramatic.

We are where we need more light and less heat!

When will we realize that the rabid instincts of the animal running with kind as against kind is no pattern for Patriotism today?

America! *Power to exercise our own creative-initiative in constructive work for humanity is our only patriotic Freedom!* Ferry us no more "sea-going" Fighters. Conscript and enslave no more the flower of our youth to murder and be murdered. Dig in while we may yet save the free way of life on this new ground upon which by native effort we may yet fairly earn the great privilege to go, not to war, but go to Work!

As individuals let us use what initiative we have to become the first great honest democratic Nation on Earth. Go to Work! Go to Work first to so improve the Individual that conscription would be impossible to us as a Nation or any other Nation and we be fit and able to give real, human assistance to other nations, but give assistance only as other

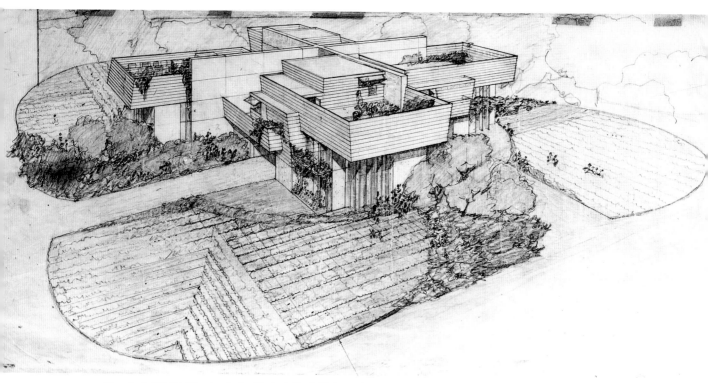

**Cloverleaf, Pittsfield Housing Project (Project), Pittsfield, Massachusetts. 1942. Perspective. Pencil and color pencil on tracing paper, 36 x 28".** FLLW Fdn#4203.002

Nations become likewise fit and ask to receive it!

That is the only Internationalism that matters to modern Democracy.

Our national ideal must no longer be quantity and the police. We must aim at Quality and Faith although ten or a hundred men—and better ones—must be employed for every one man now employed. Democracy can tolerate no substitute for *human* Quality and simply because Democracy is the highest form of Aristocracy the world has ever seen. Aristocracy intrinsic: in the nature of man. Not handed down.

Even so, Freedom is not Eternal. And Unity has strength to break down Slavery only when it is the union of free individuals strong in vital force: individuals not conscript and afraid but courageous, self confident and free.

Meantime let our New Discretion beware of the prevalent abuses of majority-rule. Men of a Democracy must never forget that the Minority of today is the Majority of tomorrow. Democracy must continually keep its enlightened minority fresh and strong or Democracy will perish in the Majority. Government is inherent neither in Majority administration nor in the questioning and proposing or appraising Minority but only in both together: the People. And we must never allow the Bureaucrat to forget that he is the employee of the whole people.

Before we, as a free Democratic Nation can look ourselves in the face at this tragic moment, a natural economic order suited to Democracy must rise, in place of the dishonest one that enslaves us, to salvage the wreck of this horrible conflagration. Organic economic order must be established to keep us sufficiently prosperous and safe *at home*. Gold or no Gold.

Inevitably this Natural Order would be all the Foreign-policy our Nation, or any other Nation, would ever need.

*Consumption must control Production and Production must control Finance.* Or we, the people, are sold out.

Money-power despotisms visible or invisible cannot stand against the enormous reactions of mechan-

**Cloverleaf, Pittsfield Housing Project (Project), Pittsfield, Massachusetts. 1942. Perspective. Pencil and color pencil on tracing paper, 36 x 30".** FLLW Fdn#4203.008

ical power from within and the growing enlightenment I see and hear from our allies and from our enemies all around the world.

I am an American.

I have had no insignificant share in putting my country where it belongs on the map of the world.

And I believe that once our Nation is truly awake and free, this whirlpool of destruction and hate in which we find ourselves will be rolled away forever by my people.

They are credulous but they are sound.

1. *Architectural Forum*, January 1948.

2. Mike Wallace Interviews, 1957.

# AN AUTOBIOGRAPHY
# BOOK FIVE: FORM

The New York publishing company Duell, Sloan and Pearce made arrangements to publish three books on Wright in three years, to include his writings, his works, and an enlarged autobiography. A square format was chosen by Wright for all three, but each had varying numbers of pages.[1]

In 1941 On Architecture was published, a volume of selected writings by Wright from 1894 to 1940, edited and with an introduction by Frederick Gutheim. In 1942 In the Nature of Materials, 1887–1941: The Buildings of Frank Lloyd Wright, an after-the-fact catalog of the retrospective exhibition of Wright's work held at The Museum of Modern Art from November 1940 through January 1941, was compiled by Henry-Russell Hitchcock. This was the first attempt to publish a complete survey in photographs and drawings of Frank Lloyd Wright's work to date. Projects not illustrated were at least cited. Accomplishing this in one volume necessitated greatly reduced images and drawings, resulting in a cramped and cut-up layout on most pages. This annoyed Wright, who was particular about graphic design, and he later admitted that the book "was and still is more now to me a perfect horror."[2]

The following year An Autobiography was published. For this volume Wright edited the first three "books" that appeared in his 1932 edition but divided the original "Book One: Family Fellowship" into two books, "Family," and "Fellowship." To these now reassigned and reedited four books, including "Work" and "Freedom," he added "Book Five: Form," which continued the story of his life and work from 1932 to 1943.

By 1942–1943 work in the studio again slowed down due to the war effort. Conscription had taken nineteen apprentices into the armed forces, and those who remained had received farm deferments. Taliesin's considerable acreage produced cash crops as well as food for the fellowship. Because of this lull in architectural work he had turned to writing. "We have shut down Hillside (drafting room) for the winter," he wrote to a former apprentice, "and with the big root cellar filled, what there is left of us expect to come forth in the spring with double chins—As for me I am a 'writer' now."[3]

"Book Five: Form" devotes more time to personal events than to architectural projects. In many respects it is a haphazard look back over his life from 1916 to 1939: his Japanese print collecting in Tokyo (1916–1922); his trip to Brazil (1931); his trips to Russia (1937) and England (1939). It also recounts the founding and the early years of the Taliesin Fellowship (with a generous portion of the narrative concerning the struggles of the Great Depression) and describes how he met his wife, Olgivanna. However, Wright

**Frank Lloyd Wright and his wife, Olgivanna, at Taliesin, Spring Green, Wisconsin. Photograph by Deiner.** FLLW Fdn FA#6202.0003

*did not adhere to a strict chronological narrative. The building of Taliesin West (1938), for example, precedes that of the Johnson Wax Administration Building (1936) and the Usonian house for Herbert Jacobs (1937). Little mention is made of Kaufmann's Fallingwater (1935), one of the most important commissions in Wright's lifetime, and one that came during a period of time when he was desperate for architectural work and its financial support. Wright's extensive commercial projects of the early 1940s, including Monona Terrace, Crystal Heights, and Florida Southern College, are not mentioned in the narrative at all. His design for Broadacre City is also omitted (1934–1940), to be addressed in "Book Six: Broadacre City." Wright received the commission for the Solomon R. Guggenheim Museum in the early part of the summer of 1943. By the time his designs were ready to show to the client,* An Autobiography *was already in the bookstores.*

*In "Book Five" are to be found poetic passages about his life at Taliesin, which describe the beauty of the building, the landscape, the terrain, and how he and his family responded to their life in Wisconsin:*

> *In Spring and Summer the windows at Taliesin are thrown wide-open. The odor of long white drifts of wild-plum bloom on the nearby hillsides drifts in—the crab apple and hawthorne in the meadows send their scent on, over the treetops. Later the sweet breath of the clover fields rises into the rooms on the morning and evening breezes. Soon the scent of new-mown hay pervades the place. So our windows, like the doors, are seldom closed in Spring and Summer. In the Autumn, when they are closed, mingling with the odor of freshly burned oak, is the smell of bowls of apples and unshelled shag-bark hickory nuts—the prince of all perfumes. And the sumach. But for the Winter, there inside the rooms is newly gathered, everlasting, cream-white antimony. This gentle odor of antimony is to the sense of smell what the flavor of slippery elm is to the young boy's sense of taste. Oak fires then start in the seventeen ever-present stone fireplaces to go out but seldom until the following Spring, unless fuel gives out.*[4]

*Following the account of his trip to Russia, he devotes the remainder of the book to an address he made in Moscow and an article he wrote for* Soviet Russia Today, *a Soviet magazine published in the United States, concluding with an exchange of letters between himself and the Faculty Branch of the Communist Party at University of Wisconsin.*

*No doubt the antiwar and isolationist articles Wright wrote prior to and even during the war, combined with his praise of the Russian people and the Russian spirit (but not its government), provided the material that Wisconsin senator Joseph McCarthy would later misinterpret in an attempt to indict Frank Lloyd Wright as an anti-American communist. Not surprisingly, McCarthy's case amounted to nothing. There were perhaps few Americans who believed more profoundly in democracy than Wright, and he devoted considerable effort to explaining this in almost everything he wrote during these years.*

*During the years from 1934 to 1940 Wright wrote often about Broadacre City; the model had toured several major cities in the United States and was finally installed in permanent exhibition in the Taliesin Fellowship buildings in Spring Green, Wisconsin. Considering the importance that Wright attributed to this model and the theories represented, it is indeed mysterious that "Book Five" contains nothing about it. On the other hand, the book ends with a promise:*

> *I wish to build a city for Democracy: the Usonian city that is nowhere yet everywhere. Since this search for* FORM *ends there, the Usonian City, Broadacres, will be the sixth book of* An Autobiography. *The natural Conclusion.*

## WORK-SONG

We have battle hymns. We have war songs, anthems, and we do have some few Negro labor-chanties. But we have no work-song of our own that is a thing of the militant work-spirit.

These T-square and triangle verses, a kind of disturbing fife-and-drum corps coming down the street—in a straight-line pattern—were spontaneously written early in my work life and should have preceded the previous book, "Work." They were omitted there because the song then seemed, and still does, to be shouting "damn." Why not? It takes an ego shouting "damn" to withstand emasculation by such imitative erudition as ours and the "cultivation" any true ego, upright, is sure to receive at our very best hands. So, here, to you is the militant work-song. Not as literature whatsoever, but for better or for worse.

Olgivanna set the lines to music and the song is now sung upon occasion by the Taliesin Fellowship.

The only time these curious verses came out of hiding was long ago, when, urged by well-meaning friends, I sent them on under the title of "The Drum" to Richard Watson Gilder, then editor of *The Century*. The Work-Song came back with a polite "The rhythm of the drum, Mr. Wright, can hardly be translated into poetry."

Life seems to disdain our very best literary measurements: especially our scholastic appraisals. Even so our approved popular standards.

All such become a frozen asset, or upset where cultural growth is earnestly sought or deeply desired.

Outside our current of conventional ideas of what constitutes literature, who knows Poetry?

The quest begun by the child in this beloved Valley, young feet woolen-warm in fresh-fallen snow; both aching arms full of "useless" dried weeds: the structure-pattern of a multitude of lives already given, the search for FORM here continues. It *is* a self-seeking—yes, of course, with what freedom I could win, or take.

Well . . . after the first four books, "Family," "Fellowship," "Work," and "Freedom," are done, like the "Freshman at the Party" I look back. Ten years later, wistful now, I imagine what I might have truly said to go deeper and come off with more

credit. Perhaps make a better book for you to read. With some chagrin I realize I have not written an autobiography at all. What I have set down is more an anti-Broadway creed. I do not regret the "anti" nor the "creed" because the "anti" is needed badly and *An Autobiography* has been with me an act of faith in what lies deeper. Every word I have written is fact, at least. But facts no more make Truth than boards, bricks and mortar make Architecture. Only Imagination using facts honestly as mere structural material can so imbue fact with Spirit as to make another life, the life of Man, take fresh, inspiring Form. The work of art.

This fifth book is the continued search for FORM.

## THE CHARACTER OF FORM

Meantime among so many disheartening discoveries stands the all-heartening important truth (something at least to "tie to") that true FORM is always organic in character. It is really nature-pattern. In nature-abstraction, therefore, lies the difficulty as well as the simple centerline of the honest ego's search for integral FORM. And since all Form is a matter of structure, it must be a matter of government as well as a matter of architecture; a matter of the framework of a society: the constitution of a civilization.

Proved by my own experience, I too can say that "every problem carries within itself its own solution," a solution to be reached only by the intense inner concentration of a sincere devotion to Truth. I can say this out of a lively personal adventure in realizations that gives true scheme, line and color to all life and, so far as Architecture goes, life to what otherwise would remain mere unrelated fact. Dust, even if stardust.

Any good architect is by nature a physicist as a matter of fact, but as a matter of reality, as things are, he must be a philosopher and a physician. So the new spiritual physiognomy of old worldwide philosophy is still at work on the pages of this belated haunted fifth book of *An Autobiography*. Here you will find the outlines of a true social pattern hidden by the realisms which may enrich but which can also obscure Reality.

What we are seeking together must be found between the lines.

An Oklahoma editor claiming to be a cousin of mine (great printer but no editor) once blazed at me in disgust and anger, "Hell, Frank, if you don't like the system on which this country's run, why don't you get out of it? Go somewhere else! Goddammit."

"Not to please you, Richard, nor any of my relatives," I said. "If I see something wrong with my country I am going to stay right here doing my damnedest to set upside-down right-side up."

Now, as a matter of course, to get my own conscience or yours on straight, or for you to get yours or mine on straight, we may trouble each other's cousins and annoy a good many good people. Such as they are, and we are. But if to you and to me Democracy really means anything at all it must mean just that kind of trouble with our cousins and our sisters. Our uncles and our aunts. Not to mention our parents and especially our dearest friends and trouble thrown in, maybe, with the Police. As things are. But, millions of consciences like yours and mine, likewise uneasy, struggling against what seems so unnecessarily stupid, so utterly inferior, are essential to the life of any honest country wherein Democracy may be after all, only that "state of unhappy consciousness," which Hegel said it was.

But no! I have a better right to stay here dissatisfied out loud than you have to stay down there in Oklahoma satisfied out louder just because you happen to own a newspaper or something, Richard.

If this country of ours (it is one of God's many good countries, either won—self-baptized in our name by our own blood—or inherited, stolen or bought, isn't it?) were incurably lame, halt or blind, the Cousin Richards of these States might be all right. To criticize would then be only cruel. But I don't think this country is *incurably* lame, halt or blind. At least, the people in it are not while I belong here and love the belonging as well as I do: loving the country not so much for what it is—no, but more for what it is meant to be and for what a good many of us still hope it is going to be. I know, with good enough reason now, there are many loving it just the way I love it: a love that means even-

tually, if not soon, a true democratic FORM not only for our buildings, but for the appropriate lives we will live in them, and even the cultivation of the ground on which they shall stand.

Meantime, in any sound—that is to say *honest*—Democracy, Peace or War, true discretion from now forward consists in the resolve to speak and act the living Truth where it concerns us as we honestly understand it and squarely face the consequences of so acting and speaking, gentle reader or reader ungentle. If we do make a general practice of such wise honesty freely, then I am sure there are enough among us with sufficiently developed intelligences to find the true social, economic (and therefore *truly architectural*) FORM normal to the culture of such Freedom as we profess. That Freedom is now the new Integrity not alone in this Nation but in all the world. We will call it, hereinafter, the new Reality.

But we are in great danger of entirely running out of ideas concerning the very simple but startling idea of human freedom we once professed, because we who ran away from the "old country" and came over here for safety, scared out of our native wits, now run back to the mother country for safety, waving not our own flag but an ism.

The Lloyd-Joneses were all handsome folk. But my mother and my maiden aunts, Aunt Nell and Aunt Jane, were, I think, the handsomest of the ten. Their five brothers, shaggy-maned, bearded, patriarchal, handsome. Four of the five: James, Enos, John and Jenkin, happening into Madison one fine day were driving along in an open rig on University Avenue (two of them were University regents) when someone shouted from the sidewalk—"Where are the other eight?"

The neighboring uncles all called the Lloyd-Jones sisters "the girls," and the boys and girls all called them Aunt Nell and Aunt Jenny. The two sisters were disciples of John Dewey by way of Francis Parker under whom they once taught school. They were nearing seventy and their school was becoming harder than ever for them to manage. Added to the naturally unprofitable nature of their enterprise, the unfortunate, tragic death of their brother James (my favorite uncle) had thrown them into acute financial distress. Bankruptcy threatened the Hillside Home School where for twenty-seven years "the Aunts" had mothered some forty to sixty boys and girls, aged seven to seventeen—preparing their forty to sixty boys and girls for college by keeping a staff of thirteen teachers in residence besides themselves. They had done a pioneer work in home-school co-education. The Hillside Home School was perhaps the first—certainly one of the first—co-educational home schools in our country: probably in the world. Mary Ellen Chase has drawn their portraits with a sympathetic hand in her book, *The Goodly Fellowship.*[1]

Meantime "the Aunts" tried manager after manager. Some of the managers were their own nephews or nieces. Some they brought in from educational enterprises in the cities. But none was ever able to do very much. And there were good reasons. My beloved Aunts themselves were those good reasons. Their plant had grown old with them and they were deeply in debt without realizing it. But, in fact, they were themselves as mentally alert and potent as ever. They simply could not reconcile themselves to be directed by others or see any of their prerogatives go into other untried hands. I myself never thought of them as old. They really had no age, these maiden sisters of five brothers and three sisters, aunts of some forty nephews and nieces, foster mothers of hundreds of other women's children. But their very strength became their weakness now. Their famous brother Jenkin had been a strength to them and he tried to help them now. It was the same with them even where he was concerned. They would take neither domination nor advice, and while he could have found money for them if control went with the money, he could not get control himself nor deliver control. So they got no financial aid at this crucial time. And some blamed me for this.

As it was with Jenkin Lloyd-Jones, so it was with their own alumni who might have been expected to come to their assistance. And I don't know why some of them didn't come to the rescue of their faithful old teacher-mothers. But none came. I believe a few hundred dollars did come in from several sources. But they needed thousands—some forty-six of them. Finally things at the school came to such a pass that Aunt Nell quite lost her mind with worry. She would wander up and down the room wherever she might happen to be, talking to herself, wringing her hands—moaning. Aunt Jane, still a quick and sympathetic soul, would try to comfort her when these fits of despair darkened the mind. Sister Anna (my mother)—a great help to them always—was especially helpful now. There seemed no way out; no one to help. So I did. To "pay up" and give them a little rest—rest they so much needed but which no one, least of all myself, believed they knew how to take. They wanted to turn everything over to me, asking me to promise that their work would continue. I promised.

That promise comforted them.

They had put their best into the advanced ideas of co-education on liberal principles which they now represented. I had found money for them before when the 1902 buildings were built. One of my clients, Mrs. Susan Lawrence Dana, gave them the little Art and Science building next the School building and equipment, complete. She loaned the Aunts twenty-seven thousand dollars more to help complete the main school building. Another client, Charles E. Roberts,[2] gave nine thousand dollars to help in a subsequent pinch. I think there were other helping hands at that time but I don't know whose.

This, partly, was why they had turned to me now when all else had failed.

About the time the new buildings were built—1902—there was some family feeling (and saying) that they would ruin the Aunts. But all the Aunts ever put into them from first to last was about half their cost plus the considerable work volunteered by the family. The new buildings were their pride and joy.

I did think of finding some schoolmaster to carry on but could not imagine anyone in their place. There could be no one.

Neither Aunt long survived after giving up active participation in the life of the school.

Aunt Jane, a gallant fiery disposition in contrast to the cool, more managerial disposition of Aunt Nell, about this time had not been so very well. I think she suffered the loss of the School most, for "loss" they both regarded it when only a promise took the place of the reality they had both so loved. Occasionally, when weather permitted, she liked to go back to sleep in her own room at the School. She was found there, dead, one morning when we all least expected it.

Aunt Nell had contracted smallpox while young. Her hair turned snow-white when she was twenty-six, but her health, subsequently, had always been good—her outdoor activity kept it so. She now lingered along for another year or two, finally losing control of the fine clear mind she always had—becoming, because of her indomitable will which had always had its way, not at all easy to manage. But finally, she too found release—in the boys' cottage of the school where the Aunts had mothered seven boys aged seven to twelve. There was where she preferred to be.

And now a strange thing concerning the "property" that was quite generally believed to be the plant of the Hillside Home School. It appeared that the individualities expressed by the glowing personalities of Aunt Nell and Aunt Jane had been all there was of the Hillside Home School except the idealistic buildings I had built for them, 1902–1903, into which went some of the enthusiasm and faith they had put into their own work. The physical side of their work was otherwise slight. The several other buildings were so ugly and worthless they were only waiting to be torn down. Out of an old metal bedstead and clean fresh bedclothes, a print on the wall, a piece of rag carpet, an improvised stand, a wash bowl and a nicked pitcher skillfully combined with a vase of flowers and a bowl of fruit, the lovely view through the windows, the living presence of the Lloyd-Jones Sisters had evoked a miracle to go with the shining waxed-boards of the floor.

With Aunt Nell and Aunt Jane gone, their "property" vanished into the surrounding air—all except their ancestral ground and the buildings standing upon it to which their spirit had given concrete form. But even these buildings were suited only to their own school work and, placed where they were, of no value unless they could be used as farm build-

ings, which they could not be. The old octagonal barn in bad repair had been badly placed, as had the dormitory and servants' building—all were carpenter-built buildings (no design) and were in such a state of disrepair that, all things considered, it seemed best to tear them down as they spoiled the buildings that did express their spirit. All of the active Hillside Home School plant other than the 140 acres of farm land (worth about eighty dollars an acre without buildings) had little or no value. There were almost no Lloyd-Jones Sisters "assets" so called. Were all such gathered into a heap they would hardly bring one thousand dollars.

What a lesson in the enlivening, characterizing, saving power of human individuality the old Hillside Home School was! The only thing in which faith should ever be placed, the only faithful "asset." Things grow old and vanish like that. But individuality once achieved, perhaps by way of the use of "things," is immortal—beyond reach of age, or better to say is developed and strengthened by age—until age itself should bring the most desirable of qualifications.

These great women possessed such individuality and to such a degree that where they were, there was consequential order out of insignificance—the usefulness of even the inferior object, atmosphere, warmth and light out of nothing.

The Hillside Home School, high-hearted in the service of a great ideal—such service is too seldom seen in this world—became toward the end of its life a kind of eleemosynary [sic] institution which the Aunts were supporting. Parents who were bereaved or had separated would send their children to the Aunts. The Aunts would become attached to the children, the dues would be paid for a little while and then as various disasters would befall the parents payments would cease, but the Aunts would keep the children on and on. And this in so many various forms was the story until at the end too many teachers were unpaid; faithful old employees had not asked for pay in years; uncollectible bills mounted to the impossible. A ledger of accounts which came along with other assets after their death shows bills due and receivable of some forty thousand dollars. Not one cent collectible.

## POST-MORTEM

For years (and even now) after the Aunts passed on (typical experience)—some old farmer would step out into the road ahead of me and say, "Frank, I never ast no pay for the forty cords o' wood I hauled 'the girls' back there February Nineteen-fifteen."

"Well," I would say, "why didn't you ask them for the money, and why have you said nothing about it to them nor to me until now?"

"Oh," he would say, "I knowed they was hard up then and I didn't need the money bad. But it's differ'nt now. Yes, *sir,* it's differ'nt."

Trying to read the man, I said, "But your bill is outlawed now."

"Oh, sure," he'd say. "Outlawed sure, but you're their nephew, Frank. You're willin' to pay me *somethin'* on the old account, ain't ye?"

"Of course," I'd say, "how much do you say?"

"Oh, pay me half—sixty dollars and I'll call her square."

"But I haven't got sixty dollars right now."

"Oh . . . ain't ye?" he would say. "All right then. I'll jest as soon come 'round sometime I'm down thet a way and pick it up. I knowed you wouldn't let your old Aunts down, Frank," said he.

And he would get the money when I got it. Such bills were outlawed, of course, but, worse, some were undoubtedly false. I used my own judgment. Grew to be less and less easy. Paid some, and told the others to go. What else?

## PERSPECTIVE

To anyone looking back over the life and work of these two dear grand maiden-aunts of mine, work of great consequence to us all is still living. I see it so cruelly set and hard beset by the circumstances of their provincial environment which is of course still our own environment at Taliesin. Age was a disqualification when the life work of these great women was endangered. They were wasted as though they were animals in a market. Their wisdom and rich experience went for nought. Just as in the provinces the age of a horse determines his useful value, or a cow her desirability, the chickens their egg-laying and edibility; so the deadly provincial American mind carries this over into human life. Instead of growing old gracefully, with the distinction and genuine honor we see it attaining in wiser ancient civilizations (the oriental, for instance), if we look about us we will see all that finer quality of living thrown away, cancelled by this characteristic animalistic view of age. Age driven to conceal its venerability under devices of the cosmetician—the plastic surgeon—devices of dress. Age tries so pitiably hard to "look" young because it *is* young and in most precious ways stronger than ever. But when the traces of use are regarded as mere wear and tear, they do become ugly indeed. A "lived in" face should be no disqualification in our provinces and even less so on the hard pavements of our urban centers. But the young have their fling and then they are flung, flung upon the scrap-heap of the Old, while youth persists and the best time of life is ahead: instead of the fruiting of the tree, a dreary waste. Our people are doing this thing to themselves, a damning count against all Western Civilization.

If age brings no great reward to others and itself in a society, something is radically wrong with the individual or the society. Perhaps with both. I remember well a great woman, friend of my mother's—Mrs. Lydia Avery Coonley-Ward, herself an example of what she was saying—"If a woman is not attractive at twenty it isn't her fault, but if she isn't at fifty, it certainly is."

## A PROMISE

I have made many promises in my life, always intending to keep them. I think I never made one that I didn't intend to keep. But my corner of hell will be paved with those that turned out to be only intentions. Time and circumstances destroy promises as distance dims one's view. But one promise would not let me go. My love for my mother and my aunts, my admiration for their grand gray heads and the dignity of their beautiful persons which age had brought were bound up in that promise as though they lived on in the promise: a promise I had made to see their educational work go on at beloved Hillside on the site of the pioneer homestead. That filial promise would go along with me wherever I went. If I settled down, it settled down with me. In course of time it became a subjective urge as well as an objective. If I lived I was sure to keep the promise whether I wanted to or not. I became an Instrument of Fate.

No matter what reason might dictate I would keep that promise in good time. And, since I was what I was, I would keep it in my own way. As yet I had no idea in what way; procrastinating as always, this time for many years, I had faith in myself or whatever it is that keeps the promises we make.

And I believed now, *from within,* that whatever I deeply enough desired I should have, because it first had me.

No, it was no longer necessary to bend my mind in that direction. Something had taken place that would simply turn circumstances and events in that direction. In good time what was desired would be there.

## ANNO DOMINI 1929

This economic, now historic nationalistic failure of the attempt by Production to control Consumption, so ignorantly termed a "depression," is here. Economic breakdown is so complete at this time that no workman's hammer is ringing in our great state of Wisconsin. Native workmen of my own countryside, laborers, carpenters and masons of Iowa County as in the next Dane County and the next Sauk County are all but starving while I watch the shingle roofs of the 1902-1903 Hillside Home

**Hillside, Taliesin, Spring Green, Wisconsin. 1940. Photograph by Pedro E. Guerrero** FLLW Fdn FA#3301.0080

**Taliesin, Spring Green, Wisconsin. 1940. Photograph by Pedro E. Guerrero.** FLLW Fdn FA#2501.0883

School buildings falling in for lack of some such labor as theirs. All of them (yes, laborers included) are rotting away. Roof water is coming in on most of the fine interiors. Waxed sand-finish walls of the rooms are completely scribbled over with proper names like some provincial privy, desecrated by this ever devastating passerby whose better name is Curiosity. Should what is still left of these buildings I so proudly built in 1902 for those gallant pioneers, my Aunts Nell and Jane, go through one more winter in this agonizing condition, then no use ever attempting to repair them. The matchless flesh-colored sand-stone walls built under my direction by twinkling-eyed, bewhiskered Timothy, the old Welsh stone mason ("and whatever-r-r") would be left standing. Not only was there no money to pay long outstanding money-debts but there was now hardly carfare to get to the big city in order to find work there, should there be any work to do. Where might work come from? None could say. Except as we could raise it ourselves there was no food. My friends were losing what money they had or had already lost it. How did I know? They knew how they knew I knew!

If he has no ground of his own and if he cannot go to work on some farm, no architect in these United States of America has anything to do unless he is "related" to someone who happens to be sitting pretty, and (because the more cautious were hit hardest) sitting pretty meant, merely, lucky. Barely subsisting from day to day the architects in our great country trying so hard to control Consumption by Production were still in "pursuit of happiness" but while living upon "savings" or money-means bought by insurance, got by marriage, or some inheritance. Or more than likely, got by borrowing something somehow from someone while Production was impatiently waiting to be consumed or trying to force Consumption. Not only my own "earnings" (merely what "they" call them) are gone, but any credit I may ever have had whatsoever is gone because of them. But we were only sharing now in all this the fate of the far more provident: mortgages, judgments, private chagrin, humiliation private and public, disgrace—nation-wide. Blackmail and slander still accumulate in the foreground of this glum national picture.

A motley horde of outstretched hands comes frequently to Taliesin's door in the valley! They come knocking in all too familiar guises: legal "repossessions," press interviews, duns, more repossessions, more threats. Private blackmail, private and public "adverse examinations" by shyster lawyers, long-distance telephone duns, duns by friends, duns by relatives, duns by employees. All desperate. No money—and at last, sabotage. Threats: some more threats. And assassination. These all stand outside the door, lit by the sinister flares of interior treachery. And the usual self-righteous "saviors" heap the sordid measure of tragic defeat to running over with well-meant (and too well-known) advice.

Worse than all, like Festus Jones, I myself, not having much conscience anyway, find that what little I have is pretty solidly guilty!

My trouble too is, I know, that I still yearn to be on good terms with myself and have never yet succeeded in getting rid of this deep-seated, inherited, tragic ancestral plague—the desire to stand well with my kind—to win the esteem and affection of my fellows. And to heap the cup, I have always been ready and willing—I still am—to do without the Necessaries of Life if only I may have the Luxuries. This has seemed the only way to do "the things that are more excellent" while the Criterion—Money—secretly calls the turn.

## A STATION FOR THE FLIGHT OF THE SOUL

Many times before, in desperate circumstances (perhaps because of them) came an Idea. I, too, can get a bad idea—but not this time. The now subjective promise came to its object as the idea? No buildings to build at the harrowing moment but, capitalizing thirty-five years of past experience, why not build the builders of buildings against the time when buildings might again be built?

Congenital Education, dormant family influence, up and out—at last! To make a promise good?

Numbers of young men were always coming from around the world to work with me at Taliesin. Several were at Taliesin now. After talking the "idea" over, pro and con, we, a son of Wisconsin Welsh pioneers and a daughter of Montenegrin dignitaries aiming to be educators, composed and sent out during the summer of 1932 the following circular letter to a small list of friends. Here is that circular letter:

### "AN EXTENSION OF THE WORK IN ARCHITECTURE AT TALIESIN TO INCLUDE APPRENTICES IN RESIDENCE

"Frank Lloyd Wright together with a number of competent assistants will be in residence at Taliesin and will there lead the work of a new Fellowship of Apprentices to be now established. Three resident associates: a sculptor, a painter, and a musician, eventually chosen for the work to be done, are contemplated. An inner-group of seven honor-apprentices having the status of senior apprentices and three technical advisors trained in industry will also be chosen to assist.

"Leaders in thought from many countries may also come to occasionally share for a time in our activities, perhaps temporarily reside there.

"We believe that a rational attempt to integrate Art and Industry should coordinate both with the everyday life we live here in America. Any such rational attempt must be *essential architecture* growing up by way of social, industrial, and economic processes natural to our way of life.

"Not only must this framework and background of future Democracy be developed in itself as a kind of organic architecture, but the very qualities most basic and worthwhile in Philosophy, Sculpture,

Painting, Music and the Industrial Crafts are also fundamentally Architecture. Principles underlying life and the arts are the same. So it is the Architecture of Life itself that must be the fundamental and therefore first concern of any true culture anywhere if the world is to be made safe for Science.

"No alliance between 'Art' and Commercial Industry is ever enough because no mere 'alliance,' however useful, can be Creative. Appropriate forms must be developed from within and they must be forms having worthwhile relation to our actual industry. The necessary original work will be best done where the workers will have not only spontaneous recourse to modern shop and working conditions but have at the same time, as workers, benefit of the inspirational fellowship of some genuinely creative architect. Constant working contacts with the nature of structure and materials, the ground, and of nature-growth itself are the only reliable texts to be used in this connection. Only as these are actual forms of daily experience directly related to daily life and work are they the texts we must now use to begin again at the beginning.

"What little creative impulse survives among us in the confusion of this machine age might thus have some chance to live uncontaminated by the old human expressions already dead or dying around us. The Big City is no longer a place for more than the exterior applications of some cliché or sterile formula, where life is concerned. Therefore the TALIESIN FELLOWSHIP chooses to live and work in the country. The FELLOWSHIP establishment is located on a fine farm forty miles west of Madison, four miles from the nearest village on State Highway 23 in beautiful Southern Wisconsin. Near the Wisconsin River.

"THE WORK IN ARCHITECTURE first done at Oak Park and Chicago, and later at Taliesin, has proved itself during the past thirty years. It has gone far enough in the world-current of contemporary change so that good work may be done in full cooperation with our more advanced producers and manufacturers: those who sincerely desire to improve the nature of their product. American industry need no longer depend for artistic excellence upon the copying of imitations nor need ever do so again if our country will learn to utilize resources such as our resources at Taliesin.

"As the TALIESIN FELLOWSHIP therefore, we now propose to extend apprenticeship from the several draughtsmen to whom it has been limited to include seventy [Note: Changed to twenty-three.] apprentices working under leadership as described.

"Each apprentice will work under the inspiration of direct architectural leadership, toward machine-craft art in this machine age. All will work together in a common daily effort to create new forms needed by machine work and modern processes if we are to have any culture of our own worth having. A number (a hundred or more) of such young workers in Architecture have already come to Taliesin from various parts of the world. Others may now be immersed in the many-sided activities of a growing Fellowship of apprentices. Our activities, we hope, will be gradually extended to include collateral arts by way of such modern machine crafts as we can establish. Living in direct personal contact with modern concepts and the currents of thought in the world now demanding new form we believe young architects, artists, and craftsmen may here find means to build up spiritual forces and a technique that will guarantee a life work in *the essential architecture of all the arts* and be enabled to practice them as the natural fulfillment of an experience and training belonging peculiarly to our own time and country.

"*SO WE BEGIN this working Fellowship as a kind of daily work-life.* Apprentices at work on buildings or in crafts which have a free individual basis: a direct work-experience made healthy and fruitful by seeing Idea as work and work as Idea take effect, actually, in the hand of the young apprentice.

"OUR HOME LIFE MUST BE SIMPLE. Meals in common. Fixed hours for work, recreation, and sleep. Each worker will have his or her room for study and rest. Suitable toilet accommodations will be made convenient to all rooms. Entertainment too will be a feature of our life at home. Plays, music in the evenings; the cinema and conferences to which musicians, literary men, artists, and scientists will sometimes be invited and (occasionally) the public. The beautiful region itself is a never failing source of inspiration and recreation for all concerned. Daily life will be planned to benefit by its beauty.

"Fellowship work in its manifold branches will come directly under the influence of an organic philosophy: organic architecture for organic life. At Taliesin this life will be lived with such sense of the Future as may belong to the present.

"The actual study of Architecture *as a kind of practice* will in this broad sense be taken into detailed studies of building designs and principles of construction. Eventually biology, typography, ceramics, woodcraft, and textiles will be further taken into consideration. These practical studies will go hand in hand with characteristic model-making and soon will go on to practical experiments in the crafts made by such apprentices as go into the workshops which we hope to build.

"*Apprenticeship* not *Scholarship* is to be the actual condition and should be the attitude of mind of the Fellowship. A fair division of labor in maintaining all branches of work will fall to the share of each member. Especial predilections or idiosyncrasies, although respected, will not be separately encouraged. There will be no age limit for apprentices but the qualifications of each will be decided finally by Mr. Wright after a month's trial in the Fellowship work. The right to reject any applicant at any time is reserved—either before or after being formally received into the Fellowship. The Fellowship, however, is not on trial. The apprentice is.

"TALIESIN AIMS to develop a well-correlated human being: the correlation between hand and the mind's eye most lacking in modern education.

"As a primary requirement therefore each member of the Fellowship will be asked to engage in all the daily work of necessary Fellowship maintenance. Wage slavery will be eliminated so far as possible.

"THE LABORATORIES AND MACHINE SHOPS are not yet built but, eventually, they will be planned next to the draughting room as shown in the accompanying illustrations. Studios and galleries are already built or being built. The first experimental units ready are those of architectural construction and design, the philosophy of architecture, typographical design, the printing of a publication *Taliesin*—organ of the Fellowship—also molding and casting adapted to modern systems of construction in glass, concrete and metal. Woodworking by modern machinery. A collateral study of philosophy and the practice of sculpture, painting, drama and rhythm. These units are to be followed by actual glass-making, pottery, weaving, modern reproduction processes in any form we may be able to establish. We believe that business men in industry will find it worthwhile to cooperate with us in setting up these crafts.

"A personal testimonial, only, will be given to each worker at the end of his or her apprenticeship. Each year will have a holiday of six weeks for each worker but arranged only as the work permits.

"THE FELLOWSHIP IS NOT YET THE 'FOUNDATION' IT HOPES TO BE but is an independent cultural enterprise and the sustaining revenue of the Fellowship for the next several years must come mainly from apprenticeship fees and maintenance work, four hours each day, of the apprentices. Added to this may be Architect's fees, compensation from industries for services rendered or to be rendered; the sale of complete art objects; a publication to be printed by the Fellowship. And the possible but not probable contribution of money or equipment from 'Friends of the Fellowship,' a group to be organized among those who believe in our work and who are able and willing to add scope to our usefulness. [Note: The group has not yet been organized.]

"Undoubtedly, prosperity of the Fellowship must depend upon the quality of its membership but more upon the spirit of cooperation felt and practiced by the members and myself in the work we do. Only the apprentices themselves can make apprenticeship useful to a master or to themselves. Therefore no apprentice will be accepted without trial: the right to terminate any Fellowship without notice, reserved.

"EACH WILL BE REQUIRED TO PAY THE FIXED FEE for tuition as stated on the application blank herewith. And as a necessary feature of their training, each will be required to contribute his or her share of work each day on the grounds or new buildings or on the farm, for the privilege of participation in the experimental work going on in the studios and workshops and such production of art objects as practical exemplars for industry and building as may be for exhibition and sale. An account will also be kept of the money had from such sales. At the end of each year a fair dividend will be paid to each member which may eventually reduce or abolish the tuition fee. *[Note: The original fee was six hundred and fifty dollars for a full year, but, next year, for cause, changed to eleven hundred dollars.]*

"A BUSINESS-LIKE ORGANIZATION will manage the affairs of the FELLOWSHIP. *[Note: This was never established because not needed.]*

"THE FARM AND GARDEN will be so managed to employ the help of the apprenticeship that a substantial portion of the living of members may come from their own labor on the ground, thus enabling apprentice fees to remain low as possible."

No sooner was this ambitious scheme proposed than we abandoned it. After sending out the circular we decided we would do better to stick to what we already had than to go too far institutional or "educational." I had certain qualifications; Olgivanna had others to add to mine. So we put our heads, as well as our hearts, together, simplified it all to come within our immediate capacities, so we thought, and wisely cut down possible membership to twenty-three. But the foregoing text—text by no means simple enough—was nevertheless sent out. It had the effect we hoped for and intended. Twenty-three young men and women brought twenty-three times six hundred and fifty dollars—one year each—to work it out at Taliesin. And a fair cross-section of Young America assembled there October 1, 1932, eager to go to work at something—ill-prepared for anything except academic study of some sort. Least of all for the Freedom Taliesin had to offer.

## TO THE ENEMY

Since we had now started something, supplementing the foregoing statement, the following letter replying to a *Manifesto* issued at that time by the Beaux-Arts of the United States was directed to the heads of the "Beaux-Arts" schools. The letter was mailed with a request to post the letter where students might see it, should the institution be so inclined. In some cases it was so posted.

The reader understands quite well by now that the servile Beaux-Arts societies in these United States would be anathema to any ideal of indigenous USONIAN culture.

"If this dull lack of indigenous culture ('pattern') in the fabric of our weaving is not wrong then should we be content with no pattern at all? Better off sterile? None will say so. As the matter stands we cannot afford to lose one single strand native or natural to our growth as a free nation or allow one fresh attempt to build it that may be destroyed by the old patterns and prejudices we jealously drag along. In this cultural lag we have completely stultified instead of inspired the to-and-fro of mere artifice that we are fond of calling Standardization. If we do allow this cultural back-drag to be 'Art' much longer, there can be no life of the Spirit left in our weaving. We can never have the inspiring culture of our own that can lift these inevitable routine standardizations above the belt, because Civilization is truly this matter of inspired and inspiring pattern (culture) in the social fabric (our society).

"Civilization is this affair of Pattern.

"A witty Frenchman has said of us: 'The United States of America is the only nation to plunge from barbarism to degeneracy with no culture in between.'"

Here is the reply to the innuendo "by circular" of the *Manifesto* of the Beaux-Arts in the U.S.A.:

"TO THE STUDENTS OF THE BEAUX-ARTS INSTITTUE OF DESIGN: ALL DEPARTMENTS

"A notice to you, taking my name in vain (together with the names of two other modern architects whom I respect, Gropius and Le Corbusier), has been sent to me. *[Note: See Notice to Students and Correspondents—Architectural Department—School Year 1931–32, April 20, 1932.]*

"If this circular is proper evidence of the quality of inspiration to which our young architects are now subject this may be the time for them to help themselves. Reading between the lines of this lively circular which contains a threat, I see that the Beaux-Arts establishment in America realizes that neither its old practices nor the old doctrines can be made to apply longer, except by force.

"But as this circular bears witness, the Beaux-Arts is now ready to speak-the-language of the new thought in architecture. Must then the Beaux-Arts leadership deny or betray modern architects before it can 'come over' to modern architecture as gracefully as it thinks becoming to its dignity? Or else, say (it does so in this circular) it won't come over to modern architecture at all and 'all the students will be pushed back to classicism'?

"And, are you, as students, reliably informed concerning what constitutes modern architecture? You are officially told that 'it is not going to become a style based upon Wright, Gropius and Le Corbusier.'

"Now . . . it *is* true that much that passes for modern architecture is not organic because it is already contaminated by American Beaux-Arts standards of imitation. To unfortunate young architects so contaminated I am a friendly enemy. But architecture as 'modern' has a future only because these modern architects, whatever their faults (from whom I am sorry to say the circular in question derives only language ), are what they are, and because they have done what they have done.

"Yet it is because of their work that the Beaux-Arts is now ready to modify its programme or 'push you all back into classicism'!

"I admit that the principles and practice of *organic* architecture are yet insufficiently familiar to some of these modern architects against whom you are officially warned. But they will be the principles you will be moved by and that you will master if you do not betray your country to the 'Beaux-Arts' as it will betray you now and everywhere if it can do so by assuming a virtue it cannot have. Unfortunately the Beaux-Arts training in architecture has been all the Academic training Young America has had a chance to get.

"But today no man able to think for himself believes in such pseudo 'training.' No training like it can aid any young man to grow into a creative architect. These very principles of an organic architecture (modern architecture) which the Beaux-Arts 'views with alarm' and from which it derives the unfamiliar language it tries to use in this circu-

lar—'the meaning of materials,' etc., etc., would blow their method and practice away were they or their students able to grasp the real meaning of that language.

"When 'in all history,' for instance, has 'the meaning of materials' or anything deeper than fine composition been found in these academic circles until the men whose work you are now officially told—'modern architecture is not going to resemble' came along? The simplest knowledge of simples, 'the meaning of materials,' my thesis in particular, would utterly destroy these native 'Beaux-Arts' establishments. It has already gone far toward doing so because of utter ignorance in the practice of the very nature of materials and the uses of modern methods and that misunderstanding of modern architecture which is a sublime American Beaux-Arts characteristic! 'Composition?' *That* only is the shrine of all Beaux-Arts training.

"Well, 'Composition' is dead.

"The silhouette of masonry mass over steel only lives as a festering feudal hangover, a false gesture. But in organic architecture, Creation still lives as the Magna Charta of your Liberty. Yet you are told your work must not resemble it!

"So it is natural and inevitable that hypocrisy should flower as the result of this system of eclectic imitation not only fostered, but now *featured* by the institution calling itself the 'American Beaux-Arts'! The result must be—no fruit.

"But, should fault be found with an ostrich because it persists in sticking its head in the sand, because no ostrich is a lion? Where, I ask you, young man—are you going to learn the truth that 'intelligent mass,' 'consideration of the three dimensional block of the building' are not *fundamentals,* and learn that merely as such, all are properties of good design no longer applying, fundamentally, to youth in architecture? These items are not principles but qualities—mere *by-products* of good design. No longer 'fundamental,' I assure you.

"So if you *are* to be 'pushed back to Classicism' (the threat is contained in the circular) and therefore confined to these old reactions referred to as 'the fundamentals of good design' which the ancient Beaux-Arts once learned and the modern institution now refuses or is unable to forget, then this moment seems the proper time to hold out to such of you as are really in love with architecture, opportunity to learn something of the principles that make 'modern architecture' so objectionable to the Beaux-Arts; and make it so chiefly because it has become a threat to their own self-preservation. The accompanying plan must explain to you what I mean by opportunity. Taliesin has already established a living, worldwide Tradition. Now it has good reason to know that Youth everywhere is hungry for this new reality. Everywhere Youth is rocking in an old academic boat no longer seaworthy. Even in the dock for repairs, that old 'classic,' the 'American Beaux-Arts' can no longer be made safe for youth. Nothing modern architecture has to give any student can reach him by way of such eclectic imitation as now captains and sails that old caravel.

"However reformed, the Beaux-Arts cannot forget that it must never learn.

—*Taliesin, January 1932*"

TRAINING for Democracy will thus always be beginning at the beginning with the young or else breaking through all training with its naturals.

The Taliesin hat was thus, without equivocation, "in the ring." Some twenty-three young men and women had already responded. Although Taliesin rambles over a good many acres of hillside, we had to make-shift to house the twenty-three—even temporarily. We could manage to feed them with outside hired help. But we had to go to work with them and forty outside workmen to get them all becomingly sheltered, bedded down and provided with adequate places to be planned, in which to work together as promised. I felt in duty bound to use what money they paid me (in the usual installments, of course) for that purpose only. And this use, notwithstanding the circumstances of importunate debt—debt well armed, as always, with lawyers, advance agents of bolted doors and barred windows, or even worse, the still small voice of Conscience that is my misfortune—steadily carried on. I suspect numbers of our young people borrowed the money to come to Taliesin.

Dankmar Adler once said to me that he got his start in life by owing money to the right people. He borrowed money to pay for his education as an architect and being unable at the time to pay it back, the people who loaned it to him (he said) felt that the only way they could ever get it back again was to give him a job—a building to build. So he got his first job. I pass this along (in confidence) to posterity for what it may be worth.

As the plan for the Taliesin Fellowship unfolded itself, I had hoped that apprentices—like the fingers on my hands—would increase not only my own interest and enthusiasm for my work as an architect, but would also widen my capacity to apply it in the field. The first came true. But the second, as yet, is a temporarily frustrated hope. We somewhat overshot the mark. But I have not yet given up hope. We are steadily improving.

We had designed a heading (one, Hillside roofs in snow; one, Taliesin roofs in snow) and started a weekly column beneath it, one in Editor Evjue's Madison paper *The Capital Times,* one in the *State Journal.* The articles, beginning in 1932 and signed by the apprentices, ran for several years. Although apprentices themselves usually wrote the articles (architects, I thought, had need to be especially articulate), occasionally Olgivanna and I would take a hand. Here follows one of mine. The articles, hundreds of them, are hard to come by now.[3]

## WHAT IS THE MATTER WITH HUMAN NATURE?

A young apprentice for a year—now an architect and young friend of mine *[Alden Dow]*—writes concerning the Taliesin Fellowship: "Your idea is good and your work should succeed, but you are asking too much of Human Nature. I wish you had attempted something in which you had a greater chance of success."

To my solicitous young friend:

Taliesin *is* preaching an unpopular gospel, I admit: preaching, by practice, the gospel of Work, and Work has been pretty well knocked out of American youth by way of inflated "Education." It is going to be no easy matter, I can see, to put the joy back into work that alone can make work creative and lift it above drudgery.

There have already been many youths here at Taliesin who had applied themselves to a college curriculum four to six years and had come out with the usual "degree." Some of them honor men. They could sufficiently concentrate to arrive at that. But they know, as I do, that this is less, much less, than half the right thing.

"Less than half" means that most college-grown men today are rather less than half-men. They are sometimes interesting, often informed, controversially conversational, pettily egotistic, but usually impotent. Any skilled labor involving their physical resources is beyond them. They imagine it is beneath them but, really, it is beyond them. To use tools well, especially a shovel, a hoe, or an axe requires at least as much Science and more Manhood than swinging a golf club on a golf ball correctly or rooting at a football game.

To stay with a good piece of work in the field or a building requires more stamina than football because football is showing off and field work or building is a kind of skilled sacrifice to nothing immediate but something stored up in the Future. The man who plants a tree knows something of this non-showing but deeply satisfying aspect of work. And if the Taliesin experiment in apprenticeship does fail, it will fail because our modern youths have been left high and dry above the capacity to surrender to work in its rich, full, manifold forms. And because the individual educated youth, where his physical nature is concerned with his head, is unable to be and continue as a good workman—per se, as such. That is to say, where his head and hands should be.

So I look with increasing disgust (alarm too) at the coddled addled product parents turn adrift upon society by way of the colleges. Yes, by hundreds of thousands, half-baked novitiates congregate in universities all looking for dignity, worth and wealth outside the only source from which either can spring for them: the creative energy of their whole manhood, projected with enjoyment into useful creative employment—work wherein physical force must be so related to mind that none can say where the one begins and the other ends.

I have the same feeling of repulsion for the one-sided development of, say, a sedentary musician, that I would have for some man with an enormous muscular right arm hanging from an undernourished, undeveloped body. I should consider that arm a spiritual deformity as well as a physical monstrosity. "Specialities" are usually developed at such expense to the health and soundness of the whole man. They offend me even more now since I have been leading youth into action by way of the axe, the saw, the plane, the hammer and the scythe, the shovel and the hoe. The stone chisel, the paint brush, as well as just cooking and washing up. And then comes the use of the T-square and triangle on the drawing board.

No more drawing-board architects at Taliesin! Not if I can help it. Nor, if I can help it, any more one-sided specialists who can't and won't take work as though their daily bread did not depend upon a modicum of sweat on the brow and some joy in their own decent skill. The sedentary specialist has had his not sufficiently brief hour in capitalism. For fifty years, at least, the academic pigeon hole has had its fill of peripatetic young human lives conditioned to capitalism and here we are as we now are, a nation of employees of some employee of an employee. We do not know who our Employer is. Increasingly few have the heart or the brains to inquire. Of what use to know?

And what "Educated" youth is worth employing as a workman on his own stark merit? Lack of correlation and stamina is what is the matter with him. Here in this work at Taliesin we are seeking to find and build up in the young lad that joy and stamina in work which will enable him to take hold of life afresh and *anywhere!* Were the world of men and things destroyed as it stands, he could take hold and make a better one in every way. If the weakness and indolent habits of sedentary American college life are incurable—well then, Taliesin hasn't much chance to succeed. But there are young men here already *enjoying* work, enough to prove that essential manhood is still potential in the *insurgent* college-man at least. But we have our Ups and Downs. Our Ins and Outs.

These several background sets—stage props?—must serve to give you some idea of what the Taliesin Fellowship meant to meet as best it could. They will also give you the attitude of the Fellowship at the time.

For weeks I had driven up and down the ramifying valleys of our matchless countryside looking for lumber and other materials to work with. We needed, and desperately, lumber, stone, lime and laborers of all sorts. As you see in the lines (and between them), we had very little or no money at all to pay for these coveted desirables at first. The search lasted for months. Finally, materials still lacking—having failed to secure most of the essential materials, I got forty workmen together from the neighboring small towns—laid my scheme before them and made them the following proposition—anxious and still wondering where I could get the materials for them to work with if I succeeded and they did come to work. I proposed to dissipate what money the apprentices brought in by putting most of it each week into the pockets of the all but starving workmen, sheltering them in comfort, feeding them well, and paying for the food they consumed. They willingly signed the following agreement. I suppose in the circumstances they would have signed anything. Most of them were a hungry-looking lot.

GENERAL NOTICE
[Note: Posted on the walls of Dining Room, Oct. 1, 1932.]
All workmen, as party of the first part, and Frank Lloyd Wright, as party of the second part, representing the Taliesin Fellowship, agree to work in partnership as follows: suitable board and lodgings are to be provided by the Fellowship and one-third of the wages as agreed upon in each individual contract as signed by each workman will be paid in cash weekly. The balances are all to be paid when the buildings now under construction are completed and ready for occupancy and increased apprenticeship fees can be obtained.
—*Frank Lloyd Wright*

Each workman was asked to sign the following contract:

INDIVIDUAL CONTRACT
Charles Curtis, as party of the first part, and Frank Lloyd Wright, as party of the second part, representing the Taliesin Fellowship, hereby agree to work in partnership as follows:

Charles Curtis is to go to work as mason on the buildings as planned for the Fellowship by Frank Lloyd Wright, and work as directed by him from the date hereof until October 15th, 1932, for the sum of four dollars ($4.00) per working day—to be paid as follows: twenty-five dollars ($25.00) a month as work progresses, the balance due to be paid to Charles Curtis, October 15, 1932, by Frank Lloyd Wright out of the funds of the Fellowship.

While Charles Curtis is with the Fellowship it is agreed that satisfactory board and room shall be provided by the Fellowship.

*Frank Lloyd Wright*

*Charles Curtis*

In some cases, Karl Jensen, secretary at the time, neglected to get some of the men on the dotted line, but when they were taken in on the work they were all told and knew well enough what the terms were upon which they were working. The general notice, lettered in black and red on a white placard, was posted in the Dining Room and in the buildings where they worked.

The men were appreciative and grateful. So I believed. Be that as it may, I soon had forty of them for partners and put all to work saving the Hillside Home School buildings. Other workmen (they were continually tramping by), learning of our set-up, asked us to take them on. Some came from as far away as San Francisco and New York City. That manpower of ours was a motley of urban, rural, married, unmarried, young and old, good, bad and indifferent America: the dregs of the system at the bottom, fairly good country workmen at the top.

We fixed up the old laundry building at Hillside with a wood range and managed running water, hot and cold. We made long board tables and covered them with white oil cloth, and put hard benches beside them. We fixed up the old place until it seemed inviting and homey, and began to feed our men comfortably. Workmen are captious where food is concerned. But we fed them so well that, believe it or not, they really admitted it. There was very little drinking on the premises. Some few of the men went to town for that and would come back and fight. We could always start a backfire. A little room near their dining room, we—the young Fellowship—set aside as a dining room for ourselves. We had our noonday meal there together every day (pretty well cooked farm produce) to consider things in general, and argue in detail when exciting problems were pressing, using the white plastered walls for illustrating details. Problems were plenty and always pressing. Activity was soon gratifying and exciting. The men were glad to get to work after long enforced idleness.

And to keep them all going on in the right order and direction was a problem mostly solved afresh each night about four in the morning and worked out on the drawing boards next day. During that wakeful early morning hour, which I have known ever since, I can remember creative work, an hour devoted to prospect, retrospect and perspective when all is still and I am rested, and I know I can turn over and rest several hours more: then things come clearest. At that time the unsolved problems seemed to work themselves out with comparatively little assistance from me.

We had man-power. About forty men.

## MATERIALS VERSUS CASH

### LUMBER

We were now where we had to have more lumber or stop work altogether. Standing around in the woods of our county, were many piles of sawed oak. I coveted them all as I coveted gravel, sand, and cement. The surrounding farmers had cut the timber on their own wooded hillsides and were keeping the lumber for barn building. I tried to buy some of these lumber piles, pay part down, part on credit. But nothing could be done. The hard financial going all around had made everyone, especially the farmers, doubly suspicious, especially so of me, the spender of so much money with no visible means of support. So far as they could see. For many weary patient weeks I met the same answer to all my propositions and petitions. "No—we must have cash." "Cash is what we need most of anything. Pay right now, or else !" They really did need "cash" desperately. Of course they did. Cash was more than ever, absolutely now, King. But I finally learned that Herb Schoenman (ten children), a decent neighboring farmer, had 400 acres of virgin oak timber standing just over the ridge from Taliesin. I drove over to see Herb, offered him a fair price and terms for his four hundred acres of timber, on the stump. And Herb accepted. (Yes—he was paid.) Then I found a good sawer on the other side of the river who agreed to saw the logs at the regular price if we cut them and brought them in. I found another farmer (a good fellow out on parole for stealing his neighbor's chickens) who would cut the trees for a price and his old father and two young sons (really nice boys) would haul them in, he said, if we would help in the logging with our caterpillar tractor and some of our Fellowship boys.

So back to first principles for us.

Forthwith, we went headlong into logging. The place became a logging camp. Soon, after overcoming innumerable difficulties of a time-consuming, painful but picturesque character, green-oak timber was going up into the walls and trusses of our coveted buildings. Sap was still running from the boards. Green twigs were still on the logs when we sawed them into boards, scantling, and beams according to Henry's lumber lists. None too evenly sawed timber either. But never mind.

We had lumber. Seventy thousand board-feet. It was our own.

The boys—yes, the girls—enjoyed the hard work as well as the painful picturesque experiences. Those experiences were consequential too, in unexpected but perfectly natural ways.

We had incurred a debt of several thousand

dollars besides our own labor and what money we had. But we now had something to build our superstructure with. Rather hard to manage but we would have taken anything that could not positively crawl off the building lot. You should have seen those inexperienced boys tackle that heavy logging job! No worldly wise, pavement-sore urban parents could ever believe their boys capable of such hard continuous physical punishment as their boys took. They liked it. I mean the boys.

Lumberyard lumber was still way beyond us. Prices were far too high. About double what we paid for the green oak. Lumber, like telephone and telegraph service and other "System" items, had not dropped one cent during the "depression" nor were any concessions made if headquarters knew what was going on. They were all holding the fort, which means prices. Meantime, work on the buildings continued. And the workmen, no longer hungry, were not grumbling. They were satisfied with what money we paid them. The framework was now there in the rough.

## A LEGAL EPISODE

After a few months, however, we again ran out of lumber and into a characteristic snag. Again I went about the country, covetous—seeking another piece of timber.

Finally, I located some logs just out. Young Richardson, another farmer some miles away, had dropped about twenty thousand feet of red oak to the ground and the logs were lying there on the slippery hillside to be hauled. We bought and paid for them! I borrowed that money from an apprentice, Alden Dow.

But unfortunately we were soon on our way to Arizona. The Fellowship is an outdoor affair. We need to be outdoors on buildings as much of the time as possible. Inasmuch as it costs thirty-five hundred dollars to heat all of Taliesin and Hillside, we go out to Phoenix, Arizona, in winter, and on into the desert to build a camp of our own to work with and work in. We called it Taliesin West.

Meantime Tom King, local attorney-banker, had accepted a collection item against me of several hundred dollars for a disputed account with an east-ern publishing house. This house was receiver-holder of Payson (*Disappearing City*) from whom I had bought back the copyright and "remainder" of that book. I disputed the account because I had returned the "remainder" when I found the books unbound.[4] Nevertheless the long arm of the law, learning of the logs (the "long arm" owned the local lumberyard too) the neighboring banker-lawyer "attached" them. We, who merely bought and paid for them, first learned of the act upon our return from Arizona the following spring when we went to haul our logs. The Law and taxes never sleep where money is at stake, and often make very little noise on the way to execution. Tom, the lawyer's banker (and the bank's lawyer), had posted a sign on the fence near the family chapel yard conforming to legal requirements (so he said), but a notice which none of us ever saw, nor could see because we were two thousand miles away.

This was a blow, hard as it was unexpected—another kind of boot with a hard heel, a hustling sort. But recovering and visiting the scene we found a few thousand feet the Law had left behind. (Overlooked.) The Law should never play that way.

We ruefully hauled these remaining logs. But no use.

## CATASTROPHE

Before we could get them into boards came the national CATASTROPHE!

Labor in the U.S.A. went on "RELIEF."

On account of "relief" we, the Taliesin Fellowship (in partnership with labor), had no more use for building materials for several years to come. Our labor had been "bid in" to rest—relieved.

I mention this entirely legal interference with our plans and specifications as the final blow, but characteristic of the very many ultra-legal, but entirely unjust interferences from first to last, partly because, though all were desperate for "money," none could be had by labor, none at all unless by gift. It would be too tedious to remember most of the circumstances to say nothing of narration. But just the same, though dashed, our work on the buildings did partly keep on for a time.

The buildings kept on growing up a little. The

Taliesin boys themselves were begging to be able to carry on.

The workmen were no longer satisfied.

All had gained weight except Will Schwanke.

Will was foreman of carpenter construction, a faithful Spring Green carpenter. He was lean because he was faithful, perhaps. Will was not half dominant enough though, for that tough gang. I had to step in continually. His wife, who told Will all about himself frequently, strongly objected to us also. She kept telling him so. It jarred him frequently, but Will stayed faithfully by us on the carpentry just as Charlie Curtis, the seventy-nine-year-old Cornish mason from Mineral Point (whose wife took it from *him*), stayed with us on the masonry.

Both stayed for the duration.

Both were fine characters. A good influence on the boys and good instruction too. Stone walls as fine (almost as fine) as Timothy's, which are the finest in the world, were nobly standing there now ready for the framing.

"I don't want you to pay me much, Mr. Wright," said Charlie. "I am a contributor to the Fellowship because I think it's a grand idea."

The boys made a lot of the old mason, while he made a good mason out of a lot of them. I liked Charlie.

John Commons, grand old man of the University of Wisconsin, came to see us discouraged and about beaten down. He declared he was all in—an old man at seventy-two. He did look as though he hadn't long to live. But we went to work on him, gathered 'round him and made much of him. I took him out to see Charlie working on a new stone fireplace in my bedroom. "John," I said, "this is Charlie Curtis. He is eighty-one years old and a grander mason than ever."

John Commons looked as though he had seen a ghost.

His jaw dropped. But the lesson went home.

He began to "come back" as the saying is. After a week or two with us he went home. His friends wanted to know what we had done to John.

"Oh, nothing," I said, "we just put him on good terms with himself, that's all." That was six

years ago, and John is still going strong. Charlie Curtis was kind and tolerant to all the amateurs except one rather elaborate traveling philosopher who came hitch-hiking in, enthusiastic, from the Colonial belt. All the screws needed for correlation were loose in him. But he had a polished mind and brilliant ideas to expound. He *would* keep on expounding them. I put him on as helper for Charlie, chipping stone and carrying mortar. One day, after a week of surplus theory and excess lack of correlation, Charlie put his hand up to my ear and said, "For God's sake, Mr. Wright, take 'im away. Take 'im away before I kill 'im. I can't stand 'im no more." I took him away and kept him in general circulation for the duration.

Charlie Curtis often used to say to the lads, "You've got to get the feel o' the rock in your 'ands, m'boys. It hain't no use 'til y'do! No use 't all."

We had stripped the ledges and again opened the old quarry from which the beautiful stone for the Hillside buildings was taken. This quarrying was a mighty experience for the inexpert—we were all amateurs but, Charlie Curtis helping, we did it. We had plenty of stone which we had quarried, hauled ourselves, and piled about the buildings. Our fellows were getting splendid in action. Blocks of flesh-colored sandstone, cords upon cords of it out of the ground, two miles away.

The buildings kept on growing up by way of more and more long fine stone walls. We now had four local masons working under Charlie.

## LIME

But we had to have lime or stop. The prideful Cord, getting tired, started traveling again. Finally I found some lime freshly burned but it was way up north in the state. However, they agreed to deliver it to us at a low price partly on credit. But weird stories were beginning to travel. They travel fast (and fixed) in "The System." So, on the way to deliver the lime, stopping at the local lumberyard in Spring Green, the up-state dealer was told by the local Spring Green dealer that if he sold us any lime at all he (the local man) would have him declared unfair by the "Association" (the Association, like the T & T and the lumber companies, hadn't relaxed a bit during the breakdown) and if he did so, he said, no lumberyard in the state would buy any more lime from him. The lime-burner came to us with the story instead of the lime—apologetic, of course, very. He really believed in us. He was willing to help us but was actually up against it.

He said, "You buy lime but once. The lumber dealers keep on buying lime." So he said he could not afford to go against them and sell lime to us.

What to do? Conspiracy in restraint of trade? Undoubtedly. But what of it? We were out on a limb.

The men were soon entirely out of lime. We couldn't afford to buy cement. The lumberyards were full of cement—but for us to keep our workmen going, deliveries were only for cash-down. The cement dealers, like the lumber dealers, all knew their way out of the scrape they were in: stick together. Keep prices up. We came up against this fine fellow-feeling of theirs for their fellow-creatures on more than this one typical occasion.

Things were pretty tightly interlocked, I can tell you. There was little or nothing lying around loose in our county or those next to it. And rarely was there an "independent" to be found anywhere. Independents were soon "brought around." It cost too much—this independence.

The principal materials were all under "production-control."

Strictly up against it again, under pressure, I remembered that lime for the original Hillside Home School buildings that old Timothy had used back in 1902 had all been burned in the hills not more than several miles away. The old kiln might be there yet! August Cupps owned the place now. So we went up over the hills to see August. "Sure," said he. "Sure," said tall awkward August, the sorghum-maker. "Sure, go ahead, fix up the old kiln. I'll sell you wood to fire it at three-fifty a cord. Cut it myself." There were yet lots of wood on the hillslopes nearby, and still plenty of limestone near the old kiln. So up went the boys to bring the old wrecked lime-kiln back to life again and themselves learn how to burn lime: a bunch of greensters. I got an old-time lime-burner from Black Earth to instruct them. We fixed up the broken grates with old ones we took from the old buildings at Hillside—

patched up the tumbled walls, stripped a section of the old stone quarry and filled the patched-up restoration with good raw lime rock; piled cords and cords of wood alongside in long ranks to feed the roaring fires. Our boys took their food up to eat beside the kiln and would also take turns sleeping there by the kilnside on the ground under blankets, getting up every two hours all night long to keep the old kiln burning.

We got good lime . . . hundreds of bushels of it. We could have gone into the lime business, and thought seriously of doing so. We were A-1 producers of an essential building material.

We burned many full kilns of lime from first to last and we all loved it.

Somehow we grew strong by it. All of us. And that old kiln there on the hillside in the woods was a sight at night—lighting up the countryside for miles around.

We watched that light in the sky from Taliesin itself. When the iron door would open to engulf more cordwood, the boys, stripped to a loincloth, looked like stokers in the hold of a battleship. That old kiln *was* a battleship. Back to the primitive again to beat the tieup—the "bottleneck."

We had good lime.

It was our own.

## SHOPPING FOR THE FELLOWSHIP

The old Auburn Cord (four thousand two hundred pounds in itself) became a beast of burden. But a handsome thing it was when not put out of sight by provender and put nearly out of commission by our weekly trips to the wholesale grocers in the neighboring towns of this Iowa County and the next, Dane County, and the next, Sauk County. The car had taken several foreign prizes for body design and it was the nearest thing to a well-designed car I had ever seen outside Europe. And right here the feeling comes to me that the Cord should be heroic in this autobiography somewhere.

On the edge of entering the Money breakdown when several large commissions loomed in the foreground, I gave up the Packard for the Cord, taking it on an installment-plan contract that ran us ragged for years. But it (the Cord) seemed to have the right principle—front-wheel drive pulling instead of pushing along, and certainly it looked becoming to my houses—the best design from my "streamline" standpoint ever put on the market. I had myself driven myself (my own hands on the wheel) some five different top makes of car (beginning with the Stoddard-Dayton roadster in 1910) the equivalent in miles of some seven times around the earth—and, believe it or not, with never an accident—not even a smashed fender. But let me say I did not drive in Japan. I had four or five different drivers during that sojourn—they are a special class and how, over there—high silk stockings (ladies'), patent-leather shoes, knickers, and a military cap. And they high-saluted each other as they passed. Owing to narrow tortuous high-on-a-bank roads of Tokio [sic] countryside, their proficiency was similar to that of a slack-wire performer in a circus.

Due to a compound fracture of the wrist got while cranking the heavy Knox roadster I owned (after the Stoddard-Dayton), I kept a driver at Oak Park for a time. He was very careful of my broken member—but eventually stole the car. He turned out to be one of a gang of auto thieves. The police finally got the car in a St. Louis barn as they were putting a coat of green paint over its beautiful gunmetal finish.

I never cared for the Knox anyway. At high speed it would settle down and shake itself almost to pieces in a perfect frenzy (the garage-doctors call it a shimmy). And they couldn't show it how not to.

I think I got almost as much enjoyment (1922, '23, '24) out of the long, low, black, specially built Cadillac as out of the Cord. Patent-leather Victoria hood over the rear seat, windshield between first and back seat, no footboards, sides built down. I drove it in L.A. when I returned from Japan. That Cadillac thus had mostly the look of the later Cord—streamlined—very compact. Wherever we parked the crowd would gather to see the "foreign" car—trying to guess the make.

But the Cord was a prideful car—an innovation along right lines that changed the whole field of body design for the better—for one thing.

I was headed for Chicago one fine morning, very early. Between Madison and Evansville a florist's truck turned up ahead. I drew aside, about to pass, honking hard, when suddenly the truck with no warning at all turned and dove directly in front of me, turned sharply left! I jammed on the brakes, but the Cord caught the already careening flower-wagon full on the side—nosed it over and over again and again and again as a hog might nose a truffle. Over and over went the Madison florist, three times, and he was well on the way to the fourth turnover before the truck finally collapsed in a heap—the head of the Madison florist coming up through the debris—cursing loud and cursing plenty.

Never were swear-words sweeter to my ear. The man was not even hurt.

He recognized me with a "G—d—it, Mr. Wright!!!! G—d!! Jesus Christ, why don't you look where you're going!!!" He got disentangled from the collapsed top, got up just a little wobbly, and galloped off to the nearby roadside station to call up—whom do you suppose? The press! He was asking them to send a photographer out to get the wreck. A left turn into traffic rarely gets damages, especially as we were three to testify to the fact that the florist had given no warning whatever; and had he perjured himself to the contrary, why, he was only one. Our journey was interrupted, but the Cord was not badly hurt.

They picked up what had been the florist's truck and threw it away.

Where were we? . . . going shopping . . . going in the Cord to German's Wholesale Warehouse at Richland Center, thirty miles away. (I was born in Richland Center.) We did all the shopping in person because long sojourn in Japan had cultivated my bargaining instincts, and my technique. We usually got good measure and good prices wherever it was possible. After selection we would start loading—sacks of flour on the fenders—crates of fruit on the bumper. Rump and back seats piled high with everything a grocer keeps, and a greengrocer as well. And when we would finally lash the load to the Cord the springs were on the bumpers. If we ever hit anything with that load we never could have been distinguished from the groceries, unless by color.

Reaching home, unloading began. The Taliesin storeroom filled up a little for a week maybe, and then again we went, sometimes West or East or North or South. We traded with the neighboring wholesalers for years—until added to my practice in Japan buying prints was so vast an experience in the lore of provender-buying that I would have made a bet with you that I could buy anything you had to sell for one-quarter less than any sum you had secretly made up your mind was the very least you would take for it.

Sometimes there was remaindering going on. That was where we would shine and the Fellowship would be fed that particular bargain—say, dried apricots or pink salmon or melons or whatever you can think of—until that particular "success" was out—which really means in.

Our rapid-fire Gatling-gun buying pleased the storekeepers. Pointing with my stick I would indicate what we wanted with little or no hesitation, and we would be off on our way loaded down (and almost out) while another customer was buying a crate or two of something or other. They used to say of me in the old family days at Oak Park that I was a "good provider." But I was a grand "good provider" now.

I have always liked to "provide"—especially luxuries, and spread them about in a decorative fashion on the tables. The apple-barrel-with-the-head-knocked-out of my boyhood, I suppose. The bushels of roasted peanuts set around in big bowls; grapes lavished in big bunches in glass semi-globes; all kinds of nuts—rare fruits like persimmons—figs—grapefruits—strawberries—from the South. Pomegranates—avocados, etc. And we were especially fond of small fruits.

I always judge a hotel by two things—do they have fresh fruit, and are the toilet accommodations clean? Many a time we have walked away both in Europe and America after the invariable preliminary inspection proved unsatisfactory.

Herb (Jacobs of Usonian House number one)[5] told me of the Elam Mills, an old brick building down on Halsted Street, Chicago, where the best cereals are ground in good old ways. Corn, wheat and oats. That delicious taste of corn, wheat and oats! And that mill ground it with all the life-giving features (vitamins, I suppose) left in. Good stuff to maintain bodily vigor, good complexion, active brain. Add, from our Guernsey herd, good milk, our own fresh eggs, fresh fruit in and out of season, and a glass of good wine on occasion, and our own inimitable Wisconsin cheese—and what have you? Well, that is about what we have.

Only now we raise most of it ourselves.

The Cord is gone.

The boys haul the provender into the root cellar at Taliesin and pile it up. We "put down" this year (1942) one thousand quarts of tomatoes, besides many hundreds each of green beans, peas, and vegetables. But that isn't much.

That underground reservoir of food can take several carloads and ask for more.

A tunnel leads to it, and at the arched door in the masonry wall you switch on the light—the sight that meets the eye is a treasure-filled cave, not unlike Aladdin's. To the left are Olgivanna's wine casks: wild grape wine, elderberry wine, chokecherry, rhubarb, dandelion, potato wines, beet, tomato, tame grape, wild grape, plum brandy, cider, chokecherry mead. Apples. Cider vinegar. Rows on rows of jams, fruits, marmalades, jellies, sauces, pickles, vegetables. Sauerkraut. To the right, on sand, are piles of potatoes, squash, beets, carrots, cabbage, onions, parsnips, and rutabagas. Melons in season. Hanging from the ceiling are dried herbs from the herb garden.

If a barbed-wire entanglement were put around Taliesin for the winter we would all come out next spring with double chins.

This fifth book of *An Autobiography* is destined to be no work of art, but actually the sorry tale of a congenital urge which found itself anew in this rash determination to make architects while making architecture: the consequent "sweat, blood and tears," and laughter, connected with that structural phase of our national revolution: a rebellious banditry itself which, instead of being merely punishable by death, is cruelly subject only to the severest social penalties and economic sacrifices our fearsome body-politic staggering under its overload of government can devise or inflict by Ignorance, by Neglect, or by Law.

Thomas Jefferson. Where are you now? Is the muddy wave of an ism closing over your gracious head?

But I am reconciled to punishment. Why should this adventure not be punishable?

Any established order must yield to growth iota by iota. And then it will yield only when well undermined or it falls by its own excess or by duress. Lucky if after yielding, it is not frightened back and forth again and again. But at Taliesin we have managed somehow to live on and keep on working appreciatively in the direction and actual service of a great Ideal, no less in these ten years past than single-mindedly for a lifetime.

We have, however, been compelled to work for the construction of an indigenous Architecture as revolutionaries in a far too uncommon War (I say, the right kind of war if war must be): earning another half million to go with the million dollars already "earned" in my lifetime. Yet, never really having any money. No . . . throughout these forty-five years an out-and-out culture-bootlegger, forced by the nature of our national tumbled house to work and live under the banner of a bandit: that is only to say, the banner of the Radical!

Never solvent as banking goes. No, but all the time and overtime, the honest counter-revolutionist where the social system under which we live is concerned for its way of life . . . concerned for what it calls its own safety! Its "safety," does it say? It too is "out on a limb." But, God! I should say that what it deems and calls its "safety" may be seen as ultimate destruction unless in common with our enemies we lose what we try so foolishly hard to win . . . not yet understanding that no world-revolution can be won as any nation's war unless it is a people's war. And then? We wouldn't like it.

Walt Whitman! Dear old Walt, we need you more than ever: your salt and savor in this dish of humble-pie we are called to eat in shame and defeat, win or lose! Your robust soul might save us even now.

We have taken the wrong way. We must wait for you on a closed road.

If you are sympathetic you may see, between these lines at least, how the Taliesin Fellowship could only come into being and get into open service of its Ideal as a threat to such smug "safety" as the current agents (broadcasters of our current "morale") advocate. I say the Taliesin Fellowship could have come into actual social service only as a special kind of social bootleggery. Yes, unhappily, not being "regular," our Fellowship has had to be thievery in some kind. At any rate, an Indigenous Architect, a Native Architecture, and the Taliesin Fellowship could have come to be in no legitimate way under the despotic Money criterion of present-day Usonian life.

## STARS AND BARS

And thus it comes to be in a new free country which has become a kind of hard-up "tour-de-force" speaking English far too fluently but none too plainly, that any Ideal above the belt or below the Bank is illegitimate! As things go, only Money can justify Work or pay for it or should ever talk above a whisper . . . if at all. Like the Administration-extraordinary of all this blood-letting money-getting, I have had, so far as the Ideal is concerned, somehow to get into unrepayable money-debt myself for everything related to me or directly related to this Cultural Ideal which we call the Taliesin Fellowship. Even the warm pioneer family-life so enjoyed by us as children in this beloved Valley by the broad sand-barred Wisconsin River—life so warm that it warms me still, eventually had to go away; go by way of the bad choice of its own numerous offspring, some forty of my cousins, to scatter in faraway towns to seek the cash-and-carry yeshood of the white collarite. So the hired man of the humanly glowing, noble family life of that pioneer day now owns most of the original family farmsteads: "own" (and so exploit regardless) the ground which my people broke and loved so greatly in the wise breaking, conserving the wooded hills and the tilth of the soil. Yes . . . my people, the Welsh pioneers lived and died for this, their Valley.

And now even the architectural forms I myself may discover honestly and try to practice around the world are themselves revolutionary.

So they, too, are a kind of banditry? They must be so because if we find a better way to build a better building and actually build it that way, we change and probably destroy existing values everywhere. Even overnight. Therefore in modern times let us say the Taliesin Fellowship *is* on the modern social level of ancient Robin Hood with his medieval band of freebooters.

We don't cut the throats of our neighbors or rape the women of the neighborhood. Nor do we ever disturb the overflowing hen roosts much as the boys—loving eggs—would like to. But if we are true to ourselves we must do violence to their most "sacred feelings." Continually we insult hallowed "tastes" and do outrage upon the established property rights and "beliefs" of our most worthy creatures of social habit. We do this whenever we build a new building, furnish it and plant the grounds. An outrage! And the educational system of our country (the greatest mass-production, by the way, next to motor cars, gadgetry, engines of war and munitions) is not that establishment, endangered, too, by this inevitably ruffian attitude when we go seriously—that is to say, naturally—to work in search of our radical Ideal? So this search of ours for democratic FORM is revolutionary. Necessarily. But a Revolution utterly essential to the life of this, our country.

If the Republic is ever going to grow up to be *itself*, a true self-supporting Democracy, independent of foreign exchange, safe from Money in the role of arch-commodity we as revolutionary are essential.

Since the Taliesin Fellowship is here (we celebrated our 520th Sunday evening—October 1942—together in the living room at Taliesin Sunday) and has actually come to be a cultural entity (it has lasted ten years to this moment), it follows that unless what we have done is a miracle, it is illegitimate. Inasmuch as I am but a halfhearted believer in miracles except as they are the uttermost commonplaces of nature, I must declare us illegitimate: myself Usonia's illegal but natural, therefore inevitable, son. Prodigal? Yes. But not contrite. Not yet. No. No revolutionary Evolutionist is ever penitent.

And yet: to look back is almost more than can be borne. An overwhelming pity rises for the defeated ones, those who aspired and are dead, those who expired in isolation, desolation and despair.

Our boys were getting a new view of things, and I was back to boyhood. They were no longer strangers to the Reality I wanted the young architects to meet and that was omitted from their college education. Taliesin was by now itself a kind of kiln—burning not cord wood but labor, materials, and food. Year in and year out. The buildings kept on growing. The roofs were going on. Tile roofs: a story in itself.

## ETTA

Standing there in the half-light of this, to you, confusing picture is a graying, gay, gray-eyed little woman—daughter of old Mr. Parsons—a fine old citizen of Dodgeville, up over there on the ridge seventeen miles away.

Olgivanna and I and the young Iovanna, tired of tough breaks and tough steaks, used to drive up to the Parsons' meat market. Father Parsons would go back into his box, take down his best, and cut off a rib roast for us. It would be the best we ever ate.

Etta was helping her father. She would wrap it up, hand it to us with a salty remark and the friendly smile that only Etta knew the secret of. The neighbors were all fascinated by or fearsome of Etta's native wit. She was kind but she was shrewd. She knew them all right and they knew she knew. She was a staunch "La Follette man." Her ideas were her own and she missed nothing of what went on. "I see Phil is getting around again speaking to the farmers. He was over at the 'Point' yesterday," she said. "It was a hot day so when he warmed up too, he threw his coat away, tore his collar off. Then he rumpled up his hair, and went after them."

Her gay, light-hearted laughter would let you know what she thought of the act that Phil had put on. Mother Parsons (the family lived back of and on a level with the shop) would look in through the door between the shop and the living room—a gentle soul with the same captivating sweet smile as

Etta's and ask us how we were. Somehow we were always all right. And sometimes we would go back and sit down by her windowsill full of plants and have a slice of bologna sausage and a cracker and tea, or a cup of coffee and a cookie.

Well—Mr. Parsons died. Etta and her husband, Hocking, carried on the shop—selling meats, groceries, a few plants in season. And seeds. They were pretty well off. But soon Etta lost Hocking. We went to his church funeral. They were greatly respected, so the whole town attended—all feeling deeply sorry for Etta, now a widow in black; her mother now in black, too.

The shop went on just the same. Etta now in a white butcher's apron behind the block, sometimes cleaver in her small hand with the plain gold wedding ring on her finger, mother still sitting by the door looking in occasionally. They didn't butcher any more now. Their meat came in by truck from "the System."

Our need of groceries and meats grew and we thought it might do Etta some good to have it, but things turned out the other way around. For years we drove seventeen miles to Dodgeville to trade with Etta, leaving everything pretty much to her. We gave her a few hundred dollars now and then, and she never sent us a bill—except, as she would say—"You are in about three hundred now." And we would pay up. She gave us pretty near wholesale prices—"Good idea you've got down there. Want to see it go through—think I'll come down and strike you for a job just as soon as you've eaten us out of house and home here." And she would gaily laugh that one off.

"Any time, Etta. Come on and run us. The place is yours that way, and anytime you want it."

Things were going fair and well enough until Relief came. Some of our Dodgeville workmen spent the money we paid them with Etta. From first to last a good deal of Fellowship money went into her till—and still no bills. We didn't ask for them.

"How many boys and girls have you got down there now?" she would say, as the groceries heaped up on the Cord and hid it from sight (I carried out the provender and stacked it).

"Oh, about twenty-five—say."

"My," said Etta, "they must eat an awful lot, don't they?"

"Guess they do—why? Are we buying an awful lot for twenty-five?"

"How many workmen now?" she would ask.

"Oh, about thirty now, I guess."

"Which eat the most?"

"Why . . . I don't know. I guess the young apprentices do," I said.

"I'll bet you're right," she said. "I'm going to bring mother down and see 'em at it myself." She did come several times, watching everything with an amused half-smile as though she had indulged them in food—herself. We got good advice from Etta. She would say, "Good work you're doing down there—but your bill's running high."

"How much?"

"Oh, about fifteen hundred," said Etta. And then panic. We would get after some money right away and turn in all we could. A stern chase is always a long chase, but we were getting even when Relief befell. Then we went behind. We were beginning to see that "the good idea down there" was a good deal of a money affair, after all. Etta didn't seem to care much. The men who got money to spend at her shop didn't get it from us now but they got it just the same from the government and gave it to her. She had a fair share of the town trade. We were in a fix though, and Etta knew it. We expected the worst—that Etta would have to cut us off. Etta was warned by friends. "Nope," she'd say, "I know they haven't got it now, but they'll get it some day—some way, I'll bet. Good work they're doing—smart people. But not too smart." And she would gaily laugh that one off.

She would never tell us any more what our balance was but our best thought on the painful subject would have been about three thousand at one time. That was the stock Etta took in the Taliesin Fellowship—the good idea she liked.

Etta is a good business woman and has plenty of good ideas herself. She is there, business as usual, to prove it.

She went into partnership with the good idea. Will Etta ever be paid in full, do you think? I'll bet she will. What do you bet?

## THE LIGHTER SIDE

Our Fellowship gatherings on Saturday and Sunday evenings began—October 1932—in the living room at Taliesin, continuing at Taliesin West in Arizona. These Fellowship gatherings for supper and a concert, or a reading and perhaps pertinent discussion (probably a little of these together), as I have said, have been going on for ten years. As for me, I have never failed to enjoy one of them. They were always happy and always fresh—not only composed of perfectly good material, good music, good food, enthusiastic young people, good company, but something rare and fine was in the air of these homely events by way of environment—atmosphere. No one felt, or looked, commonplace. The Taliesins (Middle West or West) are made by music for music and enter into the spirit of the occasion as if the one were made for the other. Eye music and ear music do go together to make a happy meeting for the mind—and the happy union charms the soul. This happy meeting is rather rare as independent intelligence is rare. We lived in it.

Olgivanna felt that the Fellowship—looking like the wrath of God during the week—should wash itself behind the ears, put on raiment for Sunday evenings and try to find its measure and its manners. Most of it had both. In the right place, too. The girls all put on becoming evening clothes, did look, and were, charming. That clothes make a difference is one of the justifications for our work as designers. On Sunday I scarcely recognized some of my own Fellows of the workday week. There was something vital and happy radiating from them all on these happy occasions when everybody served everybody else as though he were somebody, and willingly took the part in the entertainment he had been rehearsing. Part of it, of course, was because they were where they all wanted most to be—volunteers—doing what they most loved to do. Very much at home. I am sure none will ever forget his share in Fellowship life on these eventful but simple occasions, and while the fellowships change with time and circumstances—these events keep their character and charm nevertheless.

Many of these Taliesin young people would come because they had read something I had written or seen my work, probably both, and dreamed of someday working with me. They had come somehow with money begged, borrowed, or received as a gift, from all over the United States and many foreign countries, gratefully giving their best to Taliesin. And most of our boys and girls were individuals by nature with an aesthetic sense rejecting commonplace elegance. That rejection by Taliesin itself would be the natural attraction Taliesin would have for them: the artificiality that passed current for Art and had no place in Taliesin's instincts nor in theirs. To a man, the boys were naturally averse to the dull convention, either social or aesthetic. The girls were likewise. Alexander Meiklejohn[6]—himself the experiment at my old University (Wisconsin) and on several occasions a guest at Taliesin, said to me one evening, "Yours is the most alive group of young men and women I've seen together since I became an educator."

## ESPECIALLY DESIGNED

Taliesin Sunday Evening Occasions take place in the Taliesin living room number three, the third living room to stand in the same space. The most desirable work of art in modern times is a beautiful living room, or let's say a beautiful room to live in. And if perpetually designing were perpetual motion the world would have in Taliesin that much-sought-for illusion for the millennium. The Spirit of Design was pervasive, presided really, at these Taliesin events. The Saturday evening rehearsals and these Sunday night occasions were natural Fellowship festivity. But discipline at Taliesin in doing anything at all anywhere, lies in the fact that throughout, all must be especially designed. In none of anything can anything go that is not as especially designed to be perfectly natural to itself and Taliesin as sheep, crows, and butterflies are out of doors. And I want to insist that no discipline from the exterior is so severe a strain as this discipline from within.

This discipline applies to our boys and girls when they take turns providing the customary house decorations in appropriate scale or getting "especially designed" effects with native wild things or familiar trees and garden flowers, effects that were invariably as original and charming in seasonal arrangement as they were fresh in touch and idea with each individual who took charge. The seeds of good design fell about the place as naturally as apples fall from trees or thistledown drifts from the thistle crown. "Design" even in festivity—why not especially—was like air, the thistledown, because of what was around about, like the thistle crown, to fill and excite the mind. Every move in any direction is an opportunity. To be a developed designer or a designer in embryo was simply to be a natural member of the Taliesin Fellowship. Every member from the first to the last one was in active service to Organic Design.

From the very first we have had these pleasant distinguished company weekends—although guests are seldom invited because we were not really ready, we felt, but they were always welcome just the same and plenty came. Soon after the first years of professionals playing high quartets, we got our own Taliesin trio and quartet going into rehearsals. Soloists were plentiful among us from the first. Professionals from the various orchestras had come to join us for the summer but we soon got tired of playing second, ourselves merely entertained. We found, also and soon, that the musical activity of the Fellowship languished when the professionals did come. There were many reasons for this. So now, as I had desired from the first day of the Fellowship, we have our own male choir singing Palestrina, Bach, Negro spirituals, folksongs, and other good music: a repertoire of some seventy-five songs. We have a quartet, a trio, and as usual, many soloists. Svetlana has cultivated the old-fashioned recorder, too. Recorders now form a choir, and we mingle harp, piano, strings, recorders and voices. A really good Bechstein concert piano takes the corner in the Living Room, and one is in the Playhouse. A harpsichord in the blue loggia has joined the group. Iovanna's harp stands alongside. A Cesar Franck cantata last Sunday evening brought out our present resources. The young people have lately gone all-out for folk dancing Friday evenings.

You should see our grand-piano collection. We have seven appropriately and usefully placed about the buildings, not to mention the harpsichord.

About twenty-five years ago I sat playing the piano in my own way (no notes, so no pattern) letting the piano play itself for its own amazement. Carl (Sandburg) was listening. I suddenly stopped and wheeled around toward him with one of those mischievous impulses that I like to practice upon my friends and that so often ruin me. I said, "Carl, if my mother hadn't decided for me that I was to be an architect, I should have been a very great musician. It would have been my next choice. And since the mind required for greatness in either art is the same, I should have ranked with Beethoven, I am sure." I turned back to go on playing. But Carl didn't forget the episode and tells the story to this day to illustrate my colossal ego. I suspect he uses the word "egotism" when he relates the episode, as I have heard from others. Ego, yes. Egotism, no.

## BEETHOVEN

In Beethoven's music I sense the master mind, fully conscious of the qualities of heartful soaring imagination that are god-like in a man. The striving for entity, oneness in diversity, depth in design, repose in the final expression of the whole—all these are there in common pattern between architect and musician. So I am going to a delightful, inspiring school when I listen to Beethoven's music—music not "classic"—soul language never to be classified. Because of soul-depth and breadth of emotional range, Beethoven's music is in itself the greatest proof I know of divine harmony alive in the human spirit. As trees and flowering things under the changing lights of a beclouded sun pervade the all out of doors, so Beethoven pervades the universe of the soul.

When I was a small child I used to lie awake listening to the strains of the Sonata Pathétique—Father playing it on the Steinway square downstairs in the Baptist minister's house at Weymouth. It takes me back to boyhood again when I hear it now. And the other sonatas were as familiar then as the symphonies and later quartets are now. When I build I often hear his music and, yes, when Beethoven made music I am sure he sometimes saw buildings like mine in character, whatever form they may have taken then.

I am sure there is a kinship there. But my medium is even more abstract—so kindred spirits who understand the building are even more rare than in music. There is a similarity of vision in creation between Music and Architecture nevertheless. Only the nature and uses of the materials differ. The musician's facility is so much greater than the architect's can ever be. The idiosyncrasy of the client does not exist for the great composer. Utilitarian needs play a small part in his effort. The rules and regulations imposed by the laws of physics upon the performances of the architect are not present to any great extent in the scheme of things submitted to the musician. But both must meet and overcome the same prejudice—the same cultural lag. The limitations human stupidity puts upon insight and appreciation—these are the same for both.

I keep on saying that an artist's limitations are his best friends.

So perhaps the more severely limited art when success does crown creative effort is the greater and more abiding achievement—if for no other reason than that the one is the Abode while the other is the Song. Both are best when the song dwells and the abode sings: both may when creative power and the passion of love makes them glow from within.

Mastery is no mystery. Simple principles of Nature apply with peculiar emphasis and force to all the master does: a scheme in keeping always with the nature of materials (instruments), materials used in such a way as to reveal the beauty in tone and texture they possess. The strings were his, par excellence, but percussion, brass and woodwind—he knew them all so well that he never gives one away nor asks of the one what belongs to the other; continually enriching each with all and all with the character of each. But what gives *consequence* to mastery is a mystery. It is Inspiration.

And the planned progressions, thematic evolutions, the never-ending variety in differentiation of pattern, integral ornament always belonging naturally enough to the simplest statement of the prime idea upon which the superstructure is based: Beethoven's rhythms are integral like those of Nature!

Once organic character is achieved in the work of Art, that work is forever. Like sun, moon and stars, great trees, flowers and grass it *is* and stays on while and wherever man is.

Other musicians have this mastery also, and greatly, but none I understand so well, none so rich in the abstract idiom of Nature as he—whose portrait Meredith drew in the sentence: "The hand of the wind was in his hair; he seemed to hear with his eyes."

I am humble and grateful in his presence. "Who understands my music is safe from the world's hurt."

## AN "I REMEMBER"

I remember John Fiske (the great historian)[7] coming to the little brown house by the lake, coming there to dine with Father, Mother afterward remarking upon the great man's voracious appetite (as famous as his histories). I see his thick lips nesting in the great brown beard, eyes hidden from sight by the light glancing off his enormous spectacles. After dinner the great historian sang and even I could see how he loved that. In fact, Father (who played his accompaniments, of course) said that he was utterly proof against any compliment or blandishment where his powers as an historian were concerned but let anyone be so indiscreet as to compliment his singing, even a little, and he was singing on their hands thereafter. So it is with me. I love to sit in on chamber music rehearsals of the Fellowship talent and criticize—knowing as much of the particular composition probably as John Fiske knew of the art of singing but dreadfully pleased to have my criticism, regardless of the composer's notations (and perhaps sometimes his intentions too), heeded.

Such are the joys of the amateur, and far from innocent they are. I am sure Franklin Roosevelt gets much the same reaction where his command of the Army and Navy is concerned.

## THE UPKEEP OF THE CARCASS

Food under Olgivanna's guidance was excellent and very well served to the Fellowship and our guests by the Fellowship itself. Olgivanna started this. She said, one summer day, early in the second year of the Fellowship, "Frank, let's have no paid help. They don't belong here, you know. They vulgarize everything. There is no reason why these young men and women themselves can't learn to cook and serve their own meals gracefully without hiring help. Our boys and girls do their own rooms anyway and many of them do their own laundry. Do let me try! I want to see what I can do. You will see they will feel all the more at home, more a part of all this activity they are in here with us, if they take their share of the household routine upon themselves and serve each other."

Skeptical at first, I was afraid of the time consumed and the interruption it would be to our other labors. And I didn't believe in trusting our own good health and well-being to that extent to amateurs. But I soon found she was right. We fared very well indeed. Better than ever before. But it took a lot out of her from first to last. Nevertheless she made the plan work. And while there were plenty of individual breakdowns and many failures, she did succeed in making the Fellowship see the light in it and soon learn to discount the hardships. And the garbage, and the perpetual dishwashing.

There were many unexpected reactions. It appeared, for instance, that the nearer to the habitual wage-earner class a boy or girl was, the more rebellious he or she felt when doing what seemed to him "menial" labor. Just as those Fellows we would sometimes take into the Fellowship without fee, allowing them to work their way along with us, would be the least cooperative, most of them instinctively "keeping shop" with us. Being there only to "get" what they could, they gave the least and left the soonest.

But Taliesin kept on growing. The buildings were under roof. The boys had not only "the feel o' the rock in their 'ands" but the science of a board among boards, and what the stick was good for in a building, as they went from drawing board to the actual sticks and boards and learned what tools can do with them.

We put a scheme of rotation into operation in our work out in the fields and on the buildings. I named a head man for the fortnight just ahead who was free to choose his first aid or right bower. The first aid became next leader. He named the leader to follow him who chose his own aid. After consultation with me the leader each day laid out work for the others.

The work of the following day was thus planned the evening before. Something resembling this way of directing was now applied to the housework.

## MUTUAL SERVICE

Olgivanna tells of this: It takes years for the young people who join this work to throw off the old concept of academic schooling. At first they are unhappy because they are not all the time at the draughting board, they miss the class lecturing, they want formal discussions. They are suddenly dropped into a world of interior discipline, yet without a rule written down. A discipline which turns them to their own resources and makes them act with the sense of their own conscience. The concept that all work is important is new. There is no menial labor. There is no backyard. Taliesin is all front yard. The field work is as important a responsibility as the work in the draughting room, or in the garden, the kitchen or the dining rooms. This seems very difficult for young America to accept. One of our young men could not see the work in the kitchen as anything but menial work to be done by a servant. When he was told he didn't have to do it his conscience troubled him because all the others were doing that work. They began to tease him about it—'til he felt foolish in making an exception of work which was part of the whole. Later he became one of the best in making beautiful decorations in the dining room when in turn it came into his charge and the tables were arranged in new original ways, and he became a good cook. After the work in the kitchen he would sit and make drawings for the new arrangements he felt we needed. He would suggest new systems in serving, which would eliminate waste motion. He was just as interested in that work as in any other. His knowledge of the working of a kitchen and dining room on whatever scale is instilled into his very being—a knowledge earned and gained by him by way of actual experience—not by way of a superficial inadequate theory of designing.

This participation in our maintenance has a strengthening and unifying effect on the group. Taliesin has become their real home. One part of the group is headed by one with experience in planting the garden in the spring. Every morning all of the young people work in the garden for an hour or two. Afterwards the seniors go directly to the draughting room, some go planting trees (there have been hundreds of them planted about Taliesin), some go checking and fixing the electric fence, hauling gravel, grading roads. They learn how to handle stone by building the walls, laying the floors, putting up piers. They learn to work with wood, metals, and textiles. They arrange their own rooms, rebuilding the interiors according to the plan made by them which they submit to their master for approval. The large draughting room is like an abstract forest with light pouring from the ceiling in between the interwoven oak trusses. The atmosphere in it is always one of intense quiet concentration—which sometimes under pressure keeps the young people voluntarily working on drawings until the late hours of the night. Yet the draughting room responds to lively relaxation when tea is brought in at four o'clock and everyone gathers about the large fireplace, or in the stone-circle on the hill talking, discussing Fellowship problems, or getting engaged in dynamic political social discussions. The tea is prepared in weekly rotation by the young women of the Fellowship. Most intriguing recipes are tried. Those the group particularly enjoys are put into the Taliesin Cook Book, which is already a rich collection of Taliesin favorites.

It is fun to plan meals with our young people. For instance, as to what meat we shall use this week— shall we butcher the calf or the pig, or the goat-kid, geese, or chickens? We would wander together through our old cook books, some of them fifty years old: American, Russian, Yugoslav, Polish, of all nations really, and find new delicacies, always learning new exciting ways and always succeeding in getting interesting meals prepared. And when the wine-making season comes, we all go in automobiles, station wagons, trucks—taking picnic lunches with us—to gather wild grapes, chokecherries, blackberries, elderberries. Permeated with warm autumn sun we return home. The following weeks we crush and prepare our grapes and berries for wine. We gather our apples and the golden season

of apple cider sets in. Large crocks are filled with cider and tin cups hung by them stand in the court for the boys to drink while the cider press keeps on working, making more for the hard cider we will drink next spring and the vinegar we need.

About that time the rapid plans for the annual Hallowe'en masked ball are being made. The committee of entertainment is appointed. Small secret group meetings are held and all of Taliesin is sensitive to a mysterious mood that pervades everything. The party will be full of surprises—original and exciting— since each one of the young people is talented and designs with spontaneous, quick imagination.

Many of our young people, as I have said, are musicians and keep up their work in music. They have programs to prepare for every Saturday and Sunday evening. The chamber orchestra has been in existence for five years, playing Bach and Beethoven, Brahms and Haydn trios, quartets, sometimes quintets. The choir of eighteen young voices sings Palestrina and beautiful old English and American songs. On Saturday night we go to the Playhouse, where buffet supper is served, and listen to chamber music and solos. Sometimes a short play is put on the stage. Then we see moving pictures which come to us from all countries of the world. Every Sunday noon we go picnicking, exploring new places, going back to our favorite ones.

The social life of Saturday and Sunday ends the week and begins the next by an evening at Taliesin when all dress in their best clothes, and where we entertain our weekend guests, many famous artists among them. They frequently entertain us, and taking their turn, sing or play for us, or speak or read to us. The gathering usually breaks up in small groups engaged in quiet discussions gradually dispersing one by one 'til quiet descends upon Taliesin and the graceful figure of Buddha stands unperturbed in this warm human movement projected into Space.

## REHEARSALS
Meantime Fellowship life went on in the original Taliesin studio: designing, drawing. Always details

of details for the buildings steadily growing up at Hillside in spite of Relief and all other obstruction. Our own boys were learning to *build* our own buildings. Designs were perpetually made by the apprentices for the fittings and furnishings of their own rooms to be executed by themselves (if a boy's room were changed he threw out what his predecessor did and started "fresh"); perspective renderings; abstractions of plant life; studies from nature, and the nature of materials especially. And all the while our hands were in the mud of which bricks are made. We saw the designs we made take shape in the actual work of our hands and stand there before us in actual materials. But what was more important, the boys had to live with their errors or successes in building themselves into their own rooms and see the mistakes corrected. We do not learn much by our successes: we learn most by failures—our own and others', especially if we see the failures properly corrected.

To see a failure changed to a success—there is what I call Education.

Photography, too, we tried to include. Without much success, although several of the boys showed remarkable ability in that resource. We didn't have the money. As for music: at the beginning we tried several professional musicians, composers, to get that side of our work going, but it was too soon for that—we were much too engrossed in construction. Just for that perhaps, we didn't go very far or very fast. However, the intimate little Saturday evening rehearsal dinners in the Playhouse, and the Sunday evening event, music and supper in the Taliesin Living Room, went on to give relaxation its place in our lives.

Formal introductions in the Fellowship were dropped where guests were concerned. The guest would be introduced by Olgivanna or myself or one of the apprentices to the Fellowship as a body. Then the boys and girls would step up and say, if addressing a junior—I am John; or an adult, I am Lautner. The girls likewise. A little too much to expect guests or callers to carry in mind both given and surnames of thirty or more young men and women at one time. Casual guests were so frequent.

## CAPITAL INSTANCES OF THE CASUAL

Sophie Breslau, for instance (She said with a laugh, "A thousand-dollar package where singing was concerned"), coming out from Madison, bringing Ima Roubleff, her accompanist, standing up in the Living Room singing gloriously and happily there until three o'clock in the morning. There were many others from time to time.

We were all music lovers, or else mad about music, which is not quite the same thing. Many such informal occasions were thus stolen from the system—another kind of bootlegging, you see?

The most extraordinary instance of casual evaporation by translation I ever knew occurred when Mies Van der Rohe was to be inducted as Pilot into the chair of Architecture at Chicago's Armour Institute.

Mies and I have been fond of each other. He has known of me all his architectural life. I believe him a sincere man as well as an architect. He had asked me to come as speaker to a big dinner given in honor of that occasion. The dinner took place in the ballroom of the Palmer House. I sat near the center of the platform table at which were ranged various architects and dignitaries. My turn to speak, after listening to Emerson and other professional speakers reading from notes, and another lot of other bores intending eulogy of "the talented German," now their guest, taking over the helm of Armour . . . but saying nothing.

It was all most superficial blah or labored lip service, so when I rose I put my arm across Mies' shoulders (he was next to the speaker's place), and simply said, "Ladies and gentlemen, I give you Mies Van der Rohe. But for me there would have been no Mies—certainly none here tonight. I admire him as an architect and respect and love him as a man. Armour Institute, I give you my Mies Van der Rohe. You treat him well and love him as I do." I abruptly stepped down and walked out.

When Mies' turn came to speak he spoke in German, as he knows little or no English. For some five minutes he went into the origin of his discipleship and reverence for me. He told how much he was indebted to me, frankly and to the point. He was proud to stand there and say it. The German architect paid a well-considered tribute to an American architect, an affectionate tribute such as is rare in the history of the world, the architect's world at least.

The interpreter said (he was Walterdorf of the A.I.A.), after Mies had paused before going on with the rest of his speech, "Mr. Van der Rohe says he is sorry Mr. Wright left so soon." And unless you understood German, that is what you got from Mies Van der Rohe so far as he went up to that point at the crowded dinner in his honor.

The many boys and girls of Taliesin, hundreds from first to last, all behaved themselves with self-respect. And so far as Olgivanna and I could see (none too far, of course)—with circumspection. The first several years, however, there were some exceptions to the latter. But during all ten years of Fellowship-in-residence we have yet to look back and complain of an insolent act, or any unwillingness to carry on as requested—or very much shirking. While free co-operation was a hard lesson to be learned, we had only a few slackers, some with native disabilities, some dazed—not knowing what it was all about—but few real incompetents. Perhaps a dozen that I can remember. Naturally such would not last very long in our atmosphere and activity anyway. This loyal Spirit of the Fellowship in face of such handicaps of accommodation and equipment as ours was truly remarkable. I look back upon the circumstance with astonishment and no little gratification.

In the first years we had much altered and reconditioned the old buildings. We were trying to complete a large new one—our Draughting Room, flanked by sixteen small apprentice rooms, eight on either side. The old buildings had a new lease on life now—all protected under good tile roofs. The tile roofs that are a separate story. I don't want to forget it.

These first years of Fellowship went rapidly by for young and old. Young fellows would hitch-hike across the continent—and from as far away as the country was wide—to join us if they could. We were compelled, for lack of means and room, to refuse more than four hundred. Had I enough money to keep and feed them we could have filled the valley with hopeful young workers and might have started Broadacre City right then and there, ourselves. They have kept on coming in from all sides though we have never proselytized for apprentices as we never have for clients. But the sad fact is, those we were compelled to refuse were often the most desirable ones. Skilled workers they were, often.

## THE OFFICIOUS SAMARITAN

And then one day when we were looking forward to getting into our buildings the blow fell—not prohibition this time, but "RELIEF." The Administration of our government suddenly placed some forty or more of our workmen in a position where they could figure out that by doing nothing at all they could have a few dollars more in pocket from the government than they were getting from us. We had been keeping about seven families in Iowa County out of the poorhouse and about as many more in neighboring Dane County. All our men had good quarters in which to sleep. They had good food, the best, and plenty of it. They were pleased and satisfied. But now the men—several or more at a time—would decide to quit; more and more would come in to me and say, "We are going to take advantage of Relief." I had no argument to advance because the only inducement I could make would be to outbid the Administration and I couldn't. Many men probably would prefer to get their money without working anyway. Thus this matter of Money still stood with us.

Just to make this affair of money worse, of now being able to eat without working, an I.W.W. or two from New York City (I had a couple of them in on the work) got a dozen or more of the worst ones among the local men to join up in repudiating the partnership agreement, demanding that I pay up all the balances *"right now."* Someone in Madison had told Mike Lazar, the lather, about an old dead-letter law on the Wisconsin statute books to the effect that no wage laborer had a legal right to make any contract whatsoever for his labor. The worker was thus so classified that legally he was nobody but a slave to be paid in full at least every two weeks, or he and his employer, too, would go to jail. He had no right to himself. The workmen got together on this, shamefacedly at first, but the get-together soon gained headway. The men formed in queues outside my study door and then several at a time would come in to my corner of the studio to ask for "pay," reckoning the sum due them on the overall contingent wage agreement, but those sums were stipulated as wages only if they stayed on until the time came when I could get the buildings into use. *Now* this unexpected demand struck in addition to the board, room, and weekly cash payments we had agreed upon and that I had managed to pay them so far when they could do a little better by living on the U.S.A. and doing no work at all.

Of course, I had already given these men all the money I had. There was no source from which I could then get more. There was no relief for me or mine. The agreement I made with them stated that I could get the sums stipulated only when I got use of the buildings. And unless I could get those buildings we started to build together for the apprentices, I could get no money to pay the balance of their stipulated wages. The buildings were only about half-done. But all the money I had already paid for labor and materials (some forty-five thousand dollars) was tied up in unfinished buildings as useless to me as to them.

The buildings now stopped growing altogether. Instead of getting suitable places in which to work in three years, it was to take seven, until we learned to build them ourselves for ourselves.

## RELIEF

Karl Jensen was secretary at the time, and Henry Klumb was right bower. They would be with me at these trying times as I sat over there in my little corner of the old Studio by the big stone fireplace. The gang (gangsterism was what they were in now) had formed this habit of lining up outside, and kept on day after day, for months, coming in to me for this money they were really only entitled to when they had kept their word as men and performed their part of the partnership agreement.

Well, I thought of making a test case of the foolish slave-law—one of those "three laws passed to cure one flaw." But it so appeared, after appealing to the State Industrial Commission (which, I

suspected, suspected me of exploiting labor), that under this law the laborer was made a slave, and that any attempt to make an agreement with him only laid us both liable to jail, just as they had been told. And although most of the men had gone on government relief at the time, that did not stop them from tearing the agreement down and pressing me for money, which they proceeded to do. This feature of relief where wages were due was not "legal" and I might have informed the authorities of the money coming to them in the circumstances, but I felt ashamed to knock the men out of anything they could get when they had so damned little. And I have always rather shied at any appeal to "authority" anyway. No good ever came of the policeman where I am concerned. So foolishly I made promises. We kept the promises just as well as we could, all the while looking and hoping for miracles.

The miracle would be "work"—buildings to build.

There was no building. Little money was coming in to go into so many hands, and without any, some of the men began to get ugly. But they would go away with a little. During many ensuing weeks there were outrageous scenes. One, Jones, a troublesome ringleader, attacked me in the studio one late afternoon—got his hands well on towards my throat when Henry jumped at him, yelling so loud with anger that Jones was scared into "taking his hands off Mr. Wright." Human nature in the bunch and in the raw was not unfamiliar to me. But I had not yet learned *to make no promises to anyone*.

Karl was now like a secret-service man, prolific in subterfuges and stallings—untiring and resourceful. But Karl was scared—really. In Karl's mind probably was an incident that took place in an obscure street in Madison where Jimmie had driven me in the Cord to get some tools for Fellowship work. Blackhand letters had kept coming from "a nice character" every now and then—after he saw us, as he soon did, carrying on our buildings under the Fellowship banner while he—a pre-Fellowship creditor—was not yet fully paid. Evidently he felt himself entitled to desperate measures. So one hangover from pre-Fellowship days, but now a situation, was an attack upon me in the street by an angry farmer—Indian blood in him.

## A COARSE INCIDENT

Business transacted, I was about to get back in the Cord when someone came up behind me, struck me violently several times on the back of the head. Partly stunned, I turned toward the Indian farmer, saw Jimmie some distance away on the sidewalk struggling violently, his arms pinned behind by the farmer's son brought along for the purpose. A planned, well-timed assault. I took this in at a glance; as I caught other blows in the face I turned toward the assassin. Instinct warned me not to strike the man. So I clinched with him and he went down into the gutter on his back. I held him down there until he said he had enough. But, in the split second when getting off him I stepped back to let him up, he kicked backward and up at me with his heavy boot, caught me on the bridge of the nose with his boot heel. I pinned him down again. Blood spurted all over him. This time I had both knees on his chest, his head still in the mud in the gutter. While holding him down there I deliberately aimed the torrent of blood with a broken nose full in his face. His own nose, his mouth too, clotted with blood, he gagged and gasped for breath. Jimmie, meantime frantic, was unable to break away and come to the rescue. The nice character was cursing and appealing to the several astonished bystanders. . . . "God damn it, men, take him off," he shrieked. "Take the man off me, for Christ's sake! He's killing me!" But I had not struck him. I was careful not to. I was only holding him down there in his own gutter in his own mud, painting him a gorgeous red until his features were clotted with my own blood. I let him up and he disappeared in the astonished crowd, which must have thought a murder was being committed.

I didn't know but that I was disfigured for life. Jimmie now free to drive, I got in the car. "Jimmie," I said, "my nose is broken. Drive me to the Clinic."

Everything I had on was saturated in front with what the doctor assured me was remarkably young blood, and it must have been so, for the break mended with astonishing rapidity, the per-

fectly good nose showing no trace. That boot was a symbol.

So was the nose.

Never mind, dearest. . . . I know what the moral is.

This adventure with "ideas plus work" as against "money plus authority" was thus ushered in. When I got home, bandaged, unknown to me, my boys (four of them) went out after their man, got into his house to find him there on the other side of the dining table, holding his wife in front of him for protection. Later he got a kitchen knife in his hand and the ugly fellow threatened them from behind his wife, she and the daughter meanwhile screaming imprecations and calling for the police. Of course, the police came and arrested the boys and the assassin. All were in the county jail when I heard of their well-meant sympathetic "strike" and got there to take a look at them behind bars. There they were, a nice-looking lot of boys, but a nice case for the District Attorney. Before I could get the young lads released, they spent a couple of nights in the county jail. But the nice character himself stayed in for quite some time to await trial. The case was finally settled in court, the nice character leaving the state. The boys were paying a fine of several hundred dollars. On the "installment plan," of course.

The Taliesin Fellowship had got off to a very bad start. Indeed.

## DEFENSE

There were subsequent approaches now, to a similar thing until it was suggested that I employ a bodyguard or, at least, carry a weapon. Both suggestions were ignored because I believe any man is safer unguarded and unarmed in almost any emergency.

The time that perfidious gang spent standing around trying to get money out of me in such equivocal circumstances would have paid them much more in work—ten times over—than the money they now declared I owed them. But there was no work for them to do if they would work, except that which I offered them. Were they enjoying this act, sitting pretty and being paid for it while they shook me down? A situation? Yes . . . and no.

I kept on faithfully handing out to them whatever I could get—collected dues, or fees if any, sums I might still borrow somewhere, somehow (it is amazing how gullible my friends have been)—something I might sell—but still on and in came the gang. I was frequently without a cent in my pocket. But I was used to that. And I grew to believe that if I parted with my last cent more would come. And more—a little—always did come. I got rid of that gang finally, one by one, though not until black-hand letters had been in my mail for a year or two. Anonymous always. And for many years afterward, some of the men would turn up still asking for forgotten unpaid balances. But I must say that a few were really decent, a half-dozen or more, and one of the tragedies of the situation thus created by my effort to put ideas-plus-work against money-plus-authority was that the more decent the men were, the longer they had to wait for money in the circumstances. Of course, ethically the men were not entitled to be paid. Morally I suppose they were. I don't know. I knew there could be no more building until we could do it ourselves.

We had boys now who could handle carpenter's tools, do good masonry, plastering. Painting was easy. They learned to weld and use woodworking, as well as road-building and farm machinery.

Just at this high moment in our mundane affairs the Employer's Mutual Insurance moved in on us: stepped up for money for past-due protection for these men which they hadn't needed. Well, enough is enough. Let's not labor the details but say that from the advent of "RELIEF" and its innumerable consequences we hung fire on construction, except for what the boys themselves could do, for nearly five years. Then my work in Architecture began to come back, and I could add my fees as an architect to apprenticeship tuitions, pay for the materials we needed, keep some expert workmen, and go ahead to salvage what we had already done. Even this was now in a state of decay. But altogether thirty-five thousand dollars a year would not keep us going for materials—and Fellowship upkeep. I had found that I had got into something that only a multimillionaire should have attempted. But, of course, none such would have

attempted anything of the kind. That I kept up in the circumstances and was not murdered, as well as still further "disgraced" as they say (ungraced would be nearer), was a surprise even to myself.

"I don't know whether you are a saint or a fool," said my lawyer. I said, "Is there a difference?" As I've looked around me I never could see that there was. Much.

But I had made a promise worth keeping. A promise to myself. When I remember my promise to my grand old Aunts—Nell and Jane, and my mother, I often wish they, and the Lloyd-Joneses, might look in now upon what we have accomplished these ten years past, and say—fool or saint! But who cares to be either one or the other even in the fond eyes of one's own family?

I know something better, but who wants to know?

## FELLOWSHIP MARRIAGES

The current of Fellowship life flowed on.

Davy and Kay decided to be married. There was nothing we could do about that, except help celebrate. Theirs would make the sixth marriage in the cause, or is it the course, of nature since the Fellowship began. First there were Rudolph and Betty, then Vernon and Margaret. Quite an interim, then the tragedy—Wes and our own Svetlana—that turned out so well.[8] Then came Hulda and Blaine, followed by Cornelia and Peter. Now it was Davy and Kay. We conceded to all appropriate wedding parties and probably there were six happy honeymoons.

There would be other weddings—the one certainty in co-education? Another couple already in sight: My God, is propinquity necessarily fatal? Or are Olgivanna and I too good an example to set before young bachelor girls and boys?

Now came the question of the weather—we who live in the country become weatherized if we are not weatherwise. We have learned that to run from it, hoping to escape from "bad" weather (of course, we mean bad for us) is to run into worse. I have learned that everywhere in the world the weather is unusual and unless one learns to "land on one foot," so to speak, concerning it, nothing ever happens as planned. So we planned the wedding with the weather. The weather turned out to be fine. And so did the wedding part of the wedding.

Davy and Kay were both favorites. Davy, a talented, manly chap; Kay, a natural-born charmer. (Let that be sufficient introduction.) Olgivanna laid things out. Inspired, she planned another Taliesin fair-weather wedding in the little old family chapel. (Truth Against the World ᛁ) It was Spring, and we threw open the windows and doors. The birds flew clear through the chapel without stopping, and the boys went out in the big truck, as they liked to go, after wayside decorations. The old chapel walls under the high wooden ceiling of the interior which I had put there when a boy, became a festive bower of sun-splashed branching green with masses of spring flowers arranged around the pulpit where the bridal couple would stand for the simple ceremony. The auctioning of the virgin in the Roman slave mart still looked down on it all from the wall behind the pulpit. A family heirloom, our old Steinway square piano (Father rapping my fingers into proper position every time I see it) stood beside the pulpit under the golden Bible laid there as centerpiece: Olgivanna set slender stacks and groups of tall white candles (Greek Orthodox childhood—she loves candles) here and there in the foliage to burn in the shadows; they seemed somewhat religious, nevertheless they were a good decoration too (even in religion isn't that always the primary motif?); Iovanna's golden harp brought in from home was placed to the rear for pervasive incidental music. She played Debussy softly while the ceremony was taking place.

The cooks for the week were standing back there in the rear room, ready in tall white caps and white jackets and eager to carve the feast. They had baked the traditional ring into the wedding cake. Olgivanna's best wine was bottled from her big cellar casks for this especial occasion. The milieu and the menu were quite festive enough and too beautiful, I should say, even for the wedding of some Russian Lady-of-the-Bedchamber.

Then, as had Kay and Davy (Davy's little sister alongside to carry the bride's bouquet), we all got dressed up. The wedding party climbed into the old Hillside carryall to be driven in state by the old farm-team over the hills to the place where the wedding bells had been ringing for at least half an hour. The bride's headdress got pretty well jolted on the way over because the tallered canopy of that old rig had been wreathed with wild grapevines, as a substitute for split covering, and they kept coming down and mixing in. Thus embowered, beflowered and bedizened, too, we, the happy Taliesin wedding party, reached the chapel gates (Truth Against the World) without further incident. Very like the other gay weddings, although, to me, each seemed nicer than the last.

The ceremony went off with a few tears from the next of kin, but mostly there were smiles all around. The feast so attractively spread, itself a superlative decoration, we soon reduced to a mere remnant of its former self as healths were drunk in our homely wine. And then (indiscretion) the boys—Edgar in the lead as usual—in the role of the local-devil, rushed the old chapel organ out into the chapel yard, set it down in the grassy space between the graves and the road. Shaded by the gigantic cottonwood that grew by the gate, the youngsters danced old-fashioned square dances with the bride and groom. Our Fellowship talent took turns playing the dance tunes on the chapel organ. Some friendly village folk attended, standing there against the dark evergreens to watch the gaiety, and also some of the old family group were there by another group of evergreens not seeming too happy, and I soon had reason to know they publicly disapproved of this gay use of the sacred chapel and family churchyard shrine. I noticed their expressions, and they were not good. A gathering storm.

Davy and Kay disappeared after a little of this—but soon a small airplane zoomed overhead and there they were above and off on wings, for a wedding journey the modern way. The bride's bouquet had been thrown to Gene. Upstretched hands waved happiness to the bride and groom as they sailed away.

Another Taliesin man and wife.

Thereupon followed a family scene in the chapel yard. The storm broke. Bitter reproaches were lavished upon Olgivanna and myself, the guilty promoters of this violation of sacred family traditions (which I had thought I fairly well understood—and represented, too). But no, such callous disregard of family dignity! Besides (and this was true) the chapel wasn't mine anyway. It belonged to the Lloyd-Jones family.

Something well worth keeping had thus, in a self-righteous moment, been ruthlessly spoiled. Well . . . the organ was hurried back as it had been hurried out, and put into its accustomed place none the worse for the dance tunes. The music and the harp were gathered in with the remnants of the guilty feast. The tall candles (a little shorter now) were blown out and all came away from the beautifully decorated Lloyd-Jones chapel depressed.

Where happy Fellowship had been in high spirits a few moments before, chagrin was in our hearts.

Hatred had struck at Joy. The Fellowship hurried away.

Evening shadows, no longer blue but long and lengthening, had about crossed the valley to the opposite hills. The slender marble obelisk in the chapel yard gleamed tall and white against the chapel evergreens: Ein Mam, the simple legend on one side; Ein Tad on another. This simple monument marked the graves of my old Welsh Lloyd-Jones grandparents. Around this central obelisk were the surrounding headstones marking the graves of five pioneer sons and five daughters. Further away but surrounding them were the graves of the grandchildren. About all the pioneer life of the beloved Hillside valley. They—the Lloyd-Jones family—were all there safely, according to clan tradition, gathered in around the family shrine: the white ancestral marble obelisk.

I sometimes sat there under the trees and wondered and remembered, partly because Taliesin's tragedy had sent its share of graves among those of this charmed old pioneer family circle. I went there now.

The sun had set. The afterglow was dimming in the sky as again I sat there on the grass to wonder and remember. And I remembered my dear aged mother dropping to her knees, reverently pressing her lips to the cold white marble monument, to Ein Mam and Ein Tad, as I was taking her by on my arm

to stand beside the open grave then waiting for her brother Jenkin: another faithful daughter soon to join the ancestral group. And I remembered standing alone, just over there by the abounding evergreen trees, beside another open grave, at this same fading time of day; a new grave I filled to the brink with flowers and then, joined by two nephews waiting at the chapel gate, filled in with solid earth—covering the earthmound with evergreen branches. Both were grass-covered mounds now, still waiting for their headstones.

## THE ALLEGORY THAT FAILED TO CONVINCE EVEN THE AUTHOR

Read aloud in the family sitting room: Olgivanna and Iovanna listening. The title of this Allegory is "Truth Against the World," and I began to read:

"As I sat disconsolate on a low grass-covered mound in the chapel yard, I wondered, and pondered and remembered as twilight deepened to dusk and darkened under the evergreens—the sacred chapel evergreens. They were sighing, stirring to and fro in the gentle breeze. As I carelessly listened I thought I heard . . . Was it possible? A human sigh, then the whisper of my name. Listening now intently, I heard nothing more. Wondering, I still listened . . . still remembering. Silence for a time. Then the gentle human whispering of intelligible words began, extending all around me. Intent as I peered into the dusk, pale blue wraiths were wreathing upward out of the family graves like pale blue mist rising all around me, but wreathing slowly; wraiths taking on familiar human shapes. A moment more of the gentle sighing and then the whispering of the pallid shapes began again, the wraiths now quite blue, flames swaying with the breezes to and fro, to and fro as the breezes rose and fell. The ghostly company all seeming to sit there on their own headstones."

*Olgivanna: Oh, Frank dear, oh, this is too much! This Thornton Wilder graveyard thing. He got away with it but you simply can't.*

*Listen . . .*

"Nearby a shade arose in shimmering silver, head

bent forward, hands folded in her lap. A whispered name—again—my own! The ghostly family conclave rising now, one and all and standing there together in one group, swayed gently to and fro, and as gently nodded and whispered together in the dusk. I leaned, looked and listened for the secrets of the dead."

*Olgivanna: Frank, you simply can't put this sentimentality into print. They'll say of you as they did of Turgenev's later and so sentimental work, "Age is breaking in on him."*
*Listen . . .*

"Again my name. The wraiths grew more luminous as the dark deepened and their whispered words grew more distinct there on the edge of the dark. In wonder—I whispered, "Mother . . . why are you here like this . . . my mother . . . surely *you* are a spirit in heaven!"

*Olgivanna: Terrible! Terrible! Oh, Frank, how can you be so foolish! Trite—you convince no one, not even yourself as I can see.*
*Listen . . .*

"A pause . . . 'A spirit in heaven, yes, my son: but spirits in heaven cast blue shadows here on the green earth as the golden sun casts the blue shadows of the green trees. Our shades may rise and go whenever the breezes blow if they but blow gently.' The family shades gently swaying with the breeze nodded assent. Again soft whispering as before."

*Olgivanna: Pah! Frank, you are gone, gone, gone. This must never get into print, that's all.*
*Listen . . .*

"The breezes for a moment grew stronger, and I listened to all the family in chorus. They were whispering, 'If they still love us, we may rise. When breezes gently blow our earthly shades may rise. Arise and go to those who love us.' In bewilderment I looked around more curious than amazed, still listening, still wondering, as the family shades, these flickering ghostly flames in lambent blue rest-

ing on their graves were again gently swaying and nodding assent. Silence for a time, but gently as ever, timed with the breeze in the trees, the gentle swaying to and fro, to and fro, went on."

"The nearest shade, the one in shimmering silver, now whispered, 'When gentle breezes fan your cheek or stir your hair, my son, it may be the gentle touch, the caress of those whom you love but have lost on earth, those who still love you in heaven . . . their caress may be upon your head.'"

*Olgivanna: Oh! Oh! Oh! this spiritualistic thing! Frank, how can you?*

"The dusk deepening to dark the breezes now dying down. Again silence. . . ."

*(Now sweet-sixteen) Iovanna: Why, Daddy, that is something I might have written, but not you. It's not like you at all. Please don't.*

*But an author is desperately determined.*
*Listen, World . . .*

"The evergreens were now hard to see, gently stirring still, faintly sighing as before—but the sighing and whispering grew more indistinct . . . 'When you live most, then we come. . . .' The shades still slowly bent their heads and still were swaying assent."

*Oh, Daddy—Daddy! That swaying business—it's just awful. AWFUL! can't you see?*
*Listen . . .*

"The silver shade gently lifted the semblance of a beloved venerable head, eyes hidden deep in shadow as, more faintly than ever, now that the breeze was dying, scarcely audible whispered . . . 'You will know what your beloved wants you to know, my son, if you turn to look at the symbol on the chapel gate.'"

*For heaven's sake, Frank! Do wake up! This is the end. I won't listen to another word. How awful!*
*Nearly done.*
*Listen . . .*

"The breeze now barely stirring the somber ever-greens, the shades are wreathing downward into their own graves, each swaying gently and as they grew to resemble the family ones so long beloved, so now as slowly, surely sinking, wreathing away . . . vanishing as dew vanishes from the grass into nightly mist. As, utterly, all was still."

*A lurid howl from Baby Brandoch, hitherto peace-fully laying on the floor.⁹ Svetlana rushes to pick him up: Gosh, Daddy Frank, what are you up to? If it's all like the little I overheard—well, I just don't see how Mother and Iovanna stand it.*

*Listen, all of you! The idea at least is good. . . .*

"It was now dark, the wind so dreaded by ghostly shades was rising as the moon arose. I got up and went out by the way I came in. Wondering still and remembering, I looked back at the gate. There it was in stone . . . Truth Against the World, the revered, ancient Druid symbol old Timothy had carved there on the gatepost for the Lloyd-Joneses, those whose 'shades' had just wreathed upward for a ghostly gathering of the whispering clan and gone away. Had they come to give their verdict?

"Strange . . . a new meaning . . . Why had I not seen it so before? . . . The downward rays of the sun were Joy! Joy set against and dispelling the mean hatreds that were all the sorrows of this world.

"That then was what the old Druids knew? Was that what the family ghosts flickering in lam-bent blue there above the graves in the graveyard had been trying to whisper to me? 'The truth to set against the woes of this world is Joy!'

"Joy it is that elevates and transfigures Life."

*Olgivanna in despair: Pah! And you think you have discovered something? Why, the old Greeks all knew that. Everybody knows it. And here you are just picking it up! Oh, Frank, my dear, throw it away and forget it. Just stick to Architecture. You are safe there.*

Of course, my girls were right. They always are! So we all laughed and I threw the thing away. My in-nocent little excursion into "writing" was one more blasted hope.

## THE MORAL

And I here admit that like all truth, this one—the ancient Druid symbol ⚡ which the Lloyd-Jones family adopted as its own is dangerous because so few of us ever learn here on earth to know the dif-ference between Joy and Pleasure.¹⁰ The dead know. When will the Living learn?

Sentimentality is not sentiment, although if I had the skill to make the Allegory stand, sentimen-tality might have persuaded the more foolish among you otherwise. And Selfhood is not selfishness, though it is often hard for any but a Lloyd-Jones to know when the one is eating up the other. No, Joy is not pleasure. And the abuse of the good is so often taken for the good itself, that symbols are no longer good themselves.

That is truth.

And what can American wagery know of Joy when it is working so desperately hard and overtime in order to live for pleasure?

## THE FOUR SEASONS IN FOUR VERSES

Somewhat akin to the unconvincing Allegory, here is an early study in aspirates: sybillant verses to be whispered. My mother came over when she read "the study" and said gravely, "My boy, when a young man starts versifying it is a sign." She didn't say a sign of deterioration, but I knew.

This early abstraction and design in the fash-ioning of a verse to render the movement of the subject—the Breeze—into its own rhythm, starting slowly, enlivening and dying down, belongs to the same period as the Work-Song. Both, as you see, are experiments in straight-line or streamlined de-sign that really belong on the drawing board be-cause both are abstract pattern in line and color. Unfamiliar at least, and unlikely in words, although Edgar Allan Poe seemed often to come pretty close.

Emphasize the aspirates a little.

> *Slender grows the tender mesh of silken threads
> and films of green,
> Sunbeams glimmer through between the leaves in
> nestling sheen,
> Gently wavering and fluttering like
> butterfliesawing,*

*As in melody the raiment of the Spring . . .*
*Stirs and is still.*

*Languid vapors veil in torpid heat the deep of*
  *azure,*
*Lazy insects drone in drowsy bloom and glow of*
  *verdure,*
*Faintly uttering the gutturals of Summer's lush*
  *o'errun,*
*As in sultry ease the ripe of Summer's sun . . .*
*Stirs and is still.*
*Gleaming crystal overarches seas of gilded leaves,*
*Flaming vine entwines the flowing oak, and*
  *deftly weaves*
*Rustling radiance in fashioning of iridescence fair,*
*As with transient heat the rhythmic Autumn*
  *air . . .*
*Stirs and is still.*

*The frozen earth in starry night lies waiting*
  *tense and proud,*
*Glistening moonbeams shadow askance her*
  *glittering shroud,*
*Frail with frost the breath of life wreathes and*
  *rises to a shrine,*
*As the dying breeze, adream in Wintry pine . . .*
*Stirs and is still.*[11]

Meantime the buildings grew. They were worthy of what they cost us all from first to last. And there were many compensations down the line. Tough as the going mostly was, there was continual accomplishment. Both inside and outside, this thing we wanted most, a suitable, characteristic place to work and play in, grew in integrity, beauty and usefulness, kept on growing up on the hillside at "Hillside" as though it belonged there. It did belong there. We saw now ideas familiar on paper becoming useful and beautiful features of life and important effects that stood on the ground and would live long.

We worked, we sang, we played with the enthusiasm of youth undiminished. Love's creative labor well spent.

## OUR GOODTIME PLAYHOUSE

For one thing, we got our little recreation room—a

happy thing—(call it the Playhouse for lack of a better name) with the Bechstein concert grand below, and above in the balcony a fine cinema (35-mm. equipment). Operation began shortly after "Relief" had thus laid *us* in the gutter and on *our* back. That playroom was fun (on the installment plan, too—three years to pay for the piano, seven to pay for the equipment, etc., etc., etc.).

Originally we cut up the old Hillside Home School gymnasium and rearranged it into a bright nightspot in Fellowship life. Then we changed it and cut it open more. Then we changed it some more by deepening it. Ever since we have continued changing it here and there and lavishing upon it all our scheming skill to make the great oak-roofed and oak-walled room a lovely, likely place to be expectant in: sympathetic to sound as a viol.

For our events we combed the available supply of the best foreign films in the world as well as our native products.

The education I myself have received from that source alone would justify the Playhouse.

And I may as well confess right here that it appears to me that, after all has been done and said, it is my own education that the Taliesin Fellowship has undertaken—much more so than I have undertaken that of incidental Fellowships.

An amazing additional wealth of experience and broad range of travel is stored up in me, already the much-traveled traveler, as the result of those films. It would be impossible to travel about the world and see for one's self as deeply or richly the life of the strange parts of the world as the cinema in the hands of great writers and good directors working with the historic resources of the various great nations that have gathered it can now present it.

We have had from Austria and Germany thirty-three splendid features; from China, three; from Czechoslovakia, one; England, forty-four; France, fifty-nine; Ireland, two; Japan, three; Mexico, three; Norway, one; Russia, seventy-two; Sweden, two; Spain, two; and the United States, forty-four. To date a total of two hundred and sixty-nine top films of the world.

The stage curtains were the first craft-work of the

Fellowship—rectilinear, brilliant, colored-felt abstractions (I made the design) applied to a neutral coarse cotton fabric. We bled the silver screen (the screen is about eight by ten feet). The screen is luminous white instead of beaded silver.

We let the sound track play through on a red felt band about one foot wide, up and down on the left side of the picture. Straight-line sound patterns were there in light to harmonize the moving picture with our characteristic type of design.

We indulged in some interesting experiments in sound—reflexes ending up with the loud-speakers beneath the stage pointing toward the rear wall of the recess in which the screen stood. Sound to permeate the house instead of hitting hard on the ear. From this backboard wall, the sound—now a reflex—spread to the audience. Integral sound. Many guests having seen the films elsewhere which they now happened to see in our Playhouse would say they enjoyed them as though they were seeing them for the first time, discovering more in them than they had ever thought was there.

Incorporated in the Playhouse:

1. Reflex seating arrangement instead of seating on centerline with eyes directly front.

2. The stage, part of the audience room.

3. Bled screen for cinema.

4. The sound track playing through beside the picture on a red band. A straight-line decoration in light, harmonizing the picture with the house.

5. Electric lighting without glass.

6. Sound magnifiers beneath stage floor—directed against rear wood wall of stage—sound thus becoming part of the room instead of directed at the ear.

7. A dais for quartet, one for the piano, and seating for choir, arranged and related sympathetically to the stage at one side—instead of pit in front of the stage.

8. A real "Foyer"—a fireplace in the Playhouse itself. The use of architectural screens to reproportion the room and provide service for feasts and cloakroom space.

9. The top of the seat-ranks a broad ledge on which colorful table service is arranged for ear-and-eye feasts. Good interior decoration.

The whole construction in native oak aside from the supporting walls is stained dark, with a brilliant play of polychrome against the dark throughout.

## SNATCHING VICTORY FROM THE JAWS OF DEFEAT

Our special act: this "snatching victory from the jaws of defeat."

We had quite a time getting seated in this Playhouse of ours. After looking about a good deal and being refused often, we had finally decided on some movable metal chairs manufactured in Elgin, Illinois. About eight hundred dollars for about the one hundred chairs we needed. We accepted the terms offered. But nothing happened. The Company, after agreeing to deliver, refused to deliver, demanding the never-to-be-forgotten "cash." We had waited some weeks in blissful ignorance of this—setting our opening date to correspond with promised delivery. But the characteristic blow fell. So, what to do? Eight hundred wasn't much, but we couldn't spare eighty dollars at the time. We might have expected it by now; it had blocked us ad libitum—ad nauseam. But strangely, hope does spring eternal in the Taliesin breast—we still believed in Santa Claus. Though in the toils of the System, we have never yet learned how to lose hope.

Thus driven to pay for the trifle which was not trifling, in order to open on time we again sat down at the drawing boards to see what we could do with green oak boards, 1" × 9", a keg of nails, and a few screws. We evolved a system of bench seating, more appropriate than the coveted Elgin metal product. Far more interesting in character. Rough green lumber was all we had to put into it, but we fitted it all together into a new idea—the comfortable reflex seating arrangement you may see there now—where seating an audience was concerned. The girls cut up cotton bed-pads and tripled them to pad the seats and backs of the benches, which had a broad top rail to hold the supper service. We found some cheap red denim (ten cents) to cover the cushions, sewed colored cords to the covers, and tied them on to the seats. And we had seating.

Pretty hard, but not impossible if the play was really good. Most always it was.

But the Playhouse was becoming charming

entertainment in itself—entertainment that could never fail. The magic of something new and interesting appeared among us again "to snatch victory from the jaws of defeat."

I had wanted a theatre of my own ever since when, as a boy, I read of Wilhelm Meister's puppet-theatre in the attic of the house Goethe designed for him. Here it was—far beyond Wilhelm Meister's or any Goethe himself could have designed. This surely counted us *one?*

Every time we were cut off from an unexpected source of "cash-and-carry" supply, we came up smiling, really better off for the rebuff because of the demand upon our own resourceful inspiration. Of course the middlemen were all hanging by their eyebrows from sky-hooks. Their bosses were taking no chances.

Nevertheless we found generous cooperation enough so that we are not yet convinced that no one wants to go into partnership with us. We thought we were a good thing at a time when all was dead or dying. We are surer than ever now, now that dead and dying are actually here all around us and it is war in place of economic distress.

## REST FOR THE WICKED

We kept on trying to get and give cooperation whenever need for accommodation appeared, as it did, constantly. But always the risks seemed too great to those who could help us on our way if they would. So far as they went, our cause was beside their mark. It never could "pay." And (seriously) why should the System want to compromise itself by helping us anyway? What interest to the "make" of the middleman were we, or was anything whatever, if there was no cash profit in "the deal"? They had to live. So they said. So their discounts were naturally not only very few but very suspicious.

Help was spaced far apart on centers in those equivocal trying days. We might say that in the early days help was invisible. Or in reverse.

I may as well confess, at this point, however, that I was certain financial help from some source *would* appear when we really got something going to show the nature of the cultural effort to which we were committed. But we never got to the point where I was ready to show what we had done and ask anybody for financial help. We are not there yet. So all the friendly help we've had has been small and haphazard; you might say, accidental, but none the less appreciated on that account. The more welcome for that, I should say. I should like to tell the stories of several such. And some day I will write them.

I am no longer so sanguine where substantial help is concerned. This effort of ours is far too individual to attract it. No nameplates of donors nor much glory in substantial giving to us. And I guess that we must make ourselves or break. Only the Institution can get help. And we don't want to be an Institution. Neither are we "all dressed up and no place to go."

We are not much dressed up at all.

In many desirable ways we would like to be. And yet, in many respects our self-respecting poverty stands as itself by itself for the thing it is—the open countenance of principle: something out of our own soil belonging to our own time and place, naturally.

It is crude as the bark on a tree.

But the tree itself is there—under the bark the branches are springing, the green leaves spreading to the light—as the whole endeavor grows slowly, painfully but happily according to the true principles within it.

We believe that we have planted a fruit tree and that our cultivation will bring the tree into bearing.

There is no source of inspiration the West won't copy. In this substitution of experienced example and exemplar experience that we call master and apprentice, we have met certain characteristic traits of character, certain liabilities as well as assets. And while we believe we are fundamentally democratic, we are as anti-"cash-and-carry" as we are anti-war.

Here are some of our principal liabilities and, in general, they would be those of a true democracy:

When we were building Edgar Kaufman's house at Bear Run, I had one of my enthusiastic, faithful boys, Bob, "Little Sunshine," on it on the usual apprentice arrangement made with every client. "Take him away," said E. J. in despair at an early stage of the proceedings. "His blunders will cost me money. Take him away!"

"No, E. J.," I said, "not yet. Be patient. He may be, and he is, costing us both a little money, but not much. You gave me a thousand dollars to help make the models of Broadacre City. Well, it's only fair for you to pay your small share of the education of these young fellows—America's future architects. It is fair, if for no other reason than just because they are giving you and me, where your opus is concerned, something no money can buy: an alive and enthusiastic interest in our work and the eager cooperation that goes with it too, as well as they can. None of them are fools. I know it is an intangible I am talking about. I know. But your building will come out right-side up in the end, and you'll have something in the way of a building experience as well as a building that money could never pay for. And I assure you that the building won't have cost you as much either as it would have cost you were the whole thing 'regular.'"

"All right," said E. J., but unconvinced (he is a good business man as well as a good fellow, too). "We'll see." And now, to tell the truth to E. J. (and the same goes to all my clients in this struggle for superior character and integrity in building), the experienced professional would be just as much or more at sea in the way of doing things where I am concerned. And the experienced professional would be much harder to inform and convince of his error in trying the new way than my amateurs would be. He would make mistakes and he would stick to them to save his face, where one of my boys would say, "Sure, how stupid of me—I see it all now." The boys did add a lively human interest element all down the line, on every house we built. For better and some for worse. Sometimes prospective clients coming to see the work on a new building and being shown about by the boy would like him so much they would give their work to the boy!

A system was then in force allowing a Fellow to do work with his name on the plans but all designs and details to be submitted to me for approval. The same fee, ten per cent, to be charged; divided one-third to apprentice, one-third to cover the cost of plans made by the Fellowship, and one-third left in the Fellowship for it to grow up on. This was a mistake from every standpoint as I will explain in a later chapter. While authentic originals are available, why devote the resources of the Fellowship to warmed-up or warmed-over amateur productions, especially as they seemed to destroy the Fellowship rather than build it up? More on this subject later.

And it is only fair to say that on all the buildings I have built with the Fellowship alongside (there are some thirty-five or -six or -seven such buildings now), from the very first I have found quicker comprehension and more intelligent faithful cooperation, counting in all the aggravating dropping of stitches from first to last, than I ever got out of "experienced" professionals at any time. This would not apply were we doing the standard thing done by the regular architects for which the channels are all cut. I well know that. But once we do go afield from the beaten track, not for novelty—no—but for the necessarily different because it *is the better thing,* we (my clients and myself) are better off (the time limit aside) with the honest amateur than we could ever be with the conventional "expert" in the rut. The expert is usually a man who has stopped thinking and so is perfectly able to be utterly wrong for at least the rest of his lifetime. He has made up his mind, not upon principle, but upon expedient practice. So he is quite likely to be, himself, a rule of thumb already out of date where we are concerned.

As a matter of fact, during the rational pioneering of these past forty-five years, I have developed a technique of my own—still flexible—therefore still growing with each new experience, which means each new building we build. Not only is it not probable that "the practical man of experience" would be likely to grasp and apply it: he *wouldn't* do it if he could. But in all frankness, let me say he couldn't do it without more study than he can afford to give it, and on the way that study means more failures. Failures which would be more numerous, more difficult to remedy and as much more costly to apply as he was certain of his experience. Saving his face would be more costly to my clients, therefore, than the quickly corrected blunders of

Edgar J. Kaufmann House, "Fallingwater," Mill Run, Pennsylvania. 1938. Under construction. FLLW Fdn FA#3602.0019

my amateurs. But I realize that my proximity to the work done is more than ever essential. That is not likely soon to change except as I have in time trained good builders myself. The Fellowship should now have several such, and will soon have more like Harold Turner and Ben Wiltscheck. We have a score of boys though, who could already build one of our houses and build it well if backed by capital.

But the time when we can thus build our own buildings, milling our own materials, is not yet.

We are looking forward to it, however.

No more drawing-board architects if I can help it, contractors trying to build buildings they know nothing about.

To bear me out, about all my clients have testified to the joy and satisfaction they get from their own particular building, believing theirs to be the best house I have built, as indeed it is for them. Their experience with the sincere try for the organic in character—the honest experiment made in their behalf—has often opened a new world to and for them.

Were it not likely to be misleading—looking like boasting, or a plug—I should like to introduce here letters from many, even from most all of the clients, testifying to that as a fact. And my clients are a cross-section of the distinctly better type of American—I should say Usonian, to be specific—most of them with an esthetic sense of their own, many of them artistic, accomplished, and most of them traveled. They have sometimes learned about us from abroad.

We seldom get the real provincials. The provincial doesn't dare trust his own judgment as to cultural causes and effects. If he has been abroad, his education such as it is, usually confirms his instinctive eclecticism. He is the country's characteristic cultural coward.

The houses we build are usually enjoyed by people who are rich in other things than money. It seems as though the appreciation of our work is inversely proportioned to the financial standing of the person involved.

But sometimes when Usonian houses are very far away and proximity to the work therefore is not possible, after work is "practically complete," we have had to go back to the opus as a body of workmen ourselves to straighten out mistakes, meantime perhaps bettering the original, correcting faulty workmanship and materials in order to save the owner harmless trouble and generally establish or reestablish what was originally intended but perhaps in this or that particular instance, by the owner's interference, unhappily lost in execution. We do this. And we ought to have and will soon have a Fellowship follow-up group organized to help furnish and use the house after it is done, in the style intended, with the ease, grace and distinction which the new forms make possible. We are already doing this, often.

Our Fellowship method grows steadily more effective as we go along, until I am assured by my clients, comparing their own costs with the known costs of neighboring buildings, that one of our operations will result in more actual space accommodation and greater material advantages in every way than the more "regular" houses much more easily had, that abound around them. What style and distinction our buildings possess is therefore "thrown in." "No charge." But it is also only fair to say that it is more difficult to find ways and means to get our houses built.

The distinction of our buildings (the countenance of principle will stand out in any crowd) is inevitable. It marks them and makes them, should they fail at any point—temporarily leak or show defects and especially should they exceed expected costs—immediately become a common mark for the envious skeptic. Most of the skeptics are architects. Or friends and neighbors who live in fashionable homes.

We are yet, thanks to our lucky star, unfashionable.

Our faults are those, not of a common system but of an independently growing thing: a challenge to Fashion. But our faults are corrected much more easily than the faults stock-and-shop would be sure to perpetrate. Because every problem carries within itself its own solution, and, because we make the buildings what they are, thoroughbred, we are perfectly competent to cure evils and rectify errors as

they arise. We have the secrets conferred by our experience with the type we originate.

Any experiment we make is not on our part a seeking for novelty—but is sincerely and intelligently an experiment made in the client's own interest. Cure and correction are a matter of pride with us because, in a peculiarly intimate sense, every building we build is not only the client's own, but also *our* own. We must and will see that that building becomes what we intended it to be or we would soon be ashamed to look ourselves in the face. And since the building is always a public mark, the building must be maintained as intended even if we have to help. It is sometimes a matter of enough money of our own to be able to do this. But we get the money eventually. And no client who has stood by us has yet been let down. It is also only fair to say that most all of them have not let us down either. Many of them have taken a lot that seemed at the time beside the mark in order to get what they were certain was coming, glad to stand by the principles we practice, principles in which they as firmly and faithfully believe as we do.

Their investment in the building is dated some

**Edgar J. Kaufmann House, "Fallingwater," Mill Run, Pennsylvania. 1938. Under construction.** FLLW Fdn FA#3602.0006

**Taliesin West, Scottsdale, Arizona. 1939. Under construction.** FLLW Fdn FA#3803.0104

years ahead (say, ten years) and increases in value with time because our buildings cannot go out of fashion. They are not and never will be dated.

## THE CONQUEST OF THE DESERT

TALIESIN WEST is a look over the rim of the world. As a name for our far-western desert camp we arrived at it after many more romantic names were set up and knocked down. The circumstances were so picturesque that names ran wild—so we settled sensibly to the one we already had.

To live indoors with the Fellowship during a Northern winter would be hard on the Fellowship and hard on us. We are an outdoor outfit; besides it costs thirty-five hundred dollars to heat all our buildings at Taliesin, so it is cheaper to move Southwest. The trek across continent began November 1933. Each trek was an event of the first magnitude. The Fellowship's annual hegira with sleeping bags and camping-outfit, big canvas-covered truck, cars and trailers for thirty-five, *was* an event even in Fellowship life. To conquer the desert we had first to conquer the intervening two thousand miles in cold weather. The first several years we stayed at Dr. Chandler's hacienda at Chandler, Arizona.[12] Very happy there, too, but crazy to build for ourselves.

We were growing in proficiency.

A major rule in the Fellowship has always been "do something while resting." So we preferred to build something while on vacation. I was earning something again, now, as an architect, and we could get materials. But first we had to settle on a site. By this time that vast desert region, Silence and Beauty, was as familiar to us as our part of Wisconsin. There was plenty of room and plenty of superb sites, high or low—open or sequestered. Every Sunday, for a season, we swept here and there on picnics. With sleeping bags we went to and fro like the possessed from one famous place to another. Finally I learned of a site twenty-six miles from Phoenix, across the desert of the vast Paradise Valley. On up to a great mesa in the mountains. On the mesa just below McDowell Peak we stopped, turned, and looked around. The top of the world!

Magnificent—beyond words to describe! Splendid mystic desert vegetation, but what a bad road. The only trail crossing the great wash of Paradise Valley, the broad wash to the Verde River was this miserable G—d—Hell of a road that that trail across the desert was in wet weather, so we found. And there was a rainy season until later it got to raining all the time.

But roads can be improved. The site could not be. The land could be bought from Stephen Pool at the Government Land Office. Pool said he was keeping it for some fellow (he said "fool") who would fall in love with it and "do something with it." We got about eight hundred acres together finally, part pur-

**Previous pages: Taliesin West, Scottsdale, Arizona. 1938. Clearing the ground for construction.** FLLW Fdn FA#3803.0266

**Taliesin West, Scottsdale, Arizona. 1939. Under construction.** FLLW Fdn FA#3803.0102

chase, part lease. Next year we began to "do something with it." We made the plans and were all ready.

We knew about what thirty apprentices, our little family alongside, needed—one of the things was "room."

There was lots of room so we took it and didn't have to ask anything or anybody to move over. The plans were inspired by the character and beauty of that wonderful site. Just imagine what it would be like on top of the world looking over the universe at sunrise or at sunset with clear sky in between. Light and air bathing all the worlds of creation in all the color there ever was—all the shapes and outlines ever devised—neither let nor hindrance to imagination—nothing to imagine—all beyond the reach of the finite mind. Well, that was our place on the mesa and our buildings had to fit in. It was a new world to us and cleared the slate of the pastoral loveliness of our place in Southern Wisconsin. Instead came an esthetic, even ascetic, idealization of space, of breadth and height and of strange firm forms, a sweep that was a spiritual cathartic for Time if indeed Time continued to exist.

The imagination of the mind of man is an awesome thing to contemplate. Sight comes and goes in it as from an original source, illuminating life with involuntary light as flashes of lightning light up the landscape.

The Desert seems vast but the seeming is nothing compared to the reality.

But for the designing of our buildings certain forms abounded. There were simple characteristic silhouettes to go by, tremendous drifts and heaps of sunburned desert rocks were nearby to be used. We got it all together with the landscape—where God is all and man is nought—as a more permanent extension of "Ocatilla," the first canvas-topped desert camp out of Architecture by youthful enthusiasm for posterity to ponder.

Superlatives are exhausting and usually a bore—but we lived, moved, and had our being in superlatives for years. And we were never bored.

From first to last, hundreds of cords of stone, carloads of cement, carloads of redwood, acres of stout white canvas doubled over wood frames four feet by eight feet. For overhead balconies, terraces, and extended decks we devised a light canvas-covered redwood framework resting upon massive stone masonry that belonged to the mountain slopes all around. On a fair day when the white tops and side flaps were flung open the desert air and the birds flew clear through. There was a belfry and there was a big bell. There were gardens. One great prow running out onto the Mesa overlooking the world, a triangular pool nesting in it—another garden sequestered for quiet with another plunge-pool with water raining down from the wall in one corner of it.

There were play-courts for the boys, spacious rooms for them, and there were pleasant guest-quarters on a wide upper deck overlooking the garden and the Mesa.

Said the local wise-man, "No water on that side of the valley—waste of money to try."

But we tried and got wonderful water at 486 feet—85 degrees when it emerged at the pool. All went forward pretty much as usual, etc., etc., only on a less inhibited scale and upon the most marvelous site on earth.

Our Arizona camp is something one can't describe and just doesn't care to talk much about. Something like God in that respect?

And how our boys worked! Talk about hardening up for a soldier. Why, that bunch of lads could make any soldier look like a stick! They weren't killing anything either, except a rattlesnake, a tarantula, or a scorpion now and then as the season grew warmer.

No, they weren't killing anything: stripped to a pair of shorts they were just getting something born, that's all, but as excited about the birth as the soldier is in his V's when they come through. More so if my observation counts.

The reward came.

Olgivanna said the whole opus looked like something we had been excavating, not building.

That desert camp belonged to the desert as though it had stood there for centuries. And also built into Taliesin West is the best in the strong young lives of about thirty young men and women for their winter seasons of about seven years. Some local labor went in too, but not much. And the constant supervision of an architect—myself, Olgivanna inspiring and working with us all, working as hard as I—living a full life, too full, meanwhile.

The difficulty was for us that the place had to be lived in while it was being built.

We were sometimes marooned for five days at a time. The desert devils would swirl sand all over us when it was dry. We could see whole thunderstorms hanging below us over the valley, see the winds rushing the clouds toward us, and we would get the camp ready as though we were at its mercy out on a ship at sea. At times on the way to and from Phoenix for supplies I would sit in the car, Olgivanna by my side, when my feet were on the brakes under water up to my knees.

The Masselinks coming to visit their son were lost in the desert water-waste overnight, and water was up to everybody's knees until the afternoon of the next day. The son in an attempted rescue was almost carried away.

Frequently visitors trying to see us were nearly drowned in the desert.

Hardships toward the latter end of the great experiment were almost more than flesh and blood could bear. Olgivanna and I, living in the midst of a rushing building operation for seven years, began to wear down.

Otherwise our Fellowship life went on much the same, Taliesin or Taliesin West—except that the conspiracy of Time and Money was a little less against us.

Once you get the desert in your blood—look on the map of Arizona Highways for Taliesin West.

N.B. I've forgotten to speak of our desert playhouse: a "kiva," solid masonry inside and outside, with a sunken fireplace and an outside hangar for our cinema to peep in through the thick stone wall, arrangements for feasting and music. A triumph of imagination by way of simple form and limited space in the heart of a great cubical masonry block.

## FELLOWSHIP LIABILITIES OR DEMOCRATIC BACK DRAG

I have said they would not be peculiar to us but would be those common to Democracy.

### I. THE SERVANT MIND

The servant mind is a menace to us as it is a menace to Democracy. And it is a natural inheritance of the melting pot. It comes from the lower ranks of society and permeates the upper ranks to destroy them—the drag of innate servility on the struggle for independence: the congenital curse put upon the true or innate aristocracy we call Democracy, placed there by feudal servility. The servant mind is inbred and not likely to be cast off except as it is unbred.

For instance: a well-to-do country gentleman was visited by a friend. The gentleman's valet met the guest, showed him to his room, meantime complaining of his master. In small invidious ways he deprecated him until the exasperated friend, who was a true friend, said:

"Well, Michel, if you don't like the way your master treats you, why don't you leave him? Go somewhere else . . ."

"Oh," said the valet, "no, it's all right. I gets even. I spits in his coffee every morning."

Now there are as many variations and modifications of that cup of coffee as there are people and circumstances. A general example of what I mean by "the servant mind."

And, of course, since the freedom of Fellowship is impossible except on terms of self-respect and equality—some form of kick-back or treachery is the inevitable consequence of the servant mind, should it get into our midst, which is more and more unlikely.

## II. THE INFERIORITY COMPLEX

Not far removed from the servant mind, probably descended from it in some way, is this troublesome inferiority complex. But it is even more dangerous to Fellowship than the servant mind because it is harder to diagnose and deal with. It is something that will make a young fellow ashamed to pick up a walking stick dropped by an elderly man, or a companion, for fear of seeming servile; something in the boy that makes him bad-mannered and awkward in fear of his own inherent servility. And the fear makes him look as he is—cheap. That same thing prevents him from ever earning the title gentleman, and stands in the way of his ever becoming a truly manly man. We have observed it sometimes in the Fellowship in the more feminine types of young men. But the girls are not entirely exempt. In them it may stem from their attempt to throw off the domination by the male.

Of course, it is only a man who believes in himself that can ever give loyalty to an idea or be faithful to the master of one, or to one who is master of the idea.

In true apprenticeship there must be an interchange between the two which puts them into a trust with one another.

So the inferiority complex is dangerous to us.

It cannot safely be put upon a footing of equality in comradeship nor, because it cannot trust itself, is its loyalty to masterhood or to mastership to be trusted.

Always a questionable type.

Judas was probably the better sort of the type in question who sought to save his Master from himself, seeing his Master as he (Judas) saw himself. The consequences of discipleship where the complex is concerned are always dangerous.

The inferiority complex shows itself most in unnecessary unbecoming self-assertion—trying hard to make itself believe what it wants others to believe: that it is not inferior. It is the opposite of modesty and protests too much always because it wants too much so much, and fears it has too little. Nothing is more damaging to Fellowship or harder to root out, because, for one thing, it is a hangover of the umbilical cord. For another, it is the same inevitable subjective association of ideas that goes back to aristocracy not natural but false, false because hereditary.

Dr. Spivey (the hero of Florida Southern College) once said to me that the boys who came in to work their way through college were usually the malcontents, and eventually the troublemakers. Instead of gratitude for the privilege extended to them, they themselves were suspicious that they were not in the same category as the paying students, and fancied slights, soon or late, developed resentment.

The Fellowship has found that the less a boy or girl actually has had in life before coming in to the Fellowship, the more supersensitive to fancied slights or resemblances to servitude he is.

But there is something deeper than that, undermining good fellowship, that tries to set up artificial barriers in order to "even up" the score, something not openly acknowledged even to itself. Perhaps the same thing happens that happens when an article is "marked down" for sale. What we get cheap we seldom value except as something cheap.

## III. THE UMBILICAL CORD

The grown-up child seldom casts it entirely off—especially the unregenerate. Usually it is the sentimental tie-back to prejudices of the former generation: the "hold-back" of the parent who wants to see the child grow up, but suspects and dreads the consequences of enlightenment. The Father who was a conservative fears for the son who is becoming a radical. Mother instinctively hovers over her young, perhaps in the position of a hen who has hatched out a duck. Or Father is the cock who has fathered a feather. The cord drags after the offspring or coils about its neck, preventing, so far as it can, the free action of the free spirit of the child. Because, if affectionate and dutiful, the child is sentimental where Mother (sometimes Father, too) is concerned; the cord hurts them, and drags the boy or girl back if going too far or too fast ahead. So the "cord" is no asset to Fellowship. And the cure for it is always tragic. When the Spirit-parent encounters the flesh-and-blood or carnal parent, there is usually an uneasy feeling on the part of the carnal parent that parental authority is getting a bad break or being betrayed, his offspring being led astray. Usually the parents feel that the child's individuality is being sacrificed. He is being misled. Certainly the only place a young mind can or should be led when the umbilical cord remains around the neck is *"astray."*

## IV. THE PIN-FEATHER EGO
Worthless cargo. But the Fellowship falls heir to it not so much in the refugees from Education as those who come to Taliesin after four, five, or six years of fairly successful college life. These "degree" men, even more than those who break with college, come to us with a habituated mind and a tightly strung nervous system to boot. Characteristic always is premature (which is immature) criticism. On a moment's notice, categorical wisdom! The premise and the thesis. Always the stock-and-shop point of view. Disjecta membra on every subject ever catalogued. The damage thus done to Youth by the classroom authority is incalculable. This type is the Expert in embryo.

It is living what life it has on information but is never really able to learn.

Young men living the vicarious life of the devotee vicar, they are the individuals who try to escape the herd by herding.

By way of the mere association of ideas we call wishful thinking, it is easy for most of us to make ourselves believe what we want to believe. For the young man educated far beyond his capacity, it is possible to erect a complete synthetic "ivory tower" and live there in it if his experience stands still long enough to allow him to get into it. But in certain circumstances in Urbania such intellectualism does stand up. I have seen it so stand, as potato sprouts do on potatoes in a dark cellar. This vicarious character is a prematurity and eventually an utter emasculation of soul where the manly ego should be. It is the result of Education that is destined and designed to die on the vine. "Designed mis-education." But meantime it has occasionally been a Fellowship stumbling block. Time, often months, sometimes years, must be given the victim in which to relax before he becomes sufficiently receptive either to perceive or acknowledge the mastery he would meantime subconsciously emulate. Nothing can be put into hands self-conscious nervous tension has shut so tight. When the hands are open, palms upward, voluntarily held out together in the dignity of true humility, then is the time to give without fear of wasting the giver and what is given.

## V. THE EVER WOMANLY
The woman always wins.

This, the Eternal Feminine, is a Fellowship problem of no mean dimensions: the one we have not yet solved and may never solve so long as we hold to our co-educational ideal. The woman always wins. This is her civilization, her day, and her hour. When left to her choice in our country she dresses her figure to emulate the broadshouldered style of the male, and her sons grow more and more to resemble the silhouettes of her own figure. The figures of the sons of their mothers and the daughters of their fathers are thus growing more and more to resemble each other, and they trade characteristics with disconcerting, increasing frequency.

Woman is steadily winning away the Fellowship.

She can turn a Fellowship into a nursery without half trying.

To what extent co-education, under ideals like ours, can be trusted as desirable, we have no mind, as yet, except that we are not for the average woman. Certainly married companionship should be no bar to Fellowship were the average woman less possessive. But the average woman is the natural cup to be filled—to which her man is to bring not only himself, but the makings of a future for her children. She is seldom cultured to be honestly idealistic in herself. She is pragmatic because of her biological character. She is concerned, subjectively if not objectively, for the little shovelful of coals that will enable her to start a little hell of her own at the very earliest possible moment. She is cooperative only until she gets her man. Thereafter she is only waiting to establish herself wherever man can be the bringer to her, for hers.

Now the average woman is a wise provision of nature for the survival of the species. We, the Fellowship, cannot and should not quarrel with her, but we must, for the time being, go around her. The average man may still be a true servant of an Ideal, but his inspiration comes frequently from his love for a woman and so long as she sees him turning toward her, all is well. But she has to have a place for this and the place is not in Fellowship. He must make a place especially for her, so either we must include in our plans separate households, independent but associated for the purpose of raising children—which we are considering—or accept only such womanhood as has evolved the satisfactions of the artist, the philosopher, in short the Idealist who does not sacrifice but rather intensifies womanliness. Such women are rare. We hope to have them, but how are we to recognize them before it is too late?

## VI. THE CASHANDCARRY

Democracy badly needs a new Success Ideal. The present one is a form of damnation. Not only does democracy need a new one but must have it soon or democracy perishes. Cashandcarry "Success" knows no qualities nor can admit or permit of any mastership but Money. Money must be in the very nature of things as things are, the proof of Success in such as our System. So most American universities inculcate and prepare for that venal sort of Success. Inevitably our American colleges and universities are similar to enlarged Trade Schools—all qualifying the youth of the nation to cog in somewhere in the commercialized social machine, and so—earn money. We who are not so constituted find that many youths must go back into the wagery of Cashand-

carry to pay back the money they borrowed to be thus educated. So the wires get crossed. It is unfortunate for us that the trader-instinct, shopkeeping, lies in ambush everywhere: the price tags already fixed on humanity as they are fixed upon any other commodity. But so it is. We of the Fellowship can scarcely hope entirely to escape the mark-up and the mark-down continually being made by American educational institutions. The result of this institutional idiocy is what I am calling the Cashandcarry mentality we live in. That mentality is a routine, commercialized, middle-of-the-road substitute for a mind. You can move anybody in it around for a little more money than he has been getting.

But it is more than merely difficult to set up, and almost impossible to maintain, a way of life for young men and women otherwise.

Such life as ours in the Fellowship *is* otherwise and it is not only in sharp contrast, but in unfair competition with that surrounding mentality. We (the one) must come and go in the other (the many) to a certain extent. That is inevitable.

It is due to the opposing philosophy of our surroundings that we suffer most.

Just as Democracy always suffers most in War.

A Cashandcarry nation needs every man a wage-slave just as the nation in war needs every man a conscript. Because, in its false economy, production controls consumption, it would have to be so. The Commander-in-Chief of the Cashandcarry would have to be the banker as it stands now. Professional commercial propaganda, using the proper names, could make either defeat out of victory or victory out of defeat in any commercial circumstances if the prop could be kept up long enough. That faith in production and continuous unrelenting advertising propaganda is the touching faith of the average-man of our day in Peace. And so it is the same in War.

The most dangerous characteristic of the System however, from any cultural standpoint, is the short-cut to burial for the inherited inferiority complex which the System affords.

Money can do it.

Fellowship is looked upon by the Cashandcarry, and naturally, with suspicion. "You are a kind of Art Colony, ah!" Or: "You are a kind of country club for art students"; or, well, there are dozens of their own ideas of what we are. "Fellowship" sounds to them like some sect or other. Anyhow, no good can come of "getting off the beaten track." "The machine can't go there." "Stick to the boulevard, my boy, if you can." "Main traveled roads are best, you know." "No patience with this assumption of the try for something different." "It is insulting to *our* intelligence." "Who the hell are the people anyway?" "And what *is* the assumption?" "We aren't good enough for them? All right, who cares a damn about them?" Etc., etc.

If the Cashandcarry mentality (it is wage-slave) gets into Fellowship, it would probably soon be found mixed up in some kind of secret exploitation inside or outside of the Fellowship. The Cashandcarry mind is constantly worried: "What am I getting out of this?" "Will it pay?"

"Never mind what I am giving to it: let them get what they can out of me."

The natural fundamental of the profit system is here. It gets us when we get it. We don't get it if we can see it first. Often we can't. It is only under pressure that it appears.

Suggested motto for the Cashandcarry: "Let us then be up and doing"—for *me*.

Running along with this mundane membrane Money, there is another parallel invention: Time as a kind of policeman. Time, the policeman. But a policeman subsidized by money gangsterism.

## VII. THE BROADWAY CREED
BELITTLEMENT is its business.

Confusion of the best with the worst is its avocation.

Concerning the wisecracker. We have always a supply of him in the Fellowship. We laugh at his cracks and in good turn we take a crack at him. He comes most frequently from the large urban centers of the East, but he comes also from Kansas, Dakota, California, or Minnesota.

The Broadway Creed has covered the country pretty much until it has Hollywood for its other end, and is pretty much commonplace all the way between. Especially where the upper region of the

pantaloons is concerned . . . Box Office. The particular cynicism of our era is a kind of smart smut which the breed of the creed instinctively uses to besmirch the common faith of the common man.

Faith of any kind is a mark for the creed's experts, especially any surviving faith in human nature. Selfishly bred, children of pleasure herding on hard, crowded pavements in congested urban areas, the breed naturally gets the worm's-eye or lowdown view suited to the Cashandcarry mentality.

But, more important, the Broadwayman's Creed is the solace and the front line of defense for the inferiority complex. Its performances are the instinctively inferior smartboys' flag and release.

In spite of the Immigration laws, it has grown up among us as the natural product of the melting pot.

As Carlyle said of Democracy, so we say of the Broadway Creed, "It is a disease. Let us have it so we may have done with it and get on to rule by the bravest and the best." Nevertheless, human conduct may eventually grow to be a little wiser for the Broadwayman's worm's-eye view. But a sense of the ridiculous assuming the airs and graces of humor which is really what it is not, has robbed us of too much of our native salt and savor. A Winchell is a Broadway substitute for a wholesome, manly Will Rogers.

Among us there is enough punctilio to puncture. There are enough stuffed shirts to thump and enough hypocrisy to play up, infested as the country is with the flood of commercial exploits idiotically extolling their own cheap merits, hoping to knock off a good piece of business by so doing.

The rat-like perspicacity of the breed raised on the Creed is worth much where that work is to be done. How much?

Well, there's Mickey Mouse. He's amusing.

Amusement is the indispensable as things get to be in Urbania. And while the laugh provoked by ridicule and the funnies is not the same as the laugh provoked by the salt and savor of true humor, even that cheap laugh is worth something to our plight. The Creed thus serves a turn. And the breed does serve the Box Office. Its Box Office is social poison. Its laugh is a cheap laugh. But a laugh is our best medicine—that and a good physic.

Well . . . perhaps both save the day for some purpose for which neither was really intended.

But the search for FORM must reject the Broadway Creed entire, because the laugh it produces is not only a cheap laugh, but the breed itself is antiseptic, in itself sterile. It is inorganic and therefore it cannot reproduce. The future dies with it, or of it.

## THE CREATIVE CONSCIENCE

The Alter Ego is the distorted mirror (concave or convex as the case may be) in which mastership sees its own reflection. The alter ego may be a form of flattery but it is more often a distressing caricature which must be borne for the good of some cause. If any.

The young, if innocent, are hardly conscious of being guilty of alter-egoism, but the more sophisticated ones who do know they are guilty soon grow a hatred of the original of their image, the pictures they make. And in time the alter ego thus becomes the instinctive detractor of the coveted original. His trouble is that the original is there behind his cupboard door as a threat to his own sense of himself, when he himself performs. He would like to escape and to destroy his original in the short cut.

The disciple is a legitimate form of the Alter Ego. Jesus had twelve disciples, such as they were, and they were such as they always are. But, occasionally, even Jesus got up into the high mountains to be relieved of his disciples for a time. Nevertheless, I think the Alter Ego is a justified necessity. But he is an asset to Fellowship only just so long as his alter-egoship is an open door or window through which he may look out upon a natural world otherwise dark to him, a world wherein his alter-egoship will gradually grow independent by way of the sincerity of his devotion to his master; his devotion becoming the door or window through which he sees what his master sees—gaining direction at least for going, as time goes, further on: perhaps being saved years of wasted effort by the light that shines from his master, who under certain conditions can himself be the door and the window. Then the alter ego is justified. Then only is he an honest asset to Fellowship. His apprenticeship is a stepping stone to his own independence; even if his aim continues sympathetic, it continues as collateral. It is always unfair to accuse an alter ego of that type of plagiarism. He steals nothing. He gives himself to his master simple-mindedly with no reservation, while his own sense of himself in whatever is to be done by him is forming within him. I have found that those in the Fellowship who had least Individuality worried most about it. Those who had it most were seldom concerned about it. It would take care of itself naturally without offense or defense. The Cashandcarry seldom lets it come through alive.

The Alter Ego never consciously "copies" his original source of inspiration although he is usually no more than promoting a natural implication which was inherent in the masterpiece in the expression of which he participated. If he is a good disciple he is himself an implication of his master. Maybe for life. But most disciples are a weariness to the future and to the mastership which sees before very long that he has not inspired them but is only being used by them as a shield for inconstancy, or vain exploitation.

To enter sincerely into the spirit of a master, standing loyally by his side in his work is, so it has always seemed to me who have myself been such a one, the greatest privilege any novice may ever have.

Education has nothing so precious to offer to youth.

Usonia needs thousands of Taliesins, not one only.

But to go too far with the letter of any master in any implications of his own work is to insult both the master and the apprentice himself. Both become a source of grim amusement.

Men of achievement in the Arts and Sciences should continue their activities by placing themselves where their experience may serve the oncoming tide of life. But how far should the Alter Ego go with his apprenticeship? The answer is that all depends upon circumstances and the Creative Conscience. With that Conscience developed both the novice and the master are safe and happy in each other. Time is of no essence in the matter. Apprenticeship may go on five—ten—years profitably to both, perhaps for life. It all depends. The sincere search for FORM can use the honest alter ego. He can go along. He will be there when FORM becomes a matter of fact.

The Creative Conscience then lies in the artist, as in manhood, in himself. As the fashioner of FORM it demands the whole truth or suffers. It gives the whole truth—or suffers.

It is marvelous to stew, like fruit, in one's own juice and then be set back to simmer for a while.

## FELLOWSHIP ASSETS

I.    AN HONEST EGO IN A HEALTHY BODY—GOOD CORRELATION

II.   LOVE OF TRUTH AND NATURE

III.  SINCERITY AND COURAGE

IV.   ABILITY FOR ACTION

V.    THE ESTHETIC SENSE

VI.   APPRECIATION OF WORK AS IDEA AND IDEA AS WORK

VII.  FERTILITY OF IMAGINATION

VIII. CAPACITY FOR FAITH AND REBELLION

IX.   DISREGARD FOR COMMONPLACE (INORGANIC) ELEGANCE

X.    INSTINCTIVE COOPERATION

These human attributes of Fellowship when inspired by love will eventually evoke THE CREATIVE CONSCIENCE.

## THE FIRST-PERSON SINGULAR

The only thing a man has that can't be taken away from him is himself. He cannot afford to be selfish. In Selfhood the more of himself he gives the more he has to give. The less he gives the less he has to give.

As I have already said: I find that those young men who had most Individuality were troubled least about it. To be too much concerned with it is a pretty sure sign that there is little there to be concerned with. A sound man does not think or speak much of his health nor willingly speak of what he thinks most deeply. So until a man knows the difference between individuality and personality he may confound them in any issue where either is concerned. What he is worrying about is really his personality. Individuality is the essential innate character of the man. His personality is merely the way he looks, walks, speaks, his form, features and habits. Idiosyncrasies are matters of mere personality. None of these personal things is the man's Individuality. And because Individuality lies deeper and is the soul, it is probably looking out at you from the eyes of him you are looking at, looking from under the roof of his mind quite all unconscious of itself.

We don't labor the first-person singular much in the Fellowship. We let it pretty much alone, as it likes to be if it is genuine. And we have found none getting in here without enough of it to be respected. We are bored, however, with the intellectual disguise which is the abuse of the thing—mistaking mere egotistic curiosity for a thirst for knowledge but seldom able to draw the line between the curious and the beautiful. The first-person singular is always born. It grows best and becomes strongest and most fruitful when it is most unaware of itself and is not encouraged to pull itself by the roots every now and then to see how it is growing.

Walt Whitman said he loved the companionship of animals—they were not worried, or worrying others, on account of their souls.

And I like Emerson, walking out under the elms: "The great trees looked down on him and said, 'Why so hot, my little man, why so hot?'"

Why indeed!

## ALDEBARAN

Among the very first to come in to the Fellowship, a tall dark-eyed young man turned up at Taliesin. He was the son of an Evansville editor. *Who's Who* says the editor was the man who drove the Ku Klux Klan out of Indiana. He did, and practically singlehanded. The lad came from a course in engineering at Massachusetts Tech, was a fountain of energetic loyalty to the ideas for which Taliesin stood. He soon took a leading hand in whatever went on. His mind was alert, his character independent and generous. He was young—about nineteen.

Svetlana, my charming adopted daughter (she came to Taliesin with Olgivanna), was sixteen. Soon it appeared that Svetlana liked to ride in the truck Wes drove. A general sympathy amounting to a conspiracy grew up behind these young people, and everybody but Olgivanna and myself was aware of a budding romance. Not we. When we did wake up there were some accusations and unkind words. Too soon! Both too young! The budding romance which looked like a kind of treachery went underground, but partisans for the young couple formed to fight their battle for them. No use. We wouldn't have any of it. So after a while the principals and their partisans struck out for parts unknown. We had been so fond of both of them that we couldn't see the thing as other than the treachery of ungrateful, irresponsible children.

We didn't hear from them for a year or two. But we greatly missed them and the inevitable reconciliation took place after they had been married—Svetlana studying music in Chicago, Wes building buildings in Evansville. Were we happy to have them back—giving good accounts of themselves? We were. Perhaps the break was a good thing all around. Certainly both were much improved by the break on their own. And we were a good deal the wiser. I guess we had improved, too.

Wes's father died soon, and Wes had a small income and a widowed mother. Taliesin had a son-in-law as well as a devoted follower.

There is a picturesque group of hills to the West—nearby. A farm on the river next to Taliesin, a farm of about three hundred and fifty acres. Wes coveted it, and I egged him on to buy it. He seemed the kind of lad who could use ground. And I wanted to see Taliesin expand—expecting someday to see its collaterals owning as much of the countryside as together we could well use.

Wes bought the ground—named it Aldebaran (the follower), and Taliesin soon after that jumped to the control of about one thousand acres with about three miles of waterfront. The naming of the place shows the spirit of the lad. He was a genuine apprentice. His ambitions were not cheap. His individuality was strong. He didn't need to worry about that. He was glad and proud to stand by and contribute his strength to Taliesin and Taliesin appreciated him, believed in him now as much as he believed in Taliesin.

Here was apprenticeship in flower. Wes planned a good house on a nearby hill—a well-conceived house for his young wife, who gave him a young son they have named Brandoch, a name which puts it up to the boy to be a hero.

Taliesin had a son, a daughter, and a grandson. Taliesin has other faithful competent sons—many of them an asset to Fellowship, but none so close in as Wes—none with more strength or more energy and loyalty than the young man Olgivanna and I drove away years ago with the unkind assumption that he was stealing away a daughter. Well, Svetlana is now somebody in her own right. Here in the Wisconsin Hills is Aldebaran, Taliesin's first real extension—collateral human growth. But inside Taliesin Wes is a leader and the charming lively Svetlana has a large share in cultivating the music life of the Fellowship. She has an innate sense of music. Wes is so interested in farming that I can scarcely get Architecture out of him or into him anymore. But it is there. They make, I guess, a Taliesin showpiece.

Wes (now ten years at Taliesin) is a right bower, the best example of What-Taliesin-Can-Do-for-a-Young-Apprentice (his wife thrown in) and what a young apprentice can do for Taliesin.

## THE STORY OF HIBBARD THE JOHNSON WHO DID MUCH FOR THE OLD HOMETOWN— WAX OFFICIATING

Hibbard (the Hib), was an attractive young waxmaker, son of a waxmaker, who was also the son of a waxmaker. Hib's father, so they say around Racine (the old hometown), was famous for his "hunches." Not only did Hib inherit the ancestral factories but the ancestral hunches. And this now world-famous modern office building to house the administration of the ancestral wax-manufacturing company was one of Hib's hunches. Hib's remarkable house, now standing broad, wide and handsome, out in the prairie countryside near by, was . . . but of that, later. Hib's hunches made him, for one thing, the only Racine boy to do anything really worthwhile to culture that industrial ace: the big graceless Wisconsin Factory center by Lake Michigan where millionaires originate and from which they always go somewhere else for fun. And cultivation, too. If

**William Wesley Peters and son, Brandoch. Aldebaran, Spring Green, Wisconsin. 1946.**
FLLW Fdn FA#6308.0012

any. Along with Hib's family inheritances was a valuable lieutenant-general, John Ramsey by name, manager by nature. And no manufacturer, I believe, ever had a better manager or a better man than Jack. Jack, like Hibbard, had seen the education manufactured at Wisconsin U. but both refused to bite off more standard erudition than either could well digest. Hib's brother-in-law, Jack Louis by name, was head of a prosperous advertising firm in Chicago nearby, guiding the publicity side of S. C. Johnson Wax by radio. "Johnson's Wax" gave Fibber McGee and Molly a long ride, eventually greatly to the benefit of the wax-polish industry, and no doubt— Fibber and Molly McGee.

Well, this hunch of Hib's so had it that the prosperity of his now overcrowded and solidly prosperous wax concern should enable the company to do something worthwhile for the daily lives of its numerous office employees, young and old. So the limit in convenience and beauty in a building for this purpose that intelligence could find and the best in quality that the Johnson money could ever pay for, was none too good for Hib.

When the sky at Taliesin was dark and the days there gloomy, as I have described, Hib and Jack were the ones who came out to Taliesin to see about that new building.[13] They came, you might say, like messengers riding on white steeds trumpeting glad tidings. Jack Louis had been willing, but skeptical; architecture was not radio. But, some time before, a group of art directors from Chicago had visited Taliesin—egged on by good Bill Kittredge, I believe. And Willis Jones came along. Willis, a discerning and greatly appreciative young art director, was working for Jack Louis at the time, making designs for his Chicago advertising company. After his visit, of his own volition, Willis got after the Johnson folk. And also a talented young architect, Howard Raftery, put up a sacrificial fight for Taliesin. As a result, the official visit (gratifying annunciation) occurred sometime in July 1936. The occasion was pleasant all around. Next day came a note from Hib enclosing a retainer (one thousand dollars) testifying to his appreciation of what he saw on that occasion. And, the pie thus opened, the birds began to sing again below the house at Taliesin; dry grass on the hillside turned green, and the hollyhocks went gaily into a second blooming. The orchard decided to come in with a heavy crop of big red harvest apples and the whole landscape seemed to have more color; Iovanna rode more fiercely through the Valley; and both Olgivanna's responsibilities and mine were doubled—with smiles. Work was incessant. Taliesin galvanized into fresh activity.

Well . . . pretty fine sketches for the administration building, the best I could do and just about as the building stands there in its utterly unworthy environment today, went forward. Returning home after that momentous visit, the abandonment of plans resembling a fancy crematorium which some local architect had already contributed was enacted and Hib gave over the coveted commission to the architect Jones and Raftery had persistently recommended—an architect held back outside the current of building for seven years. Here and thus his feet were put back on the road to an activity almost "struck out" by the very long chain of untoward circumstances hereinbefore related. So I now look back upon that visit—July 20, 1936, with a deep and pleasant satisfaction, never ceasing to be glad that I have for friends the two men who came to see me that day.

What a release of pent-up creative energy—the making of those plans! Ideas came tumbling up and out onto paper to be thrown back in heaps—for careful scrutiny and selection. But, at once, I knew the scheme I wanted to try. I had it in mind when I drew the newspaper plant at Salem, Oregon, for Editor George Putnam, which he had been unable to build. A great simplicity.

Owing to a high ideal of simplicity, this building was bound to be an exacting piece of work. And for

quite some time I conducted myself like a pregnant mother.

There were enough headaches to go all around on all sides: the "union" universally strong in Racine, the building codes strong in Wisconsin. Also, in addition to the law of gravitation, there was the terrific time-lag of Innovation to be overcome: they are similar. But no cultural lag! None. Both Hib and Jack were at the head of the procession from start to finish. "They" say I am "hard to get along with" (meaning, really, hard to go along with), but I was never too much for these boys, even if they did finally begin to chafe a little as the inevitable began to happen and the original building kept on growing up. The opus added unto itself a vast domiculated carport, a small hemicycle for the entertainment and instruction of employees got up over the entrance and then came squash courts, garages, etc., etc. All these, and more, came knocking for admission. We started with a pal-

S.C. Johnson & Son Co. Administration Building, Racine, Wisconsin. 1936. Peters, Wright, and Johnson at building site and test column, 3 June 1937. FLLW Fdn FA#6801.0006

Above: Headline about Johnson test column, *Milwaukee Journal*, 4 June 1937. Newsprint.
FLLW Fdn FA#3601.0129/1701.037

try $250,000 in the "rock pile." Before we started, it jumped to $350,000—and as time went on landed in a pile nearer $850,000. But we had more to show for that pile than anybody who ever built a similar industrial administration building of the first rank. The entire thing thoroughly fireproof, air-conditioned, floor-heated (gravity heat), and, including appropriate furnishings designed by the architect, was built for about seventy-eight cents per cubic foot. And observe—although a building is not radio, it was the psychological world-moment for the more serious sort of thing we now did. Hib knew it (his "hunch") and he took the gaff with only a stab or two at his architect now and then just for luck.

But no stabs in the back.

Jack kicked around a little—managerially. But why not? Some kicking was a necessary feature owing to the great simplicity of that building.

Also, to preserve the great simplicity, I made some 132 trips by motor car from Taliesin to Racine (a distance of 165 miles) to superintend the structure, and over a period of two years in all weathers, just to get it built the way I thought it should be built—carrying on until, towards the end, pneumonia had me down to interrupt proceedings. More patience had to be added to infinite patiences that great simplicity had required up to that time. Perhaps only Ben, the Wiltscheck, our builder, can quite realize how much was required. Ben was no contractor's contractor. He was educated at Penn for an architect. Failing to satisfy himself with his own designs he went out to build buildings for others. Ben was "au fait." He went about everywhere in Racine society on equal terms with his employers. But more to the point, he was a careful builder—well aware of the great importance of keeping the architect right there on the job. Not one move would Ben make until the detailed drawings of the original drawings were detailed some more. And so far as I know, for once in a way the Builder did not try to destroy the Architect. There was real cooperation, confidence in each other's ability all around, and all the time. Without that circumstance no such building as that modern thoroughbred could ever have been built at all. It was, and altogether, such a Simplicity as is never found in stock. It was in no sense and nowhere—shop.

When the building was opened the world seemed to have been waiting for the event because it was there outside trying to get in to see it.[14] When finally it did get in, reams of newspaper copy began to pour from the press, and such talk!

Everyone who saw the building tried to describe it: "It is like a woman swimming naked in a stream. Cool, gliding, musical in movement and in manner. The inside of an office building like a woman swimming naked in a stream? Yes, that's right." (Leading feature article: *Life Magazine,* May 1938.)

Bill Connolley, competent "man on the job" for the advertising of the S. C. Johnson Co., calculated that (with no help from him at all) two or more millions of dollars could not have bought the front pages in newspapers and top-notch magazines which the building had attracted to itself.

And, the movie "shorts" took it up and carried on.

The radio came chiming in. Meanwhile the stream of visitors from all over the world went on and continues to go on to this hour.

Why? Because of something in the universal air, that's why. It was high time to give our hungry American public something truly "streamlined," so swift, sure of itself and clean for its purpose, clean as a hound's tooth—that *anybody* could see the virtue of this thing called Modern. Many liked it because it was not "modernistic," but seemed to them like the original from which all the "streamlining" they had ever seen might have come in the first place. As a matter of fact, the word "streamlined" had been first applied to buildings by the architect of this one.

It is a trifle hard to hit the bull's-eye *every* time *all* the while, and we expected certain minor troubles to develop. They did, but mostly as expected—annoying of course, even so. But they were remedied eventually, and also as designed. Nothing developed sufficiently important to mar the integrity of the building as a whole which was lengthwise, crosswise, and in cross section an Experiment in design and construction. An experiment, though, and mind you, in behalf of the S. C. Johnson and Son's Company. All the time. There is an important difference between the merely "experimental" and a genuine experiment. The one may be a feeling for novelty. The other is rationally based upon experience seeking a better way.

The Wisconsin Industrial Commission vexed us for some time, wouldn't say yes and didn't say no to the plans. But I've learned since from contacts with other building commissions in other states (let's say Missouri for one) how sensible and considerate that Wisconsin Commission under Mr. Wrabetz, et al. was. This was partly, I believe, because Hib himself stood up at the board meeting beside me and squarely told that commission that he wanted that building that way and he was damn well prepared to stand back of it to the limit. Finally, if we would agree to make tests as the building proceeded, should the commission require them, we were told to go ahead. We did make several important tests. We made them with such startling and gratifying success that new precedents for reinforced concrete construction were established. The Industrial Commission raised no further objection.

When I went to the Tokio Building Commission (1914) for a permit to build the international Imperial Hotel earthquake-proof, the Japanese authorities enacted a scene somewhat similar. They couldn't say yes and didn't say no because they had never seen anything like the scheme proposed, but said—"Go ahead: we will watch you with the hope that you, world-famous architect [deferential bows both sides] may have something. So we will follow carefully. Please proceed." We did. And they followed. Very carefully, let me say.

There was never a permit to build the Imperial Hotel earthquake-proof. It was all a gigantic experiment in behalf of Japan by the *Kenchiku ho* of the Imperial Household—myself. An experiment not yet understood nor fully granted success by my own people, except with a grudge. The Japanese, however, were pleased with the results.

After all, it was their affair?

And there never was more than a conditional permit to build the unique Administration Building of

Johnson's Wax; nor ever a permit to build the original textile block houses in California, nor the later board-and-brick Usonian Houses in seventeen different states. No. Nor—but we are talking about the building that Hib's "hunch" set up life-size in his native Racine partly for the edification and amazement of the hometown. But not so, too much.

Organic architecture designed this great building to be as inspiring a place to work in as any cathedral ever was in which to worship. It was meant to be a socio-architectural interpretation of modern business at its top and best.

The building was laid out upon a horizontal unit system twenty feet on centers both ways, rising into the air on a vertical unit system of three and a half inches: one especially large brick course. Glass was not used as bricks in this structure. Bricks were bricks. The building itself became—by way of long glass tubing—crystal where crystal either transparent or translucent was felt to be most appropriate. In order to make the structure monolithic the exterior enclosing wall material appeared inside wherever it was sensible for it to do so.

The main feature of construction was the simple repetition of slender hollow monolithic dendriform shafts or stems—the stems standing tip-toe in small brass shoes bedded at the floor level.

The great structure throughout is light and plastic—an open glass-filled rift is up there where the cornice might have been. Reinforcing used was mostly cold-drawn steel mesh—welded.

The entire steel-reinforced structure stands there earthquake-proof, fireproof, soundproof, and vermin-proof. Almost fool-proof but alas, no. Simplicity is never fool-proof nor is it ever for fools.

Weight herein this building by way of a natural use of steel in tension, appears to lift and float in light and air; "miraculous" light dendriforms standing up against the sky take on integral character as plastic units of a plastic building construction entire, *emphasizing* space instead of standing up in the way as mere inserts for support.

The main clerical work force was all correlated in one vast room, 228 by 228 feet. This great room, air-conditioned, besides the top lighting and rift for light at the cornice level, is daylit also by rifts in the brick walls. And the heating system of the main floor of the building is entirely beneath the floor slab. The structure is hermetically sealed and air-conditioned with this gravity heat.

The building complete, being destined to stand in unimpressive surroundings bounded by three ordinary village streets, we settled upon the main entrance as interior to the building lot; thus the motor car was provided for as a modern indispensable and with new hospitality. Ample parking facilities are under cover of this great domiculated spread of carport.

The main building itself in which the dendriform shafts are floated is set back from the street on three sides; a colorful band of planting dividing the main brick walls from the sidewalks, enlivening the dreary environment. Above, the carport, tile-paved, was to have become a playground for the workers.

The hemicycle—a cinema seating 250 for daytime lectures or entertainment, wired complete for sound, is placed at mezzanine level at the middle of the floor arrangement. An enclosed glass-roofed bridge spans and connects the officers' quarters in the penthouse to a tall wood-lined squash court rising high above the garage. President Herbert Johnson's private office, an office for his stenographer, and a private chemical laboratory ride at the apex of this penthouse; the officers, Jack Ramsey at their head, are built in on the same level (roof level) in each of the wings extending from it.

Below this penthouse arrangement of officers who, by way of the open court under the glass ceiling, have a view of the big workroom on the ground level, are the several hundred office workers sitting at especially devised desks on chairs that belong to the desks. Sub-heads of various departments function just above them in a low gallery, mezzanine to the big room where direct vision and prompt connection with the workers in the big room itself is had directly at convenient points by spiral iron stairways.

The few enclosures within the big workroom are low glass walls, screened by Aeroshades. Thus the plastic sense of the whole, most stimulating, is well preserved in various parts even to the uttermost detail.

The main toilet accommodations are located, conveniently, directly beneath the working staff and are directly reached by means of small circular iron stairs located at appropriate intervals.

The entire building operation, generally by way of cost-plus arrangements, was in the architect's hands, ably managed by Ben Wiltscheck, supervised by myself and superintended by the Taliesin Fellowship, mainly by Wesley Peters and Edgar Tafel.

To enumerate in detail or even catalogue the innovations to be found in this one building would require more time and patient attention on your part, and mine too, than either of us cares to give it. So let's say here that it is technically, and in the entire realm of the scientific art of Architecture, one of the world's remarkably successful structures. I like it. They like it. Let it go at that.

For once in a way, again an up-to-the-minute thoroughbred, daughter of the Larkin Building—1906—was born—1938—on provincial American soil. A great modern building completely furnished, planted complete in perfect keeping with the original idea of a more feminine building as a whole, was its sire, the masculine Larkin Building of Buffalo.

The legitimate offspring is now there to be seen. But, you can only see as much of the harmonious whole as your inner vision permits you to see.

And that will be however much your prescience of innate rhythm in building construction enables you to perceive. It takes a developed "someone" to see the Johnson Administration Building altogether. That is, to see it *all*. But most folks see enough to delight them or make them envious. Or make them mad.

There is no escape from the building otherwise.

Hib's hunch not only worked out in advertising returns—it began to work out in terms of increased work and morale. Work and morale increased one-tenth to a third the first year the building was in use. The officials loved the place as much as the help did, and some of both of them said they hated to leave it to go home. Jack Ramsey (who had a fine new happy home) was one of these. But there were many others. And Hib must have felt something that way himself . . . because just as I had got out of bed with pneumonia, the idea of building a house of his own, to match it, grew up in his mind. One day he had taken me out to see the tract of prairie (a small lake running its length) that he owned by the big lake (Michigan), and had for years been keeping as a kind of wild-fowl preserve. Some days after we had walked about and talked about a house on that site and I had explained a zoned house to him, Hib brought me a little sketch plan he had himself penciled of the general outlines of a house pretty much as his stands out there on the prairie now.

Just before I had come down with a devastating fever, Hib had been dining with us and, after dinner, I was demonstrating with a Victrola the essential lack of modern music as compared with Music—jumping up and down meantime to change the records. "Man," he said, "don't you know you waste a lot of energy that way when you might be resting?"

Shortly after this, an agent of the Capehart, Cushing, came out with instructions from Hib to measure the house for a complete three-station installation of that remarkable record changing and playing instrument. A superfine record player with a radio attachment just as the Scott is a superfine radio with a record-playing attachment. Hib put in the most complete installation I have ever seen. More complete than his own. He was like that sometimes—a "hunch," you see?

I respect "hunches" in others if they correspond with mine. This one—the little sketch made with T-square and triangle—did. And soon the new house for the young bride Hib was to bring in to it was designed, laid out, and under way. He had mumbled something to me in a vague sort of way about "cost," but I knew he didn't mean me to be too much interested in that. That was *his* affair—after all. So I laid the house out on a scale befitting a young industrial prince of the Johnson line, who all his life long had had about everything he wanted. Now I intended he should want something finer than he had ever seen to want. What else than a house such as that one would be, could he buy with

money or time that would yield him such large returns? This house I would build for him should be, definitely, "capital" not only safe during this lifetime, but go on as true capital into the lives of his children and their children—a joy meantime and a distinction. A proof of quality. What more capital use to make of "capital"? There were some arguments about that point later on. And some feeling about it. Not much though, because Hib is, after all, pretty much right.

Two youngsters—a charming girl and a nice boy were his own as a result of a former marriage and now his newly promised bride already had two boys of her own—hence the children's wing for four. Here was the high Wigwam (living room) under the mass of wild grape vinery at the center shooting out four independent wings—one wing (a luxurious mezzanine), with a continuous balcony toward the great lake, for Hib and wife, and one on the ground floor for the four children—another wing on the ground for workspace and help, and another on the ground also for guests and motor cars.

We called the house "Wingspread" because spread its wings it did. We set a cast bronze door plate into the wide stone slab of the doorsill with abstract wings upon it in low relief to signify the name.

This structure is of the common "prairie-type" of the earlier years. A type proving itself to be a good one for a home in the climate around the Great Lakes. It is popularly known as brick veneer. Outside upper members are wide cypress plank, roofs tiled, floors of concrete, four-foot-square concrete-slab tiles over floor heating, here as in the Administration Building itself.

Thus Wingspread, unique Herbert Johnson prairie house nearby Racine, became another zoning experiment which began in the articulation of the Coonley House at Riverside, built 1909, wherein Living Room, Dining Room, Kitchen, Family Sleeping Rooms, Guest Rooms, were separate units grouped together and connected by corridor.

The building is orientated so that sunlight falls in all rooms and the ground plan shows a completely logical expression of the Zoned House. (The first design for such a house was printed in the Taliesin Monograph, December 1934.)

At the center of four zones forming a cross, a spacious wigwam of a Living Room stands. A tall central brick chimney stack with five fireplaces on four sides divides this roomy vertical central living space into four spaces for the various domestic functions: Entrance, Family Living, Library, and Dining Room. Extending from this greatly dignified, lofty central wigwam are the four wings. This extended zoned-wing-plan lies, very much at home, quiet and integral with the prairie landscape which is, through it, made more significant and beautiful. In this case, especially, green growth will eventually claim its own: wild grapevines swinging pendent from the generously spreading trellises; extensive collateral gardens in bloom, extending beneath them; great adjoining masses of evergreens on two sides and one taller dense dark green mass set on a low mound in the middle of the entrance court—the single tall associate of this spreading dwelling on the prairie. Lake Michigan lies well off ahead but within the middle distance, and is seen over the wild-fowl pool which stretches away in the direction from just below the main terrace of the house. A charming foreground.

But this house, while resembling the Coonley House at Riverside, Illinois, is more bold, masculine, and direct in form and treatment. It is better executed in more permanent materials. The building has a heavy footing course of Kasota sandstone resting on rock ballast laid deep in broad trenches, has the best brickwork I have seen in my life, and the materials of construction and the workmanship throughout are everywhere substantial. Especially the woodwork and furniture by Gillen show fine craftsmanship.[15] The house is architecturally furnished throughout in fairly good keeping with the quiet character established by the building.

Here, because Hib rubbed his lamp and parted from a little "capital," another prairie house in 1938 came out of the blue to join the earlier ones of 1901–1910.

The young bride never lived to enter the furnished house. Out of the blue (the house three-fourths fin-

ished) one day an old workman on the house told me that a white dove we had seen frequenting the belvedere of the building—and in which both he and I were interested—had flown away and disappeared. The workman shook his head. A bad omen. "The young mistress will never live in this house," he said. And she too, as we soon learned, had passed away.

Hib's interest in our building went way down. It took good persuasion to get him interested in ever going on with the house again, although it was three-fourths done at the time this blow befell him. I, friend now as well as architect, did my best to represent to him what I thought his young wife would wish were she living. I felt sure she would want to see him finish what he had so happily begun with her; he needed, and now more than ever, a refuge such as that house would be for his children (they were fast growing up); he owed it, if not to himself, if not to her, then to Racine not to leave an empty shell of a house desecrating in desperation instead of nobly memorializing the memory of the wife he had lost. After a while I guess he began to see it something like that, because we began the work on it again. We completed the house in every particular as planned for a wife and four children. Hib seemed to sigh with relief upon seeing actually realized the building—the house they had both worked on with me and of which he had fondly dreamed. The house, not yet a home, began to justify the hopes we had from the first invested in it. It turned out a veritable thing of the Spirit: a true consort of the prairie. The "last of the prairie houses" it shall be, so I thought—though I don't know why.

Should you ever see it, observe this fact . . . the house did something remarkable to that site. The site was not stimulating before the house went up—but like developer poured over a negative, when you view the environment framed by the Architecture of the house from within, somehow, like magic—charm appears in the landscape and will be there wherever you look. The site seems to come alive.

Hib saw this. He felt it did express, in a finer sense, human feeling for the young wife lost than anything else he could have done. And soon he began to wake up really and actually live in the house. That house, more than anything else, I believe, brought Hib back again. But he might be unwilling to say so.

## HERESY

A test is usually heresy. Ever since I can remember trying to build, tests have been going on under my supervision. A test of some kind was always either in sight or just around the corner, or was just evaporating results and another necessary. The supreme test, I suppose, was the earthquake's grasp of the Imperial Hotel.[16] Leading up to that final test were foundation tests with borings and pig-iron leadings; slab tests; cantilever tests; tests of the value of continuity in heavy concrete beams; tests of stair-flights extending from floor slabs like extended arms. Not to mention plumbing tests, wiring tests. Test by test we arrived at the ultimate: the Imperial's flexible stability.

Nearly every structure I have built, large or small, required some test. Or many. Floor-heating tests; novel wall-construction tests; tests of new details of fenestration. Fireplace construction to be tested; roof construction in new materials to be tried out. Experiment following experiment. Frequently one test would require others. One experiment would lead to the next until the building process extending back over a period of forty-five years resembles the continuous test to which life itself subjects the architect himself.

It is true that nature never puts an idea of Form into practice, plants a new type or species, that she doesn't plant its natural enemy beside it. Nature has her equilibrium to maintain. She is continually maintaining her sense of proportion in all things. So when we make tests we are really trying to discover her status quo (for so it is), or, shall we say, the laws of proportion inherent in her own designs. Her equilibrium is an unknown quantity. It is probably God, and we cannot reach God on a stepladder, which is what a Code is. And probably a very short and rickety one. But lightness and strength in erection, volume and weight at the ground levels, certain obvious limited patterns, we may see make sense before our eyes. There are many variations of this. Hence the test.

An architect comes closer to certain secrets of nature in his practice if he is master of organic FORM than most artists and scientists. Although in any final analysis we are all in the same category—making tests according to calculation or better than calculation—inspiration. Testing an inspiration? An expert in building construction would declare it an absurdity.

But that "absurdity" has characterized my life.

An architect is either on the winning side grasping the laws of nature or on the losing side, the side of dead data, the idée fixe, the rules of the Code.

Most book data are the result of some testing process limited at the time by this and that circumstance. The most important of such data as we know serves only for a time, the length of time determined by how flexible the mind of the man and the formula were when the datum was fixed.

Flexibility is the only chance a mind or a datum has for survival.

Heraclitus was right.

So Codes are the mental limitations of short men, short of experience, short of imagination, short of courage, short of common sense.

A federal law should be enacted compelling the bureaucrats (those "blessed by a little brief authority") to throw the codes out of the window every five years and enact new ones. Meanwhile (as it has already been done in England) a referendum should be set up as a Court of Appeals with better mental equipment than can be expected of the administration of codes. The referendum qualified to listen to ideas and give sanction to a likely experiment in structure—proper safeguards provided—in order that the data for the next five years may be a matter of record.

Inevitably a bureaucrat is a short man, however long his legs may be. His is a mind only fit for a bureau. He is undersize in most respects. Being a limb, or out on one as some member of an Authority, he worships Authority and since the Authority is all the strength he has he cherishes what little he has with all his strength.

Justice, truth, advancement—these are not his concern.

These are his enemies. He does not feel safe with any one, not to mention several, of these vital concerns of humanity.

Tradition—the formula—this it is that invests the bureaucrat with whatever power he has. Anything irregular inverts him. So he is one of the grains of sand in the sandbags that ballast the flying ship. And that is good enough for him. It's all he asks—"but little here below." So never submit tests to a bureau or a crat. Both are in the position of the black crow who declared, after the other crow had tried hard to convince him that he could sing, "No, it's no good. No, I don't like it. No. Youse is wastin' your time—'cause I wouldn't like it, even if it was good!"

Here is the fatal weakness of Democracy: the bureaucrat. The fatal weakness of Democracy does not lie in gangsterism or political chicanery or civil disobedience or anything like them. It lies in this dumb sheep-like submission to Authority, "the drinking of the vanity of office." And especially this taking sanctuary in Authority by the bureaucrat. That is why Democracy sets Authority under Authority which is set under another Authority that can go to court and have the lower Authority reversed. But how long? O Lord, how long?

The Wisconsin Building Commission, Wrabetz, et al., is a superior building commission as commissions go, but enforcing an antique code which they revise from time to time, calling in for the purpose those architects who abide by the Code and do not make trouble for the commission by experiments. Thus the body of the politic is safeguarded.

In the story of the Johnson Administration Building, I referred to a board meeting wherein Hib and I appeared to ask the commission to give us permission to proceed on a test basis. . . . One of those tests, not because it is more important than a dozen others but because it is recent, should be recounted here.

The Code allowed a maximum height of six feet for a concrete column nine inches in diameter no matter how constructed. Concrete is concrete, n'est-ce pas?

To go to the height of the dendriform shaft twenty-four feet high, spreading into a ceiling as was now contemplated, three feet in diameter would thus have to be the senseless size at the base—for a spacing of the shafts 24' 0" on centers—because two thousand five hundred pounds was code-limit on concrete. There would still be space to sit around in the building but little visibility. Hence the scene in the board room described in that story of the building.

My dendriform shaft was predicated on cold-drawn steel-mesh reinforcements, a steel integument embedded in the outer concrete flesh of the shaft—the circular membrane of steel thus becoming one with the flesh of concrete. The resultant strength was far and away beyond anything the usual rod-reinforcing, on which the code had been framed, could do. Also by agitating the concrete while pouring, it was quite easy to raise the code-limit from twenty-five hundred pounds to an actual twelve thousand at least.

A field test was decided upon and declared open: no objection to publicity. Having the expensive steel forms already made (we were that sure of success), we set up an exact duplicate dendriform out on the site in plain view, steadied it by slight diagonal wood braces, and with a steam shovel we started dumping weighed gravel and cement bags on the extended flat floor of the top of the shaft. By the time the load appeared in sight not only the commission but the town and neighboring press were observers. I sat with several apprentices looking on—woolen shawl on my shoulders (it was cold) but was soon walking around with Hib watching for the first telltales of failure. The crane kept swinging and dumping, swinging and dumping, until the sun went down. We were still there waiting for collapse. Long ago any requirement by the commission had been passed and doubled. Still the heap up there on top kept growing.

The sight was incredible. The police had taken charge and roped the populace from the vicinity of that heroic slender stem, standing up there a graceful thing on tiptoe, standing straight and true, until sixty tons instead of the twelve tons required were on top of a shaft nine inches in diameter at the tip on the ground, and the concrete was only eight days of age. Slight cracks were now discernible in the upper part of the shaft where it splayed into the top. No more load could be put on without sliding off, so I gave the word to break it, wanting to see where failure would come first, although it was pretty evident where. A lateral push against the shaft brought the enormous overload tumbling to the ground causing a tremor felt to the surrounding streets. The shaft, still unbroken, lay on the ground. The spreading head had broken off. The commissioner, saying nothing, disappeared.

Their silence gave consent.

We went on with the building scheme that had been trembling in the balance, but in the balance only up to twelve thousand pounds. The code was satisfied at that figure of twelve thousand. Yes, silence gave consent. We proceeded.

There were other tests: An amusing one wherein the circular metal elevator and its enclosure was challenged. Could anyone get the car released from the outside? None of us could. But a clever operator appeared from the bureau, who, having had much practice in picking elevator locks by a means no layman could have thought of, did finally succeed in starting it. So we lined the car with a transparent substitute for glass.

Such is the Expert and his Bible—his good old Code.

No doubt the Code as a check for the jerry-builder has saved some lives where jerry-builders are the quarry. But it didn't save the new capitol wing at Madison where code sizes were as prescribed but superintendence was so faulty that I had my first lesson in building collapse while, in a former chapter, you have seen me hanging on to the iron fence looking in on Catastrophe.

## THE CHURCH OF THE FUTURE

Here's to the good old Reverend Dr. Burris Jenkins of Kansas City, Missouri, and his young right bower in the parish, Joe Cleveland, both wholeheartedly trying to do the right thing by the future . . . but hampered by two good Kansas City lawyers working with a zealous (not to say jealous) building commission composed of one good "old foundation man" and one ex-architect (his clerk) both strictly of Yesterday.

So far as these building-committee lawyers were concerned, they never cared much for that sort of thing anyway. But this church-of-the-future business was all right enough, if Dr. Burris wanted it, though everything must be strictly legal . . . as it is in heaven.

The church plans were hurriedly made because all were anxious to get a start. Money was insufficient for needs, but everybody, even the lawyers, thought it likely to be easier after we got going. So we tried to get going in a hurry in order to get the necessary money. The building scheme had to be simple—a thousand seats at least, Sunday School rooms, a separate chapel, offices for the church officers, kitchens, and a clubroom or two. Such a program as would have cost about five hundred thousand dollars under ordinary conditions. We had to get the congregation inside and fairly comfortable, if possible, for one hundred and fifty thousand. The scheme was therefore the simplest thing that we could imagine. Incredibly simple and economical. And, if I do say so myself, a damn good scheme. The plans called for a light *tenuous* steel frame, flexible in shape—a hex—*resting for the sake of flexibility on rock ballast foundations*. The same foundations as used in the Johnson building at Racine and all the other buildings I have built. The light steel skeleton was to be covered on each side by heavy paper strung with steel wires (Steeltex) securely wired to the skeleton and then the cement-gun process, so successful on the West Coast and used in K.C. itself to waterproof old brick buildings, was to be used to put a thin but sufficient shell over the insulating paper: the shells were 2¼" apart, held by the wires to the paper like plastering on a lathed wall. This was to go on both inside and outside. Probably, I thought (and still think), the most advanced and desirable cheap building construction yet devised for any climate. Provided the Gunite is good. There was little or no detail involved except the open framework of two shallow sloping roofs over the two channels. All surfaces were plain. All corners were slightly rounded to aid the Gunite process. The structure depended upon its shape, graceful simplicity, and lightness of treatment

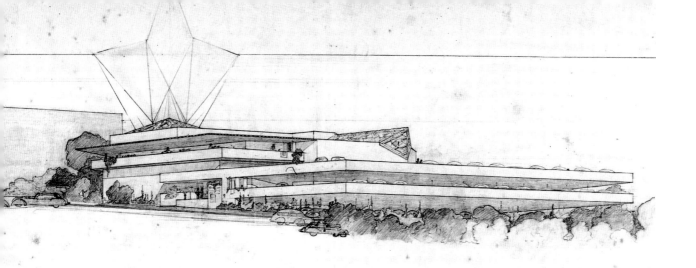

**Community Church, Kansas City, Missouri. 1940. Perspective. Pencil and color pencil on tracing paper, 36 x 22".** FLLW Fdn#4004.006

for esthetic effect. The cost figures came in finally, but only after no one in K.C. had confidence enough in the church and its architect, or faith in the novel technique, to bid.

I turned to Ben Wiltscheck in the circumstances (emergency), and in the midst of a turmoil such as conflicting interests and ideas can set up on a building built by lawyers and a building commission enforcing an antique code, Ben took on the main structure at about one hundred thirty-five thousand dollars, but leaving the chapel and the parking terraces and the block of Sunday School rooms to be built at a cost of about twenty-five thousand more. We all then felt sure that the twenty-five thousand would come in on top of the other forty thousand we needed, when the character of our effort was recognized.

We went after a building permit. Snag one. The newly elected commissioner himself said he was an old foundation man and I couldn't put anything like that foundation over on him.

"Never heard of pounded rock for foundations," he said.

Said I, "Look at the railroads of the country. Their heavy loads (moving too) have been on rock ballast for a hundred years."

Said he, "Nothing to do with Kansas City foundations; peculiar conditions in K.C. ground; cracks open in dry weather and walls settle."

"But the thick rock ballast would be just the equalizer for a thing like that, wouldn't crack nor could it harmfully settle."

"Oh, no! No! Not here in Kansas City. Nothing but concrete here. Only concrete. Nothing but concrete footings can go underground in Kansas City." This, unalterable, was a serious knockdown blow because there is a certain lateral come-and-go possible to the light superstructure in a hexagonal form when the light steel fabricated structure rests on coarse broken stone; in this case, particularly, a necessary flexibility that would be lost if the frame were fixed to solid concrete at the bottom. There is a contraction and expansion going on in solid footings that is not present in rock ballast. I protested and tried again and again with all I had, but the legal committee of disbelievers itself insisted that "all should be perfectly legal."

Well . . . the time to assert the rights of an owner to his own building had arrived. The essential scheme should have been rejected or accepted by all and sundry, right then and there, the building committee fired, and a new start made.

But Dr. Jenkins, Joe, and I wanted to save the thing and trusted to our ability to subsequently "snatch victory from the jaws of defeat." So I proposed, "Allow us to go ahead and we will make any tests you require." The lawyers hesitated, hemmed and hawed, deliberated and visited the commissioner, looked wise, and looked for compromise. They found the compromise by employing a local engineer (recommended by the commissioner himself) to design solid concrete foundations. I don't live in Kansas City and heard of it only from some reporter who dug up the story.

Some eleven thousand dollars up on building costs.

Again—right then and there—I should have stopped the building where it was and have withdrawn from any connection with it whatever. The building was, henceforth, in the hands of the enemy. The fundamental condition of success of a rational experiment in behalf of the church was gone. The flexible hex-frame could not contract and expand in its own way, so cracks were sure to appear in the envelope. But I too am an optimist. I hated to "abandon the child," hoping to find something if they did appear as expected, that would serve—perhaps another coat of Gunite after the first winter was over. It is always possible to build up the thickness of the shell indefinitely.

But no—the worst was far from over. Snag now after snag was set up. The building was soon no longer mine except in shape—the shape which had already lost some of its meaning. And "the good foundation man," egged on by the inside K.C. engineer, began stiffening up the frame. Making the frame rigid where I wanted it to be and remain flexible.

Some fifteen thousand dollars more up on the building costs.

Ben Wiltscheck had a contract and had to build the building. Ben also thought that by making these concessions he could get by and save the thing somehow at the end in spite of all legal interference. But the lawyers intended to win the case.

We made tests but were warned there must be no publicity. The commissioner suspected and the engineer challenged the strength of the balcony. On the condition he made, that there should be "no publicity," we made the tests with loads prescribed. There was no visible deflection anywhere.

The new floor construction next came under suspicion. Still specifying "no publicity," the commissioner observed that test: twice the required load and no deflection whatever.

These proofs seemed to make "Authority" thoroughly mad.

Of course, there was no way of testing the footings the building needed, except the hundred or so buildings that had been standing for generations.

But behind Ben now was no church and no architect. There was only the good old foundation man, his clerk, their stand-in, the local engineer (the blind leading the blind), and a pair of lawyers. The lawyers knew their law; masters of the profession, they were sure they could take care of anything when the time came, especially any contract they themselves made. They knew how to make them.

Now Kansas City is just about as near Taliesin as New York City, so far as accessibility goes. Had I been able to go down and live on the job, the wrecking crew might have been checked even then, if there had been a building committee less legal and more rational—faithful to the idea we started with. I offered to go down if that could be set up. Dr. Burris Jenkins had himself fallen very ill. He was a sick man. Joe, succeeding to the chief ministry, did all he could and did (eventually) do so much that he resigned, which is probably the same thing as being fired.

Dr. Burris himself, now somewhat better, was told to "keep out" and leave the affair to the lawyers. He did. Worn out, I guess. The usual game was being played. It looked as bad for Ben as it had for me.

The Church of the Future was now a row between lawyers and the K.C. building commission, their local experts, the various others that the lawyers had called in over Wiltscheck's head, and Ben Wiltscheck himself. There had been no reference by them to me in the matter since the essential foundation scheme was wrecked and the frame "strengthened," "made safe," as the K.C. engineer said. I don't know what superiority over Wisconsin-licensed engineers (we had two of the very best beside myself) the Missouri engineer (unlicensed) could have except that he was down there in Kansas City working.

I have always known that lawyers make the poorest builders in the world. They are narrow-minded dealers in and for and with the strictures of the law. And they are poor sports because they are men of opinion.

If only we could have had several forthright practical American business men as we did in Racine to back up the novel experiment in housing a deserving congregation for much less than half the usual cost of the ordinary thing, housing it with comfort, beauty, and distinction, success would have been ours. It will be yet.

Meantime . . . well . . . Joe Cleveland, elevated to the ministry by Dr. Burris Jenkins himself, wants a job. I'll never get another building to build in Kansas City, which is less than no matter at all. But Ben is out about twenty thousand he could ill afford to lose, and just because he stuck his head out. And I am now "ex-architect." Kansas City, Missouri, just missed something that might have been a jewel in the town; it will now resemble a busted pearl in a swine's snout, until finally after all the messing around is over, we do go down there ourselves to take what will be left of the whited sepulchre and make it what it was intended to be before it went all-out *"legal."*

The lawyers meantime are busy. They have their hands full of the sort of thing that makes them what lawyers are. But some lawyers I know are pretty decent fellows at that. Out of court.

There must be something, too, about "this here Missouri" that makes Kansas City what it is today—Yesterday . . . no place for the Church of the Future.

## BREAKFAST AT TALIESIN

There may be other breaks for a fast, but none so far as I know, like a Taliesin breakfast on any one of Taliesin's seven terraces, the one where the view is best or the sun is right, or the one where the wind is most agreeable, or where all are right together. Light early supper, early to bed the night before, are the conditions on which digestion is willing and happy to break-fast. Push the button of the Capehart as you pass? Haydn pouring from the built-in speaker over the hill garden this morning. But, fresh as dew themselves, the breezes are blowing the scent of sloping clover fields over our way, birds in the tree-tops below are singing as though delirious with joy, perhaps nothing at all is best. Yes, it is. Let's sit down (ourselves fresh) in comfort to a wide well-spread tastefully set low table, ample cloth of Chinese linen fancifully colored and great big napkins to match, big enough to tuck into the neckband and spread all over whatever it is you wear for breakfast. This

morning Alec (Woollcott) wears dark-blue silk pyjamas, belted coat to match, large white polka dots the size of a dime sprinkled all over his person.

The table decorations this morning? By Herbert. Unusually good. A big shallow glass platter brimming with clear water: anemones nestling in a big branch of fern brake held up by a curious yellow moss-covered stone set in the water.

Ribbons of the white mist into which the morning sun has already resolved the dew are lifting, going up to ride as clouds in the blue while the shadows are still wide and long.

Alec is just looking, not talking.

Cowbells are tinkling, gently dinning away on the meadow running up the valley by the stream. White peacocks gather nearby on the roofs and Yoo-hoo-oo!

Olgivanna, picturesque in a big hat tied on her head with strings under her chin, to shut out the sun which was shining in everybody else's eyes, presides over all. Iovanna fluffs out, coming on the breeze already dressed for school and sits down opposite. Because both of them like Alec, Svetlana, wearing bright slacks, bright ribbons perched in splendid dark blowing hair, and Wes come in for this occasion.

Me? Oh, I have on raw linen. Loose wide-sleeved jacket buttoned at the wrist, wide baggy trousers tied close around the ankles. Carl (Sandburg) once visited me when he was working on his "Lincoln." I dressed him up in similar style. Lloyd Lewis was there and got a good "shot" of us in the artistic semi-elegant negligee. For years Carl has been trying to buy that picture from Lloyd for fear someone will see it! Well, anyway, that is what I have on.

Everybody wishes everybody an affectionate "good morning" as we finally draw up to the table.

First, we all look around and listen, then look again.

A few fresh strawberry leaves laid over them, here comes a heap of noble Taliesin strawberries in a big old Chinese Celadon bowl. The stains of the strawberries are lovely on its cool pale-green surface. Just picked the berries in the garden there below, dew on them, still. With Devonshire cream perhaps?

Then some real Scotch oatmeal (Elam's)—four hours in a double boiler—with Guernsey cream? Fresh eggs with *baked* bacon—ours, too: the eggs still warm from the nest. Will you have yours, white or dark, in the original package?

And here comes Billy with a wide, old Celadon platter of fine asparagus freshly cut—he has just this moment gathered the asparagus. You cannot fail to observe how the color of asparagus agrees with Celadon. Beside each place is a tall glass of our fresh Guernsey milk—from the herd tinkling there on the green meadow. Cold? No? All right then, hot. Comb honey? Our own: Hans is a good bee man. As the honey is passed somebody tells the story of Wilde's important urban lady who asked for some more of "that extremely delicious honey" to be passed, with the remark, "Do you know! Were I too, to live in the country, I assure you that I too, should keep a bee!"

Alec looks at me more in sorrow than in anger and I feel suitably ashamed.

Novel jams and preserves of many novel sorts Olgivanna now presses upon us. She made them all herself. What color! And what flavor! We are served by ourselves, ourselves this morning meaning Kenn, Billy, and Kay of the Fellowship.

Naturally, steaming coffee is right there on the service table. And crisp original-Graham toast (one side only, please) comes from the toaster tended by Olgivanna.

After that awful break concerning the bee has somewhat evaporated, we sit back and just enjoy being there, forgiving each other everything. Eating meanwhile with appetite . . . everybody all right.

Our fast is completely broken.

There is no "Let us then be up and doing" for us this morning. As he begins to do the talking, Alec continues to sit with his hand on the handle of a special coffee pot we have set beside him (no, the pot is not Celadon nor is it distinguished) pouring out a fresh cup, now and then. (I could hardly get a word in edgewise for three or four days even if I had wanted to.) But I always prefer to listen to him. He is charming us one and all by the play of his wit— waving a fly away now and then as though he were waving a flag.

Alec is not like "the man who came to dinner" when he comes to breakfast. I can tell you that. I look at his fine square face, firm shapely chin—a distinguished mature man of a becoming age, whatever it is or ever will be . . . something very fine in Alec's face due to innate kindness of heart. His is a really warm heart-beat generosity possessed by few men I've met. I watch him now seeing that steaming coffee-bowl carrying cargo to his liver between sallies. We are enjoying the real conversation of a friend among friends, Alec making brilliant marvelous things out of commonplaces as other less gifted people make marvelous things commonplace. And we sit there oblivious of Time until it is time for lunch.

I have misgivings about such "goings on" with coffee. No physical weakling myself, perhaps because I had my first cup when I was fifty-five, I can't drink one without some slight dizziness, liver spots or something or other an hour or so afterward. So I remonstrate with Alec a little. No effect.

Lieber Meister used to come down to breakfast, pound the table for coffee, his hand shaking, and be morose until he got it. Then with it, soon pleasant, expansive as a blooming rose. Different, certainly, but good too, when in his coffee.

I've never seen a match for Alec. He makes me feel as though I had just come down from way-back yonder on a load of poles when I listen to him . . . damn him! You know.

"The Man Who Came to Dinner" can't compare with The Man Who Came to Breakfast. He too is a wit, a colorful cynic, a man of the world but a bitter smart Alec. The man who came to breakfast is a true friend, an esthetic enthusiast, lover of fine things, one who well knows why he loves them—a man of rare discrimination as well as master of a wit seldom at its end. The kindest, most generous man I know is Alec. And I know many kind and gentle men. Put that beside "The Man Who Came to Dinner," which you've probably seen. Try to figure it out.

If you get Alec straight he will be both and probably as many more in between as there are occasions. No Chameleon either. He just takes cir-

**Alexander Woollcott and the Wrights, Taliesin, Spring Green, Wisconsin.** FLLW Fdn FA#6803.0001

cumstances as a diamond takes light—that's all. And flashes.

I like the distinguished, kindly man who came to breakfast. So do we one and all. I speak for the Fellowship too.

Olgivanna put into his hands as he departed a simple little matt-glass Madonna because he admired it so much: a chef d'oeuvre a little taller than an overcoat pocket is deep. And because I don't know why Alec should have a Madonna or what he might do with one I tried to be a little jealous and failed. Somehow you can't do that to Alec.

## THE USONIAN HOUSE I

The house of moderate cost is not only America's major architectural problem but the problem most difficult for her major architects. As for me, I would rather solve it with satisfaction to myself and Usonia, than build anything I can think of at the moment except the modern theater now needed by the legitimate drama unless the stage is to be done to death by "the movies." In our country the chief obstacle to any real solution of the moderate-cost house problem is the fact that our people do not really know how to live. They imagine their idiosyncrasies to be their "tastes," their prejudices to be their predilections, and their ignorance to be virtue—where any beauty of living is concerned.

To be more specific, a small house on the side street might have charm if it didn't ape the big house on the Avenue, just as the Usonian village itself might have a great charm if it didn't ape the big town. Likewise, Marybud on the old farm, a jewel hanging from the tip of her pretty nose on a cold, cold day, might be charming in clothes befitting her state and her work, but is only silly in the Sears-Roebuck finery that imitates the clothes of her city sisters who imitate Hollywood stars: lipstick, rouge, high heels, silk stockings, bell skirt, cockeyed hat, and all. Exactly that kind of "monkey-fied" business is the obstacle to architectural achievement in our U.S.A. This provincial "culture-lag" in favor of the leg which does not allow the person, thing, or thought to be simple and naturally itself. It is the real obstacle to a genuine Usonian culture.

I am certain that any approach to the new house needed by indigenous culture—why worry about the house wanted by provincial "tasteful" ignorance!—is fundamentally different. That house must be a pattern for more simplified and, at the same time, more gracious living: necessarily new, but suitable to living conditions as they might so well be in this country we live in today.

This need of a house of moderate cost must sometime face not only expedients but Reality. Why not face it now? The expedient houses built by the million, which journals propagate, and government builds, do no such thing.

To me such houses are stupid makeshifts, putting on some style or other, really having no integrity. Style *is* important. *A* style is not. There is all the difference when we work *with* style and not for *a* style.

I have insisted on that point for forty-five years.

Notwithstanding all efforts to improve the product, the American "small house" problem is still a pressing, needy, hungry, confused issue. But where is a better thing to come from while Authority has pitched into perpetuating the old stupidities? I do not believe the needed house can come from current education, or from big business. It isn't coming by way of smart advertising experts either. Or professional streamliners. It is only super-common-sense that can take us along the road to the better thing in building.

What would be really sensible in this matter of the modest dwelling for our time and place? Let's see how far the Herbert Jacobs house at Madison, Wisconsin, is a sensible house. This house for a young journalist, his wife, and small daughter, is now under roof. Cost: Fifty-five hundred dollars, including architect's fee of four hundred and fifty. Contract let to P. B. Grove.

To give the small Jacobs family the benefit of the advantages of the era in which they live, many simplifications must take place. Mr. and Mrs. Jacobs must themselves see life in somewhat simplified terms. What are essentials in their case, a typical case? It is not only necessary to get rid of all unnecessary complications in construction, necessary to use work in the mill to good advantage, necessary to eliminate so far as possible, field labor which is always expensive: it is necessary to consolidate and simplify the three appurtenance systems—heating, lighting, and sanitation. At least this must be our economy if we are to achieve the sense of spaciousness and vista we desire in order to liberate the people living in the house. And it would be ideal to complete the building in one operation as it goes along. Inside and outside should be complete in one operation. The house finished inside as it is completed outside. There should be no complicated roofs.

Every time a hip or a valley or a dormer window is allowed to ruffle a roof the life of the building is threatened.

The way the windows are used is naturally a most useful resource to achieve the new characteristic sense of space. All this fenestration can be made ready at the factory and set up as the walls. But there is no longer sense of speaking of doors and windows. These walls are largely a system of fenestration having its own part in the building scheme—the system being as much a part of the design as eyes are part of the face.

Now what can be eliminated? These:

1. Visible roofs are expensive and unnecessary.

2. A garage is no longer necessary as cars are made. A carport will do, with liberal overhead shelter and walls on two sides. Detroit still has the livery-stable mind. It believes that the car is a horse and must be stabled.

3. The old-fashioned basement, except for a fuel and heater space, was always a plague spot. A steam-warmed concrete mat four inches thick laid directly on the ground over gravel filling, the walls set upon that, is better.

4. Interior "trim" is no longer necessary.

5. We need no radiators, no light fixtures. We will heat the house the "hypocaust" way—in or between the floors. We can make the wiring system itself be the light fixture, throwing light upon and down the ceiling. Light will thus be indirect, except for a few outlets for floor lamps.

6. Furniture, pictures and bric-a-brac are unnecessary because the walls can be made to include them or be them.

7. No painting at all. Wood best preserves itself. A coating of clear resinous oil would be enough. Only the floor mat of concrete squares needs waxing.

8. No plastering in the building.

9. No gutters, no downspouts.

To assist in general planning, what must or may we use in our new construction? In this case five materials: wood, brick, cement, paper, glass. To simplify fabrication we must use our horizontal-unit system in construction. We must also use a vertical-unit system which will be the widths of the boards and batten-bands themselves, interlocking with the brick courses. Although it is getting to be a luxury material, the walls will be wood board-walls the same inside as outside—three thicknesses of boards with paper placed between them, the boards fastened together with screws. These slab-walls of boards—a kind of plywood construction on a large scale can be high in insulating value, vermin-proof, and practically fireproof. These walls like the fenestration may be prefabricated on the floor, with any degree of insulation we can afford, and raised into place, or they may be made at the mill and shipped to the site in sections. The roof can be built first on props and these walls shoved into place under them.

The appurtenance systems, to avoid cutting and complications, must be an organic part of construction but independent of the walls. Yes, we must have polished plate glass. It is one of the things we have at hand to gratify the designer of the truly modern house and bless its occupants.

The roof framing in this instance is laminated of three 2 × 4's in depth easily making the three off-sets seen outside in the eaves of the roof, and enabling the roof span of 2 × 12" to be sufficiently pitched without the expense of "building up" the pitches. The middle offset may be left open at the eaves and fitted with flaps used to ventilate the roof spaces in summer. These 2 × 4's sheathed and insulated, then covered with a good asphalt roof, are the top of the house, shelter gratifying to the sense of shelter because of the generous eaves.

All this is in hand—no, it is in mind, as we plan the disposition of the rooms.

What must we consider essential now? We have a corner lot—say, an acre or two—with a south and west exposure? We will have a good garden. The house is planned to wrap around two sides of this garden.

1. We must have as big a living room with as much vista and garden coming in as we can afford, with a fireplace in it, and open bookshelves, a dining table in the alcove, benches, and living-room tables built in; a quiet rug on the floor.

2. Convenient cooking and dining space adjacent to if not a part of the living room. This space may be set away from the outside walls within the living area to make work easy. This is the new thought concerning a kitchen—to take it away from outside walls and let it turn up into overhead space within the chimney, thus connection to dining space is made immediate without unpleasant features and no outside wall space lost to the principal rooms. A natural current of air is thus set up toward the kitchen as toward a chimney, no cooking odors escaping back into the house. There are steps leading down from this space to a small cellar below for heater, fuel, and laundry, although no basement at all is necessary if the plan should be so made. The bathroom is usually next so that plumbing features of heating kitchen and bath may be economically combined.

3. In this case (two bedrooms and a workshop which may become a future bedroom) the single bathroom for the sake of privacy is not immediately connected to any single bedroom. Bathrooms opening directly into a bedroom occupied by more than one person or two bedrooms opening into a single bathroom have been badly overdone. We will have as much garden and space in all these space appropriations as our money allows after we have simplified construction by way of the technique we have tried out.

A modest house, this Usonian house, a dwelling place that has no feeling at all for the "grand" except as the house extends itself in the flat parallel to the ground. It will be a companion to the horizon. With floor-heating that kind of extension on the ground can hardly go too far for comfort or beauty of proportion, provided it does not cost too much in upkeep. As a matter of course a home like this is an architect's creation. It is not a builder's nor an amateur's effort. There is considerable risk in exposing the scheme to imitation or emulation.

This is true because a house of this type could not be well built and achieve its design except as an architect oversees the building.

And the building would fail of proper effect unless the furnishing and planting were all done by advice of the architect.

Thus briefly these few descriptive paragraphs instead of a floor plan may help to indicate how stuffy and stifling the little colonial hot-boxes, hallowed by government or not, really are where Usonian family life is concerned. You might easily put two of them, each costing more, into the living space of this one and not go much outside the walls. Here is a moderate-cost brick-and-wood house that by our own new technology has been greatly extended both in scale and comfort: a single house suited to prefabrication because the factory can go to the house.

Imagine how the costs would come down were the technique a familiar matter or if many houses were to be executed at one time—probably down to forty-five hundred dollars, according to number built and location.

There is a freedom of movement, and a privacy too, afforded by the general arrangement here that is unknown to the current "boxment." Let us say nothing about beauty. Beauty is an ambiguous term concerning an affair of taste in the provinces of which our big cities are the largest.

But I think a cultured American, we say Usonian, housewife will look well in it. The now inevitable car will seem a part of it.

Where does the garden leave off and the house begin? Where the garden begins and the house leaves off.

Withal, this Usonian dwelling seems a thing loving the ground with the new sense of space, light, and freedom—to which our U.S.A. is entitled.

## THE USONIAN HOUSE II

We have built some twenty-seven of them now in seventeen different states. Building costs in general in the U.S.A. were rising and are rising still. We find that seventy-five hundred dollars is about the sum needed to do what the Jacobs bought for fifty-five hundred. The Usonian house would have cost from seventy-five hundred up to ten, twelve, and in some certain extensive programs, fifteen, sixteen, and on up to twenty thousand dollars. We have built several extended in every way that cost more.

The houses cost, I should say, one-third more to build than when we started to build them in 1938. But this holds true—any comparison with the "regular" houses around them shows that they are more for the money physically for the sums they cost than the "regulars." Their freedom, distinction, and individuality are not a feature of that cost except as it does by elimination put the expenditure where it liberates the occupant in a new spaciousness. A new freedom.

It is true however that no man can have the liberation one of these houses affords with liberal outside views on three sides becoming a part of the interior, without incurring extra fuel—say twenty per cent more. Double windows cut this down—but also cost money.

## GRAVITY HEAT

Concerning floor heating. Heated air naturally rises. We call it gravity heat because the pipes filled with steam or hot water are all in a rock ballast bed beneath the concrete floor—we call the ballast with concrete top, the floor mat. If the floor is above the ground it is made of two-inch-square wood strips spaced 3' 8" apart. The heating pipes are in that case set between the floor joists.

It came to me in this way: In Japan to commence building the new Imperial Hotel, winter of 1914, we were invited to dine with Baron Okura, one of my patrons. It is desperately cold in Tokio in winter—a damp, clammy cold that almost never amounts to freezing or frost—but it is harder to keep warm there than anywhere else I have been, unless in Italy. The universal heater is the *hibachi*—a round vessel sitting on the floor filled with white ashes, several sticks of charcoal thrust down into the ashes all but a few inches. This projecting charcoal is lighted and glows—incandescent. Everyone sits around the *hibachi,* every now and then stretching out the hand over it for a moment—closing the hand as though grasping at something. The result is very unsatisfactory. To us. I marveled at Japanese fortitude until I caught sight of the typical underwear—heavy woolens, long sleeves, long legs, which they wear beneath the series of padded flowing kimono. But as they are acclimated and toughened to this native condition they suffer far less than we do.

Well, although we knew we should shiver, we accepted the invitation to dine at Baron Okura's Tokio house—he had a number of houses scattered around the Empire. As expected the dining room was so cold that I couldn't eat—pretending to eat only and for some nineteen courses. After dinner the Baron led the way below to the "Korean room," as it was called. This room was about eleven by fifteen, ceiling seven feet, I should say. A red-felt drugget covered the floor mats. The walls were severely plain, a soft pale yellow in color. We knelt there for conversation and Turkish coffee.

The climate seemed to have changed. No, it wasn't the coffee; it was Spring. We were soon warm and happy again—kneeling there on the floor, an indescribable warmth. No heating was visible nor was it felt directly as such. It was really a matter *not of heating at all* but an affair of *climate.*

The Harvard graduate who interpreted for the Baron explained: the Korean room meant a room heated under the floor. The heat of a fire outside at one corner of the floor drawn back and forth underneath the floor in and between tile ducts, the floor forming the top of the flues (or ducts), made by the partitions, the smoke and heat going up and out of a tall chimney at the corner opposite the corner where the fire was burning.

The indescribable comfort of being warmed from below was a discovery.

I immediately arranged for electric heating elements beneath the bathrooms in the Imperial Hotel—dropping the ceiling of the bathrooms to create a space beneath each in which to generate the heat. The tile floor and built-in tile baths were thus always warm. It was pleasant to go in one's bare feet into the bath. This experiment was a success. All ugly electric heat fixtures (dangerous too in a bathroom) were eliminated. I've always hated fixtures—radiators especially. Here was the complete opportunity to digest all that paraphernalia in the building—creating not a heated interior but creating climate—healthful, dustless, serene. And also, the presence of heat thus integral and beneath makes lower temperatures desirable. Sixty-five degrees seems for normal human beings sufficient. But neighbors coming in from super-heated houses would feel the cold at first. It is true that a natural climate is generated instead of an artificial forced condition—the natural condition much more healthful, as a matter of course.

I determined to try it out at home at the first opportunity. That opportunity seemed to be the Nakoma Country Club, but that Indianesque affair stayed in the form of a beautiful plan.[17]

Then came the Johnson Administration Building. Just the thing for that, and we proceeded with the installation, but all the professional heating contractors except one (Westerlin and Campbell) scoffed, refusing to have anything to do with the idea. But as chance had it, the little Jacobs House turned up meantime and was completed before that greater venture got into operation.

So the Jacobs House was the first installation to go into effect. There was great excitement and curiosity on the part of "the profession." Crane Company officials came in, dove beneath the rugs, put their hands on the concrete in places remote from the heater, got up and looked at one another as though they had seen a ghost. My God! It works. Where were radiators now?

As usual.

Articles on "radiant heat" began to appear in testimonial journals. But it was in no sense "radiant heat" or panel heating or any of the things they called it that I was now interested in. It was simply *gravity heat*—heat coming up from beneath as naturally as heat rises.

Some thirty or more Usonian buildings now have floor heating. We have had to learn to proportion the heat correctly for varying climates and conditions. We have accumulated some data that is useful.

There is no other "ideal" heat. Not even the heat of the sun.

## THE UNKIND FIREPLACE

Lloyd (Lewis) is not only my own client after my own heart but he is one of my warmest and most faithfully insulting and insulted of friends. Long ago when I was down getting a worm's-eye view of society and Lloyd was a rising young "publicity man" I engaged him to keep me out of the newspapers. He lasted a little less than three months. Then I paid him off and fired him for cause. The thing couldn't be done. He blamed me. But why blame me for my own fault?

Now his turn. He employed me to build him a house. He was a hard client. But not hard enough.

Having been there myself, often, I knew it was so damp and hot out on the prairie by the Des Plaines River that I set Lloyd well up off the ground to keep him high and dry in Spring, Fall, and Summer, his domicile winnowed by the wind . . . beneath! Thereby I exposed him in Winter not unnecessarily, but somewhat expensively. For the good of his health? Yes. But more for the good of his soul.

That type of house I believe ideal for a prairie site on low, damp land of that type. But no such proceeding could be called cheap.

So, up there off the ground, the beautiful river landscape coming in through three sides of the beautiful house and the woods showing beneath, it was hard to keep Lloyd warm in Winter. Kathryn, his wife, didn't cool off so readily as Lloyd did, but the sixty-five degrees we set for normal in a floor-heated Usonian house just didn't jibe by about twenty degrees with the Daily News office where Lloyd worked. And there was something the mat-ter with the boiler pump there which we went down to fix or else the house would have risen to seventy-five. I am glad of an excuse to go to Lloyd's home anyway.

With usual bravado, pretending to make light of the thing, I thought of various ways of keeping the writer warm. I thought of wiring him to an electric pad inside his vest, allowing lots of lead wire so he could get around. But he waved the idea aside with contempt as a passing of the "buck." No patience at all, so we dropped that. Then I suggested we appeal to Secretary Knox to turn down the heat at the Daily News from eighty-five gradually to sixty-five so he could become acclimated. But Lloyd said the cold-blooded Daily-News-men couldn't get their stuff out at that temperature. Anyway he didn't want to be educated; he said he *was* educated. So we dropped that one, too.

There was nothing left for me to do, since I had made the house part of the landscape and the landscape all around it came in on three sides (and underneath as well) but put on some double windows at Lloyd's expense just like the other folks do, in hiding around there in those fashionable woods. It was humiliating to get down thus into that clandestine society but we just had to go through with it.

Still in the same spirit of bravado, knowing that it is not at all in my own interest I now refer to the unkindest ordeal of all. The innocent, very simple little fireplace I built for Lloyd to sit by when he writes just refuses to draw . . . too simple, I guess, to know how. We have built some three thousand fireplaces that do draw and a few that didn't know how at first but that do know how now. This particular one, though, Lloyd's own, doesn't know how yet. It will. We haven't given up.

Meantime, the curious neighbors are coming

**Herbert Jacobs House, Madison, Wisconsin. 1937.**
FLLW Fdn FA#3702.0025

and parking their cars in the vicinity to watch and see if there is any smoke coming out of that part of the chimney top yet.

But was the house doing it to Lloyd or was Lloyd doing it to the house?

There it is . . . my beloved most intimate friend, the Historian, Drama Critic, Sports Editor, sitting there by that damn little fireplace, an especially unobtrusive little one I designed especially for him (brick), now so obtrusive you can hear the midget miles off by way of a sort of clinical or morbid interest on the part of the neighbors. Those who had undergone operations of their own?

Well, there it is, one out of three thousand, to speak truth, that did draw.

But I know what: should we fail to teach that fireplace the law and it still refuses, we can put a little fan, a kind of policeman, up there in the chimney with a switch down nearby where Lloyd sits so when he has enough fire he can turn it off and when he doesn't want smoke he can turn it on. In the whole galaxy (or is it phalanx) of three thousand fireplaces that little one (it is a sidekick of the successful big one) will thus be unique.

We'll let you know how everything turns out.

If we don't, the neighbors will.

Although, if it turns out well they will have lost interest and dropped the whole matter.

The house made a gardener of Kathryn and a farmer-without-a-barn out of Lloyd. You should see the boy around the place in those coveralls! He raises pigs.

There is a lot of the best in both of them built into their house because I knew and loved them so well, well enough to put it there. And they earned it and deserved the best I could do. They were up to it too. They loved the house.

Nevertheless the tragedy that befell so many of my clients happened to the Lloyd Lewises. They just liked to stay in their house and didn't care to go out anywhere unless they had to go.

Many of their friends, like the Alfred MacArthurs, for instance, just pretended to like the house because they like Lloyd. But I know some of the neighbors didn't. But those who didn't were living in period houses dated way back when and furnished "way back" to match.

In fact, the new dwelling made quite a stir in the society of that squeamish, highly stylish neck of the flat woods where Old Mexico, Norway, Ancient Sweden, and Camden village were in hiding behind the trees and to no good purpose, believe me.

Lloyd and Kathryn also furnished their exciting but very quiet Usonian House "to match" and in such good Usonian style that even I like to go back to enjoy it myself. So does Marc (Connelly). So does Alec (Woollcott). Alec wrote a nice little letter to me about the house which was fine. And generous again.

Hoping Alec won't object, if Lloyd doesn't, here is the little letter which I cherish. I'll share it with you.

Dear Frank:

I hear you will be returning to Spring Green tomorrow so I am leaving promptly for Rochester, New York, but not before making a second visit to Libertyville to see that exhilarating house you have built for Lloyd Lewis. I was there last Sunday and went to confirm, by a second visit, the impression it made upon me. On the strength of that house alone I think I could go forth and preach afresh the gospel of Frank Lloyd Wright.

I see now more fully than ever before what effect the right house can have upon the person inside it. I told Lloyd that this one makes even a group of *his* friends look distinguished.

Lloyd, whom I admire and enjoy, never did anything so wise in his life. Just to be in that house uplifts the heart and refreshes the spirit. Most houses confine their occupants. Now I understand, where before I only dimly apprehended, that such a house as this can liberate the person who lives in it.

God bless you.

A. Woollcott

April 15, 1941

## THE STAMPEDE

I refused to be stampeded by the wave of urbanism which swept the U.S.A., affecting such of our architects as Harvey Corbett, Lamb, Van Allen, Ray Hood, Bel Geddes, to name but a few, and so very many others: in fact, *all* of our commercial architects, both great and small. I could see little more in La Ville Radieuse, a greater New York by Hugh Ferris, or the soulless dreams of Bel Geddes et al. than exploitation of what was already an excess. The taller Chicago, the more-up-in-the-air San Francisco, etc., etc., were stupidities that bored me. Higher and higher up and up went the visionless race for skyscraper distinction. Skyscraperism by way of the urban man-eaters became, by way of false civic pride, popular and science monthlies, T-square and triangle clubs, a startling dream of a stunning future in which man himself as a feature of that future became a speck of no significance whatever. Except as he had brought to an apex his own abnegation in this splendiferous, hard-as-nails design for his own tomb.

The skyscraperist craze was due to our commercial vanity played upon by the false pride of Science itself in our day and hour. Or I should say the pride of false science.

The skyscraper itself, however, was the needed hallmark for modern commercial *Success!* And certain civic ambition *was* served by it. But really it was, at bottom, a mere unethical exploitation by the landlord of the profits of superconcentration. Socially a menace; architecturally, false. An exploit of the blind perverted mechanization of the period. The realtorific faith and fatalistic promotion that are the danger and the curse of this mechanistic age came to a death's head in the American skyscraper.

My faith went the other way.

I could see the very tall building only in the country. And Broadacre City, as agrarian as it was urban, was eventually the answer I found to this spectacular folly of prevalent commercial vanity. But the "man-eater" had captured the imagination of American business men to such an extent that nearly every city of the country had its skyscraper in the worst possible spot in order to keep up and be anybody at all, at least be "up to date," a "going institution." It was *on* the street but not *for* the street. Why the skyscraper so readily found so many false prophets among our American architects until their work could be seen standing up and out even on the Western prairies, under circumstances that made them similar to headstones in the cemeteries of those same places, is a question I could answer if it were really worthwhile.

Nevertheless and notwithstanding all consideration, ethical, esthetic, economic, the skyscraper was serving as the banner of American commercial success: the success that was running the nation ragged. And down and out, Anno Domini 1929. America's cow, so to speak, was, by this ruse, taken indoors, spoonfed in a stanchion behind glass for advertising purposes only. The cow was steadily declining in health and productivity in consequence. All this when the national cow from any standpoint of health or real wealth should have been turned out to grass.

## TO THE AMERICAN EAGLE

If you must have a skyscraper—he is a flyer. You will see his symbol on the back of most of our coins. And he is a square American. I sent him the following telegram: "We knew you could fly straight, but now when everywhere is equivocation and cowardice you not only think straight but you dare speak straight." You know whom I mean. And this goes for his brave little wife.

Honor, too, to the true American who put him into the service of his country for better or for worse. A staunch man, Henry Ford.

And the Usonian hat is off to John Haynes Holmes, a courageous hero fit for a sky pilot for the American Eagle.

## ON TAKING EFFECTS FOR CAUSES

For forty-five years I have seen, intimately, the origin and growth of the movement in Architecture in which the work I have done myself has been a major factor. And now that I am principal witness to its inception and subsequent development (the inception and development of that movement which is now called Modern architecture for lack of a better name), I am still seeing History made, able to compare the making as seen by our very best critics with facts with which I am myself familiar. What I have seen makes me more than ever suspicious of the critical Historian. And this applies to any Historian of himself. Yes, I am suspicious of myself sometimes. Three Scotch highballs would call for suspicion.

I have seen the original work spread worldwide as an original impulse, take general form on the surface of the globe, and increase both here at home and abroad, but take superficial general form only—a superficial resemblance.

I have contributed to it new forms, again and again—hundreds—only to see them exploited, put forward wrong end to, and if not exactly upside down—then certainly inside out. I have seen since 1910 (I then for the first time visited Europe) the European reaction to this work I have myself done and I know full well its contemporary effects on other architects at home and especially abroad. I have seen the direct and creditable obvious implications of my work often credited to others as their own original idea or impulse, although I have never seen the obvious implications of the work of others credited to me—that were creditable to me.

I have seen the critical view of what were mere effects persistently, often wilfully, mistaken for causes. And vice versa. So equivocal and confusing, so far astern were they in their necessarily posterior view of the situation so far as origins are concerned that I usually read critical reviews of my own work in relation to the work of my contemporaries with grim amusement and appropriate profanity. Since I cannot read them backward. Reviews are so far out of focus and (designedly or not) so badly out of drawing as to put effects forward as causes and set causes back into the category of mere effects.

Such, I say, is the History of the so-called Modern Movement in Architecture, "a designed miseducation" in general. Instead of growing more simple with time, the mere Effects multiply and further obscure actual Causes.

The gift of seeing a source rise, take its natural course and begin to flow—become a rivulet, then spread to a steady, broad flowing river in contemporaneous life—maintaining a just proportion in the seeing and the writing: well, it is simply not done.

Perhaps origins are entitled to the seclusion ensured by such confusion?

A nice provision of Nature?

But artificial subsequences are soon universally looked back upon as of primary consequences, and there is no remedy.

Higher education is too much a cheap conceit hoping to thrive on mere Information but never really able to learn the net result, inferiority mistaking patriotism for Honor—sacrifice for Duty—money-punctilio for Character and a hectic noisy self-assertion for a good time.

No wonder this great provincial nation has such faith in propaganda.

Perhaps there is something in the English tongue that makes it an efficient prevaricator, a natural equivocal perverter of truth. Yet how could things have been very different in other and earlier times? How can we be sure that all History is not made in the same way: effects mistaken for causes, causes mistaken for effects?

I have seen the long arm of mere coincidence thus play strange tricks on the Critic. I have seen appearances too often be the only basis for his rationalizations after the fact, and all entirely beside the mark—no more than a pleasant fiction or an interesting speculation. Amusing as well as exasperating.

I could name a long list but would only open profitless controversy because the critic, per se as such, is no respecter of an original source of information. And certainly, even were he a competent judge, no respecter of an original source of inspiration. The thing is too simple for him on any such basis. There is not room enough for his own expansion. History "à la mode" is, I suspect, mostly the personal view of reflections, a sort of mirage in a distorted mirror: the mind of the Historian. In our day true proportion in true perspective does not go with our temper or our pace *or* the effects we aim to produce. "Speed," as Meredith says, "is a kind of voracity." And voracity is by nature none too particular. That for one thing. But, for another, out of our academic pigeon-holes we are swamped by the departmental mind. A mind which has its uses but a mind that sees in parts only and patches the parts together to make a case for its own sake, or for himself and, unfortunately, for the future.

Thus any sincere search for FORM is meantime betrayed to the inimical, and worse, perhaps confused from Generation to Generation.

We need something safe to build on. Of course, that something is the Truth. But the real seeker for Truth always gets back to simples—and with rectitude, amplitude, and impartiality lets the shallow surf of erudite self-assertion break upon itself and roll back where it came from.

Bred to greatness and splendor by Art and Science, Architecture has cosmic destinies yet undreamed of . . . by the critics.

## DR. FERDINAND THE FRIEND

Did you understand me to say that the Taliesin Fellowship had received very little help from anyone? I should take that back. It was in pre-Fellowship days, to be sure, but there probably would have been no Fellowship at all, but for the occupant of the Chair of History at Chicago University—by name, Ferdinand W. Schevill. In Book Four you have been told of the incorporation of Frank Lloyd Wright: how seven of my friends and clients contributed between them some fifty-seven thousand dollars to defend and get me back to work again and keep me working at Taliesin. They were Dr. Ferdinand Schevill, Harold McCormick, Mrs. Avery Coonley, Darwin

D. Martin, the principal subscribers. Ben E. Page, Mrs. Jane Porter, and George Parker of Parker-pen contributed also.

Well—Dr. Ferdinand was president of that corporation (much against his will, I suspect), an enterprise wherein all of the fifty-seven thousand was lost in the national collapse of 1929–1930 except the objective for which the money was originally intended and subscribed. And that had a narrow escape. The purpose was getting me back to work again where, protected, I could keep at it.

Ferdinand won't like this—but most of the corporation subscribers were "rich," while he had only a good revenue from his historical textbooks and his salary as Historian at the University. Only recently I learned that he had not only subscribed his original quota, seventy-five hundred dollars, but had secretly put up five thousand more in the name of a friend who afterward became secretary of the corporation. And, moreover, to show you what use the man has for money, Ferdinand was a heavy subscriber to Sherwood Anderson's publishing venture—no more profitable, I venture to say, than my venture as an architect. Poor, great Sherwood! Ferdinand loved him more than he loved me, because Sherwood was so much more lovable.

It all goes to show, I think, that money is no stricture in the hands of a man like Ferdinand, the recluse. For he now lives and writes—retired—in a nice little home Woltersdorf built for him in the woods near Michigan City, Indiana, not far from the Carl (Sandburg), he who took a national hero to pieces, put him together again, and got rich. The true Carl was born to be a poet, a glorious failure, not a Success. "Success" is very unbecoming to Carl.

That I didn't build that house for Ferdinand hurts me more, I guess, than Ferdinand helped me—because I would gladly have given the price of his subscription to have built it for him. But at that time I was far away, the going still uncertain, and Dr. Ferdinand was in a hurry and . . . well . . . you will probably have your own idea as to why he didn't want to take the trouble to go through a building operation with me. The circumstances I admit were

not propitious. But do you know what? I believe Ferdinand didn't try to overcome the obstacles so that I might pay back to him at least that much because he is so essentially modest and retiring. He wanted a commonplace house. If I had built his house he might have been rooted out at all hours of the day by tourists and young students of architecture; he would have been exemplar, a showpiece. And having no mind to charge fifty cents for the privilege of viewing his abode, he chose the obscurity that went with Woltersdorf.

I am therefore jealous of Woltersdorf—and obscurity.

Obscurity is so much easier to live up to.

Had I followed in my own youthful, shy bent, I might have been allowed to build a house for my best friend.

They say the woman always pays. . . . Nonsense!

It is the fool who has allowed himself to be famous who pays—and pays.

## THE MERRY WIVES OF TALIESIN

While I was alone at Taliesin after coming back from Japan, I had three wives, Sylva, Dione, and Nobu, looking in on me and keeping my spirits up. But they were not mine. They were the wives respectively of Werner (Moser), Richard (Neutra), and Kameki (Tsuchiura)—apprentices from Zurich, Vienna, and Tokio. But I can't imagine what I would have done without them at the time. On the rocks mentally, morally, emotionally.

We had music in the Living Room of Taliesin II evenings as we do now in the Living Room of Taliesin III. We occasionally drove about in the countryside. Werner (Werner played the violin) and Sylva had a fine little boy, Lorenz. I liked to hold Lorenz sometimes. I loved to have him around. He was a beautiful boy. Richard and Dione had a small son, too (named for me before leaving Vienna); Kameki and Nobu were only just married. Together with Major Will (Smith) they were all my immediate family. A happy one, because they were all good to what was left of me at that bad time. The boys kept my mind on my work; the girls kept kind attentions and flowers all through the house. While they did make me feel less lonely, they only

**Christmas Concert, Taliesin, Spring Green, Wisconsin. 1924. Left to right: FLLW, Richard Neutra, Silva Moser (with baby Lorenz), Kameki Tsuchiura, Nobu Tsuchiura, Werner Moser, and Dione Neutra.** FLLW Fdn FA#2501.1114

made me feel all the more need of "the woman in my life" in these several pre-Olgivanna years. That Sylva-Werner baby especially made me long for a little soft one of my own at Taliesin. After all, what was Taliesin without young children? I guess the happiness of these young couples pushed me gently over the precipice of divorce and marriage to really live again.

The young women were three entirely differing individualities. Their young husbands were talented fellows, but not to be compared to their wives. Sylva was a true-hearted beauty; Dione was a genius, good to look at, played her cello and sang while playing, doing both with real style: her own. And like most Europeans she played the best of music. Nobu was like a petite Japanese doll—when exquisitely dressed in her native costumes. Kameki was extremely competent, blinking intelligently behind his glasses. I look back upon that period of life at Taliesin as a quiet prelude before the storm. The outside storm broke when Olgivanna appeared upon the scene, which she did some time before they had all left, two of them going home (their terms were up), and one to the West Coast to "get jobs."

Werner had come to me with a letter from his distinguished father, Herr Professor Moser of Zurich, probably then the leading architect of Europe (Herr Professor Otto Wagner gone), asking me to take his son Werner as a pupil. I was happy to have the great architect's son. Kameki came by way

of the Imperial Hotel to study with me. Richard had been knocking on my door from Vienna for admittance to Taliesin for several years, until at last, coming over anyway and finding me gone, he camped down with Holabird and Root a few months to wait until I came back. All are building reputations for themselves in, respectively, Switzerland, Japan, and California.

Autobiographers publish a good many letters, I believe. So here is one I have recently received from Herr Professor Moser's now distinguished son, Werner, himself author of many important interesting buildings in Switzerland.

"Dear Mr. Wright:

"Since we have this terrible totalitarian war in Europe there is much uncertainty, much dissatisfaction and opportunism in our European architecture. There is great need for a constructive, clear, direct mind. You can demonstrate in your life-long work one continuous line of architectural development, of course expressed in a big variety of applications of the one principle. Your work is a consolation today for every sensible architect, and an encouragement not to resign, because it shows to us the deeply rooted belief in everything which is positive today and the possibility to express it beautifully with the characteristic elements of this time.

"(It is bad English but I hope you know what I mean.) I had a great pleasure to follow your new ideas from the recent publications in preparing a lecture about your work. There were many young students and a really spontaneous interest in all your achievements. It was a good thing, in comparing it to your designs, to show up the weaknesses in Swiss architecture. The lack of thoroughness, of coordination and imagination, and so on!

"Of course, you never can replace an ingenious mind, you can only try to follow his basic idea! Sylva and I had many thoughts for you since we saw Olgivanna and you three years ago in Paris. I remember well your critical call referring to my designs: 'Werner, you need a good spanking!'

"We would enjoy strongly to hear how you and your inner-Wright family are going through these times!

"In your work we feel the never-tiring youth, which is over-shadowing everything done by the younger generation, in respect to inspiration and courage.

"You certainly know how precarious the situation in Switzerland is. We are trying very hard to keep independence.

"I would like to forward pictures of my works to get a severe critic from you! I hear of your big exhibition in New York and regret very much not to be able to see it. It is about time to have an exhibition like that in Switzerland!

"Sylva and the three children are very well, we are for a few days in the winter sports to do skiing. Lorenz is almost my size and wants to be an architect. He will be through school in a few years and I should like him to be some day apprentice to you.

"Very many thanks and sincere wishes for 1941 to Mrs. Wright and you from all the Mosers, especially from your Werner."

## LULU BETT

Zona (Gale) once told me, "I think the wisest thing you have ever done is to stay in the country."

I pondered this. She might have meant so many things. While Sylva, Dione, and Nobu were all the wives I had at Taliesin, I occasionally drove up the river to Portage with one or another of them to see Zona—in spite of the columnar village-palazzo she lived in. The old-colonial box (of course, she didn't build it) stood baldly and emptily forward on the street leaving a great lawn to the rear—a few nice trees on it—running to the Wisconsin River bank—the same sand-barred river that flows below the windows of Taliesin. My people all knew Zona. My Mother and my Aunts much admired her. While in Japan I read *Lulu Bett*.[19] Straightway I made up my mind to know Zona Gale better when I got home; if not, to know the reason why. I had met her at Taliesin with Charlotte Perkins Gilman.

We used to come in to the house with our arms full of wild flowers gathered on the way up the river. Once or twice we were compelled to throw them all out on account of the violent reactions, none too kindly, of old Father Gale. Hay fever.

Sometimes I used to take Nobu and Kameki along in costume (Japanese umbrella too, you know) and pose them on the lawn by the river—making pictures for Zona. Zona and her friend (it might be the Lulu who wrote the play *Sun-up* or some other literary celebrity—they were always around) would get a little supper together for us.

Of course, I hated her environment as utterly unworthy of her (she was an exquisite thing, Wisconsin's Zona Gale). I hadn't met Olgivanna and I thought Taliesin would be a much more appropriate place for the author of *Lulu Bett*. But I had been spoiled, or something. Perhaps I had always expected the women to make love to me. I just didn't know how to make love to Zona Gale.

But she was always glad to see us, asking me to come, although she said she valued her Regency at the University of Wisconsin too much ever to be seen with me in public. (There were other reasons I guess, because it wasn't so very long before she married.) For any woman to be seen with me in public *was* pretty dangerous for the woman (not to mention dangerous to me). So I loved the Zona who wrote *Lulu Bett*. And after I knew her a little better I told Zona that I didn't believe she ever wrote the book, she was so unlike Lulu Bett, herself. But you couldn't quarrel with Zona. She was too complete and lovely in herself. She was like something exquisitely carved out of ivory.

I wonder, though, what she meant when she said "the *wisest* thing you have ever done," because it was no *wisdom* of mine that kept *me* in the country. No, it was something constitutional. My mother so deeply loved life in the Valley that I am sure I nursed at the Valley's breast when I nursed at hers.

Terrestrial beauty so grows on me as I grow up that the longer I live the more beautiful it becomes. A walk in our countryside when the shadows are lengthening is to look and drink a poignant draught—and look and drink again. I wonder if anything there can be in "Heaven" is so lovely. If not, how tragic Death must be! Death or no death, I see our countryside as a promise never to be broken.

## THE AMERICAN CITIZEN

And here in the midst of this small trilogy of reminiscences, where and when and how she appeared in my life, between The Merry Wives of Taliesin and Lulu Bett, is Olgivanna. Fate the dealer dealt her to me at this particular moment. And since Fate so decided and this is, in a way, an autobiography, I do not have either the hardihood to fly in the face of Fate and change the place of her appearance or leave her out. These eighteen years she has been a vivid living presence, next to my heart and in the hollow of my arm, a joy and inspiration.

She is here under the casual title "The American Citizen," which, though a triumph of understatement, is a true and becoming title for Olgivanna.

Were I to keep on "growing up" I had reached a jumping-off place. At least a critical stage in the growth of this thing which is me. Things had been going pretty low so far as I was concerned. Something was past due. What was it? Was it me?

When I met her at the parting of the ways, a mad genius-of-the-pig-bristles, Jerry (Blum) was alongside. A better than good, much-traveled, diamond-in-the-rough painter but rather terrifying. His parents had spoiled him with too much easy money. There was a fury in him now damned by trouble with his wife Lucile. I myself, lower down in my own estimation than I had ever been in my life, was staying at the Congress for a night or so. Jerry of auld-lang-syne (the Midway Gardens) happened in and all unsuspecting we, "Les Misérables," strolled over a block or two to the Sunday matinee of the Russian ballet. Our tickets landed us near the stage in two balcony box-seats, by the rail. A third seat in the box was empty: apparently the only unoccupied one in the big overcrowded house. Karsavina was to dance and her performance had just begun when an usher quietly showed a dark, slender gentlewoman to the one empty seat in the house. Unobtrusive but lovely. I secretly observed her aristocratic bearing, no hat, her dark hair parted in the middle and smoothed down over her ears, a light small shawl over her shoulders, little or no makeup, very simply dressed. French, I thought—very French . . . and yet perhaps Russian? Whatever her nationality I instantly liked her looks and wondered who she was and where from. And why. Losing all interest in the stage. Although I can perfectly see Karsavina poised on one toe as she stood when the gentle stranger entered the box and my life.

Jerry, more intent on the dark, slender lady with the graceful movements who sat beside him than on Karsavina, moved a little closer—but evidently frightened the gentle stranger for she moved a little further away. I looked over the rail to see where he would land if I dropped him bodily out of the box, but he would hurt too many people down there below. He addressed a remark to me intended for her, foolishly complimenting Karsavina, so I gave him one also intended for the gentle stranger.

"No," I said. "No, Karsavina won't do. She's dead." And waving toward the audience below, "They are all dead: the dead is dancing to the dead."

A quick comprehending glance from the young Frenchwoman with the sensitive feminine brow and dark eyes . . . or was she a Russian princess?

The glance went home: a strange elation stole over me. Suddenly in my unhappy state something cleared up—what had been the matter with me came to look me in the face—it was, simply, too much passion without poetry. Starved . . . for poetry . . . that was it, the best in me for years and years wasted—starved! This strange chance meeting, was it . . . poetry? I was a hungry man.

I didn't notice Jerry after that until the intermission. Something long since out of drawing had come to life in me. The intermission came soon. Evidently Jerry intended to find out who the lady was. "Pardon me, Madam, we have met somewhere before?" She seemed unconvinced and unimpressed. "In New York, at Waldo Frank's perhaps?" She gave me a startled look. A long shot. Yes, it so happened that the gentle stranger did know Waldo Frank's wife, Margaret Naumburg. That clever knight picked out a few more names she recognized and Jerry had opened the way to introduce me: "My friend; he is Frank Lloyd Wright, the famous architect. You may have heard of him?" She hadn't, but she looked at me as though she had seen me before. So much so that I thought she had for a moment. I thought I must have met her—somewhere? But no, no one like her—that I could remember—

and yet—where? There was something . . . coming clear. She spoke in a low musical voice. In a sentence or two she criticized Karsavina from our point of view, showing unusual familiarity with dancing and dancers. No longer quite so strange, the emissary of Fate, mercy on my soul, from the other side of the known world, bowed her head to my invitation to tea at the nearby Congress. She accepted with perfect ease without artificial hesitation.

I was in love with her.

It was all as simple as that. When nature by the hand of Fate has arranged her drama all else is beside the mark. It is as it should be.

Over tea cups the obvious conversation ranged the gamut of Philosophy and Art. The implications were colorful overtones, deep undertones. She held her own in either: and "her own" was a famous architect. Manifestly well educated she was unusually well trained in self-possession in a more profound school than anyone I had ever met. And, incidentally, not so important, I learned what you already know, that Olgivanna—that was her name—was born to an official family in Cettinje, Montenegro, was educated by her sister in Batum, Russia, had just arrived from Paris with her seven-year-old little daughter, Svetlana. She had come to Chicago to confer on business matters with her husband from whom she had separated. She was intending to return to Paris as soon as possible. You already know, too, the attractive name Olgivanna was made by her friends out of Olga Ivanovna as it had been in Batum—Russian for Olga, daughter of John. The nickname Olgivanna was a respectful form of address not unlike our Mrs. or Miss.

The *Institute Gurdjieff* for the harmonious development of man, I had already heard about. The Asiatic savant had brought his group to New York the summer before and performed remarkable studies in human correlation at Carnegie Hall. She herself had been in the group, and I now learned from her more of that remarkable training. The Institute took unrhythmical neurotic human beings in all the social stratas, took them apart, and put them together again better correlated, happier, more alive and use-

Olgivanna during her first visit to Taliesin, Spring Green, Wisconsin. 1924. FLLW Fdn FA#6104.0003

ful to themselves and others. I am putting here what Olgivanna said with her own inimitable accent into my own words. It seems that Ouspensky, Orage, Lady Rothermere, Katherine Mansfield, and many others were Gurdjieff beneficiaries and disciples. Olgivanna, Jean Zartsman, Lili Galounian, the Hartmans, and Schoenvalls were all star leaders in the teachings Gurdjieff had promulgated and was preaching—nearer Dalcroze it seemed to me than any other well-known system. But more profound. It was fascinating revelation as she described it. She seemed to approve and like what I had to say about it. Between us across that tea table went more from each to each than I can ever describe. It was not in words, although the words were good. I am no novelist. Meredith might do it. But I should be dissatisfied with what he did and so would Olgivanna.

Jerry kept on gushing. Even more than her acquaintance with philosophy I admired the more than lady-like art, art is the word, with which Olgivanna let Jerry slide off without hurting his feelings too much. Jerry was a good talker though, and discussion at the table had been stimulating, so let's forgive him his trespass. After a half hour Olgivanna arose to go (arose is the word), to go to her child, she said. But I couldn't bear the thought of letting her go—I was afraid I should lose her. She hesitated, but only for a moment when I said, "Olgivanna, please leave your address so we may call on you? I want to learn more. I can't think we should let our remarkable meeting end here." But I was eager to teach as well as to learn as anyone could see. Jerry took the address because he, being a painter, had a pencil. I, being an architect, never have one.

Olgivanna (what a winning name) was gone. The light went off when she went. But I knew well enough that nothing could stop us from seeing each other again, nothing either for her or for me. I went East for a week, but sent a little note from the train. I dropped back into the aching void.

As soon as I got back I called Jerry to come over and stay with me, knowing that he would have been to see her. Poor Jerry was all broken up over the affair Lucile. I had to listen to that first.

"Jerry, have you seen Olgivanna?"

The unhappy painter-wretch had been to the address Olgivanna had given. "But," he said, "Olgivanna only wanted to talk about you and that bored me."

I felt grateful to Jerry for being bored that way, and much that pleased me more he imparted with a few characteristic curses.

I wrote another note asking when I might come. The time fixed, I went to take Olgivanna to the theater. Neither of us can remember, nor care to, what the play was. She had several faithful North Side friends, music-makers some of them, and some on whom we began to impose.

Some days later I invited Olgivanna to Taliesin to have her meet Sylva, Dione, and Nobu, and their clever husbands. Olgivanna and "the merry wives of Taliesin" had much in common, all being European. Next afternoon she left. My 1924 household, knowing full well what had happened to me, was sure that Taliesin was the place for *her*. None so sure as I. Her divorce was in court—granted. So was mine, waiting for signature—so why wait? Two fountains of arrested energy didn't wait. Waiting

was not in our natures—never was. Never has been. Isn't now.

Although we didn't know then how much would have been saved to both if we had "waited," it probably would have made no difference.

We had each other for better or for worse.

Olgivanna was mine. The night we were off to New York together I read her to sleep with Carl's fairy tale of *The White Horse Girl and The Blue Wind Boy*. I guess he so intended it. I had just discovered the "Rootabaga Stories" and they delighted me so much I wrote him a little letter, appended hereafter in gratitude.

The story of the plight that followed this brave flight into a new life—passion with poetry now— you have read in the fourth book of *An Autobiography*. What you have not read is how well the chance meeting dealt by the hand of Fate—kind for once, at least—turned out for us and for everyone else who had any right to be at all interested in how it turned out. For more than eighteen years, the perfect mistress, Olgivanna, and I have lived and worked in luck and out of luck at Taliesin, constantly together in any case. And this in sickness and in health. Mostly health. No fair-weather friend was Olgivanna. There was great work to be done there as well as a full life to be lived. But one that would have destroyed any human being less well trained for the struggle for the better thing, and less inspired by natural gifts, mutual love and understanding for that high struggle.

Just to be with her uplifts my heart and strengthens my spirit when the going gets hard or when the going is good.

We were married, certainly, but we wouldn't know it unless you insisted on the point, because we don't need to be. I found that the girl who was qualified by years of hard, patient trying to understand, inspired by ideas similar to my own, was qualified to be an imaginative vivid inspiration and a real mate.

Whatever we undertook, she never shirked.

And strangely enough—or is it so strange— she, whose parents were Montenegrin dignitaries, had pictures of her Montenegrin forebears that looked just like my Welsh forebears. They might have been of one family although we ourselves resembled each other only in spirit.

John Commons (of Wisconsin U.) told us there was nothing to wonder about in that because the Montenegrins, the Basques, and the Welsh were all a related mountain people. Her severe bringing-up was so similar to mine that we liked not only the same fundamentals, but what went with them in much the same way. There was just enough difference in the non-essentials to make whatever she did the more interesting to me. She would take a case of any kind in the Fellowship, straighten it with a grasp and effectiveness that could not be matched. She could paint, or sculpt, or cook, or dance, or play and sing. Svetlana is like her in that respect. It isn't mere versatility. There is a driving fire in it all.

Svetlana is Olgivanna's little daughter's name. After some legal difficulties which you have read about already, she came to live at Taliesin with her mother where she is now married to the stalwart Wes.

As for the little "soft one" that I wanted to complete beloved Taliesin in the valley—Iovanna? Why, she is already a lovely plus-seventeen, as tall and with as gracious a manner as her mother, a young lady with beautiful masses of brown hair, hair such as mine was at her age. She looks at you something like me, but enough like her mother to make the resemblance of not too much consequence.

This isn't much of a story. It is all too close to home to write much about it. But too long a time elapsed before Olgivanna and I finally found each other. It was pretty late. Olgivanna often says, "Oh, why didn't we meet before all the Past ever had a chance to be the Present?" Well . . . after all, that is probably a little ungrateful because Olgivanna wouldn't have liked me until I had been battered into shape by the many untoward circumstances of outraged previous experience, passion properly starved for poetry, and the harm done by too much damage and too much flattery, somewhat undone. I don't like myself much back there. And if she hadn't been properly starved too, probably I wouldn't have such faith in Olgivanna as I have now—with that serious noble look in her face of which I am proud, the graying hair drifting back from her sensitive temples that proves my point.

She is brave and has the heart of a lioness.

No, I think we mated as planned behind the stars—just right. I don't even wish I were younger because we both seem to add up to just about the right age for us, and I admire maturity much more than youth. I would prefer to die to going through my own "youth" again.

When she was "inducted" to citizenship, standing up straight in court to answer the question asked by the old judge, she answered all the questions correctly in a firm, clear voice, except one. She made one ridiculous mistake. "Mrs. Wright," said the judge, "what form of government do we live under?"

Unhesitating she said, "A democracy, sir."

The judge bent his head, smiled a little, while poking at the blotter on his desk. "No," said the judge. "No, Mrs. Wright, but we *are* a Republic."

The American Citizen . . . Olga Ivanovna.

## TO CARL SANDBURG, POET

Dear Carl:

I read your fairy tales nearly every night before I go to bed. They fill a long-felt want—Poetry.

I'll soon know them all by heart.

Have you sent the book to Lord Dunsany? It would make him feel sorry he was born a Lord and so had to fool around with Gods and Goddesses.

I've tried so long to play the guitar with my mittens on that Henry Hagglyhoagly is mine—and O Man! the beauty of the White Horse Girl and the Blue Wind Boy! And the fairies dancing on the wind-swept corn! The Wedding Procession of the Brown Stick and the Rag Doll! The Skyscraper that Decided to have a Child!

All the children that will be born into the Middle West during the next hundred years are peeping at you now, Carl—between little pink fingers—smiling, knowing in their hearts they have found a friend.

And Lucky Spink and Skabootch—to have a daddy—"fire-born" who understands blue. Blue is happy imagination. Something that wakes and sings no matter how much it hurts—or is it always singing?

Yes, Carl, only the Fire-born understand blue. You are the kind of artist for me. Stick this little posy in your hatband for a day. I fling it to you from where, as always, the tracks leave the ground for the sky and I'll be waiting for you at this station in the Rootabaga Country to bring Spink and Skabootch to play with their Uncle:

—*Frank, Taliesin*

And then Carl, the genius, had to ride to riches by way of counting the hairs on the head and fingering the buttons on the clothes of our most beloved national hero: that great leader who truly believed the Union could only live if half of it was destroyed in the name of Freedom by the other half: the agriculturists on the wrong track, slavery, wiped out by the industrialists on the wrong track, machine production controlling consumption.

The great fanatic who invented conscription-in-a-Democracy and by way of white-slavery drove black-slavery into the body-politic, instead of banishing it—enthroning the money-power and the machine to wave the stars and stripes over a wrecked and devastated South, where a culture might have taken root that would have cured its own evils from within if any real help had come from the North.

Napoleon said: "Do you know what amazes me more than anything else? The impotence of force to organize anything."

War itself is a denial of Civilization.

## THE INVITED GUEST: RIO DE JANEIRO, BRAZIL

October 1930: An invitation came from the Pan American Union to go to Rio de Janeiro, as member of the jury representing North America, to judge the accumulation of drawings in the world-wide competition for a memorial to Columbus. Herbert Kelsey (Kelsey built the Pan American building in Washington) was engineering the affair. The program included wives and we thought the excursion might be beneficial—although Olgivanna and I were both bad sailors. Perhaps this time in quiet southern seas we might do better.

All right, we packed up, caught the boat as she was casting off the pier: the Grace Line—United States built boat.

Kelsey was already in Rio.

Diplomats were on board, and Saarinen, the Finnish architect, who for some reason was representing Europe from America. The two great continents, Europe and North America, would see something of each other by way of Wisconsin and Finland. I had always resented Saarinen a little, regarding him as our most accomplished foreign eclectic—a little jealous, too, of his easy berth, bestowed by the hand of American riches, while I had to wait and work and scrape for mine, the hard way. Yes—I know, this seems pretty small. But our provincials feel that culture comes from abroad if at all, and the importation is looked upon in the provinces, especially at Detroit, with great favor. I suppose they think we can't have much at home that should be looked up to.

But it is only, of course, because they wouldn't know how to look.

Saarinen, the Finnish cosmopolite with the Norse accent, spoiled all that mild ill feeling. We became fast friends and had no basis for disagreement on anything whatsoever. I wouldn't disagree with Saarinen and he couldn't disagree with me if he would.

Which reminds me: some time ago we met at a railway restaurant in Chicago—he was on the way to a church he was building in Columbus and I on my way to a church I was building in Kansas City.[20] He had a million dollars to do his (his usual luck). I had one hundred and fifty thousand dollars (maybe) to encompass about the same thing (my usual luck). He asked me if I had seen his design. I had, in a newspaper. "What do you think of it?" he asked.

"Well, Eliel," I said, "when I saw it I thought what a great architect—I am!"

We laughed and he slapped me on the wrist. Well, that's Eliel Saarinen and that, I am afraid, is me. Saarinen was born and will die—a Finn.

By way of the British, I was born native . . . and I refuse to die.

Speaking of Saarinen always brings to mind the power behind the throne at Cranbrook, Carl Milles.[21]

Carl is a sculptor—probably the greatest.

In the hall of his house he has the whole wonderful Barberini collection of Greek sculpture which

**Frank Lloyd Wright with group of architects in Rio de Janeiro, 1931.** FLLW Fdn FA#7402.0032

he bought outright and brought home from Rome.

He will give it all to Taliesin.

Cranbrook cannot have it. I wish this simple disposition of the wonderful Barberini collection were true.

We were on the way to South America. . . . The old half-freighter pushed up to the great pier at Rio in early morning—that wonderful harbor at sunrise![22] There were a lot of boys (students, I thought) climbing on board. They surrounded us. Only one (and a half, say) spoke English.

They were a delegation from some seven hundred or more students of the Brazil Belles Artes, out on what they called (borrowing from us) a "strike." The institution was modeled by and on the French, of course. Latins for the Latins. The Beaux-Arts professors of the Belles Artes had ruled me out altogether by banning my books and forbidding magazines on modern architecture in their library, together with all of my kind.

The youths were a delegation sent by the student body to ask me for help.

Would I help?

I would.

"Look out," said Saarinen. "This is a revolutionary country—first thing you know SSSKKK [he drew his finger across his throat]—and it will be all over with you."

"Never mind," I said. "Come on. Get in and help." He stood on the sidelines, however.

But I was soon in over my head.

My head still on my shoulders I met Herbert Moses, editor of *El Globo,* one of Rio's leading newspapers, and I soon learned how to make a speech in a foreign tongue. Moses was not only remarkably intelligent, but also (an experienced editor) remarkably articulate. I filled him up with the point of view. He was enthusiastic.

The first meeting with the enemy was in the old hall of the Belles Artes. The Beaux-Arts dignitaries, myself, and the handsome president of the University of Brazil presiding. I sat next to him. "How do," he said. I did a little better, but it was in my own language. I knew less Portuguese than he knew English. He knew no more English than that. And only one and a half boys out of the seven hundred at Belles Artes spoke English! Many read it, though.

*El Globo* spoke English like a Yankee.

Our ambassador, Morgan, a genial competent one, was there and spoke.

We, the dignitaries, were all ranged at a long elevated bench such as judges use in our court rooms. The boys were massed down there below.

The meeting began with Latinesque formalities. The President offered a welcome, a professor or two chimed in. My turn—but without waiting for me to speak, bedlam broke.

When they let go a little I got *El Globo* by the arm and, standing that way, would tell him in a sentence or two what I wanted to say. He would put it over to the young rebels with such effect that they would go wild.

The Latins love to go wild.

I gave them all I could—pleaded their cause as the future of Brazil. If Brazil was to have a future, how could she deny her youth the advanced thought of the world whether or not her elders disagreed with that thought and—well, my reader knows by this time what I would say. I stopped; Moses *(El Globo)* stopped.

And then the masses of youngsters charged the judges' bench, pushed their dignitaries aside, *El Globo* and the Ambassador too, picked me up and carried me down to the street, called a taxi, and sent me off to the Copacabana with all on board who could stick.

There was now meeting after meeting.

The affair Columbus took a back seat although we finally did judge the show. And there were great dinners and celebrations galore. I wrote the opinion and the other judges politely concurred—not looking for argument. What was the use anyway? A young Englishman got the prize and deserved it. The whole mass of entries, with a half-dozen exceptions, was a bad form of grandomania and wonderful draftsmanship. Like most competitions it was all in vain. What can a competition be except an averaging upon averages by the average? The first thing the jury (a picked average usually) does is to go through and throw out all the worst ones and all the best ones, and then the jury, itself an average, averages upon some average design as it could only do. But I wouldn't have it that way.

Well, the Belles Artes "strike" began to turn on the heat. I don't remember where or how many times I spoke, or how many newspaper articles I wrote for *El Globo* and *El Manha,* the leading newspapers of Brazil.

The boys would come after me and I would go, and Herbert Moses would "interpret"—if that is what he did. He became fiery eloquent—I suspect he frequently put more into me than I had put into

him. I met the "modern" professors the boys wanted. They were good architects and excellent men. The authorities were very negligent or else indulgent because they didn't arrest me, but finally they did arrest one of the coveted professors who spoke alongside me—Araujo.

Saarinen said my turn was next.

He enjoyed the whole affair in a very refined sort of way, peculiar to the Finns.

They have a National Academy in Brazil, a medal dispensary something like the National Academie Française. The Academy tendered me an honorary meeting and subsequently an honorary membership. I accepted on condition that the society help the boys in their struggle for Freedom.

They agreed.

The Architects Society of Brazil gave us a dinner, with wives. I was in the very thick of the struggle then, and I pleaded the cause of the boys until I brought tears to their eyes to go with the seven different kinds of wine—and my own eyes came to tears without wine. They tendered me honorary membership in their National Society. I accepted conditionally: on condition that they help the boys at Belles Artes.

They agreed.

Ah—the Rio de Janeirians are a fiery, gallant folk. I never thought I would ever like the Latins so much. Olgivanna and I hardly touched the ground during our stay. We went from place to place with a grand set of fellows and their handsome wives. We weekended at Petropolis, bathed on the beach before the Copacabana, rode in the suburbs and along the marvelous Rio waterfront dominated by curious mountain silhouettes.

Kelsey must have hated me for it all—because what had it to do with the competition for the Columbus Memorial? He attended to that and made a good job of his knitting.

A famous French landscaper was there at the time with plans for the replanting of the Versailles-like gardens of the waterfront. The Rio de Janeirians brought the architect and the plans to exhibit both to me . . . for criticism.

I didn't feel competent.

The *Atlantique* came to harbor one day during our six weeks' stay and the great city turned out to meet her at the pier. Our Ambassador had a stalwart bodyguard who fought a clear-way in the crowd so we might follow the Ambassador up the gang-plank, get on board, and see what I thought was France's greatest contribution to modern architecture.

Truly, the elegance and beautiful craftsmanship of the interior of that great ship were stunning. I sat and marveled.

The Rio de Janeirians have but one social fault. They are committed, heart and soul and therefore so are you, to photography. Everywhere we went in public or in private at unexpected moments there was the puff, puff—or startling flash—of flashlights. Ambassador Morgan was usually around somewhere. Our Ambassador was popular in Rio. They couldn't have a function public or private without "El Ambassador."

After the dinner-in-honor at which everybody photographed everybody else, the architects took me over to be especially photographed again by their famous star portrait-photoist. The photographs were good and I had to sign them all for all the architects of Brazil.

Time came to come away. Things had been tremendous. The students came to say they wanted to do something for us. They said they had been "out" so long that (like me) they had no money left. Some of them wanted to bring flowers to Olgivanna but they could not afford to buy them.

Might they not then come to the Copacabana and serenade us that evening? They could. And they did—hundreds of them.

They rushed the piano out to the middle of the ballroom floor. Some of the boys improvised instruments and native costumes, sang and danced till three in the morning while we looked on from a balcony. I wish an American movie magnate could have filmed that show for our country. But down there I couldn't say *American* movie magnate without giving them offense or to think that I meant one of *their* own magnates. The Rio de Janeirians always resented any reference to ourselves as the Americans.

So I said "Usonia" when I talked about our country to them. They liked the term. They had never heard it before but thought it appropriate.

We got home after a long journey in perfect weather on an old United States steamer (why do we build them half-freight, half-passenger, I wonder?). Probably the subs have sunk it. Anyway, we were happy to get home.

Taliesin was a beautiful dream again realized. There is nothing like homecomings for that realization.

A cablegram from Ambassador Morgan, a fortnight after we were settled again, said that the boys had the professors they wanted.

The students of the Belles Artes were free to grow up to serve the future of Brazil!

We brought along such a mass of photographs, newspaper pictures, and clippings that Henry sat down and compiled an album, thirteen inches square and two inches thick, which you may see at Taliesin to this day.

## SNIFF TALIESIN

Independently of wide-open windows seldom shut, letting in the varying smells of the four seasons, Taliesin is pervaded by its own very especial smell. The visitor on coming in for the first time will sniff and remark upon it, ask what the fragrance is.

In Spring and Summer the windows at Taliesin are thrown wide-open. The odor of the long white drifts of wild-plum bloom on the nearby hillsides drifts in—the crabapple and hawthorn in the meadows send their scent on, over the treetops. Later the sweet breath of the clover fields rides in to the rooms on the morning and evening breezes. Soon the scent of new-mown hay pervades the place. So our windows, like the doors, are seldom closed in Spring and Summer. In Autumn, when they are closed, mingling with the odor of freshly burned oak, is the smell of bowls of apples and unshelled shag-bark hickory nuts—the prince of all perfumes. And the sumach. But for the Winter, there inside the rooms is newly gathered, everlasting, cream-white antimony. This gentle pervading odor of antimony is to the sense of smell what the flavor of slippery elm is to the young boy's sense of taste.

Oak fires then start in the seventeen ever-present stone fireplaces to go out but seldom until the following Spring, unless fuel gives out.

A few of the many fireplaces smoke just little enough to contribute the fumes of the burning oak when the evenings are chill in Autumn or Winter, and Taliesin is covered with its thick protecting blanket of snow, thin white wood-smoke going straight up toward the evening star.

So it is in Winter especially that Taliesin is most itself and smells best.

The Taliesin smell, then, is compounded of the acrid odor of oak-wood fires, overlaid and softened by the odor of great bundles of antimony gathered from the fields in Autumn. Great masses of the decorative creamy white herb-blossoms stand about on tables and ledges in big old Chinese jars. The tang of burned oak and the strange odor of antimony together in fresh air—this is the authentic recipe for "the Taliesin Smell."

## AGGRESSIVE FOREIGN POLICY—A FABLE

There was once a nice Johnnie on his way to school with a lot of other little Johnnies and Tommies and Jennies all around him. Johnnie saw a curious thing he hadn't noticed before—a hornet's nest hanging in the bushes. Not knowing much about hornets, he got a stick and poked the nest—whereupon the hornets swarmed out, stung all the little children except Johnnie, who went bravely on to school. At school, in the midst of the boo-hooing and wailing, Johnnie told his tale. The teacher said, "Why, Johnnie, you are a *hero!* I didn't know hornets were so dreadful." So Johnnie, the hero, sat up front. And all the children went out instructed to destroy all the hornets everywhere to make the woods safe for such as Johnnie.

## TOKIO, JAPAN

Invited to Japan to build the new Imperial Hotel, the Teikoku at Tokio—during that four years' residence, and a preliminary visit in 1906 [sic], I learned some little something of a culture that I had studied and worshipped from afar. Owing so much to Old Japan, it would be absurd for me to leave her culture to the mercy of the "patriotic" destructive "white-eyed" ignoramus who will write and rate her now. Typical trash is this dedication of a new book published by Macmillan: "Dedicated to the gentle, self-effacing and long-suffering mothers of the cruellest, most arrogant and treacherous sons who walk the earth—to the women of Japan, who will as always reap the richest harvest of suffering as their reward."

Well—there you have it—about the general, generous size of the average Western comprehension of the Orient.

Extraordinary that for so many centuries "the arrogant sons" should have sired this paragon of virtue and she should in turn have mothered "the most treacherous sons on earth"? But no common sense nor any sense of decency stays with our traveling provincials when they undertake either to underwrite or destroy Japan. The basis for any sense of proportion whatever is lacking.

Kipling said, among other things he said with a grain of truth in the saying, "East is East and West is West and never the twain shall meet."

I am sure they should not meet, at least not yet because, except for a few culture-hunters (and exploiters?) like myself, the West has no tolerant comprehension whatever to give to the East—from the first to the last. And the East has conceived a thorough, grossly exaggerated contempt for the culture, honor, and character of the West. Both China and Japan have preserved a great deal of their sense of beauty and artistry. And it is true that the Japanese have from their first knowledge of us regarded us as vulgar barbarians. From their standpoint we are.

The Commodore who fired the shot that compelled Japan to "open up" was no violet.

That rude awakening of Nippon—the Land of the Rising Sun—from the peaceful pursuit of culture for four hundred years, during which time her Art and Craft rose to high-water mark in all the culture of the world, was a terrible shock to the Sons of Heaven.

"What is the secret of this strange power? These vulgarians have neither character, manners, nor brains," said the Nipponese wisemen. And they sent their elder statesman, Count Ito, journeying around the world to find out. He was absent some two years, staying longest in Germany. Japan's

Number One statesman came back with the secret: "Explosives. In Machines."

Japan (and this is hard for the West to understand) went into hysterical self-abnegation and began to destroy her beautiful works of art, casting them upon sacrificial bonfires in the public places surrounding the palace moat in the capital, Tokio: virtually throwing her civilization upon these fires as on a funeral pyre, a national form of that *hara-kiri* which is also incomprehensible to the West. A young American at that time helped save many of the proofs of their great culture from this wanton destruction. His name was Ernest Fenollosa.

Japan, whose religion was Shinto—the severe "be clean" religion, overlaid with a colorful Buddhism, had reached the parting of the ways. She had "lost face," an Oriental spiritual tragedy which again we fail to understand. Her centuries of severe interior discipline, more severe in poverty than any the world has ever seen, had gone for nought. The culture of Dai Nippon—the Land of the Rising Sun— must have been wrong if a crude barbaric people with cold white skins, cruel noses, and white eyes that frightened their children and made them cry, had the power to destroy them; these coarse men who had no power of thought, or true spirit of courage, so they said. But they could destroy them only because they were masters of explosives in engines of destruction!

Soon after Count Ito's return, the Japanese schools were being modeled on the German. A military system was set up Germanizing the Japanese. Official Japanese delegations were for years and years continually traveling the West and picking up the details of the new power all over the world, almost invariably finding the best applications in Germany. It was such a delegation that picked me to build the second or new Imperial Hotel, a social clearing house for official Japan, after first having heard of me in Germany. So German architects built Japan's new Parliament buildings, built the first Imperial Hotel. The Imperial University became, virtually, a German university. Japanese music went "Ich liebe dich" on the stages of modernized Japanese theaters. The conviction had settled deep

in the Oriental breast and in official Japan's national conscience that the Asiatic yellow peoples must some day meet the Western white-eyed peoples on a footing that would save Asia from barbarous double-dealing England and her stooge America. They saw nothing to admire in Western culture except that as a means to an end, it would serve them better than their own in the undertaking now ahead.

Many years later, one day when an American architect, myself (almost by accident), was building the new Imperial Hotel for them at Tokio, came the news that American statesmanship had declared them an inferior race. The United States of America had denied them the privileges of civilized nations.

I remember the fury of the indignation meetings that took place at that time in Tokio.

I was not allowed abroad without protection for more than two weeks until the ancient capital quieted down again. The infuriated Sons of Heaven were now completely confirmed in their belief that Asia must prepare to save herself from the international shopkeepers and peddlers of the white variety with their gods and their goods: and *everywhere* on the Asiatic continent or on any sea that washed Asia's shores.

They did prepare with thoroughness and efficiency: preparations that seemed entirely to escape the military eye of the purblind dominant race except for one intelligent mind: the mind of the hunchback Homer Lea. His books *The Valor of Ignorance* and *The Day of the Saxons,* when issued thirty years or more ago, should have had attention which they failed to receive. His is one of the few minds—like Napoleon's—to realize that the military mind is a dead mind.

The largest populations of the world—about three to one—and the most ancient, were no longer innocent of a leader-nation who had mastered the great secret of cruel western barbaric power—explosives. The West was riding a new horse. Not only had Japan made that discovery but she learned how to ride. She felt she was therefore the savior of the sleeping, unaware Yellow races of All Asia. That leadership, even if in their ignorance of danger it had to be fought for among themselves, was her Destiny.

It is a common saying under the flag of the Rising Sun that the East is the morning land, the West the evening land. All the dirty seven hundred commercial tricks in streamlined Western commercial duplicity practiced by the worst of Westerners found apt pupils on Asiatic shores. Soon the slant-eyed yellow-men everywhere, but especially in Japan, learned another secret of Western power—the monkey moneyism of commercial empire, wherein the sophisticated whites were pitted against the unawakened, as yet untaught, yellow-men. The yellow-man was no match for the streamlined commercial experts of the West now in action. No, not yet, but coming: tricks against tricks. Being a more ancient people, the Asiatics were more easily degenerate and demoralized even than the relatively cold whites.

Two episodes seem to drop into place here of their own accord, since my persistent absorbing pursuit of the Print is so involved with Oriental experience. The first was one for me. The second was one for them.

From time to time I had collected superb Actor prints: Hosoye—about eleven hundred Hosoye of the first rank—Shunsho, Shunko, Shunyei. Single sheets, diptychs, triptychs, pentytychs [sic], and several septyptichs [sic]—iridian sheets of soft paper stained with soft colors portraying ancient famous actors in classical roles on the ancient Japanese stage. Any collector will know what that collection means. "Wrieto San" was already on the map of Tokio as the most extensive buyer of the fine antique print. Already described to you is what an avocation the pursuit of the rare print made in ancient Yedo had become to me in Tokio. The prints, extremely rare and expensive, were still going up in price at this time. It was often said, "It is finished" and "Japan had been raked with a fine-tooth comb for a quarter of a century, so give it up."

Frederick Gookin of Chicago was the foremost reliable connoisseur in our country. A fine person in himself. When I was about to return for the fifth time to the building of the Imperial Hotel, he introduced William Spaulding to me.[23] The Spauldings were cultured Boston (Beacon Street)

people who had got into this most absorbing, exciting, and expensive game known to esthetics very late. As bride and groom, William and his bride, Virginia Fairlie of the Chicago Art Institute, had tried to start a collection while on their honeymoon in Japan but they could find almost nothing. I myself had been able to find very little. Learning from Frederick Gookin of my extraordinary collection of actor prints, Mr. Spaulding came to my rooms in Orchestra Hall to see a group I had brought in for my own pleasure. Delighted with the portfolio of one hundred prints, he offered me ten thousand dollars for them. It was at the time a fair price. For a number of reasons I accepted, although, except as collections were abandoned, it was quite impossible to find first-rate prints.

A few days later, about ready to return to Japan, I received a telegram from the Spauldings inviting me to come to Beacon Street for a conference. I gladly went, and at dinner that evening the subject was broached by the Spauldings. I imagined the interest was Mr. and Mrs. William's but John also sat in with us. "Would you consent to try to find prints for us in Japan, Mr. Wright? We are both impressed by your experience and your knowledge of the subject and your opportunities in Japan and feel we can trust you completely. We know it is no longer possible for us to find prints unless you will help us." I had expected something like this and had been trying to arrive at something but had nothing definite in mind.

Suddenly I decided. I said, "I will take whatever you want to spend, spend it and divide. I'll keep what I think in the circumstances I should have and you shall have the others." "Well," said John as he laughed, "that's hardly a business proposition, is it, Mr. Wright?" I said, "No, I am not a business man, Mr. Spaulding."

They wanted to know why I would not do it on commission. I said, "Too much bookkeeping." We left it at that and went to bed.

Next morning John and William said they had all thought it all over. "We will be glad to accept your offer. You will find twenty thousand dollars to your credit in the Yokohama Specie Bank when you arrive in Tokio."

There was no scratch of a pen to record the agreement.

Neither the Spauldings nor I thought I could find enough prints worth buying to spend the money.

When I arrived after the usual tedious Pacific crossing, the fifth, I went directly to Shugio. He who was the Meiji Emperor Mutsuhito's "connoisseur" and my intimate friend. Hiromische Shugio had charge of all Japanese fine art exhibits, in the foreign expositions—a friend of nearly all the great artists of Europe, Whistler especially. He was a lover of London, which he liked to compare with Tokio. Shugio was a Japanese aristocrat (there must have been some Chinese blood in him with that name) and highly respected by everyone. He had access to court circles and enjoyed a universal reputation for integrity. I laid the case before him.

It was my feeling that, hidden away Japanese-fashion in the *go-downs* of the court beyond the approach of the merchant class, were many as yet untouched collections of the somewhat "risqué" prints.

Shugio wasn't very sanguine but agreed to talk with a few friends. He wasn't very energetic either. But finally by tactful pursuit he was moved and soon we did hear of a private collection that might, with proper circumspection, be bought. Shugio had the tact. I had the Spaulding money.

Well, it *was* simply amazing. I bought the first collection that turned up on that trial for much less than I ever thought possible. The news (a secret) got around just how and where we hoped it would. Money was very scarce then (1915–1916) in Japan. The interest rate at the banks was nine per cent.

I was getting excited. Already I had established a considerable buying power and anything available in the ordinary channels came first to me. I picked up some fine things in this way. But aristocratic Japanese people lose face if they sell their belongings, even such taboo things as the prints. But evidently Shugio had found a way. Well, it had begun. The twenty thousand was soon gone and already I had priceless things. Anything unique or superior went to the Spauldings. I kept the prints together in Shugio's own *go-down* and mounted and grouped them as I got hold of them. I would cable for money from time to time during the five-month cam-

paign. The money always came, no questions asked. And nothing from me except excited demands for more money until I had spent about one hundred and twenty-five thousand Spaulding dollars for about a million dollars' worth of prints.

Many were unique on the record.

A superb collection almost beyond price—most of it is now in the Boston Museum of Fine Arts, a gift from the Spauldings.

Finally a cable: "When are you coming home?" I cabled back: "Taking next boat," boxed the prints, and caught the next boat but one. I was to bring the prints to the Spaulding country home at Pride's Crossing. By this time both the Spauldings, William and John, and Mrs. Spaulding were proficient judges, but they had Gookin (as consultant connoisseur) present. For three days we laid out prints and prints and more prints and some more prints until neither the Spauldings nor Gookin (he was now leading expert in America) could believe their eyes. Even to me it seemed like some fantastic dream. Sated with riches in the most exquisite graphic art on earth, after three days at a marvelous feast we sat back and rested.

Gratified was hardly the word. William Spaulding, especially delighted, said, "Mr. Wright, this goes far beyond any expectations we had. You can't have much of your own after turning this over to us?"

"I have enough," I said. "I've done pretty well by myself, I assure you."

"No, I don't believe it."

He walked over to his desk and wrote a check for twenty-five thousand dollars and handed it to me. I genuinely hesitated to accept it but of course I did. And he came downstairs with an exquisite, slightly toned copy of Utamaro's Ryogoku Fireworks[24]—black sky—and said, "My brother and I want you to keep this treasure and never part with it. You have brought us a better copy—probably the finest in the world—but this is the next best, we believe. We bought it from Baron Sumitomo."

After lunch we went out for a drive in the Spaulding Stearns-Knight—top down. I was sitting on the rear seat between John and William. Not going very fast, enjoying the relaxation, we were passing the school grounds, boys playing ball, when I heard the crack of a bat on the ball: a square hit. I glanced up just in time to see the ball sailing over us. Instinctively I reached up for the ball, caught it and threw it back into the game.

"Well!" said William Spaulding in astonishment. "So that is it! Well, Mr. Wright, I know now how you got those prints! It's all clear at last !"

Hiromische Shugio got some of the twenty-five thousand, but I wish now I had given him all of it. You have here before you a perfect picture of the West looting the Orient. I make no apologies. You may judge for yourself.

A fascinating game had now developed as an avocation: this pursuit of the print—but on a scale never originally intended.

My own buying—buying for the Spauldings—for the Metropolitan, for the Buckinghams, Chicago Art Institute, had automatically, no such intention on my part, given me command of the print market in all Japan. Nothing much now got away. I had spent nearly a half million dollars in Japan at a time when money there was scarce indeed.

You may well say, the East got the money, didn't it? But what did the West get? Priceless art treasures running into millions. And it was always the same story, in either Japan or China.

Wrieto San's "avocation" was great pastime, but profitable to him and to the West. I grew ashamed of it finally.

All right. The Japanese merchants didn't like it, of course. But it went deeper.

Howard Mansfield was treasurer of the Metropolitan Museum at the time. He had asked me to pick up some treasures for him next time I got back to Tokio if anything extraordinary should turn up. Emissaries used to come to me from various country places, frequently, to offer their "finds" first to me.

Wrieto San is getting to be too much of a merchant, I thought.

I believe I lost caste a little in Japan by way of it. But one more chance came from Nikko—very secret. I went up by train with the well-known Tokio dealer, Hayashi, a name as common in Japan as Smith is common in America. Then we went by rickshaw to a little Japanese house hidden in the woods in the outskirts in the country.

There we found the "collection." My God! I thought I had seen every subject extant by now. I hadn't. There were things in that collection still unique—things like a large-size Harunobu (printed in gold leaf in heavy goffered paper) that later brought twenty-five hundred dollars at auction in New York. Kiyonagas—stunning subjects I had never seen. Noble primitives: Sharaku by the dozen, Shunsho, charming Kiyonaga, Shunko, Yeishi triptychs, Toyokuni I five-piece, the Shunman black-and-white septyptich [sic], Hokusai almost complete, the Hiroshige Saruhashi, the gorge, the snow-triptych, ah well . . . why go on? Suffice it to say that this clandestine collection beggared imagination and so description. I who had so eagerly read of Aladdin and his wonderful lamp when a boy . . . well, again this was Aladdin's cave. All the prints were of the first quality. *Ichiban*, as the Japanese say.

I, still the hungry orphan turned loose in the bakeshop, spent about two hours there and bought it all for fifty thousand dollars. They needed money badly. And I who had crowded out other buyers by now—practically had things my own way. I was accustomed to getting about three for one anyway, which was not greedy as things were going. Ten for one is about what the West expects from the East, and takes.

Again the usual tedious return voyage across the vast Pacific. The eleventh.

But I had my treasures on board to study and gloat over. Glutton? Absolutely.

When I returned I had them all classified and properly mounted and took them to New York and Howard Mansfield. Howard, really by this time our most fastidious American collector, was the center of a group of more or less wealthy but, nevertheless, very discriminating collectors. He himself was by now a veteran. The group called in experts (several of them) and excluded me from their conference, which hurt me. Why should they exclude me? I couldn't understand.

Finally Howard, pencil and paper and lists in hand, offered me forty-five thousand dollars for about half of the collection. Make it fifty thousand, I said. Agreed. Some months after returning to Tokio and back to work on the Imperial, already sick of the role I had been playing, I received a cablegram from Howard Mansfield:

WRIGHT. IMPEHO. TOKIO. KYOTO MATSUKI, NEW YORK DEALER, TURNS INFORMER ON TOKIO RING REVAMPING PRINTS. SOME FROM YOU HAVE PINPRICKS SHOWING REVAMPING. BETTER INVESTIGATE. MANSFIELD.

I investigated at once and knew where to go to do it. I found that Matsuki told the truth. Several leading dealers, the smartest in Tokio, had for years been keeping a famous craftsman with helpers working in the country on genuine old prints, as rarities in poor condition turned up, putting months of work on a single rare specimen that would bring several thousand dollars, probably. They would first discharge the color—restoring the paper to normal, soak old worthless prints to obtain the proper colors, and then, by an ingenious system of pin pricks at certain angles of the drawing, guide the reprinting of the original print from blocks cut solely for the purpose of reprinting that one print. The result was not an imitation. It was a genuine restoration and valuable. But who wanted it? No collector, certainly.

The jig was up. Staying away from me until this last trip, they had previously loaded up many collectors like Sir Edwin Walker of Canada, and a half-dozen less well-known collectors in our country, but they had fought shy of me—either not daring to try me out before or emboldened by their success with others thinking it time to retaliate.

Wrieto San had fallen. I went after the ring, wiped it out, got the ring-leader (he was Hayashi) in jail. After he had been there a year his case came up. The court sent for me. The police brought Hayashi to me where I was sitting in court at a small table to judge him. The court wanted to know what I wanted done with him. He knocked his forehead to the floor and begged for mercy as tears streamed from his eyes. I said, "Take everything of the sort he has away from him. Forbid him to ever deal in color prints

again and let him go." This was done. He had very little of anything. They would have hanged him if I had said so, for the Japanese authorities were furious.

The trickery greatly humiliated them. So I had "cleaned up the market" in quite another way than I originally intended.

The Japanese authorities openly apologized. The dealer was banished. He was last heard of in London. The print business, but not Japanese prints.

He was a product of the West and belonged there.

I dare say he is successful in London.

Was I satisfied? I was. Satisfied that the East was one up on the West. And somehow, not sorry. It was a sop to my own conscience.

But now I had to square myself with Howard Mansfield and friends. When I got home again, much later, we held at Taliesin what was known as "The Print Party." I threw open the vault at Taliesin with its collections to Howard and his friends. They were free to choose what they would in exchange for the restored prints. About one-third of the "treasures" I had brought them had been "restored."

That party cost me about thirty thousand dollars. "Wright," said Howard Mansfield, "I knew we could count on you!" "Yes, Howard," I said. "But you are as culpable as I am. You excluded me, you called on your own experts and picked out your own prints. And I had no responsibility really. But 'Wrieto San' couldn't afford to 'lose face,' as the Japanese themselves say."

"Yes, Wright, I know," said the treasurer of the Metropolitan, "I know."

The game was all played according to a pattern set by the West. And it all served me right for getting into something I had no good right to be in. I woke up. There was no one now to say to me—No, you are no American! I was a pretty good "American."

And I have always maintained, without pride, that had I ever desired to become one of the successful commercial gamblers of the West they would now be taking my money away in freight cars.

Came the Japanese war with Russia. Japan, the novice, put her schooling to the test and to the amazement of the dominant race she won that dubious prize. From that time on she began acquiring the stance in the Pacific that would some day stand her in good stead: valuable coast lines and some ten thousand islands. One of those, nearby, became a vast secret training ground for trying out Western ideas with German schooling and Japanese improvements.

At one time—it was just previous to the Exclusion Act—Japan evidently looked upon the United States as an exception. Many of her people and many of her statesmen looked upon us as a possible trustworthy friend. I do not know why, unless because of our extensive (and expensive) interest in her culture. But she soon lost that hope and with it went what little respect she ever had for us when she saw us selling coveted iron to her for war purposes at the same time that we were encouraging China to resist her. That act tallied with her firm faith in Western depravity and duplicity.

Japan has always adored the motherland, China, as we adore the motherland, England. When I went to Peking, 1918, to let contracts for the rugs for the Imperial Hotel, I learned facts regarding China and Japan from Dr. Ku Hung Ming of Peking. He had once been secretary to the Empress Dowager of China. Dr. Ku was an Oxford graduate, but wore his cue (a Manchu inheritance) curled up under his red mandarin cap as a protest against what he called the motor-car Chinaman. While in Peking (Peiping) he wrote several famous books—one, *The Spirit of the Chinese People,* I had read which so impressed me that I determined to look him up when I arrived in Peking. I had a chance to sit and learn from him.

The sage and I went about off the beaten track exploring Peking. Since he hated the motor-car Chinaman, we took a strapping young Mongolian (six feet seven for me and another smaller for Dr. Ku—he was not very tall) and we would usually take along a guide who had attached himself to me—not very welcome he, but useful often.

We saw the old palaces, the blue-tiled Temple of Heaven, the Imperial Palaces, the great Gates, dusty caravans of camels going through from the Gobi Desert—loaded with furs. And then branched off into the unknown. One day he took me to an ancient temple little known to tourists. He was continually showing me the obscure but significant, interpreting it all to me in the spirit of the Chinese people. This particular temple-roof was down, water coming in on the sculptured walls—one entire wall was covered with pottery figures in complete relief set into niches in the wall. There were several hundred in several ranks, each some two and a half feet high—brilliant in color.

Dr. Ku walked away to take in the view.

I was again like the "hungry orphan turned loose in a bakeshop" for the moment coveting the sacred images. Satan in the bulky form of the guide stole up alongside me and now that Dr. Ku's attention was on the landscape that came through the fallen walls, he said in a low voice, "You like statues very much? Yes? All right—you pick out one, two, tree. I bring you hotel tonight, you see in mornin."

I was tempted for a moment and then came a reaction—a revulsion of feeling would be it. I couldn't bribe this fellow to plunder the place—sacred to such as Ku Hung Ming—a plundering process across the years that was stripping China of her finest things. I said, "No. No, I don't buy that way. Some day this temple might be restored."

"Never," said the guide. "Soon all gone. Somebody else will get."

"Not me."

The little sage's ears must have been sharp. The dialogue had all been sotto voce, but I heard steps behind me and felt an arm laid over my shoulders as the old philosopher's voice almost down to a whisper in my ear said, "No, it is not so. *You* are no American." The token of affection and respect, for so he meant it to be, touched me, and I have never regretted abandoning those marvelous figures to the "somebody who would if I didn't."

We stood looking at the figures. Dr. Ku talked, told me about them. He too said there was not much chance of saving them. But it was better to leave them to their fate than go to perdition (or at least purgatory) with them.

The little old scholar, gray cue still curled up under his little red mandarin cap, said many wise things. He truly was a wise man—one of the few I've met. He was neither old school nor new school. He was the timeless sort so far as his mind went. I remember he said, as we walked about the ruins, there were almost no original Chinese left in China—all were now Mongolized. They had, during many, many centuries, been gradually Mongolized from the North. The only remaining original Chinese, due to an early migration by way of Korea, were the Japanese. The Japanese were Chinese who had met there on their islands the native Ainu and absorbed most of the small Ainu population. The secret of their excessive fertility was phosphorescent food, their diet of fish. And he said the rapid rate of their increase would soon raise a serious problem. A Japanese family of thirteen is a small family. A Japanese sire having sixty children to his credit was nothing unusual; of course, this would be a rich man with several wives. But the Oriental birth rate, including Russia (more largely Asiatic than is generally realized), was such as to be quite capable, were a gun put into its hand, of forming a deluge of manpower which under capable direction might easily swamp any further attempts by the West to subjugate Asia. They would multiply faster than they could possibly be killed, even by modern mechanized warfare. They could ride the wild horses of destruction three to one!

Now, he said, Japan looks upon herself as that "gun in the hand" of Asia. Both Japan and China worship at the shrine of India. Should India gain her independence, she is their natural spiritual leader. The Hindus—Buddha—conquered China and Japan. Dr. Ku said the Asiatics regard Russia as the connecting link between the East and the West. Japan, no doubt, would some day, probably by way of China as a natural bridge, join with Russia. And it was not unlikely, in the opinion of Dr. Ku, that India freed from Western domination would join with the yellow races led by Japan and China, and that all Asia would make a defensive treaty with Germany which would give a good four-fifths of the population and area of the world over to the power and uses of the yellow man. He said the Africans were sure to go with the Asiatics whenever the time came.

And in Dr. Ku's philosophic view was perhaps whatever biologic basis there was in the Emperor Wilhelm's "Yellow Peril": an overwhelming opposite, an entirely separate race genius—one which we do not and cannot, even if we cared to, understand. Dr. Ku told me that we of the West not only could not understand but could only ascribe to that genius the motives which we would ourselves have in whatever the circumstances might be, and be completely deceived every time as to whatever they might be actually. Russia and China were already, and soon Japan would be, glacial in the human mass due to the fecundity of population and limitless natural resources when modern sanitation and arms came to them.

No Asiatic nation could ever be thoroughly conquered for long by any outsider.

Never would Japanese conquest of China be the end of China or German conquest be the end of Russia.

But Japan's conquest of China *would* be the end of Japan. As the Mongolian was the end of the original Chinese, so the Mongolian-Chinese womb would be the end of Japan. Every Japanese man covets a Chinese woman. Even a well-to-do merchant will gladly take a Chinese coolie-woman for a wife. She would add at least nineteen half-castes the first generation, who would in the second generation add at least three hundred forty-four three-quarterites, etc., etc., ad infinitum. In seven generations there would be no Japanese left in China nor probably very many left in Japan itself. "Henceforth," said the tiger to the lady, "henceforth you ride inside." The fanaticism and cruelty of Orientals is something we can stay away from but that we can't change by fear of us or our power any more than we can level their eyelids to a perpendicular with their noses. Because they are not afraid and they fight not for revenge but for their own.

Now in 1942, remembering the words that Dr. Ku had spoken a quarter of a century ago and judging from my own experience, I find it utterly wrong to classify Hirohito with Mussolini and Hitler. Japan is an entirely different racial quantity and spiritual quality. She is pro-axis. That is all. She is really Asia for the Asiatics, dead or alive, and for whatever that may mean she will fight to the death. Anything that will serve that end she will embrace with indescribable Oriental faith and fatalistic fervor.

She feels the liberator's sword is in her hand and she feels free to use it in ways that seem treacherous to us of the Western world but which to her seem only good strategy.

She feels that but for the white bedevilment of China, the Indies, and India, she would even now be secure in her position as qualified leader of what she calls and feels to be the great Emancipation.

What the Western world calls and would like to believe to be the Chinese Republic was ridiculous to Dr. Ku. The Chinese Republic in his view was only a coastal strip which the great uncounted—even, to modern times, undiscovered—masses of Chinese know little and care less about. To refer to China as a Democracy was to refer to Dr. Sun Yat-sen, his remarkable family and friends, and a few million Chinese all looking to the U.S.A. for a hopeless confirmation and support, which could in any final issue only *betray* and *not* liberate the Chinese people. There was no realistic basis, not even a commercial one, for calling our support of China our fight on the side of "Freedom." No. Freedom of the Asiatics will, he said, never come by such external means. It would gradually grow from within, Japan or no Japan. And it was to be a matter of many centuries.

The West, Dr. Ku thought, failed utterly to take into account that China and Japan are of one blood. Their own natures within the range of their own fanaticism and cruelty can do best for and with each other in due course of time. He saw nothing the West could do for either nation or their collaterals except further bedevil and destroy them, postponing their inevitable future—the yellow races solidly linked by way of Russia with the West and Germany—if Germany should survive—retained as a paid schoolmaster. But the schoolmaster would probably be no longer needed.

## LONDON, ENGLAND

April 1939: An invitation came from the Sulgrave Manor Board by way of the British Ambassador to the United States to take the Sir George Watson Chair for that year and deliver the lectures that a bequest from Sir George had made possible. The lectures were to alternate, one year by an Englishman, the next by an American. The lectures were intended to serve the better acquaintance of British and American culture. Lord Bryce, Woodrow Wilson, Hadley of Yale, Theodore Roosevelt, the Governor of Canada, and many others, had delivered them.

The Sulgrave Manor Board, as you may know, took over the old home of George Washington in England and was taking good care of it—common ground in American and English history. The lecturer was free to deliver the famous lectures in any one of the English universities he might choose, and as many or as few lectures as he chose. The honorarium of twenty-five hundred dollars might be for but one lecture if the recipient of the honor so decided. The rights of publication went with acceptance by the lecturer. I accepted the honor, for so it was. I decided to give four evenings at London University. But the Royal Institute of British Architects, upon learning that I was chosen to give the lectures, proposed to join in sponsoring them, asking that they be given in the new hall of the new building of the Royal Institute in Portland Place. As a preliminary attention, the Institute made me honorary member of their body so that I might not set foot on England's soil a stranger. At least I like to think that might have been one characteristic English reason.

The most coveted honor among architects in our country is this one from the Royal Institute of Great Britain. Unlike many of our own similar societies, its honors are honorably bestowed. They do not go by fashion or by favor or prestige and are so recognized throughout the United Kingdom. The Royal Gold Medal of the Royal Institute therefore goes a long way with any Britisher anywhere on earth and so as a matter of course it should go with any American anywhere. It rounded out the honors previously received from seven other countries. This last should have been first—but that the first shall be last and the last shall be first is standard old prophecy.

We decided to take Iovanna with us. She would soon be thirteen and needed the educational experience. So we went by the *Queen Mary* again to London, this time staying at the old Garland Hotel which, standing not far from Trafalgar Square, puts an end to Suffolk Street. On the boat we met a *Manchester Guardian* man who told us enough about the hotel to decide us to visit it. Henry James had stayed there to write. Whistler and his cronies had often turned up there. I remembered that Ashbee said he stayed at the Garland when he came up from the country—Camden Town—to London. Lady Sandwich said people from the English country estates coming up to London often stayed there. We found the old place delightful. English homeliness and quaint ugliness. As English as anything in "Pickwick."

In giving lectures, if that is what they are, I've found that I do my best if I do not make preparation for them whatsoever. When I get enjoyment out of delivering them, I am sure others get some. Trying to remember spoils the delivery of what I want to say when on my feet. Since I am only talking out of myself anyway, I need no rehearsal as I would if I had collected material for the occasion. The audience is an inspiration, too, not to be forestalled. So when I wish to do my best as I always do, I am careful not to think of what I intend to say. And this was the only careful preparation I made for the lectures—four evenings at the Royal Institute—lately published by Lund Humphries under the title *Frank Lloyd Wright*. A well-illustrated and tastefully printed book issued while the bombs were dropping on London. The first copies reached us in Arizona February 1941.

While listening to the New Year's Eve broadcast at Taliesin West, 1941, that same winter I learned that among the King's birthday honors of that year, His Majesty's Royal Gold Medal for Architecture had been bestowed upon me. If my friends were astonished, you may imagine my astonishment. I think they were all startled except Russell Hitchcock, who seemed to know something about it as being in the air.

I accepted with the cablegram: YOU PROPOSE A GREAT HONOR. I ACCEPT GRATIFIED THAT DURING THIS TERRIFIC WAR ENGLAND CAN THINK OF HON-ORING AN ARCHITECT. FRANK LLOYD WRIGHT.

Former American recipients had been Richard M. Hunt, Charles McKim, and Thomas Hastings. I took it as remarkable evidence of the great change taking place in the currents of thought in the modern world. It pleased me that the young lads who had been working with me would have less opposition to overcome in the years ahead than I had met. I regarded the award as a distinct break for them although perhaps there are worse enemies than open opposition. Popular success, for example.

The British lectures in the Sir George Watson Chair I regard as a great experience: one of the most gratifying of my life. Young men came from Edinburgh, Cambridge, and in between, until there was seldom even standing room in the splendid hall. Notably, the audiences were young. The audiences increased until they were turning many away.

Said the Earl of Crawford, leaning over toward me on the platform, "What is this, Mr. Wright? The board has never seen anything like this before."

I said, "Your lordship, I can't imagine."

That same Lord, the evening on which I had taken a perhaps too gloomy view of the cultural state of things in general, got up and remarked that the proceedings had rather puzzled him. He said he felt somewhat in the position of Sandy at the funeral being held in the old Scotch churchyard. Sandy, curious to see what was going on, got too close to the edge of the grave, slipped and fell in, barking both shins on the coffin. Next day the local paper, commenting on the funeral, said, "The unfortunate incident cast a gloom over the entire proceedings."

And the good-natured laugh was on the "lecturer."

There was an affable Lord in the chair always. There is no better nor more competent company on earth than the English gentleman, but one or two of the M.P. Lords who came over to preside were, unlike the Earl, "rather a bore, don't you know." Olgivanna was present at all the lectures and many would ask her if it was true that my speaking was entirely spontaneous—not because it didn't seem so, but because it *did* seem so spontaneous. She assured them it was so: perfectly spontaneous. During post-mortem discussions of the lectures many

**George Sturges House, Brentwood, California. 1939. Perspective. Pencil and color pencil on tracing paper, 37 x 22".**
FLLW Fdn#3905.002

interesting things were heard. One ponderous Duchess next seat to a friend of mine raised her lorgnette and asked, "Who is this charlatan from Texas who comes way over here to talk us down?"

Iovanna was castle-crazy but was disappointed so much by the adding and patching that didn't "belong." She found a companion in John Gloag's little daughter who took her about. She was particularly offended by Sir Christopher Wren's additions because they so invariably ignored the original work as to be really not additions but subtractions. Nor could she reconcile the plumbing hanging over or on or showing under the ancient dignity of the outside walls. No amount of explaining squared the facts with budding Romance. She loved the Tower—but was eager to be on the trail of François Villon in Paris.

On the whole I who have the most intelligent of audiences have never had such a high level of intelligence and fine character in the audience as in London—nor such awareness and purposeful heckling. I always enjoy a heckling, and so does a British audience. I won't quote any of the many evidences of this because an old court reporter was present and got the whole thing down, so accurately that for once in my life there was little to correct in the copy he presented. The tasteful book, heckling and all, edited by Secretary of the Royal Institute Carter, came out as I have said, when London was raided, bombs exploding, and the walls of London falling or in ruins.

There is something indomitable in British pluck and splendid in British character that makes you wonder what England might have been like in the culture of this world were it not for the "white man's burden"—her Empire. Surely such qualities as hers are good for far more than war and conquest and the conduct of subjugated peoples. If England had a chance to be a free England on her own—developing slowly the characteristics and strength of Englishmen from within, the nation might have been small, but the world would have had one mighty, genuine democracy by now. A shining light, the great exemplar needed. Her great were among the world's greatest, irrespective of conquest. Empire has ruined England. Her successes for three hundred years did her, as England, no real good. A disease took root and spread by way of her success. Dismal reflection: it has now spread to us.

About a year later a telegram came from the *News-Chronicle* to the Arizona desert, asking for 1,500 words of cabled suggestions for the rebuilding of London, January 21, 1942. I sent the following:

"The greatest creature of habit on earth is London. Slums and ugliness that would have taken centuries to overcome have been blasted out of the way in a few days. While sentiment is entitled to its tears, the art and science of human habitation may get a break. If English-speaking culture by way of grit and the will of Englishmen takes the break, goes ahead, and builds in line with this age of mechanical power the Empire may die, but English dominion will survive to triumph.

"Power so capable to destroy is just as capable to create, we shall soon see. And we shall soon see whether England is humanitarian or only English, and whether Germany is humanitarian or only Germanic. If England is humanitarian London will decentralize. Even the bomb overhead points to that as a necessity. London reintegrated should be twenty-five times the area of old London. The new space-scale of our mechanical era is just about that—twenty-five feet now to one foot then.

"Human congestion is murder; murder if not of the carcass, then murder of the most desirable human sensibilities. There is room and crying need for the greater London. The plan for it should be laid down now keeping in mind that Tradition with a capital T is greater than the manifold traditions to which it gives rise. Traditions must die in order that great Tradition may live.

"Great buildings always begin at the beginning, so the necessary items are:

"1. No very rich nor very poor to build for—no gold.

"2. No idle land except for common landscape—no real estate exploiters.

"3. No holding against society the ideas by way of which society lives—no patents. In short, no speculation in money, land, or ideas; not one of them must be a speculative commodity but *must be used* as actual necessities of human life like air and water. This is the true basis for what we could honestly call Democracy. It is a necessary basis upon which to build a city of the mechanical age that will take the place of the feudal monster now being destroyed.

"This liberation of human individuality is not so terrible a leveller of human fortunes as it may seem to be. It is the only just basis for true capital, the life of human initiative. Base capital broad upon the ground, not as now with apex on the ground, base in the air. Except for the disabled, unemployment of any kind would be unthinkable in a State so founded. England could be that State and would be forever impregnable.

"The physical body of the democratic city of today would have no one center but would have many centers all well correlated, the height of the

**Frank Lloyd Wright and apprentices on construction site of Midway Barns, Taliesin, Spring Green, Wisconsin. Photograph by Lois Davidson Gottleib.** FLLW Fdn FA#6644.0002

buildings increasing as the perimeter of activity was approached.

"Were Old London to fairly accommodate the partial motorization it already had B.B. (Before Bombs), there could be no building at all in London. And London motorization had only just begun. London should be a motor-car, aeroplane London, the new spacing all laid out upon the new scale of human movement now set by car and plane.

"But the sentimentality of our elders blocks the path of true progress and continually begs for compromise. Make none. Make none whatever, because all the vision we have is not enough to prevent such sentimentality from catching up and holding us back again. Keep this static out, and keep the traffic centers all wide open. Historic London could be featured in a great central London park-system. Conduct power from the mines. Do not cramp industrial areas around piles of raw material or fuel with the usual deadly-dull collateral 'housing'-by-Government. Abolish the back-and-forth haul of people, fuel and supplies. Do not be afraid to build factories and farms as fit associates for country homes, schools, churches, theaters and parks.

"Railway arterials should be elevated with continuous storage space beneath the tracks: lorry traffic should be set low on each side so that lorries may be free to take on or take off anywhere. All traffic should be fluid and undated. Yes, it can be done. Such grandomania as survives the bombs should expend itself by extensions parallel with the ground—going up into the air only as activity thins out. Old building codes should be thrown away. New ones simplified and broadened in keeping with the opportunities of the new age should be written.

"There must be no traffic problem. That has been solved in Broadacre City. Make broad streets concave instead of convex, with underpasses for foot passengers. Provide top-turn left intersections for traffic, and over- and underpasses for the criss-cross: no traffic lights because the roads themselves would be low-lighted ribbons. For all this the likelihood of accidents is reduced to about one tenth of one per cent. And away with poles and wires forever.

"Along with speech honestly free goes free life for the individual on his own ground in his own house, all his own way, yet in no man's way.

"No, not Utopia, just a way of building from a good modern plan for a Democratic people. That's all. What luxury and pagan beauty the Greeks knew or medieval Christianity knew is, by comparison, an exterior thing, like some stage setting. There need be no difference in quality of thought between the house of a man with more and the house of a man with less: only difference in extent.

"The home is the real citadel of the human race in any democracy. And where and while the private home has the integrity I here bespeak for it there will be no war.

"All may harmonize. Individuality could inform and enliven all private homes now without mutual detriment if architecture could live again, even if it must live again because of bombs in irresponsible hands. Maybe it could yet only live because of bombs. Who knows?

"It is easy to do this with fluid power and integral architecture. The necessity for the old pigeon-holing aggregations of the horse and buggy past belong back there now with the horse and buggy mind and the manure pile. A new kind of beauty comes back to life—integrity. That is beauty. Plan for an integral economy. Integral building and economy is cemented to democratic culture. It is not a mere phrase. We are building it a little here and there, in spite of ancient codes, ignorant interference and wanton waste. Though international now, it spoke English first and can save England from bombs forever because the pressures that made war inevitable cannot exist in a Democracy so planned. Dictators would be out of luck.

"No use blinking the fact that mechanics have outrun the social and esthetic forms, the philosophy and ideas of your Yesterday. Why use Yesterday's rules for laws today? 'If we are on the side of nature we are never lawless.' We are safe. Were such organic planning executed, the Empire might disappear, but British Dominion would be safe. Were Germany to win this war it would be to lose it on any basis of a plane-and-gun future.

"Don't grieve too much, Britain. Empire is not essential."

F. LL. W.—*Taliesin West.*

"The Empire of Imagination is more enduring than any Empire of mere fact."

A note from Sir Ian McAllister said the cablegram had been published throughout the United Kingdom. In due course a *News-Chronicle* check for twenty guineas made "the crossing." In the circumstances a touching affair—that check.

## MOSCOW, RUSSIA

May 1937: An invitation came to travel as Honored Guest of the Soviet Union to attend, in Moscow, the great world conference of Architects to which a number of the great architects of the world were being invited. So again we set out. We debarked from the *Queen Mary* at Cherbourg, went by way of Paris to Berlin, and after a short stay in both capitals, finally landed at the Russian border for customs' examinations. The examination (something like looking the gift horse in the teeth) was getting acrimonious and more and more complex, when a telegram from Moscow called it all off and we took the old European leftover parlor-and-dining-car to Moscow.

There was a wide blank space at the frontier, trees all cut down, a kind of no-man's land, a barbed-wire entanglement both sides. Towers with sentries were overlooking this cleared space. Russian sentries were marching up and down the station platforms on the one side, Polish sentries on the other. I ran into one and was waved back into the Russian station.

The famous trials were just over. The Army had been purged of an army. It was said in Paris that both the frontiers were closed and we could not get into Russia. In Paris they tried to scare us out of going there at all. We wouldn't be scared.

I should like to write at length of Moscow, but this chapter of *An Autobiography* for a hundred reasons, all good, must come to an end.

The enthusiastic Russian people were wonderfully kind to us. Warm hospitality. Their works were even more wonderful. Old churches were going up in the air, dynamited to make way for wide avenues for the new Moscow. Moscow was being made ready for five million citizens. The great road-making program going on toward Leningrad, young girls with white kerchiefs over their fair hair driving great steam-rollers. Tractors and trucks were everywhere.

The old buildings, some good, contrasting sharply with the new ones, mostly bad. Of their kind, many of the old Russian Greek Orthodox churches were fine. Of course, the beautiful Kremlin.

But the modern buildings were hard and coarse, unsympathetic and badly proportioned. This would apply to all but a score of them with perfect justice. I don't wonder the Russian people reacted to them as they did, rejecting them in favor of the old classic order. The so-called modern buildings must have been hateful to the mystic emotion, the passion of the people of Russia. I met many of the Russian architects, and writing for *Soviet Russia Today* when I came home, have described them and their work.

We went over to meet our Ambassador and had luncheon with Mr. and Mrs. Joe Davies. Joe was a Madison U. boy and we enjoyed a private talk, with a glance now and then at the walls, because there was reason to believe that outsiders were under espionage. But that wore off and not a single basis for suspicion could we see from first to last during our visit.

We were allowed to buy nothing for ourselves. Even our telegrams, personal laundry, went in with the hotel bills to the Soviet. The architects carried this so far that when we wanted to bring back some antique Russian instruments to Taliesin they wouldn't hear of anything but buying them and presenting them to us.

So warmly attached did we become to the Russian Spirit that I came nearer to tears in leaving them than I remember in my life.

What a land of opportunity was Russia! In the street or in private homes, in all places public or private, it was we, *ours:* our theater, our subway, our schools, etc. Too much going into building up the defense which would inevitably have to be used, and perhaps just because it was built up to such proportions! It was a subject of which no one spoke. I don't know. The world was in a jam. Great changes coming. And there was something in the air then—May 1937—that made everyone afraid of something he couldn't define.

The American newspapers were nasty because I said publicly that they had not been telling us the

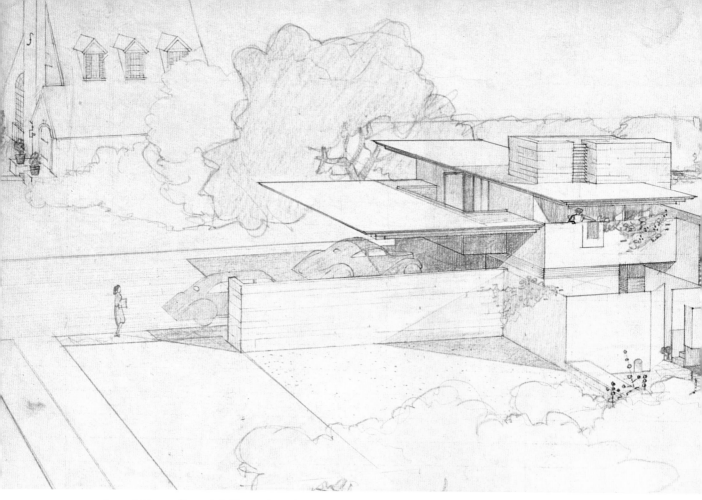

**Bernard Schwartz House, Twin Rivers, Wisconsin. 1939. Perspective. Pencil, sepia ink, and color pencil on tracing paper, 36 x 14".**
FLLW Fdn#3904.001

truth over there at home about Russia, and were I in Stalin's place I would kick them out, all correspondents, and for the good of everyone concerned. There were a few exceptions. I named them. Walter Duranty was one.

There were at the Congress architects from Spain who told us of the restoration of old Spanish buildings undertaken as soon as the bombing had ceased—long before either side had won the war. There were architects from Turkey, Ankara, Jerusalem. From Finland, Rumania, Sweden, Norway and, of course, England and France. But most interesting were the native architects from the fifty-eight Russian States stretching off toward Tibet and toward Batum on the Black Sea. In all there was an ideality, an eagerness to learn, I had never seen before. A solidarity difficult to believe in. Comradeship was everywhere as they filled the great circular

foyer of the Hall of the Nobles and gathered in groups for discussion of what had already or was just about to take place.

When we got further in to the country I was surprised to find the same flowers and trees we have here at Taliesin, and see them fighting the very same weeds at the Kolkhoz until I learned that the latitude is the same.

The belts of similar foliage, bird and animal life seem to encircle the globe in strata according to latitude. Longitude doesn't matter much.

We stopped at the Metropole—historic old Europeanized caravansary—until we went to Sukhanov. Sukhanov is the Russian Taliesin. The same rural loveliness—oaks, pines, white birches, and wild flowers. The same herds and the same birds and similar architects.

But the buildings were of the ancient order—an old palace, a big circular room with a big circular table at which the architects sat with their families and guests, to be fed from provender which they raised themselves. Their herd was twice the size of ours on four hundred acres where we have about a thousand.

We liked the Russians and they liked us. I had liked them back in 1915 to 1919 when I had invited Russian refugees from the Revolution (there were so many in Tokio) to my apartment at the old Imperial. Then it was the Russians of the old Regime I liked; now in 1937 it was the Russians of the Soviet proletariat. The women I thought much the same in both regimes. In them the Russian Spirit, regardless of circumstances, shone through. With the men it was quite different—in favor of the proletariat.

In my Tokio apartment was that rarity in Tokio, a grand piano. (I had found a fairly good one on the Ginza and bought it.) The food at the Imperial was probably as good as anywhere in the world, so I used to invite them frequently and we got to know each other pretty well. So well in fact that they would sometimes put an arm around me and say, "But no, it cannot be that you are an American! Surely you are a Russian!"

"No," I would answer, "I am very much an American. And so are you! It isn't that we are one or the other but alike, that's all."

But they would say, "We don't like Americans."

"Well, the reason for that is that you don't really know Americans. The ones you would like don't come here often. Come to America and see them where and as they really live and you will like Americans. The traveled ones aren't the natural or even the more cultivated ones. I can think of a dozen American men with whom the princess (Cheremissinof) would fall in love and the Countess C, Countess Metaxa, and Countess Lubienski, too. Perhaps you would like our American men better than our women. I don't know. The women can be awfully nice. Your men would like them. They aren't too much like the movie stars you see. The little shop girls take the stars for patterns, but our American women, those not Frenchified too much nor Anglicized out of their natural lives, would resemble Russian ladies more than any other nationality. I assure you—you would like us at home."

"Nobody likes us abroad because the best of us don't go much abroad."

And this little speech to the Russian refugees in Tokio twenty-five years ago goes for the proletariat in Moscow today. There is something native to present-day Russians which is also native to Americans. It is the simplicity of freedom. Or should I say the freedom of simplicity? Strange that I could see but little difference between the women of the old regime and the women of the new. The men? Yes, there was a difference there.

I love the Russian Spirit. I am glad my wife speaks Russian. She was a wonderful interpreter for me and frequently cleared up points for them. She

**Frank Lloyd Wright with wives of Russian architects, Moscow, June 1937.** FLLW Fdn FA#6827.0003

was educated in Russia even though it was under the old regime, so she speaks the soft, beautiful language like a native. Soviet Russia and Usonia are capable of perfect understanding and sympathy. It is inevitable. But the Russians are richer in human content and in colorful spirit owing to their Oriental heritage. I, too, think they combine the East and the West. The best of us not only have sympathy to give them, but an experience that might show them much to avoid. I guess we ought to have a revolution over here.

## TO RUSSIA

As the Honored Guest of the Russian People I had come to deliver the following speech from the speaker's box in the great Hall of the Soviets where the famous purge trials were held. Inasmuch as I couldn't speak the language, I wrote the speech and had the text translated by *Pravda*. The translation was carefully checked by Olgivanna before giving it to Colle, the President of the Institute of Architects, to read. I spoke the introduction and conclusion, leaving him to read the body of the text. The place was filled to overflowing with six hundred architects from all the states of the Soviet Union, and many from abroad. I have never had so great an ovation in my life. Many young architects crowded around Olgivanna, she who could speak to them, saying, "We know your husband's work so well, and we even knew his face before he got here." The place resembled a convention hall electing a president. Again and again I had to go back, the applause continuing until I reappeared to take my seat beside Olgivanna in the box at one side when the entire audience rose to its feet, turned our way with a new burst of applause. The Soviet fliers had just won the plaudits of the whole world by reaching Seattle across the North Pole. There was great excitement in Moscow, flares, music and triumphal marching day and night.

## ADDRESS TO THE CONGRESS OF ARCHITECTS—SOVIET RUSSIA

MY DEAR COMRADES: I have traveled across the frontiers of five nations, from one great hope of the

**Olgivanna Lloyd Wright with wives of Russian architects, Moscow, June 1937.** FLLW Fdn FA#6827.0004

world, the U.S.A., to greet another great hope of the world, the U.S.S.R. I find that I, your guest, could now go home crossing but one, and that one the frontier of my own nation. And I can return by traveling only one-third of the distance I traveled to get here. The U.S.S.R. and the U.S.A. are both moved into a central position among the nations of the Northern Hemisphere by the supreme aviation of the Soviet Union. Thanks to Science we are next-door neighbors. But the Soviets are now to build fine buildings: a very different matter. A great art. I am glad to be here because I am already familiar with your struggle to find suitable architecture for your new Soviet life. I am sympathetic because we of the new life of my own country, the U.S.A., were ourselves where you stand now. We once had the great opportunity—"a clean slate," as we say. We had to choose between crawling back into the shell of an old culture or going bravely forward to the new one we needed in order to become a strong, new culture ourselves. In our new-found freedom we made the wrong choice. We chose the inferior path of the slave.

The rapid growth of Science, apparent success of mechanical appliances and industrial technique, these achievements exploiting vast natural resources gave us great wealth, suddenly. All these advances had so far outrun our knowledge of the principles underlying the right practice of Art that, needing Architecture as much as you do now, we freely plundered such tombs of preceding civilizations as we liked, and foolishly built upon forms we took from the bargain counter of dying or decayed cultures. So today our official architecture is a disgrace to the name of freedom owing to that ignorant license.

Our official buildings only serve to betray by way of our commercial vanity our significant triumphs in the realms of Industry and Science. As it is elsewhere in the world, only now are genuine architectural forms suited to our new life breaking through. We see them, if we look for them, among these stage settings with which we ignorantly sought to camouflage our lack of growth from within: the growth that alone is worthy to be called Culture; the integrity which gave ancient nations whatever greatness they had in their day. That we have done pretty well at this prostitution is poor enough consolation. What we have done is not good enough because meantime the U.S.A. has allowed herself to learn nothing of architecture. All of the arts in our country have suffered atrophy in consequence.

Our skyscraper? What was it? A triumph of engineering but the defeat of architecture. Steel frames standing hidden by facings of thin stone tied on to the steel frame—fascinating pictures—imitating feudal towers, but Architecture as false as the civic economy that allowed them to be built in congested urban areas. I have seen a dismal reflection of that falsity in your own work palace. This work palace—only proposed, I hope—is good if we take it for a modern version of St. George slaying the Dragon: that is to say—Lenin stamping the life out of a capitalistic skyscraper.

And elsewhere among you, I see our old enemy—Grandomania. I see it even in your subways. I see you repeating underground what the nobles did for themselves (and to themselves) in this hall in which we stand now. Suitable enough, no doubt, for their parasitic life, but too far beneath the level of the new integrity we are learning to call organic architecture, naturally becoming to those ideals of freedom for which you fought.

The "palatial" will not be easily destroyed in Russia as I see. Cut grandomania down here and it lifts up its head somehow over there (which means among you over here) when and where we least expect it. But I believe it is popular here only because the finer expressions of modern architecture have been allowed scant standing room among you.

A new thought comes to us fresh from the new freedom of humanity: a more exacting and exciting ideal has come with these new freedoms than the Old Cultures ever knew. The old cultures could only flourish by externals, but the new must and may now flourish by growth from within. Slow growth, I know. But it is the only growth that is safe for Russia now.

I dread to see the Soviet Union making the same mistakes our American Union made. When buildings must be built before culture has had time to come abreast in order to make them true architecture, it is better for the Soviets to make buildings scientifically sound with as much good sense and intelligent use of good materials as possible. Then stop there!

The left wing of our new movement toward an organic architecture professes to do this but they did not do more than make flat-topped plain-wall surfaces ornamental. They will pass.

The right wing was not content to do less than make ornament of the building itself. They are therefore in senile, bad company. But the true center of the movement, organic architecture, has gone on developing the scientific, sound material conditions of building into a higher manifestation of the human spirit suited to modern life.

At this moment were the Soviets to concentrate on good proportion, good planning and construction, building great highways and bridges, great planting schemes, retaining walls and terraces, refraining from much ornamentation of her structure and refraining from any attempt to make them elaborate in form until her young architects by way of experiment gradually evolve new Russian types as true to the New Russia as the Kremlin was true to the Old Russia—then the U.S.S.R. would justify our new world hope. A genuine culture at last! I am hoping the U.S.A. will some day undo what it has so badly done, and itself not do less than this.

Comrades, in building, do not waste yourselves upon these mere affairs of "taste." Architecture, in the advanced thought of the time, is fast becoming a matter of scientific knowledge applying philosophical ideas wherein Art is again free and supreme.

Take no less than this.

Another great matter coming to light in our modern world is the inevitable decay of great cities. Urban life has served its turn even for you, and cities great or cities small are definitely dated. The factory worker's view and version of life, and his vision now especially, needs the cooperation and healthy inspiration of Russian ground. The agrarian needs the industrialist, yes, but the industrialist needs the agrarian far more. The ground is the natural and national birthright of every man and is more important to him than anything he makes out of it or puts upon it. Of that fundamental basic ingredient of the good life—Russia has plenty for all and forever to come. So it would seem to me.

Russians, make good use of your ground for the new Russia! Can the Soviets not see that electricity, machines, automobiles, radio, television—the architecture of splendid highways and spacious, farflung Agriculture—can make the old form of city (centralization) not only useless, but harmful to the future? Vertical is vertigo, in human life. The horizontal line is the life-line of humankind. An entire nation will some day be one great free extended city. Its citizens will be living broadly spaced on ground of their own in a free pattern where workers in field and factory, in art and craft, science and education, commerce and transportation, will harmoniously intermingle. Each human endeavor will be related to every other on organic lines natural to all. And human life without waste motion, distraction, dissipation, interference, or imposition will take on new

**Lloyd Burlingham House, "The Pottery House" (Project), El Paso, Texas. 1942. Perspective. Pencil and color pencil on tracing paper, 41 x 18".** FLLW Fdn#4202.001

forms—better ways of doing everything. If that is what Russia means to do, then I am a Russian. Everybody in Russia, whatever his nation, will be a free man. Organic architecture has already so far evolved the pattern of such a higher life on earth as to be able to know and show the City of the Future. I would much like the young architects of the U.S.S.R. to see, and some day they may see, Broadacre City— the city that is everywhere and nowhere.

The United States is still far from such a plan. Her economic waste and the attempt of production to control consumption prevent it. Private Owner-

ship and the Profit System supreme and raised to the *nth* degree in all branches of life prevent it. These economic follies make the greater city impossible for another half-century at least. But Russia could have that freedom of democratic form now, if she wanted it enough. Her architects have the vision and the ability.

This new freedom is the great integrity modern life lacks and needs. This integrity is the service organic architecture could render the U.S.S.R. at this critical stage in the national life of the Soviets. And later it will extend from Russia to the continental world at large—if by that time there should be any of it left.

To you architects of the Soviet Union: I, who admire and love your spirit, I say, Go slowly into the higher realm of building that we call Architecture. No matter what the pressure, prepare to begin at the true beginning! Learn structure, yes, but first study thoroughly the *principles* beneath the technique and forms of organic architecture, and by way of your own high Russian spirit, grow an architecture as true to yourselves living the new Soviet life as the forever beautiful Kremlin was true to the old life of the soil, so that the great work grew out of itself where it stands.

The Kremlin—divested of its parasitic Renaissance improvements—stands as one of the great human treasures of all time.

The Soviet must not imitate the Kremlin. But the Kremlin honors the Soviet. And it is my great hope that the Soviet will honor itself by growing up to be a true cultural entity in terms of today's tomorrow. When Architecture is really Architecture it is timeless. Out of the young Freedom that is now the U.S.S.R., other great treasures for the Future should come. But, patience. They cannot be forced. They also must humbly begin at the beginning and slowly grow.

Returning from Russia the American papers were openly hostile because of what I had said about them in Moscow. But I wrote the article below: "Architecture and Life in the U.S.S.R." in August 1937. It was published in *Soviet Russia Today*. Russia was then "red," and therefore to the entire United States, news and radio, disreputable.

No one wanted to hear anything good about the U.S.S.R.

To commend anything Russian got you in wrong with the powers-that-be—socially, financially, and especially morally.

My God, of what hypocrisy we are capable!

### ARCHITECTURE AND LIFE IN THE U.S.S.R.
Now that I am back at Taliesin again, my Moscow colleagues are far enough away for perspective to assert itself. I enjoyed them so much, was personally so much in sympathy with them while there, that appraisals made on the spot might easily have been overdrawn. They were not.

As I look back now across the Pole—my friends in Moscow and their work appear the more extraordinary. I went to them intending to do what little I could to end the confusion in the reactionary practices in Architecture I saw among them. I particularly disliked the Work Palace of the Soviets. I had hoped to alter the minds entangled with its erection. But the foundations were in.

And I found that in Russia, as in the United States long ago, the masses who had nothing and to whom the landed aristocracy appeared to have everything, now had their turn to be pleased. Nothing pleases them so much as the gleam of marble columns under high ceilings, glittering chandeliers, the unmistakable signs of luxury as they looked up to it when it decided their fate, and they ate out of luxury's hand if they ate at all.

But reassurance for me lay in the attitude of the Soviet architects themselves. I may mention Alabyan, Colle, Yofan, the Vesnins, Nikolsky, Chusev, and the editor, Arkin, as personal acquaintances in this connection. All of them took the present situation with a humor and a touch of fatalism characteristically Russian.

Just now is no time to offer the liberated ones the high simplicity which repudiates the falsity of that sort of luxury. This is not the time to insist upon something they could not understand—the higher simplicity that has turned upon that flagrant artifice as the people themselves turned upon its possessors. So in the Soviet Union I saw the cultural lag again as I have seen it and fought against it for a lifetime in these United States. With the Russians, as with the Americans, several more generations must pass before a more natural way of life and building takes the place of the old order. The Russian people see viciousness in that old order where human rights are concerned. But the masses of the Russian people are yet unable to see that viciousness in the higher realm of created things of which architecture is the highest, and that what they fought to destroy still lives on among them in the parasitic forms of the life they destroyed, to destroy them in a more subtle and far-reaching destruction.

The architects, however—at least those I have named—are men who realize this. But they are men who say, "Never mind—we will tear it down in ten years."

"It will take nearly that long to finish the Palace of the Soviets," I said.

"Never mind, we may tear that down too—even before we complete it."

"But this popular rush to get into Moscow? Are you right when you prepare Moscow to take five million country people, instead of sending Moscow out to the five million?"

"But Russia needs a cultural center for her uneducated millions for years to come. Let the city be that cultural center for a time," said they.

Such resignation would not be possible for me. I can understand it, perhaps envy it, but cannot approve it. Notwithstanding the tragedy of the first essays in the direction of the new simplicity, I would see the Russian opportunity as a mighty incentive in no way diminished by a false start.

But the attitude of the Russian architect is sincere and far in advance of the social consciousness of our own American architects. I do not know one architect among us who looks so far into the future, able to smile indulgently at his own present effort—perspective given by a fine sense of humor mingled with idealism.

Said Alabyan: "I thought I would put all the columns I would have to use for the rest of my life into this building [the new Theater] and have done with it." Said Vesnin, concerning his Palace of Culture and Rest (a very desirable improvement on Le Corbusier, et al.), "It lacks color. It is only a preliminary study. It is not yet Russian." Said young Yofan, not yet disillusioned concerning his highly decorated eclecticism, the Palace of Soviets: "Never mind, Mr. Wright, it will improve as we go along. We are studying it continually." And I saw proofs of that statement in Yofan's studio (Napoleon's old residence in Moscow by the Kremlin wall).

Who could help loving such liberal, great-hearted imaginative fellows? What colleague would not do anything he could do under heaven to help them? The result might be help *from* them. Said they

to me: "Have faith in our people. We Russians are by nature artists. We love the beautiful. Our sense of life is deep and rhythmic. We will create a new Russia. You will see."

I believe I do see in their efforts a new organic Russia slowly entering into their buildings "through closed doors." And I see no necessity for Russia to die that the Soviet Union may live.

If Comrade Stalin, as disconcerted outsiders are saying, is betraying the revolution, then, in the light of what I have seen in Moscow, I say he is betraying it into the hands of the Russian people.

In Moscow the architects enjoy a large old palace complete, as their Academy. There you find a gallery and supper rooms on the top floor. Libraries, studios, and collections below. Just before leaving Moscow we joined some of the architects I have named for retreat and recreation at their Sukhanov, a four-hundred-acre park, thirty miles from Moscow, where another old palace stands. There, their own herds and flocks around them, they are putting up new buildings. All stand in a beautiful forest with fine vistas of beautiful countryside. To this wooded retreat whenever they will, they may and do go with their families and friends for recreation. The architects are about to build small studios for preliminary study and shops for technical experiments.

There seems to be none but friendly rivalry among them. Why should there be other than willing cooperation? Worldly rewards cannot benefit them. They are economically independent for life and so are their loved ones. One man's success hurts no one else but is a stepping stone for his fellows. The sting has been taken out of competition. There is no humiliation in today's defeat because failure today may be retrieved by tomorrow's triumph. The road is open. And their "tomorrow" is today in the sense that Eternity is Now. You will feel it so when you talk to them.

Good fellowship at Sukhanov, as Olgivanna, my good interpreter, and I found, is an unforgettable human experience. Have you ever known Russian hospitality? No? Well, then, be an architect and go to visit Russian architects. They will take you to Sukhanov.

Being a farmer myself as well as an architect, I

visited a collective dairy farm. The farmers were at their work in the fields and barns, all sharing according to their contributions. They milk three times a day—at sunrise, at ten o'clock, and at sunset. All live together in a village like the farm village of the old order except that now there is the crèche filled with babies cared for while their mothers are at work. The babies are nursed by their own mothers. Nearby is a kindergarten, along modern lines. Both crèche and kindergarten are maintained by the Soviet itself. The *kolkhoz is* a nucleus characteristic of Soviet effort, but this agrarian effort is far less developed than industrial effort, as it still is with us in the U.S.A.

The factory is better built and run than the farm. For one thing, the farm requires so much more. This is partly because the Revolution first came from organized labor in the factories and the farms at first resisted the subsequent movement to collectivize their work. At one time the farmers destroyed their pigs and crops rather than turn them over to the collectives. We well know how difficult it is to bring any cooperation to bear upon American farm life, or within it, even now. The Grange came the nearest of anything we had but it does not flourish.

The agrarian hurdle seems to have been taken by the Soviets. Cooperative farming is likely to prove the same blessing that socialization proved to be in factory industry. The houses of the farm village range about a central square that might be a beautiful park, with loud-speakers there connecting each farm group with the voice of their leader and the cultural efforts of the urban centers. In time, these farm units are sure to become the most desirable of all places in which to work and live.

Plans for the new Moscow are still wrong from my standpoint but far ahead of any city planning I have seen. There is splendid opportunity to make the city over because no private property nor sentimentality can say "no" when the great plan requires the blowing up of whole sections of old buildings. Even sacred old landmarks are blown into the air to make spacious streets where dirty, obscure lanes existed. The scope and liberal character of the proposed changes and extensions are astonishing.

When completed, Moscow will inevitably be the first city in the world. But to me, that can only mean something already dated and outlived by the advanced thought of our today, Broadacres.

All of the new city will be much too high—the same premium put upon congestion that land-lordism places there. And I suppose this is partly because the industrialist, still clinging to his habits, is ahead of the agrarian in the U.S.S.R. He is still ahead in our own U.S.A. For some reason, there will be regimented areas too in the "classic" manner, where inevitable freedom should be. There will be four-story school-houses—knowledge factories—where two stories would be too high. And while the entire outer-belt is a park area, it should be the other way around. The best of the traditional and official buildings should stand in a big central park, buildings growing higher as they extended outward into the country.

But much that is splendid is already done—wide avenues and park spaces. The ancient Moscow River is being walled with cut granite blocks sweeping in a fine curve from the water to the upper levels. The ancient Kremlin walls and domes stand nobly above these great new granite-slopes.

The Moscow subway is a succession of well-planned palatial stations. I like the more simple ones, built at first, with columns containing lights, the shafts rising and spreading into the overhead. Later ones are richer and more spacious. The Moscow subway makes the New York subway look like a sewer.

But cutting across the road to culture there is a barrier—the same barrier that is here with us: the popular demand for spiritually unearned, luxurious grandeur. But in their case, no wonder or reproach. The Russians outside the aristocracy and bourgeoisie had less than nothing. Now it is their turn. Millions looking toward Moscow as a Mecca can go there at last! Of course, they go and want to stay, because the lash of unrequited toil on the land has left its scars.

Concerning new construction: their buildings are no better or worse than the best work of other countries. Misfortune befell Moscow when her modern architects took after the left wing. That mistake in direction left some very negative and foreign results—indeed, drab, lonesome, technically childish. The popular reaction from that fiasco could only be luxurious picture-making in the antique, the picture-making which the older people learned as children to admire and covet.

Chusev and I stood together in his great Soviet hotel, a huge constructed thing, done in what I told him should be called "the Metropolitan style" because you could see it with such virtues as it has and all its faults in Philadelphia or any big city of the world. A comfortable hotel though, and I exaggerated a little because in many respects it was better done, and more comfort provided for the occupant, but still the building was the type of hotel we Americans are learning to hate.

Mere size seems to captivate the Soviets as it seduced our provinces earlier. Of course, all this is the reaction in action which I was afraid I would see.

The Palace of the Soviets, to be the crowning glory of the new construction, suffers likewise from grandomania of the American type in imitating skyscraper effects way up to the soles of the enormous shoes of Lenin, where the realistic figure of that human giant begins to be three hundred feet tall. Something peculiar to the present cultural state of the Soviet is to be seen in the sharp contrast between thick shoes and workman's clothes and skyscraper elegance. These perpendicular skyscraping motives are surmounted at the characteristic New York setbacks by sculpture, pygmy by comparison.

Lenin, enormous, treads upon the whole, regardless. Nothing more incongruous could be conceived and I believe nothing more distasteful to the great man Lenin if he could see. And yet Yofan, the young architect whose design was accepted for this work seven years ago, has this year built the most dramatic and successful exhibition building at the Paris Fair. The general motive of that building is not dissimilar to that of the Palace of the Soviets. It too is a building surmounted by gigantic sculpture.

But the Paris Fair building is a low, extended, and suitable base for the dramatically realistic sculpture it carries, whereas the Palace of the Soviets itself is a case of a thoroughly unsuitable, badly over-dramatized base underneath realistic undramatic sculpture.

I went with Yofan to see a sanatorium he had done near Moscow and that too was a very well-designed, very well-built structure. Any Soviet citizen needing attention and care may go there to luxury seen only on our trans-Atlantic liners. An ingenious arrangement of balconies and rooms gives outdoor enjoyment to indoor comfort. On the whole here is a performance that could not be, has not been, excelled anywhere. The building occupied by *Pravda* I saw as the more creditable of the "modernistic" attempts by the Russians. But, because of its negative and unconstructive precedents, such building is not for the Russians—it is too laborious a stylization of too little spirit and small content. I see the Russians discontented with less than something profound, when culture catches up—say, in ten years.

The extensive Palace of Culture, a recreational center for the studious or artistically minded citizen, was better in many respects. It contains as good a design for an auditorium as I, a specialist in auditoriums, have ever seen. The scope and extent of the whole is good in conception, not bad in execution. I liked its architects. I will like their work better when it is more like them, and that means more Russian in spirit and character. Both architects are capable, invaluable to the Soviet as are many others besides the friends I have mentioned. The Soviet sent more than four hundred Russian architects to the Congress at Moscow. And invited many from other countries.

Leningrad is to be, I take it, the Soviet showpiece in cities. Nikolsky showed me his design for the new stadium at Leningrad: stadium spaciously monumental, a broad treatment employing masses of trees in an architectural way I liked much. A sensible relief from ponderous masonry, it will be a fine work on a grand scale.

The Russian cinema has made its buildings the finest good-time places for the people to be seen anywhere in the world. The Vesnins have designed some of them. Collé, my interpreter at the Congress, President of the Architect's Society—the A.I.A. of the U.S.S.R.—has a fine sense of proportion and style, at present leaning classic-ward, however. Alabyan, President of the Congress, shows himself a competent designer in the new theater, giving some life to the old mode. And so it goes on, this tremendous social construction that is calling upon Architecture for help and direction. Competent architects able to build great buildings are there. And alongside are sympathetic employers, critics, editors like Arkin, the editor of *Pravda,* and many others, among whom the heads of their fine arts academies may be included although now, as here, on the side of reaction. I hope temporarily.

What a pity that architecture in Soviet Russia is not as free as the man—so that the millennium might be born at once, where the road is still more open than anywhere else, without all this wasteful, wearisome temporizing with the old time-lag and backdrag of the human predilection for ignorance where culture is concerned. It is hard for me to be reconciled to the delays Russia is experiencing, no matter how cheerfully, in getting architecture characteristic of her new freedom.

I saw the admirable models for Soviet Russia's new towns and cities in various places—all better than good but too many concessions to the cultural time-lag. I suppose the marvel of it all is that a country so backward as Russia should have these fine things at all—at least, have them so soon. Perhaps too soon!

I grant all that and still regret.

But I saw something in the glimpses I had of the Russian people themselves which makes me smile in anticipation: the Russian Spirit!

There is nothing like that spirit anywhere in the world today.

I felt it in the air, saw it as a kind of aura about the wholesome maleness of her men and femaleness of her women; in this new gospel of work; in the glad open expressions of the faces of workmen and workwomen. Freedom already affects them unconsciously; proud they carry themselves. Especially the women. I could not help feeling, "What a mother this new Russia is going to have !"

A kind of new heroism, one more integral with humankind, is surely growing up in the world in the Soviet Union where men are men and women are women; where God has ceased to be an expensive abstraction to the people; where abortion is abolished; where there is no illegitimate child and the resources of the state stand behind the mother to reinforce her in the care of her sons and daughters. In Russia, there is a place in the sun ready for the little newcomer when conceived. Wherever and whenever the child is born, there is really another citizen with rights guaranteed by the state—education ready and waiting and opportunity to work. There is no discrimination between the sexes.

All this is surely wise.

And how wise are the premiums placed upon *quality* in work—integral industrial rewards which build up the man in his effort—the "Stakhanov Principle," they call it. Rewards of a social and substantial character devised by a wise leader to develop an entirely new Success ideal. It is hard for us *here* in our society, our Success ideal as it is, to conceive this new freedom for the individual without grasping several fundamental things totally changed there in the human objective. I find myself continually needing a more simple viewpoint than our complex order of "meum and tuum" allows. Until we get that viewpoint, however, we cannot understand Russia. We of the grasping West will marvel at her vitality and strength, her heroic growth and richness of expression, and admire especially her colorful individuality, never knowing the secret of such happiness.

That secret is too simple for us because it does not longer consist in our way of to-have or to-hold but in acceptance of a life consisting in neither except insofar as having or holding may have human benefits each to each and each to all. The relief of such release from ignoble fear, economic anxiety and false shames, you may already see in Soviet faces, Soviet acts. Heroes and heroism will glisten naturally in the fabric of this new Soviet life.

Having seen and sensed the Russian Spirit, I should say that enemies interfering with the Soviet Union would not only have to reckon with the whole male population bearing arms, but with the women, too, and every child above nine years of age.

Nothing less than total extermination could conquer Soviet Russia.

A true poet and philosopher, Dr. Ku [I have quoted him when talking about Japan], had the faculty of thinking and speaking "in simples." One day, while sitting on the edge of an old stone terrace overlooking a lotus pool, he summed up and characterized the various races of the world with what seemed to me great insight and justice—especially with regard to America. "Soul" seemed to him to be the element most lacking in all the nations—the French having a substitute. The substitute was delicacy.

But, he said, it was Russia who would give soul to the world.

At that time I knew Tolstoy, Turgenev, Dostoevsky, Pushkin, and Gogol; I knew Russian music and theater, too, somewhat. And I thought I saw what he meant.

Today I believe what he said. It is true. Russia may yet give to this money-minded, war-minded, quarreling pack of senile races that make up the Western world the soul they fail to find within themselves—and, I hope, in time to prevent the suicide the nations are so elaborately preparing to commit.

—*Taliesin, August 10, 1937*

One of the many repercussions to the foregoing article, which was copied by *The Capital Times* of Madison, was this letter:

### AN OPEN LETTER TO FRANK LLOYD WRIGHT

In the many years that your name has been associated with excellence in Architecture, you have won a reputation for honesty and fearlessness, and your opinions are listened to by many Americans. It is therefore regrettable that you should have seen fit to couple a favorable account of the Soviet Union with a serious slur on the Communist Party of the United States.

We, who have visited your Taliesin and have seen your buildings with uncompleted floors, without light, and without heating facilities, have witnessed a melancholy illustration of how art is forsaken by an economic system whose one God is profit. We have admired the integrity which has kept you from accommodating your talents to the erection of the kind of structures Capitalism is willing to buy.

We wondered what you would say of the land of socialism where art as well as industry belongs to the *whole* people, and a great architect's creations do not need to stand about without electricity, gloomy symbols of the enchainment of art under capitalism. And we were not mistaken in your integrity. You came back with frank praise, you gave the lie to the distortions of the press, you said: "If Stalin is 'betraying the Revolution, as people are constantly shouting, he's betraying it into the hands of the Russian people." We are therefore completely at a loss to fathom your assertion that the Communists in America are racketeers. Can it be that you have momentarily forgotten your distaste for "Grandomania" and disdain us, merely because as yet there are only fifty thousand of us and we are not quite in a position to do the things the Communist Party in Russia can do?

Or can it be that even after learning that a first-hand knowledge of Soviet Russia is quite different from what the capitalist press supplies us with, you are still content to get your information about the *American* Communist Party at second hand from that same press? If the statement in *The Capital Times* was not an error, we hope that you will find time to make an accusation more explicit and that the fairness you have shown in your description of Russia will prompt you to give us a chance to answer. We feel convinced that only a lack of direct acquaintance with American communists—coupled perhaps with the all too common mistake of confusing some campus bohemians with Communists—can be responsible for your statement.

—*The Faculty Branch of the Communist Party,*
*University of Wisconsin*

### REPLY TO THE FACULTY COMMUNISTS OF THE UNIVERSITY OF WISCONSIN

To our University Communists: I have read your open letter. First, let me assure you that I have not said Communists in America were Racketeers. That was a slip between the Press and the lip—over the telephone. To say that would be as untrue as foolish. I did say, Trotskyites and campus intelligentsia in mind, that the Communists in our country seemed to me, now that Racketeers were in among them as they are among the labor unions, the worst enemies of Russia.

I confess that I do not know what your "communism" is. I do not believe it is like that, but I am inclined now to see any ist or ism as alien and shun the ites.

I have lived to see the organic architecture I put my life into exploited in the name of an ism—made istic by the "ites." I refer to "international-ism," now the "modernistic." So perhaps I am too ready to believe that whatever communism may once have been, it too has been exploited by "campus sharp-wits," the lazy irreverent sharp-wits who flourish on ists and isms. Inevitable ites that curse truth by living *on* it instead of living *for* it. Theirs is the kiss of Caiaphas. For that reason, what does the term Republican mean now, or Socialist, or Democrat? Yes, or Communist? Any ideal or movement is more vulnerable from beneath and from within than it is from the outside or from above. Communism in the United States is a conspicuous example. Or that term Progressive? Already just about as ambiguous. Let's drop the corrupted and corrupting labels and be specific!

"Social Justice" sounds better to me than any ism, but that too is only a label. I could march under a banner that stood squarely upon that idea if made definite.

The United States might unite under the banner of some unequivocal idea, and win any honest social objective.

Democracy itself, like Social Credit, is no more or less than Social Justice. But even the grand term, Democracy, has been bought and oversold by party politics and fakirs until it is now merely "Americanistic."

## TO YOU, AMERICAN COMMUNISTS

From Russia to the United States and back again to Russia . . . as to "FORM":

1. Every man guaranteed the right to work.

2. No able man to eat unless he works.

3. Free ground and a free medium of exchange.

4. General decentralization: less crowding everywhere, and less government except as government consists in transacting the impersonal business of the whole people.

5. No speculation in natural resources or in the utilities common to all by way of which our people live. No exploitation of earth, water, air, or sky; of natural resources like oil, gas, coal, common carriers, or radio; no speculation in telephone and telegraph, press, or post; education and medical help to be free.

A shortcut to all this, to becoming a country owning itself; in debt to itself only government *from within itself*. A far greater simplicity than Russia. A new Success ideal would soon supplant the one that went with the old profit motive, one more organic, and therefore more *humane*.

How could this be brought about? Gradually. By taxation and some form of purchase by capitalizing the country itself over and above a fair living for every man, woman, and child in it—selling the margin back to the people as stock in their own country.

A genuine system of private ownership, a system of capital with its broad base on the ground in the lives of the whole people, instead of standing precariously on its apex for the few. Is it communism I am describing? Is it socialism? No? Well, gentlemen, if you must have an "ism" I see it as true capitalism—the organic capital of an organic Democracy: the only basis of an organic architecture or for indigenous Usonian culture.

N.B. And, comrades, please don't put my plight at Taliesin up against Russia as a reproach to my country. I've been pretty "trying," you know. I am still trying.

—*Taliesin, August 1937*

## THE SAFETY OF THE SOUL DEPENDS ON ITS COURAGE

The long view is the cool view.

"Tolerance, experiment, and change gives a culture strength."

Life always rides in strength to victory, not through internationalism or through any other "isms," but only through the direct responsibility of the individual. It bears a royal characteristic called Initiative. Where Individual initiative is active, strong and operative, there you may see the mainspring of life in abundance, operating.

Nature herself places this premium upon Individuality. And it applies to Nations. Nations are only the Individual raised to a common-power which should act as a check upon idiosyncrasy. The fact that a Nation does not so act is the weakness of the Nation.

Organic Democratic Form: TRUTH ever fresh has not yet come to our Civilization.

So we have the sorry spectacle of a venal world substituting blows for ideas: a whirlpool of destruction and hate into which our leaders draw us with too great ease.

When I returned from Russia many friends, reading what I had written and hearing me talk of our experiences there, were all curious to know how the visit had affected my "point of view." Said Lloyd (Lewis), for one, I remember, "Frank, come now, what do you really make of Communism in Moscow?" "Oh," I said, "the Russians have done remarkable things considering their start with such tremendous illiteracy. But the Revolution has been only partial; they've kept our idea of Money—the System that is destroying us and will destroy Communism, too; they still believe in great concentrations of human beings on hard pavements for educational purposes (it will probably prove to be for military purposes). She has fallen for machine worship—it will turn and rend her as it will rend us." "Then," said Lloyd, "you don't come home a convert to Communism?"

"No," I answered. "No isms, private or international, for me. I believe in a capitalist system. I only wish I could see it tried some time."

The Fifth Book of *An Autobiography* ends here.

## "KEEP THE YOUNG GENERATIONS IN HEALTH AND BEQUEATH TO THEM NO TUMBLED HOUSE."

Like Sinan, the famous Ottoman architect of Agra who, centuries ago, built a city for Babar, I wish to build a city for Democracy: the Usonian city that is nowhere yet everywhere.

Since this search for FORM ends there, the Usonian City, Broadacres, will be the sixth book of *An Autobiography*. The natural Conclusion.

## INDEX

For the writing of this work I have long ago consulted and occasionally remembered Pythagoras, Aristophanes, Socrates, Heraclitus, Laotze, Buddha, Jesus, Tolstoy, Kropotkin, Bacon, William Blake, Samuel Butler, Mazzini, Walt Whitman, Henry George, Grundvig, George Meredith, Henry Thoreau, Herman Melville, George Borrow, Goethe, Carlyle, Nietzsche, Voltaire, Cervantes, Giacosa, Shelley, Shakespeare, Milton, Thorstein Veblen, Nehru, Major Douglas, and Silvio Gesell.

Louis Sullivan's writings I have not read: he whose thought was, in his own person and presence, an open book to me for many years.

And innumerable are the various collaterals, diagonals, and opposites that went into the place where this book might have come from but did not. I said at the beginning that the real book was between the lines. It is true of any serious book concerned with culture.

Gene (Masselink) of the Fellowship and his helpers have untangled day by day, month by month, the mass of inter-lined and defaced scripts that would tease anyone, especially myself. Gene is the only one who could read them.

1. This was the first time Frank Lloyd Wright had an exclusive arrangement with a publishing company. It was to continue on to 1949 for the printing of *Genius and the Mobocracy*. But following that book Wright grew disillusioned with the royalties and eventually was outraged when Duell, Sloan and Pearce sold the rights to the autobiography, without consulting him, to an Italian publisher that came out with a poorly designed version in Italian. At that point Wright broke off with Duell, Sloan and Pearce. Later he would select another exclusive publisher, but that relationship ended, although not so dramatically, in a termination of agreement.

2. FLLW to Grant Manson, 30 April 1957. FLLW Archives.

3. FLLW to James Thomson, 5 December 1942. FLLW Archives.

4. Frank Lloyd Wright. *An Autobiography*. New York: Duell, Sloan and Pearce, 1943. p. 520.

5. Mary Ellen Chase. *A Goodly Fellowship*. New York: Macmillan Company, 1939.

6. Susan Lawrence Dana was a wealthy Springfield, Illinois, client for whom Wright designed one of his best-known early houses in 1902;

Charles E. Roberts, a client from the 1890s, sat on the building committee for Unity Temple, 1905.

7. The column "At Taliesin" began in 1934 and was published for four years, most frequently in *The Capital Times,* but also in other Wisconsin newspapers. Randolph Henning discovered 285 columns. See Henning. *At Taliesin.* Carbondale, Illinois: Southern Illinois University Press, 1992.

8. Frank Lloyd Wright. *The Disappearing City.* New York: William Farquar Payson, 1932. Reprinted in *Collected Writings Volume 3.*

9. Herbert and Katherine Jacobs built two Wright homes, the first Usonian in 1937 and the Solar Hemicycle completed in 1948. See Herbert Jacobs. *Building with Frank Lloyd Wright.* San Francisco: Chronicle Books, 1978.

10. Alexander Meiklejohn, a respected educator who was brought to the University of Wisconsin in the late 1920s to head their Experimental College. According to Jack Holzheuter of the Wisconsin State Historical Society, Wright had hoped Meiklejohn might become the director of the Hillside Home School for the Allied Arts.

11. John Fiske (1842–1901), American historian, lecturer, and author.

12. William Wesley Peters and Svetlana Wright, Olgivanna's daughter from her first marriage whom Wright adopted.

13. Brandoch Peters, Wes and Svetlana Peters's son. He was named for a protagonist in *The Worm Ouroboros* by E. R. Eddison.

14. See *An Autobiography,* reprinted in *Collected Writings Volume 2,* pages 105–106 and 113 for a discussion of the Lloyd-Joneses and this Druid symbol.

15. This poem, "The Breeze," was used by Catherine and Frank Lloyd Wright for a quite elaborate Christmas card in 1907. The design, drawn by Maginel Wright, FLLW's younger sister, had four small illustrations to accompany the calligraphed seasonal stanzas. See FLLW Fdn project number 0716.

16. Dr. Alexander Chandler had been the client for the unrealized 1929 San Marcos-in-the-Desert project.

17. S. C. Johnson & Son Administration Building, 1936, Racine, Wisconsin.

18. The Johnson Wax Administration Building was opened for public tours April 22–23, 1939. Twenty-six thousand people toured the building over this two-day weekend.

19. The Gillen Woodwork Corporation of Milwaukee, Wisconsin, made the cabinetwork for Fallingwater as well as for Wingspread.

20. See *Collected Writings Volume 1,* pp. 162–192 for Wright's articles describing the Imperial Hotel.

21. A clubhouse commissioned in the early 1920s for the Nakoma Country Club, a newly organized golf club. For a discussion of the project see Mary Jane Hamilton, "The Nakoma Country Club" in *Frank Lloyd Wright and Madison.* Madison: University of Wisconsin Press, 1990.

22. John Haynes Holmes (1879–1964), Unitarian of the Community Church in New York City. He was a founder and active member of both the National Association for the Advancement of Colored People and the American Civil Liberties Union.

23. *Miss Lulu Bett* was first published in 1920; its dramatization the next year won Zona Gale (1874–1938) the Pulitzer Prize.

24. The Tabernacle Church of Christ, Columbus, Indiana (1939–1942), designed by Eliel Saarinen (1873–1950) and his son, Eero (1910–1961).

25. The elder Saarinen not only designed the Cranbrook School for Boys (1924–1930), he also served as its director from 1932–1942.

26. The Wrights sailed for South America in September 1931, returning to the States in late October.

27. William and John Spaulding were prominent Boston print collectors and Wright bought tens of thousands of dollars worth of prints for them during his visits to Japan. The Spauldings donated their collection, considered one of the finest in the world, to the Museum of Fine Arts, Boston in 1921.

28. Wright probably meant Hiroshige, not Utamaro. *Fireworks at Ryogoku Bridge* is a famous print in the series "Toto Meisho: Famous Views of the Eastern Capital," by Hiroshige.

# AN AUTOBIOGRAPHY
# BOOK SIX: BROADACRE CITY

**P**romising, *at the end of* An Autobiography, *that the "natural conclusion" would be Book Six, "Broadacre City," Wright privately published this text during the summer of 1943 while* An Autobiography *was at the printer. In the "Preamble" he writes about his early thoughts concerning democracy:*

> *I began to think of Democracy somewhat when I began the practice of Architecture. Before that I had not thought so much about it. As a boy I was taught that a vote was a political power and that because each man had a vote he would have an equal share in determining the powers of the government. But the people who had real power, as I soon saw, were those who knew how to take advantage of the vote and of the hunger and weakness of the voters.*

*The first half of the paper is almost an autobiographical "confession" of how Wright views democracy, capitalism, the economy, and reviews other political systems, from imperialism to socialism. Step by step he explains how he came to be interested in economics and politics: "I had always been rather backward in political ideas—but idealizing Thomas Jefferson and Tom Paine." As he began to study the designs for Broadacre City (1934), he realized that he had to re-educate himself about many facets of social and political issues:*

> *Karl Marx never appealed to me because he seemed to see the world as a factory for factory workers and his view of society, with all its reality, seemed to me the worm's-eye-view. . . . Always I have loved the ground. And it interested me more than it seemed to interest Karl Marx or any of the socialists who subsequently grew up around his scientific analysis of human economy . . . chiefly industrial. I always felt the ground would be the proper universal basis for social life. Not the factory of the store.*
>
> *As an architect, never before much interested in Economics, I was compelled, now, to read much of the amazing conflict that constitutes such Science and Ethics as "Economics" assumes.*
>
> *But the exaggeration of false industrial-capitalism has intensified itself more and more as an empire within the empire of the colonial expansion of ruthless Imperialism. All over the Earth today you may see the fierce cruel grasp for this empire within the Empire by the Whites, now the Yellows, perhaps soon by the Blacks.*

*Here, then, gathering all this together follows in simple outline the base Basement of the organic Capitalistic Republic that I am calling BROADACRE CITY: THE CITY THAT IS A NATION FOUNDED IN COMMON SENSE and that subsequent chapters will present in more FORM: this great reflex concerned chiefly with what an organic co-operative capitalistic society would look like were we ourselves one. Politics, and therefore Politicians, should take a very different plan in our affairs. It is probable that no politician as such could make a living were our laws organic. Only the idiosyncracies of individuals and their quarrels would require lawyers. As one item we might well dispense with five hundred thousand of our six hundred thousand lawyers. As for future wars, any occasion for them could scarcely be trumped up by the secret molders of public-opinion.*

*In no other text did Wright more clearly define his political and economic views. He concluded with his suggestions for a cure to the ills of democracy as he saw them in 1943, even while the Second World War was in progress.*

## PREAMBLE

I am not fond of thinking: preferring to dream—until circumstances force me to think, which the circumstances in which I live are perpetually doing.

Previous to 1929, so far as I was concerned, Economics had been confined to professors and a few well-read men.

I knew that the Declaration of Independence, the Rights of Man, and the Pursuit of Happiness did not result in the people's obtaining independence or rights or happiness. And I saw clearly enough that not Economics but Religion was what the people were expected to turn to for relief from their inevitable lot of suffering and deprivations.

Charity was a virtue because a necessity.

Myself the son of a minister who came down a long line of ministers extending back to the days of the Reformation in England, I was quite familiar with deprivation and knew where to turn for relief—to my imagination which supplied me with all good and forbidden things.

I knew that the very idea of Liberty was a danger to the State and to Church and to Society if the people took it in earnest and not religiously.

I could never believe the Declaration of Independence meant that all men were born free and equal because what sense I had told me it was not so and could not be. But I thought it meant that all men, independent of the circumstances of their birth, should be given an equal chance to prove themselves equal.

I began to think of Democracy somewhat when I began the practice of Architecture. Before that I had not thought so much about it. As a boy I was taught that a vote was a political power and that because each man had a vote he would have an equal share in determining the powers of the government. But the people who had real power, as I soon saw, were those who knew how to take advantage of the vote and of the hunger and weakness of the voters.

Democracy stood in my mind for the growth and protection of individuality: stood for the rights of man as against authoritarian Kings and open or secret dictatorships. Gradually I came to see that the Christianity of my forbears, by way of their own sentimentality and credulity, had done a lot of harm in the world as well as a lot of good—but the harm was increasing and the good diminishing.

I had always been rather backward in political ideas—but idealizing Thomas Jefferson and Tom Paine.

Shelly and Goethe (by way of Carlyle) contributed much to my early sense of the thing when I was about fourteen years old. At that time I read Rousseau's *Emile,* and Carlyle's *Sartor Resartus* among other things . . . being an omnivorous reader. But, I had been most interested in the *Arabian Nights.* Of course Jules Verne and—secretly—the "Nickel Library."

The War of Independence fascinated me. All I knew of it was what the stock-and-shop Historians wrote for colonial consumption and the Civil War got to me in similar channels. I later realized that I knew nothing of either if I really wanted to know the truth.

The power of conservatism, as I have good reason to know, is tremendous, because I grew up a rationalist.

My religion so far as it went was Unitarian. After I became old enough to discriminate between dogmatism and principle, Philosophy came to me gradually and mostly by way of the farm, care of animals, the mysterious beauties and obvious cruelties of Nature—interlocking interchanges of the universe. And these began to fascinate me more when I began to build.

Then I became a seeker after Truth of Form.

Well along in the young practices of Architecture I met Mazzini, Meredith, Tolstoi, Whitman and the great humanitarians; I must have had that quality of feeling and thought—a pretty strong undercurrent from my pioneer forbears—because none of it seemed to me other than the most natural thing in the world.

Victor Hugo's *Notre Dame* affected me deeply.

But not until I had a home of my own and an independent practice did I realize the beneficent nature of the law of change—or see life in one continued flux of becoming, as Heraclitus stoned in the streets of Athens for a fool, saw it. Then and there were laid the foundations of the philosophy of a modern architecture. That Philosophy arrived in my mind, as Architecture, ten years before I had known Laotze in his own words.

I met none of all this in school.

I have often told of my meeting with the philosopher who had said what I was myself trying to build: Laotze who lived and taught five hundred years before Jesus was born.

Capitalism, Socialism, Communism were all so much water on the duck's back so far as I was concerned. There seemed nothing organic in them. Nothing began at the beginning where all thinking must begin—for itself and our own sake. If anything was to happen.

As an Architect I saw that financial prosperity and the law of Change, so far as growth went, have little or nothing in common and that I must choose between them. It cost me nothing to choose. My forbears and upbringing as well as my innate feeling were all on the side of growth, with the onward movement that is upward, toward the light. My faith in that was always a happiness.

Force and compulsion on the part of the State or any individual seemed hideous to me. Thoreau's "That government is best government which governs not at all," I accepted as a truism and felt that if men were not prepared for it yet they soon would be where they were free to feel and think for themselves as they were in my country.

I saw cooperation all around as the natural or normal thing, and not selfishness and violence. The anarchist's idea, faith in the common-wealth based on voluntary instinctive respect for the other fellow's rights, I saw as the normal thing and could never understand why it was not recognized as ideal even though unattainable in present-day society. I did realize that it was incompatible with false capitalism.

But all the various "beliefs" were so blended at the edges that it was hard for me to tell just where and when one slid into the other. The labels so confused me. And there seemed always to be a soiled fringe of disreputables clinging to every fine faith or great thought when it started to move. But the people who were "wrong" I liked. And the people who were "right" I seldom liked.

What happened to Malatesta in Italy usually happened to people who really got things moving ahead. Jail seemed always there to put a stop to anything that really meant a step up and a step forward. If not the civil-jail then it was the money-jail.

Resentment and violence seemed to attach to the law of change where human nature was concerned, although change is natural and perpetual in the nature of the Cosmos. Inextricable "interests" so involved nearly everyone in his present situation that any real forward movement was made painful beyond endurance. I began to understand why.

Karl Marx never appealed to me because he seemed to see the world as a factory for factory workers and his view of society, with all its reality, seemed to me the worm's-eye view. After all the industrial revolution was a passing phase—not God.

It seemed folly to assume that a greater measure of life for all could be had by exalting valleys so that hills, big and little, would all disappear. He seemed to me, as Christianity did at about the same time, to be the enemy of the rhythm, beauty and premium that nature places upon the quality she lays her plans, and is most patient, to secure: Individuality. Marx, notwithstanding, seemed to reduce everything to the level of crowds on hard pavements with a union card in its vest pocket versus the fat paunch of capital, silk hat on its head and a big cigar in its teeth as presented by the popular cartoons of the day.

The Marxist revolution was probably necessary if the Industrial Revolution was to continue wrong side up by way of a false Capitalism. Necessary enough. But it was not the revolution I was concerned with, and in which I wanted to fight. I never cared to sing the "Internationale." I wanted to sing the work-song of Democracy.

The science of chemistry and machines and the Industrial Revolution I accepted as new tools in the Artist's hands, a great blessing—but if the Artist were to fall into the hands of these new tools, a curse put upon life that would soon destroy human happiness. I firmly believed the aesthetic-sense to be the saving clause in a Religion, a Society, a Factory, a Store or even a Government. Especially if Democratic Government.

About this time I wrote "The Art and Craft of the Machine" and, urged by Jane Addams, read what I wrote to the group at Hull House as you probably have learned from an earlier chapter of this autobiography.

Always I have loved the ground. And it interested me more than it seemed to interest Karl Marx or any of the socialists who subsequently grew up around his scientific analysis of a human economy . . . chiefly industrial. I always felt the ground would be the proper universal basis for social life. Not the factory or the store.

A struggle against nature never appealed to me. The struggle for and with Nature thrilled me and inspired my work. The Victory of new ideas that, actually or figuratively, made the proverbial two blades of grass grow where only one or none grew before, became the motive for me in the day's work. But producing things just for the sake of producing things seemed senseless then as now. The fetters of old ideas and rigid dogma were always hateful and grew more hateful as I grew of age and new, more prolific methods of production took the place of more simple old ones and left the old cultural forms hideous artificialities. The Marxian view of all life as a class struggle put the inordinate strain of inorganic character upon the face of the swiftly changing Cosmic order, which seemed to me less important, even if more expedient, than the facts of life seen as concordant with the nature of Man on his own Earth in his new circumstances.

So Marx (that is to say, Socialism) seemed to me an orthodox negation or degradation of the organic character of Nature. Profane to my Unitarian mind because the creative-artist was left out.

The revolutionary bayonet has little in common with the evolutionary sickle although the one is supposed to have made way for the other—apparently for the purpose of making away with it eventually?

Exploitation of mankind by way of colonization in order to keep false Capitalism and its licentious Production alive (as we now see it coming to some sort of reckoning all over the world) was to me carnal sin. Coming to what conclusion? Capitalism in principle is old and strong. It is wrong only if wrong-end-to—or selfishly exploited by those who abuse it by using it for Empire instead of using it for indigenous human growth and happiness. Every age, of course, rots with its own Success. The richer a false capitalistic society becomes, the nearer bankruptcy it is. Its prosperity is a tragic thing. "Leave me undisturbed to create and cancel the financial credit of the nation and I don't care who makes its laws" said one of the great bankers.

And I could never see that what we did in the U.S.A. ever gave capital a chance to spread its base on the ground and rise naturally to an apex. Certainly it did not do so as we knew it and still know it with its apex on the ground, base up in the air—a topsy-turvy Capitalism against which Socialism and many other isms are directed for special justice and relief. Nor could I believe that Agriculture necessarily meant ignorance of beauty and a peasantry any more than I could believe that Industrialism necessarily meant ugliness and a wage slave. Unless the creative artist was left out.

Cooperation and Freedom and great Art are certainly possible to the order of true Capital. But no Capitalism is true or tolerable where cooperation and freedom of the workers and creative art do not exist and flourish. Private human initiative flowers as prosperous public enterprise only under such conditions of Capital. This I firmly believed: an artificial society based upon capital wrong-end-to and minus Art must end in weariness and war.

The elections of our Democracy have been described as "a public auction where all manner of promises are made." But that is the false democracy of the false Capitalism under which the people are content only so long as prosperity is enjoyed. Meanwhile how prosperity is had and passed around is no great matter. Apparently. The time of reckoning comes and it's always war-time. Almost all our wars are waged to keep prosperity, that is to say Success, at home under the false Capitalism which exploited (and now is itself exploited by) big money power. What can be worse than the deification of money by a whole people? Herodotus, when asked why civilizations died, said, "First Success. Then as a consequence of Success, arrogance and injustice. Then as the consequence of arrogance and injustice—overthrow!"

Probably a false Socialism or a false Communism would work just as well, or just as badly, if similarly situated in similar circumstances which would probably arise were they put in place of Capitalism. Government in either case would become an aggressive form of egotism infecting an insolent bureaucracy. Nothing would have really happened to organize the true sources of all real wealth—the creative work of a happy people.

The great money-lender nation of the world was first England but now the United States. And it is easy to see that "God has been put in his place away from earthly matters" by our System so that this supremacy of finance might happen and prosper. Religion is become a silent partner in such top-heavy prosperity as ours. But its tolerance is really only a matter of indifference. On both sides. As a matter of fact, no Science-worshipping Nation really cares much what happens to Religion. And we might go on to say that no Western nations care much either, what happens to creative art. Except as the Artist can prettify a commercial product for the eye of some prospective buyer. We may see where we stand in this throughout the world today by visiting with appraising eye the various mortuaries for the prophetic, indicative remains of ancient civilizations that we call our Art Museums. The record that is dead and not read.

And this indifference, though concealed by superficial means, eventually came to me as a profound disillusion.

True Wisdom is no earthly thing. Wisdom is a spiritual state attained by refraining from selfish competition, imitation or moralizing. And, most of all, by living in love and harmony with Nature.

But the exaggeration of false industrial-capitalism has intensified itself more and more as an empire within the empire of the colonial expansion of ruthless Imperialism. All over the Earth today you may see the fierce cruel grasp for this empire within the Empire by the Whites, now the Yellows, perhaps soon by the Blacks.

The English sang of the White Man's Burden; the French of the Mission Civilisatrice; the Germans of Kultur. "No one sings of the black-man's or the brown-man's burden"—not yet. But all of the Western Peoples seem to have lost the secret of true creative energy and, because of grossly exaggerated scientific means of production, to batten upon others less "productive" for raw materials to feed into the maw of the machine to make more and more machinery. But, actually, alchemy is turning sea water, the air we breathe, and the mud under our feet into all any nation needs for independence as a basis for true world cooperation.

What cooperation is desirable without independence? Or possible?

## DEMOCRATIC FORM

Although only begun, mechanized use of these brutalizing forces of the Industrial Revolution, and now more especially those of the Chemical Revolution, have already gone so far that no reform, nor any mere modification of these empirical systems of Capital now battening on colonies and milking them as a farmer does his cows, can do more than join the drab recessional that drags us, by force, toward the same tomb reached by ancient civilizations. Though we do reach our end by an ultra "Scientific" and so a different road: the Life-Vicarious is our degeneracy and our doom.

## THE NEW DISCRETION

If we are not satisfied with this impending disintegration, we must go to painful, unpleasant Work, my Usonians. We must go to work at a beginning that has been far too long overlaid and so long delayed by our own very best people: go to more destructive work than bombs and mass-murder can effect—go toward organic construction.

At last we ourselves, discounting all our false starts and false alarms, we, the people, although we may not be the very best, must begin. We must go by, or cast out, our popular warped-heroes and all standardized Rulers. We must get down to work at the honest beginnings of Democracy with far higher and finer courage than any courage which may be bedeviled into going to War! The consequences of constructive destruction are so much more far reaching than destructive construction. So much more devastating and beneficent.

If this Democratic Future, for which because of designed mis-education we are now to toil and plan all over again, harder than ever before, is going to be realized, our first need is for a New Discretion: true humility succeeding these excited, ignoble, angry fears.

"Whom the Gods would destroy they first make mad." That madness is fear and fear madness—is true as it ever was. And it is this peculiar consequence of Success—arrogance, that is destroying us! We need the national and rational humility that is not afraid. True humility (faith instead of fear) might serve to open the doors and windows of the Spirit of National-life to what constitutes the Democratic spirit. But, while our people are conscious of being virtuous when they are honest or conscious of being charitable when they love their neighbor—they are not virtuous nor charitable nor honest. We must begin at the beginning with a New Discretion which is not Fear nor related to it—but is Intelligent faith.

## THE DEMOCRATIC SPIRIT

As a creative artist, at first in disillusionment followed by anger and resentment but with somewhat more humility, I have been seeking, in what I have called these Broadacre City studies of our civilization, the organic-form of such Democracy.

And as a builder I have been long enough and far enough afield to know that true FORM is and must always be, Organic. I myself have actually prophesied FORM with that integrity throughout this vast undeveloped country of ours in revolutionary bricks, boards, and mortar wherever the lives of our Usonian people have come to me for a remedy. And for that matter, abroad over the whole Earth.

That is why I know now that the true architect of a social order—we would not name him an Architect but call him a Statesman—could in one lifetime lay down outlines on which we could build the Democratic State for which I would be happy to build organic buildings. For one, I would like to build these life-giving buildings as normal, no longer as revolutionary. The life of a revolutionist is not easy to sustain.

At this groaning moment of all isms—Internationalism—might we not afford a statesman with the vision and personal responsibility that characterized a Thomas Jefferson or a Thomas Paine? If only we might soon find him in the terms of our own new day!

Most of all, we ourselves need the inspiration of such vision and personal-responsibility as was theirs where the humanities are concerned.

But the mind that goes with vision of that broad humane type we do not seem to have produced by our established systems of self-interest in thought, emotion, and education—all of which have been misdirected or carried away to "produce" for the sake of inordinate Production. We have been exalting a Profit-motive pretending to work both ways. Indeed we seem to have abolished the creative mind on suspicion, or by insult or neglect.

## MISEDUCATION

The first thing our Broadacre studies taught me to see is that it is solely upon our own personal initiative as a people that we, what there is left of us, must now turn to the young. In their behalf we must politely but firmly ask higher education to get down off its stilted horse. First of all we must Decentralize and Nature-ize the education of the very young: the same effort but opposite the direction taken by State-Socialism. We must get popular, and especially higher education, down on native ground somehow. Anyhow. And keep both higher and lower education down there long enough to learn these truths: first the truth concerning this medium-of-exchange thing we keep on calling sound-money; second, the matter of the good ground. Both are neglected by us down to the present moment. And here we find Henry George for the ground and Silvio Gesell for the money.

The analysis of the basis of human poverty made by Henry George has never been refuted. His expedient for bringing a remedy to bear caused more controverts than converts because expedients are more important to academic thinking than principles. As usual the means is taken for the end. Pigeon-hole thinking.

Silvio Gesell's *Natural Economic Order* was as necessary to Henry George's success as Henry George was necessary to Gesell's success. The two men are opposite but harmonious sides of the same shield.

The preface to the *Natural Economic Order* and the preface to *Progress and Poverty* are two of the finest things in recorded English. Both are an exposition of Principle rather than panaceas: both dealing with Land and Money with a simplicity seeming naive to the prestidigitators of interest: our professional economists.

## MAMMON

"Why the conscription and control of everybody and everything except the banks and their pro-duce?" There must be a reason. What is it? And we must hold education's nose down to the native ground long enough for teachers to see that in money, that vulgar, moot root-matter, corrected lies one of the most important elements under the sun if the fundamental footing of our social structure is to reach the ground instead of the rubbish heap of bought-and-sold, dishonest Finance on which it now rests and upon which no footing can be safe. We the people can no longer afford to take "Finance" (this matter of granting a special privilege to create money out of nothing at little or no cost) for granted by way of such an education as we have received at the hands of present Education. On this basic matter of social structure we have received less than no enlightenment at all. This matter-of-ignorance might even be considered the result of designed miseducation.

We can no longer afford to regard this affair with Mammon as a sacred superstition as good old Karl Marx did, or as did the Russians, unfortunately following him by way of Lenin his disciple. Why must all Revolution be only partial and then start all over again the other way? Is it because Revolution is either ignorant of organic-law or is an explosion under too great pressure which must proceed to recover lost equilibrium?

But so far as we are concerned we cannot afford to take Money as it is now set up as any valid abstraction whatsoever. Or from God, unless we want to keep on going to War or toward Revolution, meantime maintaining Poverty as a cherished national institution decorated by "Housing."

## THE TIME HAS COME

Not for nothing is the challenger of Money in its present form soon a socio-political outcast. He is suspect. "But there is a greater service to be rendered by him," as G. Hickling of British-born *Reality* says, "than to die for his country." At bottom it is a choice between dying to retain the disastrous illusion that money is more important than men or adopting a financial policy that will serve men by enabling them to live in conditions of good will and mastery over the abundance of their own Earth.

All public offices and our entire educational system are so deeply committed and geared to the idea that Money plus Authority can rule the World, that any careful examination of this money-rot of our sociology is subversive activity. Especially if the search be at all sincere, the F. B. I. will appear. Like Sex, Money has remained the slum quarter of our human social-consciousness except when and as we realized its importance sufficiently to rebel. I found this rebellion on the trails of the Broadacre search—1929—as you too will find it when you begin to tramp those devious trails in search of either justice or organic proportion.

Long habitual mis-association of ideas kept in circulation by selfish interests conceals the vicious-character of this public enemy number one and hides from us its enormous demoralizing influence on our destiny. Our secret molders of public opinion have been skillfully concealed.

So, Power-finance now has control of our national destiny. But it has control only because designed miseducation has left us, as a Nation, ignorant. Even yet but few among us understand the imperative necessity for *consumption to control production and for production to control Finance,* nor do we understand also the "must" that *the Credit of the Nation must belong to the people to be used by them according to their will.*

Democracy must get these fundamentals straight in mind so that this Nation may be forever stopped from creating a special class living on Money; Money as something in itself. Money promoting Money as an interest-bearing speculative commodity. Thus creating not only specious values but continually building barriers against the normal creative powers of a great people: barriers that must be perpetually maintained, or destroyed, by Wars.

## MAMMON'S WIFE

It is always our business—is it not—to give an account of ourselves to ourselves? Is it not time for that accounting *now?* Official arrogance and the bureaucratic-nincompoops of National arrogance have been doing that all-important job for us so long that "Mammon's Wife" may be the proper name for our own Nation no less than for Byron's "Perfidious Albion" for which nation the term "Mammon's Wife" was originally designed by Meredith.

As we are financially established now, we are so squarely up against this affair with Mammon that in the Broadacre search for a structure and Plan-form natural to native Usonian freedom (Democracy), it soon became apparent that every man of God or man of Art or man of Benevolence in this country as things were with us then—1929 (and they are even more so today at war, Anno Domini 1943) was, first of all, and must be, a time-server, and money-raiser—or else go to Jail, go to the poor-house, go mad with frustration, or go to War.

## THE NET MISTAKE

Although results at the moment do seem far enough away from the cause to confuse it, the economic tribulation we are really in over our heads, as in England, is at bottom the net social result of the un-wisdom of taking away from the people their own Credit; legalizing that theft by act of Congress, and thus enfranchising endless spacious occupations, raising a special class (the banking class) to whom we have given money-creating privileges.

Thus, Money becomes by these acts a speculative commodity not only created by a privileged few but controlled by them. Extended by them. Contracted by them.

And on this too-easy road to subversive financial power, our so-called Capitalistic-system soon became no true Capitalistic-system at all. By way of the pool of money which has been forming behind the successful industrialists, the great industrialist himself has become a pawn of the greater money-power system, itself a great cartel with endless sub-cartels. And that power-system has gradually reduced to *mere speculative commodities all the natural means we have to live by* . . . including our own lives.

Is it easier for "rulers" to deal with human life when thus reduced to commodity status? Preferably in herds on hard-pavements. Or in factories?

## HELL

Well . . . to get back again a little out of breath but still in "simples," I hope, to this Broadacre City research undertaken soon after the nation broke down

A.D. 1929. In the search for the basis for Organic FORM I could not fail to see this despotism, Power-Finance á-la-mode, in the place where a foundation ought to be. And though as yet, it seems practically invisible to our very best miseducated manhood we can see that it is really Despotism triumphant. I soon found, as I have said before, that because of its now autocratic (now virtually automatic) power, we have no sound economic foundation whatever for our pretension to Democracy, except by this strong-arm. That is to say, exterior props and braces familiar to the ideologies that even the wielders of that power profess to despise.

We have no fundamental interior support whatever, outside the natural good intent, at heart, of the people at large to bear their burdens with blind patience. I could see that the official safeguards (external props and braces) which the administration of government set up over this privileged organ of legalized theft, were only serving to multiply popular economic-confusion until economic-fear had come as unwelcome guest to sit down at every table in this land. And now, at a time when any further concentration of humanity is mass-murder, the machine and the bomb (the industrial revolution) are carrying the work to its logical conclusion: the great war nature seems to have herself staged in the survival of the fittest—the war between white and colored.

## THE BUREAU KNOBS AND DRAWERS
The tragedy in all this terrible sacrifice of a great new nation's vitality and originality perhaps ending in its premature obsolescence or destruction, lies in the fact that just because Salvation is so simple, salvation seems politically all but impossible!

What blind absurdity this pretension to democratic government has become by putting the nation's credit in pawn to a privileged Money-system! No truly democratic nation would ever so assert self-interest of a privileged class at the expense of its own people to gain a temporary advantage.

Such Statesmanship as we have been able to put in practice here has, for many years, consisted chiefly in employing Federal Crats to take more or less money from one pocket on the one side in or-der to put more or less of it into another pocket on the other side by force of law! Meantime, "the rectifiers of the law keep on making three laws to cure one flaw." Where it will all end is not so far ahead.

It must all end in war after war, each war laying the foundation for the ultimate war, our resources wasted, perhaps the race itself ended, in vain attempts to end war by War? Probably. But, our partisan-minded legislators keep on making more laws to avert impending catastrophe until the various cogs that are the antagonistic administrations of government are already as pervasive, extensive and destructive in action as any plague of locusts. War or no war.

So many and so pervasive are they while the increasingly complicated mechanized sources of production mount (and not only in war-time) that the great Melting-pot is rapidly becoming the ultimate Grindstone.

## INTEGRITY
We have at last reached the point in this naive preface when it is to the public integrity of those troublesome few who insist upon understanding the symbols before they will consent to use the symbols that we must look for the enlightenment that is salvation.

True revolt is always founded upon the acceptance of a principle. Any hope for a true Capitalistic Democracy must therefore begin by our realization that we, the people, haven't got the proper Principles in practice, and that we are not asking ourselves the right questions.

"Ideas precede and generate facts." It is our nature so to trust in the power of Truth. With this faith at heart the people themselves must manage to proceed.

## THE SAVING CLAUSE
The original intent of the founders of our Nation was clear enough. Their intention was to found a nation of free men themselves in common possession, as individuals, of the natural resources of their nation as a Nation. Their considered statement is found in the Constitution of these United States: "Congress shall issue money and regulate the value thereof."

So, Money as a speculative commodity in itself (money as we know it) was never accepted by the pilgrim founders of this nation when making our Constitution. Imperfect as that property-loving instrument originally was, some of our statesmen forefathers must have seen ahead this impasse we are now in. Because, to enable the people independently to establish themselves by free use of their own credit, a vital clause was put into the constitution of these United States by the forefathers. Wisely they stipulated: "Congress shall have the right to issue money and regulate the value thereof": a provision for economic independence indispensable to Democracy.

But in that parlous time, Alexander Hamilton, under pressure of the ragged new republic's lack of initial faith in itself, himself sincerely imbued by the idea that Money-plus-Authority was inevitable, smiled, sailed over and sold us back again to the powerful money-changers of monarchic old England.

Thus English domination of these new United States was, by Hamilton, refounded upon our own Revolution. In the very name of Democracy, English domination was set up again to influence our destiny, gradually undo our Democratic Republic and precipitate wars. Unchallenged to this hour this money-power is now an invisible but none the less cruel despotism guided only by such peculiar, flexible, English conscience as we have ourselves inherited. And we are now ruining ourselves to perpetuate this old English doxology that Authority-plus-Money can rule the world?

In these bewildering reactions of a despotic era wherein under the influences of secret molders of public-opinion all ideologies swap sides or straddle the fence, the Chemical-revolution and Machine-production are pushed to a runaway artificiality which may never come back to earth on the white side of this planet.

## SO WHAT OF THE NIGHT

Sound *economic foundations* are simply not there to be reached.

Consequently the artificial money-props and braces now employed instead of foundations were more than merely confusing to me as they must be confusing to anyone who tries seriously to understand Money as an organic instrument, not to say basis, of human establishment.

As an Architect, never before much interested in Economics, I was compelled, now, to read much of the amazing conflict that constitutes such Science and Ethics as "Economics" assumes. And taking heed, as you have already heard (might hear to much better advantage from a less amateurish source) I have nevertheless reached views that seem to validate the Broadacre studies. The variables that are variables only because no fundamental principle appeared necessary to them, we have set aside.

The Broadacre conclusion was to dig deeper, untangle and decentralize everything—except Government, to simplify and organize Government as a matter of the people's business directly, and chiefly, then try to put all back together again in more free, flexible Form planning to use our vast mechanical powers and processes for truly humane purposes.

I believe that once we do establish ourselves as organic on organic foundations and are therefore independent of external props and braces, we can afford a far more flexible, *natural* and free social FORM than has ever been known. And *Architecturally,* therefore we will have the practical social-basis for the great, beautiful, healthy buildings of genuine human Freedom. Actual Democracy will be ours.

These new Plan-forms were neither urban nor rural, but were the outgrowth of use of the ground as a common human right equally for the tiller of the soil, the poet, the preacher and the makers of things, the shop-keeper and the trader. So the forms were into the light out of the ground and were harmoniously established each in all, all in each.

Whereas the present order is Monarchic, Feudal and from the top-down. As the matter now stands to fall our Nation will be, probably, the shortest lived on record because of the deadly accelerations afforded by inordinate use of machinery: the consequence of man's control of Monstrosity before he had obtained control of himself.

We, the people, have been hoping against hope to see the fine things our politicians have been saying to us about ourselves coming true because we wished them to be true. They have not come true. We have gone from our early hope to early bad on the way to far worse. We are concealing the worst from ourselves as we are able.

## AND YET

I believe that our Usonian society is, at heart, still sound. I believe that if we, the people, waken to our responsibility to ourselves as men and women, first, then to ourselves as a people, and therefore not only learn to know but actually *realize* the immediate need of a better (because an Organic instead of a Monarchic) world-order—we might expect to have the organic social FORM we could honestly call Democracy visible to all men within a generation or two. Say three generations at most if we began at the beginning in earnest.

This belief is not peculiar to me. It is, I believe, the growing conviction of the entire World of Thought.

As a Hope, a Dread, or a Fear this belief has incidentally reached and touched the lives of many millions of our own people. And, though more backward here in the United States than anywhere else in civilization, we too are about ready to go to work for an honest Organic Order.

My own quarrel, and I have one, with this money-affair of our own government is, as I have tried to describe it to you here, not that I have, myself, been unable to make money (I do not say "earn," because no one *earns* money as things are) but that to do anything at all worth doing I must be a shop-keeper whatever else I aspire to be. "As things are" who knows, today, what is really his own except that what a man *does, that* he has. Or we might say, *that* has him. He merely plays at a game to win or lose in a gamble with cards now stacked against him. In spite of the police he can no longer play a fair game. Or is it because of them?

Had I, myself, been free of the impositions of "the game" what might I not have accomplished for my people?

## AN ANSWER

Nevertheless, the Taliesin Fellowship has proceeded to work and plan with me the erection of a great three-dimensional model for a true Capitalist Soci-

ety. We sought a solid Democratic FORM for our modern mechanized-society that was honestly and essentially Democracy, recognizing that the Nationalism of a true Democracy would be tolerant, humanitarian and progressively liberal toward the individualities of other nations because *it greatly cherished its own*. It would regard its own individuality as its supreme asset and entertainment. Not only preserving its own but vitally concerned above all with improving its quality. A fairly certain way of improving the World.

Unless such constructive effort as this is made educational and effective at this time what but Revolution or obsolescence has ever or can ever come of such complete abnegation to money-power as ours has now become?

This compelling tide of invisible money-power dispelling our best thought and secretly aborting our honest original national-intent cannot, by way of our Science, or by singing hymns, Christmas Carols, or Cradle-songs continue to keep us wrong side up and upside down Revolution or no revolution, if we will dig down to begin at the beginning and put in a good Foundation.

## TO GATHER THE SIGNIFICANCE OF ALL THIS TOGETHER

I wish to avoid the accusation that I am too vague about it all.

So in case some too academic or too impatient reader has skipped the foregoing characterization of our economic "tribulation" and a wandering eye or two should hit the page at this point, simply as I can, let me state the fundamentals (they are all Architecture) involved in these amateur chapters on organic social-welfare: social structure as seen by one whose chief study and interest is structure: an Architect.

Unfortunately, because the so-called Science of Economics has so far been only a variable in human reactions to material things instead of the working of a known principle, all simples must seem naive to the professional economist and Broadacres will have no real help from him.

Nevertheless this summation:

*Democracy cannot become a vital force until:*

*One,* APPROPRIATE LAND IS FREE TO THOSE

WHO CAN AND DO CHOOSE TO USE IT CONSIS-
TENTLY WITH THE COMMON GOOD;

*Two,* THE CREDIT OF THE PEOPLE IS THEIR
OWN, SO ESTABLISHED BY THEIR CONSTITUTION,
AND THEIR FINANCIAL ESTABLISHMENTS ARE SUCH
THAT THEY THEMSELVES CONTROL AND FREELY USE
THE CREDIT THEY ALONE CREATE.

Until these two conditions are established we
can have no sound economic basis for this highest
form of Aristocracy the world has yet to know and
that we have here been calling Democracy.
Democracy is the highest form of Aristocracy this
world has ever seen because it will have made Quality integral. It is Manhood upright and unafraid,
achieved fresh, free, and true with each and every
generation, freely choosing to be governed by its
Bravest and Best.

When a genuine order of Capital is honestly
tried, our national economic freedom of both Land
and Money will be the safest basis yet devised for
the creative imagination of human life in this mad
world because that order of Capital will be founded
in the true nature of human egoism: founded upon
intelligent self-interest and honest selfhood encouraged, instead of the worthless by-product, egotism
and selfishness, constantly restrained.

Meanwhile, "sound-money?" Yes, absolutely
sound. Why not? What makes money "sound money"—the only true security for the investment of
Work as Idea and Idea as Work—what, indeed; except the Nation behind it?

What makes Land valuable to mankind and
constitutes its only true Ownership except appreciative use and development; no makeshifts allowed to
be devised as a substitute.

Building-construction is the most important
organic single feature of such development. Therefore building, too, should be integral. All this put
together: Building, Money, Ground and Government is Organic Architecture. All are Economics,
broadly speaking, as we use the term at Taliesin. We
see it so developing around the World.

Stripped of all Academic confusion and make-
shift, fundamental freedom of both Land and Money
is not only most important to you as a citizen home-
builder and to me as a creative-architect but even

more important to the yet unborn because both
freedoms are indispensable to the creation of a great
popular Architecture for popular Life. Such an
Architecture is the real proof of quality in any civilization.

Meantime the new Integrity, let us say *knowledge of Organic-law,* must begin with our children so
they may learn to hammer heated iron but not a
stick of dynamite. And this new Integrity must reach
them in time to teach them to be suspicious of what
any educated, or habituated, "key man" is saying or
may ever say. Our children must be grounded in a
responsible selfhood; Individuality no longer to be
confused with mere Personality. Theirs must be an
essential Character, humanitarian, liberal, tolerant,
and conciliatory. We, a truly liberal people, are
learning that world-unity as the military supremacy
of one people over all or any other people is impossible. But we have not learned well enough that
commercial-supremacy is just as mischievous and
just as impossible if we really desire Peace.

Here, then, gathering all this together follows
in simple outline the bare Basement of the organic
Capitalist Republic that I am calling BROADACRE
CITY: THE CITY THAT IS A NATION FOUNDED IN
COMMON SENSE and that subsequent chapters will
present in more graphic FORM this great reflex concerned chiefly with what an organic co-operative
capitalistic society would look like were we ourselves one.

Politics, and therefore Politicians, should take
a very different place in our affairs. It is probable
that no politician as such could make a living were
our laws organic. Only the idiosyncrasies of individuals and their quarrels would require lawyers. As
one item we might well dispense with five-hundred
thousand of our six-hundred thousand lawyers. As
for future wars, any occasion for them could scarcely be trumped up by the secret molders of public-
opinion. And, the Bureaucrat would actually be a
public servant, say an engineer, accountant, an architect or qualified agriculturist, scientist, or artist. A
poet? It is probable.

Because matters of policy would rise and rest
fairly and squarely with the people, powers, foreign
or domestic, would change completely.

THESE PARAGRAPHS, A TO G, OUTLINE THE BASEMENT:

A

ALL LAND WILL BE HAD AND HELD ONLY BY APPROPRIATE USE AND IMPROVEMENT. BUT LAND MAY BE DEVISED AND BEQUEATHED SO LONG AS BOTH USE AND IMPROVEMENTS ARE MAINTAINED BY HEIRS. SOCIAL SECURITY, INSURANCE AND INHERITANCE WOULD BE REGULATED BY THE STATES THEMSELVES.

B

THE CREDIT OF THE NATION WILL BE FREE TO THE WHOLE PEOPLE OF THE NATION AND BE EXTENDED OR CONTRACTED AT WILL BY THE NATION.

CAPITALIZED BY CONGRESS THE NATION WILL ISSUE A CONVENIENT MEDIUM OF EXCHANGE. A DEMURRAGE–CURRENCY HAVING NO COMMODITY STATUS. THE VOLUME AND VALUE OF THE MEDIUM TO BE REGULATED BY A SPECIAL BRANCH OF CONGRESS.

C

CONSUMPTION SHALL CONTROL PRODUCTION: PRODUCTION SHALL CONTROL FINANCE. NO TRADE BARRIERS. THE INFANT HERCULES HAS ALREADY STRANGLED THE SERPENT. AND PRETTY MUCH EVERYTHING ELSE.

D

INVENTIONS (IDEAS) BY WAY OF WHICH THE PEOPLE FUNCTION AS A SOCIETY BELONG TO THE PEOPLE. IDEAS THUS APPLIED TO POPULAR USE ARE TO BE APPRAISED AND COMPENSATED BY CONGRESS.

E

THE AIR, LIKE THE WATERS, IS COMMON TO ALL BUT WHEN USED AS A HIGHWAY SHALL BE SUBJECT TO THE WILL OF THE PEOPLE, AS ARE LIKEWISE ELECTROMAGNETIC CURRENTS USED AS COMMON CARRIERS OR FOR COMMUNICATION. ALL PROPAGANDA IN WHATEVER FORM WILL BE OPENLY PRESENTED AS SUCH.

F

ONLY BY TWO-THIRDS POPULAR VOTE INSTRUCTING THEIR OWN CONGRESS MAY WAR BE DECLARED. AND EVERYONE VOTING FOR WAR IS THEREBY SELF-ENLISTED REGARDLESS OF AGE OR AUTHORITY. WARS NOT FOUGHT VOLUNTARILY WILL BE IMPOSSIBLE.

CONSCRIPTION IS FOREVER ABOLISHED AS THE MODERN CRIME OF CRIMES.

G

IN ORDER TO MAKE MECHANIZATION AND ALCHEMY A HUMAN-ADVANTAGE, THE DECENTRALIZATION OF ALL LIFE-CONCERNS SO FAR AS POSSIBLE IS THE MODERN PRESSING NEED AND SCIENTIFIC OPPORTUNITY. THEREFORE MEASURES CONCERNING THE PUBLIC WELFARE SHOULD BE DETERMINED WITH THE END IN VIEW OF REINTEGRATION OF THE CONCERN, OR THE INDIVIDUAL WITH THE GROUND.

## SELF-DEFENSE FOR USONIA

THIS SHOULD BE INTEGRAL, MILITANT BUT NOT MILITARY, BECAUSE DEFENSE WOULD CONSIST IN THE INTEGRITY OF THE PATTERNS OF DEMOCRACY EQUIPPED IN PERFECT TIME, TUNE, AND CHARACTER WITH ALL-OUT MECHANIZATION TO BE USED ONLY BY FREEMEN IN EMERGENCY.

EDUCATION will be free and for freemen must develop popular ability to resist the lies that "key men" devise and in whatever circumstances, thus enabling Youth to stand up to the realities of events. Authority, instead of arising from the make-shifts of party politics and policies and scheming traders, would become, more and more, the administration of well-understood principles which the Nation would willingly die to defend if necessary.

AND NOW WE COME TO THESE MODELS which the Fellowship in 1932 began to put into tangible form. They were, for the first time so far as I know, an entire cross-section of a complete Civilization: three-dimensional models devised in relation of every part to the whole showing in detail a better way of doing nearly everything that we now do. A "better way" meaning one more in keeping with our character and the Science that is our opportunity. These models of Broadacres, making good and appropriate use of new means to escape the outworn Expedients, were designed as a broad-way into Democratic future-life for Usonians. Direct, practicable employment of organic Principles in creating the multiplicity of forms essential to modern civilization. It should be unnecessary to add, therefore strong from within to defend itself against any external attack. A great work of Art.

But these new ways should now be so modeled

and so presented that not only could the ideas of fresh plan-formation be seen by our own people but the various parts be seen in actual perspective in relation to each other by those unaccustomed to the reading of plans: the scheme as a whole should be so presented that the details, as well as the whole, might not only be touched and intelligently studied by whoever was interested, but the plans and models themselves should be extended and supplemented by recordings and cinema.

Severely limited as originally set up and seen but by several hundred thousand people, the idea of the new City that was nowhere except everywhere had not been carried far enough to be easily understood as a true basis for Capitalism consistent with Democracy: that is to say Capitalism consistent with the freedom, individuality and personal initiative of a grand fusion, such as our Nation, of essentially intelligent emotional peoples.

So "The City" was freely misunderstood and variously criticized. Criticized by some as Communism, by others as Socialism or even as Fascism. By only the few was the City recognized for what it really was—a relaxed, resilient, fundamentally free structural FORM for the life that will, some day, become one great free City so founded in common sense as to make human life not only more secure but more beautiful. More secure and beautiful because its concrete forms are organic: natural to human Life, Life really free from the feudal hangovers from which we seem to be striving in vain to escape. Held back by a false sentimentality masquerading as Sentiment, we have exhausted ourselves defending what has become indefensible.

This true Capitalist system, when we decide to honestly try it in our own behalf with the independence we once declared, July 4, 1776, will surely eventuate into living structural Forms within a Planform something like Broadacre City, the free City that is the consequence of perception and enlightened acceptance of new forces which have either already changed or are rapidly changing our lives for better or worse. Obsolescence with us has already been terrific. But the back-drag is a growing menace to Usonian life itself.

IF ONLY as a people we had permitted ourselves to learn what Organic Architecture could do to make of our private and national life great unexampled beauty by way of our own manifold resources, a greater harmony than has yet existed anywhere would now be our constant recourse and delight. But because we have fed upon already degenerate phases of the great art of Architecture which were casually washed up on our Atlantic shores instead of developing an organic culture of our own cast in the alloy of the great melting-pot, well-suited to our own time, place, and changed circumstances, we have missed the greatest most fruitful happiness of all in any civilization: a great Architecture.

For solace we have turned away from the things of the creative spirit, seeking satisfactions derived from an eclecticism ill fitted even to material things. The greatest security for those satisfactions being money as the present brokerage banking-system has established it. A false expedient we have fought to maintain.

And, since, for the moment, Science gives us more of these so-called "realisms" than Art or Religion give, both Art and Religion languish together.

Meantime the Democratic Spirit that has waited and hoped must go to work.

Victor Hugo, the great Modern of his time, in a chapter of *Notre Dame,* prophesied that Architecture, already some five hundred years moribund, would in the latter end of the nineteenth century or the beginning of the twentieth, come alive again.

This prophecy is beginning to be realized.

In the concept of Architecture as organic we not only grasp the center-line of true indigenous Culture for this era of the machine in Usonia, but we have the beginning of a better world and a more humane racial order.

# WILLIAM ALLEN WHITE

*In this warm and touching tribute to editor William Allen White of the* Emporia Gazette *(Kansas),
Wright mentions another famous Kansas editor, Henry J. Allen. Allen was governor of Kansas and an
editor of the* Wichita Beacon. *Both men were clients; Allen had built a house Wright designed for him
in 1917, and White, as the article explains, had "an animal fear of being turned out of the old one."*

*Wright's affection for White and for his widow, Sally, is apparent throughout the text. Wright refers to
the Fellowship stopping by Emporia on their trips from Wisconsin to Arizona. These cross-country treks
were done, at that time, in caravan, with the Wrights in the lead. Mrs. White not only set out a resplendent
table for the thirty or more from Taliesin, but for the occasion she brought out her best china, linen, and
silverware. One time when White noticed how the hungry Taliesin apprentices were, "wolfing" down the
roasts, vegetables, fruit, and assortment of freshly baked cakes, he turned to Wright and, smiling, remarked,
"Frank, your Taliesin Fellowship is certainly The Great American Sponge!" And the next morning
Mrs. White prepared baskets of cold roasts, cheese, fresh fruit, candies, and cakes for each of the vehicles
continuing the voyage to Arizona. [Unpublished]*

I WOULD LIKE TO LAY A GREEN BRANCH AND A FLOWER OR
two on the table in all there is of a house I once
planned for Will and Sally White—there in Emporia, Kansas. An old house that absorbed all it could
take of the new one Will said he was afraid to build
because he had an animal fear of being turned out of
the old one. Will and Sally split the difference and
made a home that is pretty thoroughly Will and Sally throughout. They loved it and all who loved
them loved them in it.

As one. Because no one ever thinks of Will
without thinking of Sally and no one would think
of thinking of Sally without Will. The two were
lovers. Always I guess. The British have Robert

Browning and Elizabeth Barrett—but the U. S. A.
has Will and Sally.

More salt and savor in our Will and Sally I believe.

I knew Will when he was a young writer
coming to my home in Oak Park occasionally with
his publisher, Chauncey Williams. Will was solid,
and handsome even then. A witty urbanite—something of a good sport. He got past it all and out West
into an editor's none too easy, chair. The world
knows what Will did from that chair which he
made his own—and Sally's.

The White home in Emporia was a Kansas
White-house with more warmth and a genial fra-

**William Allen White and his wife, Sally, on her 71st birthday, Emporia, Kansas, 1942. Photograph courtesy David Walker, *The Emporia Gazette.*** FLLW Fdn FA#6702.0006

grance of hospitality more personal than any other White-house I know about.

And what a table? Will believed in good eating and Sally saw to it that not only Will ate better than well of better than the best but so did everybody in the United States that she and Will liked. There were a lot of us.

The Taliesin boys, thirty of them, turned in there a couple of times on the way to Arizona and even they couldn't clean up the spread Sally had laid out for them in the old Dining Room made over to resemble, somewhat, the new one I planned for them.

And, one time, on the way back from Arizona, stopping to see him (a couple of years ago), Will was rather despondent. He had just got out of war-mongering committee-work in New York City. His senses had come back to him and he said with tears in his eyes, "Frank, there isn't even a little bit of it left!" holding his fingers up so close you could scarcely see

between them, "No, not even a little bit of it left."

Of course I knew that he meant the American spirit that is Jeffersonian.

And my charming young daughter Iovanna, sixteen, knowing about his daughter Mary, and seeing him sad—went up to Will, put her arms around his neck and kissed him with a smack. It was sudden and Will turned away to hide what it did to him.

But you couldn't really know Will, not only if you didn't know Sally too, but also unless you had seen him with Governor Henry (Allen) of the Wichita *Beacon.* They carried on a sort of war of wits and flow of soul all their own and for all their Kansas lives. I sat in once or twice and enjoyed the fireworks. In the wrestling match of wits first one was on top and then the other, but always in deep good humor—no matter how sharp the jibes. And they did lay each other open—as few men could do. I've never heard two men, pitted against each other, so faithfully square with each other—as were those two.

A grief came to the Whites when young Bill decided there was no place for him in his distinguished father's shadow and he went away to carve out a career of his own. His father left sitting at the Emporia desk without an heir of his own flesh and blood to carry on his work.

What a comfort it must have been to Will when young Bill did come back to go on with the *Gazette* after distinguishing himself. He came back just in time.

Will and Sally were natively cultured people who traveled much at home and much more abroad. They had acquired a sense of events worldwide—that was, no less, their own. I think Will was cautious; Sally more courageous—but you couldn't take them apart that way.

They were one—if ever two were one. And now I know that Sally isn't going to miss Will. She is so much Will herself that Will is going to keep right on living. And whatever has happened to Will—Sally is there. So it's all right.

Here is to Will's Sally and to Sally's Will—worlds without end.

Always.

# HOW SHALL WE REBUILD OUR CITIES

*The American Forum of the Air was a program broadcast by the Mutual Broadcasting System coast to coast every Tuesday evening at 9:30, Eastern War Time (1944). An announcement always prefaced the broadcast: "Since founding this institution in 1928, Chairman Theodore Granik, attorney and editor, has arranged these weekly broadcasts in which the news personalities of the day discuss the issues of the day openly and frankly in the American tradition of free speech. This is democracy in action." On 29 February 1944, Granik went on to explain that particular evening's topic: "Four and one-half years of war have brought destruction to many of the cities of Europe. In America we have been more fortunate. No enemy bombs have fallen on our cities. Nevertheless, many of them have been suffering for years from overcrowding, from blighted areas and slums, and from antiquated housing facilities." The panelists for the evening were the mayor of St. Paul, Minnesota, the chairman of the National Committee on Housing, the executive vice president of the National Association of Real Estate Boards, and Frank Lloyd Wright. Each was allotted time for a statement on "How Shall We Rebuild Our Cities?"; a roundtable discussion between the four followed. Wright's theme, expectedly, was based on his idea of decentralization: "Spared the bomb—how to proceed? Decentralization is our true answer." [Published in the* AIA Journal, *April 1944]*

THE SUCCESS OF OUR AMAZING MATERIALISM HAS MADE all our cities bottlenecks to be smashed.

To build the city we need there is no problem of production. There is only the problem of distribution.

Shall we wait for the right answer to come over here because of bombs dropped over there? Who can doubt that better cities will result for Europeans while we, spared the bomb, will be left, out-moded in the light of reconstruction?

Spared the bomb—how to proceed?

Decentralization is our true answer.

Humanity can meet the now agonizing problems of distribution in no other form. Hence the organic tree-city of the future: Broadacres. The city that is everywhere growing up in the substance of our nation as the inevitable reaction against the over-production that is our ruin.

Under-consumption is a disease with a death rate we have never faced. Cure that disease, not by sentimental tampering with symptoms trying to save "the Poor." Radical surgery removing causes is desperately needed.

Let us plan . . . but I am suspicious of all planners. Planners jump in on the middle of this or that problem, splash around and come out. All wet. To begin anything at the beginning is a lost Art in our

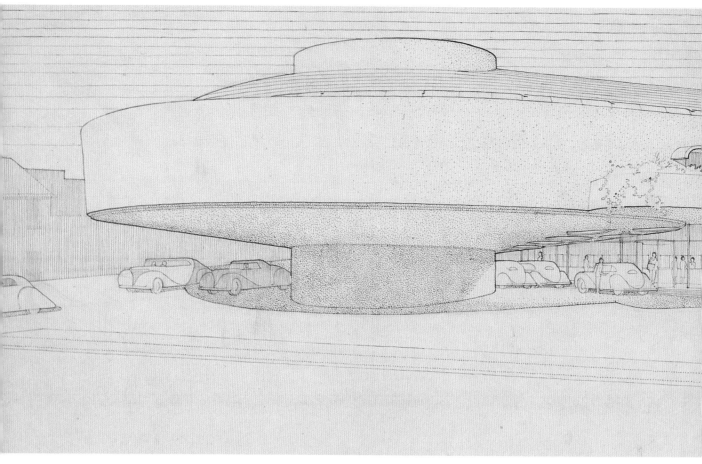

**Laundry for Benjamin Adelman (Project), Milwaukee, Wisconsin. 1945. Perspective. Pencil and color pencil on tracing paper, 55x 25".** FLLW Fdn#4507.001

country. Because we are so confused by the driving pressures of over-production we have not learned that Scientific art. But nature herself is more merciful. She is growing the city we need, unnoticed, in the body of our nation.

If we take heed, new life comes to our civilization. If no heed, then bring in the bombs for butter and go trading our butter for bombs.

The new frontier of a true culture is here but the right kind of bomb to defend us from mass-production produced for the sale of more massive production is not here.

But, at least, from the present rate of produc-

tion for war purposes, the people know this: "The age of plenty is here and poverty need never smirch the face of the globe again." The present stupendous rate of output for rations and war-fodder could easily be doubled for peace and prosperity purposes, if required.

Our cities? Well . . . is it enough that our big-production boys hire a few popular streamliners; scrape off a few barnacles; put in some gadgetry, somehow, anyhow; then subsidize the realtors for pilots and try to sail the old caravels we have kept? Can bureaucracy stop them?

There are mines sunk in that harbor!

"Crystal Heights." Hotel, apartments, shops, and theater for Roy Thurmond (Project), Washington, D.C. 1939. Perspective. Sepia ink on tracing paper, 30 x 20". FLLW Fdn#4016.004

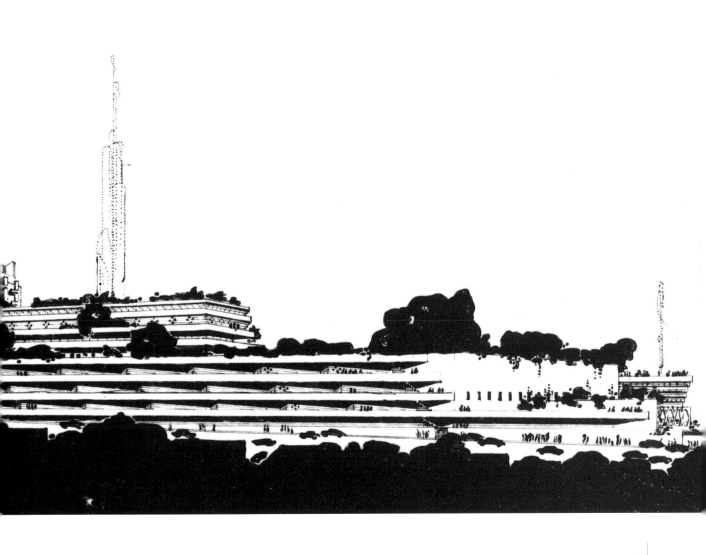

**Calico Mills Store (Project), Ahmedabad, India. 1946. Perspective. Pencil, ink, and color pencil on tracing paper, 30 x 20".**
FLLW Fdn#4508.001

**Rogers Lacy Hotel (Project), Dallas, Texas. Perspective into central atrium. Pencil, ink, and color pencil on Japan paper, 24 x 53".**
FLLW Fdn#4606.011

# TO THE MOLE

*Robert Moses, parks commissioner of the City of New York, and Frank Lloyd Wright were cousins by marriage. But that was as close as the two of them ever came. They vehemently disagreed about city planning. Wright abhorred the "planner" because he believed that all planners simply compounded the basic problem of city congestion with more congestion, burrowing under the ground with subways and springing bridges across rivers: the sin of the overcrowded urban vortex was not solved by these expedients. High-rise housing in such congestion was also anathema to Wright because he thought it merely exacerbated the problems and was less humane. When he proposed the Broadacre City plan to his cousin, Moses responded with an article in the* New York Times *Magazine on 25 June 1944, originally entitled "Mr. Moses Dissects the 'Long Haired Planners': The Park Commissioner Prefers Common Sense to Their Revolutionary Theories." This Taliesin Square Paper Number 7, printed on 14 August 1994, was Frank Lloyd Wright's counterresponse to Robert Moses.*

WHEN ROBERT MOSES AND I FIRST MET BRIEFLY, HE picked up a bronze medal which he said was from "his boys." With a smile of satisfaction on his face that showed me it was what he liked most about him, he pointed to a mole cast in relief on one side the medal and said, "you see, I am a Mole."

Then Moses the Mole disposed of me. He put me up in the air. Said he: "You are a 'Skylark'."

Of course I knew what he meant. "Brilliant but erratic" and so, quite beside the mark. The Moles-eye view?

Schopenhauer once did a valuable "piece" on the Mole. I commend it at this point. Shelley did well by the Lark—read that poem.

As instinct, the Mole noses in to whatever is where he is and goes it, blind. He gets there where he wants to be. Which after all, is only where *he* wants to go.

But, concerning "Planners": during a nation-wide broadcast, The American Forum of the Air, February 29, 1941, I, myself, had this to say:

"I am suspicious of all Planners! 'Planners' jump in on the middle of this or that problem, splash around and come out. All wet. To begin at the beginning is a lost Art in our Nation. We are so confused by the driving pressures of so-called "Production" that we have not yet learned planning as a Scientific-art. Nature herself makes no such mistake. Nature is growing right in our midst (apparently unnoticed) the Free city we need." I referred to the city I called Broadacre City. I sent a copy of that thesis to Robert Moses. For no very good reason.

Well, for the sake of argument, I grant Robert Moses the Mole. Incomparable burrower for the Boroughs of Manhattan and the Bronx, he is. I take the Skylark, but suggest that every city have a furry burrowing Mole of Moses calibre to put off the Coroner, say, fifteen to twenty-five years. No Mole could (or should) do more.

Now there are millions of intelligent Americans who have no anxiety as to when the coroner gets to New York.

I am one of them. So far as a Lark sees, all American over-grown villages are dated. To me Moses' molesome City is as definitely dated as a bouquet (pronounce it "bo-kay") out of water.

His astonishing achievements in mitigating details of dying and burial entitle him to eternal local gratitude. New York City should be given, outright, to Robert Moses. He is another Moses leading his people out of bondage—though not in just the way he intended. No. In fact, just the opposite way.

The Big City is no longer "the Glass of Fashion and Mold of Form" for this Nation that it once was.

Neither "Long-haired planner" nor Mole, I will try to suggest to the Moses boys, and Moles whatsoever, what Broadacre City meant.

First, the thesis of that future city of Democracy was no plan in either moleish or "planner" sense. It was a Vision. And very simply the Vision meant: more holeing in the dark isn't what the people of this Nation need so much as a clear view of the direction great mechanical forces we helped release into our world are taking. And more comprehension of the significance of what this deadly thing is doing to us right now.

Broadacres meant that, if, after taking a good look down into the gruesome thing we want to go on burrowing more channels for erosion in big-cities vainly hoping to save them and if, then, anyone wants to "plan," go ahead! But, as you are bound to see if you do look down, and in—why?

Anyone can make a plan or poke a fire. But, Broadacres is a window open on the inevitable Future.

Broadacres is itself a "looking down," not too far nor too wide, into an agonizing struggle, seeing a desperate clash between inordinate Mechanism and human Life, knowing that before this agony is resolved to human benefit, more blind Planning or Moleing is going to afford only more confusion to an already confused people: a people waiting (whether they know it or not) for the "Financial Disarmament" we are going to call Peace.

Further, and without shame, I say Broadacre City is a Song of Freedom. Yes, singing of the inevitable approaching City that America will recognize as the true-city if Democracy ever builds at all.

I cannot believe that a free Democracy is so much an affair of hard-pavements, wage-salary and the vicarious, gregarious-life of bigger and bigger "Production" as "Planners" would make it out to be. However vicarious it is, the good life in modern times is no less than ever *a matter of the right kind of building!*

Always, true Civilization was, exactly, a matter of the right kind of Building.

But the kind of Building we do in our America won't let the true Nature of anything come through. At terrific pace we proceed "from barbarism to degeneracy with no real Civilization of our own in between." I venture to say that the kind of building we do is the worst bottle-neck of the Ages: the way that solves nothing. A way that has no *integrity*. The Integrity of Freedom and Democracy cannot be found anywhere in our way of building. So, what civilization? We are in mortal danger of losing the Freedom we once thought we had won! Wherein then lies the occasion for more such "planning?"

If we as a people could find the way to do the right kind of Building then *the right way of building* would itself begin to find the right kind of ground in the right way in the right place for the rightkind of people. Yes: as sure as gravitation! What then is the "right kind of Building"? The answer is Organic-building, the only building that serves the inside of the man as well as the outside of him and makes this deadly mechanical equipment that has raced the young of our Nation off to War, an asset to young and old. Not a curse put upon both.

When Johnnie comes marching home, is the best "Planners" can do for him to push him into the slavery of wagery in inordinate "production" in big-ger and bigger Cities? Are plans to be made for that?

The Mole says Yes? The Lark, No.

If we could give Johnnie a clear Vision of some direct road to the right kind of building in the right place for him at home he would never again be treading in on bigger and better Wars on foreign soil.

Now it was just that Vision Broadacre City was meant to indicate to him. And, also to all "Plan-ners." With the moles thrown in. But they saw in it only a plan to rule the world by Communism or Fascism, Socialism or Capitalism. What a lot of "isms" they do have down there in the dark!

We (the people) cannot plan the Right Kind of Building yet because we are cowards. We are afraid to know what it is. Now, to present the Right Kind of Building isn't within the scope of any brief reply to criticism. Perhaps it is no matter at all for a newspaper. But the right way is mod-eled in great detail at Taliesin. Anyone interested may study it. "The Powers-that-be" could not af-ford to know what "Broadacres" meant were they to look ever so long at it because were they to know what integrity actually is in the common life of "the common man" it would be all up with both Dictator and Bureaucracy. As for the "com-mon man," I don't know who he is myself because I've never met one. Strictly speaking he is just You and Me in Broadacre City, which is a gospel of In-dividuality.

It is this seemingly trite affair of first things first in the right way of Building in the right place that must be on straight before "planning" is going to do less harm than Robert Moses sees it doing. Or as I see it doing, myself, for that matter.

*First-things must come first!* Any good Plan must have that *basis*. The Mole may be blindly nearer to that basis than the planners are because "every prob-lem carries inside itself its own solution." But are educated Planners looking inside for that solution? Or is the Mole? No, so far as I can see, neither are. And, the administration's "little people" must avoid that look inside or lose their jobs.

Why are they not looking "inside" for it? Well, because the right kind of building is radi-cal, always was, and it will always be a minority

report and so cannot originate or thrive by way of Government.

Now, until a *natural* basis for radical planning is found—an Organic basis—is any moleish makeshift whatever, or any "makeover" really worth a real man's time at this juncture? I say No.

But, what the Mole likes most about *him* is his "practical" attitude: that is to say: "first of all make the neighbors easy."

I say, let them suffer in hell and all until they know why they suffer and for what they suffer until the *Basis* for a better social contract becomes imper-ative to them. This is the view of the incorrigible Romanticist—the Skylark.

"Plan" if you feel inclined to do so. And mole. But be sure you go to work to get that bet-ter *Basis* into effect and no more of the eternal shuf-fling, infernal temporizing that is nothing more than the mere abatement of some *local* nuisance. Why fuss over that nuisance first when our Salva-tion is inherent in this fundamental, over-all view from the *inside*? That view, call it Vision, is what is needed most right up here and down there. And *right now*. Vision was left out of the education of our planners. And no administration of Govern-ment can remedy the defect. Was the omission de-signed? I believe it was.

And to hell with the voracity of our amazing materialism! *Speed is a kind of voracity.*

Planning (and the Moleing that should come only after planning) for more *VORACITY* won't help the American citizen in Jeffersonian pursuit of hap-piness.

Unless such voracity as ours is soon seen for what it is: the straight road to hell, what hope for the Freedom of Democracy in any actual City on our soil?

Then according to whose Plan is a *better* city? A city for what? A city where? And what *is* the good Democratic life?

Whose answer would Robert Moses take? Or would I. But the true answer comes first before any good planning can be done!

What then is the right answer? Is War the answer?

Yes, it is, so long as "Planning" and "Moleing" stand where they stand in our Nation. War *is* the only answer. The only answer ever yet given!

As for administration of government, it turns its back upon what is naturally our agrarian gifts, to push more specific industrialism into world competition for command of markets in other nations not so gifted with ground as ours: Britain being only one of them. What else than War can be the result? Are Planners, with a capital P, going to plan for that? They are not.

Thus immensely gifted as an agrarian Nation, we have turned from Organism to the Factitious. . . . As a Nation we are "Banking" on the Factory. We huddle in the gregarious life. So here we are, a voracious maw for world-markets when we could easily consume at home more than all we could hope to make if we looked *within* the nature-of-the-thing to find the Right-Kind-of-Building and then relentlessly smashed the sucking financial "bottlenecks" trying to prevent our building it. Always money for War and always no money for Peace. Whether prevention is by ignorance or by design I don't know. Our official "planning" is so like ignorance and our ignorance is so like "educated planning." But it is the Big-city itself that puts us down among the vicious hang-overs from Feudal times that are now our crucifixion.

We could, and would, integrate a Culture of our own worthy this great ground we inhabit if we could triumph over this stupid cupidity of arrogant, heartless "Production" by natural Distribution.

This "arsenal of Democracy" is a Nation Nature blessed otherwise.

Bigger and better exports? Well . . . either we do something sensible about that grand Voracity ruining us now or we give the country back to the Indians.

What plan then? Is that inevitable plan in the books or on record?

No, unless it is Broadacre City.

No Haphazard skyline, no park-system or playground can tell us anything.

We need this clear long look down within the Ground-plan of the right way of *Building*. If we got that look the Organic way—we would soon find

our way to the right kind of Social-contract we might call good Government. Soon we would learn to use our dangerous run-away "equipment" for our own good instead of exaggerating it as a world-murder adding machine for bigger and better exports. Or for suicide?

Are we hell-bent on this monstrous menace to ourselves? If so, that is what comes of little men getting control of Monstrosity before getting a little control of themselves! How, then, would who "plan" for this emergency?

Well—two things at least the Lark sees: first, the necessary recognition—it can never be official— of the way of *integral* or Organic-building as Ideal. Then, second, the need of men with Robert Moses' power and pertinacity to get them built. His perspicacity is not so rodent-like, either, as he sometimes likes to pretend.

I care to be neither "Planner" nor Mole.

Broadacre City was only the name I chose (for lack of a better one) for this "right-kind-of-Building in the right way in the right place" to enable us all to go to work *with* the forces we are facing instead of working dead against them. I know it is high time for our Nation to find out how to *go along with them*. I know we must enable machines to go to work for mankind or scrap both. So I know it is high time to get into action on the side of our own humanity instead of urging more Production for the sake of Production in order to insure employment to more "employables" paid for by enforced sales to foreign nations under some Strong-arm.

A far view? I only know that it is the one view most needed not only out there far away in the War but also down here in the trenches in the Big-Bedlams at home.

Now, what happens to the furrowing of moles up here in the beautiful green hills of Wisconsin?

Good rains fall. Finding the little self-seeking channels in the soil they enlarge them until the good top-soil trickles down into streams draining the green valleys. The streams carry it further along toward the great Mississippi where all goes down to the Gulf of Mexico. Soil erosion.

Big-city moleing will do something like that to these hard, sucking bottle-necks which the overgrown villages of America have become in American life; the soil being the people themselves started on their gravitational way perhaps by unpremeditated opposite intention, like Moses' moleing. What will be left to the Big-city will be only the wrong kind of Building for the "impeccable taste" of the wrong kind of people all in the wrong place. The moles will be out of jobs.

Because *"total-mechanization" is going to create "useless" people under the laws of orthodox finance at a rate not yet conceived of!* And soon. In spite of as well as because of man's Arrogance in general and the extremes of his Folly, the gigantic mechanical forces unwittingly set in motion as "Progress" are already *reactionary*! They are on the move to destroy the poor creature that gave mechanism power. The Robot will destroy the Creature unless the reaction can be used as good Tooling for getting good building in the right way in the right place for the citizen *done in time.*

Therein: "getting good building done in time," lies the simple significance of Broadacres.

Is it so hard to understand?

The Broadacre City Thesis I sent Robert Moses meant to use this reactionary Machine-force to open, in a natural way (and it can be no matter for the "Strong-arm") a free life for the Citizen which in our country the administration of government ought to be, and will be, honest enough to call Democracy.

If reaction goes unrecognized much longer as Revolution, then our educated Planners and channeling Moles will only make of this Mechanized Era one vast Tragedy!

Our transplanted youth (hoping to someday come back home from Foreign-nations) have not only the right to find their own initiative released on their own soil. They have an even better right to find their own lives in their own hands, at last.

Any planning worth more than a tinkers damn should give them the right help to take the right road to such native freedom.

Broadacres, the natural city of Democracy is no invention of mine, I assure you. That City is really by the brilliant but erratic Architect: Nature.

## THE OCCASION

Quoting Robert Moses, Park Commissioner for New York City, in the *New York Times* Sunday Edition, June 18, 1944. After disposing, summarily, of "long-haired Planners" in high places. . . .

"Now for Frank Lloyd Wright of Wisconsin, another brilliant but erratic architect and planner. Regarded in Russia as our greatest builder, he has been enormously popular everywhere abroad. He is the author of *The Disappearing City* and founder of the Taliesin Fellowship, described as a cultural experiment in the arts. Here are a few samples from Frank Lloyd Wright's *Modern Architecture:*

"Even the small town is too large. It will gradually merge into the general non-urban development. Ruralism as distinguished from Urbanism is American, and truly Democratic."

"Last year I received from Mr. Wright a copy of his book *Taliesin* with a friendly note. The understanding was that the book would be passed around among the men upon whom I lean for advice. This reply summarizes their conclusions:

"While we were generally familiar with your publications and views, my little group of earnest thinkers, or rather constructors, have read the Taliesin Pamphlet and your more recent memorandum with considerable interest. The consensus of opinion is that we do not fully understand them. Some of the implications are most interesting, and, of course, we respect your accomplishments in the field of architecture, but it seems to us you have taken on a little too much territory. Most of my boys would feel you would get further if you tried an experiment on a reasonable scale, frankly called it an experiment and refrained from announcing that it was the pattern of all future American living.

"There it is. You can't expect anything better from moles who are blind, crawl short distances under the earth, and have only the most limited objectives."

The *Times* wired to know if I cared to reply. The preceding reply was refused by the *Times* as not being a sufficiently specific reply to Moses.

# THE PRICE OF PEACE

*This article, Taliesin Square-Paper Number 8, was published in May 1945. It expresses Wright's reaction to the San Francisco Peace Conference at which the United Nations charter was drawn up. He assessed the findings of the conference as betraying the ideals of peace: "We are coming in sight of a ghastly War wherein four-fifths of the population of the Earth—(yellow)—will be solidly lined up in hatred with murderous resentment (justified) against attempted domination by one-fifth—(white)!" Wright had great foresight in predicting that the United Nations would act more as a police force than as a peaceful assembly of nations.*

THE PRICE FOR INTERNATIONAL PEACE IS FUNDAMENTAL:

No Gold;

No Tariffs;

No Conscription.

Were these, the modern crime of crimes, abolished—why arm? What for?

Disarmament follows.

Free Citizenship comes along naturally.

Empire, territorial or commercial, would dissolve . . . therefore no one wants to talk about it.

Super-officialism at the San Francisco Peace Conference ignored everything fundamental to Peace! Why? Because the less questions asked about "why a horse" in any horse-trade the better for the trade. Especially when the traders are heavily armed policemen trying to make their own horse-trade stick.

Well . . . evasion is a shabby answer to the prayers of a world in mortal agony for five years, the loss of tens of millions of sons, or more when collateral losses are counted, and monster-mortgage to be redeemed by future generations.

We, the people, see this San Francisco Conference as treacherous to Peace. To actually pay the Price for Peace would insure a world to live in with less and better politics, scant bureaucracy and fair distribution of more liberal production in a world made more free for Freemen. Democracy might rise under such circumstances and shine. But the "Interests" are not interested?

Not yet interested. But we the People are—yes, we are. But our faces are so close to the bricks that we can't see the shape of the wall? To what "Power" then must we now turn to guard against being ruthlessly used against each other, time and again and yet again, for official horse-trade after horse-trade (we are the horse) to maintain Gold—Tariffs—Conscription—all the while recklessly whipping toward ourselves in the Pacific inexorable war Nature herself staged when she made us animal.

Such "all out" surrenders as "Policemen" demand have invariably had hideous consequences for Civilization. Because of them we are coming in sight of a ghastly War wherein four-fifths of the population of the Earth—(yellow)—will be solidly lined up in hatred with murderous resentment (justified) against attempted domination by one fifth—(white)! And the four-fifths will be powered to the last notch in Mechanized-industry with consequent Man-power leverage equal or superior to our own. Man-power multiplied by five!

If the People once take the biologic view, Russia is natural leader of "Asia for the Asiatics." Why not? It is her Destiny. Germany is the school-master.

Probably one hundred million Chinese are today siding with Russia while perhaps two million favor the America-Britannic investment called the Chinese Republic. Imperial Japan was worried by growing Communism when I was working there—1915 to 1919.[1] Probably Japan is on Russia's side as largely as China when "Unconditional Surrender" does to Japan what it has done to Germany. India, all Islam, yes Liberia too, whether in Africa or the United States will inevitably follow biological race-lines.

I do not say this long dreaded European Invasion by Asia is premature. Or as things are now in the West, wholly undesirable. I say only that we made it inevitable. Perhaps within the small arc of the Cycle of Human Destiny which we can see, it is due. That Cycle seems to be: first Success—then Arrogance—then Downfall! We were unable to change that Historic Cycle at the San Francisco Conference. Was that Conference only the froth on a fatal brew?

If we the people do take the biologic look, who then are these Japanese people we are so eager to mortally wound and eventually destroy ourselves to crush? Well, for one thing, they are the only surviving Chinese. Because China herself is Mongol as Greece is Albanian. Most of Russia was Mongolized centuries ago. Genghis Khan, the Mongol, was a European nightmare during those early centuries and Kubla Khan carried on. The cry "Yellow Peril" survives today in this cry "Asia for the Asiatics." If America is for the Americans does she dare deny the justice of that cry? Why had the San Francisco Conference no inclination to see Asiatic Russia as leader of the Asiatics when it must be seen that Russia is only "Western"? That is to say along the contact strips! Nevertheless witness Western Officialism still insisting upon the three ponderous anachronisms—Gold—Tariffs—Conscription—trying to upset by shopkeeping guile organic differences of Character and consequent human Necessity and Destiny planted deep in Race. Who are we, The Melting Pot of Race, to see Asiatic domination of the world discreditable? As we pleased we have been slapping the Asiatic face for a hundred years. We now hope to break the spear-head of coming invasion of the West by the East? But we have the spear-head by the blade to wound ourselves and not our enemy.

How can any likely basis for Peace be found in any all out attempt to restore Western domination of Asia?

Call this San Francisco fiasco no more than an attempt to call in the Police to quell a big riot. Police only temporarily "big." No attention paid to the real causes of the row. None!

Meantime Asia, great, ancient heart of Civilization is going to go "all out" for herself and come back against Western *Domination* able to enforce her own kind of Unconditional Surrender. The more she is "crushed," the stronger she will rise against us. Ubiquity is hard to "crush," Mr. Military man!

Why then must the over-powering mechanized-forces of the West be so recklessly used in foolish fear; in ignorant violence, animal-hatred turned against the East?

The Industrial-Revolution on which the West rode to Power has run away to the East! Top to bottom, this very industrial-mechanization we depend upon for Salvation is much more the natural tool of what we call Stateism than it can ever be the tool of Democracy. Stateism is more in the Nature of the Oriental Character be the brand Nazi, Communist, or State Socialism than it could possibly be to Democracy! It is nearly ready there and far better adapted to conscienceless-official-uses in the Orient than it can ever be in the Occident.

Freedom of Conscientious Democracy must depend upon deeper and higher Power!

If Conscientious Democracy had ever honestly squared itself with itself by abolishing the modern crimes, Gold, Tariffs, Conscription, to firmly plant a Nation that would stand by the true Principles of Democracy, no matter how scared it got in the midst of the rising tides and coming hordes of Stateism, there might be visible here and now among us a convincing pattern for World-peace. Salvation. But at this moment the United States of America is recreant to Democracy. False to Peace.

The price of Peace does not come too high! But the cost of War is easier to pay as the "Interests" are. That is why no public official, nor anyone within reach of an "office" in the United States dare inquire today about either the *Price* or the *Foundation* of World Peace!

As a matter of Truth, this Armistice got by the great armies of the three Goliaths propping up the tri-mangled corpse of a congenital Relative, moving the helpless hand to write "Unconditional Surrender" is not even annual interest on the Price of Peace! It would seem that of all wars ever fought, this jealous War praising God while trying to knock a hole in Western Civilization itself is the most inglorious ever fought. Looking toward the Future—the most tragic! Indeed, has Mechanized Western Civilization any Future?

As Dominant factor Europe is gone? Spengler was prophetic when he wrote the "Decline of the West"?

If the King be dead, Long live the King! Yes. But why talk of Peace?

Asian invasion of Europe was the awful nightmare of European civilization for centuries (and thanks to us) at long last, accomplished fact. Is this fitting end to the vicious old family-quarrel between England and Germany?

At San Francisco no ethical thought went down square to the bottom of World-Wars or to aggravating causes of approaching Race-war. So we the people, wantonly used against each other again and again, are again and soon to be ruthlessly used against each other in this most terrible war of all wars—a War of Extermination—senselessly driven our way by insane appetite for "Unconditional Surrender"!

The official Peace Conference at San Francisco proved to be an advocate of Conscription in whatever form: all hoping to use Conscription instead of International Law to secure "Peace": evading the honest price for Peace loyal Humanity demands. So, what hope? Call in the Police.

As for Peace-time Conscription, big club in the big hand of a big policeman, well . . . what Nation ever made Peace-time Conscripts of its Citizens and did not grow so hard and arrogant that it had to do terrible violence to Peace again and again and yet again in the name of freedom. Germany is an instance. Japan is another.

1. Wright was actually working in Japan from 1915–1922.

# NATURE

*Taliesin Square-Paper Number 9, printed and published in August 1945, continues the thesis that Wright began in the preceding article, "The Price of Peace." With the ending of the Second World War, the signing of the unconditional surrender documents, and the San Francisco Peace Conference, he saw old mistakes and misconceptions about "peace" continuing. "When Rome was at perihelion how many Romans could see that because of what had become Roman success, fatal decay had set in?" By entitling his article "Nature" Wright suggests a* looking in *rather than a* looking at *to be the guiding principle in how to study the problems facing humanity at this time. "We should realize that peace has never been won and never can be won by violence. We should know that constant resource and continual reference to the principles of Nature in order to make them manifest to men is the only education—the only safe way to take with any attempt at civilization."*

WHAT IS NATURE?

Nature is fate.

Fate has a countenance. That countenance is the great countenance of principle. Sun, earth, sky and star; snow, moon and flower; storms; the forests, hills and streams; birds, fishes and the animals; all are but expressions of the great Nature Countenance as seen from the outside.

If we wish to go within to understand these expressions of the great countenance we call on the Astronomer with his telescope, the Alchemist with his knowledge of potent essences or we go to school to the Scientist with his microscope. We do get a little nearer Nature then.

But out of our own hearts the great Artist—Philosopher and Poet—must come to us to go deeper than Science can yet go if we are to know the profound significance to man of the great Na-

ture Countenance. And it is the Art, Philosophy, and Poetry of an organic architecture that goes deepest into structure to discover to us the working of Principle in the building of the great building we call a civilization.

Reality is always the nature of Nature but, to distinguish ourselves, we continue to assume and refer to a *Human Nature* because such civilization as we have known is civilization precisely in that we have made it not integral with, nor even natural to, Nature.

Civilizations, therefore, are still antagonistic assumptions?

Have all attempts to build the fruitful life of a society failed because of such antagonism?

All have ended in eventual downfall, as History and monumental ruins scattered over the face of the globe serve to prove. Appearing again and again in different guise under different names but essential thought unchanged, civilizations have followed one another to the universal tomb.

Democracy was a real first change in thought. And so democracy became the challenge to the monarchic past that stateism today feels it must meet and defeat. Yes, the old order is afraid of the new. But the new has no occasion to be afraid of the old.

Our attempt to build a democracy in order that democracy may build should result in free and independent civilization able—no matter how afraid—to hold together from within. The time has come when, if we are ever to have Peace in which to develop and cherish what the human heart holds most dear, it is only the true nature of the human ego, living, strong and noble, that will be the safe basis for our civilization. We must go nearer to fundamental Nature to learn principle and draw more simple, because more fundamental, designs. We should realize by now that peace has never been won and never can be won by violence. We should know that constant recourse and continual reference to the principles of Nature in order to make them manifest to men is the only education—the only safe way to take with any attempt at civilization. The organic way. Especially so now when mechanism more and more commercialized renders our lives more and more vicarious. Force is again, as always, able to organize nothing.

But, man sees deeper into Nature only by mind-sight—the inner-eye we call imagination. So seeing men learn that heated iron may be safely hammered but no stick of dynamite. Only by so seeing can men discover that trying to win Peace by War is like hammering dynamite. If Nature means Nature. But seeing with the inner-eye is rare seeing—even yet. The military mind is a dead mind. Militocracy sees nothing.

The inner Vision of the Creative Artist it is, still, that strips away what lies abundant (and redundant) on the surface of things: the obvious realisms everywhere exuberant. Behind this pictorial outpouring of "effects" the creative mind sees the basic patterns of construction in the FORM of whatever is. There, within, lie the patterns of being which he sees by

abstraction. And such abstractions are architecture. Organic architecture is not only symphonic: it is a synthesis inevitable to civilization. We may, therefore, now learn to build a civilization wherein all abstractions are patterns true to organic (or innate) structure. If we do not discover and demand this safe foundation for our lives destruction will continue to be the ultimate of any attempt we may make to be civilized, no matter how sophisticated and "powerful" we become.

When Rome was at perihelion how many Romans could see that because of what had become Roman success, fatal decay had set in?

Principle is the universal pulse—the ever-moving, basic inner-rhythm of all being. And so, to the creative architect the working of principle is Nature's Manifest. Principle is Cosmic Law. He sees that universal law giving sequence, validity and consequence to the immediate patterns of all life whether mineral, vegetable, animal or human; and it is principle that gives countenance to either a true building or a true civilization. We already have a word for this deeper penetration. We call it vision. Vision is prophetic. Vision grasps and unmasks, to reveal by way of abstraction interior realities behind exterior appearances. It is by this search for integral character in all things that a man discerns, perhaps discovers, the poetry of innate order. No, not the classic-order of obvious symmetry with its fixation of major and minor axis which has imprisoned man so long, but the more natural order which lies in the reflex (as in the great "in-between") and gives the great nature countenance significance, everywhere. True expressions of that countenance, however gracious or perhaps terrifying, are always humanly significant. All man-made FORM whether Architecture, Music, Poetry, Painting, or any of the many arts and crafts of our Life here on earth either betray that significance to life or betray life to that significance. Monarchy, kingship or dictatorial government saw (as stateism now sees) obvious mathematic symmetry as the divine order of life. It became and still is "classic." But democracy sees the divine order of life as deeper: to be found more humane and abundant in the vast reflex: sees the great "in-between" from which fixed points may infinitely issue as far more important to men than any points they can ever fix because once fixed life has gone out of the fixation. Men may easily measure from point to point but democracy insists upon freedom to be and to vary at will if true to principle. In that freedom of the will guided by conscience lies the vitality of a democracy. It should be and could be the salvation of civilization at this moment.

We could call organic Architecture—the mother-art of structure—the essential poetry of innate order and not go far wrong. That is why we may say that "organic Architecture is the Architecture of Democracy." And it is only by discipline from within that mankind achieves democracy. That discipline has been abandoned, now by all faiths except faith in Democracy. Democracy has not yet, built.

Great Architecture is civilization. Without it? No civilization. Art alone can give vitality and true appreciation to desire. With art alive civilization is quick. Without architecture, civilization is dead. Or dying like an animal.

The study of Nature in this deeper organic sense enables the man not only to see a brick as a brick or a board as a board but also to see a prostitute as a prostitute, a man as a man or see a politician's ideas of government as good or bad.

It is the capacity to perceive (introversion) and reveal (extroversion) plus the ability to put this interior compulsion of principle to work, that gives character to whatever may be done by men and gives to a civilization all of the value it has, or ever had, to cherish as FORM.

To the degree that principle is inviolate in the form we have beauty.

To the degree that principle is violated we have ugliness.

When principle is confused we have the curious.

That is why if our civilization is to arrive and survive we must learn to draw with surer hand the line between the merely curious and the truly beautiful. A scientist cannot be expected to draw that line. Beyond the mere mathematics of "classic" or obvious symmetry only the artist can make sure work of placing that line where it belongs for Humanity. Then only, do we have the interpretation of dynamic life which we have the right to call a safe and sane civilization. Without such inner vision made FORM by their own will the people must continue to perish. The more successful Science is, it can only hasten destruction the more. Religion is powerless to inspire a people without the Image: recourse to great Art. And constant reference to the principles of Nature is the only sure basis of a true Image. Right or wrong. Ethics in line with principles of Nature never go wrong. Morality often goes wrong because morality is only some approximation of ethics changing as customs change. There are fashions in morality. There are none in ethics.

Upon the *innate validity* of the Nature-pattern of principle which we are here calling the Abstraction whether in human thought, conduct or in our works of art depends whatever integrity of FORM has ever existed, exists or may ever exist in any civilization past, present or to come.

The ability and excellence of the artist as the prophet of his people continues to depend upon the concordant simples to which, in his work, he can resolve confusing externalities of Nature: strip appearances of redundant realisms in order to express reality simply in terms of innate character. The great artist is he who enables us to clearly see infinite rhythms of the cosmic order as a clean integrity in terms of everyday human-life.

In this inner sense it is the integrity of Individuality that is Character.

Character is fate.

Fate is principle at work as Individuality.

# TO SWITZERLAND

*In this article two statements allude to the possibility that Wright sent something to his Swiss friends other than this essay, if—indeed—this ever was sent. No record in the Frank Lloyd Wright Archives gives any further evidence to this script. However, since much of the article is devoted to the discussion of democracy and an architecture for democracy, it might well be that his newly published book* When Democracy Builds *was sent to the students of the architectural school in Zürich as well as to his longtime friends, the Swiss architect Werner Moser and his wife, Silva. The Mosers visited Taliesin in 1924, and their son Lorenz was born there during their stay. It was about the same time that Olgivanna met Wright and subsequently made her own first visit to Taliesin. Moser, as well as being an architect, was on the faculty of Zürich's architectural school and devoted a great portion of his life to education. The article commends Switzerland for its courage and extols her architects: "What an Architecture Switzerland might have for her extraordinary terrain and the independent courage of her strong people—if the fundamental principles of Organic Architecture took root and flowered over there!" [Unpublished]*

I AM HAPPY TO FLING ON THE AIR MY GREETING TO OUR boys and my own friends in little—but mighty—Switzerland: a David among the Goliaths. I am sure that my thought and work do not need to be introduced to you over there by me over here.

I am assured that the original contribution to Organic Architecture so genuinely appreciated in your Nation is growing in strength throughout the world. If there is to be a Post-war European world (which many good men seem to doubt), the Organic Architecture of years past will be the sure expression of further growth. Were the Philosophy informing Organic Architecture better understood an organic peace might be established in this world even now.

We have a hopeful sign in this modest attempt to get together upon what shall constitute good post-war building? But Government, itself, by its very nature, cannot do advanced building because government cannot act in advance of the established order. Progress is controversial always. Government depending upon the next election cannot take risks such as advanced thought in Architecture demands. But intelligent government can propagandize advanced thought as you see it now doing over there.

The Post-war building problem is a problem only to Government. If it is to be in Government hands building will remain comparatively life-less. We will look to individuals not so controlled for such buildings as will ensure honor to the future Architecture of either Switzerland or America.

Inability of Democratic Government to lead is no dishonor to Democratic Government. But it means that the matter of Organic Architecture today, tomorrow and the day after is an affair of the heart and mind of the inspired individual; he who fares badly at the hands of governments. Architecture (as a matter of course) *is* Civilization. Without an architecture of its own there is no Civilization to the credit of any Nation.

What an Architecture Switzerland might have for her extraordinary terrain and the independent courage of her strong people—if the fundamental principles of Organic Architecture took root and flowered over there!

Owing to our own official subservience the progress of an Organic Architecture over here, though initial in these United States, has been ignored by Government. In proportion to population and wealth we are behind other countries in official recognition of such Architecture. Even South America and Mexico advance more rapidly.

But this curious indifference to the growth of our own baby grows less. You are listening now to what is still a voice from our Democratic Minority. And after release from the bureaucratic majority-grip of War lets us up and going again *on our own,* you may see us building organic buildings quite generally at home.

Courageous Switzerland has much in common with us in the struggle for indigenous culture: a mixed people in love with Freedom. And I believe Culture, *if based upon the common stock of Principle* must develop already existing variety among the different peoples of the World unless we want to sacrifice true Style from within to *a* style applied by exterior compulsion of Authority. I hope the danger of exterior compulsion is passing away. It surely will pass when what Organic Architecture really means to the life of men is generally understood by Education.

Organic Architecture is the Architecture of Democracy whether Swiss, Finnish, French, Swedish or Irish: each nationality true to its own individuality. I am not one of those wanting to see the Derby hat and gaiters descend upon the world as the norm of respectability. I wish that what wisdom we have left in this world would cherish the individualities of Peoples while establishing friendship and cooperation between them. This could only be done on the basis of Principle; all Peoples free to grow their own culture from roots already planted—even though the harvest might be the common heritage of our great world.

Let us have more of individual characteristics, not more uniformity. If we love Life let us have living room for more tolerant initiative, not less. Nature herself bears me out in this desire. Study her manifest purpose in that direction.

So—our boys in Switzerland, to you! May you grow strong and stronger in your own right—Free in fact; free in every feature of your lives. Give us more *Switzerland:* give us the Switzerland that *is* Switzerland. Your Swiss comrades will, I hope, enjoy this fragment of the United States sent to you with love and gratitude.

Force can organize nothing. Out of the ignoble shambles of War no Peace ever came. Peace can only come by way of Nations such as Switzerland.

# CEILING OR NO CEILING

**W**riting in Ladies' Home Journal in December 1945, the writer Dorothy Parker took Wright to task for calling the Metropolitan Museum of Art, with its overly high, lofty ceilings, "undemocratic." He had suggested, instead, the more human scale of his proposed Solomon R. Guggenheim Museum and explained that public rooms should be only about twelve feet high. What Parker failed to notice about the Guggenheim Museum, for example, is that the spaces where the paintings and objects were to be exhibited were relatively low by the Met's standards, but the central open space, rising up six floors to the surrounding ramps and capped by a great skylight, was certainly lofty. Wright drafted this article as a rebuttal to Parker, but it remained unpublished. "Human scale," a phrase coined by him, meant that the measure of the interior of the building should be the human being: "But let me maintain that when any ceiling is evident as low or lofty, then something is gone wrong whatever feet and inches may be. The height of a ceiling should be such that appropriate human scale is maintained in a proportion that makes it unlikely (were one's attention ever directed to the matter) that anyone could guess its 'height' in feet or inches." Much of his text addresses specific points in Parker's, including references to "towering elms," a cathedral, Thomas Jefferson, democracy, Groton and Harvard, as well as redefining the essence of democracy without resorting to "Grandomania." [Unpublished]

DOROTHY THOMPSON HIT THE TWELVE-FOOT CEILING SO hard she should have attention. A safe landing on "the horizontal" is no light matter even after hitting a ceiling at twelve feet. The normal ceiling for domestic purposes is eight or nine feet. In organic architecture we prefer free horizontal movements in space to the inevitable constriction of heights. High ceilings pull the walls in. Low ceilings push them away. There is seldom money for both space and height. Now, I did not call the New York Metropolitan Museum "undemocratic" just because it is so uselessly tall but because the ponderous old stone-quarry is monarchic in derivation. Its elaborate heights and wrong emphasis on mass and detail throughout the conception should make freedom-loving citizens feel not only improperly insignificant but appropriately angry. All that gets back to the citizen for the scandalous cost of the enormous disproportion is only an empty gesture of which many of us are getting heartily sick. Let's say we are disgusted with Grandomania.

And may I respectfully ask what twelve-foot trees have to do with a twelve-foot ceiling? Since when have our trees determined the height of ourselves or of our ceilings? What has a "towering elm" seeking sustenance by spreading its branches in the free sun and air of the great overhead in common with a room intended to shelter and protect the animal moving about in it on two feet seeking protection from too much of those very blessings—Sun and Air?

What has a Cathedral in common with a modern habitat anyway? What has a skyrocket in common with a man's hat? When they hang a man they take his feet off the horizontal. No high overhead can save him.

The realization of human freedom is horizontal. Verticality is "tour de force," vertigo—or death.

Refuge for the soul of man in democratic Freedom is found in breadths: in the earth line not the sky line. Earth and sky travel together but never meet in this life. From both we may derive symbols. We are doing so now. For fun.

But let me maintain that when any ceiling is evident as low or lofty, then something is gone wrong whatever feet and inches may be.

The height of a ceiling should be such that appropriate human scale is maintained in a proportion that makes it unlikely (were one's attention ever directed to the matter) that anyone could guess its "height" in feet or inches. Now, is the terrible heresy of modern democracy to be found in this organic assertion of the human-figure as the normal scale of building heights? I assert that "the common man" is not "made into a tyrant" by anything appropriate to his soul, to his size or to his function. But he *is* made into one by such high ceiling ideology as the exemplar soldier's awestricken adulation of extremes. The democrat is safe only when his appreciations are keyed in due proportion to his understanding and his own capacities. The modern tyrant is made by the "high ceiling" of credulous hero-worship; worship of force; worship of extremes of any sort. Perhaps it would be safe to say "worship" of any sort.

Inspiration is no matter of feet and inches. Wholly an interior affair, it is a matter of character and growth from within the nature of whatever is inspiring. First quality of inspiration is interior integrity: fitness to purpose that wears the exterior countenance of principle which we call beauty.

Tall or Short has little (or nothing) to do with it all! Except as one lifts one's spirit with one's eyes to contemplate harmonious expression of the spirit either of man (or of mankind) as Entity, haven't we progressed beyond the point where a Gothic spire is needed to say that God is in his heaven and that his heaven is way off "up there"?

There was once a man who sought God on the highest mountain he could find, climbed the highest tree on the mountain top and called to God. He heard a voice saying—get down, man. Go down! Go back there where your people live. There (if anywhere) you will find God. Now the climber to the skies—"the sky the limit"—was evidently refereed back to the horizontal? To the masses therefore?

No. I too dislike this "common man" heresy. I have never met a common man. As for a common woman—well, just call for a volunteer!

And just for fun let's say the sky *is* the limit. But how many of us could stay out there beneath it if we wanted to? If we don't want to and wish a ceiling where do we put the ceiling? That will depend, of course. But depend on what beside the walls? So many things occur to any and everyone, why name them? It is nothing worth stating to say that the ceiling should be "as high as possible." Too many somethings that matter too much for that to be any answer at all. So what? More Grandomania?

William Blake said "Exuberance is Beauty." But he meant according to Nature without stint. The point at which exuberance becomes exaggeration is where Sentiment degenerates to sentimentality, where love becomes lust, and where Grandeur breaks down into grandomania. That is to say where good proportion becomes excess. High ceilings are not according to the nature and proportion of the figure of a human being. Exaggeration of the relationship is not exuberance. It is merely excess.

We as a people do love to Paul Bunyanize and are Gargantuanistic by desire. This nation *has* played enthusiastic stooge to Grandomania in all its forms from British Empire and Kingship to Arcturus and the Big Dipper. Our nation's vast, commercial educational-system (like the nation's journalese) has persistently, perversely mistaken exaggeration for greatness. No wonder we get our buildings all out of human scale. We get our government that way. We go to war that way. We write for the *Ladies' Home Journal* that way. But does that make the mania admirable? Or even democratic?

I say no. Grandomania is damnable: a fatty degeneration of soul as much the matter with our life as with our architecture. We owe to it the hypocrisy of our absurd pretensions to Democracy. It is the real curse put upon Usonian culture by the still unsuspect Anglo-European inheritance of our cultural lag.

If there is to be the height instead of breath . . . how much is enough?

The proper answer to that question is not found in Mobocracy. The answer is nothing for the man in the street nor the man in the University. The answer is for one who does make sure of his own adequacy by love of nature: a devoted study of the organic principles of building wisely and well. He alone can answer the question. The answer is a matter of Culture.

Our so-called Democracy has never yet built a single thing unless it is these buildings we are building now in the name of an entity we call organic architecture; actually building with a consistency and appropriateness to human scale and to indigenous life that makes many a sensitive soul hungry for a harmony heretofore not to be had, shed tears of happy satisfaction when they see the actual building. Deplorable as this shedding of tears certainly is, it is better than gawking on high at the sky or being hushed with awe in buildings where ceilings disappear in the chiaroscuro of oblivion. Or by ejaculating over and over "It's a miracle!"

And I maintain that our own "farm boys" who grow up to names coveted by Who's Who are the very ones to crave a ceiling just right for its purpose; appropriate to them as they live; a ceiling without waste. But a ceiling, too, with an eye to "drama." That is to say a low ceiling when low is suitable foil for the high and a high ceiling when the low ceiling makes both becoming, timely, and appropriate.

"The measure of a man" is never his "smug satisfaction" with anything less, or other, than his own individual responsibility for the creation of a better Order; the finer proportion of a better building: a better way of life for himself and his own according to his means.

"The great apostles of Democracy" never thought as much about "ceilings" as I have just

**George Sturges House, Brentwood, California. 1939.**
FLLW Fdn FA#3905.0008

written. If they had thought about them they would have wanted them appropriate, neither "clamped down" nor lifted up.

Thomas Jefferson? Well . . . Thomas Jefferson is one of my adorations, too. But in retrospect I should say that his shortcomings consisted in trying to live in a hostile wilderness with fashionable clothes, lace at his throat and wrists, adopting meantime the architecture of an effete aristocracy that never knew what organic-character was in anything and would not care if it did know. He rose above it all, though, when he built a brick wall one brick thick—laid it serpentine—so it would stand up and be attractive as well as economical.

Davy Crockett hit the eye of our modern organic architecture when he made a simple cap of coonskin and let the tail hang down over the hair he had refused to cut off behind his ears.

So "Thomas Jefferson did not believe in horizontal education?" He believed in nothing else! He himself proposed it when he asked that all children be educated according to their talents. A little mistake, however, getting his colored people in to play Mozart instead of refreshing his soul by having them sing their own spirituals to him. That "Mozart" was a little too high ceiling. Really.

And dear Emerson! He never foresaw that

some accomplished writer might take his "Hitch your wagon to a star" so literally.

Now—let me contend that if the limits of Art are *not* "set in advance" the measure of appreciation accorded the artist will be mediocre. And I assure you he will deserve the mediocrity he will achieve. Because *an artist's limitations are always his best friends*! It is *within* them by way of *his respect for them* that he rises supreme as creator.

*All* great Art *does* create in the beholder the "self-satisfaction" that was the artist's great joy in his work. That *joy* is reflected in the beholder's own satisfaction with the great artist's satisfaction.

Yes, the limits of all Art great or small, are severely set in place by the problem itself as presented to the artist for solution. Within those constitutional limits every problem carries its own solution.

When a man standing before a masterpiece emotionalizes "It's a miracle, it's a miracle!" it is miraculous only to the superstitious or sentimental observer, however wonderful the piece may be in itself.

"Walt Whitman?" Yes. Of course he knew the truth of what I am saying here if ever a man did know it. He said it much better than I can say it but no better than I can build it, thank you.

As for "the statesmen our people adore"—well . . . a proper ceiling over their heads might have saved us now from the loss of the moral leadership of a mortal world plunged into confusion and agony because "the sky was the limit." No need now to speak of "self-evident truths nor of decent respect to the opinions of mankind" in connection with what has transpired as the result.

So (an *architect* speaking) let the ceilings of Democracy be in good proportion, there where they belong! When our own good people get a chance to build for themselves more stately mansions for any democratic soul they can honestly call their own: where do ceilings belong? Well . . . certainly no longer with "the parliamentary tradition in the tongue of Groton and Harvard" nor with the "insignificances" of any man even though he be "gentle." Nor does it belong there with this chronic mediocrity that instinctively craves grandomania as we of this nation have craved it just because we

came over that way in fancy. Our infancy.

To conclude upon a plane conservatively under Dorothy Thompson's "ceiling" . . . Well . . . the Greek word *Demos* has been politically degraded to signify a government by unrestricted Majority-rule—the sky the limit! Our own word "Mobocracy" (no ceiling at all) fits that case better than the Greek word "Democracy."

Demo or Demos may be held to mean the normal man-unit: the individual—in the society of mankind. Qualities that make the man a Man (a characteristic individual—not a conscript) would, therefore, be the true basis of any social life we could honestly call Democracy. And what is it that makes the man a man as distinguished from the brute? Conscience, Creative-sensitivity, and Individual-responsibility.

With the *normal* man then, as a proper ceiling, we might build a society worthy of mankind, conceiving a government under a ceiling protecting man, *the individual*, as the cherished Norm.

As a term applied to Government a true ceiling for Democracy would mean the very gospel of manlike individuality as distinguished from the mere idiosyncrasy of the person either added up in order to rule or let loose in order to ruin.

To protect the *individuality* of the normal man would be the only province of such inhibition and expropriation by government as we could honestly call Democratic. We should keep the ceiling right there (maybe about twelve feet). A high ceiling for Government would be regarded by democrats as a necessary evil because Democracy starts with the horizontal assumption that men are created equal to living together on the ground to grow in Freedom. Not in fancied "Freedoms." Democracy would believe unselfish well-being to be *normal*; no special quality or privilege but the natural and priceless norm of all men taken into democratic citizenship by their fellows. Democratic Government would be founded in that Faith and should be so administered.

Democracy is *the ceiling appropriate to true human scale*! Therefore a natural challenge to the high ceilings of Stateism. A splendid heresy today!

# THE MODERN GALLERY

By 1946 the commission for the Guggenheim Museum had been under way for nearly three years. The first letter, from curator Hilla Rebay, asking Wright to design the building came in June 1943, but delays in procuring a site somewhere in New York City held him back from making any sketches or designs. Finally, on the "hunch" that a typical city block in Manhattan would be the choice, Wright made preliminary studies in December 1943, with more detailed presentation drawings prepared the following weeks and shown to Rebay and Guggenheim. On 13 March 1944, the property between 88th and 89th streets was obtained. The first set of working drawings was finished and signed by Frank Lloyd Wright on 7 September 1945 and countersigned by Solomon R. Guggenheim as proof of his approval of the scheme. At the same time, both Wright and Guggenheim concurred that a model of the building should be made to better illustrate the innovative use of the spiral ramp with its peripheral skylight and central court with its top lighting. Photographs of the model were published simultaneously in The Architectural Forum and the Magazine of Art in January 1946. For the latter, Wright prepared this text explaining the building. At this point in time, neither the architect nor his client could possibly foresee the myriad difficulties—delays, struggles, and creative agony—that would go on for another decade before ground was broken. This was to prove the most arduous and painful commission of Wright's entire career. [Magazine of Art, January 1946]

FOR THE FIRST TIME IN THE HISTORY OF ARCHITECTURE A true logarithmic spiral has been worked out as a complete plastic building: a building in which there is but one continuous floor surface: not one separate floor slab above another floor slab, but one single, grand, slow wide ramp, widening as it rises for about seven stories—a purely plastic development of organic structure. If pulled from the ground and tossed away the whole building would bounce intact. Starting in the theater below the ground, it would be easy to go up in a wheel chair and come safely down again without undesired interruption. Or taking the fast ramps concentrated in a tower on one side of the grand ramp, visitors go easily and quickly up and down. Two plunger elevators are located at the center of this tower and are directly connected with the grand ramp at each recurrent level. The open center of the central chamber made by the grand ramp is wider at the top than at the base by about twenty-four feet and is open to the sky, though covered by a shallow glass dome shedding night light as well as daylight.

The entire building is a completely floor-heated, air-conditioned vault, adapted throughout to the safekeeping and becoming display of not only

**Frank Lloyd Wright, Solomon R. Guggenheim, and Baroness Hilla von Rebay with model of Guggenheim Museum, New York, 1946.**
FLLW Fdn FA#6805.0002

valuable paintings by great masters but the paintings of contemporary artists and students as well. The interior is absolutely fire-proof, dust-proof, andvermin-proof. A constant moisture content will be maintained throughout the changing seasons.

As people come into the museum through the entrance vestibule they pass across a perforated metal floor through which air-conditioning apparatus, operating like a vacuum cleaner, creates suction on feet and clothes, making it less likely for dust to come into the building. All entering air is washed, filtered, tempered, and discharged at slow speed into every portion of the building. The temperature changes within will therefore be negligible throughout the course of years, enabling all glass coverings and frames to be eliminated from the paintings. The vast collection of paintings is so situated and displayed that wall surfaces of the building itself automatically frame them in a setting suitable to each and every one. Desired changes may be made with little effort and special exhibits be easily arranged to advantage in as many ways as imagination may dictate.

For the first time, purely imaginative paintings,

regardless of the representation of any natural object, will have appropriate, congenial environment suited to their character and purpose as harmonious works of art for the eye as music is for the ear.

In a corner of the first floor of the building a globular laboratory is designed wherein experiments in the sound-projection of movement and color in various forms of picturesque animation can be made and exhibited to a small group of about one hundred friends of the gallery. Experimental work in this art and the art of painting will be encouraged. Projection in this chamber for experiment will be from a pit in the floor under the center of a shallow dome. Reclining chairs will make it comfortable to view the domed ceiling as well as the walls.

The main structure is monolithic throughout, pre-stressed steel in high tension reinforcing high-pressure concrete. The exterior and interior will be faced with polished marble-aggregate. The only exception is the greatly extended ground-floor surface which will be a continuous pavement of large marble slabs. The galleries taken all together afford approximately three-quarters of a mile of day-lighted wall-surface perfectly adapted—either by daylight or night light to the convenient display of paintings. There will be no hanging of the pictures; all will rest on a prepared base which is part of the wall. Throughout the structure artificial lighting comes from the same source as daylighting and is incorporated within the construction of the building. From wells in the great rotunda under the glass dome changeable prismatic illumination plays upward and outward from electrically controlled fountains of light, not only illuminating the great open central space of the grand ramp but going outward over terraces and gardens.

Under the main gallery there is a cinema, entirely below ground, where films may be projected from behind the screen or projected upon it from the front. This inner chamber, completely insulated from exterior sounds, will seat four to five hundred persons. This novel, subterranean room is also admirably adapted to chamber music and various forms of educational entertainment. Entrance to the cinema is through the museum, and exit is directly to the street through an outside sunken garden on Fifth Avenue.

Provisions have also been made in this connection for greenrooms, experimental workshops and also for the safe storage of a choice film collection recording the work of the Foundation. For film research in many different directions, cinema workshops and research laboratories are not only provided but are equipped with the latest apparatus for experimental work; scholarships will be awarded to especially talented workers. Adequate clerical, shipping and receiving accommodations are conveniently arranged independently of the main museum.

Not only is the entire monolithic building plastic in the form of a rising spiral but it is plastic in actual construction also. Glass in the form of Pyrex tubing is extensively used to light and seal the interiors; a beautiful material in itself as well as a utility. The solid floors, ceilings, and walls are all lined with cork to insure good insulation and noiseless movement. Quiet floor surfaces and ceiling are uniform with each other, all together contributing to the great repose of the spacious interior. The whole is a well-studied background for the paintings to be displayed there.

All effects are integral parts of the building it-self, both exterior and interior. Comfortable seats are features of the design everywhere there is an interest. They are part of the general installation so that any painting may be viewed comfortably.

Quarters for general administration alongside the museum are developed in the same general character, so that conduct of the affairs of the museum can be directly under the supervision of the curator as needed. A number of studios for preparatory work for exhibitions and the research continuously sustained by the Solomon R. Guggenheim Foundation are provided for upon the upper levels of the building. These upper levels terminate in a conservatory filled with plants above which to one side, crowning the tower for the elevators and fast ramps, is an observatory where an adequate astronomical telescope will be installed for general study of the cosmic order.

**Model (cutaway) of Guggenheim Museum, New York, 1946.** FLLW Fdn FA#4305.0638

On the ground floor provision for an adequate and intimate cafe service is made. Entrance is directly from 88th Street. And a charming banquet hall and boardroom is located on an outside terrace beside the grand ramp opening to the court overlooking Fifth Avenue.

A large, high, and spacious quiet innergallery below the main floor level is concealed but partly revealed to the main gallery—in which will be shown the great masterpieces of the new movement, collected by Solomon Guggenheim and the curator, Baroness Hilla von Rebay, and which for many years have characterized the Guggenheim Foundation with no adequate place in which even to store them, not to mention showing them.

An interesting feature of the building is the fact that grandomania is discarded. All in all, it is proportioned to the scale of the human figure. This is true not only in every detail of the new gallery but of the organization and uses of the building itself as a whole.

Not only the proportions but method of construction of the building are in perfect keeping with the plastic nature of the design, so perfectly adapted to its purpose that the paintings it displays will be at home in an environment admirably adapted to their character. The entire structure will be securely founded upon bedrock fifty feet below the street level and will be of the most enduring character known to modern science. Requiring little or no maintenance, the edifice is virtually indestructible by natural forces—earthquake-proof, fireproof, and storm-proof. The building is intended to be a reposeful center for all sincerely interested in the art of painting as a source of human culture; a window open upon the future of painting as a progressive, responsible cultural art indispensable to modern life.

And finally, this building will be permanently in the heart of New York City upon one of its proudest avenues—the gift of a far sighted philanthropist—one of a great family of philanthropists, who loves his city and sees the growth that lies now at the threshold of its future.

# THE ARCHITECT

A series of lectures at the University of Chicago brought together many artists, scholars, and educators to discuss their specific professions and fields of work. The series was then published by the University of Chicago Press in 1947 as The Works of the Mind. Among the twelve contributors were Marc Chagall, Arnold Schoenberg, Robert Hutchins, and Mortimer Adler. Wright was invited to speak on behalf of architects, and gave this address. Wright began by describing his definition of the word "mind": "The Mind should not be only a matter of the head (the intellect) but an affair of the heart and of the imagination and of the hand (or what we call technique). But I believe that until those three (intellect, heart and hand) become one, become operative by inspiration, going to work together, you do not have a true work of the Mind." His address concerned itself mainly with a description of what constitutes organic architecture, and what the young, aspiring architect should look for, look into, and absorb in order to build a better architecture for the country.

Along with his 1930 lecture at the Art Institute of Chicago published under the title To the Young Man in Architecture, this essay constitutes one of Wright's finest descriptions of the architect's obligations to society: "I think Organic Architecture should begin in the American home. . . . there is where this ideal of something integral, something of life and not on it, something with which you can live with grave and intimate consideration of the things more excellent—and a feeling that you are somebody in your own right; feel like somebody yourselves because there is a harmony in the atmosphere of things you have created about you." [The Works of the Mind, University of Chicago Press, 1947]

HERE THIS EVENING IT DOES SEEM AS THOUGH YOUNG America may be waking up? At last? [Mr. Wright here refers to the overflow audience which attended his lecture when it was delivered in Leon Mandel Hall, University of Chicago.—Editor.] Am I to stand before you here tonight and defend (or am I to present) Architecture as a work of the Mind? As for my share in this discussion (or presentation) of various phases of human activity said to proceed from the mind, it is my belief that for five hundred years at least we have had no architecture which did proceed from the Mind.

So here at the beginning we might as well clear up a little ambiguity concerning what we are in the habit of calling the Mind. Some of us laughingly (and wrongly) refer to our "minds." But the Mind should be not only a matter of the head (the intellect) but an affair of the heart and of the imagination and of the hand (or what we call technique). But I believe that until those three (intellect, heart, and hand) become one, become operative by inspiration, going to work all together, you do not have a true work of the Mind. You would not call the building in which you are now sitting a work of the Mind? Would you? I don't think this great university could call its home (these cast-iron Gothic buildings in which you are being nurtured) a work of the Mind? Because, as a matter of truth—we won't say "matter of fact," since facts added up can tell the most awful lies—to speak, as a matter of truth, of the architecture we are familiar with and such as the world has had to be content with for five hundred years or more as coming from the Mind would be rank misstatement. Very little of it ever came from the Mind. And the significant thing before us here tonight for consideration is the truth that at last Architecture (I mean what we call Organic Architecture) *has* become a thing of the Mind. No—not a thing of the brain only, but of heart, intellect, imagination, as one together amounting to the perception which we call Vision and which is now (at last) capable of its own technique.

But it is true to say that, so far as technique may go (that is to say, architecture in actual practice), each man must find *his* way of doing what he wants to do. That is tragic but true. Hitherto a building has not been a living organism proceeding by way of natural inspiration from the nature of the circumstances, the nature of materials, the nature of its purpose in order to gratify the nature of Man. In each generation and in every civilized nation at each period of time in this world's history, Architecture has served its purpose fairly well. At some times better than at others. But seldom if ever has there been an architecture which proceeded outward from the within (the mind) and by way of a technique which mastered the nature of materials old and new, the actual nature of the conditions of its existence become something integral with the life of the people: an Organic Form. So Architecture has been almost always—certainly for the last five hundred years—something *on* life, not *of* life. A Renaissance—"a setting sun all Europe mistook for dawn!"

Now, whenever architecture does actually be-

come a work of the Mind, we will have what we are calling Organic Architecture. Organic Architecture can come to us only as a work of the Mind. When it does so come to us, perhaps for the first time in the civilization of the whole world our people will begin to realize the inner meaning to them of this word "Freedom." They will begin to know something of the meaning of this slogan which we have waved abroad too freely named "Democracy." Should you ever succeed in getting this old "new" sense of the thing as something inevitable to you coming from within your souls to achieve outward appropriate Form, your whole point of view would change. You could no longer tolerate the sort of buildings we live in but do not live *with* today nor call the life you live in them an affair of the "*Mind.*"

Is it a matter of course that as a nation we can claim no aesthetic sense whatever beyond a superficially educated taste? It is true that we are become grossly materialistic. But not to such a degree I hope that, were we once to get this organic point of view into our mental system, we could not realize to what an extent mere *matter* has had its heavy way with what we call our architecture. By the way of what we are pleased to call our "taste" (believe me such taste is only a matter of ignorance) came all the environment our life has to show for itself today. By way of our memory, by association of ideas or rationalization, our people have arrived at an eclectic's "choice." Well, picking and choosing in that way is no longer good enough. Believe me, such is not and never was a work of the Mind in the least. It is rather a kind of ornamental hallucination.

A great change is coming over the whole world in regard to this thing we call Architecture. Carelessly we speak of the new way of building as "modern architecture"—an insufficient term because any building built today is "modern" architecture. But when you say "Organic Architecture," you begin to get something into view that will make you try to think, even if ever so little. And it hurts, of course.

What is Organic Architecture? What—exactly—has happened? Well, what has happened is quite simple. Victor Hugo prophesied the happening, I remember, in a book he wrote, which I hope many of you may have read, *Notre Dame.* In this strange book there is a discursive chapter titled in some editions "The One Will Kill the Other." The point he made in this instance was that Printing (printing was and is the Machine) would eventually kill Architecture, then known as the great universal "writing" of humanity. And of course were that to happen, something else would have to come to take the place of architecture—building having been the great "writing" (we might say) of humanity up to that time. He was persuaded that this new writing of humanity would be the printed book. He believed that in the printed book human thought had found a new outlet more volatile, easier to preserve, and cheaper. The great novelist indulged in prophecy. He said that in the latter part of the nineteenth century (or early in the twentieth) Architecture would come alive again and that we (the people) would begin to live in buildings that were our own in more than a material sense.

Well—his "line" is mine for this evening: I assure you an Architecture of the Mind is really here. That sentiment and prophecy coming to me from Victor Hugo when I was a youngster of fourteen are more than ever alive tonight. What the great novelist said is now true. And I think he based his judgment upon the thought that by now the old Architecture would be so worn out as to be inapplicable: so uninhabitable, meaningless, and stupid that the worm (that's us) would turn, and by way of our new power (tools which, taken together, we call the Machine) we would go to work upon all these new materials which have since then come to life for us—materials like glass and steel. You may be sure that if the ancients had glass and steel, they would never have built a thing as they did. Glass and steel would have been the great liberation for them. It is now (at last) about to become the great liberator for us by way of Organic Architecture. A liberator, however, which we have not yet learned to appreciate as such, because without art it is a destroyer of Architecture.

Yes, we have never yet learned to use the Machine properly. That is to say to use it *for mankind*. The Machine has never done very much for our culture—in Architecture especially—because of this stupid classic "idea" that the art of building, as Architecture, is something out of the past; and the ed-ucational mistake that Tradition must be something old taken out of books by way of colleges and professors instead of made anew from the nature of things as time changes all. Believe me, Architecture is no longer made that academic way. Architecture (if it is Organic Architecture) is the very life you live made in the terms upon which you must live it. It is *you*; it is *all* of you. It is all of the things of your life put together by way of the means by which you live and by way of which you may live not only comfortably and happily because of the great advantages for adventure which we have today but with the new beauty of a great integrity. In our civilization that integral beauty must be Architecture. So Organic Architecture, the living thing, is not to be measured by the masquerade we see all around us everywhere we go. No. Organic Architecture is a *thing of the heart*. And such architecture comes to be ours along with all the good things we have ever known and have been able actually to think about. Thought cannot be taught. It is not from the head. God alone knows where most of it does come from. But we are surrounded by a glut of an imitation of it everywhere. If we would seek an education, we are surrounded by it—literally imbedded in it.

But, as we may see now, there is good chance that Victor Hugo was dead right. As you know, he was the great "modern" of his time. Of course, he was, like all moderns, egoistic. Easily gullible, he loved flattery. I remember reading of an occasion at the salon he held in Paris, in which now famous men were gathered around him, a group of his guests came in the with the suggestion that the name of Paris be changed to "Hugoville." He was quite satisfied to say that he thought the change a good idea.

And, as you can see here tonight, moderns are all inclined to be somewhat arrogant. Unfortunately, it is true that some of us are even inclined to be what you would call "egotistic." But I have always denied the egotistic and declared myself only "egoistic." I think you are all egoistic just as I am. And I hope you are. Because, if you are not, you aren't going to have an architecture of your own. Or maybe that is not quite true; perhaps I am stretching things a bit. At least—I will say that you are not going to have an architecture of your own until you are somebody yourselves. Now, are you? You will have no true Architecture until you have convictions; until you see where you stand, and from within you comes the something that is really you. Until you learn to see and decide independently and take the inner nature of the very thing you yourself are into account, you are nobody Architecture knows or cares about.

Do you know where you must go to study architecture? Do you know where it will come to you from? Know where the proper study of it can best be prosecuted? It would not be in colleges. No. It would not be in universities. No. It would not even be by way of the History of Art or any Tradition, because Tradition does not hold this thing we have now. There is no record anywhere in the past of these buildings that today we build from within the man, for the man himself by way of the nature of the circumstance, the nature of new materials. A new kind of Architecture that says, "Here, take me. What I am will please you, not curse you." Invariably this new simplicity does bless and not curse the householder who wants to live in a better way, beautifully.

Now, where did the thought in all this new Architecture come from? Well, we must admit that it has been lying long in the great philosophies of all the ages. But Lao-tzu, the Chinese philosopher, first called attention to the actual thing when he declared (some five hundred years before Jesus, I think it was), "The reality of the building does not consist in the four walls and the roof but in the space within to be lived in." And right there is the central core of this work of the Mind which we call "Organic Architecture." That simple assertion by Lao-tzu is the philosophic center line of our Organic Architecture. Were you to expand that central thought *naturally*, were you to take it to heart as it *is* in itself, it would turn everything you have been taught and everything you see around you upside down and inside out. It is quite impossible for me, here in the time at our disposal to give you more than a mere hint of the tremendous change, the great importance to our future that comes into the life of any individual who begins to *think* thus—*from the within outward.*

All architectures of the world, fascinating though they were, charming as examples of good craftsmanship as they are, and in some cases appropri-

ate in design to the life lived in them—well—I assure you that all of them have been fashioned from the outside inward. The so-called "classic" architectures especially adhered to in our Washington, and promiscuously disseminated by all our universities, was actually a block of sculptured building material (sometimes a stone quarry) cut into shape: wholly a semblance fashioned all on the outside and regardless.

As a matter of fact, if we had this Architecture of the Mind (this Organic Architecture which we are talking about) down there where authority now sits in our Capitol, what would we have? I am sure we would have well-proportioned buildings of gleaming glass well adapted to their purpose; beautiful buildings, glistening with stainless steel; daylight everywhere within; easy circulation. All the structures would be as well placed as they would be conveniently designed for the work to be done in them. Because, after all is done and said, even a bureaucrat has to work a little? So he ought to be able to work under circumstances that can give the people a little more for the money they now pay him. But nothing of that in Washington? People tramping about in miles on miles of empty corridors to reach big waste rooms with little holes for windows. Artificial light burning in the big, dark rooms all day long; proportions all harking back to the grandomania of the Roman Empire. Yes, farther back than that: no thought at all given to the scale of the human beings occupying them.

Now, why? I would like to be able to pass a few suggestion on to you that will enable you to pursue a line of thought for yourselves—or a line of inquiry. We won't say "thought" because, as you know, we use the word altogether too carelessly. So very few of us ever really think! As I have said, we mistake memory, association of ideas, rationalizations, ratiocination—we mistake all that hypnosis and hallucination for thinking. But none of it is thinking at all. Do you realize that a great musician, if he is a performer, does not really have to think? Very few professors ever have to think. A mathematician does not have to think. You can study mathematics all your life and never do a bit of thinking. [The mathematicians and scientists will hardly agree with Mr. Wright. Cf. Mr. von Neumann's essay in this volume in which he discusses the role of the mind in the science of mathematics.—Editor.][1] And do you realize that, so far as we can see now, you can function pretty well and get pretty far along almost any line as a "success" (especially socially or politically) and yet never think one thought? Thinking is an intense concentration of which few people are capable or even aware. It is a going-within, somehow, penetrating into the very nature of some objective: going in after gaining adequate experience of nature—study relating to that particular matter and *staying in* there until you get what you went in after. You may not get it the first time, and you may not get it the second. And you may spend half your life trying to get into that place where the thing you are seeking really is—where it lives—finally to find the plane upon which what we call Reality really lives. But once you do find it—what a reward!

Now, if we would all accept these simple precepts, which are—well, yes, they are *truisms*. But what is a truism but a tested Truth? That is why we say "truism." But often a truism is only something which, repeated often enough, reiterated with faith and conviction enough, is eventually accepted as true. But many of these old sayings so familiar to us from childhood's Sunday-school days on to manhood's success (the sayings of Jesus particularly) are the most fruitful things for the practice of an Organic Architecture that were ever said. Jesus, of all the great moderns—we must call him a modern—was, above all, the greatest exponent of this great modern thought in Architecture—this need of the building coming from within the nature of the circumstances, place, and man to outward Form, as does everything natural. It is in its very nature. And this very naturalness is the secret of its aesthetic beauty always and as well. So if you will carefully study nature in this interior sense, you will soon see how simply true Jesus was to "the lilies of the field": to Beauty. He was (his thought was), and to this day (if you could only take most of the Bible away from him, and take what his disciples tried to do in his name and leave it entirely to him) you would have in Jesus himself one of the most *convincing* advocates of an organic architecture (or organic anything else) who ever lived.

But, of course, when you begin with this inner thing, it is going to do a lot of things to you personally that are not at all pleasant. If you do not look out—if you have not good digestion and plenty of stamina—it is going to make a cynic of you; a pessimistic wise-cracker, because soon you are going to be able to *see through* things at this time in our day and generation. If we were able to see through things as they are just now, I am afraid most of us would want to go out and commit suicide. But the reward for seeing through what is around in this new light is very great—if you can take it.

So, I say that if any of you are going to really become converts to what I am preaching to you tonight, you must first be qualified "to take it." You cannot get too gay with the affair either. I did. I know boys who, when they first got outside the idea, began to swell up. Their hats were not big enough for them. Their clothes no longer fitted around the chest. They would go out and make fools of themselves. It doesn't matter at all how big a fool any man makes of himself, but—and especially (the only thing that really matters)—he should never make a fool of the thing he loves. And I find that is likely to happen to the novice who first gets into and held by this inner faith. Soon faith becomes *conviction* and a performance with him before he has safely got the necessary technique.

Now, good technique (when he does get it for himself) takes all that conceit out of him. By the time he has acquired proper technique (which is the essential justification for his having had this thought of Organic character in Architecture at all), he becomes a great deal more—I will not say "humble" because that word has been much misunderstood. A truly humble man is a very proud man. I have learned to feel that the "conceited" man is concealed beneath the most quietly modest exterior after all. He does not talk much. He will let the other fellow do the talking because he knows he is safe if he does not talk. And, of course, he is much safer.

But now let's get down to some facts. Let's talk about this inner creative impulse in more practical terms. I have been giving it to you haphazard in this random talk—trying to inspire you with an idea of the philosophical center line of this work which I have come here to present to you as Architecture of the Mind: the greatest opportunity and the means of

**Rose Pauson House, Phoenix, Arizona. 1939. Perspective. Pencil and color pencil on tracing paper, 29 x 14".** FLLW Fdn#4011.002

genuine growth. Especially so for Americans if they are ever to be a democratic people.

You must see that as we are we are the only powerful nation alive or dead with no architecture of our own? A great nation with no indigenous aesthetic tradition? Let's disregard this Georgian thing that washed up here on our shores with our English forefathers. Haphazard. We now call that importation "Colonial." But now we can well afford to disregard all that sort of thing. It is a something we are still maintaining because we do not really *know* any better. We keep on living in buildings like these we see all around us, and we have such architecture as we generally have for our universities contaminating the youth of the country with the same old sense of grandomania that went with monarchy. And all because of this curious idea that modern building all should be in league with that of the great past. Young people do become contaminated by falsehood and fakery thus built dead into their school lives in the name of Tradition. They must go away from school believing that sort of thing to be the real thing. I have found that that sort of "habituation" by education is awfully hard for an Architect to undo.

But just about all our first-class American education is living in an atmosphere thus false: atmosphere generated by things that are not essentially true or at all good. Sometimes violently bad. I be-

lieve you cannot do that to the very young minds and ever let youth get out of its education alive—not to say remain there entirely healthy. Is it too late to change the colleges?

Probably so. Therefore I think Organic Architecture should begin in the American home. I have felt that the important thing I could do myself was not to build *big* (so-called "important") buildings. And—well, to start with, a confession, I would not give ten cents for a great . . . in fact, I would accept no commission great or small from any government—to build anything. But the industrial buildings of my country? I do enjoy doing these. And big hotels? Yes—all right. But the homes in which our American people dwell—there is where this idea of something integral, something *of* life and not *on* it, something with which you can live with grave and intimate consideration of the things more excellent—and a feeling that you are somebody in your own right; feel like somebody yourselves because there is a harmony in the atmosphere of things you have created about you. And there is where all that has direct effect upon sensitive growing children. And that should be there at home where they grow up. That, I believe, is where we should first hope to find and attempt to plant this kind of building we are calling Organic.

But I know that we can never get Organic Architecture in America as national Architecture in my

**Sidney Bazett House, Hillsborough, California. 1939. Perspective. Pencil and color pencil on tracing paper, 16 x 9". FLLW Fdn#4002.001**

lifetime or in the lifetime of this generation next following mine except as certain isolated examples can be planted in our hills and in our valleys that will serve as patterns in their coming turn. No. The thing has gone too far. We cannot get a noble Architecture in your lifetime or in the second generation after mine either. Although as it seems just now, seeing so many of you young people together here tonight, perhaps you are waking up. And what a lot to be thankful for! But you will have Organic Architecture for your own when your turn comes to build, although you may be still only the few. What is impressed upon me most deeply and depresses me most is the enormous mass of this great nation; the tremendous *weight* of the thing! Our tremendous specific gravity as a people. What an amazing mass we are now. And how unqualified! When a whole nation—so massive—has its great masses of people nurtured on what can only be a mean motive (the profit motive is the main motive of our civilization), it is no wonder we have developed a materialism probably beyond anything this world has ever known since Rome. What then comes to us next?

I think the Romans had quite the same materialistic quality and pragmatic point of view that we have. Should you happen to look at Roman coins, you will see that we are really the modern Romans.

Head, face, and hair cut are the same. Incidentally, I would remind you that the Great Designer never intended the back of a man's head to be looked at. Nature designed a graceful coverage there. Look at most of our fellow-men from behind when they come out of the barber shop! It is difficult indeed to see them from behind as significant at all, especially if nature didn't paste their ears very close to their heads. Well, that type of blank ugliness is peculiarly Roman. Yes. Just like the Romans in their day, we in our day are the great materialists of the known world. We like to be that. So we look like it. Absolutely by and large, we are becoming the very portraits of the soggy sordid thing we call "Materialism."

So, it is a long ride for you. And a very long way. It will be a very long story for you too. And it will take a sincere love from the Heart. You cannot get it from the Head only or by way of the Hand alone. These will all come inside, and we will come by them all three together as one. But—most important now—let us get it here in our hearts so we may develop love for beauty and then not only feel but know that Truth is Beauty and Beauty Truth. Yes . . . . Keats was right.

And just what is this *quality* we call Beauty (it is quality) that is so lacking in American life today? Why do we have this feeling of uneasy insecurity;

why do we feel that everything we have is phony everywhere—more or less? And it is. There can be no just Fame among us. There can be only notoriety. So perhaps pessimism is justified just because nearly everything on our politico-social top is like the froth on a mug of beer. You have to blow away most of our vaunted intelligence to get to anything beneath that amounts to—say "a hoot in a rain barrel." (I learned that picturesque phrase on the farm.)

So it is important that young life like yours come to our rescue. Everywhere I go I see it. I do not go very often; I do not go for very long. But as I see young America here tonight waking up I have seen it awakening all over this vast country. I am seeing the young men and women of America up on their toes for something they know now very well they have not got. Yes, they have learned to know that they have not got it. They are becoming aware that what we call integrity is missing out of this terrible materialistic picture, however practical the soggy avalanche of Production may be. And, do believe me, there can be no integrity in any civilization without this true love of the Beauty of organic integrity, this deep inner sense of Life itself as something to be lived from the inside out by way of the things that bear the influence of the Spirit made by the Mind.

Yes—I am here tonight to assure you that this Organic Architecture I am perhaps too earnestly preaching is Architecture of the Spirit. As a people we have not known genuine Architecture. Democracy has not yet built a single thing as Architecture. And whenever "they" take a look at our Organic Architecture and I hear them say, "Well, I don't like that," I remember some small-town people who came many years ago to my new home on the hill in southern Wisconsin—Taliesin. They came at a time when I was getting a worm's-eye view of society. They were merely curious of course. That is all . . . (we no longer let people in who are merely curious) . . . well, there was a Dutch door (the upper half standing wide open), and I was lying on a seat inside by the fireplace where the peepers could not see me. In high nasal provincial twang, they commented on what they saw. They thought this and thought that—all very interesting but awfully odd. Then a pause. Quiet. And one of them said, "Well, I wonder if I would like livin' in a place like this as much as I would livin' in a reglar home."

Now, that characteristic incident brings you (and me) to the conclusion of this random but earnest talk. The conclusion shall be a few words concerning such habituation. It is a bad-sounding word—"habituation." When I was a much younger man, I decided to avoid all habits. So, as soon as I found anything I did becoming a habit, I would refrain. "Cut it out." I did. And to the extent that I almost lost my digestion.

But it is certainly true that you can too easily *habituate* a human mind. For a minor instance, look at people coming in on trains from the suburbs, faces all in the newspapers. I guess that habituation must be the dead end of the aesthetic nerve because they would have to have some such deadening were they to bear to live as they do live. That is granted? Right. But, being human, you cannot keep up that monotonous habituation and what goes with it forever. If you are good, it is not good enough. Present habits have to change, and something must come alive from *within* now. The people cannot go on forever with this living death of habituation in which we are sunk. But unfortunately the animal is still of such character and quality that, if human, it can be habituated to anything. So it seems.

I read a story (somewhere) recently about the Nazis putting prisoners of war into a yard paved with cobblestones. The prisoners slept on the paving stones, and (as the story went), after the prisoners were "liberated," for a long time they really could not sleep unless some similar kind of stone pavement were found to sleep on. This instance may seem far-fetched? But, no, it is not too far. This vast city in which you live is just as great a monument to just such *habituation* as that or anything else you can imagine.

In this long struggle to get an Architecture of the Mind born, where is the enemy? Right there. Human habit—"habituation"—is enemy No. 1. And the enemy is he who looks backward toward that to which he has become accustomed as comfort. There (next to the English conscience) is the enemy. Another we have inherited from the British is the next biggest enemy Organic Architecture has had to face. And it is the English Conscience.

Do you know what is called "the English Conscience"? It goes back very far indeed. It is simply this feeling that you can say anything you want to say if you will do things definitely enough the other way; and you can do anything you want to do if you talk the thing enough the other way. Should you have a dirty deed behind you there— so long as you keep it behind you and sing hymns and Christmas carols out in front, you believe you will get away with it. Well, the English do usually. Probably we Americans will as things are. But right there in such hypocrisy is where our next greatest enemy lies.

Now how is it in this prevailing atmosphere made by a false architecture, a phony political system, and education for some purpose or other which I have never been able to understand because it certainly is not on speaking terms with Culture—how in spite of all that footless waste does America still live? It is because America is more Middle West than East. America is not so much on the hard pavements of the East anymore. And America is no longer in Washington; no longer look for America on the coastal strip. (And, by the way, if another war is inevitable, my wife Olgivanna, after a trip east with its inevitable political contentions, suggested that it be fought between Middle West and East). America still lives because she moved west off the cinder heap and hard pavements of English industrialism onto the good ground of the still open spaces.

Now it is not only because I am a native that I am so deeply committed to indigenous character in Architecture though I do want to live to see our country worthy of an architecture of its own. I want to see life get down to something that I see coming as the New Reality—or, no, not a *New* Reality, because Reality is never (or is ever) new. But I do want to see us a great people no longer pushed around but getting something real out of the nature of our own ground by use of the very life we live: get it in our own way by way of the development of our National Mind in our own environment and not depend upon some collection of books where it is never to be found. I know indigenous culture is not going to come to those boys and girls who try to get at it or come by it through books or the present system of education. It is going to come to us from the truly human natures who truly love Nature. I do not mean "love" Nature superficially on general principles only—but those who understand that a brick is a brick and love it because it is just a brick and so use it; those who know by experience why a board is a board and think it is "swell" that it is just a board and so use it. And those few who are learning to know that stone, glass, and steel and all those blessed new things given to us to live by—yes even the machines themselves might have, in themselves, great beauty for human beings if we understood how to use them. And so our Architecture will have that great human knowledge which is imbued with that kind of sympathy for Beauty which craves that same integrity which we are calling an architecture of the mind—Organic Architecture. Let's all give it a chance here where we live. Give it a national break eventually. That break will be when Democracy builds the Architecture of Democracy.

1. John von Neumann. "The Mathematician" in *The Works of the Mind*. Chicago: University of Chicago Press, 1947. pp. 180–196.

**V. C. Morris House, "Seacliff" (Project), San Francisco, California. 1945. Perspective. Pencil and color pencil on tracing paper, 42 x 40".** FLLW Fdn#4303.002

**Solomon R. Guggenheim Museum, New York, New York. 1943. Early proposal (Hexagonal). Perspective. Water color and gouache on art paper, 24 x 20".** FLLW Fdn#4305.748

# WHY I BELIEVE IN ADVANCING UNITARIANISM

**F**rank Lloyd Wright, who himself descended from a long line of Unitarian preachers, in this essay extols the Unitarian faith and emphasizes the resources needed for the Atomic Era and Organic Architecture. Indeed, he makes an interesting amalgam of the three. [Published by the American Unitarian Association, May 1946]

As ONE UNFORESEEN CONSEQUENCE OF A MOST INGLORIOUS war, humanity now stands upon the threshold of a new era. We will probably call it the Atomic Era of the Chemical Revolution. In this revolution lies the possibility of universal power—power that may be to man as the sun overhead, the air he breathes, or the mud under his feet. The Thermodynamic Era (styled by the "West" the Industrial Revolution), out of which we now pass, took us to this threshold.

To turn this possibility of universal power over to militocracy—as a mere weapon, giving the professional politician and our unruly big-production boys a new stranglehold on the future—will never stand up in the light of Unitarian ethics, but the attempt to get the stranglehold is already well under way.

The Unitarian church, always leader in the ethical thought of humanity, is again leading. Decentralization is now as imperative to us as centralization was a century ago. The Church must learn why—and resolve to lead or we will all be led to destruction.

The Church will find that Organic Religion should be allied to Organic Architecture in order to lead the way. That is how the First Unitarian Society at Madison, Wisconsin, sees our situation. That little society is courageously going away from the deadly power-clinch, pig-piling and logrolling (still encouraged by nineteenth-century capitalism), going out to adjacent country to build the small modern "church" that is truly free.

If what we call the Church can't wake our people to the fact that they need be economic slaves no longer, it dies by its own fault. The Church must lead in teaching the why and wherefore of their new freedom to the people, now learning to practice what it preaches. If the Church does not, then Organic Architecture must.

Universal atomic power looms ahead of all our present-day institutions ready to render them all obsolete—looms not so much a danger as a *new expansion of human life on earth*. This great new implement of democratic freedom lies ahead to liberate or destroy as humanity will decide. The Church by its acts should say *Liberate*, though all the interests lining up to fight against the inevitable obsolescence of thermodynamic ways and means say *No*. The

Church must accept atomic energy as the new power of construction. The Unitarian church at Madison has already taken the first courageous step over the threshold of the Atomic Era. Perhaps the Unitarian church is the only church able to see clearly the implications of this new light that makes the promised land of democracy easier for all to see. Universal power is coming to liberate the American people and they are ready to let Mobocracy drop with the dull and sickening thud it will make. By intelligent use of such advantages as the Thermodynamic Age has already brought they will begin to establish democracy not as a potentiality merely, but as the New Reality itself.

The architecture we are calling Organic Architecture could serve the adventure of the church in this emergency at this critical juncture of the life of our civilization. The first step to take is towards *decentralization*. The next step is towards organic *reintegration*. Both steps are the immediate need if a more organic basis for our social and political structure is ever to come out of present degradation. No effort we may make to civilize ourselves now will succeed if the Church does not again assume ethical leadership and, at whatever cost, really begin to practice what it preaches.

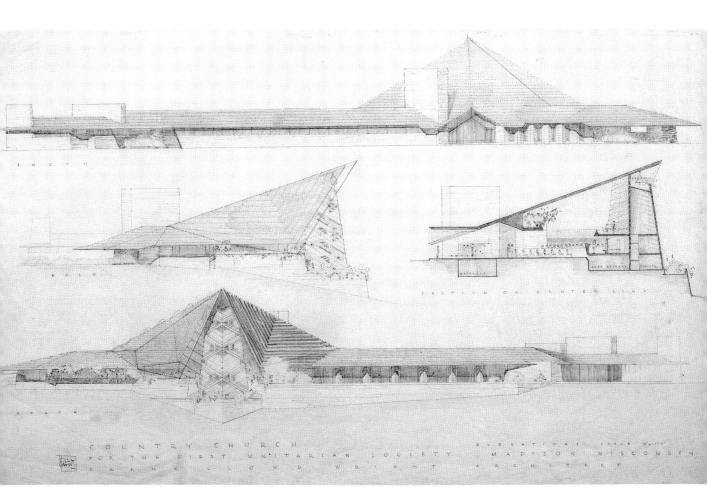

**Meeting House for the First Unitarian Society of Madison, Wisconsin. 1947. Elevations. Pencil, sepia ink, and color pencil on tracing paper, 40 x 24".** FLLW Fdn#5031.014

# STARCHED CHURCHES

*W*right *here reviews a book on present-day (1946) church architecture. As he was writing this, he was also at work on his design for the Meeting House for the First Unitarian Society in Madison, Wisconsin. His design, in every way, is the antithesis of all that he is harshly criticizing in this review. [Review of* The Church Beautiful, *published in the* Christian Register, *August 1946]*

THE BOOK *THE CHURCH BEAUTIFUL* SHOWS HOW FAR the church is today from any feeling for the beautiful, the good or the true. It shows how far anything connected with a church edifice, especially on the little accessories required by church services, is from imaginative inspiration. Have creeds dried up the source from which beauty flows? Even the symbols we see in these proper little churches are wholly insignificant. The church then has become a cliché—a pitiful and feeble repetition where life is concerned?

This little book all too plainly reveals that it has become so. The little "portico" to the tall room with a relic or remnant of the ancient altar at the far end, the pediment under the clock and belfry—the finger above pointing to heaven—the this and the that to the right and to the left, all on a center line! The moribund major and minor axis of the old totalitarian days remains. Is this trying to return and be respectable in our democracy? But what church is democratic or tolerable in the life of a genuine democracy? It is not yet built, I am afraid.

Cannot religion be brought into a human scale? Can it not be humanized and natural? Must "church architecture" be starched stiff as a hard collar and the symbols of worship be no more inspiring than a black bow tie or a pair of suspenders? What is a church? Isn't it a gratifying home for the spirit of human love and kindness? A certificate of faith in man himself as of God and for himself? "Eventually"—you may say. Well, why not now? A pleasant well-proportioned room in human scale with a big fireplace and a plain table for flowers and the Book;—the sky pilot on the floor with his flock—the whole business bright with sun and a wide prospect. I say, let down the too tidy moral tone of the regulation from all concert pitch and relax the whole thing. Why must a church, even on a small scale, crucify the congregation just because Jesus was himself crucified?

Is the painful circumstance of crucifixion, even on a very small scale, any longer appropriate? The whole business of symbols is already too cheap.

**"Memorial to the Soil," Newman Family Chapel (Project), Cooksville, Wisconsin. 1934. Perspective. Pencil and color pencil on tracing paper, 27 x 14".** FLLW Fdn#3710.002

# BUILDING A DEMOCRACY

*In this essay, published as Taliesin Square-Paper Number 10 in October 1946, Wright again professes his unwavering belief in the sovereignty of the individual. He equates organic architecture and a true sense of democracy—both grow naturally, both are from American soil, and both express the nation's ideals. He structures the building of a democracy much as he would a fine work in architecture: "Democracy is not such a form . . . as it is abiding faith in man's indivisible right to himself as himself." He expands the concept of democracy as a form of government and gives it a deeper meaning: "It is only natural or organic architecture, interior philosophy, and a living religion—not the institutionalized kind (I am talking now about the heart and the deep-seated instincts of man)—it is these three alone, organic architecture, interior philosophy, and a living religion, that can make life again creative, make men safe as is good for them, or ever make government tolerable." And once again returning to architecture as the main theme, he writes,*

> *A democratic building is at ease, it stands relaxed. A democratic building, again, is for and belongs to the people. It is of human scale, for men and women to live in and feel at home.*

DEMOCRACY AND ARCHITECTURE, IF BOTH ARE ORGANIC, cannot be two separate things. Neither can democracy nor architecture be enforced, in any sense. Both must come from within, spontaneously. In architecture, as in democracy, this organic or natural way is new to us only because the interior nature of man is still new to mankind, and democracy is still a search for organic form.

Democracy is not so much a form—even were we to find it—or a policy—even were we to make it—as it is abiding faith in man's indivisible right to himself as himself. That faith is the natural essence of manhood and is therefore the only safe foundation for creative building. In so far as the State is concerned, it is the same. It is only the man with self respect who has any respect for others, and so is capable of faith in mankind, and thus of constructing a government. Lacking this sound human foundation, no government can rise above servility and secret hate. Collective security without this foundation *first* is merely illusion. Internationalism without this foundation *first* is coercion.

Man-made codes come in to obstruct, expropriate or punish only when we lose sight of the way to live naturally, as we build, and build naturally as we live.

Unfortunately for us, and the nature of democracy at this moment as well, the way of our literate official architecture is, owing to academic education, utterly inorganic. It is by code, and our way of life therefore is no longer free nor inspired by principle. How can a man's life keep its course if he will not let it flow from within? The democratic code must be designed to *complete,* not to *prevent* the man.

The mass to which we belong calls itself Democracy while betraying the courageous idea that the soulful source of all inspiring life flows from the individual. The other mass is obsessed by the cowardly idea of taking cover under a State supreme with no individual responsibility whatever.

To overcome false ideas, bad work or violent men, democracy has only to mind its own business, stand its own ground, build its own way, the natural or organic way.

Were we genuinely a Democracy this violent division would be resolved, and there would be no adversary.

The structure Democracy must know is the living kind, and that kind of structure is of life at its best for the best of life itself. In itself, organic character is sound social foundation: integral or organic structure grown up from the ground into the light by way of the nature of man's life on earth, the method of building to show man to himself as nobly himself. The true architecture of democracy will be the externalizing of this inner seeing of the man as Jesus saw him, from within—not an animal or a robot, but a living soul. Organic life cannot grow from anything less than the independence of the individual as such—the independence of the individual: his freedom to be true to himself! And since that cannot be enforced it cannot even be standardized.

Force is futile. It can organize nothing. Nor can science help us now. Science has put miraculous tools in our toolbox, but no science can ever show us how to use these tools for humanity. It is only natural or organic architecture, interior philosophy, and a living religion—not the institutionalized kind (I am talking now about the heart and the deep-seated instincts of man)—it is these three alone, organic architecture, interior philosophy, and a living religion, that can make life again creative, make men as safe as is good for them, or ever make government tolerable. These three need each other at this crucial moment as never before. In the light of these three organic inspirations, revived and alive, we could build an organic democracy.

Here in America, if we will only discover what our vast good ground is good for, and use it to build with and build upon, a native culture would come to us from loving our own ground and allowing our ground to love us. A great integrity! The integrity! The integrity we lack!

We have no good reason here in America to give an imitation of a great industrial nation confined to a small island like England, whose only way out is manufacturing. Our entire nation from border to border and coast to coast is still just a neglected back yard while we have this cinder strip here in the East. A marvelous range of individual expression awaits us as a people when we do discover our own ground. Why are houses alike all over America? Why do we think they have to be so? Why are we as a people inhibited so early? Because we build by code. Sometimes I think we were born, live, and die by code. Give us freedom!

Let inspiration come to us the natural way. Why plant more Oxford-gothic on the plains of Oklahoma? Let us mimic no more. If we build in the desert let the house know the desert and the desert be proud of the house by making the house an extension of the desert. So that when you're in the house, the desert seems the house's own extension. The same thought, in the same feeling, goes for whatever we build wherever we build it. Organic buildings are always of the land and for the life lived in the building. They are not merely on a site, they are of it. Native materials for native life where such exist are better than plastics which have to be brought in. According to circumstances, both may be equally desirable.

And this idea that seems to have invaded our country from somewhere that architecture is one thing, landscape architecture another, and interior decoration a third is absurd. In organic architecture all three of these are one.

Whether a structure be life, a building, or a state, why buy more monstrosity?

Look at Washington. Is there a single-minded democratic, that is to say, organic, building there, one sincerely devoted to the nature of its purpose?

Bureaucrats are there to work. How can they work in these miles of stone quarries erected to satisfy a grandomania as insatiable as it is insignificant?

Not satisfied, look at Moscow. The case is much the same. A new civilization, unable to find a way of building that is its own, slavishly reproduces the buildings of the culture it overthrew. It overthrew the great high ceilings, high chandeliers, pornographic statues playing on grand terraces. Only now they want the ceilings higher, five chandeliers where there was one before, and they want it all everywhere, even in the subway!

Not liking Moscow, see London! The greatest habituation on earth sunk in its own traditions, unable to see daylight anywhere—part of its charm, of course.

If you see within at all, you will see the same degradation in all. You will find them poisoned for democracy, one and all militaristic, their columns marshaled like soldiers menacing the human spirit, their opposing major and minor center lines of classic architecture—the true crucifixion.

A democratic building is at ease, it stands relaxed. A democratic building, again, is for and belongs to the people. It is of human scale, for men and women to live in and feel at home.

No wonder we were bound as things were and must struggle to be unbound as things are.

Were we to build a building for the United Nations we could not build for an incongruous idea anything but incongruity. The attempt of the nations now to get together is a hopeful sign. All this struggle is good. I have a feeling—it is only a hunch—that we have to make mistakes; we can't come upon the ideal thing right side up all at once.

I do know that when the home for the United Nations is built it must be a modern high-spirited place of great repose, an unpretentious building, abandoning all specious symbolism, having the integrity of organic character in itself, an example of great faith in humanity. Let the Assembly room be a place of light as wide open to the sky as possible (that influence is auspicious). Make it no screen to hide ignoble fears or cherish native hypocrisy cultured anywhere by any tradition. Like the human being it would prophesy—its basis the earth, its goal the universal.

If the United Nations is to be a success, it is all up to each of us right where we now are, in the citadels of democracy, our own homes. We love to call them our own. We wish to live there the life of brotherly love and creative sensitivity with full individual responsibility. But we want to live as potent individuals craving immortality, believing in ourselves, and therefore in each other, as with worldwide hospitality we strive for the things that seem more fair to live with and to live for.

When the organic architecture of Democracy is allowed to build for democratic life the organic or natural way, we the American people will recover nobility. Our creative sensitivity will then learn from right-minded architecture to see a man noble as MAN, a brick that is a BRICK, see wood beautiful as WOOD (not falsified by some demented painter). We will wish to have a board live as a BOARD and use steel as STEEL—the spider spinning—and we want glass to be the miracle life itself is. We will see, by means of it, interior space come alive as the reality of every building. We will learn that our greatest lack as a civilization is the beauty of organic integrity and that Beauty itself is the highest and finest kind of morality. When Democracy builds it will build the organic way and every man's building—his chosen government no less—will be benign.

If we love Democracy, the way to *do* is to *be*. I can see no fight for freedoms. In a democracy there is only FREEDOM.

# TO A HERO NATION: IRELAND!

**A**lthough the title might suggest a text dealing with the nation of Ireland, that is not the case in this unpublished article. Instead Wright is once again urging decentralization and intelligent planning: "But plan suspicious of all educated planners because our planners (educated far beyond their capacity) jump in on the middle of the problem, splash around and come out. None wet above the ankles. To go deep enough, begin at the beginning, seems a lost Art." That he would entitle the piece "A Hero Nation" reflects his admiration for Ireland, as for Switzerland, for being a small nation yet surviving while being surrounded by large, empirical powers. With the end of the war, architects were atuned to the idea of planning, rebuilding, and remaking the world. Wright pleads for a more enlightened type of planning than had been witnessed in the past.

OBSERVE THE PLIGHT OF "V"! IT IS THE SUCCESS OF Western Materialism! A success that has made of the Western city a bottleneck to be smashed and the plight of that Western city the plight of the world.

But thanks to Production for War we can now see at least that to build the city we need there is no problem of Production. There is only the problem of Distribution.

Isn't Decentralization the only true answer to that problem?

Humanity can meet this now-agonizing problem of Distribution in no other form.

Inhibited distribution (like bad circulation) is now international disease: a death-rate to be faced in consequence. Cure that disease, not be governmental promise-merchants tampering with symptoms but by the structural Surgery removing three radical causes of human misery—Gold, Tariffs, Conscription. No other relief will be needed. Reconstruction will begin.

Let us plan. Yes. But plan suspicious of all educated planners because our planners (educated far beyond their capacity) jump in on the middle of the problem, splash around and come out. None wet above the ankles. To go deep enough, *begin at the beginning,* seems a lost Art. The planners are so confused by the contrary driving pressures of our day

that they have no chance to learn the Scientific Art of beginning at the beginning. But Nature is merciful over there in Ireland as over here in the States. Unnoticed, the City life needs is growing up in the midst of this congestion, abberation and confusion.

If we take heed now new life comes to Civilization. If not—then atomize us.

The New Frontier of a World Culture is very near if the right kind of architectural thinking could come to defend us from the Mass-made producers of things, mass-produced only for the sake of more massive Production: Production for trading purposes now leading only to war!

But now, at least our people know this from the rate of production for War purposes: "the age of Plenty is here and Poverty need never smirch the face of our Globe again" because even the stupendous rate of output for war-fodder could easily be doubled *if so required* and the peoples of the world were allowed freedom to work for Peace and Prosperity.

Replanning our cities? Well . . . is it enough to hire a few popular planners to scrape a few obvious barnacles off their bottoms—put in still more gadgetry somehow and then subsidize the realtors to sail the old Caravels we have kept going in spite of all modern advantages?

# CONCERNING HENRY GEORGE: FREEDOM VS. SPECULATION

*This unpublished article was subtitled "Freedom vs. Speculation," and at one point Wright might have planned to incorporate it into his various texts on Broadacre City. When Wright speaks on the subjects of economics, politics, and government, it is sometimes difficult to trace the centerline of his thoughts. Yet once he relates those topics to architecture, they are right on the mark, striking the center of the note.*

WE FOUND THAT WE MUST FIRST HAVE GROUND FREE IN the sense that Henry George, one of the greatest wise men, predicted free ground—I am not speaking of the single tax. We found that we must have not only free ground as he advocated it but free money, that is to say, money not taxed by interest but money based only upon the National Credit used only as a medium of exchange, and as Henry George specified, ground not held by absentee landlords: the good ground as free to those who could and would make good use of it as Sun and Air. Then we soon ran against another dark place, iniquity there too: we run into the fact that the ideas by way of which society lives, moves, and has its being, were all speculative commodities. A little farther on we began to realize that everything we had to live on (it was during the 1929–36 depression, remember) was some form of speculative commodity. We found that life itself had with us become practically *a speculative commodity*. The matter had, practically, gone so far as that! Of course having everything in life down upon the basis of speculative commodity, you would have naturally a Nation of gamblers. You would have gambling not only as the principle go-getting, money-making device, but see it as the great romance of being. And that is what the system (call it capitalistic—it isn't really) became in America.

# WE MUST SHAPE TRUE INSPIRATION

*When asked to comment about the proposed headquarters for the recently founded United Nations in New York City, Wright responded with this article published in the* New York Times Magazine *on 20 April 1947. The thought of housing the UN in a skyscraper seemed totally inappropriate to him: "The city skyscraper is exploitation, therefore abuse of principle . . . a sinister emblem for world power." On the other hand, he advocated a scheme that would place the building out on the landscape, "where nature speaks and the beauty of organic order shows more clearly the true pattern of all peace whatsoever."*

ENLIGHTENED DEMOCRACY IS STILL IN SEARCH OF A GREAT form and has no great official building it could honestly call home. Like the cuckoo, it nests in homes devised by its adversaries. Language may conceal thought, but when the thinker builds he cannot hide. Limitations and false reactions are then on record to stay. Anachronisms like Michelangelo's dome (a great arch high up in the air on stilts) become symbols of authority.

So, in so far as the U.N. is democratic, the U.N. is in a fix. But, with little hesitation and no embarrassment, the U.N. is willing to make shift. *The Times* wants to know what the makeshift should look like. I believe a number of architects are to answer. No doubt, being total masters of the makeshift, they can. But holding democracy an organic ideal, I believe no man entitled to build anything until individual entity is achieved. The same goes for democratic institutions established in his name.

Isn't his very building just what a man knows about "institution" in a very real sense? He knows the city skyscraper is exploitation, therefore abuse of privilege. So he must know skyscraperism to be a sinister emblem for world power. But if the policeman needs even more glory, the skyscraper would be it.

And empty monumentality like the building that was proposed for Flushing Meadow, showing architecture to be an utter sterility, would bear no comforting assurance of U.N. wisdom nor would it indicate the possession of any depth of humane feeling. So why not wait? Plant grass there on Flushing Meadow. Grass the ground where the proposed U.N. skyscraper would stand. Buy a befitting tract of land, say a thousand acres or more, not too easy to reach. On the land put a simple, adequate shelter where the U.N. mind, without artificial stimulation or immediate recourse to our popular flesh-pot—the big city—might be less likely to "mistake the

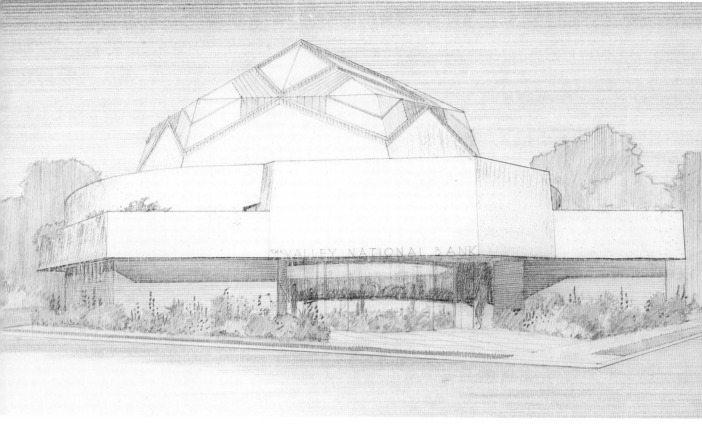

**"Daylight Bank" for the Valley National Bank (Project), Tucson, Arizona. 1947. Perspective. Pencil and color pencil on tracing paper, 25 x 27".** FLLW Fdn#4722.006

driver for the passenger or mistake the passenger for the driver" in the peace of this world.

When a man has fever he doesn't take stimulants, though he may crave them. Humanity is now man-in-a-fever and is that fix likely to yield to the sanity of order by further concentrations and excitements of the standard sort?

In short, no overcrowded urban street is a better place for humane concentration upon the ethics of human progress than a graveyard.

Sequester the U.N. Why does it not itself ask for good ground where nature speaks and the beauty of organic order shows more clearly the true pattern of all peace whatsoever? Then build there in perfect accord adequate shelter for the body and, if possible, shape some true inspiration for the shamless democratic soul of this world's greatest hope.

**Sports club and play resort for Huntington Hartford (Project), Hollywood, California. 1947. Perspective. Pencil, sepia ink, and color pencil on tracing paper, 52 x 35".** FLLW Fdn#4731.020

# PREJUDICE, SIR, IS A DISEASE

*New York City parks commissioner Robert Moses not only disapproved and lampooned Wright's concept of the city when he saw the Broadacre City model, but he also was strongly opposed to the innovative design of the Solomon R. Guggenheim Museum and its eventual construction on New York's illustrious Fifth Avenue. He frequently railed against the collection of nonobjective painting and the building Wright conceived to house it. This unpublished reply from Wright responds to Moses's objections. It seems that the parks commissioner would prefer a museum that would look like a museum, meaning all the museums he had seen in the past. "A thoroughbred like the splendid gift of Solomon R. Guggenheim Museum is bound to make the official bristle because it is no pagan idol either of ancient or modern times," Wright wrote. But being a public official, the architect reminds Moses that he must necessarily cling to the status quo and therefore be fearful of anything new or revolutionary in the way of architecture in New York City. "What he really means is that a building, regardless, should look to him like what he is used to seeing in that line." Although good friends, and cousins by marriage, Wright and Moses continued this battle over the museum for many years, until finally a permit was issued and the building went into construction in the summer of 1956. [Unpublished]*

WHEN OUT OF THEIR OWN FURROW IT IS ALL TOO characteristic of our prophetic power-boys to cling to the "good old ways" where Culture is concerned. This is politic to say the least. Therefore "safe." Perhaps Commissioner Moses is lamenting the press given "ultra modernists" because the spearhead of progress is always news whereas the amorphous avoirdupois that resists it never is until it begins to murder.

Probably that is the reason—too—why the fact that New York City has earned the reputation of being the most provincial city in these United States is not news.

But what Moses, so able in his furrow, regards as "Functionalism," also sometimes seems a fake to me. When any truth-of-being becomes ism, istic, or ite it *is* usually affected rather than organic effect. Any forward movement along lines of the Spirit is likely to have its soiled and soiling fringe. But if men lie, cheat, and steal in the name of God is there occasion to curse God and die?

It does take great natural insight or much intelligent experience for which no official has temper or time to tell good from bad in that super-realm of the Abstract from which modern architecture is derived. What the Commissioner indicates in this matter is that he has neither.

Should any power-prophet with any "edifice-complex," his very own or not, ever successfully interfere in this matter New York City would lose its only real claim to charm: freedom of choice in all human variety adding up to a picturesque human document. The vast city, by force, would settle for the lowest terms of human stupidity once and for all.

What every overgrown village in our democracy needs everywhere is not a dictator or a planner as such. Our cities need more freedom to develop from within—not less freedom. More good sense: something Authority always seems to lack. Far from becoming more simple as our facilities increase, the conditions of life have become complicated until human conflict no longer consists in fighting off the animal in us but in

**Frank Lloyd Wright and Robert Moses, New York, New York. Photograph by Maurey Garber.** FLLW Fdn FA#6804.0001

No doubt "Functionalism" can become the braggart anachronism he says it is. But the world-wide movement from which it is derived cannot. That movement is a genuine enlargement of what all buildings should mean to every human being: an invaluable movement toward a way of life and an Architecture commensurate with the times. It is easier now in the light of Moses' "carte blanche" to understand why that movement's benefits seem so tardy in reaching New York City. Should some pugnacious prophet ever succeed in interfering he will block a blessed release for millions of lives now immured in the city's false facades, fancy stacks of pancakes and downright tombs: all extravagant in the name of "the good old-fashioned."

No power-boy ever yet got out of his furrow to go against the inevitable upsurge of the human Spirit toward more freedom for the individual *when developed from within*, and lived that act down. The Commissioner is squarely up against the ground-swell right now with a prejudice of which dignity in office should be ashamed.

fighting the habits and false symbols of our so-called Civilization itself. The pagan idols of ancient times won't save us or serve us unless we understand them well enough to leave them right where they were.

A thoroughbred like the splendid gift of the Solomon R. Guggenheim Museum is bound to make the official bristle because it is no pagan idol either of ancient or modern times.

I suggest that Robert Moses (the man) actually see the model of the new museum designed as a great gift from a great New Yorker to his own great city for a great purpose. As an individual or an official Moses owed this to himself before, "carte blanche," he generalized so freely concerning this great thing which he reads about in the papers or only hears about from the boys in his backroom where there is ample reason to believe they are blind to the world-wide trend which they choose to see as "functionalism." If the worldwide trend is right the back-room boys are wrong.

But no Moses could be commissioner were he not a strong partisan with a peculiarly stark "edifice-complex" his own or not, and be the more violent as he reached his own limitations.

Sincere lovers of Truth arrive at the "demonstrably better," how? By liberty of demonstration. Should any Moses have the Future brought back to him on a silver platter ready to serve so that such as he might accept or regret it?

I admit that a good copy *is* better than a bad original until the good copy stifles originality. Then we have the inevitable evil of eclecticism: things dead or better dead.

The Commissioner and all that goes with him might have learned from the splendid gift to a backward city, the Guggenheim Museum, to take pride in so shaping the structures that America builds that their natural use and wont is identified *by their actual form*?

Why let some bad habit of association-of-ideas liken a College to a Church, a museum to a morgue or the Roman baths of Caracalla. Or urge an American's dwelling to ape some foreign Palazzo? Since we are facto minded anyway why not make the Factory a humane, attractive work-place and not so much like Warehouses or Prisons? Why make a Hospital (or even a Sanitarium) look like a Cathedral or a Fire-engine-house like a Chateau?

Solomon R. Guggenheim Museum, New York, New York. 1943. Elevation (early proposal). Pencil and color pencil on art paper, 24 x 20". FLLW Fdn#4305.007

And, by the way, why if a "Workshop for Peace" must be got into the street, should it resemble a tall Factory-for-getting-money-out-of-Office-space? Etc., etc.

In this very connection the New York Moses used language very like that used by the modern architect. But what a difference behind his words! What he really means is that a building, regardless, should look to him like what *he* is used to seeing in that line. So outside his furrow the able Commissioner (likes to liken himself to a mole) is only a standpatter or lid-sitter for the Usual.

And why—I ask—this sob over the loss of ornaments (usually the equivalent of casual earrings or nose rings or diamonds-to-market)—next breath extolling the lack of them in New Jersey?

In the course of his facetious diatribe the "Doctor" says "symbolism is almost as important as use"? Is it? Well . . . to believe that one is to reduce man to the level of an undertaker always functioning at the wrong funeral. The inventions of man have revolutionized the conditions of life even if he fails to profit by them. Does "his honor" really know where good engineering becomes architecture and where good architecture becomes engineering? If he did New York would lose him. Posterity would reach right back and snatch him for Progenitor.

And, "Sir," we have no right to think of what the reactions of "discriminating" (ergo, *habituated*) people would like any fraction of a century hence any more than we have a right to imitate those any fraction of a century past. The inventions of man have so changed all that and will so change the Future that our day is *now* or never. Already the great "revulsion" prophesied by Moses as the Future is here. But it is here as revolution and entirely the other way around. World-wide, the human mind is turning from silly symbolism, senseless association of ideas, nasty, musty or hasty lives to deeper feeling and clearer Vision. As the conditions of Life change honest Architecture is searching for Forms commensurate with the change wherever it is organic. And that search is disciplined from within by higher ideals than any quoted by New York's rash Park-commissioner in his defense of an old offense which he cannot recognize as false and, if he could, can see no remedy for but to die in it, of it, and for it, worlds without end, amen.

# PLANNING MAN'S PHYSICAL ENVIRONMENT

**B**efore proposing a plan for "man's physical environment," Wright, in this especially lucid article, addresses some of the problems facing the United States and its society. Education? "As a people we are educated far beyond our capacity." The plunge into the atomic era? "And now this cataclysm, the atomic bomb of science, has thrown us off our base, undoubtedly making all we have called progress obsolete over night. . . . The push-button civilization over which we were gloating has suddenly become a terror." As for politics, Wright recommends a brief recess of ten years for power seekers; for the State Department and the Presidency, "utter abolition"! Cities, for him, were always anathema, and he observes, "No city can maintain itself by way of its own birth rate, and a glance at history shows us that all civilizations have died of their cities." Freedom, as the nation defines it? "Men born free and equal? Before the law, yes, perhaps—but the coming man does not believe that all men are born free and equal because he cannot. . . Only a state politician out for re-election at a Fourth of July picnic could say we are all born with the same brain power." But, after tearing into the fabric of these time-worn predicaments, Wright then proposes the panacea:

> Only when the heart is open is it fit to receive teaching quick with life. Eyes must be there and be opened first. Eyes must be there as well as ears, and be opened first before illusion, superstition or prejudice may be expelled. . . . The remedy is more Freedom . . . greater growth of Individuality—more men developed by the way of self-discipline from within the man. . . . Under the watchful care of the people themselves, government must take its place down under, not up above the right of the individual to be himself.

[Journal of Modern Culture, *Berkeley, California, March 1947*]

MY FAVORITE UNIVERSITY IS PRINCETON. MEMORY OF pleasant times here long ago while delivering the Kahn lectures brings me from Arizona desert to Princetonian revels of intellectual fellowship. I have the same nostalgic love for Princeton as for the great founders of our Republic, and yet, I believe that were all education above the high school level suspended for ten years, humanity would get a better chance to be what humanitarian Princeton itself could wish it to be. Our thinking throughout the educational fabric has been so far departmentalized, over-standardized and so split that like a man facing a brick wall, counting bricks, we mistake the counting for reality—and so lose or ignore the perspective that would show us the nature and wherefore of the wall as a wall.

As a people we are educated far beyond our capacity. And we have urbanized urbanism until it is a disease—the city a vampire—unable to live by its own birthrate, living upon the fresh blood of others, sterilizing the humanity for which you, Princeton, have always stood. And now this cataclysm, the atom bomb of science, has thrown us off our base, undoubtedly making all we have called progress obsolete over night. Prone to our own destruction, we may be crucified upon our own cross! To me, an architect, the hide and seek we have played with, the further revelation of the nature of the universe we inhabit as parasites or gods (it is up to us) has been a ghastly revelation of the failure of our educational, economic and political systems. The push-button civilization over which we were gloating has suddenly become a terror. But instead of the agony appropriate in the actual circumstances, we are even more smug and heedless than usual. A little flurry—that's all. The military mind is a dead mind—so, no surprise to find that reaction as it was. The journalistic mind, a reporter's mind, left to the humorist the only real attempt to arouse the people to reality: not an explosive bomb only, but a fantastic poison-bomb that made their habitation in cities no safer than an anthill beneath a ploughshare in a field.

So, my Princeton, I say, let's pause and consider this lack of vision that not only hides from us the better nature of ourselves but makes us unable to see further than our own furrow. Weighted down by our own armor, insatiate with this voracity we call speed, huddled the more—though not suitably in panic, it is conceivable that the country we now call ours may go back to the Indians. Escaping the bombing—the probable apex of our civilization, (as they will) they might easily come and take it back again quietly in the night; proving that barbarism is, after all, better suited to human life here on earth than what we have too carelessly called civilization.

In this fearful emergency, the state (as such) has proved utterly unworthy of the allegiance accorded it by the sons and friends of American education. Politics, in any perspective afforded by this insensate clamor and clash of power-seekers is sadly in need not only of the brief recess of ten years or more, but utter abolition of the State Department and the Presidency as it now exists. We should strip the Capitol from the periphery of our nation and plant it nearer the heart of the country. We must realize there can be no real separation between Religion, Philosophy, Science and the great Art of Building. They are one or none. But in this petty partisan particularity now everywhere so prevalent we find education the more divided into petty specialities, and those most advantageous to the ignoble profit and party system we have so foolishly made the very core of our Republican life.

So let us rise for a moment from the furrow to take the view, and soon, with disgust, we will dismiss petty politics for the prostitution it really is. Instead, let us view excess urbanism. . . . This pig-piling or human-huddling we call the city. It is true that to very many the city is a stimulus similar to alcohol, ending in similar degeneracy or impotence—no city can maintain itself by way of its own birth rate, and a glance at history shows us that all civilizations have died of their cities. To others like our good old Doctor Johnson, the city is a convenience because every man is so close to his burrow. But read "hole in the wall" now for "burrow." Nevertheless, American cities were dated for our humanity long before the cataclysmic poison-bomb of the Chemical-Revolution appeared on the horizon.

Then, how now? Are not concentrations of humanity madness or murder? We might remember the Hindu proverb, "A thousand years a city and a thousand years a forest." The UN is, of course, the present hope for escape and survival. The UN itself has taken refuge in a New York skyscraper. Can it make good?

And we must view Education, wherein this salt and savor of "work as gospel" is gone out. The gymnasium has taken its place. The higher education is busy taking everything apart and strewing the pieces about in the effort to find what makes it tick; failing to put it together again, it cannot make it click. It cannot because it cannot or will not go back with the *organic* point of view to begin anything at all. Education, like the city planning of short-haired experts for short-haired moles, is either a splash in the middle of something—or else, like some tangled skein of colored worsted, seeking any desired strand, it comes out only a short piece of any particular color. Continuity and unity? They are gone. So education is almost as helpless to confront this ghastly emergency we are blindly refusing to face as is the state.

Next, if not in order, let us view our Ethics. Men born free and equal? Before the law, yes, perhaps—but the coming man does not believe that all men are born free and equal because he cannot. As a millenial aspiration? Yes, but it is fanaticism here on earth. Such a world implies total death. Struggle makes our world what it is—not struggle for equality but for supremacy. That struggle is the process of creation; inequality is the very basis of creation. In the brain lies the chief difference between men. Only a state politician out for re-election at a Fourth of July picnic could say we are all born with the same brain power.

Let us now glance askance at our "Production." Naturally, everybody, everywhere, cannot be taught to love, appreciate and assimilate Art or Religion. It is impossible to impart to any man one single grain of truth unless he has the undeveloped germs of it within him. Buddha said, "A spoon may lie in the soup for a thousand years and never know the flavor of the soup." Only when the heart is open is it fit to receive teaching quick with life. Eyes must be there and be opened first. Eyes must be there as well as ears, and be opened first before illusion, superstition or prejudice may be expelled. Architecture, the great Mother Art, is in itself the highest knowledge-in-action of which we have any knowledge and cannot be bought or even acquired from books. One good look at an actual building, and a man has found what no reams of writing or years of teaching could give him—providing he has eyes to see.

And what are our buildings? Education and two wars have all but killed this germ of creative thinking. And so, creative work for us—especially in building—is all but destroyed. This amazing avalanche of material, we call production, seems to have its eyes shut to all but destruction. The standardizations it practices are the death of the soul, just as habituation kills any imaginative spirit. So within this welter of the misapplied wealth of knowledge, with so little realization—wherein consideration and kindness are so rare, why not develop a little *integral know-how*? Only spirit affords that.

Now come our G.I.'s, devastated by war, to be further devastated by four more years of education. Why send more G.I.'s, by way of government money they will themselves repay or their children will repay, to school? Why not subsidize land and transportation for them to relieve intolerable immediate pressures instead of sending them back to hard pavements, to trample or be trampled upon further by the herd? Why not get the boys out where they can get in touch with and be touched by their own birthright: the good ground? Give each man an open chance to make his own environment beautiful, if possible, and restore to him what he most needs: the right to be himself. If, owing to the false doctrines of artificial controls or of economic scarcity—making and maintaining black markets now, they are unable to build, why not throw natural roads open to immigration from countries where the skills have not been cut back by ignorant labor unions emulating still more ignorant employers? The only requirement for immigration to our Democratic society should be only common decency and trade skills. Then not only would the G.I. learn from them and by the natural working of law of supply and demand have a home, but all Americans would soon have better ones and have them by their own efforts.

No, no assembly line is the answer either for him, for you, or for me—and that means not for our country. Decentralization of our American cities and intelligent utilization of our own ground, making natural resources more available to him, is his road, yours and mine, to any proper future as a Democracy for which we may reasonably hope. Essentially, we are a mobocracy now. Our present extreme centralization is a bid to slavery. All down the line, a bid-in by a short-sighted, all to plutocratic industrialism.

But the right to strike still belongs to the American people as well as to American labor unions. The time has come for that strike. I find it increasingly hard to believe that a free people can be so be blinded to the nature of their own power as our people have been by their own foolish credulity. Do they want to keep their eyes shut? Perhaps so.

The remedy? No remedy will be found in more statism. That is more static, truly. No, the remedy is more Freedom . . . greater growth of In-dividuality—more men developed by the way of self-discipline from within the man. Today, especially, the most cowardly lie disseminated by the congenital cowards among us, as well as by Church, School and State, is this lie that "I, the State, am the people." In a Democracy where the people remain a people, the people do not understand the State any more than the superstition that the people call "Money." In a true Democracy the people are bound to suffer the State as against their own customs and natural rights. Democracy cannot love government! Government is its policeman, privileged by the people themselves to obstruct, expropriate or punish. Under the watchful care of the people themselves, government must take its place down *under*, not up above the right of the individual to be himself.

"Butterfly-Wing Bridge" (Project) for regional development, Spring Green, Wisconsin. 1947. Perspective. Pencil, ink, and color pencil on tracing paper, 45 x 34". FLLW Fdn#4723.002

# TO HOWARD

From 1908 and through 1929 Wright published articles in the Architectural Record. But when Howard Myers, editor of the Architectural Forum, approached Wright in 1936 requesting publishing rights to the new S.C. Johnson Administration building in Racine, Wisconsin, Wright responded, "My dear Mr. Myers: I guess I will have to abdicate (I still feel obliged to my old friend Dr. Mikklesen of the Record, who when I was in deeper distress than at present gave me an all-time 'high' for a series of articles for the Record ['The Nature of Materials,' at $500.00 an article] in favor of the new Forum whose acquaintance I have yet to make. My clients have intimated that they prefer The Forum. So I accept for myself (and for them) your offer as outlined in your letter of November 27th."[1]

A strong and affectionate friendship developed between architect and editor. The monograph issue of January 1938 grew out of that relationship, and again, ten years later, Myers planned another monograph issue due to be published in January 1948. Myers, however, took ill in the summer of 1947, and Wright wrote him saying,

I have worried about you a lot and needed to know the good word. Would have written as soon as I heard you were back in again but the trouble is: already too much of us and too many too often. We (your friends) can't spare you to sickness. But we can't be greedy either when you are sick. You are a hard case, Howard, but you will come through. Your love of life and vitality is so great. Conserve your strength, man. Easy to say relax—be lazy—but I know how hard it is. . . . Affection,[2]

On 18 September 1947, Myers died. Wright dedicated the January monograph issue to him with these words. [Published in Architectural Forum, January 1948]

JUST AS THE FORUM OF JANUARY 1938 WAS YOURS SO THIS issue of January 1948 is yours. We were working on it together when I last saw you a day before you left and whatever this number of your magazine may mean is here dedicated to you. I saw no indication that you were going so soon, so had no chance and now have no need to say Goodbye. In truth I am unable to believe that you have gone—sure that what is you will see this work, as always, with the sympathetic and approving vision of an even greater spirit.

We who loved the humor in your eyes and wit upon your tongue shall miss you but Architecture will not lose you. While fashioning a magazine for "profit" in equivocal times you steadily upheld the standards of Freedom and Truth. For a needy profession you greatly served despite its sense of itself.

A heart as deep as yours we see but seldom coupled with the fine discrimination you possessed or such loyalty to friendship.

Your helping hand reached this work some ten years ago at a time when something resembling neglect at home confronted it and you helped to change all that to something resembling appreciation. The end is not yet. You made *The Forum* on paper a Forum in fact. Your devotion to Architecture as a great Cause held true to its course as you steered your charge between the shoals of avarice and false-pride toward a more generous end.

And now young men in Architecture, everywhere, owe to Howard Myers more than to any journal or any school anywhere. They looked to what you were and did with brightened hope. They look upon you now with gratitude, sure of the sympathy and understanding that is as surely, love. To them you were and are the Future that is Now.

1. FLLW to Howard Myers, 7 December 1936.

2. FLLW to Howard Myers, 19 July 1947.

**Howard Myers, *Architectural Forum*, New York. Photograph by C. W. Huston, PIX Inc.** FLLW Fdn FA#6737.0001

# HARUM-SCARUM

*There is a great deal more sarcasm in this article than in a previous address delivered at Princeton University a year earlier. Wright, seeing some of the same problems he voiced while at Princeton worsening over time, continued to react to the national fear of Communism, the ongoing struggles between the antagonists in the United Nations (U.S.A. and U.S.S.R.), and the worship of the dollar: "The American dollar was made so almighty by our expert engineering at Bretton Woods that we now have to give it away to foreign nations to enable them to buy anything at all with it." He perceived the current foreign policy as a sorry spectacle, a vicious interference into the internal lives of other nations. His cures were rather extreme, to say the least. But he concluded with a four-point program that he admitted would constitute a dangerous threat to the "Almighty Dollar." [Taliesin Square-Paper Number 12, May 1948]*

LEADING UP TO THE LAST WAR ISOLATIONIST SERVED AS smear-word for smoke-screen for war. Now leading up to the next war, Communist serves as smear-word for smoke-screen. To read the corporate press one would think that Russia invented Communism whereas—any intelligent man knows—it was a well-defined movement in every civilized country before the Soviet was born. Thirty-four years ago when I was building the Imperial Hotel in Japan the Imperial police would hide in the basement to watch communist meetings in Hibiya Park, opposite the building. But I never saw any action taken by them.

To find and hold a faith for the "Haves" and the "Have-nots" alike, in our world, has proved most difficult. Until Democracy appeared there was no such faith. But Democracy is that faith now when and if understood and lived up to. As certainly, if our Nation does understand democratic principles it does not live up to them. Every nation on earth knows this only too well. Were we ourselves actually to un-derstand Democratic principles and sincerely put them into effect there would be nothing for us to fear from Communism or any other "ism" on Earth. At bottom Soviet Russia wants what we want but believes in a different way to get it, that's all. Seeing the way the Have-nots have fared throughout the world, notwithstanding our democracy, what we brag about somehow doesn't convince her. The issue as a matter of course is as old as Government itself. Only a truly Democratic nation can solve it for the world, I believe. But just what and where now is Democracy? Were we to get that straight and get together to act upon it we would have no enemies in this world. Least of all would Russia be our enemy. If you take one good, straight look at the present political scene in these United States you will not find anywhere in it sufficient organic integrity to add up to one honest man! Hypocrisy is a taint in everything everywhere. The political parties are unwilling (or unable) to practice what they preach. Secret agreements; buying governments by putting a few dollars taken from the pockets of the Haves to put into pockets of the Have-nots just to stem for a moment their ever-rising tide, does not work! Scaring opponents with the super-secret A-bomb hasn't yet worked nor will it ever work because whoever uses it first seals the doom of Civilization.

There is more beneath the present world-situation than is allowed by the "Haves" to appear on the surface except as the stir brings it to light for a moment—now and then. The American dollar was made so almighty by our expert engineering at Bretton Woods[1] that we now have to give it away to foreign nations to enable them to buy anything at all with it. While at the same time the same dollar is worth so little at home that it now takes three to five dollars to buy what a dollar would have bought before it became almighty: say "B. V." . . . (before Victory). And as we now go head-on with our heroes we may soon discover that what we call Barbarism is better fitted to survive here on Earth than Civilization! An instance? When barbaric peoples went to war and came back with heroes (as a matter of course) they would give their heroes everything a hero might desire say for a year: the top of wine, women, song and riches to any extent. Then they took their heroes out and executed

them with suitable pomp and adequate ceremony. And that was that. Wouldn't something like that go far in the direction of Peace right now?

Because of this military pageantry the foreign policy of our Nation is so ostentatiously making toward war after war after war, are we not compelled to see some wisdom in this policy of the barbaric tribe? Least of all do we want heroes for executives. Policy should not be made by executives. If the people have no will or vision to their credit they deserve to perish and they will. Heroes won't save them.

Seeing also the entrenched position Money has taken to itself in the circumstances this malignant matter of conscription should also receive intelligent proscription. Eligible for conscription first should be the children of all Citizens living as appointees of Government; next all salaried employees of Government; next all Governors themselves of whatever description. And, finally all wealth above $25,000 per unit should be confiscated by Government to wage war wherever and when war be declared by that Government.

If Peace is ever to be put upon a Democratic basis, some such arrangement seems to come near wisdom. The three million five-hundred thousand employees, etcetera, "we-the-people" are carrying

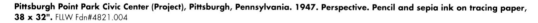

**Pittsburgh Point Park Civic Center (Project), Pittsburgh, Pennsylvania. 1947. Perspective. Pencil and sepia ink on tracing paper, 38 x 32".** FLLW Fdn#4821.004

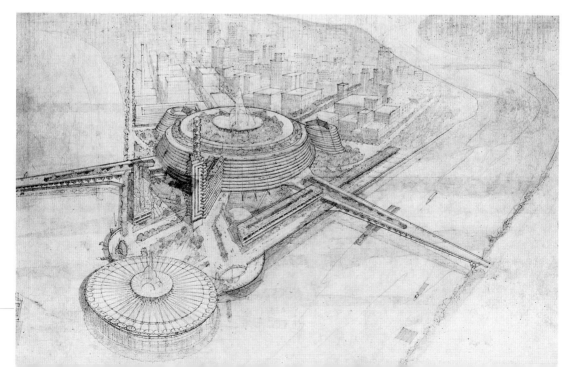

now would go far to give us any army we might really need. But the category of heroes, by all means, should come under laws similar to those so wisely adopted by barbaric tribes in behalf of tribal peace.

To deal with our ubiquitous professional propagandists and all agitators they should be required to refrain from any connection whatever with money—either their own money or the money of others. If this requirement were either secretly or obviously violated they should be taken out and condemned to Hollywood for life. This provision would not entirely prevent the evils of playing the game their way but might show it up enough to make it possible for a real citizen now and then to qualify for public office. Were the limitations herein suggested placed squarely upon the circumstance of Office they would probably operate to cut officialdom down to where it belongs in a Democracy: the least common denominator in a society that could call itself Democratic and look itself in the face.

Foreign policy has made such a spectacle of itself that it should also receive our drastic attention. This whole process of professionalized expert interference with lives of the people of other Nations should be made liable to the charge of meddling—meddling with the private affairs of others. This charge in any well-constituted Democracy would be a cardinal offense. The offending expert should be summarily handed over to the tender mercies of the foreign nations thus offended. However, mercy might be recommended because it is quite impossible for any such to learn better as "Internationalism" (such be-meddlement is now so called) is the smoke-screen of all smoke-screens for Profit in some one or another of its infinite disguises.

Since Democracy is the only open challenge ever made to the age-old Autocracy of the Haves while dealing with the Have-nots and Communism finds the worst features of Autocracy essential to dealing in favor of the Have-nots, why must we do likewise ourselves? It takes the courage of independent responsibility to become and more than common courage to live as a Democrat. Security for him must depend chiefly upon his Freedom. Why not

then instill a little world-confidence in our own Faith in ourselves instead of the police by enacting some of the more obvious rules and regulations for insuring democratic Peace?

First we should ourselves know the basis of Peace to be these fundamental Freedoms:

1. No conscription of manhood.

2. No economic constriction by gold-standard.

3. No tariffs; instead open trade agreements openly arrived at.

4. Based upon character and skills inter-immigration among all peoples of the world alike to insure world-cooperation.

These essential freedoms have never been allowed to show in any official peace talks in our country or anywhere else. I suppose these "Freedoms" are so dangerous to the Almighty Dollar that even to mention them would either seem trite or else frighten the delegates. In fact, the Dollar-fight is all that we have seen tried so far to insure the Peace of the World!

The U.N. has not been really interested in anything but this wrestle for Power. So far as I can see the spectacular prizefight staged by the U.N. between the U.S. and the U.S.S.R. that is where its interest (and such usefulness as it has) really seems to lie. And the grand prize? Well . . . when "we-the-people," credulous and timid as we are, do really find out it will be something to see the turnover—some of it in newly made graves.

Meantime one formula forever practiced alike by all Authority either autocratic or so-called benevolent is "scare the people"! If you can scare the people you can huddle them where you will. Scare them a little more and they will shoot each other. Scare them enough and they will even go out and shoot themselves.

So far, this simple formula has always worked for Government.

When will Democracy take the horns from these belligerent rams in our National ram-pasture and set them all peacefully at work upon their real business of more and better sheep?

1. United Nations Monetary and Financial Conference held July 1–22, 1944, at Bretton Woods, New Hampshire, created the International Monetary Fund and the International Bank for Reconstruction and Development.

# CONCERNING HOUSING

*In this unpublished article about housing Wright brings to the fore the faults as he sees them developing across the nation at that time. Many of his previous observations are worked into the text: cities as overgrown villages, destined to perish; a push-button civilization now threatened even more by the atomic bomb; the United Nations as a premature hope for survival; the futility of hoping that good housing could be realized under the control or mandate of government; the rush to erect enormous high-rise buildings as a cure for housing, which Wright regarded as not only compounding the urban problem but making it far worse. He often commented on these high-rise developments as doing nothing more than transforming the slums of the body into the slums of the soul. The results—general disappointment and dissatisfaction with such housing—have proven him correct. As he wrote in the article, "Government 'housing' by this insensate bureaucracy is the new slum in any perspective afforded within this clash and clamor of black-marketeers."*

WE OF THESE 48 UNITED STATES ARE FOOLISHLY URBANIZING professional urbanism until today this is our most dangerous disease and the big American City has become a vampire unable to live by its own birthrate. Our big cities—overgrown villages—are living upon rural blood and sterilizing the humanity for which Democracy has always stood. Now comes this cataclysm—the A-Bomb! Undoubtedly all we call Progress is made obsolete over-night and prone to our own destruction we may be crucified upon our own cross if our "pilots" have their way. To an architect advocating organic Architecture the game of hide-and-seek our big-production-boys play with this further revelation of the nature of the universe we inhabit as parasites or gods—(it is up to us)—has been ghastly revelation not only of utter failure of religious, economic and educational systems—our Architecture goes along—but as certainly revealing the lack of any humane *foundation* for the economic ways and means of good housing for our people. This push-button Civilization of ours over which

we foolishly gloated suddenly becomes a nameless terror! But instead of any housing activity appropriate in the circumstances we are even more "set," smug and heedless in what we do than we were before. A little scare up top—that's all. No change until "big producers" get hold of the bomb? Meantime scare the neighbors with it. An amusing slogan appeared in a recent New York parade: "Take the uniform off the bomb and put it in overalls."

As for that uniform—the military mind is a dead mind. Napoleon himself confessed this shortly before he died—so, no surprise to find that reaction what it was. Strangely enough the journalistic mind (a reporter's mind) left to the humorist (*The New Yorker*) the only real attempt to arouse the people to the ghastly reality: a fantastic poison-bomb to make habitation in cities no safer than an ant hill beneath a ploughshare in a field.

Why not, then—for God's sake—in the name of "housing"—pause? Consider this lack of vision on our part! Not only are we hiding from sight of the world the better nature of ourselves as a people with faith in their own political philosophy but we are no longer able to see out of our own furrow. We are a Nation determined to be weighed down by its own armor. Insatiate with this voracity we call speed we are huddling ourselves the more, regardless!

In this or any realistic view of our present plight, our housing increasingly subjected to the most enormous bureaucracy ever devised is what we have to show for our "blood, sweat, and fears." The State in this connection has proved utterly unworthy the allegiance accorded it by the democratic friends of indigenous culture. Government, "housing" by this insensate bureaucracy is the new slum in any perspective afforded within this clash and clamor of black-marketeers.

A glance at History will show that all industrialized civilizations died of their Cities—in other words died of Industrialism impinging and imposing upon Agrarianism.

The Chemical Revolution is here now!

Are we not then where further concentrations of humanity such as our big Cities and big housing projects are either madness or murder?

UN is—or was—our premature hope for escape and survival. But UN itself has taken refuge on New York City streets in a Nazyish New York skyscraper just like all the other money-making establishments around it. Is the Democratic culture of the world deeply concerned over this sinister symbolism? What evidence?

In any long view we must see that what we call higher Education—that is to say Education with all song, salt and savor of native work by native workmen gone out of it—is tragedy where any hope of good buildings or happy lives might be. Why all this inflation of "schooling"—when work is so badly messed up back there at home! No one there now with skills to build houses or take care of anything at all. Union or no Union we have few workmen left anywhere and mostly no good. Pride in craftsmanship is a myth or a memory.

Now acute housing-shortage might be relieved by admitting, say, three and one-half million workers from abroad: Germany? Siberia? Yes. Anywhere. Skills and decency should be the only re-

quirements for admission: much as it was in '49 when so many of our best citizens got here. But try and get this freedom while the Politicians sleep with one eye open on the Labor union!

Current Housing, on account of legislative folly, is more and more an assembly-line affair. Like current big-city-planning our efforts to go ahead with planning more humane and organic schemes is just a splash in the middle of something. I can find neither continuity nor unity anywhere in the Government effort nor in any big-boy Housing, anywhere above the belt. Useless to inquire what Foundation under the whole Housing structure! It is in the Black Market now and has been there for nearly five years.

What we are now calling Building is merely a stupid attempt at standardizing people themselves by Government and the exploiting of material big-production boys. But both big-boy and Government are quite as helpless to confront this ghastly emergency in human-life and as blindly refusing to see as the peoples are themselves.

Security? Well—the Democrat finds the security he asks for if his Freedom and fair protection for him *as an Individual* are reasonably sure: His own sense of responsibility to himself makes him respectful of others. Faith in himself is the right basis for Faith in his Fellow Man. That *Faith* standing up straight *is* Democracy.

And since we are on the subject of democratic housing, glance—askance—at this vast ocean of material, not alone what is lying on the bottom of the sea but the great deluge of production that gave us what we are trying so hard to celebrate as Victory: the "Victory" that gives us benefit of fantastic prices for our big "housing" or anything else. We are realizing that "Victory" must for its own continued salvation give us war after war after war!

Good building cannot (or ever could) be bought ready-made by machine, nor can it ever be acquired from books or prosecuted by Government—*alive*! One good look at a truly organic building scheme and a man has found what no years of teaching could ever give him—he sees building *alive*—provided he has eyes to see. Most free men have them if they dared open them.

**Cooperative Homesteads (Project), Detroit, Michigan. 1942. Perspective. Pencil, ink, and color pencil on tracing paper, 35 x 28".**
FLLW Fdn#4201.001

Well—open them now and see our cities! Yes—but see our housing! Promiscuous education and two wars, with a next one in sight, have all but killed the germ of creative-thinking so far as organic building on a good foundation goes. Creative work in building a Nation or houses for citizens is all but destroyed by this amazing avalanche of mechanized material for the total mechanization which we are now expected to learn to call "*Production,*" or else! This seems to have shut our eyes to all but destruction. Such standardizations as "authority" now wants to practice on householders or house-keepers are the death of the manliness of the man and the individuality of his home—just as any routine habituation must kill his imaginative Spirit.

Within this welter of misapplied wealth and technical knowledge rampant—technical knowledge wherein consideration and *kindness have a place is as rare as building-skills,* has no humane realization anywhere in it. So why not develop in our youths a little *integral know-how* by *inviting them to go to work* instead of giving them money to go to school, book under one arm, wife under the other in a Quonset hut, baby's diapers out on the line?

Only experience affords that know-how of the spirit which we may have already lost to sterile technique. Paper-certificates cannot substitute for experience. "What a man does *that* he has" and his own home should be something he does or at least something in which *he* is represented.

G.I.s came back devastated by the war-eye view of humanity to be further devastated by four years of school, theirs by way of government-money they must repay. Or their children must. Housing for them? Why didn't we subsidize good ground and transportation to relieve intolerable immediate pressures instead of sending them back on hard pavements to further trample on or be trampled by the herd?

Why not get the boys out there where they get faith in themselves as men; out there where instead of a book they could be taught the touch with their own birthright—the good Ground? Good individual housing for them would soon come along with that opportunity and that is the kind of *planning* we should be interested in. Why not *give* each citizen in our country an open chance to make his own environment the basis of a good livelihood and make it as beautiful as might be possible to him? No—not merely *possible*, make it *probable*! Why not restore and protect what he most needs: the right to be himself? If, owing to Fascist doctrines of artificial controls—the false economic-scarcity of a money-system now chiefly interested in maintaining more military establishments—neither the men nor we are able to build houses for ourselves, why not open our doors to immigration from all countries where skills have not been cut back by ignorant labor-unions emulating penny-wise employers? Unions by killing off apprenticeship to keep wages high have already put themselves on "the assembly-line." *They are there to stay!* At this moment but for political chicanery the only requirements for immigration to our Democratic society should be common decency and trade-skills. Not only would the G.I. then have a chance to learn from the skilled immigrant something so fundamental to his immediate need, but soon, by the natural working of the law-of-supply-and-demand, he, we, (and they) would all be living in better homes *of our own*. These 48 United States we call "America" would soon have beautiful organic homes by way of our own attitude toward all human life.

No "assembly-line" can be the right answer for laborer, G.I., you or me. That means, not for

our country! If Democracy is to prevail *we must practice what we preach*. First comes decentralization of our big American cities; the subsidizing of transport for the needy to the open spaces; intelligent sponsoring of agrarianism on individual ground thus making the natural resources of life more available to every good man. Decentralization is the nearest open road to any probable future for which we, as a democracy, may reasonably hope. Or else—bring in fascism to stay and the big Bomb will drop. Democracy is the only form of society able to eventually reconcile the haves and have-nots without force. Democracy therefore is the new challenge to the old-order if we practice what we preach.

The right kind of housing? None will be found in the expedients of state-ism. We could find there only more "static" just as bad in socio-economic life as on the salesman's radio. No, my governors, generals, columnists, publishers, professors and all capitalists—the remedy is more *freedom*! Greater trust in the growth of more individuals—more faith in voluntary discipline from within *the man himself*. Today the most cowardly lie disseminated by socialist, communist, or fascist (they are the congenital cowards among us), and especially by our own vast bureaucracy as well as Church, School, and State is this lie that "I the State, am the people!" In any democracy the people not only hate the army but are bound to suffer the state as against their own customs and natural rights. Democracy cannot love government! Government is only its policeman, privileged by the people themselves to obstruct, expropriate, or punish them. More than that and Democracy flies out the window; the isms get foot in the door. So let us go and build and so build that we mimic Imperialism, Mobocracy, or Cowardice no more.

# AIA ACCEPTANCE ADDRESS FOR THE GOLD MEDAL

**F**rank Lloyd Wright *never joined the American Institute of Architects. Often he maintained that the organization was founded to protect the members of the profession rather than to uphold the quality of architecture. In fact, he claimed that he would have joined had the organization been called "The American Institute of Architecture." But regardless of his opposition to the institute, on 6 December 1948 Douglas William Orr, president of the AIA, wrote to Wright informing him that the board of directors had voted to award the Gold Medal to him "in recognition of most distinguished service to the profession of architecture. It is our sincere hopes that you will accept this award and be present to receive it in person during the Convention of the Institute in Houston, Texas, March 15–18, 1949."[1]*

*At first Wright had doubts about accepting, in view of his longtime disagreement with the institute. But his wife, Olgivanna, interceded, reminding him that many of the architects were his friends and colleagues and he could not insult them thus. Her advice prevailed, and he responded: "My dear President Orr: I am deeply touched by this token of esteem from the home-boys and assure you that I will attend the Houston convention to say so in person. This token coming, as it does, to one who has constantly remained outside the ranks of the institute proves me wrong in not having joined that body long ago to work from within it for the things I have been consistently working for outside it. . . . Kindly convey my appreciation to your members. I am glad to be counted as one of you."[2]*

*In his address, published in Taliesin Square-Paper Number 13, Wright graciously accepted the honor and the medal, and then spoke of the other honor, from the Royal Institute of British Architects, that he had received almost a decade earlier: "Honors have reached me from almost every great nation in the world. Honor has, however, been a long time coming from home. But here it is at last. Handsomely, indeed. Yes . . . I am extremely grateful." He reminded his fellow architects of his own professional ethics in the field of architecture and building an architecture suitable to democracy, to freedom. "We have built nothing in the spirit of the great freedom that is ours. No. Look at Washington—well—look anywhere. . . . We put ourselves on a hill here in the highlight, we talk about the highest standard of living the world has ever seen: yes—we have boasted much about all these things. But, my fellow architects, as least we don't deliver! Well . . . now how are we—as men and architects going to learn better?" He continually reminded his fellow architects in the audience of their responsibility to build something finer, to look deeper, to search for honor in the art of architecture: "However," he spoke, "I do wish to call your attention to one thing. I have built this kind of democratic building for the free man. Therein lies the original source of my effort here with you tonight. . . . Why I can stand before you, look you square in the face, smile and insult you? All this because. . . . well, I don't think very many of you realize just what is happening in the world coming toward us in the little out of the way places where Mrs. Wright and I are living with some 60 youngsters. They keep on coming to us from 26 or more different nations. . . . All came to Taliesin as volunteers because this thought which I am calling Organic Architecture here tonight, has gone, so long ago, so very far abroad."*

*Shortly after the address was delivered, a recording of the event was sent to Taliesin. Wright gathered his apprentices in the theater in Wisconsin and together we listened to the recording. There was no sense of arrogance about him, and he was obviously greatly pleased and gratified by the occasion. Douglas Orr's opening lines comparing Wright to Prometheus moved him, and when the audience was heard breaking into applause, we looked over to where he was seated and saw there were tears in his eyes. [Taliesin Square-Paper Number 13]*

## THE SPEECH OF ACCEPTANCE

(To Mr. Douglas Orr) Mr. President . . .

I thank you for this splendid citation and golden token.

(Turning to the assembly) . . .

Ladies and Gentlemen . . .

No man climbs so high or sinks so low that he isn't eager to receive the good will and admiration of his fellow men. He may be reprehensible in many ways; he may seem to care nothing about it; he may hitch his wagon to his star, but however he may be circumstanced or whatever his ideals or his actions, he never loses desire for the approbation of his kind.

So I feel humble and grateful.

Upon this really fine occasion of our presence here I don't think humility a very becoming state for me.

But I really feel deeply touched by this token of esteem from the home boys.

Honors have reached me from almost every great nation in the world.

Honor has, however, been a long time coming from home.

But here it is at last. Handsomely indeed.

Yes . . . I am extremely grateful.

How is it going to change my course in the future? I don't know. It is bound to have an effect? I am not going to be quite the same man when I walk out of here that I was when I came in tonight, because, by the citation that put this token in my pocket it would seem that a battle has been won.

I felt much the same when, as I was sitting by the fire in my desert home in Arizona New Year's Eve '41, news came over the international radio that the coveted Gold Medal of the Royal Institute of British Architects—incorruptible honor—had fallen to me—a lad grown up out there, Middle West, in the tall grass. Well, I felt then that these youngsters who have held (yes, we will say) with me; those who have believed and made sacrifices, "taking the gaff" with me, well . . . *we* had won a world-wide fight. But we hadn't yet won at home. The Cape Cod Colonial still continued, but (by the way boys, observe what "we young fellows" have already done to "Old Colonial") have you seen its false front come down and open to the view; its wings extend? Have you seen its proportions becoming more and more reconciled to the ground? Well . . . you notice it!

Anyway, it is unbecoming, on an occasion like this, to boast—isn't it?

But I do want to say to you tonight something that may account in some measure for the fact that I have not been a member of your professional body—that I have consistently maintained amateur status.

Long ago, way back in the days of Oak Park, I set up a standard of payment for my services of ten per cent. I have consistently maintained it and I have always felt that competition by the architect in order to sell his services (I felt he should be a great

Y.W.C.A. (Project), Racine, Wisconsin. 1949. Perspective. Pencil, sepia ink, and color pencil on tracing paper, 36 x 25".
FLLW Fdn#4920.001

*creative artist*) was sacrilege. A shame. I have often pointed to history to prove that nothing good ever came of a competition. I still think nothing good ever *will* come of one.

Also, I think that for you to make sketches; prospect for anybody for nothing, that is, to tender your services, "hawk yourself on the curb," you might say, is reprehensible in any circumstances.

The top payment demanded then was seven per cent.

Oh yes, I know the *ideals* of this Institute very well. I took them to heart years ago, and believe me, with this your token in my breast pocket, I can say, and truthfully, that never have I since sacrificed one iota of those ideals in any connection whatsoever. The man does not live who can say that I compromised and sought his work.[3]

I remember that in the very early days when my children were running around the streets without proper shoes, Mr. Moore, across the way, wanted to build a house—a fine house.[4] A fine man; a great opportunity for a youngster like me. Well, I had these ideals at heart even then. I never went to see Mr. Moore and never asked anybody to say a word for me, because who was there who could say an honest one? They didn't know anything about me!

But, glancing up one day through the plate-glass door to my office (and, by the way, *I* started the plate-glass door) there stood Mr. and Mrs. Moore. Imagine how this heart of mine, then so young, went pitty-pat! The Moores came in and sat down at the big table, opposite me.

Said Mr. Moore, "Now, Mr. Wright, I want

to know why every architect I have ever heard of, and a great many I've never heard of, came to ask me for the job of building my house?"

I said, "I can't answer that question Mr. Moore. But—I am curious to know—did Mr. Patton come?" (Mr. Patton was President of The Institute—that is, of your A.I.A. at that time.)

"Why yes," he said. "Mr. Patton was the very first man to come."

Then Mr. Moore said, "Why haven't you come to ask me to build my house? You live right across the road."

"Well Mr. Moore—you see—you are a lawyer aren't you? You are a professional man. If you heard that someone was in trouble, would you go to him and offer him your services?"

"Ah!" he said, "I thought that was it. You are going to build our house."

That was the way it began that day in Oak Park—and began, too, to get noised about. Several months later the next man was a Mr. Baldwin. He was also a lawyer, who wanted me to build his house. Mr. Baldwin appeared and laid a check on the office table. It was not a big check. (It was for $350—Oh yes, I remember the sum because it would be about $3,500 now.) Then Mr. Baldwin said, "Here is your *retainer*, Mr. Wright."

Can you imagine what that did to me?

Now, that is exactly how *my* clientele began and *it has all been that way, or better, ever since!* Never in my life have I asked one man to say a good word for me to another man who was going to build.

As a consequence, I've been sitting around working hard at waiting. I have spent a good many too many years of my life hoping somebody would come to me and give me buildings to do. So every job I've ever had hit me out of the blue on the back of the head. That's true. Nor have I ever sought "publicity." Publicity sought me. Therefore, this Gold Medal (let's forget all about superior design, let's forget all about contributions to building-construction; all the rest of it) I feel I can keep your token in my pocket and walk away with it justly because I worked so hard just *waiting for a job!*

Now—of course Architecture—capital A—is in the gutter.

Yes, there it is.

Yet, I have seen myself referred to more and more often as a great architect. I have heard myself referred to as the greatest living architect. Concerning myself I have heard reference to "the greatest architect who ever lived." Wouldn't you think that ought to move one? Well, not me, because in the first place they couldn't know. In the next place, no architect, in the sense that a man now has to be one, has ever lived.

And that's what so many of these enthusiastic boys down there in front of me, some of whom make these well-meant statements, don't seem to know.

Architects as they existed in ancient times were in possession of an established state of society as an instrument with which to build. The guilds, who then did almost all the building, were well organized. Style itself was predetermined. All was well established, especially during the Gothic period. So an architect in those days was pretty well furnished with everything in the way of ideas he needed to work with. He didn't have to be a *creator*. He merely had to be a sentient artist, with fine perception let's say, and some practical knowledge of building, especially if he was going to engage in some monumental enterprise. But he didn't have to *create* as he must do now.

We live under entirely different conditions. We live by this leverage we call the Machine. Most of us are machines ourselves; not much higher in consciousness and mentality than the man in the garage. Anyhow, *we do live by the machine* and we do have the enormous product of all modern sciences in our toolbox.

But as a matter of fact it is Science that is ruining us in Architecture and Art as it has already ruined Religion, as it has made a monkey of Philosophy. Already Science has practically destroyed us spiritually and is sending us into perpetual war.

You may say all that isn't our fault. But where, I ask you, is the virtue of these boasted advantages that to us are proving so disadvantageous? From where comes the new way of life? Who, I ask you, is going to conceive the new buildings we need? How come unless from Architecture? Architecture must come from Architects?

A great pity, isn't it, that the Greeks didn't have glass? A great pity they didn't have steel (the spider spinning) because if they had them both we wouldn't have to do any thinking, even now. We would copy them with gratitude. But no—not with gratitude. We would not even know we *were* copying them. No, we wouldn't know. Nor would we have the least gratitude. No copyist has any.

But today what must an architect do if he is going to be really worthwhile; if he is really going to be true to his great social privilege? Well—he *must* be a *creator*. He must perceive beyond the present. He must see things pretty far ahead . . . let's not merely say that because we can all do *that* more or less, but the Architect must *see into the life of these new things with prophetic eyes* if he is going to build anything worth building at all in this day and generation.

Do you know—do you realize that we ought to be the greatest builders the world has ever seen? We have the riches, we have the materials. In steel and glass, we have the *greatest* range of riches ever found by man. We have everything, *but*. We have a freedom, too, that never existed before; we profess Democracy but live in a "mobocracy" that is insult, astounding and arresting. Meanwhile *we have built nothing for the Democracy we profess.*

We have built *nothing* in the spirit of the great freedom that has been ours. No. Look at Washington—well—look anywhere. You can even go out down here on the Texas prairie and see the new Shamrock. And, by the way, I want to record (right here and now) that the builders themselves told me the building was "International-Modern" style. So let's give that devil what's due. Let's put the style of the Shamrock right where they say its style belongs: "International-Modern." And anyhow, while we are speaking of that mad exploit, I say there should be written in front of it, in great tall letters, in electric lights, W-H-Y . . . Why?

Well, Houston has this miracle. And Houston itself is a good example of *the typical pattern* of the capitalist city: a single broad pavement, skyscrapers erected along each side on one end, and way out there in the country at the other end, a skyscraper—the Shamrock. (You may see the sham but look for the rock!) Each side, alongside, on the prairie somewhere there in the mud are the people: shanties—no pavement.

Nevertheless "we the people" are prosecuting a cold war with a people who have no faith in the haves when they act, while their faith in the have-nots is pitiful to us. When we talk we declare a faith in the beneficial union of the have-nots and the haves, equally pitiful to them. We call our faith Democracy—but when are we, ourselves, going to learn to understand this faith and ourselves practice which we preach? *When* are we going to learn to *build for Democracy?* When are we going to learn the true significance of Democracy? If ever we do understand it, will we then live up to that courageous faith in mankind? Are we ever going to be willing to work hard and *wait for a better kind of success?* When are we going to be willing to work to make out of our desire the great deed we need to be able to look ourselves in the face—that is, to really build for Democracy?

I believe we could do it. We already have enough building "on the ball" (as the slang phrase goes) to go on in that direction if we would go.

But to me, the most serious lack is this "something" we haven't got—no not yet. If you look over the political scene (of course it is obscene) then *where* is the Democracy we are all talking about? Where, in it all, is our own Honor? Nowhere.

Now, what about this missing sense of honor? What would it be in our architecture? What would it be in the building of the free buildings needed by a free people? What would our honor be in the living of a life in a true democracy, under freedom—not mistaking license for freedom, not mistaking personality for individuality, our greatest error, one that characterizes us as a mobocracy instead of a true democracy. Yes, as a people what would our sense of honor be—I mean that sense of honor that might save us in our world now. As Science has mowed us down and we are lying ready to be raked, over the brink, what could save us but an *innate sense of honor*—and now how would that sense of honor work?

Well—what would be the honor of, say, a brick? To be a *brick* brick, wouldn't it? A *good brick*. What would be the honor of a board? It would be to be a good board, wouldn't it? Now—what the honor of the man? To be a true man—*an individual*. To live up to this ideal of individuality we call Democracy as a man rather than to keep giving ourselves away to a mere sense of personality. Were we ever to get that distinction between individuality and personality straight in our minds we might be able to go up. We could at least last a very long time. If we can't get it, we might just as well prepare for the brink. We are going over and down—not as men either, but as machines.

I have been right about a good many things in my lifetime—therein lies the basis of a good deal of my error. But at least *my* error *has had that basis*—one thing I can honestly say for myself.

And now I say I do believe *we can* save ourselves! We're smart. We have a rat-like perspicacity . . . but we have the same courage! That's what's the matter. I don't know of a more cowardly howl than this howl for security—well—I'm getting in far too deep tonight and I cannot swear—not now—not here. But, certainly, we are a great brand of the moral-coward in our grand America. We've got (if only we could get them in hand) the greatest of opportunities to live nobly a spiritual life with great interior strength and honesty of purpose. But our *minds* go continually by the board! Why?

All these years I have asked myself "why" all this futile dishonesty. Why afraid—so long? You've all seen this recourse to weapons: Fear. I am not telling you anything new. Art and Architecture? Churches—Religion—what have all become? Western Philosophy—where is it? Education? What have you?

Cowardice in all.

What else are these vast Universities of ours today as they overflow with the hungry-minded GI? And yet, standing here before you I am perfectly willing to admit, to confess, that our moral cowardice is not the fault of our universities. It's not the fault of our education. None of our moral failure is the fault of *systems* as they exist among us. *The systems are our fault*. This capitalist city, of which Houston is so good an example: we did it. That city came to us *from* us because we-the-people are what we are. . . . Don't forget that!

If we are ever going to deserve anything better—and get it—we are going to work to come by a more honorable expression of ourselves as a civilization, one such as the world is entitled to from us. We put ourselves on a hill here in highlight, we talk about the highest standard of living the world has ever seen: yes—we have boasted much about all these things. But, my fellow architect, as least *we* don't deliver! Well . . . now how are we—as men and architects going to learn better?

No, why we don't know our own honor better is not so much the initial fault of our *institutions*. No, nor is it the fault of any class . . . it is not even the fault of the *big boys* that make the big money: big money that makes most of these blunders that shove us over the brink (like this one out here on the Texas prairie that we bespoke a minute ago.) No.

How then could we-the-people learn better? How is the architect who consented to build that foolish building out there going to know any better? How are "they all" going to find out? Well . . . "they" can only find out by "your" disapproval! "They" can only find out by your telling the *truth*, first to yourselves and then out loud, wherever you get a chance to tell it.

Yes, as architects—we have soon got to find our own honor. You all know well enough the old saws and sayings. We dislike them now because most of them are a reproach to us. We don't honor "the people" really. We do not really honor ourselves. So how honor the men who came over here with a new ideal of manhood in their hearts? They couldn't foresee, in their day, our sudden riches and these new scientific powers put into childish unfit hands nor foretell that by way of them we would all so soon be disintegrate. No, they were rebels not prophets.

Were we now to wake up, take a good look at ourselves *as ourselves*, without "passing the buck"; without trying to blame other people for what really are our own shortcomings, shirking responsibility or lying about our own lack of character we could well be the due example to the world that the world needs *right now*.

With a good conscience we wouldn't be pursuing a cold war—we would be pursuing a great endeavor to plant, rear and nurture a true civilization at no matter what cost. We would then soon have the kind of culture that would be sure to convince the whole world that we had the right idea. We'd have all the Russians coming in here on us, learning from us, willing to work for us or with us, not afraid that we were going to destroy them or destroy anybody else.

It is because of our own fearsome cowardice, the constant political chicanery and a guilty conscience—this degradation by fear into which we have fallen as a nation that we are—well, a wisecrack by a witty Frenchman comes to mind. But this time—I'll refrain. My wife knows what it is. I am not going to quote it here tonight.[5]

Now—this is all probably far too serious for this occasion and more than all I think I ought to say.

However—I do wish to call your attention to one thing. I have built this kind of democratic building for the free man. Therein lies the original source of my effort here with you tonight . . . why I can stand before you, look you square in the face, smile and insult you? All this because . . . well, I don't think very many of you realize just what has happened to us or is happening in the world coming toward us today in the little out of the way places where Mrs. Wright and I are living with some 60 youngsters. They keep on coming to us from 26 or more different nations (we keep turning some of them away).

All came to Taliesin as volunteers because this thought which I am calling Organic Architecture here tonight, has gone, so long ago, so very far

abroad. It has won respect and admiration there under different names. A singular thing these names! Why will "they" never take an original thought or an idea until they have diluted it among themselves and passed it around under a good many different names? After that diversion or disintegration has taken place, then we can go with the idea. And we go—toward insignificance.

What then is really happening to our Architecture? This thing—Organic Architecture—keeps coming back home. I use the word *home*. I say "keeps coming back home" advisedly—because here is where the idea was born. Here it was born, in this cradle—as we are fond of calling it—of Liberty. Liberty so easily degenerating into license.

What are we as architects going to do with this practice of Architecture as Organic? Are we going to let this democratic ideal become just another commonplace of autocracy—see it shoved into the gutter by imitation, by popular commercial expedients—by mere fashion—or are we really going to look into its philosophy and use it—honor ourselves by honoring it? Believe me, if we do thus honor ourselves by understanding we will have found the center-line of true Democracy, because the principles of Organic Architecture naturally grow and expand into this great Freedom of the mind we, so carelessly, are calling a Democracy.

Well . . . again far enough? Far too serious for now . . . isn't it? Good night. . . .

1. William Orr to FLLW, 6 December 1948. *Letters to Architects*, p. 211.

2. FLLW to Orr, 13 December 1948. *Letters to Architects*, p. 216.

3. FLLW footnote from original text: I have perfect contempt for "Success" as it appears in our country. As publicity is now arranged to be had, invariably the "pushing architect" easily wins. The prizes that he wants are an infection—mostly going his way.

4. Nathan Moore, Wright's Oak Park neighbor. For him, Wright designed his only Tudor-style house in 1895.

5. FLLW footnote from original text: "The United States is the only nation to have proceeded from barbarism to degeneracy with no civilization in between."

# WHAT'S WRONG WITH THE UNIVERSITY

*Frank Lloyd Wright was a strong advocate for the small college, the small university—this by reason of his belief in the individual. So much of higher education he regarded as nothing more than a gathering of the masses: students by the tens of thousands herded into education whether they desired it or not. The "system" requiring a college degree brought this on, and Wright believed it to be a false standard. He often called the college diploma nothing more than "a pink slip signifying a four-year loaf." In this unpublished essay he voices his opinions candidly. But at the same time he qualifies the desire for higher education: "Were desire burning in the heart of the student as an honorable individual for more and better life he would soon have help by way of a better University."*

WHAT'S WRONG WITH THE UNIVERSITY?

The Students.

Of course.

There is no university otherwise. All there is otherwise is up to the students and I hear no voice proceeding from them concerning the matter.

Naturally, patriotic regents and their sitters in armchairs have to pinch-hit for them as they are able. No home-runs possible.

I know of nothing more inadequate than characteristic college education is now—nothing more pitiful. A trampling herd of frustrating and frustrated men-wives in Quonset huts, baby's diapers out on the line, book under papa's arm, books, books and apparatus. The entire herd evading the real issue which is clearly a better life there back home. Back there where their own people live and where they themselves should now be at work building, little by little, a better place to live in. Building an independent life for themselves square with what good ground there is. Making "home" a better place for Pa and Ma and for little brothers and sisters to grow up in. Books, outside those by the prophetic poets, will only keep the cart in front of the horse. Science is so badly overdone by premature techniques that knowledge of oneself, the true basis of education, is a sham. Were desire burning in the heart of the student as an honorable individual for more and better life he would soon have help by way of a better University.

But such eager integrity is missing because Honor is lacking.

What is Honor?

Well—here is a brick. What would be the honor of a brick? Its brickness . . . its quality as a brick? Yes. Here is a board. Its honor is its quality as a board. Now a man. What would be the honor of a man? His honor would be his *quality as an individual*. I do not mean his mere personality. I mean himself.

Isn't lack of this innate quality in the student what ails our University?

The lack became preponderant long ago as Science increased it and winners blinded us, until the city became a vampire and University-life became either a good four-years loaf or a paper license for book-futility where the acts of life itself are concerned.

Attitudes are not good enough.

What we call "Education" should end at seventeen with high school; university only for those who show special aptitude for universal Truths.

Success now is mostly proof of failure.

Go home, boys. Go home!

Or go to work.

# WE WANT THE TRUTH

*Published as Taliesin Square-Paper 14, the following text was not the actual speech that Wright had prepared. But as he wanted this original text to "go on record," it was printed and circulated on 2 November 1949. He postulated from the vantage point of Peter Cooper returning and seeing what has happened in the United States since the mid-nineteenth century: "Peter Cooper today would surely wonder why we cannot see for ourselves that Capitalism without sharing in robbery; Industrialism without Beauty is blasphemy; and that the Wars becoming more and more necessary to each are only murder." The issues and ills that Wright once again highlighted here are a further reinstatement of his talk two years earlier at Princeton, of "Harum-Scarum," and of the unpublished "Concerning Housing." All these writings reveal Wright's sad disillusionment with what had transpired in the nation following the Second World War. Yet, ever hopeful, Wright still professed great faith when he wrote, "To see things in their eternal significance is all that can ever really matter to us as true individuals and we must never forget that the individual free is the norm of Democracy." [Taliesin Square-Paper Number 14]*

WE ARE HERE TOGETHER THIS EVENING TO HONOR A GREAT American—the founder of this most honorable and useful Peter Cooper Union, of New York. So here tonight might it not be "in keeping" with this occasion to imagine what Peter Cooper would feel about the present State of this Union of these United States of America to which he entrusted his Union.★

Peter Cooper would see that "we the people" have come to believe that our very life depends upon commercialized industry. So, as War is inevitable to such ideals of Industry as ours have now become, we take War for granted. We are satisfied to continually *choose between evil*—which is all the choice the politics of the life we now live seem to offer us?

Peter Cooper would see that we are officially reconciled to let Beauty go, which is the sign of our degeneracy and proof enough that we are in danger of being the tail end of a civilization and not the beginning of a great one. Pictures, picture-galleries, museums for foreign art, movies and television take the place of the creative artists and Cathedrals of former times. Imitation is our rule and imitation is always base.

As in Peter Cooper's day, we are *essentially* an agrarian nation enormously gifted with land, but the commercial industrialism we have assumed now is, and in its very nature has proved to be destructive of enthusiasm for the beauty of our land itself. We have laid this land of ours to waste wherever "eminent-domain" has touched it and we have this wasteland that is—always—*the West!*

As a matter of policy, our principles have been generally abandoned by us in order that we may run with the pack. Popular patriotism today is just that "running with the pack."

Man alone of all created beings can take part in Creation and yet his creativeness is dying of elaborate contrivances increasing speed or production: a voracity avoiding labor.

Peter Cooper might well ask, "What has happened to our new Republic that so bravely declared itself a Democracy?"

The first call to Man is to the Land—and the time has come when the city should exist for the country, not the country for the city. Before Democracy can be born to the United States of America it must be born again among us to a love of the land upon which we live.

There is now no sacred money. There is no more a Holy City. The new space-scale of an Organic-architecture clearly shows us that the salvation of our Nation can be brought about not by improving cities but by destroying them; by now returning them to nourish the good life of the soil they drained: the soil which is itself threatened by unbalanced industrialism—everywhere subjected to impoverishment and erosion or depredation by the mechanics and chemistry of a needlessly Commercialized industry. More basic is the ruin that all this capitalist-industrial world we now try to live in is bringing to humanity. More and more the factory is destroying the home. The prideful refuge for the unit of Democracy is—primarily the Family. The home, our vital refuge itself is in danger of "housing" and it is in good family homes that the breakaway from out-moded city-life must first be made. The war inevitable to capitalist-industrialism such as ours makes motherhood despicable—a mere provision of gun-fodder however we may patriotize and rationalize concerning Motherhood. Even now our best young men are to be again "conscript" as they have already been and our workingmen are satisfied to be conscript in labor "unions" with little and less thought of craftsmanlike excellence or honor.

Peter Cooper would see the Nations of the whole world struggling with one another in fear for material possessions and material advantages one over another regardless of justice. And he would see that the greater the material success they win the more frightful is the loss eventually to the winner.

The ceaseless spurring on of man's prowess of invention which we see all around us only ends in man himself becoming a perfected tool of mechanized warfare. And so men are again to perish in the ruins of their ever-enlarging degenerating cities: perish impotent with secret damnation in their hearts and open curses on their lips for a life of misery ending in the frightful fear that now continually drives Nations to extremity.

Because the whole Christianized world itself is deadened by mechanical materialism the good people who compose it all seem doomed to the fearful selfishness of a perishable civilization.

Peter Cooper would see us waging mechanized warfare or cold wars as a means to preserve such living and achieve more worthless success and yet he would see us filled with admiration and enthusiasm for these great material advantages by which all kinds of Science and Machinery have seduced us from the great Art, Philosophy and Religion of a truly great Democratic life.

Peter Cooper today would surely wonder why we cannot see for ourselves that Capitalism without sharing is robbery; Industrialism without Beauty is blasphemy; and that the Wars becoming more and more necessary to each are only murder. For one kind of property-value we preserve by force we destroy inevitably hundreds of values to us infinitely more valuable.

Can we not see for ourselves that so long as we are content to use man's labour only as something to be bought and sold—and see all the features of human life made subject to speculation, to be openly bought and sold, we are truly blind to the monstrous inhumanity of this way of life we boast? All the practices we have founded upon or allowed to grow up on the competitive system of capitalized industrialism which we declare has given us the highest standard of living in the world is becoming apparent to the world as a modern inhumanity.

Can we treat human beings as mechanism and ourselves survive as human?

Peter Cooper might well ask that question here tonight.

Modern total war has become a far different affair from wars waged in his time.

Both the War and no less the Wage-system we practice have become monstrous, indefensible on any ethical grounds, yet we not only practice both enthusiastically but doggedly extol and defend both. Why?

Why does a soiled and spoiling materialism underlie and inspire all modern government with militarism? What is more ungodly than modern mechanized machine-making or war-making? But is either worse than our politics—this confused business of dollar ramps and rackets, pretended quarrels and dishonest diplomacy designed to ruin the real affairs of the real interests of the people in favor of their rulers? What is it all, at best, but a grandiose commercialized human fraud—ending in a kind of megalomania.

Peter Cooper would today see the practical professionalism of our age without honor—although he would see it served by devoted and honest men all aware of it but seeming unable to save it. . . .

. . . and Peter Cooper the radical would see us now believing we won and can win inglorious wars which may become by way of the next war which each war is always breeding—the decisive victory of despotic materialism over humanity. Such is modern militaristic enterprise however we camouflage it from the outside in or from the top-side down.

This feverish general activity in our cities as well as the industrial fruits of our vaunted scientific research is irrelevant to the real problem of Man in which Peter Cooper was himself so interested as to found and provide for this Union.

It is the *quality* in things that should make them desirable and beautiful, the joy forever that is ever and will always be the most important thing to mankind.

It is this inner human *Quality* that physical science, by its very nature, can never touch. We no more know what one inch of space really is than we know what a watt of electricity is. We cultivate little or no idea of what relation the Fact bears to the Truth and none at all of what *Solid* means, because though we may be expert in the fact we are afraid of the Truth.

To see things in their eternal significance is all that can ever really matter to us as true individuals and we must ever forget that the individual *free* is the norm of Democracy.

To justify the Faith which men like Peter Cooper placed in our future by founding this useful Union—an act of faith in the future of his Nation— we must again put our minds to work upon these causes of fear, skepticism and ugliness that so spoil our modern life and try to find where lie the causes of this everpresent threat of universal destruction, and the insensate damnation that follows our every "Success" with increased human anguish. What would Peter Cooper answer—now?

★The occasion seemed so happy and optimistic that I refrained from delivering this paper and my brief remarks fell in more with the spirit of the evening. FLW

# GENIUS AND THE MOBOCRACY

**A** *few days before his death in April 1924, Louis Sullivan gave Wright a collection of original drawings: exquisite freehand sketches for buildings, ornamental details, as well as studies of nudes made while he was at the Ecole des Beaux-Arts in Paris in 1880. The end of Sullivan's life found him in poverty, and these drawings and the clothes on his back were about the only personal items he had left. When he presented Wright with the drawings, he told him that he would be writing about them sometime, and Wright promised him he would. A quarter century later, the book* Genius and the Mobocracy *was the fulfillment of that promise. "Who, then, was this Louis H. Sullivan I still call lieber-meister so long after he is gone because he is still an inspiration to me? How did this 'pencil' come into his hand? This book is my attempt to answer. . . . This book is 'in memoriam' because of a promise."*

*Wright came to the firm of Adler and Sullivan in 1887, when he was twenty years old. For nearly seven years he worked as a draftsman for Sullivan, quickly rising to the position of chief of design. Eventually an argument over his accepting outside work on his own time led to a violent scene—and as a result, Wright quit. But twenty-five years later they came together in a reconciliation that held firm until the end of Sullivan's life.*

*Sullivan's partnership with Dankmar Adler had long since been abolished. His architectural practice, famous for noble office buildings and skyscrapers, had dwindled to an occasional bank in the Midwest. His finances plummeted and he found himself in abject poverty during the last years of his life. Although only thirteen years older than Wright, sickness and despair had taken a toll on him. He had become weak and frail. Wright visited him in Chicago as often as he could, bought him clothes, saw to it that his rooming-house bills were paid, and, although himself in difficult straits financially, supported his Lieber Meister as best he could.*

Genius and the Mobocracy *is far more than an account of the association of Louis Henri Sullivan and Frank Lloyd Wright. It is also the study of the creative genius in a democratic society. Wright makes amply clear that he was* not *Sullivan's disciple, but rather his draftsman. Yet he absorbed from Sullivan much more than architecture. He saw in Sullivan poetic genius and fed from that illusive source: "In that creative realm of ideas where all must be induced and nothing can be enforced, or taught, we find the great master—a living source. A flame." Sullivan, in turn, was impressed by Wright's work, especially the Imperial Hotel in Japan and its glorious survival during the disastrous earthquake of 1923. "Frank," Sullivan once told him, "you have never been my disciple—but you are the only one who ever worked with me who understood. I couldn't do what you've done, nor could you have done what you've done but for me!" One of the last things that Sullivan wrote, and he was a prolific writer, was a treatise on the hotel that appeared in the* Architectural Record *in April 1923.*

*In conclusion to this often touching account of Sullivan's tragic life, of the genius in a "mobocracy," and of his own place in it as well, Wright observes:*

*Furthermore it is in the art of building wherein aesthetic and construction not only approve and prove each other. In organic sense such building is an entity of the human spirit as that of any tree or flower is of the ground. A natural, human circumstance—possible only to the complete architect. There will never be too many of them. He is the master of the elements: earth, air, fire, light, and water. Space, motion, and gravitation are his palette: the sun his brush. His concern is the heart of humanity. He, of all men, must see into the life of things; know their honor.*

[Genius and the Mobocracy. *New York: Duell, Sloan and Pearce, 1949*]

## PREFACE

TIME WAS WHEN ARCHITECTURE WAS GENUINE CONstruction, its effects noble because true to causes. The forms were sculptured from materials according to the nature of construction and the life of the time—decorated by indigenous carving and painting. This integrity disappeared among the latter Greeks and the Romans. Time came when Christianity appeared upon the scene and architecture again arose closer to the plastic character of inspired architecture and came alive again for a time. But in the Gothic architecture of the Middle Ages we see the last of architecture as a great style of structure. Gothic architecture approached the organic in character. Sculpture and painting became even more a part of it and music entered it. Then the Renaissance appeared—a rebirth of the ancient forms of Greek and Roman architecture, construction more and more pretended. Features of the old orders of construction like pedestals, pilasters, cornices, and columns, piers and arches or wall masses, domes and pendentives; any effects the architects of that period had seen or now thought impressive were assembled as architecture. Architects proceeded to mix them all up, not according to nature but according to "taste." Instead of creators, architects became operators. All conscientious care for causes disappeared as caution did. Architects now only arranged, composed and the "classic" was soon ready for our inheritance. The laws of creation were not defied because they were not understood but they were not even considered beyond getting whatever picturesque effects architects desired: making the "effects" stick together and stand up.

The picture had now triumphed over architecture, and symbolism took the place of original inspiration.

A certain knowledge of the laws of gravitation was still necessary even for this affair of mere effects, especially if monumental.

But gradually all sense of building as genuine construction became a matter of an inside with independent outer facing to make a picture. The facade, or facing, need have no particular meaning whatever where either interior or purpose were concerned.

For five centuries the great art of architecture, in spite of many earnest attempts at revival, declined.

The Renaissance, in Europe "a setting sun all Europe mistook for dawn," was imported by us to bring our architecture up to the level of a democratic civilization dedicated to freedom. But the spirit of architecture was dead. Human thought had found the printed book. The other arts had fled. Printing was the Machine. In spite of sporadic attempts at "rebirth" by special kinds of abortion, the ancient forms of architecture could only be outraged by the Machine.

Meantime the Machine became the monstrous power that moves us now. All our timely materials like glass and steel came to hand as a great new means of building. But there were no architectural forms suited to their use. The practice of architecture was so far gone to the composer of the picture that we had no architects able to conceive the radical new forms needed to use the new tools and materials with nobility, inspiration, or even intelligence. So our own architects in this new world further falsified symbols and again prostituted the new materials not only by a kind of mimicry but by outrage that made our architecture what it is today—servile, insignificant refuse or puerile nostalgia.

When I speak of architecture as organic I mean

the great art of structure coming back to its early integrity: again alive as a great reality.

What forms shall buildings take if the glory of the great edifice is to come back to man again and he be blessed with the great beauty of truth in the way of his life we call his environment: so meretricious, so inappropriate now. How is the sap of human life which we call culture—escaping from autocratic monarchy to democratic freedom—going to establish itself?

It was evident long ago that we must no longer picturize, compose, or in any way pretend. We must conceive and integrate: begin again at the beginning to build the right kind of building in the right way in the right place for the right kind of people. An affair of genius.

Organic architecture is the right answer and the effort to establish it is really what this book is about. Organic building is natural building: construction proceeding harmoniously from the nature of a planned or organized inside outward to a consistent outside. The space to be lived in is now the human reality of any building and in terms of space we will find the new forms we seek. Or lose them. The old order called "classic" is therefore reversed and where so many of our basic building materials are wholly new, we must search again for the natural way to build buildings appropriate to the unprecedented life now to be lived in them. Our modern advantages should no longer be disadvantageous, as they are.

That we be enamored by the negation brought by the Machine may be inevitable for a time. But I like to imagine this novel negation to be only a platform underfoot to enable a greater splendor of life to be ours than any known to Greek or Roman, Goth or Moor. We should know a life beside which the life they knew would seem not only limited in scale and narrow in range but pale in richness of the color of imagination and integrity of spirit.

As the matter stands, the pallor is ours. The giant leverage the machine might be for human good may fall by its own weight from helpless, human hands, far short of our hope.

Spirit only can control it. Spirit is a science mobocracy does not know.

## BOOK ONE: BACKGROUND

## CHAPTER ONE: THE UNAWAKENED DISCIPLE

### THE ARCHITECT WHO IS HE AND WHY

He is a relentless observer. He is always active and effective in the investigation of Nature.

He sees that all forms of Nature are interdependent and arise out of each other, according to the laws of Creation.

In his every design a bit of Nature enters into building.

His perceptions (insight) science later verifies.

Intimacy with Nature is the great friendship.

He sees ideas as also manifest actions of Nature.

It is the poet in him that is the great quality in him.

The profound naturalness of his own being is the essential condition of a great architect and the condition of greatness in the man.

Expect from him a system of philosophy and ethics which is a synthesis of society and civilization.

Such an architect was he who invariably signed himself Louis H. Sullivan—our great native genius. He died penniless and, but for the several friends who for one reason or another were almost as poor as he was—alone. During his lifetime he—the master—was the hero of innumerable disciples. They imitated him but to so flatter him was to misunderstand and betray him. Imitation is never flattery. It is insult. They helped themselves liberally to the work of the genius and left the man to die.

Potentates were insignificant by comparison with this hostage given to fate by fate. How richly he might have been supported in his extremity because of what his disciples received from him even though he might have brought misfortune upon himself.

But a disciple is, by comparison and by circumstance, a graft.

A graft does not support anything.

A graft takes sap from a parent stem.

A true graft will give it back in leaves and fruit according to Nature, but, sympathetic or not, a graft is a graft. No graft can support the tree even if it would. The result would be dry sticks—dead leaves and dust.

The profession to which Louis H. Sullivan belonged, unable to value him, neglected him. But professionalism is parasitic—a body of men unable to do more than band together to protect themselves.

So far as the life of what they profess is concerned they have it by the throat as a jealous husband might strangle an unfaithful wife.

I am not writing this belated book as a disciple and I am not willingly a professional. A lineal descendant from seed—perhaps. But the disciple for good or ill is the ever present feature of our strange Usonian substitute for a civilization—call it a mentality. We are a graft upon a graft. Does that mean by grafters *for* grafters? We are a republic but nonetheless the greatest disciple of King George's empire: an empire with Gallic decoration, itself the great living disciple of the brutal Roman Empire. Is it therefore inevitable that everyone in this never ceasing Usonian struggle for release from autocracy and escape from these commonplace hangovers or branches of all phases of European culture should be a disciple of some disciple of a disciple, distorting or obscuring original character and virtue by imitation? If inevitable, why then must we see discipleship in our country so flippantly negative, impotent, or unpleasantly treacherous? What is the use of such commonplace falsifications as we see practiced in the name of art? Wherefore comes this craze on the part of the neophyte to be thought original in character at some master's expense but so willing to settle for a paper "degree" or run for any other short-cut to a job?

The truth is, we need originality more than it was ever needed to make good our claim to democratic freedom. Why can't we be honest about it? If one must steal it—steal it. Take it straight! Why fake it and spoil it?

In any country in any century great individuals like Louis H. Sullivan have been few. Although basic motives (Goethe so reminds us) are but several, the flow of consequential ideas may persist, infinite in variety and great in effect. So, moved by precedent (or trying to get on good terms with themselves), aspiring disciples congregate at the individual font they call

MASTER. From mastership precious streams of the "great idea," as they flowed to the master—a temper of his soul—now flow from him to devotees each eager to conduct such small share as he can to little branchlets here and there from which other little twigs by way of other similar diversions meander to little flowers. But no fruit. In any pseudo-civilization such as ours all sap—culture—seems to trickle up and out to inconsequence but dimly conscious, if at all, of the reality that originally sparkled with the vitality of truth—not as a mere mentality but as the temper of a serene and blessed mood: a source. What was with the master a savor of reality in the nature of the man—a quality of his individual self—is an entirely different thing in the hands of the disciple. No longer a reality, it is a ghost. Our environment is haunted and disciplined by these drab ghosts. It is made up of them.

In the shady affair our deeper concern is this: such attraction as the master's while it should expand the tree and develop more of them is, instead, mortal enemy of the creative spirit that is the tree. It is by way of this mass-demoralization by imitation on a vast scale that we, as a nation, reached our present servility in the art of architecture and in its natural children the fine arts, with consequent dubiety in our way of life. The ugliness of all servile effort surrounds us as a kind of matter out of place in our man-made environment: a kind of dishonor. Trees thus become fruitless; mountains become the plain; cascades the sea. All eminence becomes insignificant.

Yes, the substance may increase by such fatuous habituation as ours but man's faith dwindles as his inspiration grows dim or dies as his light goes out. So by way of irresponsible discipleship as by way of eclecticism of the styles, a native culture seems doomed to be stillborn. Meanwhile if a man, being unable to see into causes, must disqualify himself and dishonor an original by the imitation of effects—it is probably better for posterity that he emulate an admirable contemporary than an outlived style.

Neither custom nor habit of imitation exist in the world of the spirit. There, man's faith in himself—alone—has credit.

In that creative realm of ideas where all must be induced and nothing can be enforced, or taught, we find the great master—a living source. A flame.

Centuries have come and passed with none. But there was never a period wherein prevailing distortion or downright perversion of the master's truth has not been occasioned by discipleship shallow as a mirror. Owing to a foolish, ignorant competition for technique before there is or can be any idea for which to use it, recourse to "the ready-made" takes the place of the self-sacrifice of interior discipline. The matter is not peculiar to us but is especially unbecoming and ungrateful.

It was the Buddha who noticed that the spoon may lie in the soup for a thousand years and never know the flavor of the soup.

Well . . . here I am giving you the great mother-art of architecture awaiting the return of her prodigal children—painting, sculpture, music— gone away five hundred years ago in search of a temple, each for itself. But "Christianity" is the prime example of how lovers of spirit have been betrayed by the desirous but unawakened disciple. Are we then, as a civilization, condemned to a graft upon a graft—for grafters?

## INCAPABLE OF CONCEPTION THEY ARE MASTERS OF APPROPRIATION

I have heard those who were most indebted to the master deny him the loudest, and even those who would honor him most, distort, and so, torture his memory. Unawakened to conception as the gratuitous disciple seems to be by Nature, he is an ever-present detriment. And, where his human reactions as "artist" lie exposed for sale hidden under his own name, a cheat. He is the product of a foolish effort to put himself before his art—to put technique before developed sense. Even where, inspired by a creative mind like that of "lieber-meister," some of us have developed a mind of our own and honestly tried to live up to the clear beauty of truth according to the greatness to which we subscribed, these petty self-salesman appear to make imitations of effects by way of borrowed technique—that is to say, technique lifted or learned by rote, not by experience. Now, *each man's technique must be his own, his own way of getting his way with an idea.* But between the streamlining exploiter, the ignoramus, the canting critic, intelligentsia (men educated far beyond capacity) and

this inflated peddler who calls himself an artist, we soon find even these undersellers of the ideas of others undersold by each other. Soon a smear of ready-made techniques erases all trace of spontaneous originality and our environment becomes a caricature of culture in the enlightened sight of men. Nor will any trace of the virtue—honor—of an original idea be found alive in the avoirdupois of our stupendous mass-education. By its capacious ministry insignificance becomes dear to the common herd and true significance disturbing to authority. The stupidity of academic authority like the cupidity of the average merchant, serves only to confirm a tragic *lack of integrity* in our curiosity whenever we get out of the everyday rubbish heap to search for something superior. The true basis of every living culture will be found above and beyond this sham wherein both authority and education, for their own safety, are ever ready to combine against the inspiration of a man like Louis H. Sullivan. The net result to you and me is what? The waste of what might be the best of our lives. We, therefore, no longer have access to inspiration in this promiscuous prodigality of the vast commonplace; the massive mentality we presume to call "America" when we are but a small proportion of the Americas. Why not be modest and say USONIA? How quietly, almost imperceptibly, the great changes in Nature take place! How absolutely the great idealists who founded this country have disappeared from it except as memorials!

## HONOR

The nature of a building material is its honor. The individuality of the man, his Nature and his stature, is his honor! No imitator knows honor. Supported by the brief authority which we call, with distrust, "government," our dishonor is our mobocracy. Its main support is imitation. Mobocracy swarms, and swamps what genuine democracy we have built into our commonplace, and our commonplace becomes a battlefield for divided interests.

No wonder we come to think upon innate honesty with pleasure and respectful reticence with delight.

No wonder Louis H. Sullivan died as he did. All great sayers and doers tire of the voluntary flattery of irresponsible disciples prematurely conspicuous, instead of finding joy in work kept alive by the faithful enthusiasm of devoted youth content to deepen to maturity by the interior discipline of voluntary sacrifice to an ideal. Sacrifice is no less necessary today than yesterday if there is to be a worthy tomorrow. There is no short-cut to the profound. The poignant Jesus himself was sick of discipleship with its taste for miracles. Would wisdom, then, dictate that the master be never generous but always wary? Well . . . it all lies beyond his control. His function is not to teach but to inspire. Instead of a "form follows function" scientist, I shall give you a great lyric poet.

## DEEPER THAN THE TRUTHS OF PHILOSOPHER OR THE LAWS OF MORALITY IS THE SENSE OF HONOR

What is honor? Not the rules of a code—but the nature of honor. What would be the honor of a brick? That in the brick which made the brick a brick. What the honor of a board? Likewise—that in it that made the board a true board. Any material the same. Now mankind? A man's honor would be that which made the man true to himself as a man. What is his true self if not his individuality? Then what is the *quality* of his individual self but his honor? Now what would happen to him were he to imitate another? He would dishonor himself as himself. What would happen to the man he imitated? He would be diminished so far as could be, not expanded, and so be cheated. The imitator would steal twice: one theft from himself, the other theft from another. Often I have heard lieber-meister quote his paraphrase of Shakespeare's 'Who steals my purse steals trash,'— "Who steals my work steals my 'honor.'"[1]

The more subtle and brilliant the disciple the sooner he will either mutilate the original form, while remaining unconcerned with the technique of the man who made it, or make a sorry mess of the master's technique while imitating "the look-of-the-thing," because where there is imitation there can be no understanding; that is to say, no love. There may be infatuation without honor.

In this continuous warfare of ambitions in which we live and are condemned to die a strange death in skepticism, a resentment or suspicion grows concerning success if other than money-success. Is such success felt as a reproach by the less successful? Consequently, a popular tendency results on the part of average people to patronize the imitator. He *is* nearer to them to be sure. A good enough practice were the imitator good, but bad because all imitation is bad. We have here another characteristic submoral pest—our provincial "patron-of-the-arts." Patronage, to be sure, but always at expense to someone else—probably to the master himself. Here we see a trait worthy of our mobocracy: wealth maintaining questionable imitations of genius as a kind of friendship or merchandise. Superior discrimination is not yet trustworthy enough for that foolhardy act and cannot be until the basis of good judgment has a better foundation than it can ever have on the basis of patronage, friendship, or "taste." The day is gone by when an artist could only be one if some prince or potentate sponsored him. In all great art in a free democracy *the nature of the thing is its honor* and art is its own patron.

But there are more damaging factors at work. To demoralize native cultural effort we have our kind of education. Schools everywhere encouraging the fool's race by rote for ready-made technique, a race for knowledge encouraged by the egotistic rationalizing of professors themselves near-failures as artists. But more especially, by the professed artist who in point of fact is but a routine scientist. As scientist he is no artist. So, why expect grapes from thorns?

## THE FUNCTION OF EDUCATION IS TO TEACH MEN TO UNDERSTAND THEMSELVES

When men do understand themselves they may dedicate themselves to causes—they will never copy effects because then they will have their own, but by no short-cut. By becoming a self-evolving human being.

Unfortunately, if "educated" respectably no layman can *know* where the heart of the matter in architecture now lies unless he sees the work built and those living in it, for whom it was built. The whole matter of causes has been left out of his education. He lives wholly in effects. Nor can any routine scientist be able to teach him. Just as truth concerning the elusive depth-dimension involved in organic architecture defies the camera (being no cliché whatever), it will continue to elude the scientist and the intellectualist—the -gentsia. The great scientist may continue to furnish marvelous tools for the creative artist and the competent architect's tool-box but is himself impotent to make use of any one of them for humanity. Until architecture, philosophy, and religion become one as they are in organic architecture we are not going to be able to make such fruits of science as we already know in abundance, really constructive. We will remain disqualified by our own advantages. What hope then have we for indigenous *culture* when even our "universities" are not founded upon study of the principles and aesthetics of innate—or organic structure and their architectural courses are therefore as wholly superficial as their own buildings would indicate, were all else adequate? Is art education itself a matter of ancient history because of the expediency to which we are committed on this battleground of divided interests, and are we therefore compelled to submit to ignorance of principle or equivocation wherever principles come into question? The affair has not changed much for the better these fifty-six years past since the master's time. We are living more than ever on the printed page. More and more our national life becomes vicarious. Is such mental distortion as ours, where reality is concerned, the inferior fruit peculiar to ever-present fear because we feel ourselves untrustworthy—a bad conscience being the price of our kind of "success"? Is there real necessity to make a dishonest success out of some division, subtraction, or multiplication of the so dubious means now afforded by our economic system? Is the so-called capitalist debt-system a fault to blame for this warfare of divided interests—where head and heart, soul and intellect, come in constant conflict and war is the necessary clearing house? Fear is the state of mind that gives the dictator power and war opportunity. Not physical but moral courage is the only trustworthy integral basis or ornament for an ethical democracy. Democracy is no faith for a moral coward.

But if an organic architecture is to grow it cannot subsist on effects, neglecting or hiding the causes of those effects in order to save the faces of pseudo-disciples. Whenever derivation is open and honest, eclecticism was its name in educational circles, and

eclecticism still is the result of education itself. But even if discipleship were outright and honest, there is still neglect of a "cause" whenever the master is hung on the line "with the wash" at popular exhibitions. The quality of any original is so confused for the avid but ignorant public by odious comparisons so made by imitators with direct imitations, as to amount to a shameful or thankless exploitation of the original. The master is there but, to an ignorant public, he is already thrown in with outright backwash. Compelled to eat his own regurgitation he is with it on the way to obsolescence instead of on the way to the preservation of his quality as master. So the museum has become a morgue for the master and for the disciple a haven.

In all phases of our native cultural-endeavor the ingenuity we call "invention" is at a premium because we cannot now run our show or pursue our complicated existence without it. So by this substitution of prolix professionalism, prostitution of the "idea," and mere invention for creative art, we do get much of the dead-sea fruit—in the name of art— now so peculiar to our kind of life. In fact, mechanization is at bottom our fundamental "investment." So we are all one with the mechanics in a garage.

Whatever the cause of our "efficiency" may be or wherever remedy may lie, throughout our social fabric all forms of art-schooling or art-exposition have become unwholesome, infested by these agents of "effects." So everywhere we find the faithless disciple a handy "expedient" for "business"—a kind of growing of the fleece for the shears!

The habitual disintegration of the great value (a quality of the spirit) of any original is the inevitable consequence. How many trite or offensive things we are condemned to be and compelled to see because some venal verbalizer is deliberately confusing popular vision by playing down to fools until one might think the selling of some gadget or the clowning of a Picasso was our modern substitute for religion. By the very prevalence of constant super-emotionalized plugging for everything from a war hero to a cold cream by press, radio, and class-room, the visible environment in which we must live becomes—what it is: an insignificance at best— a shameful lie at worst. These establishments of our civilization, all too indicative of their insignificance, grow more dishonest day by day and stay that way.

Even now it is remarkable to me—as during all these past fifty-six years facing it on my own—to still see our so cocksure nation agreeably accept and proudly exhibit this plainly dishonest state of affairs, meantime calling this insignificance (which is its own tragic defeat where culture is concerned) *conservative*!

Any discipline when obsolete is a heresy.

Is heresy now conservative?

By way of the prefabricated disciple, the code-made and code-making expert, the synthetic professors of the so numerous "educated" neophytes with paper degrees in hand, or hoped for, architecture has become not a work of art at all but a technical makeshift: more than ever a mere piece of property. As for kindred "production," our big industrialists are so busily "streamlining" standardizations that we are not only compelled to see some egregious makeshift passed along as creation but also superficial effects instead of causes accepted as euthenics by the "higher education" and the officialdom it must please to live.

With the very temple thus profane what is our art? No more to us than the persistence of a desire to make the thing—whatever be the thing—seem like something not our own. Such creative sensitivity as we have, unless heroic, must soon be pervert to the sensational, the "monumental"—now a kind of "ham"; or the artist be induced by some business-man to "invent" something merchants can "sell" cheap to the credulous; or else the artist be destroyed. Artists themselves, most of whom are more ingenious than creative anyway, are willing to see invention as creation even when the "invention," though ingenious, is pernicious. Science, of course, receives the same sensations from the curious as from the beautiful. So does "invention." Lacking qualities of heart—therefore lacking the deep springs of true creation—neither science nor invention are now on good terms with art. Impelled by hope of profit or vicarious glory we see scientific invention released to our civilization and accepted by our institutions as a substitute for creative power. Who knows the difference? Therein, by help of the cheap services of the dishonest disciples of some creative mind, we have the present deluge of "box office": cheap old abuses maintained in new thousand-dollar gilt frames or old

frames for new abuses, to "pack them in." "They" do not know when they are cheated or by whom. Is it by themselves? Of course, it is.

So, restlessly, we as a tirelessly exploited—and exploiting—people must find some release, if not refreshment, for whatever native love of beauty the god of creative impulse passed along to us by Nature. As the preceding generations found it in symbolism and the empty pretension called monumentality, so we find it in shoddy sensationalism, in newfangled inventions or superficial beautifications by the commercial "designer" no higher than those of the professional beauty parlor or a cigarette in the fingers. "We" think we find—and we try to find—beauty in urbanism's streamlined machination; satisfaction in push-bottom power; entertainment in gadgetry, gag-ism; and happiness in preoccupation with so-called utilities of every kind that have no more spiritual significance than gangsterism itself, a trip hammer or an all-day sucker in a baby's mouth.

At last—but not least—the line between the curious and the beautiful is become so confused by "modern architecture" itself that the dividing line between the curious and the beautiful which marks civilization itself from savagery or degeneracy—grows dim indeed. What recourse is there for the deeper more essential Usonian-self—(that self has a soul), should it be tempted to search for great repose: a serene and blessed mood? Say, peace. I refer not only to a political peace but to organic peace. Were we to find peace, a native culture true to democracy would be sure of some chance to emerge.

After all is said and done, I believe our missing native culture is due more to the lack of what constitutes a clear sense of honor than to any adverse material conditions. Youth is so soon old by ready-made techniques that any fresh inspiration of the ill-favored or even the unversed human interest is unlikely. Bewildered, the human being knows no true recreation, so no renewal, but must live, a surge of excitement in a splash of harsh, hot noise occasioned by the deluge of ingenious gadgetry to which our dated urbanism is now impelled to so completely surrender. But notwithstanding the desperate final recourse to "invention," see how many cherished (nevertheless impoverished) "inventors" are being washed up in the back yards of our world-challenging "successes"? Like our "artists" they are posthumously glorified, if glorified at all. Our favorite insult to our inventors as to our artists? These monuments we build to ourselves in their names! Throw in the statesmen.

Again—"*theories divorced from realities are bound to produce failures*"! But even our best people—our teachers ought to be our best—teaching premature techniques as though they were creative power itself, are unaware that the creative spirit and science are not even related except as an artist and his tool-box are related. Here in this ignorant—if innocent—assassination of spirit by science lies opportunity for the dishonest disciple, ruin to sincere apprenticeship, and the confusion of all true educationists where a native culture happens to be their real concern. Unless a miracle occurs, standard education today means eventual ruin to any true experiment which great art might try to make on its own account. Credit is gone. Science has destroyed it as it has religion. Perhaps this was no less so in times past in the older countries. But among us today, owing to so much greater opportunity and the vast spread of a lower level of promiscuous intelligence, any original impression that inspired art and architecture may make is like the print of a foot in the sand washed away by the next wave.

Of course, this sinister economic "system" (ours) in which without foundation we have at last so completely invested our future—and that of the world at Bretton Woods—*is* better served that way. Mobocracy *does* thrive thus and the economic unit, the buyer, is already so far conditioned in the direction of quantity instead of quality that the merchant's real profit lies in this oblique direction, and who in this attempted civilization (so tempted) is not a merchant?

The noble quality of a true original is so rare that its chief good is for the uses of these professional dealers in the infinite substitute—we call them our universities. But strangely enough—should "nature to her custom hold" and a true master appear among us today, as in the case of Louis H. Sullivan himself, he would first be suspect. Then he would be generally denied and ridiculed (but secretly envied) until his own individual creative force had been sufficiently diluted—that is to say, until the genius was plucked of the fruit of his ideas by disciples and the disciples, plucked by their disciples, had broken all down and divided it up among themselves until "the look-of-the-thing" became less strange and more easy for merchants of the ideas of others to propagate and "sell." Must the fount of original inspiration we call master be thus diminished or obscured? Yes. In a sense, a contemptible, unconfessed revenge for the kind of independent "success" a master himself is must—not in democracy but in mobocracy—take place. No one particularly to blame? The genius does not "belong." He will not "stay in line." In the place where guardianship of his inspiration should be found, there is only the artist himself. And the artist himself is a starveling.

The great master? Well . . . by now he is done. He is dead. Retribution to us for using him up, giving him away, or leaving him to die ignored is no longer likely. Nevertheless we are not through with him. Mobocratic "art" having a chronic bad conscience, if any, is more than ever likely to join the popular tendency to mob the tribe up by mobbing the master down. If the master has been much acclaimed, assassination by the tribe can be quite sure of mobocratic sympathy.

Admitting our society to be worse than tainted by this reverse (or abuse) of the democratic instinct, we are so far compromised concerning this social use of the genius and disrespect for his work, *as his own,* that not many of us (as we run in the pile) can "afford" to respect or would be able honestly to recognize our own origins. It is "bad taste" to even consider them, publicly. The truth is we only need keep silent, look as though we did it, and "the big wind" the master was is sure to go down in us. You see, we ourselves are becoming unable to recognize origins anyhow, even where feeble gratitude is moving us to do so. So why make such a foolish sacrifice? And even were we still able to recognize them why give ourselves away? For what? "We might have thought of it all ourselves anyway, but for 'him.'"

Perhaps—as we are now set—there is no other means than grafting disciples to leaven, even a little, the inert lump of human ineptitude everywhere parasite upon art by way of this vanishing *ist* we call the art-*ist*? This creeping paralysis is chiefly in evidence in what we call "the higher learning."

Perfectly good fresh young lives—like perfectly good plums destined to be turned out perfectly good prunes.

Unenlightened "business," knowing it or not, freely patronizes this idea-deflation. Because it is cheap it is encouraged—and cheapens everybody. But how can we continue to call the deflation *conservative* and get away with it? By acting upon it (buying it), business actually cuts itself off from any radical progress in design beyond the petty gadgetry of the "streamlining" gentry, masters of "that new look" for *et cetera* and women. A radical architect sickens of the very word art if the professionalized streamliner, hired by the shrewd industrialist, gets "arty" to make more money for production by spitting on the apple and polishing it.

The master dead, sporadic attempts will be made to immortalize the poor man who died that the tribe might live. The memory of the great master should, by this time, be safely out of reach. But, as popular habit in Usonia is going, the master's "remains" are subject to disinterment and "debunking" to profit or please the swarms of those propagandists-for-the-literal, scribes of the pharisees—the Critics.

The literal will now be groomed to pass for the real; the shredded fact will become, by constant re-iteration, preferred to the truth. Soon—who knows the difference between myth and truth? Now is the time when by getting out the brass band, making commemorative speeches, staging exhibitions, and throwing their hats in the air, they will only be making louder and bigger the mistake which neglect was in the first place. This demonstration will in itself only exaggerate betrayal and make celebration even more contemptible than neglect.

## NOW HISTORY?

No matter how sincere the effort history may now be moved to make on behalf of the dead master, history is at best autopsy. Should the historian understand, interpret, or evaluate the mind of any great work individually inspired—the view is posterior for detractor and canonizer alike: the rump view! Inevitably these posterior views from the afterward are impressionistic distortion because naturally confined to rear-end perspective; or they are the personal slant of some personal sycophant or eru-edited partisan who doesn't know the difference—looking backward to see forward? As any critic is in his own nature, so in this supreme act of egotism—criticism—he not only now sees *as* himself but often sees as he does because he cannot see himself.

In the procession of posthumous academic "honors" that now proceeds, all will march together to a kind of popular entertainment or will help to maintain an expedient "museum" for mediocrity to be safely, if not infinitely, born into. Call this museum the university. Museums are what universities are becoming. These two have too much in common already.

Well, my confreres, if it moves us to compassion, anger, or pity to see what the multitudes of Usonian disciples settle for, a cheap synthetic that is themselves—how pitifully tragic it is to see what their patrons must settle for!

Education is far from the reality of education under the primitive conditions known as barbarism or even savagery. There at least the educator recognized the varying potentialities of the individual whether hunter, potter, weaver, or medicine man—and by actual experience his education proceeded.

Why do we try to make medicine men of hunters, potters, and weavers?

The artificiality of our mechanized society is helplessly drifting toward a bureaucracy so top-heavy that the bureaucracy of Soviet Russia will seem honest and innocent by comparison.

## BOOK TWO: MIDDLE GROUND

### CHAPTER ONE
### THE ARTIST'S PERCEPTION SCIENCE
### LATER VERIFIES

Next to the science of profit-taking in our system and to science itself, the greatest current of mass production cherished in this union of states, which I am modestly calling Usonia, is education. "Education" is our heaviest investment in plant, money, personnel and time. Looking at results, I would give you this as the main reason why our country is not yet on speaking terms with whatever there might still be living of its own organic culture. Popular education is served by patterns preaccepted by authority as most certainly *respectable*. Preferably dead. Anything alive is dangerous. "Respectable" patterns, in the ceaseless turmoil of such vast mobocracy as ours, have become the prefixed patterns of either provincial-Colonial, *papier-maché* French, Oxfordian or pansy Greek, German Bauhaus, or the stencilized cliché for sterility now called "modern," though modified Italian or even German Baroque might do. There are so many other names to fill in with or (literally) fall back upon! Or, because our universities, judging by the damage they do to truth and beauty by their prefabricated "respectability"—such as the buildings they build for themselves—education has neither independent will nor the least taste for the affirmation that is *inception*. Should we say, then, that our universities are being served as education *must* be served in order to keep on being our leading standardized industry? Above the cherished processes of standardized mimicry which I have described, what else can be done by such overgrown knowledge-factories as we continue to propagate at this time, swollen by millions of the boys from our villages and farms and now overflowing with the G.I.? Wholesale barter of freedom for intellectual slavery is what we are calling "the higher education." See in it, all but a little corner, the complete capitalization of our fears and deepest prejudices. We are continually mistaking both for our holiest feelings. By ministration of the "higher education" our mentality lives on the quote and manages to be as easily scared by originality as it is easily pleased to defend standard insignificance.

Instead of the good old advertising slogan we used to see along the American roadsides, "Quality knows no substitute"—let's present regents of the "higher education" A.D. 1948 with this one: "Give us quality, O genius, because we—swearing by the armchairs of the select in behalf of future armchairs—can make quality good for any quantity of substitutes." Yes . . . our greatest national industry thrives on the substitute for all other substitutions: the great god expedient. "They" are in the habit of calling this—their god—the practical!

Meantime the manners and morals of higher education are expedient. Its regents are expedient.

See the pestiferous scholastic locutions of Oxford-Gothic they plan, plant, and cultivate ad libitum ad museum! They are all too, too expedient! Cast-iron Gothic or symbolic Traditional. Cape Cod Colonial, L'Enfant Classic, or Jeffersonian-homesick—the flat-bosomed, wide-bottomed stencil (the box on stilts)—or the international quilt: any one of them will show how it all works, and what really is the difference between them?

Schooling once so "fixed," great issues dwindle in this nation or stew in our own bigotry. By way of the servility of the imported university professor or the native factory-made school our once great and original hope for a democracy seems doomed. The struggle for power by immoral international power-politics, conscription, bureaucratic proscription, fraudulent "service," and flat-minded "brass," all of which have come up from behind to overtake us and be democracy's well-meaning, if not holy, executioners.

Yes . . . great master, with patiently moderated invective I cite here what I have heard, immoderate, from your own lips. You a lyric poet born too soon, frustrated, starved back to the back room in a cheap hotel in an urban rubbish heap at a time when our cultural establishments were heedlessly, as needlessly—even greedily, servile to mass money-power, perpetuating by easy billions the materialism that grips us now! Materialism so dense that even then the consequences of originality were like those of criminality! So this new democratic architecture we call organic and is original may again be swamped by the same heedless mobocracy or more likely by official statism (the two gangsterisms do work together) and our hope of organic culture will be left to die with principle in this Western wasteland! But more dangerous to any quiet hope for our cause is the congenital copying of superficial effects and persistent neglect of fundamental causes. Yes . . . all down the line!

But, dear master, you know it to be in the nature of the ideas of great men and their causes to "die" only to be born again! Ignorant of its own destructive character where human nature is our real concern, the enormous money-power we derived from exploiting a new land by the great "industrial revolution" is power on the wane. Illusion! Its doom is its own assembly line! The chemical revolution is here to make even that vast matter of power powerless. The more amazing its establishments the sooner obsolete.

Born of the industrial revolution comes, now, another—the chemical revolution. Again a demand that our architecture dig deeper and broaden anew. But the old moral, economic, political pretensions (they were never essence truly humanized) were already failing. They were dated and going before the A-bomb appeared to mock them, mock this external type of building we inherited from a dead past and erect by the mile in facades like Radio City. Now the city is within a city. An internal turnover deliberately ingrown to intensify the folly of centralization so far as humanity is concerned. Another crucifixion! This time by the private richman. Recrucifixion of the general crucifixion by patronage of vast, conscienceless machine-power.

If in the light of this latest involution our present state of civilization is going to prove more fit for human life here on earth than barbarism, we are where decentralization is, more than ever, democracy's right challenge to the old order! That challenge is now made one with democratic ideology itself. Democracy, to survive, must mimic no more! Certainly not mimic its own past! Mimicry is not emulation. Sentimentality is not sense.

Traditions? Yes, beloved master! Scores of them will die in order that major Tradition have a chance to live! Codes? Yes, they too are stubborn impediments to great work but were they true abstractions—patterns of truth—they might be truly useful. Because they are not essential, but mostly the routine habit of mind of small-minded experts for fools, codes will die or drastic revisions be made in them by Nature herself. In our multitudes of ready-made or canned techniques, why not try to make the code at least honest? Do not try to make it "foolproof." A "foolproof" code would always be murder of the future by fools for fools. Even though yet unable to make codes true democratic abstractions—that is to say, flexible enough to stand as genuine "essence"—at least provide for timely appeal! Not as architects nor as men can we fail to pos-

sess the individual courage necessary to face the divided interests of the baudy "balance of trade." We cannot do this manly spadework short of wholehearted affirmation of the same principles put to work on codes and their framers that are now characterizing our vision of an organic architecture. *The new reality*? Yes, citizen. If we want to really live in fruitful peace instead of frightful conflict, the simple principles of organic architecture not only contain the basis but are the center line of any possible establishment of a form for a true democratic order.

Instead of allowing education to condone or promote more confusion by glorified propaganda—trying to enforce any symbolic abstraction whatever, however sacred (even the dollar sign), let us allow no more heartless mechanical techniques to pass for human artistry on the strength of any authority however "high," remembering the law is always stretched in favor of the official against the citizen.

## CHAPTER TWO
## ARE WE AS WE SEE?

Sitting alone so far away from the master, yet so near, for a page or two just for the view, come along with me beyond that now ancient incident (fifty-nine years ago) to speculate somewhat upon the why and wherefore of heretic seeking heretic by instinct amounting to intelligent choice. Why did the older novice and the neophyte not only find each other but find themselves congenial from that first moment?

Well . . . I have always regarded "birth" as inevitable invocation (blood lines tracing far back beyond slumbering instinct or living memory). So to go into this seemingly haphazard vis-à-vis might not only be amusing but informative?

In mind, this question: is there always something of archaic impulse still alive in us to reshape the ever-present confusion disconcerting our immediate present? As have men themselves, so have their architectural forms, once individual and noble at the beginning, grown weaker and weaker instead of stronger and stronger owing to strictures of geometric time? This complex limitation we call "age" seems to have come along to make materialism the more inexorable. Is our mathematics a mental device to so fix upon the human mind its "one, two, three" dimensions as to construct a prison house of and for that mind: a finality devised regardless of the benign nature of the human soul?

Sometimes I wonder if "time" was devised only to make this "one, two, three" life that scientists will themselves someday know so much more about, a life not of childlike limitations but one of childish imitation? Was time, as we now account it, designed for the shopkeeper and the counting house, eventuating in machinery, standardizing, and "age"; or were shopkeeper, counting house, machinery, and age designed for time?

Length! Breadth! Thickness! Three dimensions only? For the creative individual they are not enough. At least we must expand the third to a fourth capable of integral concepts like "form and function are one" in order to encounter the feeling for principle in this imminent search of the innate self for selfhood. Manhood not selfish. The feeling for principle was the valid source then, is now and hereafter the true source of creative sensibility.

What I am trying to say amounts to something like this: life itself is a splendid unfolding—a coherent plasticity: so there can be no real *beginning* in this or any mortal conjunction on this earth. Nor—according to the principle of organic change as we may sense it in organic architecture—end to be foreseen. Master and worshipful workman are sitting together at this moment still of and yet amid countless unperfected or perverted lives in this ever vital continuous affair of environment.

The perversions of great ideas, if not all hope, surround these two. To confound them? No, to *condemn* them! Because this moment is (the present always seems to be) a most degenerate moment when all truth is dangerously radical. Yes, this is a moment far down if not the lowest moment in the twentieth-century poetry-crushing era in which Usonians live. Life is again deformed by a more violent divorce from nature than ever before. This time the divorce is had by way of licentious abuse of new power; machines. Humane life is so used in consequence that whatever existed for man above the belt he stupidly betrays by lack of integrity in the curiosity of his "intellect" and the cupidity of his

instincts. He is calling this curiosity science, and his cupidity—business. His reward is—at bottom—ugly waste misnamed progress. Sanitation and hygiene of the body it is, but soul slaughter such as no god-of-things-as-really-made ever looked down upon among the children swarming on this infested, ravished earth. Earth, "where every prospect pleases and only man is vile."[2]

## GLANCE AT THE SCENE

Unspoiled Usonian landscape is already drawn and quartered, literally, by the old-time surveyors putting immediate convenience above future benefits. We inherit the land from them piecemeal in rectilinear "pieces," regardless of topography. The pieces are called plots. Division lines, great and small, run due North to South and East to West, dooming every structure (placed parallel to them) to one hot and bright side and one cold and black side. Natural features of our fresh beautiful Usonian landscape are thus, at the beginning, crucified by commonplace efficiency.

Notwithstanding limitless, available space in our vast new domain where population is only beginning, every single building in town (dwelling or otherwise) toes the street line—close up, according to old London town. Coal is fuel here as there, so all houses huddle straight up and stick tight. The monarch passed on the street, so—eyes front! Buildings in Chicago, as in London, were there and then adapted to "His Highness." Now, his highness is the "passer-by." Coach and horse or the Foot and Walker line, perhaps the horse-car or a hansom cab came along the London street. So all this over here took place as was the ancient habit "over there." Habit was again shamelessly taking root where it could never belong if men were men with faith instead of nostalgia.

Should more freedom be wanted by some man—impractical, intractable dweller ("Why ever would the man want it?"), more space if and when found was put into a bigger front-yard on the street!—dedicated yes, as always, to the "passer-by"—now his lordship. Few town or country residents ever thought or even dreamed of individual privacy as charm. Except as it was a slum affair (rectal or concerned with the upper region of the pantaloons), privacy was no moving concern.

The resultant pattern of an "American" village, subsequently of our cities (they are all only over grown villages), became the familiar one of a pair of scissors or the cast-iron criss-cross of dressy, military rank-and-file: eyes always front; "fronts" always obediently facing their commanding officer—the "passer-by." The "front porch" was our local improvement of the imported features of our domesticity. (We invented pie, porches, and ice water.) For the underdog, as monarchic hangover, came along the twenty-five-foot "lot." Hangdog fate for the lesser man stalling him in ranks and stanchions by the mile. Party walls in the circumstances became the brutal raw-brick masses we now see everywhere glooming against the sky, cutting human habitation to pieces: indiscriminate crucifixion of the criss-cross itself.

Bedeck this whole prisoned, regulated, but inchoate hash of fresh opportunity with loud-screaming signs—come-on-in signs everywhere urging competition, the bigger and noisier the "sign" the better—and what have you? You have what we had then to work in, work with, and work upon. In it all not one attempt at a thought-built building. No one had ever seen one!

Dwellings, high and low, each in all and all in all, were trying hard to be different from each other, each craving distinction; and by trying so hard to be "different" all succeeded in being only the same in a general fiasco. All are bastardized echoes of bad old King George's court; or, if preferred, take a little Italianate palazzo in scagliola, caricaturing in Chicago the aristocrats of the now futile monarchic era of the Italian magnificent, Lorenzo. But from George came the pseudo-manor's wooden posts, imitating marble columns under classic wooden pedimentia, while we fought so hard to be free from him and all his courtiers represented. Queen Anne fronts were for Mary Ann behinds fashionable at this time. The fallacious "front" was all that mattered anyway. The "dickie" or false shirt-bosom, the celluloid detachable collar and cuffs went along with the ornate facade, or "front." Have you seen—from behind—the "fronts" worn in the parlors by the women of that period to match the architecture?

The women beckon. Step within and see the fussified boxes they inhabit: boxes stacked or pushed together by climbing or descending stairs—boxes partitioned off into little boxies, boxlets, or boxettes—pigeonholes for every domestic function imaginable: water-tight and nearly airtight. Yes—and soon you will see every domestic function fitted for and into only some box. Great mansions? Yes—plenty of them. But they were only bigger, more extravagant boxing. The box better brushed and stuffed—that's all. The more ornate everything was, the better. It took a heavy dose to move that era to aesthetic emotion! Outsides were freely, most expensively bedeviled by the gift of ignorance called taste. Do you know why the word taste? The small windowed box even then belonged to a bygone age when glass was taxed and modern heating was nonexistent.

The wood-butcher's cut-and-butt carpentry was everywhere seen stiffly sticking up over "rock-face" masonry, all according to the elect—and alert—"classic" designers of that lost period. This "classic" went to the plasterers for any tune they might care to play with a trowel on its insides. The witchery of the interior decorator (inferior desecrator) ran away in every direction to dress and overstuff the whole thing: ultra-insides for ultra-outsides. In really fashionable circles, all materials for furnishing, good or bad, went into the hands of the "draper" and their nature either died there of ruthless rape or committed suicide in shame. The murdered woodwork had already met an especially savage death by turning lathe, shaper, or jigsaw. What craftsmen were left—they were destroyers of good material—were even then limiting apprenticeship and—knowingly or not—turning themselves as well as their "unions" over to the assembly line. This wholesale crucifixion of human nature on the outside was habitually shunted to the "inside"-architect for beautification. It was the inside-architect who presided over the "stuffings" and crowded the hangings. The result resembled an overdressed woman of the period half dressed for a party. The inside-architect never once thought to venture outside the inside, nor the outside-architect inside the outside. I used to wonder why not? Was it because woman's place was in the "home" and so the inside was usually left to the "taste" of some necessitous or ambitious "society" woman?

So far as buildings then went, or now go on the restless realtors' merciless rounds, the "lousy bastard" (even then the realtor's pet name) was always there first. The *"mise en scène"* not only made no sense but had no mercy on the desired eye and was proud of it. Total abortion by way of purposefully deformed materials in artful effort to make them appear like some other material—the first rule of the game—ruled out both sense and aesthetic sensibility. Honest? No matter! Dishonesty was more "artistic"! Is yet. Gables, dormers, minarets, bays, porches, oodles of jiggered woodwork ruthlessly painted, poking in or peeking out of piles of fancified stonework and both playing idiotic tricks with each other, just to captivate that desired eye? Oh, no: just to inflate some well-to-do owner's sense of himself—the owneress as she saw "himself." Believe me, physical torture was merciful to man in comparison with this irrepressible, badly managed desire to evacuate illicit excrescence. The prevailing motive seemed to be not only to kill by way of terrible "taste" the simple nature of man but to kill everything that touched him—especially whatever materials he touched—by making them all belie or belittle themselves, and do a caricature of the property-instinct for posterity. "Himself" seemed to want, desperately, to become somebody or something else. Man, the executioner, now not only killed to eat and killed for sport—he killed for culture.

No wonder I prayed—then—for negation!

Big or little houses, schools, banks, stores, churches—even privies—were thus badly, even madly, excrescent. All life connected with this excited bedevilment was utterly bedizened. The pernicious social fabric so excruciated by adornment was a moral, social aesthetic excrement that was only the rubbish heap of a nation-wide waste of all natural resources. As for sensitive aesthetics, the whole town from any sane point of view was obscene of everybody in it and all truths of being except one: vulgarity. *Even that had a bad time being honest!* Public buildings were only worse. They exaggerated the demand for this uxorious shamelessness and raised it to the *n*th degree. A kind of outrageous grandomania prevailed wherever money could be found or debt incurred. But these showpieces of sham were only the canned relics of monarchic grandeur; the "classic" the very best people still called for. But even at best it was callow, or canned, ornamentia. The authors of this downright dementia kept clear of the insane asylum only by the foolish pride of their clients in collecting the fifty-seven varieties of banal sentimentality that could, even then, be bought ready-made. Especially the wisdom of the "shrewd" became idiotic when they dared "show off" their idea of ornamentalitis. Even the worthy could not resist this orgy of the ornate.

Stupid? No. Just wicked *extravagance* passing for luxury—advertising to posterity that its owners were not on speaking terms with either scholars or gentlemen.

To begin the town and end it like a boy hankering for the circus there was actually a preference by the best people for contortion. This act on the flying trapeze seemed to entail that recklessness which marked this period of magnificence and expense. Chicago loved it and maintained it in the name of a "good society," mainly the prostitute relic of King George's court. And how did the patterns of this flotsam and jetsam get to "George" in the first place? To him from "Louie" in Paris, of course! Where to Louie from Paris? Probably from the Italian, "Lorenzo." In any case, all that was hallowed in English landscape or tasteful in the Renaissance itself was completely left out. Here where bountiful opportunity existed for dignified indigenous culture in freedom of space and beauty of materials, the avid license of a foolish, hungry orphan turned loose in a bakeshop was mistaken by riches for freedom!

Throughout this rebirth of so many rebirths of the Renaissance no item of horrendous misuse of wealth had ever been dignified by Nature's innate significance. *Nature was just "outdoors"!* Inner significance of architecture had been lost to symbolism some five hundred years before. Yes, and here now at home, with a new people in a new land for a fresh start, was this defamation of native character by riotous excess in the name of respectability—and respectability meant the bastardy of any and every outlived European style. Defiant of good sense or repose, here came "taste" with the Pig and the Poet on either side of the Chicago tripartite shield—both rampant! Outrageous license had found the machine and the machine had quickly won it over to its side. Again democratic freedom went under to mobocratic license. The ulterior mission of machinery now seemed to be to make the baudy showy; to crucify even vulgarity itself on its own terms—to see it squirm and hear it scream. So good machines in the hands of sudden wealth ground, tore, and bound. Or rode the lives they might have served to save but for their prostitution to this ignorant showmanship of too easy, irresponsible ownership. The great unmoral power of the modern industrial revolution had come to give meum and tuum all they could take for the grand gesture and waste the rest—to keep prices high, if for no other reason! Gigantic leverage was here in childish men's hands before even good men were qualified to use it to human advantage. Here came the newly discovered short-cuts to promiscuous power that gave the grand short-circuit to (and for) modern culture and landed us right where we are: "the only great nation to have proceeded directly from barbarism to degeneracy with no culture of our own in between."

To further crucify this gladsome celebration of wealth accelerating the grand crucifixion by machinery, came now our ever-present "modern advantages": corporate machines set up in palatial offices by vested interests (bankers), sitting behind massive Corinthian columns to control the masses of machinery. *"Public-service"* corporations were already entering upon the fresh landscape with meters, poles, and wires instead of bayonets and guns. Wherever people "settled" came these new strictures of the "investment" to devastate the future in the name of taxed human convenience. Poles and wires came to be to the investment that was the human being what the wire fence was to the investment that was cattle. Stark poles were bestrung with miles on miles of endless wiring. They marched alongside the streets to be looked through or to look by or look at. In towns a devastating forest, in the country a searing slash at the eye that would look upon whatever there was left to contemplate of beauty of Nature that had been let alone. Now came these corporate "follow-ups" of the tin can and barbed wire that had "conquered" and bound the wastelands of the west, hand and foot. Poles and wires in that pioneer day became the irredeemable mortgage on our landscape which they still are *a century later!* The entire *"mise en scène"* was being ruthlessly ravished by "power." The modern Goliath was on the job. The measured tread of the Golem was heard in the streets. Voracity had become speed. By grace of "public service," here came ruthless crucifixion of all the crucifixions gone before.

The already habituate internal-combustion engine is running away with any coordinate humane planning the scene was ever going to know: these antique spacings of the village which now made the entire arrangement of the town are becoming dangerous and a farce in the cities. Excess gadgetry, too, is beginning to sneak or leak into the old order which was stranger to them than they were to it. There in the buildings of the old "classic" dispensation now a heresy, the gadgets were like so many shiny new brass buttons on some old derby hat. In truth, the derby hat, kimono, and gaiters were harmonious compared to this violent revel of infelicity. Barbarous? No. Not so good! Man's abode on earth *dehumanized* in the name of an idealized but already licentious motive for a civilization? Profit. A game? Ah, yes . . . that was it! Nothing we had to live by or could now live with or live for had such simple integrity as barbarism, although this was a kind of pseudo-barbarism itself. The main feature of human associations today is that the vast majority prefer strife to fearless frankness. Is that degeneracy? Why then look back and call this a civilization? Let us look forward beyond glorified hypocrisy.

## CHAPTER THREE
## THE GLIMMER AND THE COURAGE

Our human aesthetic sensibility? Well—as we all know now—the cutworm forgave the plow! "They" all, or nearly all, forgave the corp that crucified them and bought stock in the enterprise that nailed them together with their own democracy upon the criss-cross. This plain cupidity and the stupid curiosity called scientific were both looked upon as *progress*! The swift march of the machine was no longer stealthy but pageantry in the streets. Disorder, dissonance, and discord composed this stunning symphony for the necessitous convenience of the human animal. Do men rise above such degradation of themselves, by themselves, by their own effort? If they do, it must be because of the slender thread of light—this glimmer or gleam of sensibility sure to be left somewhere to cheer the man: the sweating, straining artifex.

The immortal future of mortal humankind not only now depends upon that immemorial glimmer which we must call the sensitivity of the creative artist but upon his courage. Our peace as a whole people lies there too, in need of courage—in that same light. No science can substitute for Nature without foreign wars as a clearing house.

A nation industrialized beyond proper balance with its own agronomy is a menace to its own peace and the peace of the world. It is a house in a chronic state of civil war always divided against itself.

BOOK THREE: FOREGROUND

CHAPTER ONE
THE STRUCTURE OF THE FIRM

To go back to the "glimmer and the gleam"—the master sitting there so immediate; absorbed in a pattern for integral ornament before him on his drawing board: he was untroubled by any of this. He took it in his stride. I could never see that "liebermeister" had more or less than a creative conscience. He was born Bostonian but primarily of a Spanish dancer and an Irish dancing master. Sensitivity to beauty was thus in his immediate background although Boston was his foreground. As luck would have it he inherited money enough to enable him to go about as he pleased. Time came he went to the Beaux Arts in Paris where the young urbanite might become a sophisticate Parisite. Neither knowledge of nor any desire for the warm simple ways of country life were ever seen in him. He accepted the economic situation as he found it. I never heard him mention "the machine."

But I, the designing partner's "pencil" flung there beside him, inherited a troublesome Puritan strain. I was Bostonian too, but only in passing. Taken to that hallowed vicinity at the age of three by a music-loving lawyer-doctor-preacher-father I lived in a Weymouth parsonage from the age of three to the age of eleven: there to be kindergartened (the Froebel way) by my Unitarian teacher-mother. She wanted an architect for a son. It is perhaps significant that golden curls beloved by mother were down on my shoulders until, when eleven, I was sent to work on the farm. Aged six I had been sent to Miss Williams's handpicked private school, devoted, I guess, to bringing up little Lord Fauntleroys. But returning West eventually to enter Wisconsin's university, I—aged eleven—was sent to work spring and summer with my unitarian farmer-uncles in their "valley," near Spring Green, there by the beautiful sand-barred Wisconsin River. These Welsh relatives of mine were called "free thinkers." They were Unitarians. Up to and including this time, when I have looked over at ourselves and tried to glimpse fate, I was usually having difficulty raising carfare. My father was intellectual preacher-musician at this time so, and therefore, indigent. But mother's people were fairly prosperous yeomen, gladly supplying any missing sustenance for this roving, Sanskrit-writing, music-loving parent's family. Owing to my mother's prenatal wish I had, all my life long, looked forward to being (at first to me because of my mother) that sacred-hero: the architect! Dissatisfied with college training there, where architecture was not; impatient by nature, I had said goodbye to Dean Conover, a few callow fellow-"engineers" and walked out of Wisconsin U. Three months more and "they" would have given me a degree as civil engineer. I have had the same contempt for "degrees" ever since.

The designing partner left Paris disgusted with the grandiloquent Beaux Arts "projects" which, by this time, he seemed to have shed completely. But while in Paris, besides the standard vices of the "immortal city" (those tragic ones that eventually cut him down before his time), he had met John Edelman.[3] I believe John was the first real educational influence Louis H. Sullivan ever found. And John was Bostonian too. John from now on was quoted to me. Often. The master-to-be had evidently fallen under "John's" influence and seemed to share many sentiments which

"John" habitually expressed, and expressed with forcible profanity. Both despised Boston for some reason. And so, for some reason, I thought I did.

Nor had I any brief for my own education at the University of Wisconsin except outside work afternoons in the private offices of the dean of the engineering department, Allan D. Conover. The kind-hearted dean generously paid me a then-no-mean stipend of thirty dollars each month. But now, I, the unwilling "engineer," country-loving heretic (but no rustic), was in under a far more sophisticated heretic. If in me Louis H. Sullivan had found a serviceable pencil in his hand for better or for worse, I had found in him the ideal iconoclast. Nevertheless, in my credulous adoring breast was disquieting disapproval of the private ways of the master-to-be.

Although he did seem untroubled by a social conscience, he but seldom swore and in money matters was immaculate. Seeing only moral no ethical quality in either, I was heedless in both, believing punctilio with money tied up with meanness; "Were they trying to make the damned thing sacred so they could keep on playing their game safely?" Well . . . I've learned a lot about "money" since. I regarded swearing as I was taught: as unbecoming—ugly, a bad noise, repulsive like a bad smell; ventilation really. I despised smoking, then, drinking, whoring, and do now. I despised *the habitual in any form*. And L. H. S. practiced them in their many forms to a dreadful extreme. Poison himself to lose his real self just for what? Why go around following a filthy incendiary sticking out of his face? Just to give an imitation of something on fire inside? I guess the cigarette is something of a relief to paws disengaged when the human animal rose upon its feet. But the animal in me wanted and expected more from him than just that! Ah—arrogance! Of course, and—I see it now—I was a disagreeable character too.

I know the popular reaction to this confession, but I make it on no moral grounds whatsoever. Nor do I make it with a sense of superiority. Am I making it as evidence of my good luck?

By Louis H. Sullivan's side in those now far-away days, he thirty-four, "Wright" the young draughtsmen nineteen, he would often say to me with undisguised contempt: "Wright! I have no respect at all for a draughtsman!" Certainly he so conducted himself toward them but, as the other draughtsmen quickly noted, never so toward me. His haughty disregard had already offended most of the Adler and Sullivan employees. Embarrassing episodes were frequent. His contempt may have been due to the fact that he was so marvelous a draughtsman himself. But I knew what he really meant.

In the offices on the top floor of the old Borden block, "Wright!" "Wright!" rang out over the draughting room whenever he needed me, which was pretty often. With no hesitation whatever, "Wright" came whenever "Mr. Sullivan" called. Only long years after I had left the Adler and Sullivan office did he ever call me "Frank."

He taught me nothing nor did he ever pretend to do so except as he was himself the thing he did and as I could see it for myself. He ("the designing partner") was the educational document in evidence. I learned to read him with certainty just as you shall see him and see me if you are a good reader between the lines. I am sure he would prefer it—that way.

## THE PENCIL IN HIS HAND

Regularly Saturday night, this now regular (but markedly favored) employee of Adler and Sullivan would pick up at the outer office an envelope with sixty dollars in gold pieces, minus the stipend to pay off for the funny little house ("they" used to ask me if it were Seaside or Colonial) which a subsequent contract with the "firm" had enabled me to build in Oak Park. The sum was high wage in those more innocent (or less exploited) days: about two hundred and fifty dollars now? I would take the firm's gold with me to "saints' rest," as the self-righteous, fast-growing suburb "Oak Park" was nicknamed. I was still twenty-one, with a wife seventeen, when a son was born. In my name, altogether too fast, a premature little family began to grow up in that "funny little house." In exchange for the firm's gold advanced to build the house, without reading it I signed a lawyer's five-year contract with the "firm of Adler and Sullivan." This contract after working in their office for nearly two years.

To see Mr. Sullivan (the designing partner) you must know him not only by the pencil in his hand that was me, but you must also know Dankmar Adler, the senior partner! "The big chief" we called him. And, too, you must remember the way firms practicing architecture were made up about fifty-five years ago. They are still made that way. First, there was the manifest *success*, outstanding member of the concern, senior partner. Next came the "designing partner"—he in the back room behind the scenes—who, at least, must know how to draw well and (turn out plans, maybe) certainly make the *pictures*. And often there was the front or "contact" man—a "mixer"; probably a well-heeled socialite. The mixer it was who brought in the "jobs" and kept the firm in the club window for sale.

In order to "get the job" (the first principle of architecture as laid down by great-big H.H. Richardson), this more decorative "intermediate," Dankmar Adler never seemed to need. The big chief was so well provided with "jobs." But he did need the designing partner—desperately—for the great engineer-constructor had graduated into architecture from the army. The designing partner had appeared at the moment when Adler's prowess and practice as an architect were both established and rapidly growing. Many important Chicago clients, merchants like Alexander Revell, manufacturers like Martin Ryerson, wholesale merchandisers like Selz-Schwab, theatre magnates like Horace McVicker, and big industrialists like Andrew Carnegie were his clients. Several rabbis (and numerous wealthy Jewish clients, all of whom would have only Adler) came to sit waiting in his outer office. Also Adler's personal influence in the ranks of the A.I.A., at that time an honorable body of proven practitioners, was immense. Dankmar Adler was a solid block of manhood, inspiring the confidence of everyone, a terror to any recalcitrant or shifty contractor. His ideas throughout were advanced far beyond his time, as his choice of a partner would indicate, and he was known even in those more liberal days (before architecture became obsessed by college degrees) as a liberal, original thinker. Reading (or rereading) some of the papers he prepared and read to the A.I.A. at that time, for instance, the paper, "Modifying Buildings by the Use of Steel," would astonish most modernites.

One day there came to this liberal strongman in the profession still a noble one, a not so tall young man with a stride seeming quite too long for the length of his legs. The net result of the stride was a pompous strut. Carrying a dark pointed beard well out in front of a dark-brown head of hair trimmed fairly short, already "losing" at the crown, he came immaculately—as always—dressed in brown. His eyes were large, also brown; burning, "seeing" eyes that had a glint of humor in them to make the arrogance of his bearing—bearable. He had offered himself to the big chief because—well, the Bostonian novice hadn't been too successful since he returned from marking time in bad company at the Paris Beaux-Arts for a term of about two years. John Edelman, his mentor there and friend now in this country, had announced Adler to him and (I suspect) him to Adler. Sullivanian virtuosity at the time was entirely that of the amateur draughtsman-designer.[4] But in that respect he had won Adler's instant recognition as virtuoso and the young Spanish-Irishman from Boston (yes, and Paris too) was installed in the Adler back room. The long-coveted and now welcome "designer" had arrived. Adler never lost faith in that growing phase of Sullivan's genius nor ever failed him but once. Of that? More later.

Anyway, the grand chief knew enough building construction for two or more. And the Sullivan schooling in practical planning of buildings actually built began then and there under ideal auspices: ideal because the chief was not only an experienced engineer but was also a splendid planner himself; a good critic, as his choice of a "designer" was to prove. He was one of the few farsighted men in the free-for-all catch-as-catch-can "classic" of these late nineties. But the grand chief was never classic. He was independent. Inexorably honorable, he possessed an architect's practice already so well established in his favor that his clientele resented the young Irishman. "Adler was good enough for them." Some few left the chief on account of Sullivan. But soon curiosity became appreciation and designs proceeding from the young sophisticate in the back room began to please not only Adler but Adler's captious clients. Chicago, a city rapidly rising to greatness, down there on the prairie—or in the swamp where the wild onions grew that gave the city its Indian name—was already a gigantic railroad center, a vast stockyards serving the entire U.S.A. Big crude Chicago—destined to become the most beautiful American city! A few years later Chicago began to take notice not only of Adler but to exhibit a friendly curiosity concerning his new "designer."

Prompted by Ferdinand Peck, when the matter came up, Adler was naturally the man to be entrusted with a great civic enterprise like the Chicago Auditorium to seat five thousand people. So the "big job" was given to Adler for good reasons. He had built the Exposition Buildings on the lake front, Central Music Hall on Randolph and State Streets, and many commercial buildings beside the several Chicago theatres. All have now disappeared. The five million dollars that great building was to cost then would be about ten or fifteen million now. After several years on comparative "chicken feed" (store and loft buildings because the firm steadfastly refused to build residences), Louis H. Sullivan came into this important commission by way of Dankmar Adler's prowess in his chosen profession.

At this great moment in his own life as well as in the life of the "firm" the designing partner was looking for someone to help him with the "Auditorium" drawings. The great building project was casually called "The Auditorium."

I appeared before Mr. Sullivan soon after my initial year in Chicago with residence architect J. L. Silsbee: Silsbee—rising star in the residential work of that day. A fellow draughtsman working at Syracuse aristocrat Silsbee's office, by name Wilcox (he was one of five minister's sons working for Silsbee at the time—Silsbee himself was a minister's son), said he had bragged of me a little to Mr. Sullivan. Wilcox had himself tried for the job but failing to qualify he asked me to respond to an invitation to come to see him which he carried to me from Mr. Sullivan. I went. Mr. Sullivan seemed to like me but tossed aside the drawings (manifestly made under Silsbee's influence) which I had with me.

"No! No!" said he. "Silsbee draws well but draw something of *your own* and bring it to me after I get back from the A.I.A. conference in St. Louis."

Congenital, and now congenial heretic (I liked so much the knowing way he looked me through

and through), I wanted to work for him above all others because already the firm of Adler and Sullivan was known as revolutionary even in the architecture of that unconsciously—but naturally, thank God!—revolutionary time. So with great excitement I worked in my room at the Watermans' (where I was lodging) and brought a dozen or more drawings to show him. He glanced at them, studied a few intently for a moment, and said:

"Wright, you have a good touch . . . and you'll do. How much do you want?"

Doubling on what I was getting from Silsbee, I told him, surprising him by the moderation of the demand.

"All right," said the incipient master indulgently, "we can fix that up as you go along." And the relationship began that was to last about seven years. Designing partner thirty-four. "Pencil" nearly twenty.

In Dankmar Adler, Louis H. Sullivan had a heavy champion. In me, Louis H. Sullivan had a good pencil in his hand. So I then intended and still believe.

## CHAPTER TWO
## BY SELF-SACRIFICE THE HONEST DISCIPLE MUST HIMSELF BEGET THE DEEPER EXPERIENCE THAT MAKES HIM MASTER

I was quite lonesome in that strange, unfriendly, daily routine of the office that would often break into open rows. So, during the first two lonely years I was in hostile office environment. To keep me company at first, and later in order to train him into lieber-meister's way with me in case anything were to happen to deprive him of my trained help, I had brought into the Adler and Sullivan office to qualify—by work under me—a young draughtsman I had known at Silsbee's: the novice Elmslie—I called him "George." He was a conscientious Scotch lad, slow of speech and movement, who had never been really "young" as he then seemed to me. His character was fine, our comradeship perfect, and some of my much too much work I now began to pass along to the faithful George.

So, when the firm moved from the Borden block to the new quarters (we had planned them for the Auditorium tower), George was alongside in my room which had the best of the wide "guillotine" windows to the east overlooking the lake: Lake Michigan. At the master's own request, this room next his was partitioned off and ceiled over for myself. The room completed the east end of the big draughting room with the continuous row of big windows to the north. His desk was visible from my big draughting table. George, who had come over to the Borden block to work, for about six years thereafter now worked at his drawing board next my own big table in this small private office in order to continue with the master should anything happen to me.

At the same time some thirty confirmed—a few peripatetic—draughtsmen, young and old, were, by now, working under me. The draughtsmen worked in the open space between my place and a similar place partitioned off at the opposite end of the tower draughting room (the west end) for Paul Mueller, the young German engineer educated at Stuttgart. He was in charge of engineering drawings and the several superintendents coming daily in from the field reported to him. Tall, young Paul Mueller, the structural engineer, grew a black beard to give him more authority. He was directly under Dankmar Adler. I, with no graduation or architectural degrees to speak of as such, was not only directly under Louis H. Sullivan but more and more, because of Mr. Sullivan's absences, I was under Dankmar Adler.

This plan of the Adler and Sullivan offices in the Auditorium tower was made for the firm by myself while we were still in the old Borden block. It was later published by Adler and Sullivan in the Engineering Record of June 7, 1890 and explains pretty well the status of work in the office at that time.

The first designs for the Auditorium were made just before I came to the office. The first studies were brick and efflorescent terra cotta—a pointed tile roof on the tower—but under the Adler influence the design had become more the severe fenestration crowned by the nobly frowning tower we now see. But the Walker wholesale—a Bedford stone structure on West Adams Street—was done while we were still in the Borden block. This building, though a prominent one, seems lost to sight as I have seldom seen it illustrated. It was a facade in Romanesque terms (not rock-face, however), an arched cut-stone structure much in keeping with the Auditorium facade and of the same Bedford stone—with a fatal defect: great twin-arches landed on a pier dividing the building in the middle. The master brought the manila stretch with the elevation penciled upon it, laid it over my board with the remark, "Wright, there is the last word in the Romanesque." I puzzled over that remark a lot. What business had he with the Romanesque? "Wright, there is the last word in Romanesque." I have never forgotten the remark.

## THE GRAND OPENING

Let's say the great Auditorium is now about completed. Adelina Patti—incredibly famous then—and a long line of better than star-musicians like the Italian Tamagno, had made the opening an occasion never to be forgotten. Benjamin Harrison, the President of the United States, was present and prime promoter Peck had the President's words of praise for the great civic enterprise carved on the broad paneled wooden tablet to be put in the foyer of the Auditorium. I had been instructed to design the tablet. Promoter Peck bowed his pearl-gray top hat right and left. He, too, was enjoying his role of conquering hero. All the carping usual in every novel building enterprise had come to a timely end when the great edifice came to proof.

The "greatest" musicians' names (to myself had carelessly fallen the choice, by instinct, of "the greatest") were cast in high relief in plaster upon the side wings of the reducing curtain of the great proscenium arch. The choice (it included Berlioz) passed unchallenged—and I felt no longer uneasy. Wagner's name was there—of course—and my haphazard choice of names seemed to matter little so long as Wagner's was included. Great fame is exciting up to a certain point—a hackneyed affair beyond that point—but on the occasion of this grand opening there was the greatest outpouring of Chicago's most important and best, memorable and comparable in my mind now only to the opening about twenty-three years later of Chicago's Midway Gardens on the Plaisance just below the cast-iron

Gothic of the Rockefeller Chicago University. But whole editions of local newspapers celebrated this Auditorium event. And, for weeks, there was no other compatible subject of conversation to be found. As the name of Adler and Sullivan skyrocketed to an unparalleled fame-of-the-moment, everyone connected with this establishment shone in the reflected glory of an adversely criticized great work finally come to tremendously high approval. No one who shared the occasion will ever forget the fortnight of grand opera which then came on. Opera had a new lease on Chicago life by way of this golden place in which to see and hear it. Though never myself convinced that as an art form opera was more than a ponderous anachronism, the enthusiasm now evoked was contagious and we all floated upon it like small ships in a grand pageant. The big chief walked about with his hands clutched well back under his coattails. The chief's designer was drowning the greatest success of his life but one, with his old Beaux Arts friends and lifetime favorites Tom Healy and Louis Millet, his sympathetic "decorators" on the big project. They might be found together now at the great, wide, unique Auditorium bar, which I had to design for the great building owing to last-moment pressure on L. H. S. himself. This item may indicate how well versed in the technique of the master "his pencil" had become.

From now forward the fame of Louis H. Sullivan was secure—as one might have thought—and he seemed to be drowning the thought. It was like him.

But no fame is ever secure.

Yes. A great genius had appeared in the world of architecture. His triumph was complete. And provincial, professional envy immediately got out its dull little hatchet, whetted it, and went to work on him. Disciples arose and shone.

The great room for music began to be copied everywhere. It was surely his. Sentences from his "Hymn to Nature" were blazoned in gold on a great mural surmounting the elliptical arch of the great proscenium—"The utterance of life is a song—the symphony of nature"; from other hymns of his other sentences were inscribed on poetic murals painted within the blind semicircular archways set in the great side-walls of the room. (I remember I won-

dered why these were circular rather than elliptical like the proscenium.) Electric lighting (at that time in infancy) was a revelation as the lights centering in relief patterns were sunk into the relief ornament of the building itself. Lighting was thus for the first time made more or less integral with the building. Hitherto, chandeliers had made of artificial lighting something added to the building: a pleasant "fixture" only. The exquisite cream-colored delicate imaginative reliefs, by the master hand, of the interior were thus high-lighted where not wholly emblazoned with gold leaf. Intricate gilded reliefs swept over the succession of elliptical arches forming the vast ceiling. Exquisitely modeled ornament was everywhere delicately glistening and dancing overhead and to be found in unexpected places almost anywhere alongside. The catenary curve of the main floor on which the audience rested wore all this as a golden aura.

Acoustics had now come to architecture. Owing to this repeated recession of elliptical arches forming the great overhead and extending from the proscenium (widest in the world) into the body of the house like a magnified trumpet, the big chief had struck a principle that created a miracle in the projection and extension of sound. To aid in this respect, the overhead arches themselves were charged with warm air flowing out from the stage toward the audience through perforated pattern in each face and soffit of the great elliptical arches. Air was thus flowing toward the audience from the source of sound to be drawn out beneath the seats under the audience. Thus sound rode along to the listeners upon air-conditioning. Air-conditioning arrived as a carrier of sound! All opposing wall surfaces to the rear of the grand room itself were deadened by soft lime-mortar an inch thick (the chief believed only in good lime-mortar for such purposes) and sand finished so as to offer no echoing reflections anywhere. Not alone had a miracle of appropriate beauty arrived but also a great triumph in acoustics. Adler and Sullivan were now authority in a field hitherto largely ruled by academic superstition codified. In spite of the "authorities," the firm could now build all the theatres and opera houses they wanted to build. Opportunity to build them began to come along to the offices in the tower proudly rising now above all this glamorous, golden splendor.

As for these Adler and Sullivan offices—well . . . it was something in the eyes of the by-and-large to be there at all in any capacity whatsoever! Genial, bald old Weaton, office factotum with the purse (which I used often to tap between weekends), twinkled his shrewd blue eyes. The office cub, noisy Anton, hushed himself up. A new "hush" had come over the entire establishment. The lineaments of gratified desire were showing. There was less noise at the entrance, more quiet in the private rooms. Success with all her gleaming harness had moved in to awe the entourage of "Adler and Sullivan." The big chief, taking things happily as a matter of course, was there in his place as always. But the designing partner had gone south to cast off the strain of the mad rush to the finish considered fit for the grand opening. He remained away for six weeks at Ocean Springs, Mississippi, in the country house I had designed for him. The chief, meantime, came to sit and talk with me more often than usual. His generous heart and salty wisdom never seemed dearer and clearer to us all than now. The great event seemed rather to have sobered than excited him.

He was like that. His casual salutation a twinkle in his eye as he would come into my room—"Ah, Wright—I see! Still snatching victory from the jaws of defeat?"

The master was working away in his rose garden down there at Biloxi by the Gulf, next door to his beloved friends the James Charnleys, for whom I had drawn a cottage which I liked better than lieber-meister's. Both were experiments that seem tame enough now. Later I designed the Charnley townhouse on Astor Street.

Well . . . who would not want to be an architect conceived in glory such as this! I suppose Alexander when he had conquered the world knew some such sense of pride.

But soon the work in the tower offices proceeded to fall back again into something like routine. The procession of commissions included not only loft buildings, skyscraper office buildings, hotels, and factories, but more theatres and opera houses. All were turned out by the "office," ready to build. In all ensuing activity the congenial partners, except for the occasional Southern interim at Biloxi, worked together like hand in glove. The office force doubled and doubled again. Many young men, later to become well-known practicing architects, moved through the scene. In particular, I remember Irving Gill of California. I had taken him on as one of my squad. Running against him some months later, when I was getting out of the elevator into the office and he was about to get in to it, I noticed my habit of hair and flowing black tie had been adopted by him. This had been the case with others often enough, but in this instance the affair suddenly seemed to me more like caricature. I regarded him for a moment and said, "Gill, for Christ's sake, get your hair cut." The common enough exhortation, to which I have myself been subjected in nearly every province of the United States, was not pleasantly said. Gill was as rank an individualist as I and he quit then and there. But his individual character came out to good purpose in the good work he did later in San Diego and Los Angeles. His work was a kind of elimination which if coupled with a finer sense of proportion would have been—I think it was, anyway—a real contribution to our so-called modern movement. There were many others no doubt giving a good account of themselves but I do not recall them now. "George," meantime, was the steady understudy alongside—a quiet nondemanding comrade. Later when I was independent he would come out to the Oak Park studio to help me when work got out of hand. A good deal of backwash accordingly got into the later buildings of the Sullivan office which was then almost solely in his charge.

As I write I see through the glass screen that cuts me off from them the Adler and Sullivan rank-and-file, sprawling over drawing boards. Familiar faces lifted occasionally, looking to see if I was looking or faces looking dreamily out of the windows—the draughtsmen. They were a small army from first to last. I sometimes wonder what became of them as I recall lieber-meister's "Wright, I have no respect at all for a draughtsman."

But, to cut this story shorter (it could go on from building to building indefinitely), the partnership under pressure of depression—and financial loss inevitable to the kind of ground-breaking work the firm was continuously doing on every job that came in—competition also keen—had made some immediate move in the direction of money, necessary. Paul Mueller had left several years before to go into partnership with a contractor, the Probst Construction Company. This grieved the big chief at the time. He had trained Mueller thoroughly. Mueller had become his man Friday. The chief lamented him for years. First, after him, came Sickles from New York, a grandstander. The boys all looked upon him as a stuffed shirt from the McKim, Mead and White offices. Conscientious hardworking Kleinpell came next (after Sickles was confined for paresis) to take Paul Mueller's place. But the office was never the same. After Mueller left, many changes began to take place in that end of the work.

We will go forward, now, to the time when I had left the office and had been practicing building for many years—say, twenty—on my own, but, owing to a worm's-eye view I was getting of society at that moment, about out on the street myself.

## CHAPTER THREE
## A MASTER VENERATES ONLY TRUTH

Louis H. Sullivan venerated none except Adler, Herbert Spencer, Richard Wagner, Walt Whitman, John Edelman, and himself. I didn't know of anyone else and I don't know now whether he knew God in the depths of his heart or not. Nor did I ever hear a good word for any contemporary of his unless almost nothing for John Root. But later I discovered his secret respect, leaning a little toward envy (I was ashamed to suspect), for H. H. Richardson. Just the same and nevertheless he had liked and trusted *me* and I, loving poetry, adored the lyric poet I had instinctively felt him to be and later actually came to know as the great philosopher he was. As through the years I grew and listened to him, I learned because, though disinclined to teach at all, he would talk to me much and long about his resentments—hates—loves—of his contemporaries, of Wagner, Whitman, and his ideas of art and artists. Like his feeling toward his draughtsmen, he despised his disciples. Sometimes—forgetting me entirely—next him there in my enclosure—wide windows overlooking the vast lighted city lying peacefully by the lake—he would talk until I could arrive home on the last suburban train only way past a decent bedtime. He seemed to have found in me what he seemed to lack . . . the natural human sympathy and steadfast adoration of the young every great egoist needs. He did not like to work unless drawing designs for ornament. I think I did like to work: thanks to the farm? And soon (after a year or two) I could draw so well that later in his life "lieber-meister" sometimes failed to distinguish between my work and his own.

Meantime the designing partner, as he developed toward mastery, soon found it satisfactory—so much easier—not to draw so much himself. All architects arrive there soon or late.

## POINT, LINE, AND PLANE

Beginning at the draughting board, it was my natural tendency to draw away from the mastery of his efflorescence toward the straight line and rectangular pattern, working my own rectilinear way with T-square and triangle toward the more severe rhythms of point, line, and plane. Never having been a painter I had never drawn more than a little "free-hand." So at this time not only was it my instinct to go away from free-hand exercise, but my technique (such as it was) condemned me to T-square and triangle, which I came to love and prefer, but they compelled me to stay behind the sensuous expressions the master so much loved and mastered so surpassingly well.

And by now he would sometimes reproach me, his accepted chief draughtsman.

"Wright," he would say, concerning details which I was trying (as yet by instinct) to work with T-square and triangle more simply into the materials of building construction itself, "bring it alive, man! Make it live!"

He would sit down at my board for a moment, take the "HB" pencil from my hand and, sure enough, there it would be. Alive!

*"Take care of the terminals, Wright. The rest will take care of itself."*

He did "make it live." And I learned to do it his way. But that extraordinary gift I somehow then regarded (do now) as peculiarly his own. I enjoyed emulation—as a challenge—and loved being useful to him in any way I could be. But no one ever had or could ever equal this, his gift, in the peculiar field that was his unique efflorescence. Where before, I ask, in surroundings so peculiarly poetry-crushing (or, for that matter, in felicitous circumstances either) was there ever a man who *out of himself* devised a complete beautiful language of self-expression as complete in itself as Wagner's music or the period ornamentation of any of the great styles which time took so many ages to perfect? The Sullivanian philosophy, so far as it was personal to him, is written in that chosen language of his most clearly and if you are going to read *him* at all, it is there to be read at level best. Not in the remarkable buildings built by the firm nor in his own writings (so I felt then and now think) were the perfect expressions of Louis H. Sullivan to be found. As I could see even then, the buildings were often far from it. His writing at that time (let's mention "Inspiration—A Spring Song," which he read to me) seemed to me a kind of "baying at the moon," as I once risked telling him with no good results where I was concerned. Or where he was concerned either. So I seldom read what he wrote. There was no need. He would sometimes read passages to me or, better still, talk about himself in his own way. Probably "trying it out on the 'pup'"? But always I preferred his drawings. Naturally enough, because I shared in them. He may have been ridiculous when he wrote: I didn't know. He was miraculous when he drew. I always wanted him to *"draw"!* But soon he began to draw less and less.

As for his literary "tastes"—he loved Walt Whitman's "Leaves of Grass" and read Herbert Spencer. Early in my life with him he gave me Spencer and Walt Whitman to read. Not so strange a pair to draw to as one might think. I read enough to show me the color of the particular tub of dye that was the Spencerian synthetic philosophy and threw the book away. But I loved Whitman although I preferred Bach—and Beethoven especially—to Wagner. Most of all I *preferred* that he "draw." I never had occasion to be ashamed of myself with him then.

## CHAPTER FOUR
## OF THE GROUND, NOT ON IT

In any honest search for an ideal to stand firm against the "classic" (or "exterior") ideal—that inspires the super-elegance of Greek art by aiming at contrast to nature and becoming the servile pseudo-classic of our day—were we to search among the expressions of the interior (or organic) ideal as anciently set forth by Laotze, Moti, Jesus, and the Buddha (more recently by poet-philosophers like Shakespeare, Cervantes, Unamuno, Whitman, Emerson, Thoreau, Nietzsche, Goethe, Rousseau, Mark Twain, Melville, Lecomte du Noüy and so many others), a high place in modern times should inevitably go to Louis H. Sullivan.

As a complete expression of himself the master left to us not only printed volumes expounding his philosophy, but by his own more enhancing terms in his own drawings as he collected, signed, and dated them himself—reproduced here for the first time. In these little masterpieces of poetic imagination, the poet in him shines forth on the record as a free, independent spirit characteristic of the free of all time. Why could his own time only pass him by? But a handsome folio was published in his lifetime by the A.I.A. at the instigation of a friend of his named Whitaker. The prophet of a democratic architecture was recognized under the imprint of his own profession. But, too late for him. Claude Bragdon, an enthusiastic, sincere disciple of the master, had also been trying to get his writing printed in his lifetime but without success.

This work published by the A.I.A. might well have been called his last will and testament but should never be. The drawings I have used here as illustration by his own bequest—and implied request—bear eloquent witness to whatever I have said of him or could say. The publication of these poignantly beautiful rhythms tardily fulfills the promise I made to him. Even then the trembling hand with its nicotine-stained forefinger, his heart pounding, recovering for a moment, would regain much of the perfect poise, push, and touch of former days. This ornament was his unquenchable gift! The drawings he made for the late work published by the A.I.A.—though less spontaneous—show but little falling off from the power and grace of the performances included here, made when I knew him at the height of his power. But as you will see they are no longer so spontaneous. The beloved master was illustrating a "thesis." The earlier drawings he gave to me are dated by him—and, out of so many, I have chosen the few I think he would have chosen himself.

Not until toward the end of my service to Adler and Sullivan did I perceive that the nature of materials meant no more to lieber-meister than their nature had meant to the ancient Greeks but with a nameless difference. Materials, all alike, were only grist for the marvelous sensuous rhythmic power of imagination he possessed. His spirit was deeply involved in the fluent organic expressions of form naturally appropriate to a plastic—and clay was (it is forever) the ideal "plastic." But, whether executed in stone, wood, or iron, all materials were "clay" in the master's hands and—well—that was enough? Because of this effulgent sense of sympathy he possessed—for all he cared or anything he seemed to want to know materials were pretty much all *one* to him. In the primal plastic—clay—his opulent imagery could triumph, and did so. As might have been the case with the Greeks had they the gift he had. But this inconsistency by its very constancy began to disturb me. Not much at first but an uneasy little. More and more, though, as years went by I would instinctively draw toward expressions more appropriate to other building materials by way of T-square and triangle: just as purely instinctively rhythmic—so it seemed to me—but more architectural ones. Or so I thought. I now know that "architectural" is not exactly the right word because the basis of architectural thought was there in what he did, but I know now that many a long lifetime must be spent to find the proper technique—each man for himself—to put into actual building practice the implications of the great philosophy to which the lyric poet dedicated himself in this sensuous efflorescence so peculiarly and absolutely his own. But if a building was ever to be organic in the same sense that this deeply individual expression of himself was so and prophesied it, this lifetime, at least, is only a beginning. I felt this

rather than knew it—then. Now I realize it and acknowledge it.

Nevertheless, given a novel problem of that moment—like the troublesome skyscraper—his fine mind instantly saw its chief characteristic. *Aware of its nature* he got its real sense. It was tall! Why not, then, nobly tall instead of a simpering super-imposition of several or many low buildings to arrive at height in the manner that "skyscrapers" were being practiced by his contemporaries? By all except one: John Root. Root's Monadnock was a noble building. It was later but even further along. The Wainwright went very far—a splendid performance on the record for all time. Although the frontal divisions were still artificial, they were at least, and at last, effective. But the flat roof-slab overhung the street, you say? Well, you may also say that these frontal divisions were no less eclecticisms for being fresh. But a new countenance had come to light! He had conceived it as still a column, as I came to see many years later. Base, shaft, and capital were there with no direct or apparent relation to actual construction. The picturesque verticality with which he did emphasize its height, although appropriate, was still a mere facade. Where and how was the actual nature of this building construction? Equivocation in this respect by the Wainwright. Yes, but far less than in most contemporary building effort. This revolt and departure from the insignificant academicisms of that day wore a genuinely fresh countenance and was prophetic if not profound. As he threw the "stretch," with the first three bays outlined in pencil upon it, I sensed what had happened. In his vision, here beyond doubt, was the dawn of a new day in skyscraper architecture. The "countenance" then was all anyone ever thought to ask of any building anyway. I never heard the master once refer to Greek architecture, but again see the Greeks, see Richardson, see the painter-architects of the Renaissance. See the stencilists' cliché of today. See them all for five centuries previous and past! Look back and see the interminable vistas of interior structure ignored or falsified in exteriors without any sense of the nature of the problem as you see a type in the Wainwright. But other lifetimes yet to come would have to be expended upon the task of making the countenance of building authentic of structure—in order to finally make that countenance of construction integral: innate architecture. We can honestly call only an organic type of performance the new architecture of this era that I am calling organic. I "felt" this then. I realize it now because he was then what he was.

Yes. It is only fair to say, now, that in none of these Adler and Sullivan buildings are "form and function" one or, excepting clay (called "terra cotta"), is the nature-of-materials considered at all, either as a matter of fact or as determining organic form. But the buildings if considered on their own in time and place went so far beyond contemporaries in point of enlightened countenance as to prophesy a new integrity so far in advance of the work of the period as to arrest the sentient passer-by with prescience of a new world.

Perhaps, owing to a long line of ministerial primogeniture and later a frugal Unitarian upbringing, I was quick to appreciate and adore this "unitarian" aspect of simplicity. But, never yet satisfied with simplicity as "exterior" (in two dimensions only), I longed to see the thing go through and "button at the back," become genuinely unitarian. But how? The then still-mysterious third dimension was essential. Or to come through from within and button at the front would do as well, if that was any easier. And though the master so spoke and practiced when designing his ornament, the buildings the firm did were seldom far along the road of organic character until they were compared with the buildings of the robust Romanist in "rock-face"—H. H. Richardson. Richardson was the grand exteriorist and what a commotion *he* created! In the later Adler and Sullivan days more and more often in mischief my "T-square and furtive triangle"—steadier now—began to push a little here and there into the few things that circumstances left to me. Push in the direction which I *felt* (not then knowing) was Nature worship—out of which was to come "in-the-nature-of-materials," not yet clear to me. The technique of that interior philosophy of materials was then more instinct than knowledge where I was concerned. But I continued experience in that direction by means of a more rectilinear and obvious schematic abstrac-

tion—which I felt and later thought suited to the machine—wherever I could do so.

It was my good luck that the refusal of the firm to build residences gave me a number of important chances like the urban Charnley House which I did at home "overtime" for the firm. It helped pay debts due to the excess cost of the "funny little house." At this time let the Charnley dwelling on Astor Street stand as instance. There were others like MacHargs', the master's own house, and his brother Albert's—all not so good. But now the machine began to push into my consciousness—to come out later when I began to work for myself.

By a little here and a little there beneath his livelier more expressive manner, without knowing it, I was corrupting his work as in that eclecticism—the Wainwright tomb at St. Louis, the Schiller Building, the Stock Exchange, Chicago, the Meyer Building which lost its cornice, and some minor things on which his hand had no time to dwell. Or should I say I was "interrupting" results as he would have had them? He did better when he would go all the way alone, as it would be easy for me to point out in the executed work. The amateur hand shows in details that the master would have done better—otherwise.

Yes, the significant implication of lieber-meister's gift to me was his practice "*of-the-thing-not-on-it*," which I recognized and saw most clearly realized in his unique sense of ornament. Seeing this in his use of clay, when modeled under his supervision from the plastic mud itself, was always to me a prophecy and sheer joy. His sentient integral modulation by imaginative reason proceeding from generals to particulars always inspired me, as it must inspire anyone who can see into it as he drew it—or read the record when his designs were modeled as he wished them modeled. If he attended to the modeling himself (he usually did): perfection! His own soul's philosophy incarnate. Music its only paraphrase and peer.

Nevertheless and because of this music, in course of time I grew eager to go further. The matter had now ceased to be Louis H. Sullivan or Frank Lloyd Wright with me: not the aim of his gift or mine but of the giver. I began to ask myself—why not this eternal principle harmonizing any and every building anywhere with environment and for every purpose? Why not the edifice symphonic throughout from footing to coping of the *structure* itself—a harmony like music? My father taught me that a symphony was an *edifice* of sound. I wanted to see, someday, a building continuously plastic from inside to outside, and exterior from outside to inside. No stopping anywhere once the eternal "principle" prophesied anew by him so clearly in the immediate field of his symphonic eloquence was recognized. Assertion of pure form as *integral* rhythmic movement was what made him a lyric poet. Almost all ornamentation up to and especially in the time in which he worked—had degenerated to mere applied surface decoration. Ornament was "appliqué"—even as lace curtains are hung. From the first, "*of-the-thing-not-on-it*" was inimical to the thought and the way of our times. But I saw it as the norm of creative work of all and every kind. It was that *quality* in him which fired my imagination. Perhaps because the "interior" character of his sense of "efflorescence" gibed with my own wrestle with nature circumstance out there on the farm? It was square with the *unit*-arianism of my old Welsh grandfather. The Froebel kindergartening my mother discovered at the Centennial, and herself took to give to me, pointed that way. All this background now came forward a step and began to "click." The letters my mother wrote at the time—"Keep close to earth, my boy, and should you have to choose between truth and success, be sure to choose truth." This probably helped. So the philosophy of which Louis H. Sullivan was now champion was not Greek to me in that early day but easily prophetic. He must live up to it always. I will help him do it—I thought. Arrogance? Yes. You see—even so early not humble. Well "I have not yet so much to be humble about."

A gentle war thus came up and went on over ways and means. I sat in on some of the last moments of this war between the rapidly developing master and the impatient curiosity of an enthusiastic, developing "pencil in his hand." The designing partner grew more frequently absent or disinterested and this was more and more license for the T-square and triangle I now wielded as second nature. Both became a great opportunity for the eager, egoistic novice that

I was. Great sensuousness to form and especially integration—the "third dimension" as integer—gradually began to come clearer, not only useful but why not vital in the creative employment of all materials in all the arts? I was growing up beside the master to see them that way—that's all, and thanks be to himself. But the machine kept worrying me. The master hadn't mentioned it and I didn't until I was on my own. At Hull House I brought the matter to a head in "The Art and Craft of the Machine," a paper I wrote and read there.

When these rare but steadily increasing chances to experiment came my way, I made (I suppose I stole them) continual minor ones. Some were disastrous: riding hard on my conscience then. I did not know (nor do I know now) how much of this thing was wrong. The master did sometimes disapprove. He would reproach me, occasionally, and sometimes too I was in deep trouble with the chief himself as in the height of windowsills in the Schiller Building which I raised six inches to get the plastic flow of the surrounding frames complete. There were other devastating details there is no need to mention. Anshe Maariv[5] is still there in Chicago on South Michigan Avenue to attest the folly of the experiments I made in violent changes of scale in actual building construction as I had seen lieber-meister practice it in ornament with startling success.

But the magic element of plasticity—which is what this attempt at exposition amounts to—I believed to be the property in building I was capable of using someday. Just as surely, integrity of form and idea was the great need of our time if the phase of his philosophy that I could absorb was sound. Here was the practical way to give integrity to anything of useful beauty or beautiful use in life on this earth. If beauty in this mortal phase of our lives is ever to be the fine morality or happy result of conscious human effort. Give all the forms of our civilization organic integrity and you will save ours from the periodic destruction overtaking all other civilizations. This I grew to believe then. I believe it now more strongly than ever.

But need for salvation by proper use of the machine came clearer to me then as my turn to build on my own drew near, and it was my first thought when I began to practice. So I began to study the *Nature* of things more and more and "all down the line." What was the Nature of this machine we must use, above all? Why not use it creatively as an artist's tool! Everything everywhere—not only in building—true to the ground and nature of materials but true as well to the new tools and new methods that produced the thing. In due course if buildings were so built the thought in them would change the ugly circumstances under which we were all living—even react and ennoble the purpose for which the buildings were built. Buildings react for good or ill upon the human lives lived in them more directly than church, school, or state. Buildings are a synthesis of society and civilization in a system of philosophy and ethics, if they are organic architecture.

This Unitarian (transcendental?) train of thought, getting into architecture, found in the suggestions of Louis H. Sullivan's philosophy as it came through his theory of ornament, made effective impact upon my own upbringing. The consequences are still in action and the end is not yet.

Many years later as I lived, drew, and built I found in what I conceived and drew that the element I now called plasticity (the master had rendered it so completely in clay) carried in its own nature implications of unexplored structural continuity and could exemplify, simplify, and even prove the *aesthetic* validity of structural forms themselves. This *innate* or organic property of all form, if not merely looked *at* but looked *into* as structure, absorbed me soon after I had left my work with the "firm." This absorbs me now and will absorb the more sentient young mind in architecture for centuries to come. Plastic continuity is a product of these instructive spatial properties implicit in the work emanating from his own beautiful drawings. These drawings were his genuine, deepest enjoyment. So far as they went they were the embodiment of the philosophy personal to him. As I look back upon it I can see the drawings were no less truly graph of the ancient philosophy of Laotze, Jesus, or the thought of great moderns like Walt Whitman, Unamuno, Nietzsche, Goethe, Victor Hugo, Bach, Beethoven, and the integrity of so many of the early

Germans, Spaniards, and Italians, Chinese, Japanese, and (yes, for that matter) all the spirits loving honor and sincerely serving to express it in work from the beginning of time.

We have unwittingly passed by many great sayers and doers whose music or painting or poetry is still fallow in the great "in-betweens" of universal knowledge that is poetry, yet unidentified but nevertheless someday to speak out what lieber-meister's own eager enjoyment with his pencil was saying to me when he drew. But, not in buildings, because if buildings had ever been built accordingly we could not have passed them by. We would not now be compelled to originate our own in changed and changing circumstances. Buildings that became architecture in this interior sense would be the incontestable record of man's culture in his own time. A little of it has clung through the ages to various buildings. So it is still truth universal that shines forth in the life of these rhythmic developments of surface. Yes, when conceived in plastic material like clay and modeled beneath the touch of sympathetic sentient fingers at his express command, Sullivanian ornament was not only a fresh emotional phase of inner rhythm in his own name but prophecy. Therefore his drawings are not alone lyric poems but as a matter of course they perfectly illustrate the *universality* of the philosophy the master loved, declared, and to which I—the novice—wholeheartedly subscribed as it flowed from beneath his magic "touch."

Subsequent years flew by.

As my work went on, gradually, I saw more clearly the spiritual implications of plasticity where space was a quality to be realized in building construction. I learned the stimulating values of its implication wherever the life of the free individual might be served by the building. Of course, such objective outward expression of subjective inner life can only survive in the freedom of genuine democracy; the highest form of aristocracy ever seen—that of the innate aristocrat, aristocracy not hereditary but of the man himself—as himself. Inspiration for the way of building appropriate to that inner man is what came to me by way of my own choice of direct apprenticeship to a great master. I believe voluntary apprenticeship of that kind is the way an artist-to-be can really become an architect in his own right. He can learn most from one who *is* himself an architect. But I remember that sometimes (emotionally impatient in those latter days) I would ask myself, "Doesn't 'lieber-meister' know his own when he sees it?," although my "better nature" would obtain and I would stay on pretty well in line, though doing work out of hours for some friends to whom I had occasion to feel grateful. But the master was compelled by various pressures to leave more and more to the voluntary apprentice as the years went by. Sometimes the "argument"—if such it were—would come my way by his own default. Then I would try to practice in structure by way of point, line, and plane the rhythms that he preached so well in the plastic clay whenever he was completely free of the complex restraints of the actual building process. Could I wait? During this seventh year with him I began to be impatient now and then—sometimes he with me. There was but a short time to go to complete the five-year term of my lawyer-contract but I felt I owed him too much even to think of wanting to leave him: owing him as much then as now the master owes to me. A statement unbecoming? But only due in course of that "plastic continuity" of human relationship which should be the natural accession and succession of "pencil" to master if the relationship is right; or of discipleship to masterhood, if honest. But I was rudely to awaken to the fact that my status was neither. I was just a draughtsman.

Circumstances do not wait. The "funny little house" was already paid for and the deed due from the firm. I asked for the deed only to be surprised by refusal from Mr. Sullivan. Why? "Read your contract, Wright. I have seen the house you are doing for Dr. Harlan. Your contract expressly forbids doing work outside office hours." I read the contract. It did. My assumption was that, if I could plan houses at home for the firm to pay my debts without impairing my usefulness to my employers, I could go on with it. But I now saw that was juvenile and probably dishonest. Had I stolen the Harlan house from the firm? This put me on bad terms with myself. There were other similar sins the master hadn't mentioned. I appeared before him to ar-

gue the case—instead of to confess frankly and apologize, as I should have done. This angered him and, being so manifestly in the wrong myself, angered me. I reacted like any other draughtsman—as a matter of fact, I was. Like Weatherwax, I threw down my pencil, turned my back on the master, and walked away never to go back to him again. He had never talked to me in that tone of voice before. The deed duly followed from the hand of the chief. This deed in my hand and having read the contract, I wanted to go back not to resume work but to apologize and confess a grave fault to the master. Swallowing my shame hard I went back to see him. I was astonished to hear him say, "Wright, your conduct has been so perfidious there is nothing I care to hear you say." I was cut back and down in the very flower of my relationship to him. Inasmuch as I saw the fault as only taking too much for granted, I felt surely this was exaggeration. I went home, my shame doubled. Although I often felt drawn to him in following years, I never went near him after that. It was nearly twenty years before I saw him again. This bad end to a glorious relationship has been a dark shadow to stay with me the days of my life.

You see, when I signed that contract I became a draughtsman. Now he was treating me like one. The fact is I was facing the fact that facts are facts. A case where the fact was far from the truth.

CHAPTER FIVE
THE BREAKUP OF THE FIRM
Sometime after the destruction of Taliesin I—about 1919—lieber-meister and I came together again.

Returning from work on the Imperial in Japan, I found things had not been going so well with him. Since the breakup of the firm, separation from Dankmar Adler several years after that triumphant disaster to American architecture the Columbian "Fair," had left him to carry on alone in the tower offices. The Guarantee Building, Buffalo, had just come into the office when I left. This building was the last one built under the Adler and Sullivan partnership, but a group of minor bank buildings went on afterward under his aegis by way of the faithful George.

To go back to the earlier years of Adler and

Sullivan history: owing to the nature of such creative work as theirs Adler and Sullivan, Architects, had made little or no money. Their work cost them as much, often more, than they ever received for it, although they were paid as well as any first-class architects of that time—probably better paid than most. The depression following the great success of the Columbian Fair therefore hit the firm of Adler and Sullivan particularly hard. At this psychological moment Richard Crane, the magnate owner of the Crane Company, manufacturers of pipe and plumbing, came along as tempter. As a client his respect for Adler was boundless and now he offered Dankmar Adler, Architect, $25,000 a year to sell Crane elevators. (About $75,000 now?) In a fit of despondency the chief accepted. Some money had to be earned by someone. Sullivan, left alone in the tower offices, was resentful.

As a matter of course the clientele had been mostly Adler's, as Sullivan now had reason to know. Louis H. Sullivan, Architect, soon faced the fact that he was where he must take what was left to him from the Adler connection and start to build a practice for himself. Only one Adler and Sullivan client stayed on with lonely Sullivan: Mayer, of Schlesinger and Mayer. Dave Mayer employed him to design his new retail store building on State Street, Chicago. I remember the master's sense of outrage because Uncle Dan—D. H. Burnham (make no little plans)—by tactics usual to the profession—had tried to take this commission away from him.

Meantime, as I got the story, a curious mishap had befallen Crane's new lion. The chief duly went to New York to sell Crane elevators for the new Siegel Cooper Building. The opposing bidder, Sprague Electric, simply pulled out a report Adler the architect had made concerning their elevator as proposed for use in the Auditorium Building some years previous. It gave the Electric everything—yes, including the Siegel Cooper work. Mr. Adler came home. Some words from Crane. The big chief was unused to be talked to in that tone of voice, especially from a man who had hitherto come to him for justice or for favors. The result of the interview was a cheque from Crane to Adler for $25,000—a year's salary, and a contract canceled.

All now hoped to see the two partners together again. But no, the master was still resentful. The big chief had had enough, he said.

As yet I had not once communicated with Mr. Sullivan since I had left the firm. Sometime later Mr. Adler, now much at the Union League Club, called me. I went to talk things over with him. The old chief seemed morose. He had been greatly worried by the risks he had taken to please his clients: in the matter of the added height of the tower (three times) to please Mr. Sullivan; in certain other features of the Auditorium Building, such as the addition of the banquet hall over the steel trusses that spanned the big auditorium itself, to please his client Peck. It was the addition to the height of the tower (ingeniously reinforcing the foundations) to please Sullivan that was causing most concern. In the affair of the addition of the banquet hall over the trusses spanning the big Auditorium movement had not yet stopped. The settlement of the side-walls into which the steel cantilever beams were set, (carrying the cast-iron box-fronts between them like something between the points of a pair of closing shears), would sometimes crack the cast-iron shells of these box-fronts with reports like cannon going off. The tower itself was still settling, causing cracks in adjoining portions of the building. There never was real danger. Collapse was impossible but the continuous movements caused some damage and more talk. This situation Adler had to bear. No doubt a great humiliation to him.

When I came to see him at his invitation I noticed a great change in the old chief. He was thinner; seemed unhappy. For the first time I heard him speak bitterly of his partner who, it seemed, had published the Guarantee Building of Buffalo, New York, with Adler's name deleted from the plans. This act seemed to hurt the old chief terribly.

"But for me, Wright, there never would have been a Guarantee Building."

"But, Mr. Adler," I said, "I am sure you will find there's some mistake. You will find the omission was not Mr. Sullivan's fault; probably the publisher's. Why don't you make sure?"

"I'm sure enough, Wright," he said.

But I tried him in and out concerning his former partner; pleaded the master's case with him. Told him truly how much and where there was such great disappointment over their separation— we all believed each needed the other. If ever two men did, they did—had done such great work together—the depression we were in couldn't last; and many private arguments I thought I knew for resuming the old relationship. It was all useless. I was impotent.

Thrusting his head forward, his gray beard in characteristic fashion down on his chest, looking out at me from under shaggy eyebrows, "No, Wright, I am going to keep my office in my hat now so far as I can. There's nothing in the big office with its big rent and a big salary list. I'll do the few buildings I can do, and instead of earning fifty thousand, keeping one thousand, I'll earn, by myself, five thousand and keep two thousand."

Looking at me again sharply, deep-set eyes under shaggy eyebrows: "Wright, take this from me, you do the same. Keep your office in your hat so far as you can!"

He added, "No architect on that individual basis ever needs a partner."

I saw that something that had lived between the two men—who so needed each other always and even more so now—had already burned out. Again a world of high thought and fine feeling had come to a tragic end.

We walked over from the Union League to the several small rooms the chief had taken on the Wabash Avenue side of the Auditorium, while his partner—now alone—was still carrying on up in the old offices of the tower. A heartbreaking situation. But I still believed they would come together.

I said this when I left—feeling utterly futile. Worry and disappointment had already done something to the grand old chief. This was no way of life for him.

In a short time he was dead.

I have never regretted taking his advice.

Many years later (about twenty after I had left him), with no communication between us meantime, the master and I met again in response to a telephone call from him. Friends of both had urged me to go and see him. I saw instantly that he too

had gone from reported bad to far worse than I could imagine. Going to the Auditorium management I found they had finally refused to carry him further in the splendid tower offices—offered him two rooms below, next those Adler had formerly occupied on the Wabash Avenue front. He had accepted, but now a few years later even those were closed to the master. It was on that occasion that he had called me over long-distance.

I was in deep trouble myself but, luckily, able to reinstate him. Bad habits engendered by his early life in Paris had gone on and on to finally make havoc with him. Caffeine had added to his distress and now he had come to bromides. His physician said his heart was bulging between his ribs. He had "gone off," as they say, frightfully.

Notwithstanding all this havoc, he was much softened and deepened too, I thought. He gently called me "Frank." I loved the way the word came from him because before that I had heard always only "Wright."

Even now neither his courage nor his hope had gone. His were not of the going kind. His eyes burned as brightly as ever. The old gleam of humor would come into them, flicker and go. He was breaking up. His carriage was that of an old man. The body was disintegrating; his heart irretrievably damaged. But his spirit was unchanged.

I remember sitting on his desk noticing how in contrast to former neatness it was littered with dusty material-samples and old useless papers. There were some photographs of the small bank buildings he had been doing—the best one at Owatonna, Minnesota—except for the addition of the side-wing. There were other small banks. But these were tainted with backwash and showed only pitiful remnants of the great genius that flashed from him in the old days in the tower. I saw he had been leaning heavily on George Elmslie who was still with him at the time these last buildings were being done. But for George at this time he could have done little or nothing. Loyal George! I succeeded in getting the master reinstated again but the Auditorium agents were annoyed by him and wanted him out. I saw that, too.

But he was at least safe in an armchair by a fireside. He was made a life member of the Cliff

Dwellers, a congenial Chicago "club" founded by D. H. Burnham and Hamlin Garland and in which I was myself a charter member. It is one of the great virtues of that organization that it did this for him.

Some years earlier I had corresponded with him a little while I was in Japan, and later from Los Angeles. Whenever I got to Chicago I took a room for him at the Congress next mine. But Wallace Rice had got him a room in a hotel on the South Side and he was now staying at the old Hotel Warner way down on Cottage Grove Avenue: an old haunt of his own also, with but little else to recommend it. A loyal little henna-haired milliner came often to see him there and so did the several young men who idolized him. He had taken great pride in the performance of the Imperial Hotel, volunteered to write articles concerning it for the Architectural Record. "At last, Frank," he said, "something they can't take away from you." I wonder why he thought "they" couldn't take it away from me? "They" can take anything away from anybody.

Several architects in Chicago also befriended him. They had been kind to him. Andrew Rebori, Max Dunning, and there was Gates of the American Terra Cotta Company, and Lucas, Hottinger, and others of the Northwestern Terra Cotta Company. Both manufacturers had especially good reasons to befriend him. Terra cotta in him had found a prophet! But he was no more tolerant of his contemporaries in architecture now than ever before. Rather less so. And much of the bitterness I have penned here concerning the disciple, as I too have seen him, fell from his own lips then with even less patience.

Because his personal habits had given professional jealousy and provincial prejudice a chance to "view with alarm" or to "dislike and deplore," though the matter involved was no concern of theirs nor—in the earlier days of his need—too much connected with his efficiency as an architect, for many years he, the master, all but starving, had been compelled to see great opportunities for work he could do so much better as to make comparison absurd—cruelly getting by him to go to inferior men. Competitors or disciples. A genius? Yes—well, that term was enough. It damned him, as it

was intended to do by the lesser men who used the term to scare the sheep. "Genius"—the word will write any man off the heedless scene we live in and by huddling the sheep in alarm give work rightfully his to those who imitate him.

Money? Tiptoe to the banker to put it away when the word genius comes through! That bogeyman will get you, and failure push you around.

But by now lieber-meister was actually far gone—finally impaired, yes—much by himself. He had increasingly sought refuge from loneliness, frustration, and the petty betrayals of the professional life he detested—now driven where and as so many of his gifted brothers have been heedlessly driven by themselves since time ever was.

Nevertheless, had gracious opportunity really opened, even thus late in his life he might have been saved for some years of remarkable usefulness. But popular timidity and popular prejudice encouraged by the jealousy of his "respectable" professional contemporaries had built a wall of myth around about him so high that their timid ignorance kept his countrymen from wanting to know him. His countrymen might only have wasted him had they known him. I believe he was timely but too soon. At times despondency would overcome his natural pride and buoyancy. Even his high courage would give way to fear for his continued livelihood. Then all would clear and come up again. But only for a little while. It was at this time that he gave me the drawings you see reproduced here and said, "Frank, you will be writing about these someday?" A question in his swift glance.

But he was still caustic when in the mood, was the old master. A dozen or so of his more "successful" contemporaries would come tumbling from their perches top-side down, seamy-side out. His blade could cut and flash as it cut, even to the very last.

Some long time before all this disability closed in upon him, from his chair at the Cliff Dwellers he had been continuing the writing of *The Autobiography of an Idea*. He would occasionally read a chapter to me. He had always loved to write. There, completely shut off from his natural medium of expression, he had turned more and more from the pencil to the pen. Soon he was the master there. The book meant life to him now. That I saw, and he was eagerly looking forward to the first copy from the press.

He had visited Taliesin, some years before, but the visit proved a strenuous experience for him—a bad cold was the result. Now (years later) his breath was shorter and shorter. After several cups of strong coffee he loved too much (impatient, he would pound the table if coffee was delayed), his breath was so short he would have to take my arm to walk—even very slowly. At the street crossings to step up from the street level to the sidewalk would make him pause for breath.

So I continued to see him oftener than every week if I could. But I was myself desperately involved otherwise at that dreadful time. I too was getting the worm's-eye view of society.

Some weeks passed. A telephone call to Taliesin from the Hotel Warner. I immediately took the train for Chicago and found the Warner place up in arms against him. He had now fallen worse than sick. Spells of violence came over him more and more often. This time I made peace with the manager—after raising Cain over the condition I found his room in. The manager was really devoted to Sullivan as he said he was, but he was now at his wit's end. We finally got a nurse who would stay. His devoted comrade, the little henna-haired milliner who understood him and could do almost anything with him, was absent. She herself was in the hospital at the time. She had kept in faithful touch with him.

"Don't leave me, Frank," he begged. "Stay."

I stayed and he seemed to be himself again toward evening. We talked about his forthcoming book, *The Autobiography of an Idea.* He hoped there might be some income in it—for him. Hope—always hope.

I saw that he had everything to make him comfortable. So, late that evening after he had fallen asleep, I went back to Taliesin again with a promise from the nurse to call me if I were needed.

In town a few days later, I went to see him again.

He seemed better. There—at last—the first bound copy of the *Autobiography!* The book had just come in and was lying on the table by his bed. He wanted to get up. I helped him, put my overcoat round his shoulders as he sat on the bed with his feet covered up on the floor. He looked over at the book.

"There it is, Frank."

I was sitting by him, my arm around him to keep him warm and steady him. I could feel every vertebra in his backbone as I rubbed my hand up and down his spine to comfort him; and I could feel his enlarged heart pounding.

"Give me the book! The first copy to you, Frank! A pencil?" He couldn't lift his arm. Gave it up with an attempt to smile.

I could never regard the book without a strange resentment. I know it only by what he read to me himself. It had failed him as I had failed him. It was too late to do him any good. The copy he gave me was soon lost, later, in the tragic destruction of Taliesin II, and I was out on the street. But I am able to read it now and someday I will.

But yes—he the master was still there. Was he cursing a little? Gently enough. His eyes were still deeper in their wan sockets, but still burning bright. He joked about the end he saw now, and—under his breath—something. For the first time he would admit to himself that the end was near. But to me he looked as though he were better notwithstanding that helpless arm. But the man in him seemed indifferent. He didn't want to talk about it anymore, either way. Life had been pretty hard on him. Such friends as he had could do but little to make up for the deep tragedy of his frustration as the greatest architect of his time. But his ornament was his inextinguishable gift to the last and he had thrust the drawings you see here into my hands several days before when he was all but dying.

I had passed through many situations with him that looked worse than this one. So I put him back to bed again—covered him up—and sat there by him on the edge of the bed. He fell asleep. Another crisis had apparently passed. He seemed to be sleeping well, to breathe deeply enough and more easily. Once more. The nurse stepped out for a moment. An imperative call for me came in—a tragic crisis at Taliesin! I left a note for the nurse to call me immediately if there was any change in him for the worse.

At Taliesin, in the midst of disgraceful commotion, I listened anxiously for the telephone. No call coming through, I felt reassured.

But the day after the next I learned of the death of the master from the newspapers. A long-distance call from Max Dunning said that he died the day after I left him.

Several architects, warm-hearted little Max Dunning one of them, happened to come just at the end to see him and they had taken charge.

The master had nothing left in the world that he could call his own but the new clothes it had been a pleasure of my life to see him in—these and a beautiful old daguerreotype of his lovely mother, himself and his brother, aged about nine, seen standing on either side of her. These were his only worldly possessions.

Knowing he was dying he had given the prized daguerreotype to the nurse to give to "Frank."

His few remaining friends picked up his body, planned a funeral at Graceland Cemetery at which Wallace Rice, his crony at the Cliff Dwellers, spoke. I attended but stayed outside. Later "they" designed a monument for him . . . a slab of ornament designed by George Elmslie in the master's own vein to put upon his grave: the young understudy I had brought over to Sullivan from Silsbee's because the master wanted me to train someone to take my place in case anything should happen to me. George had taken my place when I left. He was faithful to the master and stayed on with him ten years or more. But to me, who had loved the master—and loving him was understanding him—this idea of imitating his work as a monument to him was worse than ironic. There was nothing to be done about it worth doing. It was his friends' best thought for the man now, and no monument is ever more than a monument to those who erect it. Is it?

By the eternal. These indecent exposures we call monuments! Will we never make an end of them? Such banality (profanity—the word nearer the truth) as they represent in our country!

But what great man ever lived whose memory was not traduced, made ridiculous, or unwittingly insulted by the *monument* "they" erected to their sense of themselves in his name after he was dead? Abraham Lincoln and Thomas Jefferson again to mind. Such monuments are made by those who, voluntarily or not, never did anything but betray the thing the great man they professed to honor loved most. Those "friends" who were charitable when he was in need; officious when he died. By a gravestone—seeking to be on good terms with themselves at his expense now that he is dead.

I wrote something in the fullness of my heart at the time, to be published somewhere. I forget where. This is it. A funeral "oration"? I suppose so. But, such as it was, my farewell to lieber-meister:

## THE MASTER'S WORK

The new in the old and old in the new is ever principle.

Principle is all and single the reality the beloved master, Louis Sullivan, ever loved. It gave to the man stature and to his work true significance.

His loyalty to principle was the more remarkable as *vision* when all around him poisonous cultural mists hung low to obscure or blight any bright hope of finer beauty in the matter of this world.

The buildings he has left with us for a brief time are the least of him. In the heart of him he was of infinite value to the countrymen who wasted him not because they would; but because *they could not know him.*

Any work, great as human expression, must be studied in relation to the time in which it insisted upon its own virtues and got itself into human view.

So it is with the work he has left to us.

Remember, you who can, the contemporaries of the Chicago Auditorium, his first great building.

They were the hectic Pullman Building, W. W. Boyington's chamfered "Board of Trade," the hideous Union Station and many other survivors in the idiom of that harsh, insensate period.

Outside the initial impetus of John Edelman in his early days, H. H. Richardson (great emotionalist of the Romanesque revival) was the one whose influence the master most felt. And John Root, another fertile rival of that time who knew less than the master but felt almost as much. The master admitted he sometimes shot very straight indeed.

They were his only peers. And they were only feeling their way. But he was thinking *and* feeling—far in advance of either—to the new.

The Auditorium Building is largely what it is, physically, owing to Dankmar Adler's good judgment and restraining influence. It was Louis Sullivan who made it sing; made it music for Music.

The Getty Tomb in Graceland Cemetery was entirely his own; fine sculpture. A statue. A great poem addressed to human sensibilities as such. Outside the realm of music what finer requiem?

But—when he brought the drawing board with the motive for the Wainwright outlined in profile and elevation upon it and threw the board down on my table I was perfectly aware of what had happened.

This was a great Louis H. Sullivan moment. The tall building was born tall. His greatest effort? No. But here was the "skyscraper": a new thing beneath the sun, entity imperfect, but with virtue, individuality, beauty all its own. Until Louis Sullivan showed the way, high buildings lacked unity. They were built-up in layers. All were fighting height instead of gracefully and honestly accepting it. What unity those false masonry masses have that now pile up toward big-city skies is due to the master mind that first perceived the high building as a harmonious unit—its height triumphant.

The Wainwright Building was *tall*. It prophesied the way for these tall office-building effects we now point to with pride. And so to this day the Wainwright remains the master key to the "skyscraper" so far as "skyscraper" is a matter of architecture.

Only the golden interior of the Chicago Auditorium, the golden doorway of the purely pictorial Transportation Building (for what it is worth), the Getty Tomb, and the Wainwright Building are necessary to show the great reach of creative activity that was Louis Sullivan's. Other buildings the firm did, but all were more or less on these stems. Some were grafted upon these, some were grown from alongside them. But all were relatively inferior in point of the quality which we finally associate with the primitive strength of the thing that got itself born regardless, *true* to the idea.

The capacity for love—ardent, true, poetic— was great in him as his system of ornament, alone—

with no buildings—proves. Say this greatest feature of his work was esoteric. Is it the less precious for that?

Do you realize that here, in his own way, is no body of culture evolving through centuries of time but a scheme and "style" of plastic expression which an individual, working away in the poetry-crushing environment of a more cruel materialism than any seen since the days of the brutal Romans, had made out of himself? Here was a sentient individual who evoked the goddess whole civilizations strove in vain for centuries to win, and wooed her with this charming interior smile—all on his own in one lifetime all too brief.

Regarding his achievement we may see the time coming when every man may have that precious quality called style for his very own.

Ah, that supreme erotic adventure of the mind that was his fascinating ornament!

Genius the master had, or rather, genius had him. Genius possessed him. It reveled in him and squandered him because he squandered genius.

The effect of any genius is seldom seen in his own time. Nor can the full effects of genius ever be traced or seen. Human affairs are continually flowing. What we call Life is, in everything eventful—plastic. It is a becoming and is so in spite of all efforts to fix it with names; all endeavors to make it static to man's will. As a pebble cast into the ocean sets up reactions lost in the faint encircling ripples of vast distances of eternity so does a man's genius go on forever. For genius *is but an expression of* principle. Therefore in no way does genius ever run counter to genius nor ever could. It is itself a human *element:* Nature.

We may be sure that the intuitions and expressions of such a nature as his in any work to which he lovingly put his hand is more conservative of the future where architecture of our country is concerned than all the schools of all time ever were even when combined with all the salesmanship of all the functioneers everywhere.

Now long ago, weak, weary, in a despondent moment not long before he died, he said to me, "Frank, our people have stopped thinking! It would be harder now to do radical work and more difficult to get radical work accepted than it ever was."

The drift toward mediocrity, taking the name of democracy in vain, had already set in. I see it now myself. It seems inevitable? No! great master. There is no such "inevitable." There is never an "inevitable" contrary to the life of the human soul—the life of love. The torch flung to your master hand from depths of antiquity kept alight and held aloft by you as long as you could breathe, shall not go out! It has ever been flung from hand to hand—since time began for man. Never yet have men been able to put it out!

## CHAPTER SIX
## THE UNITARIAN ABSTRACT:
## THE MODERN ESSENCE

Against threatening forces of Nature and the merciless passions of our fellow men, only a cultivated sense of organic form can build for democratic man an appropriate state, a deeper—therefore stronger—culture than mankind has yet known.

But observe how little of ORGANIC FORM is yet seen in our civilization! The cold abstractions of Western philosophy, scholastic materialism, the degenerate, because expedient, religions of our immediate world. All these have attributed the innate affirmations of the individual soul to the mysticism of a pseudo-romantic order! But modern thought is rapidly shifting. The old center-line, Romance, is to be found now in organic search for the organic reality that is poetic. And poetic is organic. This shift in the centerline of our utmost thought in philosophy or architecture (they now go together) comes in time to shame the expediency of our sham civilization for the lack of any culture at all. The one word necessary to deal with reality is the word *organic*—but like the word Nature it is the word least understood of any root-word in English. The deeper significance of the word is least known where the dictum, "a house is a machine for living," lies in ambush; there where the disparate fascist nature of our body-politic is becoming more evident. As the new source of physical power comes in a military uniform instead of overalls to supplant or supplement the old order, we may look for the end of all freedom: subjection of all men to standardization as themselves a kind of machinery.

## FORM AND IDEA ARE INSEPARABLE

The cult of the unitarian abstraction is now salvation. But if divorced from realities it, too, is bound to produce failures, so let us turn the dogma—"Form Follows Function"—inward. Use both the word organic and the word Nature in deeper sense—essence instead of fact: say *form and function are one*. Form and idea then do become inseparable; the consequence not material at all except as spiritual and material are naturally *of* each other. Organic architecture does prove the unity of structure and the unity of the nature of aesthetics with principle. Instead of an aesthetician we have a constructor worthy to be an architect. It is in the new reality we now call romance to believe they become so.

But if form and idea are really one almost all the architectures of our known world would wither to be—so far as the life of today is concerned—topical makeshifts. Because glass and steel and the machine, until today, were unknown. So rare are the exceptions that we will find no buildings to imitate! The now "classic" architecture of ancient Greece or any fruit of the Greeks' successful search for the elegant solution is especially useless to us. Their aesthetic search gave us the vase as an objective complete in itself—now "classic"; gave us real sculpture and was the model of what we call "classic architecture." Both vase and sculpture were not too regardful of the nature of environment and their buildings were built by the chattel slave for a more concentrated slavery—that of the mind. In our hands, both became more and more oblivious of any use, oblivious to the nature of materials and to men as man.

## THE PRISON HOUSE FOR THE MIND

In the new light of "use" as a basis for ORGANIC FORM we must find Grecian building to be without organic sense, ignorant of the nature of materials and careless of the Nature of humane purpose. Greece was wholly ignorant of organic principle in conceiving a building. The Greeks painted everything they produced as architecture, regardless of the beauty of materials used, and to them buildings were only a kind of sculpture more and more fashioned from outside inward. Intellectual? They were. But the question now arises why should we with a deeper philosophy of our own use their abstractions (coming over to us by way of such utter disciples, such grafts, as the Paris Beaux Arts, Oxford, Harvard, or Yale)—all boulevards. These new-world disciples of old-world slavery make a virtue of trying to live, build, and shine by imitation; sowing distrust of originality. Disciples we all are to some degree. It is hard to be an honorable one either way—good or bad. But in this affair with the Greeks we do reveal our inferiority complex as a bad (dishonest) disciple if we mean to build for democracy.

Well . . . this pseudo-search of the Greeks for the elegant imposition rather than a search for the more natural solution—preferably the exception that proves the rule—dazzled and demoralized us while these ideals of organic architecture were yet either absent or too novel. The nature of organic character as a matter of the third dimension is still scarcely understood. Greek culture (as were most of the great antique cultures) was imbued by imposing sense of the complete altogether. By rationalizing superficiality they reduced architecture to a science but did not evolve a building as great art. If—as we are now using the word *Nature* in interior sense—we were once to apprehend the lack of this inward *Nature* of their thought where building is the concern, and therefore become able to see the superficial character of Oxfordian-Greek abstractions, therefore the structures derived from them to form the basis of our education; we would regard imitation of the Greeks as voluntarily going to prison. Prison because, excepting primitive Dorian temples honestly built in wood, the "modern" Greeks were incapable of free—that is to say, true—building. Their later stone (marble) structures were all false structures by way of imitations of early wood temples. The stone itself—a beautiful translucence in that climate—was completely painted. They painted everything, regardless of materials. Even their life itself became an elegant form of painted sculpture. In many respects very beautiful sculpture. Yes, but based upon no truly spiritual life concept. Theirs was a civilization that died because it was Grecian to live upon elegance as a substitute for soul. Greek philosophy did contribute to modern discipleship the intellectual abstraction which Plato saw as "the eternal idea of the thing." But their own "idea"

of the thing was as viewed from outside. Their splendidly sculptural externality became "the glory that was Greece," therefore "the grandeur that was Rome." As a consequence, Greek culture became the aim or pretense of all subsequent monarchic rule and empire. So, stately Greece—exquisite as a statue—was inevitable parent of the degenerate *ism*, the consequent *ist*, and ever present *ite* to which we have dedicated the intellectual life of our nation in our universities. Thomas Jefferson is thus memorialized; Abraham Lincoln so entombed; our best minds falsely prisoned or ignored by the modern temples of universal knowledge.

No—there could be nothing in the culture of incestuous Greece or bloody Rome to inspire organic structure in building, statesmanship, or philosophy—or for a culture true to democracy in the realm of aesthetics, the realm of ethics, or religion. Unless our attempt to propagate a culture of our own is vain we cannot follow the Greeks until we understand them better than we do.

Should our democracy now determine to build for the freedom peculiar to itself, our ideology could well serve for the emancipation of humanity. I believe this nation *will* so build. Our cities will spread thin; our schools will become natural; our lives not reckoned in "freedoms" will be basically free; disciples will become more honest even though presumptive followers; and the apprentice will be a true workman with proper pride in the doing, loving to see that doing well done. To be able to work at and for what one most wants to do well should be gospel in our democracy. For a democratic slogan try "What a man does *that* he has."

Were we now to apprehend innate limitations of Greek culture that culture might become as useful to us as it has hindered us in this affair of mass-education and made (is still making) of the Greek abstraction a prison house for the mind. The freedom of the new romance? Well . . . you *will not* find it in Grecian art or mythology. Find it inside the modern democratic man: "What a man does—*that* is his." His vitality as an individual is *his reality* in the new romance; his honor and therefore the basis for creation. Organic architecture comes with that romantic reality to you today. As a man is, so he must build. Just as a nation builds—so that nation is. We have the buildings we deserve to have either as men or as man. There are many ways in life to conceal a man's true nature but when he builds he cannot hide. You have him as he is.

Within these paragraphs concerning the Grecian myth you may find why democracy has, as yet, built nothing for itself?

## CHAPTER SEVEN
## MOBOCRACY AND GENIUS

Demoralization of the creative instinct—O Lord, be merciful—lies in this universified, governmentalized substitution of a falsely decorated *mobocracy* for the thought-built *democracy* we might have. This wretched graft of which we are inordinately proud has so blinded us that already it is difficult for us even to recognize the dishonesty from which we spring and in which we live, and from which we will have suffered the greatest of all losses in this passing era of the omnipresent borrower, arrant physicist, and this ismic salesman—the artist. It is he who is primarily to blame! The weakling has not been equal to his true place. He has been a coward when and wherever his people needed his vision and courage most. Throw him in with the professionals, journalists, and the art critic (with his camera) and for good measure throw in the "history of art" as usually taught. They all belong together. Of such sham are the implements by which we work our intolerable waste: the misuse or abuse of our bravest and best; the chronic substitution of quantity for quality; guesswork instead of interior discipline and no instruction in organic construction on a good foundation, all down the line! These add up to the ruin of the creative instinct of any nation. This defect is now either the entertainment or the popular punishment meted out to the fire-born by our false success-ideal. By odious comparison genius is today just about where Louis H. Sullivan was yesterday; the life of the human spirit is wasted more securely than ever: waste sustained by authority for our already enormously increasing masses of "ownership." Even as in that day the stronger the property habit in the life of the masses—the more our bias is totalitarian. Ownership unless unusually natural and enlightened does not tend

democratic. Our young men are not urged, they are hunger-driven by false standards of success toward standardization, first, and ideas based on principle—if any—afterward. *To oppose this trend toward makeshift lives more and more standardized* is where we find the same old human frontier upon which organic architecture as great art must now go to work. Science—as inspiration—is through. In any long view science cannot substitute for Nature. It may take Nature apart but cannot put Nature together again for the growth of the human soul.

A dense conspiracy of the matter-of-fact against the human spirit is what monitors this science mentality we are calling a civilization—one which science has presented and promoted. Meantime we are miscalling our confused art and sterilized education "culture" when both destroyed by science are mainly tools for money-making. Invention? Only another tool for the same purpose. As a matter of course, such "art," "education," and "invention" allow us no fundamental architecture of our own. How, then, can democracy build? We have brains enough. We have the tools. But we have no true mind at this crucial moment in this matter of the structure of a native architecture natural to us. An affair of genuine culture, it lies far beyond the cowardly revival of the classics versus the two-dimensional patterns of the "modernist" and we have little deep conviction concerning the reality of anything if *we can't see* it work by being taught to see only in the "flat"; spiritual integrity—*depth*—always the unwelcome intruder. We do not dare to think for fear we might feel our insignificance? We are afraid to feel for fear of our thought otherwise. Nor have we deep enough faith in ourselves as ourselves to realize that the basis of democracy is—teaching men, or allowing them "to know themselves." No. Wherever the deeper essentials of life are concerned, we are craven cowards. A rat-like perspicacity? We have it, and the same courage.

It has always been difficult for me to see the grandeur of promiscuity. The horse there, too, is behind the cart. Honor hides behind the barn.

But at least so long as we are not yet committed to the mobocrat's idea of "the common man" there is hope. I have never yet met this "common man." In a democracy it is you and it is I who are the protagonists of any future that is now—democratic or fascist. And that means no future for us as a democratic nation is to be found by condoning imitations by disciples, to live in, or in sending youth to standardized schools; perfectly good plums to get back prunes.

## THE SENSE OF GUILT

Now, to say that the ideal disciple—man or nation—is hard to find may of course be only a way of saying that the ideal master does not exist?

Somehow I've always felt that were the master ideal his disciple would be so—even if in spite of himself. Does the disciple not reflect the master and exaggerate his mortality just as he does his immortality?

Did not Judas personify these forces? Probably he did.

Is there no ideal discipleship because the relationship is wrong? Is it all too human to be ideal discipline for the son of a technocracy without soul so far going, going, gone from democracy as this one of ours? To look to *any* disciple for *his own integrity* due to experience by interior discipline? Is this like looking for light in a place inevitably in the dark shadow of false eminence? But if not false, why dark; eminence should be luminous? Why is it not so for the youths of our modern world? Is it because we continue to propagate them and murder them by conscription, vast mass-education, and bad politics? Where does the faith of the neophyte lie now? I don't know . . . of course, the mechanical pace is fast; competition in this and that, meum and tuum, is more and more keen. The higher the education, the more grossly expedient it is. Life by imitation like a sickness spreads wide and thin over the vast surface of a continent. Government is becoming enormity, mostly burdensome bureaucratic expropriation, punishment, or propaganda for the business of war and the preservation of the "to-have-and-to-hold" we call "security." Such intensity as we know is mostly the voracity we call speed and the desperation we call "efficiency." Both are objectionable just as light on a purposely hidden crime would be.

But I do know by the flippant attitudes of arrant, national egotism that nobility of spirit is condemned to die by unimaginative reason or worse—the arrogant humility of our very best people. In what we call production and success there is no longer the spirit of youth because there is no firm platform nor any springboard at all for truly creative imagination. In this civilization, premature by way of science and sudden riches—probably proceeding from barbarism to degeneracy with stunning waste of power—genius is a sin against the mob! It is the calamity of our time that no master, were he to come to us today, could survive to enjoy true, that is to say, secure fame. Notoriety—no end—would be all he could hope for during his lifetime. If any post-mortem "halo" for him, dead, it would have to be carefully adjusted, by experts, to shed agreeable light on the establishments endorsed by the canonizers themselves. Their name is legion.

Something very like this massacre upon the life of imaginative reason, an assassination of which I write with unsympathetic patience and moderated invective, lieber-meister had many times more bitterly described to me. Some day some other original, wishful lover of a liberal architecture for the coming of age of our democracy, will be writing of it all as happening to him.

In due course when some *qualified* historian—a barbarian perhaps now that we hoard and hide the atom bomb—may refer to the architecture of the late nineteenth and early twentieth centuries, what honor it has will be found so far as the life of architecture is new—not renewed—to stem directly from one Louis H. Sullivan of Adler and Sullivan, Architects, Chicago, Illinois, say, in the late eighteen-nineties?

As a matter of course, only the higher discipleship which it is fair to say education is could have missed the master's own good book, *The Autobiography of an Idea*? I find many high-school boys have read it, also the Mayor of Louisville, Kentucky. His name is Farnsley.

Now, as for my place in the practice of that idea—with my inside eyes wide-open I chose to go with Louis H. Sullivan at the proper time to be "the pencil in his hand." Later I left him to carry on my work in my way as I best could. I came back to him as an architect and a friend about twenty years later, not long enough before he dropped by the wayside. Leaving that wayside with contempt, but hope, I have persistently worked. I remember the master once saying to me, sadly (he was writing something about the apparently miraculous survival of the Imperial Hotel in the Tokio temblor of 1922): "Frank, you have never been my disciple—but you are the only one who ever worked with me who understood. I couldn't do what you've done, nor could you have done what you've done but for me!"[6]

What did the master mean? He meant that though inspired by him I had not copied his work. I have never imitated him or anyone. He was great enough to be proud of me because I wasn't his disciple. He had no more respect for disciples than for a draughtsman.

I am proud to have worked by his side inspired to this day by him. A master! Yes. But no more mine than yours or anyone's who will *understand* what he understood and be faithful to that comprehension. This entire aftermath we call history, and are taught to teach to teachers to teach, must have been mismade in some such equivocal fashion as I have seen history made of his work and my own in architecture. More hapless "text" mis-made to be mis-read. I have seen the whole "movement" since inception trickle in little by little, the mere "look-of-the-thing" meantime so manipulated as to confuse and confound the simple truth because to some unqualified but all the more presumptuous writer it seemed unpleasant, or expedient, to disagree. I have seen the long arm of coincidence manipulated to reflect borrowed credit where it could not belong—and lived to see this expedient remouthed as prejudiced propaganda. Pretentious or ignorant personalities writing in the name of art in all nations have taken a fling at the subject, all professing advanced perspective from bad matter-of-fact or none. I have seen this "civilization" of ours itself excel in such conscience-less equivocation and by way of unlimited exercises of equivocal character become unanimously exterior, quite satisfied to be merely careerist. More shameless evasion or shallow pretense characterizes the phase of our mentality we call "art" than any I know—but perhaps only because I have seen this phase of our disgrace grow up.

Sophisticates obsessed by the notion that culture with a capital C for our lives must come from "abroad," play upon this weakness of ours. The exhibitionist criticism of the museum seems unaware that most of the modernist movements it presents, imagining them good for a sensation, derive from monarchy and are consciously or unconsciously bound to the roots of fascism. A bitter smile from me—to see the "trend" wherever the driver spoke with suitable foreign accent. I have come to see for myself—finally—what the master himself said with extreme disgust (and unusual profanity): "Wright! . . . why are they [the American people] so g—— d—— credulous?" Many years later when he always called me "Frank" he would say wearily, "Frank, our people don't think any more." But let me here confess: imported endorsements are nearer the truth than our own authorities ever were on the subject. But if our own crop of disciples is without honor, what of the country itself that produces them in school, in art, in politics, in religion, "ad libitum ad nauseam"? Such a state would have to die not as Louis H. Sullivan died with honor, unsuccessful, alone, but dishonored in the mass by its own kind of "success."

Now, why all this attention to the specious disciple? For one thing, reflections from the master to whom I listened a half-century ago now verified by my own experience.

For another (maybe an attempt to unscramble eggs), on account of the way I have seen history "scrambled" by disciples and come down the line deformed in respect to Louis H. Sullivan, myself, and the new architecture. In books, pamphlets, magazines, newspapers, and in all languages it has come until all history—for me—assumes a spurious aspect. With complete skepticism I now read whatever is written not only on the new architecture but any other subject. I want to know "written by whom," then "what about the writer"? When I feel I know the thing as pretentious or the usual posterior-personal slant, I throw the equivocal mass away and try to form an opinion from between the lines. I suggest that you, kind reader, do the same here. No self-portrait or portrayal of one person by another nor any report of a cause however great or small—or of both put together—as is the case here—can be impersonal. Nor should be. As for fame—fame will always mean more to posterity than it can ever mean to the recipient alive or dead. Thought by callow youth to be fun—to the famous man fame is likely to be only funny.

## CONCERNING THE APPRENTICE

Now that we have looked this gift horse, the disciple, in the mouth—the apprentice! What about the volunteer apprentice? It is my feeling and experience that the volunteer apprentice is a better basis for a future architecture for democracy than the selective disciple. Probably the only way we will achieve a great architecture. We can make best use of our best youth that way. The apprentice comes next to the doing of the thing to put his hand to it. What quality he has is soon put to test. He makes good or he loses out. As he is situated, next to spirit, character counts most. He has a chance to develop kindness, understanding, encouragement, and companionship by way of sacrifice to his ideal. Pretense is vain. Presumption is upset. By his performance he is known, and the shirker is soon shown up by the worker. In quality the apprentice is likely to remain fresh and honest because he shares by his own ability in creative effort of unquestioned superiority or else he would be no voluntary apprentice.

## A GOOD APPRENTICE IS ABLE TO SERVE WITHOUT BECOMING A VASSAL

As distinguished from the disciple the apprentice confronts his preference and is in position to serve reality. But he may become a disciple, lose contact with his conscience, and so lower his character in selfish pursuit of his own consequence at expense to his art. But as a creative force his chance of survival in his chosen field is far greater than any chance due the ambiguous disciple. There may be infinite disciples but comparatively few apprentices. The psychology of the modern apprentice therefore differs radically from that of the disciple although the apprentice may become a disciple, deceive himself, and disintegrate. To the apprentice belongs the responsible, direct approach; the approach of the disciple is intuitive, mainly selfish, and irresponsible. The apprentice works with direct responsibility to and for his inspiration. The disciple presumes upon whatever relationship he has to the master. Of the two—the apprentice has foundation in actual service to his ideal. The disciple has at best assumed elevation without any sacrificial foundation. He has tried to take the short-cut. Hence the apprentice will realize what the disciple may only surmise. Withal the apprentice is straightforward, proceeding by experience from Nature to ethics and back again to the drawing board. The disciple is equivocal and knows no ethics. If and when both are men these comparisons are fair enough. The disciple has already sold his exemplar to his client in his own name. The apprentice will not so sell until he becomes a disciple. He would lose his credit and so his self-respect. To license him to build eventually would build up a profession being torn down now by favored sons with paper degrees.

The apprentice in a democracy does not differ so much from the apprentice of *"le moyen age,"* except that, instead of the slave he then was, he is the comrade of his master, and to any extent he is able to live up to.

To detach oneself from the nature of the doing is the greatest calamity that can befall an apprentice. But the apprentice also is "loaded." The man who takes one is either brave or an incorrigible egoist. But his duty is clear. He must share himself with those who admire and trust him.

At the height of his power I knew Louis H. Sullivan—Master—as his right-hand man. And it is in the nature of what I have said that all I could honestly tell of him is personal to me. I can give the master to you only by way of his draughtsman, myself. Inasmuch as you can only see him here through me, if intimately of him this "writing" is inevitably intimate of me. So you know him by way of this willing pencil in his hand for nearly seven years. Who, then, was this Louis H. Sullivan I still call liebermeister so long after he is gone because he is still an inspiration to me? How did this "pencil" come to his hand? This book is my attempt to answer.

From me at this time the first-person singular will offend many, surprise some, and disappoint more. But in this whole matter, at risk of rousing resentment among skeptical or unwilling readers (becoming myself liable to the charge of bad "taste" by hurting the feelings of others), wherever liebermeister is concerned with me or I with him I have repeated complimentary or condemnatory words, both, as I well remember them. Because while this work is authentic it is no documentary treatise. I prefer the humble arrogance of sincerity to the arrogant humility of self-deception; so hypercriticism averse to the first-person singular would better not try to read it. I am more concerned with truth than fact. But when I use a fact the fact is fact.

This book is "in memoriam" because of a promise.

I do not like to write it because—but for the promise—it should be unnecessary to do so. Louis H. Sullivan—lyric poet—no functionalist—should, by now, be well known and cherished for *what his gift truly was*; his "gift" at the same time so much more (and other) than is on the record.

The profound naturalness of one's own being is the essential condition of a great architect, and the condition of greatness in the man. It has been the ambition of my life to achieve it with glass and steel—bricks, boards, a hod of mortar, a "client," and "the union."

So, wherever the practice of architecture today rises to the dignity of an idea in harmony with place and time, independent of ism, ist, or ite, the origin of that practice is middle-West to our courageous national experiment in freedom and stems from one, Louis H. Sullivan—beginning about 1889. But the pen is a tricky tool—fascinating but treacherous.

## BOOK FOUR: PERSPECTIVE

If there be a poet possessed of knowledge without bias—an old Welshman free from perverseness—let him answer me.

—Taliesin, Bard of Britain

## RETROSPECT

I have only partly succeeded in doing what I would do if I could.

Not having so much to be humble about, I have tried—with honest arrogance—to describe the tragedy, triumph, and significance of the great man who invariably signed himself Louis H. Sullivan; to tell you why I, though never his disciple—nor that of any man—called him "lieber-meister." His own

beautiful drawings, from which I have selected those you have seen used here, are better testimony than any I could offer in words. He had been dating the drawings (some wrongly but who really knows?) and as he put the collection of a hundred or more into my hands he said with a questioning look—I can see his glance as I write—"Frank, you will be writing about these some day?"

"Yes, lieber-meister, I will."

And I remember that, in his weakness, he seemed relieved and pleased. These drawings were the dearest treasure of his heart and this book is the true story of a personal experience now necessary to put on the record, no more for his sake than for my own, because the historical view of each where the other is concerned is getting so badly out of focus that only I can right it. I meant to write not *as* the disciple I never was, nor the pupil he never wanted, but write as the capable workman who understood (that is to say, loved) the man he served—a man who loved him in return. From me should come appreciation of the master's work as the master himself saw his own work and as I saw him. But this book is not about him—it is about our work-life and struggle while we were together.

True appreciation of his contribution if not of his true quality goes further and further astray both ways. This is partly owing to the blind-spots inevitable to badly conceived history but somewhat more to a tribe of imported self-styled "functionalists."

Form does follow function as a matter of fact. But what of it? The term "functionalism" which so many Europeans—and their gallery in this country—use as a mere term seems to be about all that came of it for them or for anyone.

## FORM FOLLOWS FUNCTION

Form follows function? Well . . . this simple fact basic to ecologist, physicist, biologist, and almost any other "ist" except the artist, has by way of discipleship to derivatives, devotees, and exploiters been razed to the level of mere dogma. The latest effects of the already trite cliché appeared as novel at the Museum of Modern Art about 1932. As this phrase was then used, we had but the latest camouflage of the old shopworn formula, "Art for art's sake." But, as said in the foreword to which this afterword is corollary, the old dogma—streamlined now—got into circulation over a hurdle of names: "cubist," "futurist," "purist," and finally "internationalist." No doubt, more names are coming. Out of the European cubo-purist or puro-cubist the modernists profess to have come into the architecture called modern—soon dubbed "internationalist." They were thrown in with me. Or vice-versa? All, originally, were minor European mirror-sects leading into or out of one bauhaus until finally, having a cart but no horse, the new slogan "form follows function" was picked up here to be used for a horse over there. Three-dimensional ideology was thus, soon by other painter-sects, degraded to sectarianism in the obvious patterns of the ever useful stencil. Instead of the new depth, another two-dimensional affair had arrived, actually no more architecture than a painter's stencil would be. But it became another aestheticism when discovered by the provincial "art elite" in our country. Call this elite the favored academic arbiters of our industrialism; of our upper haves-and-holders tending naturally, then as now, toward fascism. This elite immediately saw the stencil as the latest style and easy to use for prefabricated teaching. As promptly, the universities (advance guardians of the aesthetic and mental phases of our mass-produced imitation of a culture) imported more of it, professionalized its adoption by putting it into armchairs, and adapted its too easy (easy because superficial) advantages. Easy to learn, a cliché (or stencil) is quite as easy to forget. But nevertheless because individuality—innate sensibility—was sufficiently left out of the affair to make further academic conscription of youth quite safe (perhaps therefore), it was a great educational convenience. So, its nature not yet fully comprehended, collegiate mass-consumption of a definitely undemocratic pattern was begun in our universities and museums. It is going on there yet.

As a matter of course, to be an expedient is in the nature of what the stencil is. So in our country the stencil was soon regarded by "higher education"—itself one—as ideal. It was seen to be sufficiently "depersonalized" (to use their word for de-individual-ized) to be regarded as "safe"; that is to say, not sufficiently alive to be dangerous to handle or hard to teach. Nor is it yet clear to academic authority that the slogan, "form follows function," thus made available to negation by abnegation, was originally derived from a homemade affirmation of renunciation which subsequently returned to us from abroad a deformed, and so probably dangerous, import.

Now, for the sake of argument, let's again say that "form does follow function." Well . . . so does the sun rise tomorrow morning; so every bright has its dark, just as night is but a shadow cast by the sun. In all physical Nature form follows function! That is the simple fact. But too many misty cults for prestidigitators of fine-art "movements" are already fashioned of similiar simples—without due reference to their spiritual significance in Nature—for it to be ethical to let these too numerous stencilites, so recently and readily made, get away with another at expense to organic architecture.

Louis H. Sullivan would have been first to gleefully kick these self-styled functioneers—with their "A house is a machine for living" (but only if a human heart is a suction pump)—from his doorstep. In so far as his doorstep was mine I did it myself when they appeared with their dead-sea fruit, "the whited-sepulchre" (call it the flat-bosomed facade), at the Museum of Modern Art about 1932. But the affair was then far behindhand. So far behind, indeed, that where useful negation was implied it was definitely recorded by myself in so many words in the *Architectural Record* of February 1906[7] and in the many buildings which I had, by that time, designed and built. How did this fact also escape detection by "the authorities"—our own proprietary museums and learned educationists—when in 1910 it went so widely abroad as to be actually international today? Except by the circumstances peculiar to the posterior concept of culture as habitual from abroad it cannot be explained. Let us then blame the lack of vision and wisdom in the circumstances on the cross-eyed view, or jargon, and receive the return of the prodigal with a welcome proper to the wayward.

For any wanton sect to understand Louis H. Sullivan at all is to know that not then was he, nor ever would he be, for any such. His greatness for all lies in that at heart and in deed he was the great, human lyric poet whose creation out of himself of the poetic efflorescence of LOUIS H. SULLIVAN —great individual—was unique. Of course, he is best seen where happiest—seen in what he loved best: the primal plastic. Clay.

Although seeming at times a nature-ism (his danger), the idea is there: *of* the thing not *on* it; and therefore SULLIVANIAN self-expression contained the elements and prophesied organic architecture. To look down upon such efflorescence as mere "ornament" is disgraceful ignorance. We do so because we have only known ornament as self-indulgent excrescence ignorantly *applied* to some surface as a mere prettification. But, with the master, "ornament" was, like music, a matter of the soul—"of" the nature of man–inevitable to him: (natural) as leaves on trees or any fruit announced by the blossoms on the stems that carry both. It was this man that Louis H. Sullivan was and felt himself to be, that he expected me to write about someday: a far greater man than the functionalist he has been wishfully and willfully made to appear.

Actually ignorant of the proper depth of the word *Nature* as a term of the spirit, so-called internationalists dedicated the bare box to the machine god regardless and threw him in with it. These flat boxes on stilts—to further emphasize contrast to Nature (and ignorance of her quality)—were painted white to further mark aloofness not only to Nature but to man. This factish, leftish derivation of the old dictum, "Art is art precisely in that it is not Nature," by wrongly interpreting the word Nature, utterly betrayed the master's poetic sense. The third dimension which Sullivanian ornament prophesied never entered with the worshippers of "next-to-nothing" into their shrine, the whited sepulchre. When they do refer to "Nature," they deny truth by fact.

Where they build we have no place for a real man to live in unless he be purged of his own individuality. Just as in fascism we have submission of the man to exterior authority, so in this latest conventionalizing of fascist import, growing more and more mechanistic in concept and grasp, we have but a "sec." A dry next-to-nothing instead of quite something.

But negations are by nature dry. We do have a form of "restatement" of the negation of the Larkin Building, 1906,[8] to use in the new architecture (but not to live with) in this rebottled old formula: "Art for art's sake"; in other words, a revival of the old formula, "Art is art precisely in that it is not Nature." But wholesome rejection of this certificate of divorce from Nature now posing as artistic "contrast" is our present need. Failing to match a given sample the clerk is trained to say, "Then, madam, how would you like a contrast." Concerning these old dictums, we see in them all this childish (not childlike) *misuse of the word Nature*, the use of the word as mere fact instead of a great truth, and in that misuse lies the basis for every negative sect: the expedient excuse for the architect's "Then, madam, how would you like a contrast?" The proper use of the word Nature, as *the innate character of anything or everything*, would not only void such underdone (or overdone) abstraction in the future but be useful as the spiritual cathartic necessary in times so badly underdone or overstuffed as ours.

All but a few of these negativities seem to be—or once were—painters making their advent into architecture regardless of the dignity, difficulty, and profound character of the third dimensions of actual experience in structure; therefore no sure foundation for a new aesthetic in architecture. To bring architecture alive again as the great mother-art, negation has had its place. But its place is no longer creative. The time for affirmation is now. Nor can architecture thrive on the present. If not dated at least a decade ahead, it is born to be and stay behind its time.

Abuses notwithstanding, we must learn to use the word Nature in the proper romantic (or integral) sense of the word. Its proper use becomes indispensable if we would be free ourselves and put the true spiritual use of the word ORGANIC into the use of our language.

In this ultra-materialist era our life in Usonia needs the word used in real sense to develop honest culture of our own, or we go dry. Sap fails the graft. To take advantage of our excessive advantages our culture must be based upon decentralization and not on the major and minor axes of any grandomaniac past or modern pig-pile. Our architecture will then be in the reflex; monarchic major and minor axes no longer dominating our lives by way of any revival of any kind of "classicism," we have a chance to become a democracy. But I do not mean that organic reality—a spiritual concept—will ever degenerate to the merely realistic. The distinctions between real and realistic—between sentiment and sentimentality—between truth and fact are as important as those between the curious and the beautiful or between science and art.

## HERESY

To illustrate: a great sculptor, Michael Angelo (painter), ignorant of the depth-dimensions of good construction, visualized and isolated high up in air the great masonry arch we architects call a dome. The painter—as a matter of course—provided no more to take the inevitable thrust of the mighty arched masonry-mass than the plain air over a series of tall slender upended stilts (call them columns) set up around beneath the outer rim of the great arch. The structure had to be bound with a great iron chain at a crucial moment or all would have come to the ground. Inorganic (as might be expected), this gorgeous *"tour de force"* of the painter was extraordinarily picturesque. And perhaps this rape of the arch by the picture was so extremely successful because, for most of the time before the great Angelo and totally, except for music and painting, for about five hundred years, the "Renaissance" had all but destroyed, in favor of symbolism, any integrity—that is to say, any true inner significance of architecture as sublimated structure.

How "the picture" has damaged architecture! Such pretentious artificiality as architecture had in Buonarotti's time has now got to go. Prevalent fashions in exterior symbolism already becoming less relevant came with a rush to fill the gap made as architecture became empty *"tour de force."* We now see the dome as a symbol of authority all over the world. Cultural decline has gone so far "sky-dome" by the time in which I write, the Capitol at Washington for an instance, that perhaps only some such *tour de force* could be "extraordinarily successful." The expressions of the exterior mask aided by symbolism, the long period of the rebirths of the rebirth (history calls the rebirth the Renaissance), were in this respect similar to our own period: they were going empty of Nature significance.

Organic quality in things natural to man and the earth supporting him, though likely to be miraculous, are not necessarily "mystic" and should have been less extraordinary in the thought-world of that time: a world then not yet so degenerate. But as thought (organic) was almost as rare in that day as it is in ours, the great Italian painter's rape of the arch by picture is still sensational. This ponderous anachronism styled (shall we say "streamlined") by Michael Angelo still flourishes as the symbol of authority among us so many centuries later. But now this masonry symbol is simulated—imitated—by casting iron plates in the image of the original masonry arch and bolting the iron plates securely together. The chain thus crept up to supplant the dome.

Thus—the dome is a heresy. Throw in the pilaster, column, capital and cornice—all now Western, advertising to the world a total lack of fundamental integrity in architecture all down the line, and you will see the triumph not only of the artificial symbol of authority but the ascendancy of temporal authority over the principles of democracy. With this new integrity which we call the "third dimension" (call the third "depth") in mind—and—yes—you *are* on the way to a fourth dimension; headed for dimensions at will. Structural integrity seems even more than ever absent from the so-called modern architecture of our national scene. Is this because the third dimension inevitable to organic structure has so defied the camera eye (or the glass eye of the classicist) that it has also defied, or is derided by the flat vision of our stencilists? Their sentimental worship of the Greeks would so indicate. Nevertheless the sense of *depth* which we are here calling the third dimension—a spiritual quality that cannot be forced but must be wooed—marries the building to human life and weds both to the ground. Architecture in this deeper sense is not formidable but is truly fundamental to democracy. We will find the democratic home to be integral part of the man himself, placed upon his own share of earth, and building there a hearth he can call his own and look himself in the face. To that prophetic expression of himself man must cling for salvation in the heedless voracity of this epidemic, machine-